TERRORISM

Documents of International and Local Control

VOLUME 99

TERRORISM

Documents of International and Local Control

VOLUME 99

TERRORISM IN PAKISTAN

Douglas C. Lovelace Jr., Esquire
Senior National Security Strategist

Oceana®
NEW YORK

OXFORD
UNIVERSITY PRESS

Oxford University Press, Inc., publishes works that further Oxford University's objective of excellence in research, scholarship, and education.

Published by Oxford University Press, Inc.
198 Madison Avenue, New York, New York 10016

Cataloging-in-Publication information is available from the Library of Congress.

ISSN 1062-4007
Terrorism: Documents of International and Local Control

ISBN: 978-0-19-538307-2 (v. 99)

Note to Readers:
This publication is designed to provide accurate and authoritative information in regard to the subject matter covered. It is based upon sources believed to be accurate and reliable and is intended to be current as of the time it was written. It is sold with the understanding that the publisher is not engaged in rendering legal, accounting, or other professional services. If legal advice or other expert assistance is required, the services of a competent professional person should be sought. Also, to confirm that the information has not been affected or changed by recent developments, traditional legal research techniques should be used, including checking primary sources where appropriate.

(Based on the Declaration of Principles jointly adopted by a Committee of the American Bar Association and a Committee of Publishers and Associations.)

TABLE OF CONTENTS

VOLUME 99

TERRORISM IN PAKISTAN

DOCUMENTS

A. PAKISTANI LEGISLATION, AGREEMENTS, STATEMENTS, AND REPORTS

DOCUMENT NO. 1: Durand Line Agreement, November 12, 1893 1

DOCUMENT NO. 2: Tashkent Declaration, January 10, 1966 5

DOCUMENT NO. 3: Pakistan Anti-Terrorism (Amendment) Ordinance, 1999, April 29, 1999 7

DOCUMENT NO. 4: Anti-terrorism (Amendment) Ordinance, 2002, November 18, 2002 13

DOCUMENT NO. 5: Anti-terrorism (Second Amendment) Act, 2004, Act No. II of 2005, November 1, 2005 17

DOCUMENT NO. 6: North West Frontier Province Government's Agreement with the Taliban, May 22, 2008 21

DOCUMENT NO. 7: India-Pakistan Joint Statement, May 21, 2008 23

B. PAKISTAN'S REPORTS TO THE UN

DOCUMENT NO. 8: Pakistan's 2005 Report to the UN on Its Counter-Terrorism Efforts, Part 1, UN Security Council Resolution, S/2001/1310, January 10, 2002. 27

DOCUMENT NO. 9: Pakistan's 2005 Report to the UN on Its Counter-Terrorism Efforts, Part 2, UN Security Council Resolution, S/2002/797, July 19, 2002. 39

DOCUMENT NO. 10: Report of Pakistan to the UNSC on Implementation of UNSC Resolution 1373, UN Security Council Resolution, S/2003/307, March 12, 2003 71

DOCUMENT NO. 11: Pakistan's 2002 Report to the UN on Its Counter-Terrorism Efforts, UN Security Council Resolution, S/2004/21, January 13, 2004 81

DOCUMENT NO. 12: Pakistan's 2003 Report to the UN on Its Counter-Terrorism Efforts, UN Security Council Resolution, S/AC.44/2004/(02)/22, November 5, 2004 91

DOCUMENT NO. 13: Pakistan's 2004 Report to the UN on Its Counter-Terrorism Efforts, Part 1, UN Security Council Resolution, S/2005/524, August 11, 2005. 103

DOCUMENT NO. 14: Pakistan's 2004 Report to the UN on Its Counter-Terrorism Efforts, Part 2, UN Security Council Resolution, S/AC.44/2004/(02)/22/Add. 1, September 27, 2005 113

C. UN RESOLUTIONS

DOCUMENT NO. 15: UN Resolutions on Kashmir 319

D. U.S. PERSPECTIVES

DOCUMENT NO. 16: Pakistan-U.S. Relations, CRS Reports, IB94041, K. Alan Kronstadt, Foreign Affairs, Defense, and Trade Division, September 5, 2002. 335

DOCUMENT NO. 17: Pakistan-U.S. Anti-Terrorism Cooperation, CRS Report, RL31624, K. Alan Kronstadt, Analyst in Asian Affairs, Foreign Affairs, Defense, and Trade Division, March 28, 2003. 355

DOCUMENT NO. 18: Terrorism in South Asia, CRS Report, RL32259, K. Alan Kronstadt, Coordinator, Analyst in Asian Affairs, Foreign Affairs, Defense, and Trade Division, Bruce Vaughn, Analyst in Southeast and South Asian Affairs, Foreign Affairs, Defense, and Trade Division, August 31, 2005 381

DOCUMENT NO. 19: U.S.-Pakistan Engagement: The War on Terrorism and Beyond, United States Institute of Peace Special Report, August 2005 435

DOCUMENT NO. 20: Expert Testimony in United States v. Hamid Hayat, by Evan F. Kohlmann, February 2006. 459

DOCUMENT NO. 21: Resolving the Pakistan-Afghanistan Stalemate, United States Institute of Peace Special Report, Barnett R. Rubin and Abubakar Siddique, October 2006 477

DOCUMENT NO. 22: Indictment of Sabri Benkahla, February 9, 2006 507

DOCUMENT NO. 23: United States of America v. Sabri Benkahla, 4th cir. June 23, 2008 519

DOCUMENT NO. 24: Pakistan and Terrorism: A Summary, CRS Report, RS22632, K. Alan Kronstadt, Specialist in Asian Affairs, Foreign Affairs, Defense, and Trade Division, March 27, 2007 533

DOCUMENT NO. 25: Testimony of C. Christine Fair on U.S.-Pakistan Relations, CT-297, January 16, 2008 541

DOCUMENT NO. 26: Pakistani Public Opinion on Democracy, Islamist Militancy, and Relations with the U.S., United States Instituteof Peace Report, C. Christine Fair, RAND Corporation, Clay Ramsay, WorldPublicOpinion.org, Steve Kull, WorldPublicOpinion.org, February 2008 555

DOCUMENT NO. 27: Combating Terrorism: The United States Lacks Comprehensive Plan to Destroy the Terrorist Threat and Close the Safe Haven in Pakistan's Federally Administered Tribal Areas, GAO Report, GAO-08-622, April 2008. 593

E. OTHER PERSPECTIVES

DOCUMENT NO. 28: IAEA Report on Pakistan's National Legislation, Information Circular, INFCIRC/636, November 23, 2004 625

DOCUMENT NO. 29: Regional Implications of the Rise of Islamic Fundamentalism in Pakistan, Institute for Defence Studies Report, Kalim Bahadur, January 2006 633

DOCUMENT NO. 30: Pakistan's Political and Security Challenges, Research Paper 07/68, September 13, 2007. 653

DOCUMENT NO. 31: A Message from Sheikh Ayman al-Zawahiri to Pakistan, August 10, 2008 723

DOCUMENT NO. 32: Violence in Pakistan: Trend Analysis, IDSA Report, Alok Bansal, T. Khurshchev Singh, December 02, 2008. 739

SUBJECT INDEX 745

A. PAKISTANI LEGISLATION, AGREEMENTS, STATEMENTS, AND REPORTS

DOCUMENT NO. 1

DURAND LINE AGREEMENT

November 12, 1893

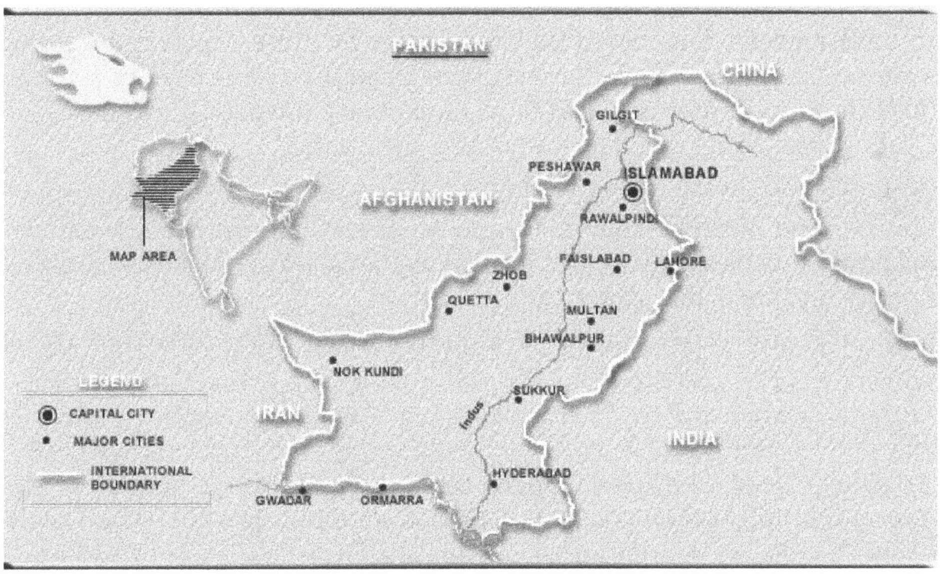

Agreement between Amir Abdur Rahman Khan, G. C. S. I., and Sir Henry Mortimer Durand, K. C. I. E., C. S. I.

Whereas certain questions have arisen regarding the frontier of Afghanistan on the side of India, and whereas both His Highness the Amir and the Government of India are desirous of settling these questions by friendly understanding, and of fixing the limit of their respective spheres of influence, so that for the future there may be no difference of opinion on the subject between the allied Governments, it is hereby agreed as follows:

The eastern and southern frontier of his Highness's dominions, from Wakhan to the Persian border, shall follow the line shown in the map attached to this agreement.

The Government of India will at no time exercise interference in the territories lying beyond this line on the side of Afghanistan, and His Highness the Amir will at no time exercise interference in the territories lying beyond this line on the side of India.

The British Government thus agrees to His Highness the Amir retaining Asmar and the valley above it, as far as Chanak. His Highness agrees, on the other hand, that he will at no time exercise interference in Swat, Bajaur, or Chitral, including the Arnawai or Bashgal valley. The British Government also agrees to leave to His Highness the Birmal tract as shown in the detailed map already given to his Highness, who relinquishes his claim to the rest of the Waziri country and Dawar. His Highness also relinquishes his claim to Chageh.

The frontier line will hereafter be laid down in detail and demarcated, wherever this may be practicable and desirable, by joint British and Afghan commissioners, whose object will be to arrive by mutual understanding at a boundary which shall adhere with the greatest possible exactness to the line shown in the map attached to this agreement, having due regard to the existing local rights of villages adjoining the frontier.

With reference to the question of Chaman, the Amir withdraws his objection to the new British cantonment and concedes to the British Governmeni the rights purchased by him in the Sirkai Tilerai water. At this part of the frontier the line will be drawn as follows:

From the crest of the Khwaja Amran range near the Psha Kotal, which remains in British territory, the line will run in such a direction as to leave Murgha Chaman and the Sharobo spring to Afghanistan, and to pass half-way between the New Chaman Fort and the Afghan outpost known locally as Lashkar Dand. The line will then pass half-way between the railway station and the hill known as the Mian Baldak, and, turning south-wards, will rejoin the Khwaja Amran range, leaving the Gwasha Post in British territory, and the road to Shorawak to the west and south of Gwasha in Afghanistan. The British Government will not exercise any interference within half a mile of the road.

The above articles of' agreement are regarded by the Government of India and His Highness the Amir of Afghanistan as a full and satisfactory settlement of all the principal differences of opinion which have arisen between them in regard to the frontier; and both the Government of India and His Highness the Amir undertake that any differences of detail, such as those which will have to be considered hereafter by the officers appointed to demarcate the boundary line, shall be settled in a friendly spirit, so as to remove for the future as far as possible all causes of doubt and misunderstanding between the two Governments.

Being fully satisfied of His Highness's goodwill to the British Government, and wishing to see Afghanistan independent and strong, the Government of India will raise no objection to the purchase and import by His Highness of munitions of war, and they will themselves grant him some help in this respect. Further, in order to mark their sense of the friendly spirit in which His Highness the Amir has entered into these negotiations, the Government of India undertake to increase by the sum of six lakhs of rupees a year the subsidy of twelve lakhs now granted to His Highness.

H. M. Durand,
Amir Abdur Rahman Khan.
Kabul, November 12, 1893.

DOCUMENT NO. 2

TASHKENT DECLARATION

January 10, 1966

The Prime Minister of India and the President of Pakistan, having met at Tashkent and having discussed the existing relations between India and Pakistan hereby declare their firm resolve to restore normal and peaceful relations between their countries and to promote understanding and friendly relations between their peoples. They consider the attainment of these objectives of vital importance for the welfare of the 600 million people of India and Pakistan.

i. The Prime Minister of India and the President of Pakistan agree that both sides will exert all efforts to create good neighbourly relations between India and Pakistan in accordance with the United Nations Charter. They reaffirm their obligation under the Charter not to have recourse to force and to settle their disputes through peaceful means. They considered that the interests of peace in their region and particularly in the Indo-Pakistan sub-continent and, indeed, the interests of the people of India and Pakistan were not served by the continuance of tension between the two countries. It was against this background that Jammu and Kashmir was discussed, and each of the sides set forth its respective position.

ii. The Prime Minister of India and the President of Pakistan have agreed that all armed personnel of the two countries shall be withdrawn not later than 25 February, 1966 to the positions they held prior to 5 August, 1965, and both sides shall observe the cease-fire terms on the cease-fire line.

iii. The Prime Minister of India and the President of Pakistan have agreed that relations between India and Pakistan shall be based on the principle of non-interference in the internal affairs of each other.

iv. The Prime Minister of India and the President of Pakistan have agreed that both sides will discourage any propaganda directed against the other country and will encourage propaganda which promotes the development of friendly relations between the two countries.

v. The Prime Minister of India and the President of Pakistan have agreed that High Commissioner of India to Pakistan and the High Commissioner of Pakistan to India will return to their posts and that the normal functioning of diplomatic missions of both countries will be restored. Both Governments shall observe the Vienna Convention of 1961 on Diplomatic Intercourse.

vi. The Prime Minister of India and the President of Pakistan have agreed to consider measures towards the restoration of economic and trade relations, communications as well as cultural exchanges between India and Pakistan, and to take measures to implement the existing agreements between India and Pakistan.

vii. The Prime Minister of India and the President of Pakistan have agreed that they will give instructions to their respective authorities to carry out the repatriation of the prisoners of war.

viii. The Prime Minister of India and the President of Pakistan have agreed that the two sides will continue the discussions of questions relating to the problems of refugees and evictions/illegal immigrations. They also agreed that both sides will create conditions which will prevent the exodus of people. They further agree to discuss the return of the property and assets taken over by either side in connection with the conflict.

ix. The Prime Minister of India and the President of Pakistan have agreed that the two sides will continue meetings both at highest and at other levels matters of direct concern to both countries. Both sides have recognised the need to set up joint Indian-Pakistani bodies which will report to their Governments in order to decide what further steps should be taken. The Prime Minister of India and the President of Pakistan record their feelings, deep appreciation and gratitude to the leaders of the Soviet Union, the Soviet Government and personally to the Chairman of the Council of Ministers of the USSR for their constructive, friendly and noble part in bringing about the present meeting which has resulted in mutually satisfactory results. They also express to the Government and friendly people of Uzbekistan their sincere thankfulness for their overwhelming reception and generous hospitality. They invite the Chairman of the Council of Ministers of the USSR to witness this declaration

Prime Minister of India
Lal Bahadur Shastri
Tashkent, 10 January 1966

President of Pakistan
Mohammad Ayub Khan

DOCUMENT NO. 3

PAKISTAN ANTI-TERRORISM (AMENDMENT) ORDINANCE, 1999

April 29, 1999

Full text of Anti-Terrorism (Amendment) Ordinance 1999, promulgated by President Rafiq Tarar on April 29, 1999

The original Anti-Terrorism Act was promulgated by then President Farooq Ahmed Leghari on August 18, 1997

We regret, the text of the original Act is not available on this site.

Whereas it is expedient to amend the Anti-terrorism Act, (XXVII of 1997), for the purposes hereinafter appearing;

And whereas the National Assembly is not in session and the President is satisfied that circumstances exist which render it necessary to take immediate action;

Now, therefore, in exercise of the powers conferred by clause (1) of Article 89 of the Constitution of the Islamic Republic of Pakistan, the President is pleased to make and promulgate the following Ordinance:-

1. Short title and commencement—

(1) This Ordinance may be called the Anti-terrorism (Amendment) Ordinance, 1999.

(2) It shall come into force at once and shall be deemed to have taken effect on the twenty-fourth day of February, 1999.

2. General Amendments, Act XXVII of 1997—In the Anti-terrorism Act, 1997 (XXVII of 1997), hereinafter referred to as the said Act,—

(a) for the words "Special Court", "a Special Court" or "the Special Court" wherever occurring the words "Anti-terrorism Court", "an Anti-terrorism Court" or "the Anti-terrorism Court" shall be substituted respectively; and

(b) for the words "Appellate Tribunal", "an Appellate Tribunal" or "the Appellate Tribunal" wherever occurring the words "High Court," "a High Court" or "the High Court" shall be substituted respectively.

3. Amendment of section 2, Act XXVII of 1997—In the said Act, in section 2,—

(a) after clause (d) the following new clause shall be inserted, namely:—

"(d, a)" "High Court" means the High Court having territorial jurisdiction in respect of the area for which an anti-terrorism court has been established; and

(b) for clause (e), the following shall be substituted, namely:-

"(e) "scheduled offence" means a terrorist or sectarian related offence as set out in this Act or the Schedule hereto."

4. Amendment of section 5, Act XXVII of 1997—In the said Act, in section 5, in sub-section (2), in clause (i), the comma and words", or in all probability is likely to commit" shall be omitted.

5. Amendment of section 6, Act XXVII of 1997—In the said Act, for section 6, the following shall be substituted, namely:—

"6. Terrorist Act—A person is said to commit a terrorist act if he,

(a) in order to, or if the effect of his actions will be to, strike terror or create a sense of fear and insecurity in the people, or any section of the people, does any act or thing by using bombs, dynamite or other explosive or inflammable substances, or such fire-arms or other lethal weapons as may be notified, or poisons or noxious gases or chemicals, in such a manner as to cause, or be likely to cause, the death of, or injury to, any person or persons, or damage to, or destruction of, property on a large scale, or a widespread disruption of supplies of services essential to the life of the community, or threatens with the use of force public servants in order to prevent them from discharging their lawful duties; or

(b) commits a scheduled offence, the effect of which will be, or be likely to be, to strike terror, or create a sense of fear and insecurity in the people, or any section of the people, or to adversely affect harmony among different sections of the people; or

(c) commits an act of gang rape, child molestation, or robbery coupled with rape as specified in the Schedule to this Act; or

(d) commits an act of civil commotion as specified in section &A."

6. Amendment of section 7, Act XXVII of 1997—In the said Act, for section 7, the following shall be substituted, namely:—

"7. Punishment for terrorist act—Whoever commits a terrorist act,—

(i) referred to in paragraph (a) of section 6, shall—

(a) if such act has resulted in the death of any person be punished with death; and

(b) in any other case, be punishable with imprisonment for a term which shall not be less than seven years but may extend to life imprisonment, and shall also be liable to fine; and

(ii) referred to in paragraphs (b) and (c) of section 6 be liable to the punishment prescribed under the relevant law."

7. Insertion of sections 7A and 7B, Act XXVII of 1997—In the said Act, after section 7, the following new sections shall be inserted, namely:—

"7A. Creation of civil commotion—"Civil commotion" means creation of internal disturbances in violation of law or intended to violate law, commencement or continuation of illegal strikes, go-slows, lock-outs, vehicles snatching or lifting, damage to or destruction of State or private property, random firing to create panic, charging *bhatta*, acts of criminal trespass (illegal *qabza*), distributing, publishing or pasting of a handbill or making graffiti or wall-chalking intended to create unrest or fear or create a threat to the security of law and order or to incite the commission of an offence punishable under Chapter VI of the Pakistan Penal Code (Act (XLV of 1860)).

7B. Punishment for creating civil commotion—Whoever commits an act of civil commotion shall be punished with rigorous imprisonment for a term which may extend to seven years, or with fine, or with both."

8. Amendment of section 10, Act XXVII of 1997—In the said Act, in section 10, the full stop at the end shall be replaced by a colon and thereafter the following proviso shall be added, namely:—

"Provided that the concerned officer shall first record in writing his reasons for such belief and serve a copy thereof either on the person or on the premises".

9. Amendment of section 13, Act XXVII of 1997—In the said Act, for section 13, the following shall be substituted, namely:—

"13. Establishment of Anti-terrorism Court—

(1) For the purpose of providing for the speedy trial of the cases referred to in sub-section (2) and sub-section (3) of section 39A, as well as of scheduled offences, the Federal Government, or if so directed by the Government, the Provincial Government may establish by notification one or more anti-terrorism courts in relation to each area.

(2) Notwithstanding anything contained in sub-section (1), if, having regard to the exigencies of the situation prevailing in a Province, the Government is of the opinion that it is expedient to establish in relation to an area, or in relation to two or more areas, in the Province, an anti-terrorism court outside the said area or areas, for the trial of offences committed in the area, or areas, it may, by notification, establish in relation to such area or areas an anti-terrorism court at such place outside the said area, or areas as may be specified in the notification.

(3) Where more anti-terrorism courts than one have been established in any area, the Government in consultation with the Chief Justice of the High Court shall designate a judge of any such court to be an administrative judge and all cases triable under this Act pertaining to the said area shall be filed before the said court and such judge may either try the cases himself, or assign any case, or cases, for trial to any other anti-terrorism court at any time prior to the framing of the charge. The cases shall be assigned to a court one case at a time:

Provided that in order to ensure that the time of the court is not wasted if for some reason a given case cannot proceed more than one case can be assigned to it at any time or from time to time.

(4) In respect of a case assigned to a court under sub-section (3), all orders made or proceedings taken before the assignment shall be deemed to have been made or taken by the court to which the case has been assigned."

10. Amendment of section 14, Act XXVII of 1997.—In the said Act, in section 14,—

(a) in sub-section (1), in clause (iii) after the word "advocate" at the end the words "of a High Court" shall be added; and

(b) for sub-section (2), the following shall be substituted, namely:-

"(2) A Judge shall be appointed for a period of two and a half years after consultation with the Chief Justice of the High Court:.

Provided that the Judge may be removed from office prior to the expiry of the said period in consultation with the Chief Justice."

11. Amendment of section 16, Act XXVII of 1997.—In the said Act, in section 16, for the words "his faith to the effect that he will decide the case honestly, faithfully according to his conscience and belief" the words "the Constitution, law and his conscience" shall be substituted.

12. Amendment of section 19, Act XXVII of 1997.—In the said Act, in section 19,—(i) for sub-section (10), the following shall be substituted, namely:-

"(10) Any accused person may be tried in his absence if the anti-terrorism court, after such inquiry as it deems fit, is satisfied that such absence is deliberate and brought about with a view to impeding the course of justice:

Provided that the accused person shall not be tried under this sub-section unless a proclamation has been published in respect of him in at least three national daily newspapers out of which one shall be in the Urdu language requiring him to appear at a specified place within seven days failing which action may also be taken against him under section 88 of the Code:

Provided further that the Court shall proceed with the trial after taking the necessary steps to appoint an advocate at the expense of the State to defend the accused person who is not before the Court.

Explanation.—An accused who is tried in his absence under this sub-section shall be deemed not to have admitted the commission of any offence for which he has been charged."; and (ii) after sub-section (11), the following new sub-section shall be inserted, namely:-

"(11A) Nothing contained in sub-section (10) or sub-section (11) shall be construed to deny the accused the right to consult or be defended by a legal practitioner of his own choice."

13. Amendment of section 24, Act XXVII of 1997.—In the said Act, section 24 shall be omitted.

14. Amendment of section 25, Act XXVII of 1997.—In the said Act, in section 25, sub-section (6) and (7) shall be omitted.

15. Amendment of section 26, Act XXVII of 1997.—In the said Act, section 26 shall be omitted.

16. Amendment of section 28, Act XXVII of 1997.—In the said Act, in section 28, in sub-section (2) the full stop at the end shall be replaced by a colon and thereafter the following proviso shall be added, namely:-

"Provided that nothing herein contained shall affect the powers of the presiding officer of the Special Court to call any witness as is available under the law."

17. Substitution of section 37, Act XXVII of 1997.—In the said Act, for section 37, the following shall be substituted, namely;-

"37. Contempt of Court.—An anti-terrorism court shall have the power to punish with imprisonment for a term which may extend to six months and with fine any person who- (a) abuses, interferes with or obstructs the process of the Court in any way or disobeys and order or direction of the Court; (b) scandalises the Court otherwise does anything which tends to bring the court or a person constituting the Court into hatred, ridicule or contempt; (c) does anything which tends to prejudice the determination of a matter pending or most likely to come up before the Court; or (d) does anything which, by any other law, constitutes contempt of court.

Explanation.—In this section, "Court" means anti-terrorism court."

18. Insertion of section 39A, Act XXVII of 1997.—In the said Act, after section 39, the following new section shall be inserted, namely:-

"39A. Repeal—(1) The Pakistan Armed Forces (Acting in Aid of the Civil Power) Ordinance 1998 (XII of 1998), as amended by the Pakistan Armed Forces (Acting in aid of the Civil Power) (Amendment) Ordinance, 1998 (XIII of 1998), and the Pakistan Armed Forces (Acting in Aid the Civil Power) Second Amendment) Ordinance, 1998 (XVII of 1997) (hereinafter referred to as the repealed Ordinance), is hereby repealed.

(2) All cases, including cases before a court of appeals, which were pending under the repealed Ordinance shall stand transferred to the anti-terrorism

court having jurisdiction under the Act and such court shall, (a) in cases which have been transferred from a trial court, continue the trial from the stage which the cases had reached; and (b) in cases which have been transferred from a court of appeals decide the same other basis of the evidence earlier recorded after hearing the parties.

(3) Any judgement given or sentence passed by a trial court or a court of appeals convened under section 3 of the repealed Ordinance, except cases in which sentence of death was passed and has been executed, shall have no effect and all such cases shall stand transferred to the anti-terrorism court having jurisdiction under the Act for decision after hearing the parties on the basis of the evidence earlier recorded.

(4) In respect of a case transferred to a court by virtue of sub-section (2) or sub-section (3), the court shall not, by reason of the said transfer, be bound to recall and rehear any witness who have given evidence before the transfer and may act on the evidence already recorded by or produced before the court from which the case is so transferred.

(5) Nothing contained in sub-section (4) shall affect the power of the court to recall any witness or rehear any evidence as is available under the law."

19. Amendment of the Schedule Act XXVII of 1997.—In the said Act, in the Schedule, after entry at serial No. 4, the following new entry shall be added, namely:-

"5. Any offence including an offence punishable under the Pakistan Arms Ordinance, 1965

(W. P. Ord. XX of 1965), committed conjointly with any other offence punishable under this Act."

DOCUMENT NO. 4

ANTI-TERRORISM (AMENDMENT) ORDINANCE, 2002

November 18, 2002

[President Pervez Musharraf on November 16, 2002, promulgated the Anti-Terrorism (Amendment) Ordinance 2002. Following is the text of the Ordinance that came into force immediately]

WHEREAS it is expedient further to amend the Anti-terrorism Act, 1997 (XXVII of 1997), for the purposes hereinafter appearing; AND WHEREAS the President is satisfied that circumstances exists which render it necessary to take immediate action;

NOW, THEREFORE, in pursuance of the Proclamation of Emergency of the fourteenth day of October, 1999, and the Provisional Constitution Order No. 1 of 1999, read with the Provisional Constitution (Amendment) Order No. 9 of 1999, and in exercise of all powers enabling him in that behalf, the President of the Islamic Republic of Pakistan is pleased to make and promulgate the following Ordinance:

1 - Short title and commencement: (1) This Ordinance may be called the Anti-terrorism (Amendment) Ordinance, 2002. (2) It shall come into force at once.

2 - Insertion of new section, Act XVII of 1997.—In the Anti terrorism Act, 1997 (XXVII of 1997), hereinafter referred to as the said Act, after section 11E, the following new Section shall be inserted, namely:- "11EE. Security for good behaviour.—

(1) Whenever the Federal or Provincial Government on an information received from any source that any person is an activist, office-bearer or an associate of an organisation kept under observation under section 11D or proscribed under section 11E, or in any way concerned or suspected to be concerned with such organisation or affiliated with any group or organisation suspected to be involved in terrorism or sectarianism, such Government may notify the name of such person or person in a list entered in the Fourth Schedule.

(2) Where a person's name is listed in the Fourth Schedule, the Federal or Provincial Government, as the case may be, without prejudice to any other action which may lie against such person under this Act or any other law for the time being in force, may take following actions and exercise following powers, namely:- (a) require such person to execute a bond with one or more sureties to the satisfaction of the District police Officer in the territorial limits of which the said person ordinarily resides, or carried on business, for his good behaviour and not to involve in any act of terrorism or in any manner advance the objectives of the organisation referred to in sub-section (1) for such period not exceeding three years and in such amount as may be specified: Provided that where he fails to execute the bond or cannot produce a surety or sureties to the satisfaction of the District Police Officer order him to be detained and produced within twenty-four hours before a court which shall order him to be detained in prison until he executes the bond or until a satisfactory surety or sureties if required, are available, or failing that the term of the order under clause (a) expires: Provided further that where he is a minor, the bond executed by a surety or sureties only may be accepted; (b) require any such person to seek prior permission from the officer in charge of the Police Station of the concerned area before moving from his permanent place of residence for any period of time and to keep him informed about the place he would be visiting and the persons, he would be meeting during the stay; (c) require: (i) that his movements to be restricted to any place or area specified in the order; (ii) him to report himself at such times and places and in such mode as may be specified in the order; (iii) him to comply with both the directions; and (iv) that he shall not reside within areas specified in the order; (d) direct that he shall not visit or go within surroundings specified in the order including any of the under mentioned places, without the written permission of the officer in charge of the Police Station within whose jurisdiction such place is situated, namely:- (i) schools, colleges and other institutions where persons under twenty-one years of age or women are given education or other training or are housed permanently or temporarily; (ii) theatres, cinemas, fairs, amusement parks, hotels, clubs, restaurants, tea shops and other place of public entertainment or resort; (iii) airports, railway stations, bus stands, telephone exchanges, television stations, radio stations and other such places; (iv) public or private parks and gardens and public or private playing fields; and (v) the scene of any public meeting or procession of any assemblage of the public whether in an enclosed place or otherwise in connection with any public event festival or other celebrations; (e) check and probe the assets of such persons or their immediate family members i.e., parents, wives and children through police or any other Government agency, which

shall exercise the powers as are available to it under the relevant law for the purposes of the investigation, to ascertain whether assets and sources off income are legitimate and are being spent on lawful objectives: Provided that no order under clause (d) or (e) above shall be made operative for a period of more than three years; and (f) monitor and keep surveillance over the activities of such person through police or any other government agency or any person or authority designated for the purpose.

(3) Any person whose name has been notified in the list entered in the Fourth Schedule under sub-section (1) or is aggrieved by any direction or order of the Federal or Provincial Government made under sub-section (2), may within thirty days of such notification, direction or order, prefer an appeal to the Federal or Provincial Government, as the case may be, and such Government after providing an opportunity of being heard to such person decide the appeal within thirty days.

(4) Any person who violates any direction or order of the Federal or Provincial Government or any terms of bond referred to in sub-section (2), shall be punishable with imprisonment of either description for a term which may extend to three years, or with fine, or with both."

3 - Insertion of new section, Act XXVII of 1997.—In the said Act, after section 11EE, the following new section shall be inserted, namely:- "11EE. Power to arrest and detain suspected persons. (1) Government if satisfied that with a view to prevent any person whose name is included in the list referred to section 11EE, it is necessary so to do, may, by order in writing, direct to arrest and detain, in such custody as may be specified, such person for such period as may be specified in the order, and Government if satisfied that for the aforesaid reasons it is necessary so to do, may, extend from time to time the period of such detention for a total period not exceeding twelve months. (2) The provisions of Article 10 of the Constitution of the Islamic Republic of Pakistan shall mutatis mutandis apply to the arrest and detention of a person ordered under sub-section (1)."

4 - Insertion of new Schedule, Act, XXVII of 1997. In the said Act, after the Third Schedule and the entries relating thereto, the following shall be added, namely:- THE FOURTH SCHEDULE (See section 11EE).

General Pervez Musharraf
President
Source: ***Jang***, November 18, 2002

DOCUMENT NO. 5

ANTI-TERRORISM (SECOND AMENDMENT) ACT, 2004

ACT No. II of 2005

November 1, 2005

An Act further to amend the Anti-terrorism Act. 1997

WHEREAS it is expedient further to amend the Anti-terrorism Act, 1997 (XXVII of 1997), for the purposes hereinafter appearing;

It is hereby enacted as follows:

1. **Short title and commencement.**—

(1) This Act may be called the Anti-terrorism (Second Amendment) Act, 2004.

(2) It shall come into force at once.

2. **Amendment of section 6, Act XXVII of 1997.**—In the Antiterrorism Act; 1997 (XXVII of 1997), hereinafter referred to as the said Act, in section 6, in sub-section (2), after clause (e), the following new clause shall be inserted, namely:-

"(ee) involves use of explosives by any device including bomb blast;".

3. **Amendment of section 7, Act XXVII of 1997.**—In the said Act, in section 7,—

(i) in clause (b), for the words "five years" the words "ten years" shall be substituted and for the words "fourteen years" the words "imprisonment for life" shall be substituted;

(ii) in clause (c), for the words "seven years" the words "ten years" shall be substituted;

(iii) in clause (d), for the words "and not exceeding fourteen years" the words "but may extend to imprisonment for life" shall be substituted;

(iv) after clause (f), the following new clause shall be inserted, namely:

"(ff) the act of terrorism committed falls under section 6(2) (ee), shall be punishable with imprisonment which shall not be less than fourteen years but may extend to imprisonment for life;"

(v) in clause (g), for the words "six months" the words "two years" shall be substituted and for the words "three years" the words "five years" shall be substituted;

(vi) in clause (h), for the words "one year" the words "five years" shall be substituted and for the words "and not more than ten years" the words "but may extend to imprisonment for life" shall be substituted; and

(vii) in clause (i), for the words "six months" the words "five years" shall be substituted and for the words "five years" the words "ten years" shall be substituted.

4. **Amendment of section 11G, Act XXVII of 1997.**—In the said Act, in section IIG, for sub-section (2), the following shall be substituted, namely:-

"(2) A person who commits an offence under sub-section (1) shall be liable to imprisonment for a term which may extend to five years, or with fine, or with both.".

5. **Amendment of section 11N, Act XXVII of 1997.**—In the said Act, in section 11 N, for the words "six months" the words "five years" shall be substituted and for the words "five years" the words "ten years" shall be substituted.

6. **Amendment of section 11V, Act XXVII of 1997.**—In the said Act, in section 11 V, in sub-section (2), for the words "imprisonment for a maximum term of seven years" the words "imprisonment for life" shall be substituted.

7. **Amendment of section 11 W, Act XXVII of 1997.**—In the said Act, in section 11 W, for sub-section (2), the following shall be substituted, namely:-

"(2) Any person quality of an offence under sub-section (1) shall be punishable on conviction with imprisonment which may extend to five years and with fine.".

8. **Amendment of section 11X, Act XXVII of 1997.**—In the said Act, in section 11 X,—

(i) in sub section (2), for the words "six months" the words "five years" shall be substituted and for the words "five years" the words "ten years" shall be substituted; and

(ii) in sub-section (3), for the words "six months", the words "five years" shall be substituted and for the words "three years" the words "ten years" shall be substituted.

9. Amendment of section 19, Act XXVII of 1997.—In the said Act, in section 19,—

(i) for sub-section (8), the following shall be substituted, namely:-

"(8) An anti-terrorism Court shall not give more than two consecutive adjournments during the trial of the case. If the defence counsel does not appear after two consecutive adjournments, the Court may appoint a State Counsel with at least seven years standing in criminal matters for the defence of the accused from the panel of. advocates maintained by the Court for the purpose in consultation with the Government and shall proceed with the trial of the case.".

(ii) after sub-section (8) substituted as aforesaid, the following new sub-section shall be inserted, namely:-

"(8a) Non-compliance with the provisions of sub-section (8) may render the presiding officer of the Court liable to disciplinary action by the concerned High Court.

(8b) Notwithstanding anything contained in section 7 of the Explosive Substances Act, 1908 (VI of 1908), or any other law for the time being in force, if the consent or sanction of the appropriate authority, where required, is not received within thirty days of the submission of challan in the Court, the same shall be deemed to have been given or accorded and the Court shall proceed with the trial of the case.".

10. Substitution of section 21G, Act XXVII of 1997.—In the said Act, in section 21 G, after the word "tried" the word "exclusively" shall be inserted.

11. Amendment of section 21L, Act XXVII of 1997.—In the said Act, in section 21 L, for the words "six months" the words "five years" and for the words "five years" the words "ten years" shall be substituted.

12. Amendment of section 25, Act XXVII of 1997.— In the said Act, in section 25, after sub-section (8), the following new sub-sections shall be added, namely:-

"(9) For the purposes of hearing appeals under this section each High Court shall establish a Special Bench of Benches consisting of not less than two Judges.

(10) While hearing an appeal, the Bench shall not grant more than two consecutive adjournments.".

13. Insertion of new section, act XXVII of 1997.—In the said Act, after section 28, the following new section shall be inserted, namely:-

"28A. Impounding of passport of person charge-sheeted under the Act.—Notwithstanding anything contained in any other law for the time being in force, the passport of a person, who is accused of an offence under this Act, shall be deemed to have been impounded for such period as the Court may deem fit.".

14. Amendment of the Third Schedule, Act XXVII of 1997.—In the said Act, in the Third Schedule, after paragraph 3, the following new paragraph shall be added, namely:-

"4. Without prejudice to the generality of the above paragraphs, the Antiterrorism Court to the exclusion of any other Court shall try the offences relating to the following, namely:-

(i) Abduction or kidnapping for ransom;

(ii) use of fire arms or explosives by any device, including bomb blast in a mosque, imambargah, church, temple or any other place of worship, whether or not any hurt or damage is caused thereby; or

(iii) firing or use of explosives by any device, including bomb blast in the court premises."

———

SHAHIQ A. KHAN,
Secretary.

DOCUMENT NO. 6

NORTH WEST FRONTIER PROVINCE GOVERNMENT'S AGREEMENT WITH THE TALIBAN

May 22, 2008

Presented below are points of the peace agreement between the North West Frontier Province Government and Swat-based Taliban militants on May 21, 2008:

1: Taliban of Swat will accept the writ of the provincial and central governments of Pakistan and will remain in the ambit of that

2: Shariat-e-Muhammadi will be implemented in Malakand Division

3: No one will attack other's religion

4: Prisoners will be released after reviewing the cases against them

5: Government machinery, law enforcement agencies, government officials, buildings and installations, police stations, policemen, police lines, army, Frontier Corps, Frontier Constabulary, bridges, roads, and electricity installations will not be attacked; there will be a complete ban on keeping private militias, there will be no suicide attacks, there will be no blasts in personal or governmental buildings, and there will be no remote-controlled bomb blasts

6: Army withdrawal will be gradual keeping in view the security situation in the area

7: Non-local militants will be immediately handed over to the government. Attacks on barber shops and markets visited by women should be stopped

8: Government will compensate the deserving people affected by the operation in Swat

9: There will be no ban on health teams administering vaccination or drops to children against diseases like polio. There will be no ban on girls' education

10: There will be complete ban on display of arms and only arms having licence would be allowed

11: Kidnapping and car lifting should be condemned and eliminated. All centres used for training militants and use of explosives must be eliminated

12: Speeches will be allowed only on that FM radio having licence

13: Local Taliban will cooperate with government in investigations of cases against those involved in murders, dacoities and kidnapping

14: The government will take action against thieves, dacoits, kidnappers and others involved in such crimes

15: Imam Dheri will be converted into an Islamic university under the management of a committee comprising representatives of government and Taliban

16: Minister for Environment Wajid Ali Khan, Dr Shamsher Ali Khan, DIG of Malakand, and DPO of Swat from the government's side and Muhammad Amin, Ali Bakht, Muslim Khan, Mehmood Khan and Nisar Khan from Taliban side are members of the committee to oversee implementation of the agreement.

Source: ***Daily Times***, May 22, 2008

DOCUMENT NO. 7

INDIA-PAKISTAN JOINT STATEMENT

May 21, 2008

A Joint Statement was issued in Islamabad on May 21, 2008 after the Foreign Minister level review of the Fourth Round of Composite Dialogue between India and Pakistan. Presented below is the full text of the statement:

1. The Foreign Minister of Pakistan, Makhdoom Shah Mahmood Qureshi, and External Affairs Minister of India, Mr. Pranab Mukherjee, met in Islamabad on 21 May 2008 to review the progress made in the Fourth Round of Pakistan-India Composite Dialogue. This was preceded by a meeting between the Foreign Secretary of Pakistan, Mr. Salman Bashir and Foreign Secretary of India, Mr. Shivshankar Menon, on 20 May 2008.

2. The talks were held in a friendly and constructive atmosphere.

3. They reviewed the progress made in the Fourth Round of the Composite Dialogue encompassing (i) Peace and Security, including CBMs; (ii) Jammu and Kashmir; (iii) Siachen; (iv) Sir Creek; (v) Wullar Barrage/Tulbul Navigation Project; (vi) Terrorism and Drug Trafficking; (vii) Economic and Commercial Cooperation; and (viii) Promotion of Friendly Exchanges in Various Fields.

4. They noted the positive contribution to improvement of relations by the Composite Dialogue process since its resumption after the joint statement of 6 January 2004 and the subsequent Summit Statements of 25 September 2004, 18 April 2005, 14 September 2005 and 16 September 2006. The Ministers reaffirmed their determination not to let terrorism impede the peace process and take all necessary steps to eliminate this scourge against humanity. They further resolved to carry forward the peace process and to maintain its momentum.

5. The Ministers noted that in 2007 and over the course of the Fourth Round of Composite Dialogue there had been a number of important bilateral achievements, including:

- MoU to increase the frequencies, designated airlines and points of call in either country.

- Agreement for the trucks from one side to cross the border up to designated points on the other side at the Wagah-Attari border.
- Increase in frequency of Delhi- Lahore bus service from two to three trips per week.
- Signing of Agreement on 'Reducing the Risk from Accidents relating to Nuclear Weapons'.
- MoU between the Securities and Exchange Board of India (SEBI) and Securities and Exchange Commission of Pakistan (SECP) to facilitate the sharing of information between two agencies.
- Completion of the Joint Survey of Sir Creek and adjoining areas.
- Two meetings of the Joint Anti-Terrorism Mechanism.

6. The two sides signed the Agreement on Consular Access, which was finalised during the Fourth round of Composite Dialogue.

7. They exchanged views on the issue of Jammu and Kashmir and agreed to continue discussions to build on convergences and narrow down divergences. They also agreed to continue with the implementation of Cross-LoC CBMs with a view to enhancing interaction and cooperation across the LoC. In this regard, they decided:

a) To increase the frequency of Muzaffarabad-Srinagar and Rawalkot-Poonch Bus service from a fortnightly to a weekly basis.

b) To finalize modalities for intra-Kashmir trade and truck service as early as possible.

c) To implement other measures to expand and facilitate travel a meeting of Working Group on Cross-LoC CBMs would be convened within two months.

8. They reaffirmed the importance of ceasefire in place since November 2003 and the commitment of both sides to cooperate to safeguard it.

9. They agreed that progress has been made under the Composite Dialogue process on promoting a stable environment of Peace and Security including CBMs. The Expert Groups on Nuclear and Conventional CBMs should consider existing and additional proposals by both sides with a view to developing further confidence building measures in the nuclear and conventional fields.

10. Both sides exchanged views on Siachen and reiterated their commitment to seeking an early amicable solution.

11. Both sides expressed satisfaction on the progress made on Sir Creek, with the completion of the joint survey, the exchange of maps, and the discussions thereafter. They agreed to further facilitate the process for an early resolution of this issue.

12. Both sides reiterated their commitment to fight terrorism in all its forms and manifestations, and re-emphasized the need for effective steps for the complete elimination of this menace. In this context, it was agreed to continue cooperation in the Joint Anti-Terrorism Mechanism whose next meeting would be held within two months. Both sides agreed to refrain from hostile propaganda.

13. Both sides emphasized the need for further strengthening cooperation to eliminate drug trafficking and welcomed the finalization of an MOU on Cooperation between Pakistan's Anti-Narcotics Force and Narcotics Control Board of India.

14. Both sides reiterated the importance of enhancing mutually beneficial economic and commercial cooperation and agreed to discuss further steps for facilitating trade and redressing the trade imbalance. In this regard, Indian and Pakistan Railway officials would meet in June for resolving all technical issues to enable increase in to and fro freight movement. They also agreed to facilitate the process of early opening of bank branches in the two countries.

15. Both sides appreciated the work being done by the Judicial Committee on Prisoners, which will meet in Pakistan shortly; welcomed the finalization of the Consular Access Agreement that will help addressing humanitarian aspects relating to persons under detention in each other's country and; agreed to provide on a regular basis updated and comprehensive list of prisoners in each other jails.

16. Both sides agreed to the need for promoting friendly exchanges between the two countries.

17. Both sides agreed to the early finalization of the Visa Agreement which will help liberalize the visa regime and facilitate people-to-people contacts.

18. The two Ministers reiterated their commitment to the Iran-Pakistan-India gas pipeline project and had a useful exchange of views in this regard.

19. The two Foreign Ministers also exchanged views on promoting the Pakistan-India peace process, reinvigoration of SAARC and agreed to work towards promoting regional cooperation for enabling South Asia to realize its full development potential. It was agreed to work for promoting sustainable development and food and energy security.

20. It was decided that the two Foreign Secretaries will launch the Fifth Round of the Composite Dialogue in New Delhi in July 2008.

21. The External Affairs Minister of India, Mr. Pranab Mukherjee, called on the President and the Prime Minister of Pakistan.

Islamabad
May 21, 2008
Source: Ministry of External Affairs, Government of India, Delhi.

DOCUMENT NO. 8

PAKISTAN'S 2005 REPORT TO THE UN ON ITS COUNTER-TERRORISM EFFORTS, PART 1

UN Security Council Resolution S/2001/1310

January 10, 2002

Distr.: General
10 January 2002
English
Original: French

Letter dated 27 December 2001 from the Chairman of the Security Council Committee established pursuant to resolution 1373 (2001) concerning counter-terrorism addressed to the President of the Security Council

The Counter-Terrorism Committee has received the attached report from Pakistan, submitted pursuant to paragraph 6 of resolution 1373 (2001) (see annex).

I should be grateful if you would arrange for this letter and its annex to be circulated as a document of the Security Council.

(*Signed*) Jeremy **Greenstock**
Chairman
Counter-Terrorism Committee

Annex

[Original: English]

Letter dated 27 December 2001 from the Permanent Representative of Pakistan to the United Nations addressed to the Chairman of the Committee established pursuant to resolution 1373 (2001) concerning counter-terrorism

On instructions from my Government, I have the honour to enclose the report of the Islamic Republic of Pakistan to the Counter-Terrorism Committee pursuant to paragraph 6 of Security Council resolution 1373 (2001) (see enclosure).

(*Signed*) Shamshad **Ahmad**

Enclosure

Report of the Islamic Republic of Pakistan to the UNSC Counter Terrorism Committee on Implementation of UNSC Resolution 1373

I. Preliminary Remarks

Pakistan is committed to combating terrorism in all its forms and manifestations as a matter of national policy and has undertaken to fully implement UNSC Resolution 1373.

Being itself a victim of terrorism for over last two decades, Pakistan had taken the following anti-terrorism measures prior to the events of 11 September 2001:

a) Enactment of Anti-Terrorism Act in 1997 which was later amended in August 2001. Under this Act, special courts have been established for speedy trial of those involved in terrorist activities.

b) Signing of extradition treaties with twenty-seven countries. Pursuant to the treaties, Pakistan is cooperating actively in tracking down and nabbing terrorists and other criminals. In recent years, wanted terrorists have been arrested and handed over to the United States, Jordan and Egypt.

c) Sharing of relevant information with other countries in the fight against terrorism as well as active liaison with the Interpol.

d) Cracking down on extremist elements. Two organizations involved in sectarian violence, namely, Lashkar-e-Jhangvi and Sipah-e-Muhammad were banned in August 2001. The activities of other suspected organizations have been monitored.

e) Launching of a de-weaponization programme this year. Under this drive, over 125,990 illegal small weapons have been collected so far.

f) Of the twelve United Nations anti-terrorism Conventions, Pakistan has ratified/acceded to nine. The remaining three Conventions are being examined by an inter-Ministerial Committee.

Pakistan condemned the 11 September terrorist attacks in the United States of America in the strongest terms. President Pervez Musharraf assured President George Bush of Pakistan's unstinted support and cooperation in the fight against terrorism. Pakistan, despite the anticipated economic costs to itself, decided to play the role of a frontline state in the fight against terrorism and has taken the following measures since the events of September 11:

a) The security agencies throughout the country have been put on high alert to prevent possible terrorist acts.

b) Border security has been tightened. Pakistan's borders are long, porous and mostly run through inhospitable and harsh terrain. Despite these factors and severe resource constraints, Pakistan has beefed up security along the borders, especially along the Tora Bora region of the Pakistan-Afghanistan border. A number of terrorists belonging to the Al-Qaida group and other suspects were arrested recently by Pakistan's border guards. While doing so, a number of them lost their lives.

c) Security at the airports has been strengthened. Security measures include more rigorous checking of passengers and careful screening of cargo. Now a more restrictive visa policy has been enforced.

d) Pursuant to UNSC resolutions 1267,1333 and 1373, Pakistan has frozen the assets and accounts of a number of entities found involved in terrorist activities. The State Bank has issued directives and advisories toward this end.

e) A Working Group to curb money laundering has been established comprising representatives from the Ministry of Finance, Ministry of Law and Justice, Ministry of Foreign Affairs, Ministry of Interior, State Bank of Pakistan, the Securities and Exchange Commission (SECP), National Accountability Bureau and Federal Investigating Agency.

f) A plan is being prepared to bring Deeni Madaris/religious schools in the mainstream of the education system. In this context, a separate Board has been instituted in 2001 through an ordinance with the task of preparing contemporary curriculum for Deeni Madaris/religious schools.

g) A national focal point has been established in the Ministry of Foreign Affairs headed by Additional Foreign Secretary in charge of United Nations Affairs to coordinate efforts for implementation of the United Nations resolutions on terrorism and to maintain liaison with the Counter Terrorism Committee (CTC) of the UN Security Council through Pakistan's Permanent Mission to the United Nations in New York.

II. Detailed Implementation Report

Information according to the format outlined in the guidance note dated 29 October 2001 of the Chairman, CTC is as follows:

Operative Paragraph 1

Sub-paragraph (a)—What measures if any have been taken to prevent and suppress the financing of terrorist acts in addition to those listed in your responses to questions on 1(b) to (d)?

The following measures have been taken for the suppression of financing of terrorism:

a) Administrative orders have been issued by the State Bank of Pakistan (SBP) to all commercial banks to freeze accounts of the organizations suspected of involvement in terrorist activities as per the lists received from the UN Security Council, Asian Development Bank (ADB) and from United States Embassy in Pakistan.

b) To evolve a legal framework for effectively curbing money laundering, the Ministry of Finance has constituted a Working Group comprising representatives of Ministry of Law and Justice, Ministry of Foreign Affairs, Ministry of Interior, State Bank of Pakistan, the Securities and Exchange Commission (SECP), National Accountability Bureau and Federal Investigating Agency. The Working Group has following terms of reference:

(i) To define the term money laundering and identify the loopholes in the system, including channels used for questionable cash transactions.

(ii) To examine international anti-money laundering standards with the aim of drafting a legal framework against money laundering.

(iii) To establish a Suspicious Transaction Detecting System (STDS) within banking industry for monitoring of accounts on regular basis and to devise explicit policy to ensure transparent business transactions.

(iv) To develop an effective monitoring system within State Bank of Pakistan to curb money laundering.

The first meeting of the Working Group was held on 10 December 2001 in Islamabad, which decided that the State Bank of Pakistan (SBP) will develop a draft legislation based on the recommendations of the Financial Action Task Force (FATF).

Sub-paragraph (b-d)

State Bank of Pakistan, being the country's regulatory and supervisory authority, has been initiating measures and regulating the banks as well as Non-Banking Financial Institutions (NBFIs) that fall within its jurisdiction. With a view to prevent, suppress and curtail terrorism and money laundering activities, the State Bank has focused both on formulating rules and regulations and ensuring compliance thereto. The measures taken include issuance of prudential regulation for banks, formulation of NBFIs Rules of Business, issuance of directives and advisories on freezing of accounts, educating the supervisory staff of banks, coordinating action with Ministry of Finance and Ministry of Foreign Affairs on relevant issues, ensuring that the banks and the NBFIs possess *'know your customer rules*, etc. The on-site examiners evaluate the 'Know Your Customer' policies and procedures during on-site inspection of the institutions and report any deviations/ violations from the Prudential Regulations and Rules of Business. Given below is the summary of the measures initiated so far:

Prudential Regulation No. XI

a. Under this regulation, banks have been directed to make all reasonable efforts to determine the true identity of every would-be account holder and to institute effective procedures and methods for obtaining proper identification from new customers.

Prudential Regulation No. XII

b. This regulation provides guidelines to safeguard banks against their involvement in money laundering activities and other unlawful trades. It stresses upon the banks to make reasonable efforts to identify the customer. Such efforts include formulation of policies and procedures. The regulation emphasizes on the banks to ensure that business is conducted in conformity with high ethical standards. It advises the banks not to offer services or provide active assistance in transactions which in their opinion are associated with money derived from illegal activities.

The regulation asks the banks to establish specific procedures for ascertaining customer's status and their source of earnings, for monitoring of accounts on regular basis. It also requires the banks to view with suspicion and properly investigate transactions which are out of character with the normal operation of the account involving heavy deposits/ withdrawals/transfers. It not only advises the banks to arrange suitable training to the staff for effective implementation of bank's policy and procedures but also to make arrangements for setting up internal audit systems to ensure test checking and compliance. The regulation contains the instructions, framed on these principles, which are the essence of FATF recommendations.

Rules of Business for Non-Banking Financial Institutions 22

c. The rule provides for similar guidelines for NBFIs as provided for in the above-mentioned Prudential Regulation for banks for the prevention of criminal use of NBFIs for the purpose of money laundering and other unlawful trade.

Freezing of Accounts

d. The State Bank of Pakistan has been issuing directives/advisories to Banks/NBFIs for freezing of accounts in compliance with UN Security Council resolutions. All Banks and NBFIs are advised to confirm compliance with the instructions of SBP.

Any Bank/NBFI found violating regulations, rules of business and directives is penalized. Violation may also lead to calling of explanation from the Chief Executive/President of Banks/NBFIs and initiation of administrative and legal action against violators.

Compliance with Core Principles

e. The Core Principles (CPs) for effective Banking Supervision developed by the Basel Committee on Banking Supervision have become a global standard for prudential regulation and supervision. Core Principle 15 requires banking supervisors to determine that banks have adequate policies, practices and procedures in place, including strict "know your customer" rule, which promote high ethical and professional standards in the financial sector and prevent the Banks being used, intentionally or unintentionally, by criminal elements. All the Banks are compliant with the said principle.

Working Group

f. On the initiative and suggestion of Governor SBP, a Working Group has been constituted. This Working Group is headed by Ministry of Finance and includes representatives of Ministry of Law and Justice, Ministry of Foreign Affairs, Ministry of Interior, State Bank of Pakistan, the Securities and Exchange Commission (SECP), National Accountability Bureau and Federal Investigating Agency. The Working Group has been assigned the task to draft legal provisions in order to establish an institutional framework for curbing money laundering. The group will provide platform for the cooperation/coordination of different agencies engaged in combating money laundering and related activities. It will also facilitate international cooperation with anti-money laundering institutions.

Operative Paragraph 2

Sub-paragraph (a)—What legislation or other measures are in place to give effect to this sub-paragraph? In particular, what offences in your country prohibit (i) recruitment to terrorist groups and (ii) the supply of weapons to terrorists? What other measures help prevent such activities?

The Anti-Terrorism Act of 1997 was adopted with the aim of preventing terrorist acts, sectarian violence and in order to ensure speedy trials of those involved in heinous offences. In August 2001, the Act was further amended to enlarge its scope.

Under the amended Act, terrorism is a punishable offence and abetting terrorism, including membership of terrorist groups and recruitment and support for such groups, is an offence.

Since last year, the Government has taken a number of arms control measures, the salient points of which are summarized below:

a. On 1 March 2000, a ban was imposed on brandishing/display of weapons in public. Cases were registered against defaulters and strict punishments administered.

b. On 15 February 2001, a ban was imposed on the issuance of arms licenses.

c. On 1 June 2001, an arms recovery campaign was launched. During the amnesty period from 5-20 June 2001, 87,000 weapons were surrendered voluntarily, while 38,990 weapons were recovered during post amnesty period.

d. In the post amnesty period, 21,163 raids have been conducted and 22,936 cases have been registered and 24,081 arrests have been made. So far 445 cases have been disposed off (Convicted 354 & acquitted 91). 19,826 cases are still pending.

e. A positive list of weapons has been approved. In future arms licenses will be issued only for the weapons mentioned in the positive list.

f. Surrender of illicit Arms Act, 1991 has been strictly enforced throughout Pakistan from 20 June 2001. Severe punishments have been prescribed under the Act, which includes life imprisonment and confiscation of property both moveable and immovable. Minimum punishment is three years imprisonment. Under this Act, illicit arms include cannons, all types of explosive substances, containers, grenades, bombs and shells, fire-arms, rifles, carbines, muskets, shotguns, revolvers, pistols and appliances used for the silencing of fire-arms. The Act contains provisions for reward for those who help in the successful recovery of illicit arms.

g. Re-registration/revalidation of arms in Islamabad and the Province of Punjab will be started as model projects with the assistance of UNDP. The following actions will be completed before issuance of new arms licenses:

i. Creation of database of Arms Dealers.

ii. Computerization of old record of Arms Licenses.

iii. Re-registration /revalidation of existing Arms Licenses.

iv. Introduction of new License book with security features.

h. In the third phase, licenses issued in the past in respect of all Prohibited Bore Arms will be cancelled.

Sub-paragraph (b)—What other steps are being taken to prevent the commission of terrorist acts, and in particular, what early warning mechanisms exist to allow exchange of information with other states?

The Anti-Terrorism Act of 1997 as amended in August 2001 provides the legal framework to deal with terrorism in all aspects. The Government has taken further steps against sectarian violence in the country which are as follows:

a. A Task Force has been constituted by the Ministry of Interior on sectarian harmony. On the recommendation of the Task Force, the Federal Cabinet recently approved the following Plan of Action:

i) Setting up of Commission on Religious Harmony comprising the Minister for Religious Affairs, religious scholars and heads of religious institutions;

ii) Constitution of Boards consisting of different sects at Provincial level for promotion of sectarian/communal harmony;

iii) Reactivation of Provincial Intelligence Coordination Committees;

iv) Establishment of Provincial Special Task Forces;

v) Establishment of Provincial Conciliation Committees comprising leaders of Shia and Sunni sects as members to seek the release of innocent persons falsely implicated in sectarian cases;

vi) Launching of a sustained media campaign to foster sectarian harmony;

vii) Building national consensus against sectarian militancy through open and candid debates with the involvement of NGOs;

viii) Constitution of a group of religious and security experts to work in coordination with the National Crisis Management and Control Centre (NCM & CC) set up in the Ministry of Interior;

ix) Creation of National Data Base on sectarian issues containing complete information about sectarian parties, leaders, activists, criminals, sectarian cases etc. NCM & CC has been tasked to prepare a blue print;

x) Review of old cases under Blasphemy laws by the conciliation committees along with other sectarian cases;

xi) Requiring of prior permission from local administration for convening religious functions outside Mosques and other religious places;

xii) Taking action against extremist religious leaders and workers;

xiii) Strict enforcement of law against provocative religious writings;

xiv) Strict enforcement of the provisions of Regulation and Control of Loudspeakers and Sound Amplifier Ordinance 1965;

xv) Ensuring strict enforcement of the provisions of Chapter 15 of the Pakistan Penal Code relating to offenses against religion.

Measures taken for sharing information and early warning mechanisms are listed under response to Operative Para 2 (f).

Sub-paragraph (c)—What legislation or procedures exist for denying safe haven to terrorists, such as laws for excluding or expelling the types of individuals referred to in this sub-paragraph? It would be helpful if States supplied examples of any relevant action taken.

The Anti-Terrorism Act, 1997 (as amended in August 2001) contains detailed provisions for the suppression of terrorism. In particular, Sections 11(A) to 11(X) prohibit organizations involved in terrorist activities and bars membership and support to such organizations. The Act also provides for the establishment of anti-terrorist courts for conducting speedy trials of those involved in sabotage, subversion and terrorist offences.

Sub-paragraph (d)—What legislation or procedures exist to prevent terrorists acting from your territory against other states or citizens? It would be helpful if States supplied examples of any relevant action taken.

The financial measures taken by the Government of Pakistan have been mentioned at Operative Para 1. The Anti-Terrorism Act of 1997 (Amended in 2001) provides a legal framework for the suppression of terrorist offences.

As earlier discussed, Pakistan has extradition treaties with twenty-seven countries. It has been actively cooperating with the international community, especially the United States, in combating terrorism. A number of suspected terrorists have been extradited/deported to the United States and Jordan. Besides, extremist organizations like Lashkar-e-Jhangvi and Sipah-e-Muhammad have been banned and the accounts of Ummah Tameer-e-Nau and Lashkar-e-Taiba have been frozen.

Sub-paragraph (e)—What steps have been taken to establish terrorist acts as serious criminal offences and to ensure that the punishment reflects the seriousness of such terrorist acts? Please supply examples of any convictions obtained and the sentence given.

Reply to this paragraph has been given under response to Operative Para 2 (a, b, c, d).

Sub-paragraph (f)—What procedures and mechanisms are in place to assist other states? Please provide any available details of how these have been used in practice.

Pakistan is a member of ICPO – INTERPOL. According to Article 32 of the Constitution of ICPO-INTERPOL, National Central Bureau (NCB), Pakistan, maintains liaison with various departments in Pakistan, national central bureaus of other countries and the Secretariat General of ICPO-INTERPOL. National Central Bureau, Islamabad has been exchanging information and sharing intelligence concerning criminal matters, with the above-mentioned bodies. The Bureau has been declared national focal point for international crime prevention and sharing information with United Nations Center for International Crime Prevention and Drug Control.

Since 1999, Pakistan has been connected with INTERPOL communication network/x-100 system for exchanging information through e-mails.

In the recent past NCB, Pakistan has been responding to references relating to terrorism received from foreign missions in Islamabad and INTERPOL.

Sub-paragraph (g)—How do border controls in your country prevent the movement of terrorists? How do your procedures for issuance of identity papers and travel documents support this? What measures exist to prevent their forgery etc.?

Following the terrorist attacks of 11 September 2001, security measures and border controls along the Pakistan-Afghanistan border have been tightened. Entry of foreigners is being strictly regulated through visas issued by Pakistan Embassies.

In case of suspicion, foreign nationals arriving in Pakistan on valid visas are directed to report to nearest Foreigners Registration Office for registration as provided in the registration of Foreigners Rules. A stamp to this effect is affixed on their passports. They are also required to obtain exit permit from the Foreigners Registration Office before leaving the country. Such persons are subjected to strict scrutiny at airports at the time of departure.

Special Procedures to deal with persons arriving from Afghanistan

In order to prevent illegal border crossings along the Pakistan-Afghanistan border, Joint Interrogative Teams (JIT) have been set up and Standing Operating Procedures have been instituted. These measures are designed to arrest and detain criminals wanted under national and international law. Home Departments of the NWFP and Baluchistan Provinces are maintaining records of all foreigners as well as Pakistanis returning from Afghanistan.

In addition to these measures, regular troops have been deployed along the Pakistan-Afghanistan border and air surveillance is being carried out to prevent the entry into Pakistan of any terrorist from Afghanistan.

Operative Paragraph 3

Sub-paragraph (a & b)

These issues have already been answered under Operative Para 2 (f).

Sub-paragraph (c)—What steps have been taken to cooperate in the areas indicated in this sub-paragraph?

As discussed in the preceding paragraph, Pakistan is cooperating with other countries in combating terrorism. It has signed extradition treaties with twenty-seven countries. Suspected terrorists involved in the 1993 bombing of the World Trade Center (WTC), killing of two CIA officials in Virginia and the bombing of the US Embassies in Kenya and Tanzania were deported to the United States.

Pakistan has extended full cooperation to the international coalition against terrorism and the coalition operations inside Afghanistan. The cooperation included information sharing, use of Pakistani air space and provision of logistical facilities in Pakistan. Pakistan has also deployed thousands of regular troops in addition to the paramilitary forces to seal its 2450 km long border with Afghanistan. Our forces along this border, specially in the Parachinar area which is adjacent to Tora Bora mountain region of Afghanistan, were under immense pressure in recent weeks as Al-Qaida members tried to escape into Pakistan. Scores of Al-Qaida members have been captured and are in detention for interrogation.

Sub-paragraph (d)—What are your government's intentions regarding signing and/or ratifying the Conventions and Protocols referred to in this sub-paragraph?

Pakistan has ratified/acceded to the following nine UN anti-terrorism Conventions:

(a) Tokyo Convention on Offences and Certain Other Acts vrCommitted on Board Aircraft (ratified on 11th September 1973).

(b) Convention for the Suppression of Unlawful Seizure of Aircraft (ratified on 29th November, 1973).

(c) Multilateral Convention for the Suppression of Unlawful Acts against the Safety of Civil Aviation (ratified on 16th January, 1974).

(d) Convention on the Prevention and Punishment of Crimes against Internationally Protected Persons, including Diplomatic Agents (acceded to on 29th March, 1976).

(e) International Convention against the Taking of Hostages (acceded to on 30th August, 2000).

(f) Convention on the Physical Protection of Nuclear Material (acceded to on 30th August, 2000).

(g) Protocol for the Suppression of Unlawful Acts of Violence at Airports Serving International Civil Aviation, Supplementary to the Convention for the Suppression of Unlawful Acts against the Safety of Civil Aviation (acceded to on 30th August, 2000).

(h) Convention for the Suppression of Unlawful Acts Against the Safety of Maritime Navigation (acceded to on 30th August, 2002).

(i) Protocol for the Suppression of Unlawful Acts against the Safety of Fixed Platforms Located on the Continental Shelf (acceded to on 30th August 2000).

The remaining three Conventions are being examined at inter-Ministerial level. The next inter-Ministerial meeting is scheduled to be held in the first half of January, 2002.

Sub-paragraph (e)—Provide any relevant information on the implementation of the Conventions, Protocols and Resolutions referred to in this sub-paragraph.

Pakistan is fulfilling its obligations under the various UN anti-terrorism Conventions to which it is a party. It is also lending its full support to the international community in the fight against terrorism.

Sub-paragraph (f & g)—What legislation, procedures and mechanisms are in place for ensuring asylum seekers have not been involved in terrorist activity before granting refugee status. Please supply examples of any relevant cases.

Pakistan provides refugee status to only those individuals who are registered with the United Nations High Commissioner for Refugees (UNHCR). In this context an agreement was concluded with UNHCR in July 2001 for joint screening of Afghan refugees.

In order to deal with illegal immigrants, a National Aliens Registration Authority (NARA) was set up in January 2001 under the Foreigners (Amendment) Ordinance 2000. This authority is responsible for the registration of foreigners and issuance of work permits to aliens seeking employment in Pakistan.

Please also refer to measures relating to persons arriving from Afghanistan mentioned in Operative Para 2 (g).

III. Technical Cooperation

As a frontline State in the fight against terrorism, Pakistan has suffered economically with a sharp decline in our trade, in particular our exports, subsequent to 11 September terrorist attacks and military operations in Afghanistan.

Pakistan is in the process of assessing its needs for technical assistance to combat terrorism. A consolidated list of our requirements would be forwarded to the Counter Terrorism Committee in the first half of January, 2002.

DOCUMENT NO. 9

PAKISTAN'S 2005 REPORT TO THE UN ON ITS COUNTER-TERRORISM EFFORTS, PART 2

UN Security Council Resolution S/2002/797

July 19, 2002

Distr.: General
19 July 2002
Original: English

Letter dated 18 July 2002 from the Chairman of the Security Council Committee established pursuant to resolution 1373 (2001) concerning counter-terrorism addressed to the President of the Security Council

I write with reference to my letter of 12 April 2002 (S/2002/460).

The Counter-Terrorism Committee has received the attached supplementary report from Pakistan, submitted pursuant to paragraph 6 of resolution 1373 (2001) (see annex).

I should be grateful if you could arrange for this letter and its annex to be circulated as a document of the Security Council.

(*Signed*) Jeremy **Greenstock**
Chairman
Security Council Committee established
pursuant to resolution 1373 (2001)
concerning counter-terrorism

Annex

Letter dated 11 July 2002 from the Permanent Representative of Pakistan to the United Nations addressed to the Chairman of the Security Council Committee established pursuant to resolution 1373 (2001) concerning counter-terrorism

With reference to your letter dated 18 April 2002, I am enclosing additional information sought by the Counter-Terrorism Committee pursuant to paragraph 6 of Security Council resolution 1373 (2001).

(*Signed*) Munir **Akram**

Enclosure

Additional information requested by the Chairman of the Counter-Terrorism Committee

Sub-paragraph 1(a)

Q.1 Could Pakistan please outline the legislation and procedures which exist for the monitoring, by banks and other intermediaries operating in the main financial sector, of suspicious financial transactions, in addition to the recent State Bank regulations related to the US terrorists lists.

A.1 The following legislation and procedures exist for monitoring by banks of suspicious financial transactions:

I. State Bank of Pakistan—Prudential Regulation XII

State Bank of Pakistan (SBP) which is the Central Bank of the country has been entrusted with the responsibility for an ongoing effective supervision of the financial sector. The relevant provisions of law which vest powers in State Bank of Pakistan (SBP) to carry out inspection of banks are contained in the Banking Companies Ordinance (BCO), 1962. Under Section 40(A) of the said Ordinance it is the responsibility of State Bank to systematically monitor the performance of every banking company to ensure its compliance with the statutory criteria, and banking rules & regulations.

The State Bank has framed Prudential Regulations for banks, which present a prudent operating framework within which banks are expected to conduct their business in a safe and sound manner taking into account the risks associated with their activities. These Regulations are issued under Section 41 of the BCO and have the force of law. Prudential Regulation XII requires banks to monitor suspicious financial transactions as follows:

a) Before extending banking services, bank shall make reasonable efforts to determine the true identity of customers. Particular care should be taken, to identify ownership of all accounts and those using safe-custody facilities. Effective procedures should be instituted for obtaining identification from new customers. An explicit policy should be devised to ensure that significant business transactions are not conducted with customers who fail to provide evidence of their identity.

b) Banks shall ensure that banking business is conducted in conformity with high ethical standards and that banking laws and regulations are adhered to. Banks should not set out to offer services or provide active assistance in transactions, which in their opinion are associated with money derived from illegal activities.

c) Specific procedures be established for ascertaining customer's status and his source of earnings, for monitoring of accounts on a regular basis, for checking identities and bonafides of remitters and beneficiaries, for retaining internal record of transactions for future reference. The transactions which are out of character with the normal operation of the account involving heavy deposits/withdrawals/transfers should be viewed with suspicion and properly investigated.

d) For an effective implementation of banks' policy and procedures, suitable training be imparted to members of staff and they be informed of their responsibility in this regard.

e) Banks may make arrangements for setting up an Internal Audit System in order to establish an effective means of testing/checking and compliance with the Bank Policy and procedures established by it.

II. The Anti Money Laundering and Terrorist Financing Law

The proposed draft law on Anti Money Laundering has a very broad scope, covering money laundering as well as terrorist financing. The law aims at setting up a National Financial Intelligence Centre (NFIC), which will be headed by a Director-General, appointed by the President of Pakistan. It will operate under the general supervision of the Minister of Finance. NFIC will exercise independent decision-making authority on day-do-day matters and will have the following functions:

- Act as an intermediary/buffer between the financial institutions, which will be required to file Suspicious Activity Reports (SAR) and the police who will be investigating the reports.
- Once the NFIC receives a Suspicious Activity Report (SAR) from the banks and other financial institutions it will collect other information from the government as necessary to determine whether the SAR should be turned over to the Federal Investigation Agency (FIA), National Accountability Bureau (NAB) or Anti Narcotics Force (ANF), for further investigation.

- NFIC will have the authority to share and receive information from other financial intelligence units around the world; and will represent Pakistan in money laundering related international meetings.
- It will be a criminal offence punishable by a maximum of five years imprisonment for anyone working in NFIC or having access to its information to pass it on to anyone not authorized to receive it.

Q.2 Are financial intermediaries outside the main financial sector (e.g. lawyers) required to report suspicious transactions to the public authorities? If so, what penalties apply if such persons omit to report either willfully or negligence? Have any penalties already been imposed?

A.2 The concept of Privileged Communication between a lawyer and a client serves as the basis of judicial propriety the world over. At present there are no laws in Pakistan requiring lawyers to report suspicious transactions to public authorities.

Q.3 Do the regulations issued by the State Bank of Pakistan have the force of law?

A.3 Yes. Prudential Regulations are issued under Section 41 of the Banking Companies Ordinance 1962, and have the force of law.

Q.4 When is the Working Group mentioned in the report expected to deliver its proposals to the Government? The CTC would be grateful for an update on the report when it issues.

A.4 The Working Group has submitted a draft law on Money Laundering and Terrorist Financing to the Government. The draft law is being examined by the Government and will be promulgated after due process.

Q.5 When is the draft legislation based on the FATF recommendations expected to be presented to the Parliament? Please outline the content of the law.

A.5 As stated above the draft law on Money Laundering and Terrorist Financing, which is based on the FATF recommendations, has been submitted to the Government. The draft law is being examined by the Government and will be promulgated after due process.

Some of the salient features of the draft law are as under:

- The draft law represents a compendium of items drawn from UN Conventions, model laws, the Core Principles (CPs) for effective Banking Supervision developed by the Basel Committee on Banking Supervision, the FATF Recommendations and several individual country laws.
- The draft law has been designed to encompass the laws necessary to meet international standards.

- In addition to legal and natural persons, the law applies to 12 different types of financial institutions or operations.
- The law defines the offence of terrorist financing and makes it a predicate offence for purposes of money laundering.
- The National Accountability Bureau (NAB), the Federal Investigation Agency (FIA) and the Anti-Narcotics Force (ANF) will be legally authorized to investigate and prosecute money-laundering offences in the special courts of those agencies.
- The Attorney General of Pakistan, the Governor of the SBP and the Chairman of the Securities and Exchange Commission of Pakistan (SECP), will also have significant responsibilities under the law.
- The law proposes to set up a National Financial Intelligence Centre (NFIC), which will be headed by a Director-General, appointed by the President of Pakistan. It will operate under the general supervision of the Minister of Finance. NFIC will exercise independent decision-making authority on day-do-day matters. (For details of NFIC, see A.1).
- The Governor of the State Bank and the Chairman of the SECP will issue rules and regulations to all the financial institutions under their control, regarding minimum standards for all customer identification, and scrutiny of high risk accounts like politically exposed persons ("PEPS"); and to satisfy themselves about the source of the funds and identity of the beneficial owners of the funds before opening or maintaining accounts. In the event that the financial institution does not receive appropriate information, it must close the suspect account.
- The financial institutions will take special measures regarding the originators of wire transfers in and out of Pakistan and set up special anti- money laundering programs.
- Charities will be required to maintain bank accounts and disburse funds through cheques or wire transfers, for knowing how the funds have been spent and the purpose for which they have been spent. Periodic field audit will be conducted for verifying the accounts of the charities.
- All financial institutions will be required to make Suspicious Activity Reports (SARs) regarding their customers. They must file the reports when there is an attempted or completed transaction which they know, suspect, or have reason to believe, it involves the proceeds of crime, appears designed to evade the SBP regulations or requirements of the law, has no apparent economic purpose, or is not consistent with the customer's normal activities.

- The law authorizes criminal forfeiture against specific tainted properties, against substitute assets if that property is not available or for the entry of a money judgment against the defendant.
- The law authorizes civil forfeiture against properties involved in offences where the defendant has died, absconded, or is otherwise unavailable for prosecution.

Subparagraph 1(b):

Q.6 Please outline the provisions existing in Pakistan for the suppression of the financing of terrorism. Please also report on the progress and content of the "new legal framework" issued by the Government of Pakistan.

A.6 The following provisions exist in Pakistan for suppressing the financing of terrorism:

Anti Terrorism Act 1997

The Anti Terrorism Act 1997, contains the following provisions for suppressing the financing of terrorism (copy enclosed):

- Section 2(aa) gives a definition of "terrorist property".
- Section 11E(2) requires Proscribed Organization to submit all accounts of its income and expenditure for its political and social welfare activities and disclose all funding sources to the competent authority designated by the Federal Government.
- Section 11F(5) makes it an offence for a person to solicit, collect or raise funds for a proscribed organization.
- Section 11H to 11K specifically criminalize various forms of terrorism financing, including directly and indirectly, inciting others to finance and aiding and abetting. The text is as under:

Section 11H:

(1) A person commits an offence if he:

(a) invites another to provide money or other property; and

(b) intends that it should be used, or has reasonable cause to suspect that it may be used, for the purpose of terrorism.

(2) A person commits an offence if:

(a) he receives money or other property, and

(b) intends that it should be used, or has reasonable cause to suspect that it may be used, for the purposes of terrorism.

(3) A person commits an offence if he:

(a) provides money or other property, and

(b) knows or has reasonable cause to suspect that it will or may be used for the purposes of terrorism.

(4) In this section a reference to the provision of money or other property is a reference to its being given, lent or otherwise made available, whether or not for consideration.

Section 11I:

A person commits an office if—

(1) he uses money or other property for the purposes of terrorism, or

(2) he—

(a) possesses money or other property; and

(b) intends that it should be used, or has reasonable cause to suspect that it may be used, for the purposes of terrorism.

Section 11J:

A person commits an offence if he—

(a) enters into or becomes concerned in an arrangement as a result of which money or other property is made available or is to be made available to another, and

(b) has reasonable cause to suspect that it will or may be used for the purposes of terrorism.

Section 11K:

(1) A person commits an offence if he enters into or becomes concerned in any arrangement which facilitates the retention or control, by or on behalf of another person, of terrorist property:

(a) by concealment;

(b) by removal from the jurisdiction;

(c) by transfer to nominees, or

(d) in any other way.

(2) It is a defence for a person charged with an offence under subsection (1) to prove that he did not know and had no reasonable cause to suspect that the arrangement related to terrorist property.

Draft Law on Money Laundering and Terrorist Financing

As discussed in answers to Subparagraph 1, the draft law also contains provisions for monitoring of funds of charities and others for preventing any terrorist financing.

Q.7 Could Pakistan please provide information on any successful prosecutions involving the provision of financial assistance for the carrying out of terrorist acts, whether within or outside the territory of Pakistan.

A.7 The Anti-terrorist Courts established under the Anti Terrorism Act 1997, started function in Punjab and Sindh Provinces since 24th March, 2002. Out of 89 terrorist cases notified for priority hearing, 47 cases have been disposed off with conviction in 28 cases. Details with regard to forfeiture of assets for carrying out terrorist acts are as under:

i. Rawalpindi Court No. 1, FIR No. 639/98, Police Station Wah Cantt, State Vs Aurangzeb etc. Case finalized on 25 April 2002.

ii. Rawalpindi Court No. 2, FIR No. 104/2000, Police Station Airport Rawalpindi, State Vs Muhammad Rawab etc. Case finalized on 4 June 2002.

iii. Rawalpindi Court No. 2, FIR No. 82/99 Police Station Chotala, District Jhelum, State Vs Khalid Mahmood etc. Case finalized on 21 June 2002.

Sub-paragraph 1 (c):

Q.8 Does Pakistan have any generally applicable procedures for the freezing and provisional seizure of funds and assets likely to be used in the commission of offences relating to terrorism and its financing? When answering this question, please distinguish between seizures occurring in the course of investigations and confiscations ordered upon sentencing. Please also outline the procedures, which pertain to the provision of support within Pakistan to acts of terrorism carried out or proposed to be carried out elsewhere.

A.8 *Legislation and procedures for freezing and provisional seizure of funds and assets*

The following legislation and procedures exist for freezing and provisional seizure of assets:

State Bank of Pakistan

The State Bank of Pakistan issues directives/advisories to banks/NBFIs for freezing of accounts in compliance with UN Security Council resolutions. All Banks and NBFIs are advised to confirm compliance with the instructions of SBP.

Any bank/NBFI found violating regulations, rules of business and directives is penalized. Violation may also lead to calling of explanation from the Chief Executive/President of banks/NBFIs and initiation of administrative and legal action against violators.

Anti Terrorism Act 1997

The Anti Terrorism Act 1997 contains the following provisions for provisional seizure of assets likely to be used in the commission of offences relating to terrorism and its financing:

Section 11O:

An officer authorized by the Provincial Government in this behalf, hereinafter referred to as the "authorized officer", may seize and detain any cash recovered, if he has reasonable grounds for suspecting that:

(a) it is intended to be used for the purposes of terrorism;

(b) it forms the whole or part of the resources of a proscribed organization, and includes any cash which is applied or made available, or is to be applied or made available, for use by the organization whether being imported into, or exported from, Pakistan; or

(c) it is terrorist property within the meaning given in section 2 (aa):

Provided that any cash seized under this section shall be released not later than the end of the period of 48 hours beginning with the time when it is seized, unless an application has been made to the court under section 11P and an order has been obtained for its detention for a further specified period.

Section 11P

Allows the authorized officer to obtain an order from the court for further detention of the cash pending completion of an investigation of its origin or derivation.

Legislation and Procedure for Forfeiture of Assets

The Anti Terrorism Act 1997 contains the following provisions for forfeiture of assets after the conviction of an offence relating to terrorism:

Section 11Q

(1) The Court by or before which a person is convicted of an offence under any of the sections 11H to 11M may make a forfeiture order in accordance with the provisions of this section.

(2) Where a person is convicted of an offence under section 11H (1) or (2) or section 11-1, the Court may order the forfeiture of any money or other property:

(a) which, at the time of the offence, he had in his possession or under his control; and

(b) which, at that time, he intended should be used, or had reasonable cause to suspect might be used, for the purposes of terrorism.

(3) Where a person has been convicted under Section 11H(3), the court may order the forfeiture of any money or other property:

(a) which, at the time, of the offence, he had in his possession or under his control, and

(b) which, at the time he knew or had reasonable cause to suspect would or might be used for the purposes of terrorism.

(4) Where a person is convicted of an offence under section 11J, the court may order the forfeiture of the money or other property:

(a) to which the arrangement in question related; and

(b) which, at the time of the offence, he knew or had reasonable cause to suspect would or might be used for the purposes of terrorism.

(5) Where a person is convicted of an offence under section 11K, the court may order the forfeiture of the money or other property to which the arrangement in question related.

(6) Where a person is convicted of an offence under any of the sections 11H to 11K, the Court may order forfeiture of any money or other property which wholly or partly, and directly or indirectly, is received by any person as a payment or other reward in connection with the commission of the offence.

Prevention of Support Within Pakistan to Acts of Terrorism Proposed to be Carried out Elsewhere

Section 11V of the Anti Terrorism Act 1997 read with Section 4 of the Pakistan Penal Code (PPC) and Section 188 of the Criminal Code of Pakistan (CrPC) prevent support within Pakistan to acts of terrorism carried out or proposed to be carried out elsewhere. The texts of the relevant provisions is as under:

Section 11V

(1) A person commits an offence if he:

(a) directs, at any level, whilst resident in Pakistan or abroad, activities of an organization concerned with the preparation, instigation or commission of acts of terrorism; or

(b) directs, from within the country or abroad, activities connected with the commission, preparation or investigation of an act of terrorism.

(2) A person guilty of an offence under sub-section (1) shall be liable on conviction to imprisonment for a maximum term of seven years and to forfeiture or confiscation of his assets within or outside Pakistan.

Section 4 of PPC

Extension of code to extra-territorial offences.

The provisions of this code apply also to any offence committed by:

1. any citizen of Pakistan or any person in the service of Pakistan in any place without and beyond Pakistan;
2. Any person on any ship of aircraft registered in Pakistan wherever it may be.

Explanation. In this section the word "offence" includes every act committed outside Pakistan which, if committed in Pakistan, would be punishable under this Code.

Section 188 of CrPC

Liability for offences committed outside Pakistan.

When a citizen of Pakistan commits an offence at any place without and beyond the limits of Pakistan, or

when a servant of the State (whether a citizen of Pakistan or not) commits an offence in (a tribal area,) or

when any person commits an offence on any ship of aircraft registered in Pakistan wherever it may be,

he may be dealt with in respect of such offence as if it had been committed at any place within Pakistan at which he may be found:

Provided further that any proceedings taken against any person under this section which would be a bar to subsequent proceedings against such person for the same offence if such offence had been committed in Pakistan shall be bar to further proceedings against him under the Extradition Act 1972, in respect of the same offence in any territory beyond the limits of Pakistan.

Q.9 Could Pakistan please indicate how these procedures are carried out. Please describe the role of responsible authorities or institutions.

A.9. Pakistan is a Federation comprising of Provinces. In this federal setup the responsibility for maintenance of law and order rests with the Provincial Governments.

The Ministry of Interior, at the Federal level, issues broad policy guidelines and conveys the decisions of the Federal Cabinet. Provincial Governments are responsible for maintaining law and order in consultation with the Ministry of Interior. Field formations evolve independent strategies to combat acts of terrorism under the supervision of Inspectors General of Police, heading the Provincial Police Departments and the Provincial Home Departments.

The Federal Government determines the effectiveness of the policy after receiving inputs from Provincial Governments and Agencies.

Q.10 Does Pakistan have any provisions for regulating alternative money transfer agencies such as the 'Hawalah' system? Please outline these provisions.

A.10 The private foreign exchange and money changing business is being taken care of by introduction of Exchange Companies. A draft Ordinance to amend the Foreign Exchange Regulation Act 1947 is being prepared.

The main objective behind the formulation of Exchange Companies is to provide a proper corporate structure to the money changing business in the country, while ensuring that various types of risks associated with this business are properly addressed. Another objective is to get all money changing and remitting transactions fully documented.

Salient features of the proposed Ordinance are as follows:

- Definition of Exchange Companies.
- Description of Exchange Companies' scope of dealing/business.
- Restriction on Money Changers to deals only in foreign currency notes and coins.
- Exchange Companies to deal in foreign currency notes, coins, postal notes, money orders, bank drafts, travelers cheques and transfers.
- Exchange Companies to have certain minimum paid-up capital requirement with mandatory SLR.
- Exchange Companies to observe Exposure Limits specified by State Bank.
- Each Director of an Exchange Company to meet the eligibility criteria specified by State Bank.
- Transactions of the Exchange Companies to be fully documented.
- Exchange Companies to report their transactions to State Bank in the form of periodic returns.

Sub-paragraph 1(d):

Q.11 Please outline the preventive controls and surveillance measures which ensure that funds received by charitable, religious or cultural organizations are not diverted from their stated purpose to terrorist activities.

A.11 The following provisions exist for preventive controls and surveillance measures, for ensuring that funds received by charitable, religious or cultural organizations are not diverted from their stated purpose to terrorist activities.

Anti Terrorism Act 1997

Sections 11H to 11K of the Anti Terrorism Act 1997, serve to specifically criminalize various forms of terrorism financing, including directly and indirectly, inciting others to finance and aiding and abetting (details have been given in the reply to question 6).

Anti Money Laundering and Terrorist Financing Law

Under the proposed Anti Money Laundering and Terrorist Financing Law, Charities will be required to maintain bank accounts and disburse funds through cheques or wire transfers, for knowing how the funds have been spent and the purpose for which they have been spent. Periodic field audit will be conducted for verifying the accounts of the charities.

Madresah Ordinance

The Federal Cabinet approved the promulgation of 'Madresah Registration Ordinance 2002' on 20 June 2002 to bring the country's religious schools (madresahs) under a regulatory framework. The ordinance contains the following provisions for monitoring the funds of the madresahs:

- Every registered madresah will be required to maintain accounts and submit annual report to the respective board.
- Registered madresahs shall not receive any grant donation or aid from any foreign source or allow admission to foreign students or make appointment of teachers without valid work visa and NOC from the Ministry of Interior.

Q.12 Please outline in more detail Pakistan's anti-terrorist legislation and provide copies of the relevant texts, including, in particular, the Anti-terrorism Act of 1997. Please make clear, in particular, what types of acts preparatory to an act of terrorism are criminalized by laws of Pakistan, and outline these laws.

A.12 Copy of the Anti Terrorism Act 1997 is enclosed.

The following acts of terrorism have been criminalized in the Anti Terrorism Act 1997:

Section 6

(1) In this Act, "terrorism" means the use or threat of action where:

a) the action falls within the meaning of sub-section (2), and

b) the use of threat is designed to coerce and intimidate or overawe the Government or the public or a section of the public or community or sect or create a sense fear or insecurity in society; or

c) the use of threat is made for the purpose of advancing a religious, sectarian or ethnic cause.

(2) An "action" shall fall within the meaning of sub-section (1), if it:

a) involves the doing of anything that causes death;

b) involves grievous violence against a person or grievous bodily injury or harm to a person;

c) involves grievous damage to property;

d) involves the doing of anything that is likely to cause death or endangers a person's life;

e) involves kidnapping for ransom, hostage-taking or hijacking;

f) incites hatred and contempt on religious, sectarian or ethnic basis to stir up violence or cause internal disturbance;

g) involves stoning, brick-batting or any other form of mischief to spread panic;

h) involves firing on religious congregations, mosques, 'imambargahs', churches, temples and all other places of worship, or random firing to spread panic, or involves any forcible takeover of mosques or other places of worship;

i) creates a serious risk to safety of the public or a section of the public, or is designed to frighten the general public and thereby prevent them from coming out and carrying on their lawful trade and daily business, and disrupts civic life.

j) involves the burning of vehicles or any other serious form of arson;

k) involves extortion of money ("bhatta") or property;

l) is designed to seriously interfere with or seriously disrupt a communications system or public utility service;

m) involves serious coercion or intimidation of a public servant in order to force him to discharge or to refrain from discharging his lawful duties; or

n) involves serious violence against a member of the police force, armed forces, civil armed forces, or a public servant.

(3) The use or threat of use of any action falling within subsection (2) which involves the use of firearms, explosives or any other weapon is terrorism, whether or not sub-section 1(c) is satisfied.

(4) In this section "action" includes an act or a series of acts.

(5) In this Act, terrorism includes any act done for the benefit of a proscribed organization.

(6) A person who commits an offence under this section or any other provision of this Act, shall be guilty of an act of terrorism.

(7) In this Act, a "terrorist" means:

a) a person who has committed an offence of terrorism under this Act, and is or has been concerned in the commission, preparation or instigation of acts of terrorism:

b) a person who is or has been, whether before or after the coming into force of this Act, concerned in the commission, preparation or instigation of acts of terrorism, shall also be included in the meaning given in clause (a) above.

- Section 11F makes it an offence for a person to be a member of a proscribed organization; solicit support; attend, arrange, manage or address meetings; and raise funds for that organization.
- Section 11G makes it an offence to wear, carry, display, any article, symbol, flag or banner and uniform connected with a proscribed organization.
- Sections 11H to 1K of the Anti Terrorism Act 1997, serve to specifically criminalize various forms of terrorism financing, including directly and indirectly, inciting others to finance and aiding and abetting (details have been given in the reply to question 6).
- Section 11V makes the directing of an act of terrorism an offence. The text of the section is as follows:

(1) A person commits an offence if he:

a) directs, at any level, whilst resident in Pakistan or abroad, activities of an organization concerned with the preparation, instigation or commission of acts of terrorism; or

b) directs, from within the country or abroad, activities connected with the commission, preparation or investigation of an act of terrorism.

(2) A person guilty of an offence under sub-section (1) shall be liable on conviction to imprisonment for a maximum term of seven years and to forfeiture or confiscation of his assets within or outside Pakistan.

- Section 21C makes it an offence to provide or receive training in the making or use of firearms, explosives or chemical, biological and other weapons and provide or receive training in acts of terrorism.
- Section 21I makes it offence to aid or abet any offence under this Act.
- Section 21J makes it offence to harbour any person who committed an offence under this Act.

Q.13 Could Pakistan please describe in more detail how the Antiterrorism Act is implemented in practice and the manner in which it contributes to full compliance with the Resolution.

A.13 Covered in the reply of Q.9.

Q.14 Please outline the measures, both legislative and practical, preventing entities and individuals from recruiting, collecting funds or soliciting other forms of support for terrorist activities to be carried out inside or outside Pakistan, including, in particular:

- The carrying out, within or from Pakistan, of recruiting collecting of funds and soliciting of other forms of support from other countries; and
- Deceptive activities such as recruitment based on a representation to the recruit that the purpose of the recruitment is one (e.g. teaching) different from the true purposes and collection of funds through front organizations.

A.14 Covered in replies to questions 5, 6, 8, 11 and 12.

Sub-paragraph 2 (a):

Q.15 Please outline in more detail Pakistan's legislation aimed at prohibiting the establishment of paramilitary groups that have the potential to engage in terrorist activities either inside or outside Pakistan. Please also outline any legislation aimed at prohibiting or limiting the acquisition or possession of weapons both within and outside Pakistan.

A.15 The following provisions of the Anti Terrorism Act 1997 are aimed at organizations concerned with terrorism:

- Section 11A outlines the following acts for which the organization is concerned with terrorism:

  a) commits or participates in acts of terrorism;

  b) prepares for terrorism;

  c) promotes or encourages terrorism;

  d) supports and assists any organization concerned with terrorism;

  e) patronizes and assists in the incitement of hatred and contempt on religious, sectarian or ethnic lines that stir up disorder;

  f) fails to expel from its ranks or ostracize those who commit acts of terrorism and presents them as heroic persons; or

  g) is otherwise concerned in terrorism.

- Section 11B allows the Federal Government to proscribe an organization concerned with terrorism.

- Section 11D allows the Federal Government to place an organization under observation where it has reason to believe that it is concerned with terrorism.

The Pakistan Arms Ordinance is aimed at controlling the sale, transport, bearing or possession of arms, ammunition or military stores.

Sub-paragraph 2 (b):

Q.16 Please report on progress with the implementation of the "Action Plan" recently adopted by the Federal Cabinet in order to prevent sectarian violence in Pakistan.

A. 16 The following progress has been achieved on the implementation of the "Action Plan":-

- Seven sectarian militant organizations have been proscribed and one kept on watch list.
- A total number of 2167 activists belonging to 6 extremist religious organizations/proscribed organizations were arrested.
- 624 offices of these organizations have been sealed.
- Subsequent to the Karachi bomb blast incident of 8th May 2002, a crack down was launched against the proscribed militants in which 411 activists were apprehended by Provincial Governments, taking the total figure of arrested activist to 2578.

Q.17 Does Pakistan have a body that specializes in counter-terrorism, or is that the responsibility of a number of departments or agencies? In the latter case, how is co-ordination between the various entities effected?

A. 17 Pakistan is a Federation comprising of Provinces. In this federal setup the responsibility for maintenance of law and order rests with the Provincial Governments.

The Ministry of Interior, at the Federal level, issues broad policy guidelines and conveys the decisions of the Federal Cabinet. Provincial Governments are responsible for maintaining law and order in consultation with the Ministry of Interior. Field formations evolve independent strategies to combat acts of terrorism under the supervision of Inspectors General of Police, heading the Provincial Police Departments and the Provincial Home Departments.

The Federal Government determines the effectiveness of the policy after receiving inputs from Provincial Governments and Agencies.

Q.18 Does each agency define its strategy independently, or does it carry out measures that have been established at a high level? Who determines that policy and, if applicable, the distribution of tasks among agencies?

A.18 Covered in the reply to question 17.

Q.19 Besides exchanges of information, are other steps being taken to prevent the commission of terrorist acts in accordance with the Resolution?

A. 19 Yes. These include border control measures, check on financing, denial of safe heaven, etc., as conveyed vide Pakistan's main report and this supplementary report.

Q.20 Please describe any mechanism aimed at providing early warning to other countries on terrorist acts that could be committed in the countries concerned.

A.20 Pakistan exchanges information with countries having extradition treaties with Pakistan. As a coalition partner Pakistan is exchanging information with other coalition member countries.

Sub-paragraph 2(c)

Q.21 Please outline the main provisions of Pakistan's legislation relating to immigration control and the granting of the right of asylum, and indicate the means for preventing criminal groups abusing those provisions. Please also outline the conditions for the issuance of identity documents, particularly passports, to aliens.

A.21 The following provisions of the Foreigners Act, 1946 deal with immigration control:

Section 3 of the Act empowers the Government to make provisions for prohibiting, regulation or restricting the entry of foreigners into Pakistan, or their departure there from or their presence or continued presence therein. The orders provide that a foreigner:

a) shall not enter Pakistan or shall enter Pakistan only at such times and by such route and at such port or place and subject to the observance of such conditions on arrival as may be prescribed;

b) shall not depart from Pakistan or shall depart only at such times and by such route and from such port or place and subject to the observance of such conditions on departure as may be prescribed;

c) shall not remain in Pakistan, or in any prescribed area therein;

d) shall remove himself to, and remain in, such area in Pakistan as may be prescribed;

e) shall comply with such conditions as may be prescribed or specified—

i) requiring him to reside in a particular place;

ii) imposing any restriction on his movements;

iii) requiring him to furnish such proof of his identity and to report such particulars to such authority in such manner and at such time and place as may be prescribed or specified;

iv) requiring him to allow his photograph and finger-impressions to be taken and to furnish specimens of his handwriting and signature to such authority and at such time and place as may be prescribed or specified;

v) requiring him to submit himself to such medical examination by such authority and at such time and place as may be prescribed or specified;

vi) prohibiting him from association with persons of a prescribed or specified description;

vii) prohibiting him from engaging in activities of a prescribed or specified description;

viii) prohibiting him from using or possessing prescribed or specified articles;

ix) otherwise regulating his conduct in any such particular as may be prescribed or specified;

f) shall enter into a bond with or without sureties for the due observance of or as an alternative to the enforcement of any of all prescribed or specified restrictions or conditions;

g) shall be arrested and, in the interest of the security of Pakistan, detained or confined.

Sections 3 & 20 of the Pakistan Citizenship Act, 1951 outline those persons who can become citizens of Pakistan.

Section 3 of the Naturalization Act 1926, lists the persons who are eligible to become citizens of Pakistan by naturalization. The text of the section is as follows:

Section 3.—(1) The (Federal Government) may grant a certificate of naturalization to any person who makes an application in this behalf and satisfies the (Federal Government)—

(a) that he is not a minor;

(b) that he is neither a citizen of Pakistan nor a subject of any state of which a citizen of Pakistan is prevented by or under any law from becoming a subject by naturalization;)

(c) that he has resided in Pakistan throughout the period of twelve months immediately preceding the date of the application, and has, during the seven years immediately preceding the said period of twelve months, resided in Pakistan for a period of amounting in the aggregate to not less than four years;)

(d) that he is of good character;

(e) that he has an adequate knowledge of a language which has been declared by the (Federal Government) by notification in the (official Gazette,) to be (one of the principal vernaculars of Pakistan); and

(f) that he intends, if the application is granted, to reside in (Pakistan) or to enter or continue in the service of the (State) (in Pakistan):

Provided that nothing in clause (e) or clause (f) shall apply in the case of a woman who was a (citizen of Pakistan) previously to her marriage to a person not a (citizen of Pakistan) and whose husband has died or whose marriage has been dissolved.

(2) Nothing in this section shall be deemed to prevent the grant of a certificate of naturalization to any person to whom a certificate of naturalization has been issued under the Indian Naturalization Act, 1852).

Q.22 Does the legislation apply to all terrorist groups and individuals or only those mentioned in the report?

A.22 The legislation mentioned in the previous question applies to all foreigners.

Sub-paragraph 2 (d):

Q.23 Does the Anti-terrorism Act specifically prohibit Pakistan territory from being used as a base for terrorist acts outside Pakistan?

A.23 Yes. The relevant provisions have been discussed in the previous questions.

Sub-paragraph 2 (e):

Q.24 What is the extent of the competence of the courts of Pakistan to deal with terrorist acts, or preparations for terrorist acts, that occur outside its territory?

A.24 The relevant provisions dealing with the competence of Pakistani courts are as follows:

Pakistan Penal Code

Section 3. Punishment of offences committed beyond, but which by law may be tried within Pakistan.

Any person liable, by any Pakistani Law, to be tried for an offence committed beyond Pakistan shall be dealt with according to the provisions of this

Code for any act committed beyond Pakistan in the same manner as if such act had been committed within Pakistan.

Q.25 Are the relevant provisions of the Penal Code of Pakistan applicable in all of the following circumstances:

- Acts committed outside Pakistan by a person who is a citizen of, or habitually resident in, Pakistan (whether that person is currently present in Pakistan or not);
- Acts committed outside Pakistan by a foreign national who is currently in Pakistan?

A.25 Yes, Section 3 of PPC covers both situations. This section has been reproduced above.

Sub-paragraph 2 (g):

Q.26 How does Pakistan secure its extensive borders against unauthorized crossings?

A.26 Pakistan secures its borders through its Border Security Force, Levies, Anti Narcotics Force, Rangers, Frontier Corps and the Armed Forces (Each agency is regulated by its respective laws).

Following the terrorist attacks of 11 September 2001, security measures and border controls along the Pakistan-Afghanistan border have been tightened. Entry of foreigners is being strictly regulated through visas issued by Pakistan Embassies.

In case of suspicion, foreign nationals arriving in Pakistan are directed to report to nearest Foreigners Registration Office for registration as provided in the registration of Foreigners Rules. A stamp to this effect is affixed on their passports. They are also required to obtain exit permit from the Foreigners Registration Office before leaving the country. Such persons are subjected to strict scrutiny at airports at the time of departure.

Special Procedures to Deal with Persons Arriving from Afghanistan

In order to prevent illegal border crossings along the Pakistan-Afghanistan border, Joint Interrogative Teams (JIT) have been setup and Standing Operating Procedures have been instituted. These measures are designed to arrest and detain criminals wanted under national and international law. Home Departments of the NWFP and Baluchistan Provinces are maintaining records of all foreigners as well as Pakistanis returning from Afghanistan.

In addition to these measures, regular troops have been deployed along the Pakistan-Afghanistan border and air surveillance is being carried out to prevent the entry into Pakistan of any terrorist from Afghanistan.

Q.27 Please provide information on the mechanism for inter-agency cooperation between the federal and provincial authorities responsible for narcotics control, financial tracking and security with particular regard to the border controls preventing the movement of terrorists.

A.27 A National Crisis Management Centre (NCMC), fully equipped with telephones, faxes, and computers, has been established in the Ministry of Interior. The Provincial Governments have also set up similar Crisis Management Centres. The Federal and the Provincial Crises Management Centres have been interlinked for round the clock collection and collation of information of all incidents occurring in any part of the country and reporting to the higher authorities. The coordination agencies are Crime Investigation Departments, Intelligence Agencies, Frontier Corps, Rangers and Anti Narcotics Force.

Sub-paragraph 3 (b):

Q.28 Does Pakistan have any legislation for providing mutual assistance to other countries in relations to criminal investigations and judicial proceedings? Please outline any relevant provisions.

A.28 Yes, Pakistan is a signatory of Extradition Treaties with 27 countries under which there are provisions for mutual assistance in relation to criminal investigation and judicial proceedings.

Q.29 To what types of bilateral or multilateral agreements in the field of judicial assistance and extradition is Pakistan a party? What are the legal procedures required by Pakistan for the execution of a request by another country for assistance or extradition?

A.29 As stated above Pakistan is a signatory of Extradition Treaties with 27 countries, in which there are provisions for judicial assistance.

The Extradition Act 1972 provides the following procedure for the surrender of a fugitive:

- Requisition for surrender of a fugitive has to be made to the Federal Government through diplomatic representative in Pakistan or Pakistan's mission abroad or through other agreed channel (Section 6).
- Federal Government may, if it thinks fit, conduct an enquiry through a First Class Magistrate having jurisdiction (Section 7).
- On receipt of an enquiry order, summon or warrants of the arrest of the accused will be issued in accordance with Pakistan's law. The Magistrate's enquiry should be according to the procedure of a Court of Session and should consider all evidence produced in support of the requisition and in favour of the fugitive to show that offence is of a political character and is not an extradition offence (Section 8).

- Section 9 provides a list of documents that can be produced as evidence in support of the requisition.
- If the enquiry report established that a prima facie case has not been made in support of requisition for the fugitive, he would be discharged. If charges are established a report would be sent to the Government and the fugitive would be committed to prison subject to any provision related to bail to await the orders of the Federal Government (Section 10).
- If the Federal Government decides to surrender the fugitive, it may issue a warrant for the custody and removal of the fugitive for his delivery at a place and to a person to be named in the warrant. The delivery is to take place only after 15 days of issuance of the warrant (Section 11).
- If a fugitive is not delivered for two months, the High Court may consider the request of the accused for discharge (Section 12).
- In case of request of extradition by more than one treaty State, the Federal Government may decide to surrender the fugitive to such State, as it may think fit (Section 14).

Sub-paragraph 3 (c):

Q.30 Could Pakistan please provide a list of the extradition and mutual legal assistance treaties to which it is party.

A.30 Pakistan is a party to extradition treaties with the following countries:

Sl. No.	Country	Date of Adoption of the Treaty	
1.	Argentina	20.2.1973	Adopted Under Ministry of Foreign Affairs SRO No.211(1)/73 dated 20.2.1973.
2.	Belgium	20.2.1973	-do-
3.	France	20.2.1973	-do-
4.	Greece	20.2.1973	-do-
5.	Switzerland	20.2.1973	-do-
6.	U.S.A.	20.2.1973	-do-
7.	San Marino	20.4.1980	Adopted Under Ministry of Foreign Affairs SRO No.427(1)/80 dated 20.4.1980
8.	Monaco	20.4.1980	-do-
9.	Netherlands	20.4.1980	-do-
10.	Denmark	20.4.1980	-do-
11.	Austria	20.4.1980	-do-
12.	Yugoslavia	20.4.1980	-do-

Sl. No.	Country	Date of Adoption of the Treaty	
13.	Iraq	20.4.1980	-do-
14.	Ecuador	20.4.1980	-do-
15.	Portugal	20.4.1980	-do-
16.	Luxembourg	20.4.1980	-do-
17.	Columbia	20.4.1980	-do-
18.	Liberia	20.4.1980	-do-
19.	Cuba	20.4.1980	-do-
20.	Italy	20.4.1980	-do-
21.	Iran	20.4.1959	
22.	Turkey	30.8.1983	
23.	Saudi Arabia	03.4.1983	
24.	Maldives	12.7.1984	
25.	Egypt	23.8.1994	
26.	Australia	16.3.2000	
27.	Uzbekistan	25.1.2001	

Sub-paragraph 3 (e):

Q.31 Please outline the provisions of domestic law which give effect to the nine relevant international conventions and protocols relating to terrorism to which Pakistan is already a party and which are mentioned in the report.

A.31 The issue is under examination.

Q.32 Please provide a "progress report" on the ratifications of the relevant international conventions and protocols relating to terrorism which Pakistan has not yet ratified.

A.32 On 26 June 2002, the Federal Cabinet gave the approval for the following:

i) Pakistan's accession to the "International Convention on the Suppression of Terrorist Bombings."

ii) Pakistan's signature of the "Organization of Islamic Countries Convention on Combating International Terrorism

The instruments of accession and signature in respect of the above Conventions will be deposited shortly.

Pakistan will ratify the "Convention on the Marking of Plastic Explosives for the Purpose of Detection", once the technical requirements for its ratification are met.

The International Convention for the Suppression of the Financing of Terrorism, is being examined by an inter Ministerial Committee.

Q.33 Have the crimes set forth in the relevant international conventions and protocols been included as extraditable offences in the bilateral treaties to which Pakistan is party?

A.33 Pakistan is bound by the relevant articles of those Conventions and Protocols which stipulate that the offences set forth in the relevant international Conventions and Protocols are deemed to be included as extraditable offences in any extradition treaty existing between States Parties and any extradition treaty to be concluded between them.

Sub-paragraph 3 (g):

Q.34 Please outline the legislation, procedures and mechanisms which give effect to this sub-paragraph. Please clarify whether political motivation is recognized as a ground for refusing requests for the extradition of alleged terrorists.

A.34 Pakistan provides refugee status to only those individuals who are registered with the United Nations High Commissioner for Refugees (UNHCR). In this context an agreement was concluded with UNHCR in July 2001 for joint screening of Afghan refugees. Further details for admission of foreigners into Pakistan can be seen in the replies to questions 21 and 26.

Section 5(2)(a) of the Extradition Act 1972 states that a fugitive shall not be surrendered if the offence in respect of which his surrender is sought is of a political character. However, for this, the Federal Government or the Magistrate or Court before whom the fugitive is produced, has to be satisfied that the requisition for his surrender has, in fact been made with a view to his being tried or punished for an offence of a political character.

Paragraph 4:

Q.35 Has Pakistan addressed any of the concerns expressed in paragraph 4 of the Resolution?

A.35 Pakistan is a signatory of the UN Convention Against Transnational Organized Crime, which demonstrates Pakistan's commitment to fight transnational crime.

Pakistan has been in the forefront in the fight against narcotic drugs. At the national level, Pakistan has taken several legislative and institutional measures to combat the narcotics menace which has assumed alarming proportions in recent years. These include the following:

a. Establishment of the Narcotics Control Division to exclusively deal with drug related matters.

b. Establishment of an Anti Narcotics Force, a premier anti drug agency which is actively engaged in seizure of drugs as well as arrests and prosecution of drug traffickers.

c. Prevention of smuggling or transshipment of chemical precursors, particularly acetic anhydride, into Afghanistan.

d. Prevention of smuggling/transshipment of narcotics particularly opiates from Afghanistan into Pakistan.

e. Prevention of trafficking/smuggling of narcotics outside Pakistan.

f. Enactment of various laws that include death penalty for drug traffickers/financiers and forfeiture of their assets.

g. Establishment of special courts having exclusive jurisdiction to try offenses cognizable under the Anti Narcotics Ordinance.

h. Effective measures to eliminate suspicious financial transactions through banks and other financial institutions.

Pakistan has strongly supported international efforts to combat the illicit drug problem. Pakistan is a party to all the three UN Conventions, namely, the 1961 Single Convention on Narcotics Drugs, the 1971 UN Convention on Psychotropic Substances and the 1988 UN Convention against Illicit Trafficking in Narcotic Drugs and Psychotropic Substances. In August 1999, Pakistan also ratified the 1972 Protocol amending the 1961 Single Convention on Narcotic drugs.

In the regional context, Pakistan is a party to the SAARC Convention on Narcotic Drugs and Psychotropic Substances and the ECO Protocol against drugs. Pakistan has also been actively involved in the setting up of an ECO Committee on Narcotics Control.

At the bi-lateral level, Pakistan has an on-going arrangement with a large number of countries for exchange of information on drug-related issues.

As a follow-up to the implementation of the outcome of the 20th Special Session of the UN General Assembly, the Government of Pakistan, with the active collaboration of United Nations Drugs Control Programme (UNDCP), private sector, as well as relevant NGO's, launched its Master Plan for Drug Abuse Control in February 1999. The major focus of the Master Plan is on demand reduction and involves public awareness about the negative effects of drugs through print and electronic media, preventive education campaigns through training of teachers and social workers and establishment of mobile drug information teams to reach rural and remote areas.

Pakistan is a State Party to the Chemical Weapons Convention and the Biological Weapons Convention. These treaties completely prohibit the development, stockpiling and use of chemical and biological weapons. As a State Party, Pakistan is in full compliance with its Treaty obligations. Pakistan also supports international efforts to implement the provisions on cooperation contained in these Treaties, which inter alia, would also strengthen the goals of Resolution 1373.

Pakistan's national authorities responsible for physical protection of its nuclear material, implement internationally agreed guidelines for the safety of nuclear materials and facilities. Pakistan has established fail-safe procedures in the area of nuclear materials safety with oversight of highly responsible national organizations.

In the area of arms trafficking, the Government of Pakistan is implementing a serious and long-term, programme of de-weaponisation. Eliminating illicit trade in small arms and light weapons is an essential goal of this programme. Pakistan also participated actively in the UN Conference on the Illicit Trade in Small Arms and Light Weapons in All its Aspects held in New York in July 2001 and will continue to support the Programme of Action adopted by the Conference, which also provides for international cooperation on this issue.

Other matters:

Q.36 Could Pakistan please provide an organizational chart of its administrative machinery, such as police, immigration control, customs, taxation and financial supervision authorities, established to give practical effect to the laws, regulations and other documents that are seen as contribution to compliance with the Resolution.

A.36 Organization charts are enclosed.

ORGANIZATIONAL CHART OF CENTRAL BOARD OF REVENUE/REVENUE DIVISION
(As on 15th May, 2002)

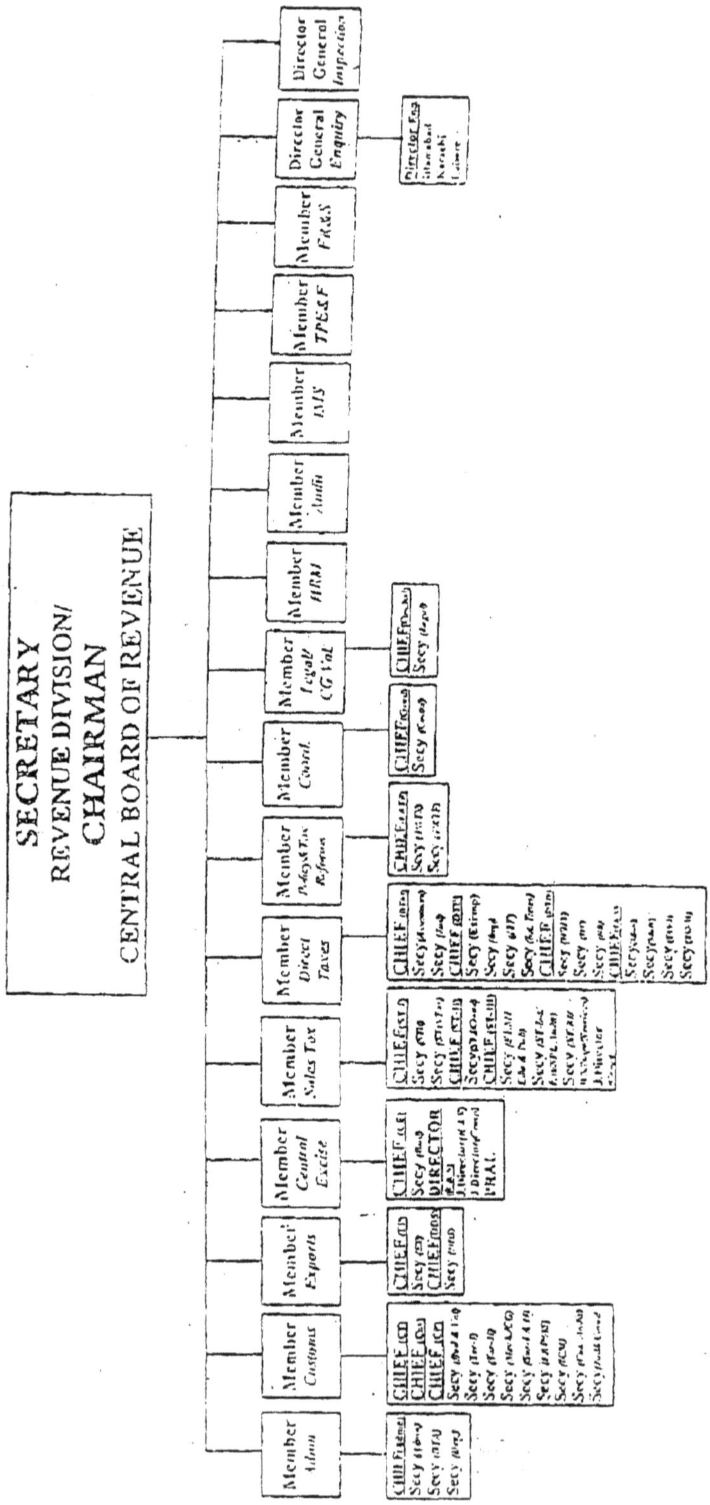

ORGANIZATIONAL CHART OF CENTRAL EXCISE DEPARTMENT

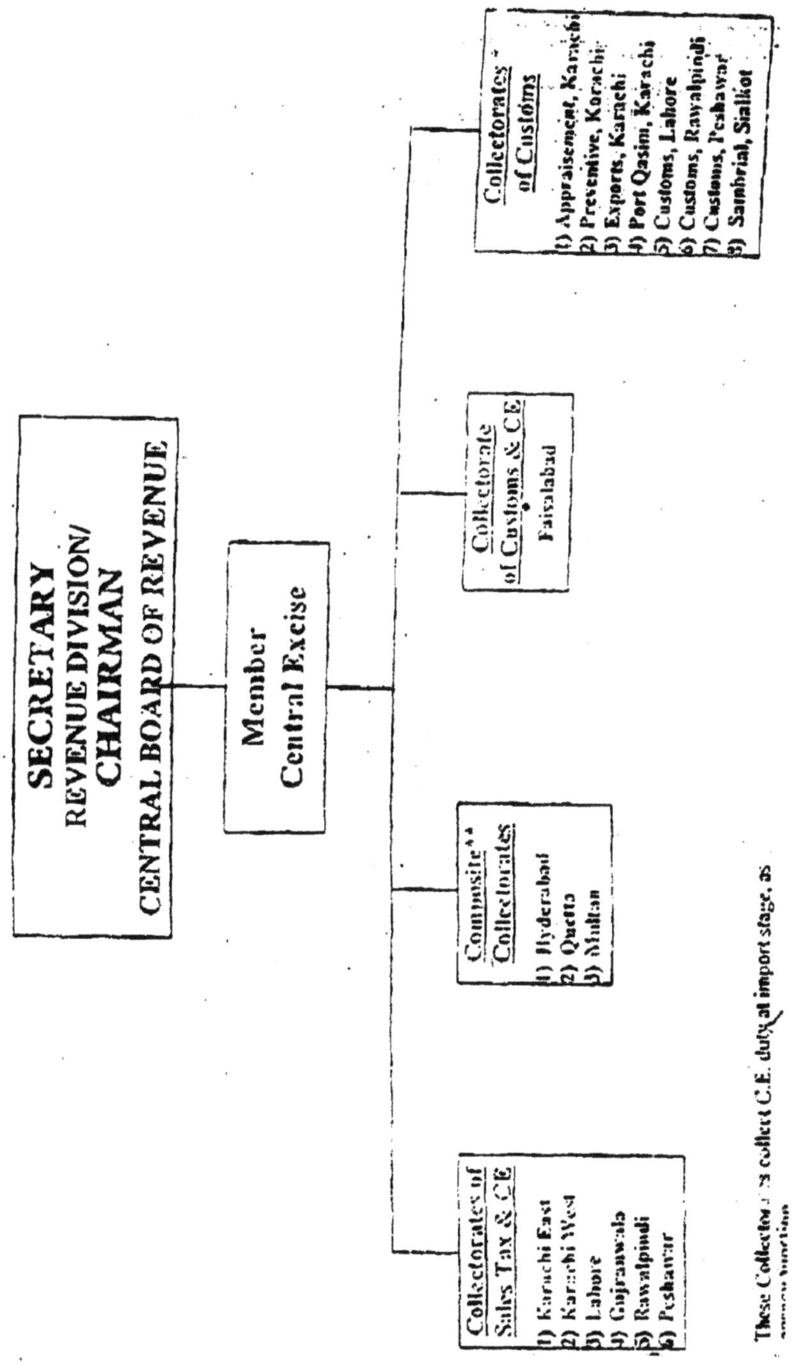

ORGANIZATIONAL CHART OF INCOME TAX DEPARTMENT

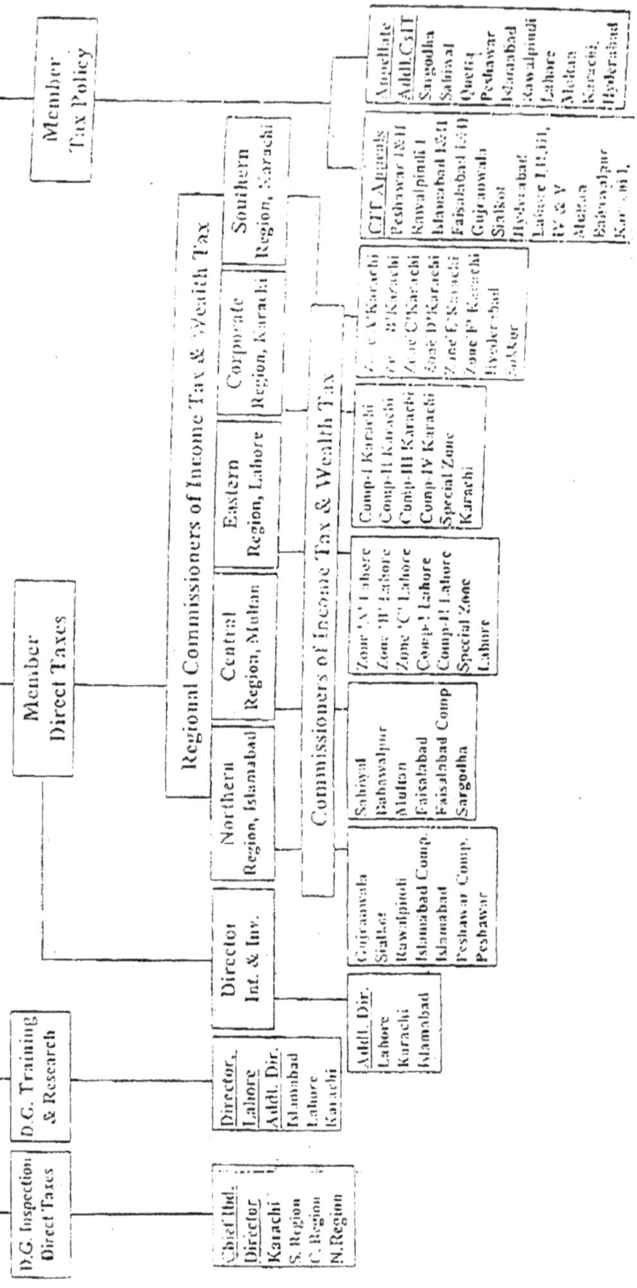

Organizational Chart of Sales Tax Department

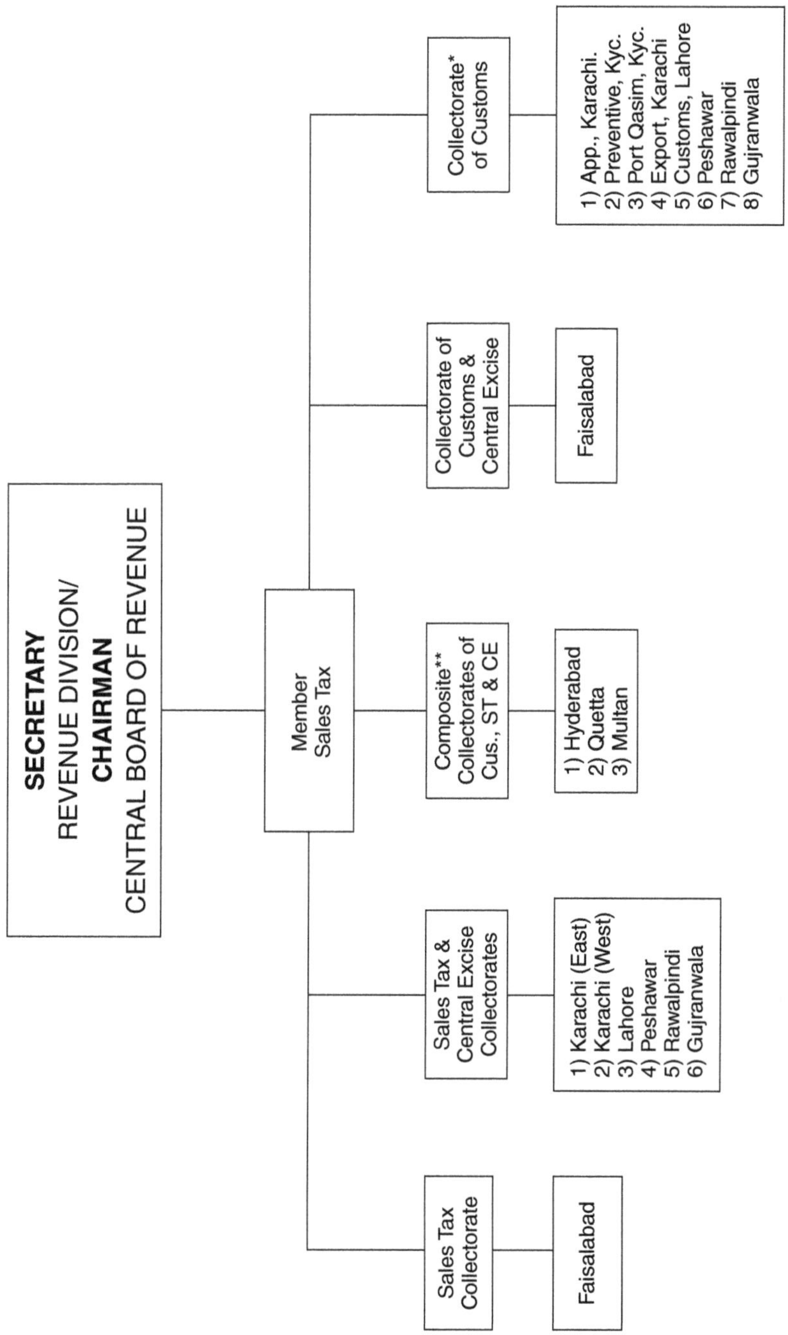

Organizational Chart of the Customs Department

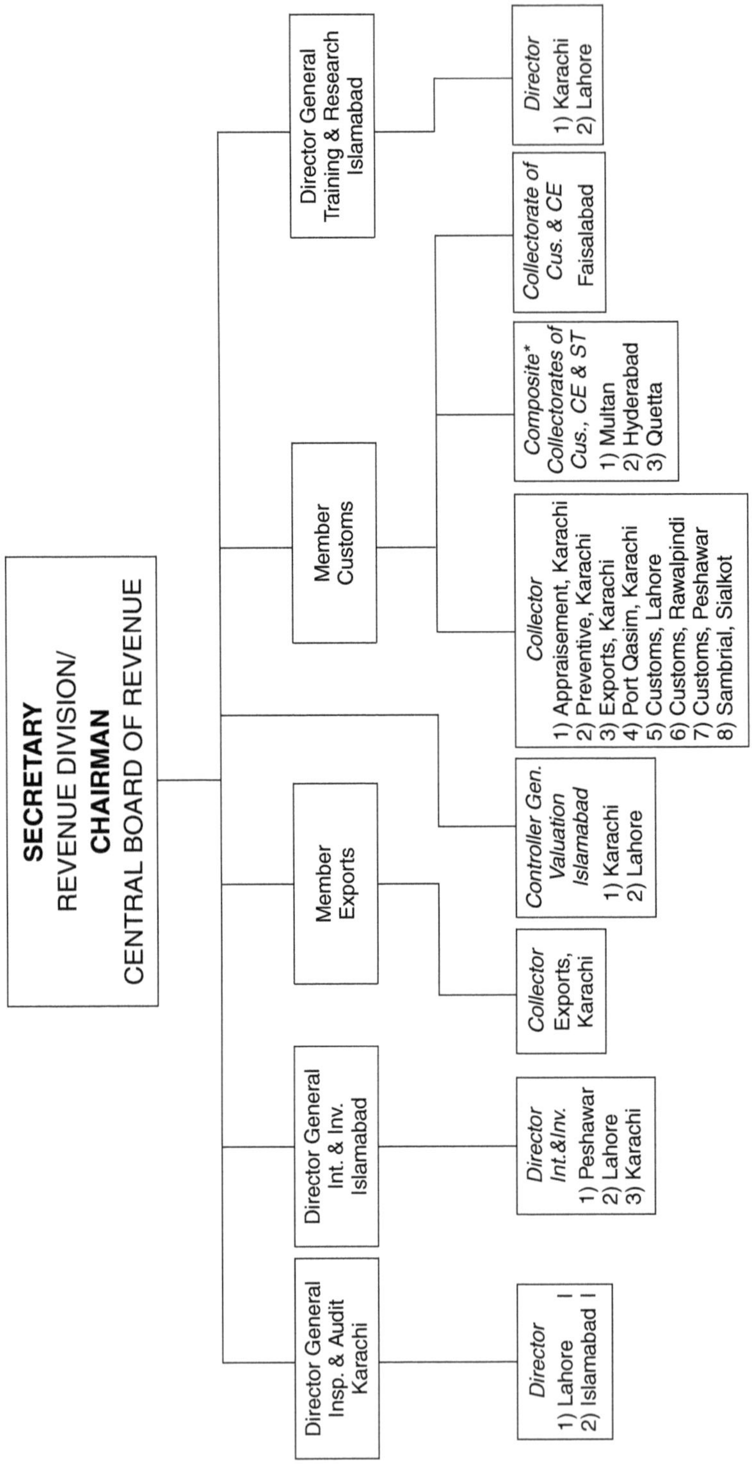

The Composite Collectorates collect Customs Duties, Sales Tax & Central Excise Duties and are administered by Member (C.E).

DOCUMENT NO. 10

REPORT OF PAKISTAN TO THE UNSC ON IMPLEMENTATION OF UNSC RESOLUTION 1373

UN Security Council Resolution S/2003/307

March 12, 2003

Distr.: General
12 March 2003
Original: English

Letter dated 10 March 2003 from the Chairman of the Security Council Committee established pursuant to resolution 1373 (2001) concerning counter-terrorism addressed to the President of the Security Council

I write with reference to my letter of 2 January 2003 (S/2003/26).

The Counter-Terrorism Committee has received the attached third report from Pakistan submitted pursuant to paragraph 6 of resolution 1373 (2001) (see annex).

I would be grateful if you could arrange for the present letter and its annex to be circulated as a document of the Security Council.

(*Signed*) Jeremy **Greenstock**
Chairman
Security Council Committee established pursuant to
resolution 1373 (2001) concerning counter-terrorism

Annex

Annex to the letter dated 10 March 2003 from the Chairman of the Security Council Committee established pursuant to resolution 1373 (2001) concerning counter-terrorism addressed to the President of the Security Council

Letter dated 25 February 2003 from the Permanent Representative of Pakistan to the United Nations addressed to the Chairman of the Security Council Committee established pursuant to resolution 1373 (2001) concerning counter-terrorism

With reference to your letter dated 25 November 2002, I am enclosing additional information sought by the Counter-Terrorism Committee pursuant to paragraph 6 of resolution 1373 (2001) of the United Nations Security Council (see enclosure). It may be noted that our reply to question 1.15 will be provided later.

(*Signed*) Munir **Akram**

Enclosure

Supplementary Report of Pakistan to the Counter-Terrorism Committee of the Security Council

Following are responses to the questions based on additional information provided by Pakistan to the Counter-Terrorism Committee on 11 July 2003

Paragraph 1.2

Q. Effective implementation of paragraph 1 requires that funds and other financial assets or economic resources of persons who commit or attempt to commit terrorist acts or participate in or facilitate the commission of terrorist acts are frozen without delay. Section 11 E of the Anti Terrorism Act 1997 provides for the freezing of the accounts of a 'proscribed organization' but depends for its operation on the making of an order adding the name of the organization to the First Schedule and does not, therefore apply to persons or entities identified generically. Section 110 of that Act enables an 'authorized officer' to detain only 'cash recovered' that is intended, or suspected of being intended, for terrorism but does not appear to allow the officer to deal with other property, such as financial instruments and other valuables, that can be cashed and used for terrorism or with cash that is not actually 'recovered', such as cash in a bank account. Is it the intention of Pakistan to include provisions addressing these aspects in the proposed law on money laundering and terrorist financing so as to fully comply with the requirements of paragraph 1 of the Resolution?

Response:

The subject of terrorist financing has been removed from the scope of the draft anti-money laundering law after much consideration, since conceptually money laundering and terrorist financing are different issues.

- The proscription of an organization under the Anti Terrorism Act 1997 involves its notification by the Federal Government for including the name of the organization in the First Schedule of the Act. This is administrative action that is an effective and efficient method of proscribing an organization.
- Section 11O (c) of the Anti Terrorism Act 1997 read with Section 2 (z) (aa) (i) (a) & ii (b) of the Act defines terrorist property to include "any money or other property which is applied or made available, or is to be applied or made available, for use by the organization, and includes assets of any kind, whether tangible or intangible, movable or immovable, and legal documents or instruments in any form, whether written electronic or digital, and shares, securities, bonds, drafts and letters of credit."
- The above definition, therefore, comprehensively covers all financial instruments and other valuables that can be cashed and used for terrorism.
- Cash at the bank of organizations is frozen pursuant to their designation as terrorist organizations by the Security Council under its Consolidated List of Individuals and Entities pursuant to Resolutions 1267, 1333 and 1390. Also, it is frozen under Section 11 E of the Anti Terrorism Act 1997 after proscription of the organizations under the Act.

Paragraph 1.3

Q. The report mentioned that the draft law on Money Laundering and Terrorist Financing 'defines the offence of terrorist financing and makes it a predicate offence for purposes of money laundering'. The CTC would be grateful for confirmation that:

- *The provisions defining the offence of terrorist financing will extend to financial activity that relates to actual, proposed or potential acts of terrorism outside, as well as within, Pakistan, and,*
- *The provisions that make terrorist financing a predicate offence for money-laundering purposes will apply whether the acts of terrorist financing take place within Pakistan or outside.*

Response:

As stated above the subject of terrorist financing has been removed from the scope of the draft anti-money laundering law.

- Sections 11J and 11K of the Anti Terrorism Act 1997 make terrorist financing a predicate offence for actual, proposed or potential acts of terrorism.
- The above sections of the Anti Terrorism Act 1997 when read with Section 3 of the Penal Code of Pakistan (PPC) extend the application of the above Sections to offences committed outside Pakistan.

Paragraph 1.4

Q. Could Pakistan please explain whether the existing provisions or the proposed law would enable the authorities in Pakistan to freeze funds, financial assets or economic resources of persons or entities, either resident or non-resident, on the request of another member state on the grounds that they are linked to terrorist acts or in those cases where they are linked to terrorism even though no terrorist act has yet been attempted or committed.

Response:

At present there is no provision in Law that allows the Government to freeze funds, financial assets or economic resources of suspected persons or entities, either resident or non-resident, on the request of another State. In any case, in all countries, where this may be possible, the laws and the courts are involved to authorise such procedures to give them local cover, and appeals are also part of this process, of the rule of law.

Paragraph 1.5

Q. The CTC would be grateful for a progress report on:

- *the enactment of the law on money laundering and terrorist financing;*
- *the issue of the Ordinance to amend the Exchange Regulation Act; and*
- *the establishment, and commencement of operations, of the proposed national Financial Intelligence Center; and*
- *a copy of, or an Internet reference for, the texts of those proposed laws as soon as practicable after they become available for release into the public domain.*

Response:

As stated above the subject of terrorist financing has been removed from the scope of the draft anti-money laundering law.

- Anti-Money Laundering (AML) law is still under process.
- The amendment allowing for formulation of exchange companies is now in place with the enactment of the Ordinance to amend the Foreign Exchange Regulation Act.
- The establishment of Financial Intelligence Unit (FIU) will be under the provisions of the AML law. The proposed law under section 14 states that "the Federal Government shall establish, by notification in

official gazette, the Financial Intelligence Bureau under the general supervision of the Minister of Finance".

Paragraph 1.6

Q. In response to the question in the letter of 18 April 2002 whether financial intermediaries outside the main financial sector (e.g lawyers) are required to report suspicious financial transactions to the authorities, the supplementary report states that, on the bases of the concept of the privileged lawyer-client communication, there are, at present, no laws in Pakistan requiring lawyers to report suspicious transactions. Since there are situations in which lawyers act for clients in the role of brokers rather specifically as legal advisers and their other professions (e.g accountants, stockbrokers) who act on occasion as financial sector, the CTC would be grateful for information on any existing or proposed requirements in Pakistan for the reporting by those intermediaries of suspicious transactions that come to their notice outside a privileged relationship.

Response:

Section 11(L) of the Anti Terrorism Act 1997 provides for disclosure of information regarding the commission of terrorist offences. The Section, however, is not applicable to professional legal advisors who obtain any such information in privileged circumstances. The text of the provision is given as under:

(1) Where a person—

(a) believes or suspects that another person has committed an offence under this Act; and

(b) bases his belief or suspicion on information which comes to his attention in the course of a trade, profession, business or employment, he commits an offence if he does not disclose to a police officer as soon as is reasonably practicable his belief or suspicion, and the information on which it is based.

(2) It is a defence for a person charged with an offence under sub-section (1) of this section to prove that he had a reasonable excuse for not making the disclosure:

Provided that this sub-section does not require disclosure by a professional legal advisor of any information which he obtains in privileged circumstances.

(3) A person may disclose to a police officer:

(i) A suspicion or belief that any money or other property is terrorist property, or is derived from terrorist property; or

(ii) any matter on which the suspicion is based.

(4) Sub-section (3) shall have effect notwithstanding any restriction on the disclosure of information imposed by any law for the time being in force.

Paragraph 1.7

Q. Please confirm whether Madressah Registration Ordinance 2002 is now in force. Does it, as an Ordinance, have effect for only a limited time? If so, what plans are there for longer-term legislation regulating madressahs?

Response:

Ministry of Religious Affairs, in consultation with the Ministry of Interior, prepared the Deeni Madaris Ordinance. Following recent elections and the formation of the National Assembly, the draft law has to be approved by the Parliament.

The institution of the Madrassah, has historically, in Islamic culture, played an important role in the educational development of Muslims. In Pakistan, Madrassah's also perform an important social service of providing education. In order to avoid, the misuse of the Madrassah, while awaiting the enactment of the law, the Government has implemented far reaching administrative actions to regulate and streamline their activities through compulsory audits to determine the exact sources of finances at the disposal of the Madaris.

Paragraph 1.8

Q. Effective implementation of paragraph 2 of the Resolution requires that recruitment to terrorist groups and supply of weapons to them be suppressed. The definition of 'terrorism' contained in section 6 of the Anti-terrorism Act 1997 does not appear to extend to acts that are directed against other Member States or their citizens. Similarly, Section 11V of the Anti-terrorism Act refers to the 'instigation or the commission of acts of terrorism'. In terms of definition in section 6, these acts are criminalized only if they are directed against the Government or the public. 'Government' is defined in paragraph (i) of section 2 as 'the Federal or, as the case may be, the Provincial Government'. The CTC would be grateful to know how Pakistan would deal with the recruitment of persons, or the supply of weapons, in Pakistan to terrorists or terrorist groups operating outside the territory of Pakistan.

Response:

The application of Section 11V of the 1997 Anti Terrorist Act adequately covers all such situations where terrorist activity is suspected whether undertaken against the State or outside the state to other areas and territories not directly controlled by Pakistan. The Government of Pakistan is not allowing any terrorist unit or cell to operate from its territory against another state. This has been reiterated on countless occasions at the highest of levels. It would also be important to take into consideration Section 121 and 125 of the Penal Code that deals with commission of crimes outside the jurisdiction of Pakistan.

As regards disarmament of the terrorist groups, the Government launched a deweaponization campaign, especially of illegal weapons/arms and has imposed a ban on the display of weapons to discourage an arms culture. So far 230216 illegal weapons have been recovered (January 2003). The campaign is continuing and has helped reduce weapon possession in Pakistan.

Paragraph 1.9

Q. As regards provision of early warning on anticipated terrorist acts, it is stated in the first report that Pakistan exchanges information through INTERPOL and, in the supplementary report, that Pakistan exchanges information with countries with which it has extradition treaties and with "other coalition member countries." How, and in what circumstances, would Pakistan directly exchange of information with other countries, as contemplated by sub-paragraph 2(b)?

Response:

Pakistan regularly exchanges information with all friendly and non hostile States, whether they are coalition partners and have signed extradition treaties with Pakistan or not. Such information is provided to these countries through their embassies/consulates in Pakistan and through our embassies in these countries as well as in accordance with arrangements under various international organizations such as INTERPOL and the United Nations.

Pakistan is always ready to cooperate with all states towards furthering the international objectives against illegal transactions of dangerous substances, technology, scientists, equipment and information against terrorists indulging in such and other illegal activities. These actions of the Pakistan Government also help in tracing and subsequent arrests of criminals involved in terrorist activities.

Paragraph 1.10

Q. Effective implementation of Sub-paragraphs 2(d) & (e) requires the criminalization of the use of Pakistan territory for the purpose of committing terrorist acts against other states or their citizens or for the purpose of financing, planning and facilitating of terrorist acts against other states or their citizens, even if the related terrorist acts have not been attempted or committed. Please provide an outline of the provisions, if any in this regard or, if there are none, of the action that Pakistan proposes to take in this regard.

Response:

Pakistan has been a victim of terrorist acts. We are against all kinds of terrorism that is state-terrorism, cross-border terrorism and international terrorism and are committed not to allow any person or organization to use Pakistan's soil for the acts of terrorism.

Sections 11-H to 11-K of the Anti Terrorism Act 1997 specifically criminalize various forms of terrorist financing, including directly and indirectly inciting others to finance and aiding and abetting. In order to make the anti-terrorism Act more effective, further amendments in Anti-Terrorism Act 1997 are being made.

Paragraph 1.11

Q. The supplementary report mentions, in response to the question in the letter of 18th April 2002 regarding the competence of Pakistan courts, that section 3 of the Penal Code provides that 'any person liable, by any Pakistani Law, to be tried for any offence committed beyond Pakistan shall be dealt with according to the provisions of this Court for any act committed beyond Pakistan in the same manner as if such act had been committed within Pakistan'. By what provisions are persons who are neither Pakistani citizens nor servants of the Government of Pakistan made "liable . . . to be tried for {an} offence committed beyond Pakistan" that is not committed against Pakistan? Please confirm that foreign fugitives found in Pakistan who are alleged to have committed or attempted terrorist crimes outside Pakistan will be either brought to justice in Pakistan or extradited.

Response:

As regards the question that the foreign fugitives found in Pakistan who are alleged to have committed or attempted terrorist crimes outside Pakistan will be either brought to justice in Pakistan or extradited, it is stated that Section 11 V of the Anti Terrorism Act, 1997 read with Section 4 of the Pakistan Penal Code (PPC) and Section 188 of Criminal Code of Pakistan (Cr. PC) prevent support within Pakistan to acts of terrorism carried out or proposed to be carried out elsewhere. Under Section 11 V(2) of the Anti Terrorism Act, 1997, a person guilty of an offence under sub section (1) shall be liable on conviction to imprisonment for a maximum term of 07 years and to forfeiture or confiscation of his assets within or outside Pakistan. Besides Pakistan has Extradition Agreements with 27 countries, and, therefore, may extradite the person who is found to have committed or attempted terrorist crimes outside Pakistan."

Paragraph 1.12

Q. Sub paragraph 2 (f) requires Member States to afford one another the greatest measure of assistance in connection with criminal investigations or criminal proceedings relating to the financing or support to terrorist acts, including assistance to obtaining evidence in their possession necessary for the proceedings. What plans does Pakistan have for making it possible to render such assistance to Member States with which it has no extradition treaty, should such a request be made?

Response:

Pakistan, in all such circumstances where sufficient evidence has been provided justifying recourse to such action, can adopt the following procedure if required:

- Extradite the person to a third country with which it has an extradition treaty;
- Extradite the person to the requesting state under a specific bilateral arrangement; or
- Act on behalf of the requesting state to obtain and provide the necessary information.

Paragraph 1.13

Q. The CTC would be grateful to be informed how the international Conventions against terrorism ratified by Pakistan have been implemented through domestic legislation and the progress that Pakistan has made in regard to the ratification and implementation of the Conventions to which it has not yet become a party?

Response:

Out of 12 UN Conventions Pakistan has already ratified/acceded to/signed eleven Conventions and in order to implement these Conventions, appropriate provisions are available in our laws. However, wherever necessary, appropriate amendments would be made to cover the specific situation.

The two Conventions (International Convention for the Suppression of the Financing of Terrorism, and Convention on the Marking of Plastic Explosives for the Purpose of Detection), which have not been ratified/acceded to by Pakistan so far are being actively considered for ratification. In the mean time certain amendments are already being processed in the Anti-Terrorism Act, 1997 which deal with Terrorist Financing.

Paragraph 1.14

Q. In response to the question whether the crimes set forth in the relevant international conventions and protocols have been included as extraditable offences in the bilateral treaties to which Pakistan is a party, the supplementary report states that 'Pakistan is bound by the relevant articles of those Conventions and Protocols which stipulate that the offences set forth in the relevant Conventions and Protocols are deemed to be included as extraditable offences in any extradition treaty existing between States Parties and any extradition treaty to be concluded between them.' The CTC notes that, while the 'relevant articles' (for example, paragraph 1 of Article 9 of the International Convention for the Suppression of Terrorist Bombings) provide that the relevant offences 'shall be deemed to be included as extraditable offences in any extradition treaty existing between any of the States

Parties before the entry into force of this Convention', they also provide that 'States Parties undertake to include such offences as extraditable offences in every extradition treaty to be subsequently concluded between them.' The CTC would therefore be grateful for confirmation that extradition concluded by Pakistan after the entry into force of any relevant Convention or Protocol made the required provision.

Response:

Pakistan signs extradition treaties with other countries in the light of the provisions of Extradition Act 1972. Pakistan has so far signed Extradition Treaties with 27 countries. The Extradition Offences are given in the Schedule of this Act. So far 23 offences are listed in the Schedule and others are being examined for incorporation, if required.

Paragraph 1.15

Q. Sub-paragraph 3 (g) of the Resolution contemplates that definitive provision will be made to ensure that claims of political motivation are not recognized as grounds for refusing requests for the extradition of alleged terrorists. The supplementary report indicates that a 'political exception' is provided for in section 5 (2) (a) of the Extradition Act 1972 but, for it to apply, an authority 'has to be satisfied that requisition for (the fugitive's) surrender has, in fact been made with a view to his being tried or punished for an offence of a political character'. Does Pakistan intend to amend the law to provide definitively that the relevant offences are not political in character for the purposes of section 5 (2) (a)?

Response:

To be provided later.

DOCUMENT NO. 11

PAKISTAN'S 2002 REPORT TO THE UN ON ITS COUNTER-TERRORISM EFFORTS

UN Security Council Resolution S/2004/21

January 13, 2004

Distr.: General
13 January 2004
Original: English

Letter dated 5 January 2004 from the Chairman of the Security Council Committee established pursuant to resolution 1373 (2001) concerning counter-terrorism addressed to the President of the Security Council

I write with reference to my letter of 9 October 2003 (S/2003/1012). The Counter-Terrorism Committee has received the attached fourth report from Pakistan submitted pursuant to paragraph 6 of resolution 1373 (2001) (see annex). I would be grateful if you could arrange for the present letter and its annex to be circulated as a document of the Security Council.

(*Signed*) Inocencio F. **Arias**
Chairman
Security Council Committee established pursuant to
resolution 1373 (2001) concerning counter-terrorism

Annex

Letter dated 2 January 2004 from the Permanent Representative of Pakistan to the United Nations addressed to the Chairman of the Counter-Terrorism Committee

With reference to your letter dated 3 October 2003, I enclose Pakistan's interim response to the additional information sought by the Counter-Terrorism Committee pursuant to paragraph 6 of resolution 1373 (2001) (see enclosure). Replies to questions 1.8 and 1.10 will be provided later.

(*Signed*) Masood **Khalid**
Acting Permanent Representative

Enclosure

Pakistan's Interim Response to the Counter Terrorism Committee of the UN Security Council

1. Implementation Measures

Effectiveness in the Protection of the Financial System

Paragraph 1.1

Q. In its third report, Pakistan explains that the definition provided by the Anti-Terrorism Act 1997 covers all financial instruments and other valuables that can be "cashed" by an 'authorized officer' as provided for under section 110(c) read in conjunction with Section 2(z) (aa) (i) (a) & (ii) (b) of the said Act. The CTC would therefore welcome examples of cases in which the relevant sections of the said Act were applied since this statute came into force.

Response:

The Government of Pakistan has put the names of activities of banned organizations in Schedule IV of Anti Terrorist Act 1997. An effective monitoring mechanism has been devised and put in place at grass root level to keep the activities of the extremists under observation. This monitoring has contributed positively to the law and order situation in general and reduced the risks of freedom of action of the extremists.

Paragraph 1.2

With regards to the extraterritorial jurisdiction of Pakistan's national courts in relation to the crime of the financing of terrorism, the CTC notes that Section 11J of the Anti-Terrorism Act establishes the financing of terrorism as a criminal offence under the law of Pakistan (at page 4 of the third report). The CTC also notes that section 3 of the Penal Code of Pakistan provides that "any persons liable, by any Pakistani Law, to be tried for an offence committed beyond Pakistan shall be dealt with according to the provisions of this Code for any act committed beyond Pakistan in the same manner as if such act had been committed within Pakistan" (at page 25 of the supplementary report of Pakistan). The CTC would, therefore, be grateful if Pakistan could outline the relevant provisions under its Anti-Terrorism Act 1997 which establish jurisdiction for Pakistani courts over the financing of terrorism when committed beyond Pakistan by any person who is subsequently found in Pakistan?

Response:

Section 11EE of Anti Terrorist Act 1997 provides vast powers to Law Enforcing Agencies for keeping surveillance on abettors, perpetrators, financers, trainers, instigators and the principal accused. The implementation of these provisions is extended up to the entire territory of Pakistan and applicable to every citizen of Pakistan.

Paragraph 1.3

The CTC notes that Pakistan, at present, does not have statutory provisions in place which allow the Government of Pakistan to freeze funds, financial assets or economic resources of suspected persons or entities, either resident or non-resident, at the request of another State (at page 4 of the third report). However, the effective implementation of subparagraph 1(c) of the resolution requires the establishment of such provisions. The CTC would therefore be grateful to learn the steps undertaken by the Government of Pakistan to introduce those provisions into its domestic law?

Response:

If the Government of Pakistan has substantial evidence against individuals/organizations for their involvement in terrorist related activities, then they are proscribed under the Anti-Terrorism Act, 1997 and eventually their accounts/funds are frozen.

Paragraph 1.4

The CTC would welcome a progress report on the enactment of the Anti-Money-Laundering Law, and the establishment of a Financial Intelligence Unit (see page 5 of the third report). In that regard, please indicate the date on which it is anticipated that the new law will come into force. If the law is already in force, please outline the relevant provisions.

Response:

The Government of Pakistan is actively seized with the early enactment of draft Anti-Money Laundering (AML) and Proceeds of Crimes Bill, which is currently under thorough review by the relevant government departments. The draft would be submitted to the Cabinet for approval shortly, thereafter it would have to be passed by the Parliament before its implementation. It is, therefore, difficult to put a definite date on which the law will come into force, however, it is expected to be enforced in the first half of 2004. The Financial Intelligence Unit (FIU) will be established under the provisions of the AML law.

Effectiveness of Counter-terrorism Machinery

Paragraph 1.5

In relation to subparagraph 2(b) of the resolution and its response thereto, Pakistan indicates that the two main channels for the exchange of information between Pakistan and other countries are Interpol and Pakistan's bilateral treaties on extradition. The CTC would appreciate receiving figures indicating the number of cases in which information was exchanged as well the number of times in which the exchange of information was significant in determining the outcome of particular cases.

Response:

Pakistan has been actively cooperating and exchanging information with many countries around the world, with positive outcome in a significant number of cases.

Paragraph 1.6

The CTC would welcome receiving a progress report in relation to the amendments introduced in order to make the Anti-Terrorism Act 1997 more effective as regards the implementation of subparagraphs 2 (d) and (e) of the Resolution (see page 7 of the third report).

Response:

Various amendments have been made in Sections 6, 7, 11, 19, 21 and 39 of the Anti-Terrorism Act, 1997. Section 11H is being further amended to include the act of financing terrorism as an offence.

Paragraph 1.7

The CTC notes that Pakistan's courts have jurisdiction over persons 'directing' the activities of an organization concerned with the preparation, instigation or commission of acts of terrorism whilst outside the Pakistani territory as provided for under 11V(2) of the Anti-Terrorism Act 1997. Could Pakistan provide the CTC with examples of cases where this provision was employed? In addition, could Pakistan outline other similar provision(s) under its domestic law which extend(s) the jurisdiction of its national courts over acts of terrorism committed outside Pakistan, other than the above-mentioned act of 'directing', such as the financing and the commission of terrorist acts:

(i) By non-citizens who are also not in the service of Pakistan as provided for under Section 4 of the Pakistan's Penal Law (see page 13 of the supplementary report).

(ii) In places other than tribal areas or on any ship or aircraft registered in Pakistan, as provided for under Section 188 of the Criminal Code of Pakistan

(at page 13 of the supplementary report). The CTC would appreciate receiving an account of the legal provisions concerning persons who are not citizens of Pakistan.

Response:

Section 3 of PPC fulfils the requirements regarding jurisdiction of Pakistan's courts over acts of terrorism committed outside Pakistan. The provisions of anti-terrorism act of 1997 are equally applicable to the Pakistani nationals or otherwise.

Paragraph 1.8

Could Pakistan provide the CTC with the relevant domestic legal provisions (see page 8 of the third report) which give effect to the terms of the international conventions and protocols related to the prevention and suppression of international terrorism to which Pakistan is already a party?

Paragraph 1.9

The CTC would also welcome receiving a progress report in relation to the ratification of or accession to the international instruments related to the prevention and suppression of international terrorism, to which Pakistan is not yet a party.

Response:

The two Conventions (International Convention for the Suppression of the Financing of Terrorism, and Convention on the Marking of Plastic Explosives for the Purpose of Detection), which have not been ratified/ acceded to by Pakistan so far are still under consideration for ratification/ accession.

Paragraph 1.10

Please indicate to the Committee whether the Extradition Act 1972 of Pakistan applies the principle aut dedere aut judicare in relation to the offences referred to in sub-paragraph 2(c) of the Resolution? Are those offences listed in the Schedule of the Extradition Act 1972? If the answer to the last question is in the affirmative, please outline the crimes set out in the list? If the answer is in the negative, the CTC would appreciate receiving a progress report on the examination referred to at page 9 of the third report with a view to incorporating those offences in the Schedule of the Extradition Act 1972.

Paragraph 1.11

Could Pakistan provide the CTC with the criteria applicable in its domestic law for determining what constitutes a political offence? Are any of the offences, referred to in sub-paragraph 2(c) of the Resolution or in the international conventions and protocols related to the prevention and suppression of international terrorism, considered to constitute "political offences" under the domestic law of Pakistan? If such is not the case, the CTC would appreciate receiving an outline of the relevant domestic provisions.

Response:

The concept of political offence does not exist in our laws. The relevant provisions are covered under the Anti-terrorism Act of 1997, sufficient details of which have already been provided to the CTC.

Paragraph 1.12

Is there a special law in force in Pakistan concerning mutual assistance in criminal matters? Are the principles of reciprocity and/or comity applied in that regard?

Response:

Pakistan has bilateral agreements with a number of countries for mutual assistance in criminal matters. Principal of reciprocity is applied in all such cases.

Effectiveness of Customs, Immigration and Border Controls

Paragraph 1.13

The effective implementation of subparagraph 2(g) requires that borders be efficiently controlled in order to prevent the movement of terrorist or terrorist groups. With a view to achieving this efficiency, has Pakistan put in place a unified data system for use at all entry/exit points? If such is not the case, how many entry/exit points, whether by air, land, or sea are currently included in the data system. Does Pakistan's system register traveller data immediately upon entry/exit, or is this data entered later (i.e. by hand on the basis of data gathered by filling in handwritten cards at all entry and exit points)?

Response:

Personal Identification Secure Comparison Evaluation System (PISCES) is being implemented under phased programme. In 1st phase; the system was implemented in November 2001 at Karachi Airport, in 2nd phase; the system was implemented in November—December 2002 at four other major airports i.e. Islamabad, Lahore, Peshawar and Quetta. In total there are 20 Ports of Immigration including sea and land routes. In the 3rd phase the system will be implemented at seven ports out of which three are seaports at Karachi and remaining four are airports. This phase is to be completed by 31 December 2003. All the remaining ports of embarkation/ disembarkation would have PISCES system by 31st December 2004, after which a countrywide border control system would become functional. After the implementation of the system, the hand written cards procedure has been stopped, seaports are being processed through automated system and travel documents are being scanned also. Countrywide database of travellers is being stored in the FIA Headquarters on a dedicated network.

Paragraph 1.14

If "traveller data systems" are maintained at all border points, do these systems incorporate information of a 'watch list' nature? If such is the case, is the information in question updated regularly taking account of all relevant sources?

Response:

The PISCES system functions against pre-defined watch lists including Exist Control list, Stolen Passport list, Lost Passports list, Black Listed individuals etc, with reference to issuance of Passport and other Proclaimed Offenders of local Police/International Organizations. These watch lists are updated regularly.

Paragraph 1.15

Does Pakistan have laws and regulations in place imposing an obligation on common carriers to meet the cost of returning travellers, who have arrived at Pakistan's borders without adequate documentation, to their point of departure?

Response:

Pakistan is signatory to all IATA Rules and Regulations, under which common carriers are under obligation to take back illegal immigrants.

Paragraph 1.16

As regards the effective control on the issuance of identity papers and travel documents referred to in subparagraph 2 (g) of the Resolution, does Pakistan issue national identity documents? If so, who is entitled to receive the document? Is the system employed for issuing identity documents computerized? In that regard, could Pakistan also provide the CTC with information as to the type of data stored and the agencies with which such information is shared?

Response:

Following identity documents are issued by the Government of Pakistan:-

i) National Identity Card (NIC) is issued to resident Pakistanis of the age of 18 years and above.

ii) National Identity for Overseas Pakistanis (NICOP) is issued to non-resident Pakistanis whose stay abroad exceeds six months and Pakistanis holding dual nationality.

iii) Pakistan origin card (POC) is issued to Pakistan origin foreigners, their spouses and children.

iv) Children Registration Certificate (CRC) is issued on demand to Pakistanis below 18 years.

The system employed for issuing identity documents is computerized. The data collected and stored consists of complete identification and contact details of a person. The information is shared with all the law enforcing agencies of Pakistan.

Paragraph 1.17

Does Pakistan allow for the routine entry into or exit out of its territory by its nationals or by nationals from other States on production of a national identity card (as opposed to a passport)?

Response:

No. Pakistan does not allow entry into/exit out of Pakistan without passports/valid travel documents.

Effectiveness of Controls Preventing Access to Weapons by Terrorists

Paragraph 1.18

With regards to the disarmaments measures referred to at page 6 of its third report, could Pakistan provide the CTC with an outline of the mechanism which it employs to disarm persons who are in possession of illegal weapons inside its territory?

Response:

A number of measures are taken to disarm persons who are in possession of illegal weapons such as:

- Intelligence Agencies are tasked to forewarn relevant authorities about presence of illegal weapons.
- Raids are conducted on suspected sites.
- Check posts are established on major transportation routes to check the flow of illegal weapons.
- Sources of illegal weapons are blocked.

Paragraph 1.19

In its first report (S/2001/1310) dated 27 December 2001, Pakistan mentions that it had banned the issuing of licenses to bear arms. It also mentioned that it had approved "a positive list" of weapons for which a license would be required in future (see pages 6 and 7 of the first report). In that regard, could Pakistan please indicate the types of weapons which have been included in the approved "positive list" referred to in its first report?

Response:

The types of weapons included in the approved "positive list" are as under:

- Shotgun-12/14/16 bore
- Revolver/Pistol –All bores
- Rifle- 22 bore (non-automatic)

Paragraph 1.20

In relation to the new licensing system for weapons mentioned in the "positive" list [at page 7 of the first report]:

i. Please outline the conditions which an individual has to meet under Pakistan's licensing system so as to be legally entitled to purchase a firearm(s).

ii. How many weapons of a particular type may be licensed for each individual? Are there any exemptions or exceptions in that regard?

iii. Does the licensing system allow for transfers of licenses? If yes, under what conditions?

iv. How long is a license valid? Is a specific agency or department responsible for monitoring the validity and/or expiry of individual licenses?

Response:

The sale and purchase of arms and explosives is strictly regulated in Pakistan. The arms are sold only by the authorized dealers to those individuals who have been issued arms licences. The un-authorized possession and sale of weapons leads to serious legal action against the defaulters. The issuance of licences for prohibited bore weapons has been banned. However, non-prohibited arms licences, on a limited scale, are issued to the gazetted officers of the Government and tax payer citizens. These licences are periodically renewed.

Paragraph 1.21

The CTC is aware that Pakistan may have covered some or all of the points in the preceding paragraphs in reports or questionnaires submitted to other organisations involved in monitoring international standards. The CTC would be content to receive a copy of any such report or questionnaire as part of Pakistan's response to these matters as well as details of any efforts to implement international best practices, codes and standards which are relevant to the implementation of resolution 1373.

2. Assistance and guidance

With the gradual build-up of database in PISCES Programme, the Law Enforcing Agencies have shown their interest in utilizing the information available in PISCES system. There is a genuine requirement to extend the system to the law enforcement organizations enabling them to monitor the movement of suspected individuals. CTC is requested to provide assistance in early implementation of this programme.

The CTC is also requested to provide updated copies of central directory for identification of targets.

DOCUMENT NO. 12

PAKISTAN'S 2003 REPORT TO THE UN ON ITS COUNTER-TERRORISM EFFORTS

UN Security Council Resolution
S/AC.44/2004/(02)/22

November 5, 2004

Distr.: General
5 November 2004
Original: English

Security Council Committee established pursuant to resolution 1540 (2004)

Note verbale dated 27 October 2004 from the Permanent Mission of Pakistan to the United Nations addressed to the Chairman of the Committee

The Permanent Mission of Pakistan to the United Nations presents its compliments to the Chairman of the Security Council Committee established pursuant to resolution 1540 (2004), and has the honour to transmit herewith the national report of the Government of Pakistan in accordance with paragraph 4 of the Security Council resolution 1540 (2004) (see annex).

Annex

Annex to the note verbale dated 27 October 2004 from the Permanent Mission of Pakistan to the United Nations addressed to the Chairman of the Committee

Pakistan's national report on national measures on the implementation of Security Council resolution 1540 (2004)

Consistent with its strong commitment to the objectives of disarmament and non-proliferation, Pakistan fully supports appropriate and effective measures to prevent non-state actors from gaining access to weapons of mass destruction and their means of delivery. This has been reiterated in public pronouncements of the Pakistan's leadership and the government. Nationally, Pakistan has instituted comprehensive administrative, legislative and security measure to ensure the safety and security of sensitive materials, facilities, technologies and equipment. Internationally, Pakistan remains a partner in efforts to stem proliferation and illicit trafficking of WMD-related materials.

Pakistan believes that the objectives of non-proliferation of weapons of mass destruction to non-state actors can be effectively promoted through freely negotiated, non-discriminatory and cooperative multilateral efforts. Pakistan stands ready to contribute constructively to all efforts that strengthen global non-proliferation within the framework of existing treaty regimes and bodies.

Pakistan has taken general and specific steps in implementation of Resolution 1540 (2004). This report, being submitted pursuant to paragraph 4 of Resolution 1540, elaborates such steps. The Government of Pakistan regularly reviews its policies and measures and would continue to strengthen them, where appropriate or necessary.

Operative Paragraph 1

1. Decides that all States shall refrain from providing any form of support to non-State actors that attempt to develop, acquire, manufacture, possess, transport, transfer or use nuclear, chemical or biological weapons and their means of delivery;

This objective is realized through the existence of appropriate policy, administrative and legislative framework detailed below.

Operative Paragraph 2

2. Decides also that all States, in accordance with their national procedures, shall adopt and enforce appropriate effective laws which prohibit any non-State actor to manufacture, acquire, possess, develop, transport, transfer or use nuclear, chemical or biological weapons and their means of delivery, in particular for terrorist purposes, as well as attempts to engage in any of the foregoing activities, participate in them as an accomplice, assist or finance them;

Elaborate legal, administrative and law enforcement measures are in place to prohibit non-State actors to manufacture, acquire, possess, develop, transport, transfer or use nuclear, chemical or biological weapons and their means of delivery. Where required, these measures have been further strengthened.

Legal Framework

Pakistan's export controls framework is governed by the following legal and administrative instruments:

i) *The Import and Exports (Control) Act, 1950 Act No. XXXIX of 1950.* This Act authorizes the Federal Government to prohibit, restrict or control the import or export of goods and regulate all practices and procedures connected therewith. Section 5(1) of the Act provides for penalty of an individual, without prejudice to any confiscation to which he may be liable under the provisions of the Customs Act 1969-(IV 0f 1969), as applied by sub-section (3) of this Act, be punishable with imprisonment for a term which may extend to one year, or with fine, or with both.

ii) *Pakistan Nuclear Safety and Radiation Protection (PNSRP) Ordinance of 1984 and Regulation of 1990* which contains provisions for control of import/export of nuclear substances and radioactive materials, extending to whole of Pakistan, has been further strengthened with Pakistan Nuclear Regulatory Authority Ordinance 2001.

iii) *Pakistan's Trade Policy 2004–05:* This encompasses Import Policy Order and Export Policy Order to regulate trade on all items. These orders take into account all previous Statutory Regulation Orders (SROs) and Ordinances issued by the Government of Pakistan from time to time. Under (a) Import Policy Order 2004 and (b) Export Policy Order 2004 (EPO), import and export of sensitive materials is regulated.

iv) *Chemical Weapons Convention Implementation Ordinance - 2000, Ordinance No. LIV of 2000.* The law enables the full implementation and enforcement of the provisions of the Chemical Weapons Convention and fulfills Pakistan's obligations under Article VII of the Convention mandating national implementing measures. This legislative framework regulates and controls the import and export of chemicals in accordance with the CWC and provides for criminal penalties in case of violations. Para 12 of the EPO 2000 pertains to export control of chemicals as required under the Chemical Weapons Convention. The National Authority established in the Ministry of Foreign Affairs is the focal point for the implementation and enforcement of the provisions of the Ordinance. These measures constitute fulfillment of the requirements of resolution 1540 in the context of CWC.

v) *Pakistan Nuclear Regulatory Authority Ordinance (PNRA), 2001. Ordinance_No. III of 2001.* Under this Ordinance, PNRA issues the required "no objection certificate" (NOC) for all imports and exports of any radioactive materials or radiation sources. The PNRA is responsible for controlling, regulating and supervising all maters related to nuclear safety and radiation protection measures in Pakistan. Any person who contravenes any of the provisions of sections 19, 20, 21, 22 or 23 of the Ordinance shall be punishable with imprisonment for a term which may extend to 7 years, or with fine which may extend to one million rupees, or with both. Notification SRO.III(1)2004 as amended on 16 February 2004; Nuclear substances, Radioactive Materials and any other substance or item covered by PNRA Ordinance, 2001 (III Of 2001); and Equipment used for production, use, or application of nuclear energy or activity, including generation of electricity and spares, are subject to NOC from PNRA as per procedure notified by the Pakistan Nuclear Regulatory Authority (PNRA).

New Legislation

A new comprehensive national legislation entitled "Export Control on Goods, Technologies, Material and Equipment related to Nuclear and Biological Weapons and their Delivery Systems Act, 2004" was passed by National Assembly on 14th September, 2004 and by the Senate on 18th September, 2004. The Act received the assent of the President on 23rd September, 2004 and entered into force the same day. The Act further strengthens controls on export of sensitive technologies particularly related to nuclear and biological weapons and their means of delivery. Salient elements of the new Export Control Act include:

- Controls over export, re-export, transshipment and transit of goods, technologies, material and equipment covered. Prohibition of diversion of controlled goods and technologies.
- Wide jurisdiction (also includes Pakistanis visiting or working abroad).
- Provide for an authority to administer rules and regulations framed under this legislation. Also provides for the establishment of an Oversight Board to monitor the implementation of this legislation.
- Comprehensive control lists and catch all provisions.
- Licensing and record keeping provisions.
- Penal provisions: Up to 14 years imprisonment and Rs.5 million fine or both, and on conviction, offender's property and assets, wherever they may be, shall be forfeited to the Federal Government. Right of appeal provided for.

- For the purposes of the Export Control Act, the authority rests with the Federal Government and the Federal Government, as and when necessary, may—

  (a) make such rules and regulations as are necessary for implementation of this Act;

  (b) delegate authority to administer all activities under this Act to such Ministries, Division, Departments and Agencies as it may deem appropriate;

  (c) establish a government Authority to administer export controls established under this Act;

  (d) designate the agency or agencies authorized to enforce this Act;

  (e) establish an Oversight Board to monitor the implementation of this Act; and

  (f) require licenses for exports from Pakistan of goods and technology, and the re-export of goods and technology that originated in Pakistan.

- Moreover, officials of the designated agency or agencies are authorized to inspect consignments declared for export and review, acquire or confiscate records or withholding an export license under this Act. The Federal Government may vest any investigatory powers and powers of arrest authorized by law in officials of the customs administration or other appropriate agencies.

Operative Para 3

3. Decides also that all States shall take and enforce effective measures to establish domestic controls to prevent the proliferation of nuclear, chemical or biological weapons and their means of delivery, including by establishing appropriate controls over related materials and to this end shall:

a) Develop and maintain appropriate effective measures to account for and secure such items in production, use, storage or transport.

Action Taken

- In accordance with Pakistan's laws, effective measures have been taken to account for and secure sensitive materials in production, use, storage or transport.
- Pakistan Nuclear Regulatory Authority (PNRA) has an established system for the safety and security of nuclear and radioactive materials and installations during use, storage and transport. PNRA regulations (i.e. PAK/904-Regulations on Nuclear Protection, PAK/909-Regulations

for Licensing of Nuclear Installations, PAK/911-Regulations on the Safety of Nuclear Power Plants Design, PAK/916-Regulations for the Safe Transport of Radioactive Material) contain necessary clauses, which obligates the licensee to take appropriate measures for the security of the nuclear/radioactive materials and the installations under its jurisdiction. Pakistan is also a Party to the Convention on Physical Protection of Nuclear Material (CPPNM) and has formally informed the IAEA regarding its voluntary commitment to follow the requirements of the Code of Conduct for the Safety and Security of Radioactive Sources.

b) Develop and maintain appropriate effective physical protection measures;

Action Taken

- The Government has put in place effective physical protection measures for the safety and security of its installations, equipment, material and personnel.
- Under the Chemical Weapons Convention Implementation Ordinance – 2000, Ordinance No. LIV of 2000, effective controls have been established to regulate and control the import and export of chemicals in accordance with the CWC and provides for criminal penalties in case of violations. The National Authority established in the Ministry of Foreign Affairs is the focal agency for the implementation and enforcement of the provisions of the Ordinance. The Ordinance includes implementation of reporting requirements for all chemicals contained in the schedules I, II & III of the CWC.
- Pakistan is a party to the Convention on Physical Protection of Nuclear Material and Nuclear Facilities since September 2000. PNSRP Regulations 1990 as amended in 1998 provides that "Licensee shall be responsible to organize and ensure the physical protection of nuclear material in use, storage and during transport and of nuclear facilities, including radioactive waste belonging to these facilities in accordance with the provisions of these regulations and guidelines issued from time to time". PNRA has advised the licensees to implement the above-mentioned regulation by following the latest version of the IAEA document—INFCIRC/225/Rev-4-Physical Protection of Nuclear Material and Nuclear Facilities. Pakistan Nuclear Regulatory Authority Ordinance, 2001 (III of 2001) Section 16-f, empowers PNRA to ensure that appropriate measures for physical protection of nuclear installations and nuclear materials are taken.
- The promulgation of Export Control Act 2004 will further stren-gthen the export regime on goods, technologies material and equipment related to nuclear and biological weapons and their means of delivery.

c) Develop and maintain appropriate effective border controls and law enforcement efforts to detect, deter, prevent and combat, including through international cooperation when necessary, the illicit trafficking and brokering in such items in accordance with their national legal authorities and legislation and consistent with international law;

Action Taken

- Customs and other law enforcement agencies keep a tight vigil along borders, seaports and airports.
- Special training to detect sensitive materials is being imparted to the customs and law enforcement officials.

d) Establish, develop, review and maintain appropriate effective national export and trans-ship controls over such items, including appropriate laws and regulations to control export, transit, trans-shipment and re-export and controls on providing funds and services related to such export and transshipment such as financing, and transporting that would contribute to proliferation as well as establishing end-user controls; and establishing and enforcing appropriate criminal or civil penalties for violations of such export control laws and regulations;

Action Taken

- The Chemical Weapons Convention Implementation Ordinance 2000 and the Export Control on Goods, Technology, Material and Equipment related to Nuclear and Biological Weapons and their Delivery Systems Act, 2004 provides a comprehensive framework for effective national export and trans-shipment control over goods and technologies that may contribute to proliferation.
- Under the Export Control Act 2004, appropriate End-user certificate as well as catch-all clauses have been included. Violators are liable to be punished with imprisonment and fine, or with both.
- Border controls have been further strengthened and scanners and detection equipment is being installed on entry/exit points.

Operative Paragraph 5

5. Decides that none of the obligations set forth in this resolution shall be interpreted so as to conflict with or alter the rights and obligations of State Parties to the Nuclear Non-Proliferation Treaty, the Chemical Weapons Convention and the Biological and Toxin Weapons Convention or alter the responsibilities of the International Atomic Energy Agency or the Organization for the Prohibition of Chemical Weapons;

- Pakistan is a state party to the Chemical Weapons Convention (CWC) and the Biological Weapons Convention (BWC) — Pakistan is in full compliance of these conventions. Pakistan is also an active member of OPCW activities. Pakistan fully supports the establishment of a Verification Protocol of BWC in order to strengthen the full implementation of the Biological Weapons Convention.
- Pakistan is not a party to the NPT. Pakistan is a member of the IAEA and of several Treaties and agreements evolved under the aegis of the Agency which promote nuclear safety, physical protection and technical cooperation for peaceful purposes. Pakistan fulfills its obligations as a responsible nuclear state through the administrative and legislative controls in the field of nuclear technology as detailed in this report.

Operative Paragraph 6

6. Recognizes the utility in implementing this resolution of effective national control lists and calls upon all member States, when necessary, to pursue at the earliest opportunity the development of such lists;

Action Taken

- Pakistan maintains a control list as provided for in the Chemical Weapons Convention (CWC). Such a list is maintained under Section 2(k) in Schedules I, II and III of the Chemical Weapons Convention Implementation Ordinance 2000.
- Section 4 of the Export Control on Goods, Technology, Material and Equipment related to Nuclear and Biological Weapons and their Delivery Systems Act, 2004 provides for development/updating, as necessary, of Control Lists of goods and technologies subject to licensing requirements under the Act.

Operative Paragraph 7

7. Recognizes that some States may require assistance in implementing the provisions of this resolution within their territories and invites States in a position to do so to offer assistance as appropriate in response to specific requests to the States lacking the legal and regulatory infrastructure, implementation experience and/or resources for fulfilling the above provisions;

Action Taken

- In view of Pakistan's experience in implementation of various treaties regimes including CWC, CPPNM and BWC and its elaborate legislative framework in the safety and security of nuclear technology and material, Pakistan is in a position to provide assistance, as appropriate, in response to specific requests, to the states lacking the legal and regulatory infrastructure, implementation experience and/or resources for fulfilling the provisions of the Security Council Resolution 1540 (2004).

- Requests for assistance from the Government of Pakistan should be sent through the Permanent Mission of Pakistan to the United Nations, New York.

Operative Paragraph 8

8. *Calls upon all States:*

a) To promote the universal adoption and full implementation, and where necessary, strengthening of multilateral treaties to which they are parties, whose aim is to prevent the proliferation of nuclear, biological or chemical weapons;

Action Taken

i. Pakistan fully complies with Chemical Weapons Convention (CWC) and Biological Weapons Convention (BWC)—both are non-discriminatory disarmament treaties.

ii. Pakistan is not a party to the Nuclear Non-Proliferation Treaty (NPT). As a nuclear state, Pakistan fully supports the objective of non-proliferation and as outlined in this report, has taken adequate measures to implement its policies of restraint and responsibility in nuclear matters. Pakistan also believes that all states should fulfill their obligations under the treaties to which they are a party.

b) To adopt national rules and regulations, where it has not yet been done, to ensure compliance with their commitments under the key multilateral non-proliferation treaties;

Action Taken

- See OP 8-a above.

c) To renew and fulfill their commitment to multilateral cooperation, in particular within the framework of the International Atomic Energy Agency, the Organization for the Prohibition of Chemical Weapons and the Biological and Toxin Weapons Convention, as important means of pursuing and achieving their common objectives in the area of non-proliferation and of promoting international cooperation for peaceful purposes;

Action Taken

- Pakistan extends full support to the activities of the IAEA as a member of the Board of Governors. It has always fulfilled its budgetary obligations to the Agency and has rendered technical assistance to Member States under the auspices of the IAEA's Technical Assistance and Technical Cooperation programmes. Pakistan fully supports IAEA's role to render assistance to member states involved in the development of nuclear technology for peaceful purposes.

- Pakistan actively participates in the activities of the OPCW, both as a state party and a member of the Executive Council.
- Pakistan remains fully committed to the strengthening of the Biological Weapons Convention including the establishment of a Compliance regime through a Protocol. Pakistan will continue to follow up the discussions at the 2006 Review Conference.

d) To develop appropriate ways to work with and inform industry and the public regarding their obligations under such laws;

Action Taken

- The Government of Pakistan maintains a close working relationship with industry, particularly chemical industry through official interaction, seminars and workshops. More such activities are envisaged.
- Inspection of the private chemical industry is regularly carried out.
- Officials of National Authority on CWC also interact with the concerned chambers of commerce and industries to keep them informed of the obligations of chemical industry with regard to implementation of the CWC.

Operative Paragraph 9 & 10

9. Calls upon all States to promote dialogue and cooperation on non-proliferation so as to address the threat posed by proliferation of nuclear, chemical or biological weapons and their means of delivery;

10. Further to counter that threat, calls upon all States, in accordance with their national legal authorities and legislation and consistent with international law, to take cooperative action to prevent illicit trafficking in nuclear, chemical or biological weapons, their means of delivery and related materials;

- Pakistan fully supports dialogue and cooperation on non-proliferation amongst states and has been playing an active role in this context at the regional and international level. Pakistan believes that the Conference on Disarmament (CD) provides the best forum to address the threat posed by proliferation of nuclear, chemical or biological weapons and their means of delivery, where the member states could participate in negotiations in a non-discriminatory manner. The objective of non-proliferation could be achieved by breaking the deadlock in the Conference on Disarmament.

- Pakistan believes that there is no substitute for multilaterally negotiated legal norms enjoying universal application and voluntary adherence. This role can be effectively performed by the Conference on Disarmament, which is the sole forum for negotiating treaty law.
- Such negotiations should encompass critical issues like global nuclear disarmament, missiles, anti-ballistic missile systems and their impact on global and regional stability and militarization of Outer Space.

DOCUMENT NO. 13

PAKISTAN'S 2004 REPORT TO THE UN ON ITS COUNTER-TERRORISM EFFORTS, PART 1

UN Security Council Resolution S/2005/524

August 11, 2005

Distr.: General
11 August 2005
Original: English

Letter dated 10 August 2005 from the Acting Chairman of the Security Council Committee established pursuant to resolution 1373 (2001) concerning counter-terrorism addressed to the President of the Security Council

I write with reference to the Chairman's letter of 3 May 2005 (S/2005/290). The Counter-Terrorism Committee has received the attached fifth report from Pakistan submitted pursuant to paragraph 6 of resolution 1373 (2001) (see annex). I would be grateful if you could arrange for the present letter and its annex to be circulated as a document of the Security Council.

(*Signed*) Ronaldo Mota **Sardenberg**
Acting Chairman
Security Council Committee established pursuant to
resolution 1373 (2001) concerning counter-terrorism

Annex

Letter dated 25 July 2005 from the Permanent Representative of Pakistan to the United Nations addressed to the Chairman of the Counter-Terrorism Committee

Kindly refer to your letter dated 6 April 2005 and this Mission's note verbale dated 13 July 2005.

I am enclosing Pakistan's fifth report on counter-terrorism pursuant to paragraph 6 of resolution 1373 (2001) (see enclosure).

(*Signed*) Munir **Akram**
Permanent Representative

Enclosure

Fifth Report by Pakistan to the Counter-Terrorism Committee

Following are replies to the questions raised by the CTC on the Fourth Report provided by Pakistan.

1. Implementation Measures

Q.1.1 In Pakistan's Reports, references are made to drafts of legislation under consideration that would amend the Anti-Terrorism Act 1972 and would provide for an Anti-Money Laundering law and a Proceeds of Crime Bill with a view to bringing Pakistan fully into compliance with the legislative requirements to implement Resolution 1373 and the 12 international conventions and protocols, including to specifically make the financing of terrorism and other forms of support to terrorism prohibited offences. It is also indicated that such legislation would allow Pakistan to become a party to the International Convention for the Suppression of the Financing of Terrorism. The CTC should appreciate it if Pakistan would provide it with an update on the status of the proposed legislation. Also, if already enacted, the CTC should appreciate it if Pakistan would provide it with an outline of the relevant provisions.

Answer:

Anti-Terrorism Act, 1997

The Anti-Terrorism Act, 1997 (erroneously referred as Anti Terrorism Act 1972 in the question) and its subsequent amendments mainly deal with prevention of terrorism, sectarian violence, terrorist financing, and speedy trial of such crimes. Pakistan has criminalized the financing of terrorism, terrorist acts and terrorist organizations; and designated such offences as predicate offence for money laundering.

In Anti-Terrorism Act, following sections specifically deal with the terrorist financing and money laundering.

Section 2(z)(aa)—Terrorist Property
Section 11F-(5) & 11H—Fund Raising
Section III—Use and Possession
Section 11J—Funding Arrangements
Section 11K—Money laundering
Section 11N—Punishment under Sections 11H to 11K
Section 11O—Seizure and Detention
Section 11Q—Forfeiture

Draft Anti-Money Laundering Bill, 2005

The draft Anti-Money Laundering Bill, 2005 has been approved by the Cabinet. Now as a next step, the Bill shall be submitted to the Parliament through Ministry of Parliamentary Affairs.

Q.1.2 Pakistan further indicated that relevant provisions of the 10 international anti-terrorism instruments of which it is a party are covered in its current laws. The CTC should appreciate it if Pakistan would provide it with an outline of the relevant laws specifically as they apply to each of the referenced activities.

Answer:

A) Pakistan is a common law jurisdiction. The main statute that creates the penal liability is the Pakistan Penal Code of 1860. It has 511 provisions criminalizing conduct under numerous heads. The statutory language used for formulation of offences is general. It thus allows coverage of wide range of crimes. There have been changes in the Code but the essential character and structure has remained the same. The main statute that controls and regulates the procedure of the criminal trial is the Pakistan Criminal Procedure Code (Cr.P.C). This spells out provisions for the manner of investigation, search, seizure, conduct of trial, evidence, procedural rights of the accused, nature and manner of convictions etc. Apart from PPC, there has been a history of special statutes enacted to reinforce the then existing regimes and to make the criminal justice system in Pakistan more efficient and effective. Cr.P.C is invariably applicable to the investigative and trial proceedings under these special laws unless there are specific provisions that overrule its application. The "Qanun-e-Shahadat Order, 1984 (Evidence Act) entails the procedures involved in procurement, admissibility, and recording of evidence.

B) Accordingly, there exist provisions in general law as well as special laws, which provides for the legal framework for catering to the requirements of various terrorism related conventions. For example, in relation to **'International Convention against the Taking of the Hostages'**, some of the relevant provisions are under:

Anti-Terrorism Act, 1997
Section 2(m)—Hostage Taking

Section 2(n)—"Kidnapping for Ransom"
Section 6(2)(e)—Kidnapping for ransom, hostage-taking or hijacking as act of terrorism

Pakistan Penal Code, 1860
Section 365-A—Kidnapping or abduction for extorting property, valuable security, etc

Moreover, for **'Tokyo Convention on Offences and Certain other Acts Committed on Board Aircraft'**; and **'Convention for the Suppression of Unlawful Seizure of Aircraft'**, some of the relevant provisions are under:

Pakistan Penal Code, 1860
Section 402-A—Hijacking
Section 402-B—Punishment for Hijacking
Section 402-C— Harbouring Hijacker, etc

Explosive Substance Act, 1884
Section 8, 9
Anti-Terrorism Act, 1997
Section 2(1)—Hijacking
Section 6(2)(e)— Kidnapping for ransom, hostage-taking or hijacking as act of terrorism

C) Similarly, provisions exists both in general as well as in special laws providing the implementation mechanism in connection with various terrorism related Conventions.

Q.1.3 Pakistan has indicated that the draft Anti-Money Laundering law, when enacted, will bring Pakistan's money laundering law into conformity with international standards, including the establishment of the National Financial Intelligence Centre, Pakistan's financial intelligence unit. In addition, the law will: make the financing of terrorism a predicate offence for money laundering; extend the banking and financial laws to alternative money transfer systems; and, regulate charitable, religious, and other non-governmental organizations. In that regard, the CTC should appreciate it if Pakistan would provide it with an outline of the relevant provisions of the law as enacted.

Answer:

A. A) Money Laundering is an offence vis-à-vis three predicate offences i.e., Drug-trafficking, Corruption & Corrupt Practices and Financing of Terrorism in respective statutes. i.e., Control of Narcotics Substances Act, 1997; National Accountability Ordinance, 1999; and Anti-Terrorism Act, 1997. While National Accountability Bureau is presently functioning as a Financial Intelligence Unit based upon its legal and operational framework.

In order to strengthen the existing legal framework and especially to include the other serious offences as predicate for the offence of money laundering, the draft Anti-Money Laundering Bill 2005 is presently in the process of enactment. Consequent upon the enactment, a Financial Monitoring Unit (FMU) will be established so as to consolidate the existing suspicious transactions reporting regime.

B) As far as financing of terrorism is concerned, it is a predicate offence for Money Laundering in terms of Anti-Terrorism Act, 1997 (Section 11K read with Section 2z(aa)).

C) Through an amendment in Foreign Exchange Act 1947, State Bank of Pakistan (SBP) has issued directives whereby the money changers have been transformed into the Exchange Companies duly regulated by SBP having a minimum capital of Rupees 100 million. The companies are required to maintain proper record of transactions and also submit periodic returns to SBP. The activities of these companies are subject to SBP onsite inspection.

D) Charitable organizations are administered separately. There are a number of statutes that administer these organizations which include:-

1. Societies Registration Act 1860.
2. Religious Endowment Act 1863
3. Trusts Act 1882
4. The Charitable Endowment Act 1890.
5. Musalman Waqaf Validation Act 1890
6. Charitable and Religious Trusts Act 1920
7. The Musalman Waqf Act 1923
8. The Cooperative Societies Act 1925.
9. The Musalman Waqf Validating Act 1930.
10. The Voluntary Social welfare agencies (registration and control) Ordinance 1961
11. Companies Ordinance 1984.

Q.1.4 Pakistan has indicated that there is no specific legal requirement for lawyers to report suspicious financial transactions. Also, it appears from the information provided so far that there may be certain circumstances under which lawyers might be obligated to do so. Could Pakistan please outline under what circumstances lawyers would be required to report suspicious financial transactions, and what effect, if any, the proposed Anti-Money Laundering law would have on the obligation of legal advisors to report suspicious financial transactions.

Answer:

A) Communications between a lawyer and his client has the status of 'Professional Communications' under article 9 of Qanun-e Shahadat Order 1984 (Evidence Act). However, there is a very significant proviso in the article:

Quote "Professional Communications

> No advocate shall at any time be permitted, unless with his clients' express consent, to disclose any communication made to him in the course and for the purpose of his employment as such . . . **provided that** nothing in this article shall protect from disclosure;
>
> (1) any such communication made in furtherance of any illegal purpose; or
>
> (2) any fact observed by any advocate, in the course of his employment as such, showing that any crime or fraud has been committed since the commencement of his employment, whether the attention of such advocate was or was not directed to such fact by or on behalf of his client".

Unquote

B) Moreover, in terms of draft AML Bill 2005, Non-Financial Businesses & Professions, which include lawyers as well, may be required to report suspicious transactions to FMU.

Q.1.5 Pakistan indicated in its reports that it has the legal and administrative capacity to freeze cash held in banks belonging to groups that are on a UN designated list pursuant to Security Council resolutions or of a proscribed organization. Does Pakistan have the legal capacity to "freeze without delay" suspected terrorist-related funds upon request from another State? Please explain the circumstances under which such action would be carried out, the procedures for doing so, and the legal basis, if any, for taking such action.

Answer:

The Government of Pakistan is empowered under the Anti-Terrorism Act, 1997 to take action against any terrorist related funds under its jurisdiction. Under section 11-B of the Anti-Terrorism Act, 1997, the Government could proscribe any organization on the ground that it is involved in promotion of terrorism. After proscribing the said fund/entity/individual, the Government of Pakistan under section 11-E of the said Act amongst other measures issue Gazette Notification for freezing the funds/accounts of the said outfit. Accordingly State Bank of Pakistan directs all banks/development financial institutions for freezing of those funds/accounts and reporting to SBP of funds/accounts so frozen.

Q.1.6 Pakistan indicated that it was in the process of implementing a Personal Identification Secure Comparison Evaluation System (PISCES) at all international air – and sea-ports under a phased programme. The CTC should appreciate it if Pakistan would provide it with an update of the progress of implementation of the PISCES and its effectiveness to date in preventing the entry and exist from Pakistan of persons suspected of acts of terrorism or providing support to terrorism and related criminal activities.

PISCES was initially deployed at Karachi and Islamabad Airports in 1997. After 11 September 2001, the scope of the project was extended to all ports of embarkation and disembarkation including Seaports, Land ports and Airport.

Countrywide Status of PISCES Sites

No.	Operational	Under Process	Pending
1.	Islamabad Airport	Taftan land route	Sust land route
2.	Karachi Airport	Port Bin Qasim	Pasni airport
3.	Lahore Airport		Gawader airport
4.	Peshawar Airport		Gawader airport
5.	Quetta Airport		
6.	Multan Airport		
7.	Faisalabad airport		
8.	Wahga land route		
9.	Wahga railway station		
10.	Karachi seaport (KPT)		
11.	Ghaas Bander seaport		
12.	Chyamman land route		
13.	Torkham land route		
Total	13	2	4

Target for 2005

May–June 2005:

- Site survey of Turbat and Pasni.
- Deployment of PISCES Project at Torkham.
- Establishment of WAN connectivity between FIA (HQ) and Gawdar airport/seaport

3rd Quarter (July–September)

- Site Survey of Sust border.
- Deployment of PISCES Project at Turbat and Pasni.

September 2005:

- Establishment of WAN connectivity between FIA (HQ) and Turbat/ Pasni.
- Deployment of PISCES Project and Sust.

4th Quarter (October–December)

October–November 2005:

- Beef up the Immigration Staff by posting sixty newly recruited lady ASI's
- Establishment of WAN connectivity between FIA (HQ) and three seaports of Karachi.

December 2005:

- Enhancement of bandwidth between major cities of Pakistan

Q.1.7 The CTC should appreciate it if Pakistan would provide it with information concerning any further action taken by Pakistan, since its last report to the CTC, to strengthen its counter-terrorism capacity and modalities for cooperation with other States to combat terrorism.

Answer:

Pakistan is an active partner in the war against terrorism. Pakistan Government and its security agencies are vigorously pursuing objectives of relevant UNSC resolutions on counter terrorism. In this connection, the banned organizations and their activities in Pakistan are under strict watch. Meanwhile, efforts to arrest Al-Qaeda/Taliban operatives in Pakistan have been redoubled. A number of Al-Qaeda operatives have been arrested and their cases are being processed under relevant laws. Important Al-Qaeda operatives, like Ahmed Khalfan and Abu Farraj Al Libbi have been arrested in the recent past. Besides, Pakistan also launched a military operation in Tribal Areas of Pakistan to flush-out Al Qaeda/Taliban miscreants. Their hide-outs were destroyed and a number of foreign Al-Qaeda elements and their local collaborators were killed during the military operation. Over 700 casualties of security officials highlight Pakistan's resolve to eliminate terrorism from the world root and branch.

Pakistan is closely cooperating with International community to eradicate the menace of terrorism. The areas of cooperation include sharing and exchange of information, sharing of interrogation reports of various apprehended terrorists and repatriation/rendition of foreign miscreants to their respective countries. This pro-active cooperation has enabled us to bust certain important networks and apprehend certain important terrorists.

Q.1.8 The CTC should further appreciate it if Pakistan would share with it any assessments or evaluations, especially those related to operational measures, in connection with the implementation of the Resolution, that are carried out by any international or regional institution or organization.

Answer:

Pakistan is closely cooperating with the international community to eradicate the menace of terrorism. In the same spirit, Pakistan actively participates in various regional/international forums on global fight against money laundering and terrorist financing in accordance with the requirements of these forums.

Q.2.1 The CTC wishes to emphasize once more the importance that it attaches to the provision of assistance and advice in connection with the implementation of the Resolution. In that regard, the CTC wishes to remind Pakistan of the CTC's Directory of Assistance (www.un.org/sc/etc), which is frequently updated to include new, relevant information on available assistance. The CTC should appreciate receiving information from Pakistan concerning areas where it believes it can benefit further from assistance, and an update on the effectiveness of resolution 1373-related anti-terrorism technical assistance it has received so far in fulfilling those needs already identified by Pakistan.

Answer:

Effectiveness of UNSC Resolution 1373 can be increased through increased cooperation between Pakistan and the developed partners in capacity building projects for security agencies as well as civil institutions. Education in Maddrassahs could be modernized through innovative programmes.

Government's resolve notwithstanding, the technical capability of the security agencies and their inaccessibility to requisite technologies continues to impede security operations in troubled areas. The international community should consider providing the following:

a. Unarmed aerial vehicles for border surveillance.

b. GSM mobile and satellite band monitoring and jamming systems.

c. Internet protocol (IP) monitoring systems.

d. Scanning equipment for detection of weapons, explosives and narcotics fitted on mobile platform.

e. Forensic Laboratories.

DOCUMENT NO. 14

PAKISTAN'S 2004 REPORT TO THE UN ON ITS COUNTER-TERRORISM EFFORTS, PART 2

UN Security Council Resolution S/AC.44/2004/(02)/22/Add.1

September 27, 2005

Distr.: General
27 September 2005
Original: English

Security Council Committee established pursuant to resolution 1540 (2004)

Note verbale dated 19 September 2005 from the Permanent Mission of Pakistan to the United Nations addressed to the Chairman of the Committee

The Permanent Mission of Pakistan to the United Nations presents its compliments to the Chairman of the Security Council Committee established pursuant to resolution 1540 (2004) and, with reference to his letter dated 18 July 2005, has the honour to transmit the matrix of the Pakistan report on Security Council resolution 1540 (2004) (see annex).

Annex

Annex to the note verbale dated 19 September 2005 from the Permanent Mission of Pakistan to the United Nations addressed to the Chairman of the Committee

OP 1 and related matters from OP 5, OP 6, OP 8 (a), (b), (c) and OP 10

State: **Pakistan**
Date of Report: 27 October 2005

Did you make one of the following statements or is your country a State Party to or Member State of one of the following Conventions, Treaties and Arrangements?	**Yes**	**If YES, indicate relevant information (i.e. signing, accession, ratification, entering into force, etc)**	**Remarks**
General statement on non-possession of WMD	X	Pakistan is a party to Chemical Weapons Convention as well as the Biological Weapons Convention as a non-possessor state. It does not possess Biological Weapons or Chemical Weapons. Pakistan is a declared Nuclear Weapon State and not a Party to the NPT.	
General statement on commitment to Disarmament and non-proliferation	X	Strong long-standing commitment to the objectives of disarmament and non-proliferation 1. Statement by the Foreign Minister at the Conference on Disarmament, Geneva, 28 March 2002 2. Statement by the Permanent Representative of Pakistan to the United Nations, Geneva, at the 57th Session of the UN General Assembly 3. Statement by the Permanent Representative of Pakistan to the United Nations, Geneva, in the General Debate of the First Committee of the 59th Session of the UN General Assembly on 12 October 2004	Page 2 of the 1540 National Report

		4. Text of the Foreign Secretary's Key Note Address to the Conference on Disarmament in Geneva, 26 May 2003 5. Text of the Foreign Minister's Address to the Royal Institute of International Affairs, London on "Pakistan's Security Perspectives", 3 November 2003 6. Text of an Official Release on Pakistan's Resolution on "Confidence Building Measures in the Regional and Sub-Regional Context in the UNGA on 4 November 2003 7. Speech by President, General Pervez Musharraf at the Institute for Foreign Affairs and National Security (IFANS): Seoul, 6 November 2003 8. "Pakistan's Foreign Policy: Responding to Current Global and Regional Dynamics", Foreign Secretary's Speech at Sarah Lawrence College on 12 November 2003 9. Excerpts from President Musharraf's Address to the 50th Anniversary of All Pakistan Newspapers Society (APNS) on 30 December 2003 10. Text of a Joint Press Talk by Pakistan Foreign Minister and India's National Security Advisor, at the Close of a Security Conference in Munich on 8 February 2004 11. Address by the President of Pakistan at the Inaugural Session of the 3rd National Security Workshop Help at the National Defence College, Islamabad, 12 February 2004 12. Address by Foreign Minister to the Members of the Foreign Affairs Committee of the National Assembly and Senate of Pakistan on "Major Foreign Policy Issues Facing the Country", 13 April 2004 13. Explanation of Vote by the Permanent Representative of Pakistan to the United Nations, on the Security Council Resolutions on Non-Proliferation of Weapons of Mass Destruction, New York, 28 April 2004	

Did you make one of the following statements or is your country a State Party to or Member State of one of the following Conventions, Treaties and Arrangements?	Yes	If YES, indicate relevant information (i.e. signing, accession, ratification, entering into force, etc)	Remarks
		14. Address by the Foreign Minister at the Italian Institute of International Conciliation on "Foreign Policy of Pakistan, Challenges and Response", Rome, 7 July 2004 15. Statement by the Foreign Secretary and Leader Of Pakistan Delegation, at the XIV NAM Ministerial Conference, on "Challenges of Multilateralism in the 21st Century, Durban, South Africa, 19 August 2004 16. Address to the Nation by Prime Minister Islamic Republic of Pakistan Shaukat Aziz on 19 November 2004	
General statement on non-provision of WMD and related materials to non-state actors	X	1. Preambular para of Pakistan's National Report. 2. Explanation of Vote by the Permanent Representative of Pakistan to the United Nations, on the Security Council Resolutions on Non-Proliferation of Weapons of Mass Destruction, New York, 28 April 2004 3. Speech by the Foreign Minister at a Seminar on "Emerging Security Challenges and Opportunities", Organized by the Institute of Regional Studies, Islamabad on 14 October 2004 4. Transcript of the Press Conference Addressed by the Foreign Office Spokesman on 21 March 2005 5. Statement by the Permanent Representative of Pakistan at the Conference on Disarmament: Geneva, 24 March 2005	Para 1 of National Report
Biological Weapons Convention (BWC)	X	Signed on 10 April, 1972. Ratified on 25 September, 1974 Entered into force on 6 March, 1975	Page 8 of the report

Chemical Weapons Convention (CWC)	X	Signed on 13 January, 1993 Ratification on 28 October, 1997 Entered into force on 27 November, 1997	Page 8 of the report
Nuclear Non-Proliferation Treaty (NPT)	X	Although Pakistan is not a state party to NPT, it is strongly committed to the objectives of Non-Proliferation	
Comprehensive Nuclear Test Ban Treaty (CTBT)			
Convention on Physical Protection of Nuclear Material (CPPNM)	X	Entered into force on 12 October 2000 Deposited on 12 September 2000	Page 6 of the report
Hague Code of Conduct (HCOC)		There is no international multilaterally negotiated agreement on missiles. Pakistan supports the negotiation of such an agreement at the Conference on Disarmament and has made a proposal at the CD in this regard.	

Geneva Protocol of 1925	X	Entered into force on 8 February,1928 Deposited on 15 April 1960	http://disarmament.un.org:8080/TreatyStatus.nsf
International Atomic Energy Agency (IAEA)	X	Since 2000. **Pakistan is one of the founding members of IAEA. It is a member since 1957 and not 2000 as indicated in the matrix.** **Pakistan is fully abiding be the Statutes of the IAEA and has closely cooperated with it.**	
Nuclear Weapons Free Zone/Protocol(s)	X	Has proposed Strategic Restraint Regime for South Asia.	
Other Conventions/Treaties	X	1. Convention on Assistance in the Case of a Nuclear Accident or Radiological Emergency-Entered into force 12 October 1989 2. Convention on Nuclear Safety Entry in to force 29 December 1997 3. Convention on Early Notification of a Nuclear Accident. 4. The Treaty on Principles Governing the Activities of States in the Exploration and Use of Outer Space.	

Did you make one of the following statements or is your country a State Party to or Member State of one of the following Conventions, Treaties and Arrangements?	Yes	If YES, indicate relevant information (i.e. signing, accession, ratification, entering into force, etc)	Remarks
Other Arrangements	X	India–Pakistan Agreement of Non–Attack on each other's nuclear installations. Pakistan is a state party to various international conventions on terrorism.	
Other	X	CD is the best forum for negotiating disarmament and arms control treaties and to address the threat posed by proliferation of nuclear, chemical or biological weapons and their means of delivery. The interim arrangement of resolution 1540 which seeks to prevent non-state actors from acquiring WMDs should be replaced by initiating negotiations on a multilateral treaty in the Conference on Disarmament, where the member states could participate in a non-discriminatory manner.	Page 11 of the report

OP 2–Biological Weapons (BW)

State: **Pakistan**

Date of Report: 27 October 2005

Does national legislation exist which prohibits persons or entities to engage in one of the following activities? Can violators be penalized?	National legal framework		Enforcement: civil/criminal penalties and others		Remarks
	Yes	If YES, indicate source document of national implementation law	Yes	If YES, indicate source documents	

Manufacture/ produce	X	• Pakistan Bio-safety Rules 2005 **Rule 19** The Production in which living modified engineered organisms—are generated or used shall not be commenced except with the consent of National Biosafety committee. This also applies to production taking place in connection with the development, testing and experiment • The Drugs Act 1976 **3. (a) "adulterated drug" means a drug—(i)** which consists in whole or in part of any . . . which contains any foreign matter, . . . or(ii)Which has been *manufactured, packed,* or: held under . . . any other *foreign matter or whereby it, may have been rendered injurious to health; or* (iii)The container of which releases any *poisonous or deleterious substance* which may render the contents injurious to health,		**Section 23 read with 27** **23.-(1)** No person shall him self or by any by any other person on his behalf- **(a)** export, import or *manufacture* for sale or sell **(iv)** any *adulterated drug;* **27. (1)** Whoever himself or by any by any other person on his behalf- **(a)** export, imports *manufactures* for sale or sell any spurious drug or any drug which is not registered. **(b)** manufacture for sale any drug without a license; or **(c)** import without license any drug for the import of which a license is required; Shall be punished with imprisonment Which shall not be less than 3 years or more than 10 years and fine which may extend to 1 lakh rupees	Pakistan is a non-possessor state. The specific implementing national legislation regarding BWC is in process however Pakistan has other legislation that can prevent and control the use of biological agents and noxious substances that can lead to production and manufacture of BW and prosecution can be maintained in respect of any person who is found guilty of manufacturing or producing.

Does national legislation exist which prohibits persons or entities to engage in one of the following activities? Can violators be penalized?	National legal framework		Enforcement: civil/criminal penalties and others		Remarks
	Yes	**If YES, indicate source document of national implementation law**	**Yes**	**If YES, indicate source documents**	
		• Export Control on goods, technologies, material and equipment related to nuclear and biological weapons and their delivery system Act 2004 **Section 4(4)** (4) The Federal Govt shall control export, re export, *transshipment, transit of goods,* technologies material and equipment . . . which may contribute to designing, development, production, stockpiling, . . . use of nuclear and biological weapons and the delivery systems		**Section 8(1)** 8(1) Any person who contravenes . . . shall be guilty for an offence punishable on conviction by imprisonment for a term which may extend to 14 years and with fine not exceeding 5 million rupees or both and—. Property and assets where ever they may be shall be forfeited to Federal Government	

Acquire	X	• Export Control on goods, technologies, material and equipment related to nuclear and biological weapons and their delivery system Act 2004 **Section 4(4) read with 8(1) ibid** • Anti Terrorism Act 1997, Sec 6 • Surrender of Illicit Arms Act, 1991, Sec 4		
Possess	X	• Surrender of Illicit Arms Act 1991 **Section 2 (iii)** defines poisonous or noxious gases or other chemicals or substances as illicit arms **Section 4** . . . . person in possession or control of any illicit arms shall surrender such arms to . . . . • Anti Terrorism Act 1997 **Section(2bb) read with, 6** 2(bb)"weapons" means any item which can be used to injure or cause bodily harm, and includes any type of firearm, explosive, sword, dagger, knuckle-duster, stengun, bomb, grenade, rocket launcher, mortar or any chemical, biological weapon or any other thing which can be used for causing injury, hurt, harm or destruction of person or property, and includes 'illicit arms' as defined in the surrender of illicit Arms Act 1991 (XXI of 1991). **6 (2)a involves** doing of any thing that causes death		

Does national legislation exist which prohibits persons or entities to engage in one of the following activities? Can violators be penalized?	National legal framework		Enforcement: civil/criminal penalties and others		Remarks
	Yes	If YES, indicate source document of national implementation law	Yes	If YES, indicate source documents	
		b involves the doing of any thing that is likely to cause death or endangers a person's life.			
Stockpile/store	X	• Surrender of Illicit Arms Act 1991 **Section 2** (iii) defines poisonous or noxious gases or other chemicals or substances as illicit arms **Section 4** . . . person in possession or control of any illicit arms shall surrender such arms to. . . • The Drugs Act 1976 **Section 23 read with 27 ibid** Anti Terrorism Act 1997, Sec 2	X	**Section 7(3)**	

Develop	X	• Export Control on goods, technologies, material and equipment related to nuclear and biological weapons and their delivery system Act 2004 **Section 4 (4) ibid** • The Pakistan BioSafety Rules 2005 **Rule 19** The Production in which living modified engineered organisms—are generated or used shall not be commenced except with the consent of National Biosafety committee. This also applies to production taking place in connection with the development, testing and experiment		**Section 8(1) ibid**	Specific Statutes in process.
Transport	X	• Export Control on goods, technologies, material and equipment related to nuclear and biological weapons and their delivery system Act 2004 **Section 4** (4) The Federal Govt shall control export, re export, *transshipment, transit of goods*, technologies material and equipment—	X	**Section 8(1)** 8(1) Any person who contravenes- . . . shall be guilty for an offence punishable on conviction by imprisonment for a term which may extend to 14 years and with fine not exceeding 5 million rupees or both and—. Property and assets where ever they may be shall be forfeited to Federal Government	This is a mechanism available to the Government through which it can control transport of any material that can be used in BW. Any person who contravenes is liable to be prosecuted under this legislation.

Does national legislation exist which prohibits persons or entities to engage in one of the following activities? Can violators be penalized?	National legal framework		Enforcement: civil/criminal penalties and others		Remarks
	Yes	**If YES, indicate source document of national implementation law**	**Yes**	**If YES, indicate source documents**	
		which may contribute to designing, development, production, stockpiling,— use of nuclear and biological weapons and the delivery systems • Pakistan Plant Quarantine Act 1976		**Section 6 read with 5** 5. when a Notification has been issued under section 3 then, notwithstanding anything contained in any other law for the time being in force,the person responsible for the booking of goods or parcels at any port, railway station, airport or other places – (i) where the notification prohibits import, shall refuse *to receive for carriage at or to forward*, or knowingly allow to be carried by sea,air, land, rail or other carriers from that port, station, airport or place anything of which import is prohibited; and (ii) where the notification imposes any conditions upon import, shall so refuse unless the prescribed documents showing that the conditions have been fulfilled are produced.	

				6. **Whoever contravene or attempts** to contravenes any of the provision of this Act, or any of the rules made or notification issued there under, shall, without prejudice to any confiscation or penalty to which he may be liable under the provisions of the Custom Act 1969 as applied by section 4, be. punishable with fine which may extend to five thousand rupees and upon any subsequent conviction with imprisonment up to six months or with fine which may extend to two thousand rupees, or with both.	
Transfer	**X**	• Export Control on goods, technologies, material and equipment related to nuclear and biological weapons and their delivery system Act 2004 • Pakistan Plant Quarantine Act 1976	**X**	**Section 4 read with 8 Ibid** **Section 6 read with 5 ibid**	
Use	**X**	• Anti Terrorism Act 1997	X	**Section 2bb read with 6 (2)(a)(d) and 7 (a)(b)** 2(bb)"weapons" *means any item which can be used to injure or cause bodily harm*, and includes any type of firearm, explosive, sword, dagger, knuckle-duster, stengun,	

Does national legislation exist which prohibits persons or entities to engage in one of the following activities? Can violators be penalized?	National legal framework		Enforcement: civil/criminal penalties and others		Remarks
	Yes	If YES, indicate source document of national implementation law	Yes	If YES, indicate source documents	
				bomb, grenade, rocket launcher, mortar or any chemical, ***biological weapon*** or any other thing which can be used for causing injury, hurt, harm or destruction of person or property, and includes 'illicit arms' as defined in the surrender of illicit Arms Act 1991 (XXI of 1991).	
		• Pakistan Penal Code 1860		**6 (2)a involves** doing of any thing that causes death **b** involves the doing of any thing that is likely to cause death or endangers a person's life. **7(a)** . . . lshall be punished—with death or imprisonment for life and with fine. (b) . . . shall be punished—with imprisonment—not less than 5 years—may extend to 14 years and with fine.	

				Section 270 **Malignant act likely to spread infection of disease dangerous to life**. Whoever malignantly does any act which he knows or has the reason to believe to be, likely to spread disease dangerous to life, shall be punished with imprisonment of either description for a term which may extend to two years, or fine, with both.	
Participate as an accomplice in a.m. activities	X	• Anti Terrorism Act 1997	X	**Section 21 I . . . 21J** 21-I **Aid and Abetment.—** Whoever aids or abets any offence under this Act shall be punishable with the maximum term of imprisonment provided for the offence or fine provided for such or with both.	
		• Pakistan Penal Code 1860		21-J **Harbouring.**—(1) A person commits an offence if he harbours any person who commits an offence under this Act. (2) A person guilty of an offence under sub-section (1) shall be liable on conviction to punishment as provided in Section 216 and 216-A of Pakistan Penal Code (Act XLV of 1860).	

Does national legislation exist which prohibits persons or entities to engage in one of the following activities? Can violators be penalized?	National legal framework		Enforcement: civil/criminal penalties and others		Remarks
	Yes	If YES, indicate source document of national implementation law	Yes	If YES, indicate source documents	
				Section 107 read with 108A 107. Abetment of a thing. A person abets the doing of a thing, who— *First:* Instigates any person to do that thing; or ***Secondly:*** Engages with one or more other person or persons in any conspiracy for the doing of that thing, if an act or illegal omission takes place in pursuance of that conspiracy, and in order to the doing of that thing; or ***Thirdly:*** Intentionally aids by any act or illegal omission, the doing of that thing. **Explanation 1:** A person who, by willful misrepresentation, or by willful concealment of a material fact, which is bound to disclose, voluntarily causes or procures, or attempts to cause or procures, a thing to be done, is said to	

				instigate the doing of that thing. **Explanation 2:** Whoever, either prior to or at the time of the commission of an act, does anything in order to facilitate the commission of that act, and thereby facilitates the commission thereof, is said to aid the doing of that act. **108A Abetment in Pakistan, of offences outside it**. A person abets an offence within the meaning of this Code who, in Pakistan, abets the commission of any act without and beyond Pakistan which would constitute an offence committed in Pakistan.	
Assist in a.m. activities	X	• Export Control on goods, technologies, material and equipment related to nuclear and biological weapons and their delivery system Act 2004 • Anti Terrorism Act 1997 • Pakistan Penal Code 1860	X	**Section 8 (2)** Any person who attempts to commits or abets the commission of an offense under this Act shall be proceeded against in the same manners as if he has committed such offence. **Section 21 I . . . 21J ibid** **Section 107 read with 108A ibid**	
Finance a.m. activities	X	• Anti Terrorism Act 1997 **Section 11-J read with 11-N** 11-J **Funding Arrangements.**—A person commits an offence if	X	**11-N Punishment under section** 11-H to 11-K . . . shall be punishable on conviction with imprisonment for a term not less	

Does national legislation exist which prohibits persons or entities to engage in one of the following activities? Can violators be penalized?	National legal framework		Enforcement: civil/criminal penalties and others		Remarks
	Yes	If YES, indicate source document of national implementation law	Yes	If YES, indicate source documents	
		(a) enters into or becomes concerned in an arrangement as a result of which money or other property is made available or is to be made available to another, and (b) has reasonable cause to suspect that it will or may be used for the purposes of terrorism • Pakistan Penal Code 1860		than six months and not exceeding five years and with fine. **Section 213 & 214** **213. Taking gift, etc., to screen an offender from punishment:** Whoever accept or attempts to obtain, or agrees to accept, any gratification for himself or any other person, or any restitution of property to himself or any other person, in consideration of his concealing an offence or of his screening any person from legal punishment for any offence, or of his not proceeding against any person for the purpose of bring him to legal punishment. **if a capital offence:** shall, if the offence is punishable with death, be punished with imprisonment of either description for a term which may extend to seven years, and shall also be liable to fine:	

				if punishable with imprisonment for life, or with imprisonment: and if the offence is punishable with imprisonment for life or with imprisonment which may extend to ten years, shall be punished with imprisonment of either description for a term which may extend to three years, shall also be liable to fine:and if the offence is punishable with imprisonment not extending to ten years, shall be punished with description provided for the offence for a term which may extend to one-fourth part of the longest term of imprisonment provided for the offence, or with fine, or with both. **214 Offering gift or restoration of property in consideration of screening offender:** Whoever gives or causes or offers or agrees to give or cause, any gratification to any person, or to restore or cause to restoration of any property to any person, in consideration of that person's concealing an offence, or of his screening any person form legal punishment for any offence, or his not proceeding against any person for the purpose of bringing him to legal punishment;	

Does national legislation exist which prohibits persons or entities to engage in one of the following activities? Can violators be penalized?	National legal framework		Enforcement: civil/criminal penalties and others		Remarks
	Yes	If YES, indicate source document of national implementation law	Yes	If YES, indicate source documents	
				if the a capital offence: shall, if the offence is punishable with death, be punished with imprisonment of either description for a term which may extend to seven years and shall also be liable to fine; **if punishable with imprisonment for life or with imprisonment:** and the offence is punishable with imprisonment for life, or with imprisonment which may extend to three years, shall be punished with imprisonment of either description for a term may extend to three years, and shall also be liable to and if the offence is punishable with imprisonment not extending to ten years, shall be punishable with imprisonment of the description provided for the offence for a term which may extend to one-fourth part of the longest term of imprisonment provided for the offence, or with fine, or with or with both.	

Above mentioned activities related to means of delivery	X	• Export Control on goods, technologies, material and equipment related to nuclear and biological weapons and their delivery system Act 2004	X	**Section 4 read with 8 ibid**	
Involvement of non-state actors in a.m. activities	X	• Export Control on goods, technologies, material and equipment related to nuclear and biological weapons and their delivery system Act 2004 • Pakistan Penal Code 1860	X	**Section 8 Ibid** **Section 126** **126 Committing depredation on territories of power at peace with Pakistan**. Whoever commits depredation, or makes preparations to commit depredation, on territories of any Power in alliance or at peace with Pakistan, shall be punished with imprisonment of either description for a term which may extend to seven years, and shall also be liable to fine and forfeiture of any property used or intended to be used in committing such depredation, or acquired by such depredation. **Section 213 and 214 ibid**	Person is defined to include a natural person and thus includes a non-state actor according to common law jurisprudence. It means that any non state actor can be proceeded against any law of Pakistan that extends to person's
Other					

OP 2–Chemical Weapons (CW)

State: **Pakistan**
Date of Report: 27 October 2005

Does national legislation exist which prohibits persons or entities to engage in one of the following activities? Can violators be penalized?	**National legal framework**		**Enforcement: civil/criminal penalties and others**		**Remarks**
	Yes	**If YES, indicate source document of national implementation law**	**Yes**	**If YES, indicate source documents**	
Manufacture/produce	X	• Chemical Weapons Convention implementation Ordinance – 2000 **Section 3 read with 5** **3.Prohibition on development, etc of chemical weapons.**—(1) No person shall- (a) *develop, produce*, otherwise, acquire, or stockpile or retain in chemical weapon, or transfer, directly or indirectly, a chemical weapon to anyone; (b) use a chemical weapon; (c) engage in any military preparation to use chemical weapon (d) assist, encourage or induce, in any way, any other person to engage in any activity prohibited to a State party under the Convention; (e) use a riot control agent as a method of warfare.		(3) Whoever contravenes the provisions of this section shall be guilty of an offence punishable with imprisonment for a term which may extend to twenty five years. (2)) Whoever contravenes the provisions of this section shall be guilty of an offence punishable with fine which may extend to ten thousand rupees **Section 5 Punishment for making or possessing explosive under suspicious circumstances**. *Any person who makes* or knowingly has in his possession or under his control any explosive substance, under such circumstances as to give rise to a reasonable suspicion that he is not making it or does not have it in his possession or under his	Pages 3 and 8 of the report. http://www. opcw. org/docs/ lanatempleg/ Pakistan.pdf

		5.Prohibition on production, etc., of toxic chemical and precursor.— (1) No person shall produce, use, acquire, possess, transfer, import or export–any schedule chemical; (a)any discrete organic chemical not being schedule chemical; or (b)any chemical containing the elements of phosphorous, sulphur or fluorine . . . • The Explosives Act 1908	X	control for a lawful object, shall, unless he can show that he made it or had it in his possession or under his control for a lawful object, be punishable with imprisonment for a term which may extend to [fourteen years]. 5-A. **Forfeiture of property**. A Court convicting a person for an offence against this Act shall direct that the whole of his property shall stand forfeited to Government.	
Acquire	X	• Chemical Weapons Convention Implementation Ordinance – 2000 • Surrender of Illicit Arms Act 1991	X	**Section 3 read with 5 ibid** **Section 2(iii),4 read with 7(I)(a)(b)(c) ibid**	
Possess	X	• Chemical Weapons Convention Implementation Ordinance – 2000 • Surrender of Illicit Arms Act 1991 **2 (a) illicit arms' includes;** (iii)All types of explosive substances as defined in the Explosive Substances Act, 1908 (VI of 1908), and the Explosives Act (IV of 1884), including mines of all types; that discharge provisions or noxious gases *or other chemicals or substances which cause damage to human body;* **Section 4**.....person in possession or control of any illicit arms shall surrender such arms to.......	X	**Section 3 read with 5 Ibid** **Section 2(iii),4 read with 7(I)(a)(b)(c)** **7 Punishments**. (1) Whoever contravenes the provisions of Section 4 or Section 5 of fails to surrender illicit arms shall— a. in respect of illicit arms defined in sub-clauses (i) to (iii) of clause (a) of Section 2, be punished with imprisonment for life and forfeiture of property, both movable and immovable; b. in respect of illicit arms defined in sub-clause (iv) of clause	

Does national legislation exist which prohibits persons or entities to engage in one of the following activities? Can violators be penalized?	National legal framework		Enforcement: civil/criminal penalties and others		Remarks
	Yes	If YES, indicate source document of national implementation law	Yes	If YES, indicate source documents	
				(a) of Section 2, be punished with imprisonment for life or with imprisonment for a term which shall not be less than ten years having regard to the antecedents of the accused; and c. in respect of illicit arms defined in sub-clause (v) of Clause (a) of Section 2, be punished with imprisonment for a term which may extend to fourteen years but shall; not be less than tree years, having regard to the antecedents of the accused;	
Stockpile/store	X	• Chemical Weapons Convention Implementation Ordinance–2000	X	**Section 3 ibid**	
Develop	X	• Chemical Weapons Convention Implementation Ordinance–2000	X	**Section 3 ibid**	
Transport	X	**Chemical Weapons Convention Implementation Ordinance–2000 Surrender of Illicit Arms Act 1991**	X	**Section 3ibid** **Section7(3)**. Punishments.(1)Whoever contravenes the provisions of Section 4 or Section 5 of fails to surrender illicit arms shall . . . (3) Any conveyance used for the transportation of any illicit arms shall also be liable to confiscation.	

Transfer	X	• Chemical Weapons Convention Implementation Ordinance–2000 **3.Prohibition on development, etc of chemical weapons.**—(1) No person shall (a) develop, produce, otherwise, acquire, or stockpile or retain in chemical weapon, *or transfer, directly or indirectly*, a chemical weapon to anyone; (b) use a chemical weapon; (c) engage in any military preparation to use chemical weapon (d) assist, encourage or induce, in any way, any other person to engage in any activity prohibited to a State party under the Convention; (e) use a riot control agent as a method of warfare	X	(3) Whoever contravenes the provisions of this section shall be guilty of an offence punishable with imprisonment for a term which may extend to twenty five years.	Pages 3 and 8 of the report. *http://www. ocw. org/docs/lanatmpleg/ Pakistan.pdf*
Use	X	• Chemical Weapons Convention Implementation Ordinance–2000 Anti Terrorism Act 1997 **Section 2bb read with 6 (2)(a)(d) and 7 (a)(b)** 2(bb)"weapons" means any item which can be used to injure or cause bodily harm, and includes any type of firearm, explosive, sword, dagger, knuckle-duster, stengun, bomb, grenade, rocket launcher, mortar or any ***chemical***, biological ***weapon*** or any other thing which can be used for causing injury, hurt, harm or destruction of person or property, and includes 'illicit arms' as defined in the surrender of illicit Arms Act 1991 (XXI of 1991).	X	**Section 3 and 4 ibid** **6 (2)a involves** doing of any thing that causes death **b** involves the doing of any thing that is likely to cause death or endangers a person's life. 7(a) . . . shall be punished—with death or imprisonment for life and with fine. (b) . . . shall be punished—with imprisonment—not less than 5 years—may extend to 14 years and with fine.	

Does national legislation exist which prohibits persons or entities to engage in one of the following activities? Can violators be penalized?	National legal framework		Enforcement: civil/criminal penalties and others		Remarks
	Yes	If YES, indicate source document of national implementation law	Yes	If YES, indicate source documents	
Participate as an accomplice in a.m. activities	X	• Anti Terrorism Act 1997	X	**Section 21 I—21J** 21-I **Aid and Abetment.**— Whoever aids or abets any offence under this Act shall be punishable with the maximum term of imprisonment provided for the offence or fine provided for such or with both. 21-J **Harbouring.**—(1) A person commits an offence if he harbours any person who commits an offence under this Act. (2) A person guilty of an offence under sub-section (1) shall be liable on conviction to punishment as provided in Section 216 and 216-A of Pakistan Penal Code (Act XLV of 1860).	
		• Pakistan Penal Code 1860		**Section 107 read with 108A 107. Abetment of a thing**. A person abets the doing of a thing, who— ***First:*** Instigates any person to do that thing; or ***Secondly:*** Engages with one or more other person or persons in any conspiracy for the doing of that thing, if an act or illegal omission	

		• Chemical Weapons Convention Implementation Ordinance–2000		takes place in pursuance of that conspiracy, and in order to the doing of that thing; or ***Thirdly:*** Intentionally aids by any act or illegal omission, the doing of that thing. **Explanation 1**: A person who, by willful misrepresentation, or by willful concealment of a material fact, which is bound to disclose, voluntarily causes or procures, or attempts to cause or procures, a thing to be done, is said to instigate the doing of that thing. **Explanation 2:** Whoever, either prior to or at the time of the commission of an act, does anything in order to facilitate the commission of that act, and thereby facilitates the commission thereof, is said to aid the doing of that act. 108A **Abetment in Pakistan, of offences outside it**. A person abets an offence within the meaning of this Code who, in Pakistan, abets the commission of any act without and beyond Pakistan which would constitute an offence committed in Pakistan. **Section 3(d)** **3.Prohibition on development, etc of chemical weapons.**—(1) No person shall (d) *assist, encourage or induce, in any way*, any other person to engage in	

Does national legislation exist which prohibits persons or entities to engage in one of the following activities? Can violators be penalized?	National legal framework		Enforcement: civil/criminal penalties and others		Remarks
	Yes	If YES, indicate source document of national implementation law	Yes	If YES, indicate source documents	
		• The Explosives Act 1884		any activity prohibited to a State party under the Convention; **Section 12** **12.Abetment and attempts**. Whoever abets, within the meaning of the Pakistan Penal Code, the commission of an offence punishable under this Act, or the rules made under this Act, or attempts to commit any such offence and in such attempt does any act towards to commission of the same, shall be punishable as if he had committed the offence.	
Assist in a.m. activities	X	• Pakistan Penal Code 1860 • Chemical Weapons Convention Implementation Ordinance–2000 • The Explosives Act 1884	X	**Section 107 read with 108A ibid** **Section 3(1)(d) ibid** **Section 12 ibid**	Pages 3 and 8 of the report http://ww. opcw.org/docs/la natmplea/Pakistan. pdf
Finance a.m. activities	X	• Chemical Weapons Convention Implementation Ordinance–2000 • Anti Terrorism Act 1997 **Section 11-J and 11-N** 11-J **Funding Arrangements.**—A person commits an offence if	X	**Section 3(1)(d) ibid** **11-N** Punishment under section 11-H to 11-K . . . shall be punishable on conviction with imprisonment for a term not less than six months and not exceeding five years and with fine.	

		(a) enters into or becomes conc erned in an arrangement as a result of which money or other property is made available or is to be made available to another, and
		(b) has reasonable cause to suspect that it will or may be used for the purposes of terrorism.
		• Pakistan Penal Code 1860
				Section 213 & 214
				213. Taking gift, etc., to screen an offender from punishment:
				Whoever accept or attempts to obtain, or agrees to accept, any gratification for himself or any other person, or any restitution of property to himself or any other person, in consideration of his concealing an offence or of his screening any person from legal punishment for any offence, or of his not proceeding against any person for the purpose of bring him to legal punishment.
				if a capital offence: shall, if the offence is punishable with death, be punished with imprisonment of either description for a term which may extend to seven years, and shall also be liable to fine:
				if punishable with imprisonment for life, or with imprisonment: and if the offence is punishable with imprisonment for life or with imprisonment which may extend to ten years, shall be punished with imprisonment of either description for a term which may extend to three years, shall also be liable to fine:	

Does national legislation exist which prohibits persons or entities to engage in one of the following activities? Can violators be penalized?	National legal framework		Enforcement: civil/criminal penalties and others		Remarks
	Yes	If YES, indicate source document of national implementation law	Yes	If YES, indicate source documents	
				and if the offence is punishable with imprisonment not extending to ten years, shall be punished with description provided for the offence for a term which may extend to one-fourth part of the longest term of imprisonment provided for the offence, or with fine, or with both. 214 Offering gift or restoration of property in consideration of screening offender: Whoever gives or causes or offers or agrees to give or cause, any gratification to any person, or to restore or cause to restoration of any property to any person, in consideration of that person's concealing an offence, or of his screening any person form legal punishment for any offence, or his not proceeding against any person for the purpose of bringing him to legal punishment; if the a capital offence: shall, if the offence is punishable with death, be punished with imprisonment of either description for a term which may extend to seven years and shall also be liable to fine;	

				if punishable with imprisonment for life or with imprisonment: and the offence is punishable with imprisonment for life, or with imprisonment which may extend to three years, shall be punished with imprisonment of either description for a term may extend to three years, and shall also be liable to and if the offence is punishable with imprisonment not extending to ten years, shall be punishable with imprisonment of the description provided for the offence for a term which may extend to one-fourth part of the longest term of imprisonment provided for the offence, or with fine, or with or with both.	
Above mentioned activities related to means of delivery	X	• Chemical Weapons Convention Implementation Ordinance–2000 **Section 2 (c)(ii) read with (iii)..a** munition or device, specifically designed . . . Definition of Chemical Weapons also include their means of delivery. **Section 5** **5. Prohibition on production, etc., of toxic chemical and precursor . . . .** 1) No person shall produce, use, acquire, possess, transfer, import or export–any schedule chemical; (a) any discrete organic chemical not being schedule chemical; or	X	(2) Whoever contravenes the provisions of this section shall be guilty of an offence punishable with fine which may extend to ten thousand rupees	

Does national legislation exist which prohibits persons or entities to engage in one of the following activities? Can violators be penalized?	National legal framework		Enforcement: civil/criminal penalties and others		Remarks
	Yes	**If YES, indicate source document of national implementation law**	**Yes**	**If YES, indicate source documents**	
		(b)any chemical containing the elements of phosphorous, sulphur or fluorine . . .			
Involvement of non-state actors in a.m. activities	X	• Chemical Weapons Convention Implementation Ordinance–2000 • Pakistan Penal Code 1860	X	**Section 3(1) ibid** **Section 126** **126 Committing depredation on territories of power at peace with Pakistan**. Whoever commits depredation, or makes preparations to commit depredation, on territories of any Power in alliance or at peace with Pakistan, shall be punished with imprisonment of either description for a term which may extend to seven years, and shall also be liable to fine and forfeiture of any property used or intended to be used in committing such depredation, or acquired by such depredation.	In all the statutes non-state actor is covered because the definition of person in most of the statute will include a non -state actor
Other	X	• Measures taken to account for and secure sensitive materials in production, use, storage and transport.			Page 6 of the report

		• Physical protection measures for safety and security of installations, equipment, materials and personnel.			

OP 2–Nuclear Weapons (NW)

State: **Pakistan**
Date of Report: 27 October 2005

Does national legislation exist which prohibits persons or entities to engage in one of the following activities? Can violators be penalized?	**National legal framework**		**Enforcement: civil/criminal penalties and others**		**Remarks**
	Yes	**If YES, indicate source document of national implementation law**	**Yes**	**If YES, indicate source document**	
Manufacture/produce	X	• Pakistan Nuclear Regulatory Authority Ordinance 2001. **Section 19 (c) read with 44 (1)** **Section 19.** Power to issue Licence.—(1) No person shall, unless he is exempted as may prescribed by the regulations, or unless he is the holder of a licence issued by the Authority . . . (c) explore for mines and mill, extract acquire handle use, . . .	X		

Does national legislation exist which prohibits persons or entities to engage in one of the following activities? Can violators be penalized?	National legal framework		Enforcement: civil/criminal penalties and others		Remarks
	Yes	If YES, indicate source document of national implementation law	Yes	If YES, indicate source document	
		sell, lease lend by transfer import export convert enrich, produce, store, process, reprocess, fabricate, transport, dispose of any radioactive ore, radio active material, nuclear substance or any other substance as the authority may by notification . . . specify • Export Control on goods, technologies, material and equipment related to nuclear and biological weapons and their delivery system Act 2004 **Section 4(4) read with 8** (4) The Federal Govt shall control export, re export, transshipment, transit of goods, technologies material and equipment . . .		**Section 44(1)** 44(1) Any person who contravenes . . . shall be punished—or a term . . . extend to 7 years or with fine which may extend to 1 million or with both **Section 8** 8(1) Any person who contravenes . . . shall be guilty for an offence punishable on conviction by imprisonment for a term which may extend to 14 years and with fine not exceeding 5 million rupees or both and . . . Property and assets where ever they may be shall be forfeited to Federal Government.	"keeping" it or use in secret care will over lap production / manufacturing, therefore, given the clear penalty it will be an important option in this kind of prosecution

		which may contribute to designing development, *production*, stockpiling, . . . *use of nuclear and biological weapons* and the delivery systems. **The Pakistan Arms Ordinance 1965 Section 13A 13-A. Penalty for transportation of arms, etc(2) Whoever**: . . . (a)transports, sells or keeps, offers or exposes for sale, any arms or ammunition other than those referred to in clause (a) of sub-section (1), in contravention of the provisions of this Ordinance, or		**Section 13A** **13-A. Penalty for transportation of arms, etc(2) Whoever**:. . . (a)transports, sells or keeps, offers or exposes for sale, any aims or ammunition other than those referred to in clause (a) of sub-section (1), in contravention of the provisions of this Ordinance, or (c)has in his possession or under his control any of the arms referred to in clause (a) or ammunition which can be fired from such arms, in contravention of the provisions of Section 9,	
Acquire	X	• Pakistan Nuclear Regulatory Authority Ordinance 2001. **Section 19 (c) ibid** • The Pakistan Arms Ordinance 1965 **Section 13A ibid**	X	**Section 44(1) ibid** **Section 13A(c) ibid**	
Possess	X	• Pakistan Nuclear Regulatory Authority Ordinance 2001. **Section 19 ibid** • The Explosives Substances Act 1908 • The Pakistan Arms Ordinance 1965 **Section 13A ibid**	X	**Section 44(1) ibid** **Sections and 5 A** **Section 5 Punishment for making or possessing explosive under suspicious circumstances**. Any person who makes or knowingly has in his possession or under his control any explosive substance, under such circumstances as to give rise to a *t*	

Does national legislation exist which prohibits persons or entities to engage in one of the following activities? Can violators be penalized?	National legal framework		Enforcement: civil/criminal penalties and others		Remarks
	Yes	**If YES, indicate source document of national implementation law**	**Yes**	**If YES, indicate source document**	
				reasonable suspicion that *he is not making it* or does not have it in his possession or under his control for a lawful object, shall, unless he can show that he made it or had it in his possession or under his control for a lawful object, be punishable with imprisonment for a term which may extend *to [fourteen years]*.5 **5-A. Forfeiture of property**. A Court convicting a person for an offence against this Act shall direct that the whole of his [property shall stand forfeited to Government].	
Stockpile/store	X	• Pakistan Nuclear Regulatory Authority Ordinance 2001. **Section 19 (c) read with 44 (1)** **Section 19.**Power to issue Licence.__(1)No person shall, unless he is exempted as may prescribed by the regulations, or unless he is the holder of a licence issued by the Authority . . .	X	**Section 44(1)** 44(1) Any person who contravenes . . . shall be punished – for a term—extend to 7 years or with fine which may extend to 1 million or with both **Section 8 (1)** **8 (1)** Any person who contravenes . . . shall be guilty for an offence	(If applicable)

		(c) explore for mines and mill, extract acquire handle use, . . . sell, lease lend by transfer import export convert enrich, produce, store, process, reprocess, fabricate, transport, dispose of any radioactive ore, radio active material, nuclear substance or any other substance as the authority may by notification . . . specify • Pakistan Nuclear Safety and Radiation Protection Regulations 1990 **Rule 58** Storage of radioactive material—(1) the licensee shall provide adequate facilities for storage of any radioactive material within his possession in such a manner that . . . (a) special containers and secure places approved by the Radiation Protection Officer are used; (b) it is kept away from inflammable substances; (c) no person is exposed to radiation resulting in doses in excess of the authorized limits; and (d) in the event of breakage or		punishable on conviction by imprisonment for a term which may extend to 14 years and with fine not exceeding 5 million rupees or both and . . . Property and assets where ever they may be shall be forfeited to Federal Government. **Section 13A ibid**	

Does national legislation exist which prohibits persons or entities to engage in one of the following activities? Can violators be penalized?	National legal framework		Enforcement: civil/criminal penalties and others		Remarks
	Yes	If YES, indicate source document of national implementation law	Yes	If YES, indicate source document	
		rupture of the container, its entire contents are retained in the appropriately designed receptacle. (2) Every container used for storage of any radioactive material shall affixed to it in addition to the symbol of ionizing radiation, a label indicating— (a) nature and activity of the contents: (b) data measurement of activity; (c) name of the person in-charge of the containers; and (d) special safety instructions. • Export Control on goods, technologies, material and equipment related to nuclear and biological weapons and their delivery system Act 2004			

		Section 4 **4.(1)** The Federal Govt shall maintain a Control Lists, to be notified separately, of goods and Technologies subject to licensing requirements under this Act. (2) The control lists shall be reviewed periodically, and revised or updated, as required by the Federal Govt and notified accordingly. (3) The Federal Govt shall notify all licensing requirements and procedures. (4) The Federal Govt *shall control* export, re export, transshipment, transit of goods, technologies material and equipment . . . which may contribute to designing, development, production, *stockpiling*, . . . use of nuclear and biological weapons and the delivery systems. • The Pakistan Arms Ordinance 1965			
Develop	**X**	• Pakistan Nuclear Regulatory Authority Ordinance 2001	X	**Section 44 (1) ibid**	

Does national legislation exist which prohibits persons or entities to engage in one of the following activities? Can violators be penalized?	National legal framework		Enforcement: civil/criminal penalties and others		Remarks
	Yes	If YES, indicate source document of national implementation law	Yes	If YES, indicate source document	
		Section 16 (c) To Regulate the radiation safety aspect of . . . (ii) *production* import export, transport, possession, processing, reprocessing, sale, transfer, storage or disposal of nuclear substance **Section 19 (c) ibid**	X		
Transport		• Pakistan Nuclear Regulatory Authority Ordinance 2001 **Section 19 (c) ibid** • Export Control on Goods, Technologies, Material and Equipment related to Nuclear and Biological Weapons and their Delivery System Act 2004 **Section 4(4) ibid** • The Pakistan Arms Ordinance 1965	X	**Section 44(1) ibid** **Section 8 ibid** **Section 13A ibid**	

Transfer		• Pakistan Nuclear Regulatory Authority Ordinance 2001 **Section 19(c) ibid**. • Export Control on goods, technologies, material and equipment related to nuclear and biological weapons and their delivery system Act 2004 **Section 5** 5.The Federal Govt shall control export, re-export, transshipment, transit of goods, technologies, material and equipment, subject to the provisions of this Act, which may contribute to the designing, development, production, stockpiling, maintenance or use of nuclear and biological weapons and their delivery systems.		**Section 44(1) Ibid** **Section 8** 8(1) Any person who contravenes . . . shall be guilty for an offence punishable on conviction by imprisonment for a term which may extend to 14 years and with fine not exceeding 5 million rupees or both and . . . Property and assets where ever they may be shall be forfeited to Federal Government.	
Use		• Pakistan Nuclear Regulatory Authority Ordinance 2001 **Section 19 (c) Ibid** • The Anti Terrorism Act 1997 **Read with;** • The Pakistan Arms Ordinance 1965		**Section 2bb read with 6 (2)(a)(d) and 7 (a)(b)** 2(bb)"weapons" means any item which can be used to injure or cause bodily harm, and includes any type of firearm, explosive, sword, dagger, knuckle-duster, stengun, bomb, grenade, rocket launcher, mortar or any ***chemical***, biological ***weapon*** or any other thing which can be used	Prosecution against any person can be maintained for use or attempt to use any NW under Anti terrorism Act 1997 because weapons "therein are defined to include Surrender

Does national legislation exist which prohibits persons or entities to engage in one of the following activities? Can violators be penalized?	National legal framework		Enforcement: civil/criminal penalties and others		Remarks
	Yes	**If YES, indicate source document of national implementation law**	**Yes**	**If YES, indicate source document**	
		2(c) "cannon" includes *(v)nuclear weapons of all types;* • The Pakistan Penal Code 1860		for causing injury, hurt, harm or destruction of person or property, and includes 'illicit arms' as defined in the surrender of illicit Arms Act 1991 (XXI of 1991). **6 (2)a involves** doing of any thing that causes death **b** involves the doing of any thing that is likely to cause death or endangers a person's life. 7(a) . . . shall be punished . . . with death or imprisonment for life and with fine. (b) . . . shall be punished . . . with imprisonment . . . not less than 5 years. . . may extend to 14 years and with fine **Section 126** **Committing depredation on territories of power at peace with Pakistan**. Whoever commits depredation, or makes preparations to commit depredation, on territories of any Power in alliance or at peace with Pakistan, shall be punished with	of Illicit Arms Act 1991 which in turn refer to Pakistan Arms Ordinance 1965 that defines NW. So prosecution can be maintained with reference to the consequences of use of NW under section 6(2) of this Act. General statute provision that creates an over arching criminal liability.

				imprisonment of either description for a term which may extend to seven years, and shall also be liable to fine and forfeiture of any property used or intended to be used in committing such depredation, or acquired by such depredation.	
Assist in a.m. activities	X	• Export Control on goods, technologies, material and equipment related to nuclear and biological weapons and their delivery system Act 2004 **Section 8 (2)** Any person who attempts to commits or abets to commission of an offense under this Act shall be proceeded against in the same manners as if he has committed such offence. • The Pakistan Penal Code 1860 **Section 107, 108** **107. Abetment of a thing**. A person abets the doing of a thing, who . . . ***First:*** Instigates any person to do that thing; or ***Secondly:*** Engages with one or more other person or persons in any conspiracy for the doing of that thing, if	X	**Section 6** **6. Punishment of abettors:** Any person who by the supply of or solicitation for money, the providing of premises, the supply of material, or in any manner whatsoever, procures counsels, aids, abets, or is accessory to, the commission of any offence under this Act shall be punished with the punishment provided for the offence.	

Does national legislation exist which prohibits persons or entities to engage in one of the following activities? Can violators be penalized?	National legal framework		Enforcement: civil/criminal penalties and others		Remarks
	Yes	If YES, indicate source document of national implementation law	Yes	If YES, indicate source document	
		an act or illegal omission takes place in pursuance of that conspiracy, and in order to the doing of that thing; or ***Thirdly:*** Intentionally aids by any act or illegal omission, the doing of that thing. **Explanation 1:** A person who, by willful misrepresentation, or by willful concealment of a material fact, which is bound to disclose, voluntarily causes or procures, or attempts to cause or procures, a thing to be done, is said to instigate the doing of that thing. **Explanation 2:** Whoever, either prior to or at the time of the commission of an act, does anything in order to facilitate the commission of that act, and thereby facilitates the commission thereof, is said to aid the doing of that act.			

		108. Abettor. A person abets an offence, who abets either the commission of an offence, or the commission of an act which would be an offence, if committed by a person capable by law of committing an offence with the same intention or knowledge as that of the abettor. **Explanation 1:** The abetment of the illegal omission of an act may amount to an offence although the abettor may not himself be bound to do that act. **Explanation 2:** To constitute the offence of abetment it is not necessary that the act abetted should be committed, or that the effect requisite to constitute the offence should be caused. • The Explosives Substances Act 1908			
Finance a.m. activities	**X**	• Export Control on goods, technologies, material and equipment related to nuclear and biological weapons and their delivery system Act 2004	X	**Section 8(2) ibid** **11-N Punishment under section 11-H to 11-K** . . . shall be punishable on conviction with imprisonment for a term not less than six months and not exceeding five years and with fine.	

Does national legislation exist which prohibits persons or entities to engage in one of the following activities? Can violators be penalized?	National legal framework		Enforcement: civil/criminal penalties and others		Remarks
	Yes	If YES, indicate source document of national implementation law	Yes	If YES, indicate source document	
		• Anti Terrorism Act 1997 **Section 11-J and 11-N** 11-J **Funding Arrangements.**—A person commits an offence if (a)enters into or becomes concerned in an arrangement as a result of which money or other property is made available or is to be made available to another, and (b)has reasonable cause to suspect that it will or may be used for the purposes of terrorism. • The Pakistan Penal Code 1860		**Section 213 & 214** **213. Taking gift, etc., to screen an offender from punishment:** Whoever accept or attempts to obtain, or agrees to accept, any gratification for himself or any other person, or any restitution of property to himself or any other person, in consideration of his concealing an offence or of his screening any person from legal punishment for any offence, or of his not proceeding against any person for the purpose of bring him to legal punishment. **if a capital offence:** shall, if the offence is punishable with death, be punished with imprisonment of either description for a term which may extend to seven years, and shall also be liable to fine: **if punishable with imprisonment for life, or with imprisonment:** and if the offence is punishable with imprisonment for life or with imprisonment which may extend to	

				ten years, shall be punished with imprisonment of either description for a term which may extend to three years, shall also be liable to fine: and if the offence is punishable with imprisonment not extending to ten years, shall be punished with description provided for the offence for a term which may extend to one-fourth part of the longest term of imprisonment provided for the offence, or with fine, or with both. **214 Offering gift or restoration of property in consideration of screening offender**: Whoever gives or causes or offers or agrees to give or cause, any gratification to any person, or to restore or cause to restoration of any property to any person, in consideration of that person's concealing an offence, or of his screening any person form legal punishment for any offence, or his not proceeding against any person for the purpose of bringing him to legal punishment; **if the a capital offence:** shall, if the offence is punishable with death, be punished with imprisonment of either description for a term which may extend to seven years and shall also be liable to fine; **if punishable with imprisonment for life or with imprisonment:** and the offence is punishable with	

Does national legislation exist which prohibits persons or entities to engage in one of the following activities? Can violators be penalized?	National legal framework		Enforcement: civil/criminal penalties and others		Remarks
	Yes	**If YES, indicate source document of national implementation law**	**Yes**	**If YES, indicate source document**	
				imprisonment for life, or with imprisonment which may extend to three years, shall be punished with imprisonment of either description for a term may extend to three years, and shall also be liable to and if the offence is punishable with imprisonment not extending to ten years, shall be punishable with imprisonment of the description provided for the offence for a term which may extend to one-fourth part of the longest term of imprisonment provided for the offence, or with fine, or with or with both.	
Above mentioned activities related to means of delivery.	**X**	• Pakistan Nuclear Regulatory Authority Ordinance 2001 **Section 19 Ibid** • Export Control on goods, technologies, material and equipment related to nuclear and biological weapons and their delivery system Act 2004	X	**Section 44 ibid** **Section 8 ibid**	

		Section4 ibid • Surrender of Illicit Arms Act 1991		**Section 7 (3)** Any conveyance used for the transportation of illicit arms shall also be liable to confiscation.	
Involvement of non-state actors in a.m. activities		• Pakistan Nuclear Regulatory Authority Ordinance 2001 **Section 19 ibid** • Export Control on goods, technologies, material and equipment related to nuclear and biological weapons and their delivery system Act 2004 • The Pakistan Penal Code 1860. • Anti Terrorism Act, 1997.		**Section 44 ibid** **Section 8 ibid** **Section 126** **126 Committing depredation on territories of power at peace with Pakistan**. Whoever commits depredation, or makes preparations to commit depredation, on territories of any Power in alliance or at peace with Pakistan, shall be punished with imprisonment of either description for a term which may extend to seven years, and shall also be liable to fine and forfeiture of any property used or intended to be used in committing such depredation, or acquired by such depredation.	
Other					

OP 3(a) and (b)—Account for/Secure/Physically Protect BW Including Related Materials

State: **Pakistan**
Date of Report: 27 October 2005

Are any of the following measures, procedures or legislation in place to account for, secure or otherwise protect BW and Related Materials? Can violators be penalized?	National legal framework		Enforcement: civil/criminal penalties and others		Remarks
	YES	If YES, indicate source document	YES	If YES, indicate source document	
Measures to account for production	X	• Pakistan Bio-safety Rules 2005 Rule 17(1) and (2) **Rule 19** The Production in which living modified engineered organisms . . . are generated or used shall not be commenced except with the consent of National Biosafety committee. This also applies to production taking place in connection with the development, testing and experiment			The Pakistan Biosafety Rules 2005 setup a new Biosafety committee which has been given a very wide jurisdiction in technical areas.
Measures to account for use	X	• The Pakistan BioSafety Rules 2005 Rule 17 ibid. **Rule 19 ibid**.			
Measures to account for storage	X	• Export Control on goods, technologies, material and equipment related to nuclear and biological weapons and their delivery system Act 2004		**Section 17** Penalizes contraventions of rules.	

		Section 4(4) read with 6 (4) The Federal Govt shall *control* export, re export, transshipment, transit of goods, technologies material and equipment . . . which may contribute to designing, development, production, *stockpiling*, . . . use of nuclear and biological weapons and the delivery systems. **Section 6** Record keeping (1) All exporters shall maintain records of all Transactions . . . 2) Any Government agency or department involved in export—shall keep records of their recommendations and decisions . . . . • The Pakistan Environmental Protection Act 1997 **Section 14** . . . , no person shall generate, collect, consign, transport, treat, dispose of, *store*, handle or import any hazardous substance . . .			
Measures to account for transport	**X**	• The Pakistan Environmental Protection Act 1997 **Section 14 ibid**			
Other measures for accounting					

Are any of the following measures, procedures or legislation in place to account for, secure or otherwise protect BW and Related Materials? Can violators be penalized?	National legal framework		Enforcement: civil/criminal penalties and others		Remarks
	YES	If YES, indicate source document	YES	If YES, indicate source document	
Measures to secure production	X	• The Pakistan BioSafety Rules 2005 **Rule 19, 21 and 22** **19. The Production** in which living modified engineered organisms . . . are generated or used shall not be commenced except with the consent of National Biosafety committee. This also applies to production taking place in connection with the development, testing and experiment **21. Permissio1n** and approval for certain substances and products which contained genetically engineered organisms . . . shall not be produced imported or used except with the approval of . . . **22. Permission** and approval for food stuffs, ingredients in food stuffs and additives including processing aids containing or consisting or having modified organisms substances or cells			

		there shall not be produced sold imported except with the approval . . .			
Measures to secure use	X	• The Pakistan BioSafety Rules 2005 **Rule 19 ibid** • Export Control on goods, technologies, material and equipment related to nuclear and biological weapons and their delivery system Act 2004 **Section 4 (4) ibid**			
Measures to secure storage					
Measures to secure transport	X	• The Pakistan Environmental Protection Act 1997 **Section 14 ibid** • Carriage of Goods by Sea Act 1925 **Schedule Article IV item(6)** Goods of inflammable, explosive or dangerous nature to the shipment whereof The carrier, master or agent of the carrier, has not consented, with the knowledge of their nature and characters, may at any time before discharge be landed at any place or be destroyed........			

Are any of the following measures, procedures or legislation in place to account for, secure or otherwise protect BW and Related Materials? Can violators be penalized?	National legal framework		Enforcement: civil/criminal penalties and others		Remarks
	YES	**If YES, indicate source document**	**YES**	**If YES, indicate source document**	
Other measures for securing	X	• Export Control on goods, technologies, material and equipment related to nuclear and biological weapons and their delivery system Act 2004 **Section 4(4) ibid**			
Regulations for physical protection of facilities/ materials/transports	X	• The Pakistan BioSafety Rules 2005 **Rule 11** Prohibition and license requirements No person shall import export, sell, purchase or trade living modified organisms . . . without the prior obtaining of license from the Federal Agency			
Licensing/registration of facilities/persons handling biological materials	X	• The Pakistan BioSafety Rules 2005 **Rule 11 ibid**	X	In certain cases.	
Reliability check of personnel		Civil Servants (Efficiency & Discipline) Rules 1975			
Measures to account for/ secure/Physically protect means of delivery					

Regulations for genetic engineering work	X	• The Pakistan BioSafety Rules 2005 SRO 336(I)/2005 • The Pakistan Council of Scientific and Industrial Research Act 1973 **Section 6** **The functions of the Council shall be . . .** (d) to undertake such special scientific and technological surveys and investigations as may be referred to it by the Federal Government from time to time. • Center of Excellence In Molecular Biology Established Under the Directives of Ministry of Science and Technology			
Other legislation/ regulations related to safety and security of biological materials					
Other	X	• The Pakistan Penal Code 1860	X	**Chapter XIV** **Section 271, 274, 275, 276, 277.** **Disobedience to quarantine rule.** Whoever knowingly disobeys any rule made and promulgated by Federal or any Provincial Govt for putting any vessel into state of quarantine or for regulating the intercourse of vessel in a State of	

Are any of the following measures, procedures or legislation in place to account for, secure or otherwise protect BW and Related Materials? Can violators be penalized?	National legal framework		Enforcement: civil/criminal penalties and others		Remarks
	YES	If YES, indicate source document	YES	If YES, indicate source document	
				quarantine with the shore or with other vessels, or for regulating the intercourse between places where an infectious disease prevails and other places, shall be punished with imprisonment of either description for a term which may extend to six months, or with fine or with both. 274 **Adulteration of drugs**. Whoever adulterates any drug or medical preparation in such a manner as to lessen the efficacy or change the operation of such drug or medical preparation, or to make it noxious, intending that it shall be sold or used for, or knowing it to be likely that it will be sold or used for, any medical purpose, as if it had not undergone such adulteration, shall be punishable with imprisonment of either description for term which may extend to six months or with fine which extends to three thousand or with both. 275 **Sale of adulterated drugs**. Whoever, knowing any drug or medical preparation to have been	

				adulterated in such a manner as to lessen its efficacy, to change its operation, or to render it noxious, sells the same, or offers or exposes or causes it to be used for medical purposes by any person not knowing of the adulteration, shall be punished with imprisonment of either description which may extend to six months, or with fine which extends to three thousand or with both. 276 **Sale of drug as a different drug or preparation**. Whoever knowingly sells, or offers or exposes for sale, or issue from any dispensary for medical purposes, any drug or medical preparation, as a different drug or medical preparation, shall be punished with imprisonment of either description which may extend to six months, or with fine which extends to three thousand or with both. 277 **Fouling water of public spring or reservoir**. Whoever voluntarily corrupts or fouls the water of any public spring or reservoir, so as to render it less fit for the purposes for which it is ordinarily used, shall be punished with imprisonment of either description which may extend to three months, or with fine which extends to one thousand or with both.	

OP 3(a) and (b)—Account for/Secure/Phvsicallv Protect CW Including Related Materials

State: **Pakistan**
Date of Report: 27 October 2005

Are any of the following measures, procedures or legislation in place to account for, secure or otherwise protect CW and Related Materials? Can violators be penalized?	**National legal framework**		**Enforcement: civil/criminal penalties and others**		**Remarks**
	YES	**If YES, indicate source document**	**YES**	**If YES, indicate source document**	
Measures to account for production	**X**	• Chemical Weapons Convention Implementation Ordinance–2000 **Section 2,7 read with schedule I, II, III and IV 7. Production, etc., for permitted purposes.**— (1). . . (2) The production, use, acquisition, export or import of any discrete organic chemical not being a schedule chemical containing phosphorous, sulphur or fluorine and facilities specified in Part IX of the Verification Annex shall be subject to data monitoring and eventual on site verification in accordance with that part of the Verification Annex unless decided otherwise by the Conference of States Parties- . . .			• Pakistan is a declared non possessor state. • Page 6 of the report

Measures to account for use	X	• Chemical Weapons Convention Implementation Ordinance–2000 **Section 7 read with schedule I, II, III and IV** The CWC Authority under the Act is preparing detailed guidelines/Rules			
Measures to account for storage	X	• Chemical Weapons Convention Implementation Ordinance–2000 **Section 7 and schedule I, II, III and IV Read with Section 12, 13 of the Custom Act 1969 regarding ware house licensing (in case where applicable)** • The Explosive Act 1884 **Section 6 ibid**		**Custom Act 1969** Section 156	
Measures to account for transport	X	• Chemical Weapons Convention Implementation Ordinance–2000 **Section 7 ibid** • The Dangerous Cargoes Act 1953 **Section 10 read with 2 & 3** **2** "dangerous cargoes" means any cargoes containing …	X	**10**. The police may arrest without warrant any person committing an offence under this Act	

Are any of the following measures, procedures or legislation in place to account for, secure or otherwise protect CW and Related Materials? Can violators be penalized?	National legal framework		Enforcement: civil/criminal penalties and others		Remarks
	YES	If YES, indicate source document	YES	If YES, indicate source document	
		(a) any goods shown as explosives in the Comprehensive Classified List of Government Explosives (c) prohibited dangerous goods, that is to say, goods classified as dangerous (d) any cargoes which are liable to fire or explosion and which are declared by the Central Government by notification in the official Gazette to be dangerous cargoes for the purposes of this Act. **3**. The Central Government may make such orders as appears to it to be necessary or expedient for securing the safety of any port and preventing or dealing with explosions and fires on vessels carrying dangerous cargoes within the limit of any port, generally for the transit working and storage of dangerous cargoes and matter incidental thereto.			

Other measures for accounting	X	• Chemical Weapons Convention Implementation Ordinance–2000 **Section 2, 7 read with schedule I, II, III and IV**			
Measures to secure production	X	• Chemical Weapons Convention Implementation Ordinance–2000 **Section 2, 7 read with schedule I, II, III and IV** • The Explosive Act 1884 **Section 5** (In selective cases)			
Measures to secure use	X	• Chemical Weapons Convention Implementation Ordinance–2000 **Section 7 along with schedule I, II, III and IV** • The Explosive Act 1884 **Section 5** (In selective cases)			
Measures to secure storage	X	• Chemical Weapons Convention Implementation Ordinance–2000 **Section 7 with all the schedule to the Act.**			

Are any of the following measures, procedures or legislation in place to account for, secure or otherwise protect CW and Related Materials? Can violators be penalized?	National legal framework		Enforcement: civil/criminal penalties and others		Remarks
	YES	If YES, indicate source document	YES	If YES, indicate source document	
Measures to secure transport	X	• Chemical Weapons Convention Implementation Ordinance–2000 **Section 7 ibid** • The Explosive Act 1884 **Section 5 ibid** • The Dangerous Cargoes Act 1953 **Section 10 read with 2 & 3 ibid**			
Other measures for securing	X	• Chemical Weapons Convention Implementation Ordinance–2000 **Section 10** **Functions of the Authority.**—In particular and without prejudice to the generality of functions under this Ordinance, the function of the Authority shall be to— (a) ensure effective operation of this Ordinance; (b) carry out, on behalf of Pakistan, such obligations which Pakistan has under the Convention;	X		

		(c) facilitate inspections of the premises in Pakistan, in case compliance of Pakistan with the Convention is challenged; and (d) do anything incidental or conducive to the performance of the foresaid functions • The Explosive Act 1884		**Section 13** **13. Power to arrest without warrant persons committing dangerous** offences. Whoever is found committing any act for which he is punishable under this Act or the rules under this Act, and which tends to cause explosion or fire in or about any place where an explosive is manufactured or stored or any railway or port, or any carriage, aircraft or vessel, may be apprehended without warrant by a Police Officer or by the occupier of, or the agent or servant of, or other person authorized by the occupier … and be removed from the place where he is arrested and conveyed as soon as conveniently may be before a Magistrate	

Are any of the following measures, procedures or legislation in place to account for, secure or otherwise protect CW and Related Materials? Can violators be penalized?	National legal framework		Enforcement: civil/criminal penalties and others		Remarks
	YES	If YES, indicate source document	YES	If YES, indicate source document	
Regulations for physical protection of facilities/materials/transports	X	• Chemical Weapons Convention Implementation Ordinance–2000			
Licensing of Chemical installations/entities/use of materials	X	• Chemical Weapons Convention Implementation Ordinance–2000 **Section 23 Registration.—(1) The National Authority may**, directly or through notice, require an individual or organization involved in production, processing, consumption, transfer, import or export of any schedule chemical or any discrete organic chemical not being a schedule chemical, or a chemical containing elements of phosphorous, sulfur, or fluorine, to register themselves with the National Authority or any other office as may be prescribed within a specified time period.	X	2) Whoever contravenes the provisions of this section shall be guilty of an offence punishable with imprisonment for a term, which may extent to two years, or with fine, or with both.	

Reliability check of personnel	**X**	• Chemical Weapons Convention Implementation Ordinance–2000 **Schedule V** **A**. General Principles for the Handling of Confidential Information. **B**. Employment and Conduct of Personnel in the Technical Secretariat. **C**. Measure to Protect Sensitive Installation and Prevention Disclosure of Confidential data in the Course of on site Verification Activities. **D**. Procedure in case of Breach or Alleged Breach of Confidentiality Civil Servant Efficiency and Discipline Rules 1973 • Official Secrets Act of 1923			
Measures to account for/secure/ Physically protect means of delivery	**X**	• Chemical Weapons Convention Implementation Ordinance–2000 **Section 2(c)(iii)(m) Schedule IV (2) A (8) (c)(iii)** any equipment specifically designed for use directly or in connection with the employment of the munition or device specified …			

Are any of the following measures, procedures or legislation in place to account for, secure or otherwise protect CW and Related Materials? Can violators be penalized?	National legal framework		Enforcement: civil/criminal penalties and others		Remarks
	YES	If YES, indicate source document	YES	If YES, indicate source document	
		(e) The purposes for which the chemical was or will be produced, processed or consumed;… (ii) Sale or transfer within the territory or to any other place under the jurisdiction or control of the State Party, with a specification whether to other industry, trade or other destination and, if possible, of final product ….(iii)(iv) … Declaration on the past production of schedule 2 chemicals for chemical weapon purposes:			
National CWC authority	X	Ministry of Foreign Affairs (Chemical Weapons Convention Implementation Ordinance–2000.			National Authority on CWC under the Ministry of Foreign Affairs.
Reporting Schedule I, II and III chemicals to OPCW	X	Chemical Weapons Convention Implementation Ordinance –2000			National Authority on CWC is responsible for reporting.

Account for, secure or physically protect old chemical weapons	X	The Explosive Rules 1940 **Rule 107** Power to destroy illicit explosive (1)the Chief Inspector or an Inspector of Explosives (a) shall destroy any explosive where ever found (i) the manufacture possession, or importation of which has been prohibited absolutely under section 6 of the Act................... Chemical Weapons Convention Implementation Ordinance–2000 **Section 24** Power to enter a premises and search, remove or immobilize object. . . .(1) If the national Authority has reasonable cause to believe that. . . (a) an object is on a premises to which the public has the access or which are occupied by a person who consents to action being taken under this subsection; and (b) the object is a chemical weapon, the National authority may authorize any person to enter the premises and to search them. . . (2). . .(3). . .			Pakistan is a non-possessor CW state. However, appropriate measures are being developed to protect against chemical weapons.

Are any of the following measures, procedures or legislation in place to account for, secure or otherwise protect CW and Related Materials? Can violators be penalized?	National legal framework		Enforcement: civil/criminal penalties and others		Remarks
	YES	If YES, indicate source document	YES	If YES, indicate source document	
		(4) if the person enters the premises. . . (a) he may seize and remove it, if it is reasonable practice to do so; or (b) he may, in any other case, affix a warning on the object. . . not to moved or inferred with. . .			
Other legislation/regulations controlling chemical materials	X	• Surrender of Illicit Arms Act 1991 • The Explosives Substances Act 1908	X	**Section 7** **7. Punishments.** (1) Whoever contravenes the provisions of Section 4 or Section 5 of fails to surrender illicit arms shall—(a) in respect of illicit arms defined in sub-clauses (i) to (iii) of clause (a) of Section 2, be punished with imprisonment for life and forfeiture of property, both movable and immovable; (b) in respect of illicit arms defined in sub-clause (iv) of	Depending on facts, offenders of CW's are prosecutable under these laws as well.

				imprisonment for life clause (a) of Section 2, be punished with or with imprisonment for a term which shall not be less than ten years having regard to the antecedents of the accused; and (c) in respect of illicit arms defined in sub-clause (v) of Clause (a) of Section 2, be punished with imprisonment for a term which may extend to fourteen years but shall; not be less than three years, having regard to the antecedents of the accused; (2) Any illicit arms in respect of which a person is convicted and sentenced under sub-section (1) shall stand forfeited to the Federal Government. (3) Any conveyance used for the transportation of any illicit arms shall also be liable to confiscation.	

Are any of the following measures, procedures or legislation in place to account for, secure or otherwise protect CW and Related Materials? Can violators be penalized?	National legal framework		Enforcement: civil/criminal penalties and others		Remarks
	YES	If YES, indicate source document	YES	If YES, indicate source document	
				Section 5-5A **5.Punishment for making or possessing explosive under suspicious circumstances.** Any person who makes or knowingly has in his possession or under his control any explosive substance, under such circumstances as to give rise to a reasonable suspicion that he is not making it or does not have it in his possession or under his control for a lawful object, shall, unless he can show that he made it or had it in his possession or under his control for a lawful object, be punishable with imprisonment for a term which may extend to [fourteen years]8.	

				5-A. **Forfeiture of property**. A Court convicting a person for an offence against this Act shall direct that the whole of his [property shall stand forfeited to Government].	
Other	X	• Challenge Inspections • Routine Inspections • Awareness of masses			

OP 3(a) and (b)—Account for/Secure/Physically protect NW Including Related Materials

State: **Pakistan**

Date of Report: 27 October 2005

Are any of the following measures, procedures or legislation in place to account for, secure or otherwise protect NW and Related Materials? Can violators be penalized?	**National legal framework**		**Enforcement: civil/criminal penalties and others**		**Remarks**
	Yes	**If YES, indicate source document**	**Yes**	**If YES, indicate source documents**	
Measure to account for production	X	• INFIRC/418(Chasma II) • INFIRC/116(KANUPP) • INFIRC/135(KANUPP) • Pakistan Nuclear Regulatory Authority Ordinance 2001 • Pakistan Nuclear safety and Radiation protection Regulations 1990 **Rule 59(1)** 1. Records of the radioactive material as stored shall be kept by the licensee in a form and in a manner prescribed by the Directorate **Rule 22** Maintenance of records—Every licensee shall- (a) Maintain the record showing the nature, form and quantity of radioactive material obtained and used monthly;	X	**Section 44(1)** 44(1) Any person who contravenes . . . shall be punished – for a term. . . extend to 7 years or with fine which may extend to 1 million or with both	

		b) Keep a record of the names, addresses, designations, qualifications and status of all the persons involved in use or handling or connected with the use or handling of radioactive material, radiation apparatus or nuclear installations: Record full particulars of disposal, decay and loss of radioactive material and intimate the Directorate about such loss and efforts made by him for the recovery. . . • Pakistan Nuclear Regulatory Authority Ordinance 2001 **Section 19 (4)** Power to issue licence.__(1) No person shall, unless he is exempted as may prescribed by the regulations, or unless he is the holder of a licence issued by the Authority. . . (2) Subject to sub-section (1), the Authority may, on application made to it accompanied by such fee, information and documents, as may be prescribed by the regulations, issued a licence for carrying out of such activities as are specified in the licence for such period as may . . . (4) the Authority may prescribe terms and condition that may be attached to a licence			

Are any of the following measures, procedures or legislation in place to account for, secure or otherwise protect NW and Related Materials? Can violators be penalized?	National legal framework		Enforcement: civil/criminal penalties and others		Remarks
	Yes	If YES, indicate source document	Yes	If YES, indicate source documents	
Measures to account for use	X	• Pakistan Nuclear Regulatory Authority Ordinance 2001 • Pakistan Nuclear Safety and Radiation Protection Regulations 1990 **Rule 22 ibid**	X	**Section 44 ibid**	http://www.iaea.org/Our Work SV/Safeguards/sir table.pdf
Measures to account for storage	X	• Pakistan Nuclear Safety and Radiation Protection Regulations 1990 **Rule 59 (i) ibid** • Export Control on goods, technologies, material and equipment related to nuclear and biological weapons and their delivery system Act 2004 **Section 4(4)** (4) The Federal Govt shall *control* export, re export, transshipment, transit of goods, technologies material and equipment . . . which may contribute to designing, development, production, stockpiling, . . . use of nuclear and biological weapons and the delivery systems.	X	**Section 44 ibid**	http://www.iaea.org/Our Work SV/Safeguards/sir table.pdf

Measures to account for transport	X	• Pakistan Nuclear Regulatory Authority Ordinance 2001 • Pakistan Nuclear Safety and Radiation Protection Regulations 1990 **Rule 62** Transport of radioactive material—The transport of radioactive material shall be regulated by the guidelines issued by the Directorate. **Rule 63** Additional requirement . . .During the transport of the radioactive materials any other hazardous characteristics . . . shall be taken in to account in such a manner as to be in conformity with the regulation already in force for the transport of dangerous goods. **Rule 70** Physical protection of nuclear material and nuclear facilities __ the licensee shall be responsible to organize and ensure the physical protection of the nuclear material in use and storage and during transport and of nuclear facilities, including radioactive waste belonging to these facilities in accordance with the provisions of these regulations and guidelines to be issued by PNRB from time to time.	X	**Section 44 ibid** **Customs Act 1969** **Section 156** 10. The police may arrest without warrant any person committing an offence under this Act	

Are any of the following measures, procedures or legislation in place to account for, secure or otherwise protect NW and Related Materials? Can violators be penalized?	National legal framework		Enforcement: civil/criminal penalties and others		Remarks
	Yes	If YES, indicate source document	Yes	If YES, indicate source documents	
		• Custom Rules and Notifications, 2001 333. Goods not permitted for transshipment.—The following goods shall not be allowed transshipment to up-country customs port or stations— a. . . . b. . . . c. . . . d. explosive, as defined in the Explosive Act, 1884 e. arms and ammunition. . . . • The Dangerous Cargoes Act 1953 **Section 10 read with 2 &3** **2** "dangerous cargoes" means any cargoes containing. . . (a) any goods shown as explosives in the Comprehensive Classified List of Government Explosives (c) prohibited dangerous goods, that is to say, goods classified as dangerous			

		(d) any cargoes which are liable to fire or explosion and which are declared by the Central Government by notification in the official Gazette to be dangerous cargoes for the purposes of this Act. **3**. The Central Government may make such orders as appears to it to be necessary or expedient for securing the safety of any port and preventing or dealing with explosions and fires on vessels carrying dangerous cargoes within the limit of any port, generally for the transit working and storage of dangerous cargoes and matter incidental thereto.			
Other measures for accounting	X	• Pakistan Nuclear Safety and Radiation Protection Regulations 1990 **Rule 9** Loss of radioactive material etc.— (1) Where, in opinion of an Inspector— (a)any loss, theft, or destruction of any radioactive material or radiation apparatus has occurred or the same has fallen into the possession of some unauthorized person or is so suspected;	X	**7.Punishments**. (1) Whoever contravenes the provisions of Section 4 or Section 5 of fails to surrender illicit arms shall— a) in respect of illicit arms defined in sub-clauses (i) to (iii) of clause (a) of Section 2, be punished with imprisonment for life and forfeiture of property, both movable and immovable;	

Are any of the following measures, procedures or legislation in place to account for, secure or otherwise protect NW and Related Materials? Can violators be penalized?	National legal framework		Enforcement: civil/criminal penalties and others		Remarks
	Yes	If YES, indicate source document	Yes	If YES, indicate source documents	
		(b)(c). . . (2) If in his opinion a violation of terms and conditions of the licence or breach of these regulation has taken place in any premises or installation, Inspector may with approval of the Director order work to be stopped or suspended. . . unless satisfied that the risk. . .is not greater than when the licence was granted • Surrender of Illicit Arms Act 1991 **Section 7 read with 4** **Surrender of illicit arms.**(1) on commencement of this Act, all persons in possession or control of any illicit arms shall surrender such arms to the District Coordination Officer, Deputy District Officer (Revenue) or officer-in-charge of a police station within whose jurisdiction such person ordinarily resides or to such other authority as may be specified by the Federal Govt. by notification – • The Explosives Act 1884		b) in respect of illicit arms defined in sub-clause (iv) of clause (a) of Section 2, be punished with imprisonment for life or with imprisonment for a term which shall not be less than ten years having regard to the antecedents of the accused; and c) in respect of illicit arms defined in sub-clause (v) of Clause (a) of Section 2, be punished with imprisonment for a term which may extend to fourteen years but shall; not be less than tree years, having regard to the antecedents of the accused; (2) Any illicit arms in respect of which a person is convicted and sentenced under sub-section (1) shall stand forfeited to the Federal Government. (3) Any conveyance used for the transportation of any illicit arms shall also be liable to confiscation.	

		Section 6 **6.Power for appropriate Government to prohibit the manufacture, possession or importation of specially dangerous explosives** . . .(1) Notwithstanding anything contained in this Act, the Federal Govt may from time to time, by notification in the official Gazette, prohibit, either absolutely or subject to conditions, the manufacture, possession, use, transport, import or export of any explosive which is of so dangerous a character that, in the opinion of the Federal Govt, it is expedient for the public safety to issue such information (2) The Custom Act, 1969 shall have effect in relation to any explosive with regard to the importation of which a notification has been issued. . . (3) Any person manufacturing, possession, using, selling, transporting, importing or exporting any explosive. . .shall be punished with fine which may extend to thirty thousand rupees. . .			

Are any of the following measures, procedures or legislation in place to account for, secure or otherwise protect NW and Related Materials? Can violators be penalized?	National legal framework		Enforcement: civil/criminal penalties and others		Remarks
	Yes	**If YES, indicate source document**	**Yes**	**If YES, indicate source documents**	
Measures to secure production	X	• Pakistan Nuclear Safety and Radiation Protection Regulations 1990 **Rule 22** Maintenance of records—Every licensee shall (e Not sell transfer dispose of any radiation apparatus or radio active material without prior approval of Directorate			
Measures to secure use	X	• Pakistan Nuclear Regulatory Authority Ordinance 2001 • PNRA Regulation PAK/904 • Pakistan Nuclear Safety and Radiation Protection Regulations 1990 **Rule 70** Physical protection of nuclear material and nuclear facilities the ____ licensee shall be responsible to organize and ensure the physical protection of the nuclear material in use and storage and during transport and of nuclear facilities, including		**Section 44 ibid**	Page 6 of the report

		radioactive waste belonging to these facilities in accordance with the provisions of these regulations and guidelines to be issued by PNRB from time to time.			
Measures to secure storage	X	• PNRA Regulation PAK/904 • Pakistan Nuclear Safety and Radiation Protection Regulations 1990 **Rule 2(e) ibid** **Rule 45** **Duties and functions of the Radiation Protection Office**–The Radiations Protection Officer shall (a) . . . (d) (e) organize the safe transport, storage and disposal of all radioactive materials including waste containing radioactive materials; . . . **Rule 58** **Storage of radioactive material—** **(1)** the licensee shall provide adequate facilities for storage of any radioactive material within his possession in such a manner that . . . a)special containers and secure places approved by the Radiation Protection Officer are used; b)it is kept away from inflammable substances; c)no person is exposed to radiation resulting in doses in excess of the authorized limits; and			Page 6 of the report

Are any of the following measures, procedures or legislation in place to account for, secure or otherwise protect NW and Related Materials? Can violators be penalized?	National legal framework		Enforcement: civil/criminal penalties and others		Remarks
	Yes	If YES, indicate source document	Yes	If YES, indicate source documents	
		d) in the event of breakage or rupture of the container, its entire contents are retained in the appropriately designed receptacle. (2) Every container used for storage of any radioactive material shall affixed to it in addition to the symbol of ionizing radiation, a label indicating— a) nature and activity of the contents: b) data measurement of activity; c) name of the person in-charge of the containers; and d) special safety instructions. **Rule 70** Physical protection of nuclear material and nuclear facilities ___ the licensee shall be responsible to organize and ensure the physical protection of the nuclear material in use and storage and during transport and of nuclear facilities, including radioactive waste belonging to these facilities in accordance with the provisions of these regulations and guidelines to be issued by PNRB from time to time.			

Measures to secure transport	X	• PNRA Regulation PAK/916 • Pakistan Nuclear Safety and Radiation Protection Regulations 1990 **Rule 45(e) & 62,63 59 (2) ibid** **45 Duties and functions of the Radiation Protection Office**—The Radiations Protection Officer shall (a) . . . (d) (e) organize the safe transport, storage and disposal of all radioactive materials including waste containing radioactive materials; . . . **62. Transport of radioactive** material—The transport of radioactive material shall be regulated by the guidelines issued by the Directorate. **Rule 63** Additional requirement—During the transport of the radioactive materials any other hazardous characteristics . . . shall be taken in to account in such a manner as to be in conformity with the regulation already in force for the transport of dangerous goods. **Rule 70** Physical protection of nuclear material and nuclear facilities ___ the licensee shall be responsible to organize and ensure the physical			Page 6 of the report

Are any of the following measures, procedures or legislation in place to account for, secure or otherwise protect NW and Related Materials? Can violators be penalized?	National legal framework		Enforcement: civil/criminal penalties and others		Remarks
	Yes	If YES, indicate source document	Yes	If YES, indicate source documents	
		protection of the nuclear material in use and storage and during transport and of nuclear facilities, including radioactive waste belonging to these facilities in accordance with the provisions of these regulations and guidelines to be issued by PNRB from time to time.			
Other measures for securing	X	• Pakistan Arms Ordinance 1965			
Regulations for physical protection of facilities/ materials/transports	X	• PNRA Regulation PAK/911 • Licensees to follow IAEA INFCIRC/224/Rev.4-Physical Protection of Nuclear Material and Nuclear Facilities • Pakistan Nuclear Regulatory Authority Ordinance 2001-Ordinance No. III of 2001, • Pakistan Nuclear Safety and Radiation Protection Regulations 1990		Sec. 16-f	Page 6 and 7 of the report

		Rule 43 **Physical surveillance of radiation workers.**—(1) The licensee shall establish a system of physical surveillance to ensure compliance with the system of dose limitation. (2) . . . (3) . . . (4) The Physical surveillance programme include— a) correctly established and implemented radiation protection procedures; b) correctly performed analysis; c) correctly maintain records; d) limitation of errors; e) maintenance of the measurement accuracy; and f) properly trained personnel. **Rule 62 ibid** **Rule 44** **Duties of the physical surveillance service**—The physical surveillance service shall provide – (a) facilities located within the site for the decontamination of personnel, equipment and areas; (b) all persons who carry out remedial actins, with individual dosimeters, suitable protective clothing and respiratory protective equipment as appropriate to the situation;			

Are any of the following measures, procedures or legislation in place to account for, secure or otherwise protect NW and Related Materials? Can violators be penalized?	National legal framework		Enforcement: civil/criminal penalties and others		Remarks
	Yes	If YES, indicate source document	Yes	If YES, indicate source documents	
		(c) sufficient quantities of various protective equipment, readily available to meet at least the minimum requirements for seen emergency plan; (d) . . .(e) . . . **Rule 70 ibid**			
Licensing of nuclear installations/entities/use of materials	X	• PNRA Regulation PAK/909 • Pakistan Nuclear Regulatory Authority Ordinance 2001 **Section 19 deals at length with power to issue licenses.** • Pakistan Nuclear Safety and Radiation Protection Regulations 1990 **Rule 11** Issuance of a licence—(1) After registration, any person desirous of obtaining a licence for any purpose for which a licence is required under the Ordinance shall apply in writing to the Director for such licence.			Page 6 of the report

		(2) Every application for a licence shall be accompanied . . . such information and documentary evidence which may be required by the Director . . . (3) . . . (4) . . . (5) In case of application for a licence to cause a nuclear-powered vehicle to enter Pakistan, the applicant shall also furnish with the application. a) Type, make and capacity of the vehicle and machinery; b) Type and make of nuclear installation carried on the vehicle; c) Quantity and quality of the fuel stored and used in the vehicle and installation; d) Origin and destination including the purpose journey and previous station where stopped in transit, including the period of stay; e) An undertaking that the applicant shall not discharge or dispose- of radioactive waste in the territorial limits of Pakistan; f) Purpose if stay and period for which license is required. (1) The Director may make such further inquiries, inspections or investigations . . . require an applicant to demonstrate by submitting the required			

Are any of the following measures, procedures or legislation in place to account for, secure or otherwise protect NW and Related Materials? Can violators be penalized?	National legal framework		Enforcement: civil/criminal penalties and others		Remarks
	Yes	If YES, indicate source document	Yes	If YES, indicate source documents	
		information that the purpose for which the licence is required would not be hazardous to the workers, the public and the environment If the applicant does not furnish all the information or the evidence required . . . his application for grant of licence shall be deemed to have been rejected.			
Reliability check of personnel	X	• The Pakistan Atomic Energy Commission Employees (Service) Regulations 2004 **Chapter VII** **General Conduct And Discipline** 1. Conduct And Discipline. The Employees for the purpose of Conduct And Discipline will be governed as per Government rules. 2. Compliance with Orders Every employee shall conform to and abide by these Regulations and shall comply with and obey all orders and directions, which may from time to time replaced/ amended.			

		• The Pakistan Atomic Energy Commission Ordinance 1965. **Section 3A** Employment under Commission to be employment under the Federal Government.—Every employment under the Commission shall, for the purpose of the Essential Service (Maintenance) Act, 1952 (LIII of the said Act shall have the effect accordingly) • The Pakistan Essential Services (Maintenance) Act 1952 **3. Employment to which this Act applies.—(1) This Act shall apply** to every employment under the Federal Government and, subject to the provisions of sub-section (2), to any employment or class of employment which the Federal Government may, by notification in the official Gazette, declare to be an employment or class of employment to which this act apply. • Pakistan Nuclear Regulatory Authority Ordinance 2001 **Section 51 & 52** **51.Declaration of fidelity** and secrecy.___the chairman, every member, advisor, consultant, officer or any other employee of the Authority shall, before			

Are any of the following measures, procedures or legislation in place to account for, secure or otherwise protect NW and Related Materials? Can violators be penalized?	National legal framework		Enforcement: civil/criminal penalties and others		Remarks
	Yes	If YES, indicate source document	Yes	If YES, indicate source documents	
		entering upon his duties, shall make declaration of fidelity and secrecy as may be prescribed by the rules **52. Chairman, members**, etc., to public servants.—The Chairman, members, officers and employees of the authority shall, when acting or purporting to act in pursuance of any of the provisions of this Ordinance, be deemed to be public servants within the meaning of section 21 of the Pakistan Penal Code (Act XLV of 1860) Pakistan Nuclear Safety and Radiation Protection Regulation, 1990, Rule 22.			
Measures to account for/ secure/ Physically protect means of delivery	X	• All production, stockpiling, security and safety etc of delivery means are under strict governmental controls. Private production etc is prohibited. • The Pakistan Penal Code 1860 • PNRA–National Radiation Coordination Center 1988	X	**Section 407** **Criminal breach of trust by the carrier, etc**. Whoever, being entrusted with such property as a carrier, wharfinger or ware house-keeper, commits criminal breach of trust in respect of such property, shall be punished with imprisonment of either description which may extend	

		EMERGENCY CATEGORIZATION Response to a nuclear accident or radiological emergency requires rapid and coordinated response in association with public authorities, as in case of conventional emergency. Emergency categorization is composed of emergency conditions that trigger certain level/mode of response. Emergency not specified to nuclear installations like Missing dangerous radiation source or transport accident.		to seven years, and shall also be liable to fine.	
National Regulatory Authority	X	• Pakistan Nuclear Regulatory Authority (PNRA)			Page 6 of the report
IAEA Safeguards Agreement	X	• INFIRC/418(Chasma I) • INFIRC/116(KANUPP) • INFIRC/135(KANUPP)			http://www.iaea.org/OurWork/SV/Safeauards/sirtable.pdf
IAEA Code of Conduct on Safety and Security of Radioactive Source		Pakistan subscribes to the non-legally binding code.			
IAEA database on Illicit Trafficking of Nuclear Materials and other Radioactive Sources					

Are any of the following measures, procedures or legislation in place to account for, secure or otherwise protect NW and Related Materials? Can violators be penalized?	National legal framework		Enforcement: civil/criminal penalties and others		Remarks
	Yes	If YES, indicate source document	Yes	If YES, indicate source documents	
Other Agreements related to IAEA	X	• Convention on Nuclear Safety. • Convention on Assistance in case of a Nuclear Accident. • Convention on Early Notification of Nuclear Accident. • Convention on the Physical Protection of Nuclear Material.			
Additional national legislation/regulations related to nuclear materials including CPPNM	X	• PNRA–National Radiation Coordination Center 1988 • Pakistan Nuclear Safety and Radiation Protection Regulations 1990 • The Explosives Substances Act 1908 • Surrender of Illicit Arms Act 1991 • The Explosives Act 1884 • The Pakistan Atomic Energy Commission Employees (Service) Regulations 2005 • Pakistan Atomic Energy Commission Ordinance 1965			

Other	X	Consistent with the strong commitment to the objectives of disarmament and non-proliferation, Pakistan fully supports appropriate and effective measures to prevent non state actors from gaining assess to weapons of mass destruction and their means of delivery. Nationally, Pakistan has instituted comprehensive administrative, legislative and security measure to ensure the safety and security of sensitive material facilities, technologies and equipment. Internationally, Pakistan remains a partner in efforts to stem Proliferation and illicit trafficking of WMD-related materials.			

OP 3 (c) and (d) and related matters from OP 6 and OP 10—Controls of BW Including Related Materials

State: Pakistan
Date of Report: 27 October 2004

Which of the following legislation, procedures, measures, agencies exist to control border crossings, export/import and other transfers of BW and Related Materials? Can violators be penalized?	**National legal framework**		**Enforcement: civil/criminal penalties, and measures of implementation, etc**		**Remarks**
	YES	**If YES, indicate source document**	**YES**	**If YES, indicate source document**	
Border control	X	• Export Control on goods, technologies, material and equipment related to nuclear and biological weapons and their delivery system Act 2004. • Sec 3(c) Federal Govt to designate agency or agencies for enforcement. **Section 4(4)** (4) The Federal Govt shall control export, re export, *transshipment, transit of goods*, technologies material and equipment . . . which may contribute to designing, development, production, stockpiling, . . . use of nuclear and biological weapons and the delivery systems	X	**Section 8(1)** 8(1) Any person who contravenes . . . shall be guilty for an offence punishable on conviction by imprisonment for a term which may extend to 14 yeasrs and with fine not exceeding 5 million rupees or both and . . . . Property and assets where ever they may be shall be forfeited to Federal Government. **Section 156**	

		• Customs Act 1969 • Imports and Exports (Control) Act 1950 • West Pakistan Rangers Ordinance 1959 **Section 13 read with 6** 6. The Force shall perform the following functions:- a. protection of persons and property in the border areas; b. Apprehension of persons unlawfully entering into or going out of Pakistan territory c. Organization of village Defence in the border areas; d. Prevention of smuggling e. Collection of intelligence in the border areas f. Coordinate of activities of Police and other civil agencies in the prevention and detection of smuggling 13(g)(vi) quits his guard, piquet, party or patrol, without being regularly relieved or without leave, shall be punished with rigorous imprisonment for a term which may extend to fourteen years . . .			

Which of the following legislation, procedures, measures, agencies exist to control border crossings, export/import and other transfers of BW and Related Materials? Can violators be penalized?	National legal framework		Enforcement: civil/criminal penalties, and measures of implementation, etc		Remarks
	YES	If YES, indicate source document	YES	If YES, indicate source document	
		• Airport Security Force Ordinance 1975 **Section 7 read with 6(e)(f)(g)** **6. Powers** and duties of officers and members.— (e) take effective measures for prevention hijacking, sabotage, placement of car bombs, letter bombs and dangerous articles, smuggling of precious metals, stones, arms, ammunition, narcotics and any other goods the brining into, or taking out of, Pakistan of which is prohibited by or under nay law for the time being in face; (f) use such arms and ammunition of equipment as may be; authorized by the Force Commander for the purpose of this Ordinance;			

		(g) search and arrest without warrant any person who he suspects of endangering, or attempting to endanger, or having endangered, the safety of an aerodrome or airport or an aircraft or a civil aviation installation and may use such force as may be necessary in the discharge of Station under the Police Act, 1861 (V of 1861), and the Code of Criminal Procedure, 1898 (Act V of 1898). **7. Liabilities of officers and members.—(1)** it shall be the duty of every officer and member promptly to obey and to obey and to execute all orders and instructions issued to him by any competent authority. (2) Every officer and member shall be liable to serve wherever he is required to serve by the competent authority. • Pakistan Coast Guards Act 1973 • **Section 3**			

Which of the following legislation, procedures, measures, agencies exist to control border crossings, export/import and other transfers of BW and Related Materials? Can violators be penalized?	National legal framework		Enforcement: civil/criminal penalties, and measures of implementation, etc		Remarks
	YES	If YES, indicate source document	YES	If YES, indicate source document	
		3. Powers to constitute and maintain the force and its functions.—The Federal Government may constitute and maintain a Force to be called the Pakistan Coast Guards for performing the following functions, namely:- (a) prevention of smuggling; (b) prevention of illegal immigration to and migration from the country; (c) stopping enemy agents or saboteurs from Infiltrating into the country along the coastal areas; and (d) supplementing defense in war. • The Pakistan Railway Police Act 1977 **Section 11 read with 3** **3.(1)** Notwithstanding anything contained in any other law for the time being in force, the Federal Government may constitute,			

		control and maintain a force to be called the Pakistan Railways Police for performing, within such territorial limits as the Federal Government may, by notification in the official Gazette, specify the following functions, namely:- a) preventing loss to Railway property and property consigned to the Railways and prevention of offences in respect thereof; b) ensuring proper conduct of persons on the Railways; c) general maintenance of law and order on the Railways and taking cognizance of offences committed on them; d) to render all possible assistance to passengers and railway servants; e) to protect travelers from injury to person or property; f) to keep Railway platforms and other Railway premises clear of idlers and beggars and to keep a lookout for suspicious persons, smugglers and persons traveling with arms without a license or in contravention			

Which of the following legislation, procedures, measures, agencies exist to control border crossings, export/import and other transfers of BW and Related Materials? Can violators be penalized?	National legal framework		Enforcement: civil/criminal penalties, and measures of implementation, etc		Remarks
	YES	If YES, indicate source document	YES	If YES, indicate source document	
		of rules, regulations or orders for the time being in force 11.—(1) It shall be the duty of every officer and member promptly to obey and to execute all orders and instructions issued to him by the competent authority. • Police Order 2002 **Section 5** Emergency duties of police with regard to essential services.—(1) The Government may, in an emergency, by notification in the Official Gazette, declare any specified services to be an essential service to the community. (2) upon a declaration being made under clause (1) and so long as it remains in force, it shall be the duty of every police officer to obey			

		any lawful order given by a senior police officer in relation to the declaration. • Maritime Security Act 1994 **Section 9 read with 10,11,12** 9. Application of the Pakistan Navy ordinance, 1961, etc.—(1) Subject to the provisions of this Act, every officer and member of the staff shall, whether appointed through initial recruitment or otherwise, unless he is already so subject, be subject to the Pakistan Navy Ordinance, 1961 (XXXV of 1961), hereinafter referred to as the said Ordinance. 10. Powers and functions of the Agency.—(1) The Agency shall be responsible for the regulation and protection of the maritime interests of Pakistan and to assert and enforce national jurisdiction and jurisdiction and sovereignty in the Maritime Zones. 2) Without prejudice to the generality of the provisions of sub-section (1), the functions of the Agency shall be to–			

Which of the following legislation, procedures, measures, agencies exist to control border crossings, export/import and other transfers of BW and Related Materials? Can violators be penalized?	National legal framework		Enforcement: civil/criminal penalties, and measures of implementation, etc		Remarks
	YES	If YES, indicate source document	YES	If YES, indicate source document	
		(c) enforce the national and international laws agreements and conventions on and under the water in the Maritime Zones; . . . (j) cooperate with, and provide assistance to Customs, Coast Guards and other departments, agencies and authorities in Maritime Zones in the discharge of their duties and functions; (k) provide an effective secondary maritime force for deployment in any emergency, war or conflict; and (l) perform such other functions as may be assigned to it by the Federal Government, from time to time, to protect maritime interests of Pakistan. 11.Other functions of the officers of Agency, etc.—(1) in addition to the powers			

		and functions as officers of the Agency, such officers may perform functions of– (i) Officers of customs as may be entrusted to them and exercise such powers under the Customs Act, 1969 (IV of 1969), as may be delegated to them under Section 6 of that Act; and (iii) Police Officer, and exercise all the powers conferred on an officer in charge of a Police Station under the Police Act, 1861 (V of 1861), and under the Code of Criminal Procedure, 1898 (Act V of 1898). (2)The Government may, at any time, assign or delegate any other functions or powers upon any officer of the Agency under any law for the time being in force in the Maritime Zones. 12. Power of searches, arrest, etc.—In exercise of the powers and performance of their functions under this Act, the officers and members of the staff may make inquiries, examinations, inspections, investigations, searches, seizures, and arrests for			

Which of the following legislation, procedures, measures, agencies exist to control border crossings, export/import and other transfers of BW and Related Materials? Can violators be penalized?	National legal framework		Enforcement: civil/criminal penalties, and measures of implementation, etc		Remarks
	YES	If YES, indicate source document	YES	if YES, indicate source document	
		prevention, detection suppression of contravention of any law for the time being in force within the Maritime Zones and for that purpose the officers and members of the staff may board any vessel except ships, vessel or crafts of Pakistan Armed Forces. • Karachi Port Trust Security Force Ordinance 2002 **Section 3 Establishment, constitution and maintenance of the force, its powers and functions.**—(1) The chairman with the approval of the Federal Government shall establish, constitute and maintain a force to be called the Karachi Port Security Force to maintain security and safety of the Karachi			

		Port Area for performing of the following functions, namely:- (a) maintain law and order in the Port Area and take cognizance of offences committed therein or connected thereto; (k) prevent pollution; spillage, waste fire hazards, chemical hazards, water hazards, biological hazards, hazardous waste and hazardous substances and also prevent the generation, collection transport treatment, disposal, storage, handling import, export of the same may be prescribed; and • Frontier Corp Ordinance 1959 **3. Powers** to maintain Frontier Corps.—There shall continue to be maintained by the Central Government the Frontier Corps forces or units as listed in the First Schedule, primarily for the better protection and administration of the external frontiers of Pakistan within the limits of or adjoining the Special Areas of West Pakistan;			

Which of the following legislation, procedures, measures, agencies exist to control border crossings, export/import and other transfers of BW and Related Materials? Can violators be penalized?	National legal framework		Enforcement: civil/criminal penalties, and measures of implementation, etc		Remarks
	YES	**If YES, indicate source document**	**YES**	**If YES, indicate source document**	
		• Civil/Armed Forces Entrustment of Power Through Custom Rules, Notifications & SRO's SRO 29 (I)/73 **ENTRUSTMENT OF THE FUNCTIONS OF CUSTOMS OFFICERS TO OFFICERS OF WEST PAKISTAN RANGERS** Notification No.SRO 29(I)/73 dated 3rd January, 1973.—In exercise of the powers conferred by section 6 of the Customs Act, 1969 (IV of 1969), and in suppression of its Notifications No.SRO 314 and 315, dated the 11th July, 1959, the Central Board of Revenue is pleased to entrust; the functions of officers of customers under sections 157, 158, 159, 160,			

		161, 162, 163, 164, 165, 166, 167,m sub-sections (1), (3) and (4) of section 168, sections 169 and 171 of the said Act to all officers of the West Pakistan Rangers not below the rank of Sub-Inspector (and all officers of the West Pakistan Rangers not below the rank of Havildar only the Powers under sections 158, 159, 161 and 164 of the said act). SRO 524(I)/74 **ENTRUSTMENT OF POWERS TO THE OFFICERS OF THE FRONTIER CONSTABULARY** Notification No.SRO 524(I)/74, dated 23rd April, 1974.—In exercise of the powers conferred by section 6 of the Customs Act, 1969 (IV of 1969), the Central Board of Revenue is pleased to entrust, subject to such limitations and restrictions as are laid down in the Rules made under the said Act, to the officers of the Frontier Constabulary specified in the first column of the Table below, the functions of officers of			

Which of the following legislation, procedures, measures, agencies exist to control border crossings, export/import and other transfers of BW and Related Materials? Can violators be penalized?	National legal framework		Enforcement: civil/criminal penalties, and measures of implementation, etc		Remarks
	YES	If YES, indicate source document	YES	If YES, indicate source document	
		Customs under the provisions of the said Act . . . SRO 1017(I)/74 **ENTRUSTMENT TO POWERS OF THE OFFICERS OF CUSTOMS TO THE OFFICERS OF THE FRONTIER CORP** Notification No.SRO 1017(I)/74, dated 26th July, 1974.—In exercise of the powers conferred by section 6 of the Customs Act, 1969 (IV of 1969), the Central Board of revenue is pleased to entrust to the officers of the Frontier Corps, operating within 2(sixty kilometers) along the international borders adjoining the Province of Baluchistan 3(and North Western Frontier Province), as specified in the first column of the Table below the functions of officers of			

		customs under the provisions of the said Act specified . . . Customs or other law enforcement agencies keep tight vigil.			
Technical support of border control measures	X	• Bilateral, technical cooperation with different countries. • Capacity building technical courses. • Special training to detect sensitive materials • Deployment of scanners, etc. • Collaboration with international organizations. • Custom General Order 2005 **Chapter –IX STORAGE, DISPOSAL & SAMPLING OF SEIZED AND CONFISCATION GOODS — INSTRUCTIONS REGARDING** 32.Storage by law enforcing agencies.—For Law Enforcement agencies hereinafter referred to as Agencies, including the	X		Page 7 of the report.

Which of the following legislation, procedures, measures, agencies exist to control border crossings, export/import and other transfers of BW and Related Materials? Can violators be penalized?	**National legal framework**		**Enforcement: civil/criminal penalties, and measures of implementation, etc**		**Remarks**
	YES	**If YES, indicate source document**	**YES**	**If YES, indicate source document**	
		Civil Armed Forces of Pakistan who have delegated anti- smuggling powers under the Custom act, 1969. The following directions are issued for strict compliance:- I. Appointment of State-warehouses II. Appointment of custodians III. Working of the State-warehouses IV. . . . V. . . . VI. Inspection of seized goods and sampling thereof. VII . . . • Pakistan Council of Scientific and Industrial Research Act 1973 **Section 6** **The functions of the Council shall be—**			

		d) undertake such special scientific and technological surveys and investigations as may be referred to it by the Federal Government from time to time			PCSIR provides technical assistance in investigating the material found during Border Control operations that can facilitate prosecution.
Control of brokering, trading in, negotiating, otherwise assisting in sale of goods and technology	X	• Export Control on goods, technologies, material and equipment related to nuclear and biological weapons and their delivery system Act 2004 **Section 2(f)(i)** shipment, transfer, transmission of goods or technologies out of the territory of Pakistan and (ii) a transfer of goods or technology within Pakistan with the knowledge or intent that the goods or technology will be shipped, transferred or transmitted to an unauthorized recipient out side Pakistan **Section 4(4)** (4) The Federal Govt shall control export, re export, *transshipment, transit of goods*, technologies material and equipment . . . which	X	**Section 8(1)** 8(1) Any person who contravenes. . .shall be guilty for an offence punishable on conviction by imprisonment for a term which may extend to 14 years and with fine not exceeding 5 million rupees or both and—. Property and assets where ever they may be shall be forfeited to Federal Government.	

Which of the following legislation, procedures, measures, agencies exist to control border crossings, export/import and other transfers of BW and Related Materials? Can violators be penalized?	National legal framework		Enforcement: civil/criminal penalties, and measures of implementation, etc		Remarks
	YES	If YES, indicate source document	YES	If YES, indicate source document	
		may contribute to designing, development, production, stockpiling, . . . use of nuclear and biological weapons and the delivery systems • Officials Secrets Act 1923 **Section 5** 1. Wrongful communication, etc., of information: (1) If any person having in his possession or control any secret official code or pass word or any sketch, plan, model, article, note, document or information which relate to or is used in a prohibited place or relates to anything in such a place, or which has been made or obtained in contravention of this Act, or which has been entrusted in confidence to him by any person holding office under Government, . . .		(3) A person guilty of an offence under this section shall be punishable,. . . a) where offence committed. . . directly or indirectly in benefit of foreign power. . . shall be punishable with death or with imprisonment which may extend to fourteen years.; b) in any other case, with imprisonment for a term which may extend to two years, or fine,. . .both.	

		(a) willfully communicates the code or pass word (b) uses information in his possession (c) retain the sketch. . . (d) fail to take reasonable care . . . shall be guilty of the offence under this section (2) If a person voluntarily receive any secret official code . . . shall be guilty of the offence under this section • Telegraphic Act 1885 • Defence of Pakistan Ordinance 1965 **Section 3(2)** 3(2)(xxv) prohibiting or regulating the possession, use or disposal of— a) explosives, inflammable substances, corrosive and other dangerous substances or articles, arms and ammunitions of war; b) vessels, c) wireless telegraphic apparatus, or any other apparatus capable of transmitting messages, d) aircraft, and e) photographic and signaling apparatus and any means of recording information		**Section 25** If any person intending. . . (a) to prevent or obstruct the transmission or delivery of any message, or (b) to intercept or to acquaint himself with the content of the message or, (c) to commit mischief, damages, removes, tampers. . .shall be punished with imprisonment for a term which may extend to three years or with fine or with both. Imprisonment for a term which may extend to five years and also be liable to fine—	

Which of the following legislation, procedures, measures, agencies exist to control border crossings, export/import and other transfers of BW and Related Materials? Can violators be penalized?	National legal framework		Enforcement: civil/criminal penalties, and measures of implementation, etc		Remarks
	YES	If YES, indicate source document	YES	If YES, indicate source document	
Enforcement agencies/ authorities	X	• Pakistan Customs. • Federal Investigation Agency Act 1974 • West Pakistan Rangers Ordinance 1959 • The Pakistan Railway Police Act 1977 • Pakistan Coast Guards Act 1973 • Airport Security Force Ordinance 1975 • Police Order 2002 • Maritime Security Act 1994 • Karachi Port Trust Security Force Ordinance 2002 • Frontier Corps Ordinance 1959			Page 5 of the report.

Export control legislation in place	X	• Export Control on Goods, Technology, Material and Equipment related to Nuclear and Biological Weapons and their Delivery Systems Act 2004 • The Import and Export (Control) Act 1950 • Export Policy Order 2004 (EPO)			
Licensing Provisions	X	• Export Control on Goods, Technology, Material and Equipment related to Nuclear and Biological Weapons and their Delivery Systems Act, 2004 **Section 5** Licensing (1) The Federal Government shall frame and notify the Licenses required under this Act, and also adopt and notify the procedure under which such Licenses shall be approved or rejected. (2) licenses for export and import of goods and technologies for peaceful application may be approved unless the Government determines that the Export would be in			Page 3 and 4 of the report.

Which of the following legislation, procedures, measures, agencies exist to control border crossings, export/import and other transfers of BW and Related Materials? Can violators be penalized?	**National legal framework**		**Enforcement: civil/criminal penalties, and measures of implementation, etc**		**Remarks**
	YES	**If YES, indicate source document**	**YES**	**If YES, indicate source document**	
		contravention of the provision of the Act. (3) An exporter is under a legal obligation to notify to the competent authority if the exporter is.......... (4) Nothing in this Act shall be taken to prohibit the export.......			
Individual Licensing	X	• Export Control on goods, technologies, material and equipment related to nuclear and biological weapons and their delivery system Act 2004 **Section 5 ibid** • The Pakistan BioSafety Rules 2005 **Rule 11** Prohibition and license requirements No person shall import export, sell, purchase or trade living modified organisms—without the prior obtaining of license from the	X	**Section 5 ibid**	

General Licensing	X	• Export Control on Goods, Technology, Material and equipment related to Nuclear and Biological Weapons and their Delivery Systems Act, 2004 **Section 5 ibid**			
Exceptions from licensing					
Licensing of deemed export/ visa					
National Licensing Authority		National Biosafety committee is a Federal Agency			Page 4 and 5 of the report.
Interagency review for licenses		Practice exists to that effect.			
Control Lists	X	• Export Control on Goods, Technology, Material and Equipment related to Nuclear and Biological Weapons and their Delivery Systems Act 2004 **Section 4** 4.(1) The Federal Government shall maintain a Control Lists, to be notified separately, of goods and Technologies subject to licensing requirements under this Act.			Page 4 and 5 of the report.

Which of the following legislation, procedures, measures, agencies exist to control border crossings, export/import and other transfers of BW and Related Materials? Can violators be penalized?	National legal framework		Enforcement: civil/criminal penalties, and measures of implementation, etc		Remarks
	YES	If YES, indicate source document	YES	if YES, indicate source document	
		(2) The control lists shall be reviewed periodically, and revised or updated, as required by the Federal Government and notified accordingly. (3) The Federal Government shall notify all licensing requirements and procedures. (4) The Federal Government shall control export, re-export, transshipment, transit of goods, technologies, material and equipment, subject to the provisions of this Act, which may contribute to the designing, development, production, stockpiling, maintenance or use of nuclear and biological weapons and their delivery systems.			
Updating of Lists	X				

Inclusion of technologies Inclusion of means of delivery	X	• Export Control on Goods, Technology, Material and Equipment related to Nuclear and Biological Weapons and their Delivery Systems Act 2004 **Section 2 (1)** technology means any documents including blue prints, plans, diagram, models, formulae, tables, engineering, design or specifications, manuals or instructions, necessary for development and production of nuclear or biological weapons and their delivery system, . . . **Section 4 ibid**			Page 4 and 5 of the report.
End-user controls	X				
Catch all clause	X				
Intangible transfers	X	• Export Control on Goods, Technology, Material and Equipment related to Nuclear and Biological Weapons and their Delivery Systems Act 2004 **Section 2 (I)(i)** Any document or information that is in public domain or is related to basic scientific research. . . **Section 4(4) ibid** • Officials Secrets Act 1923	X	**Section 8 ibid** (3)A person guilty of an offence under this section shall be punishable, . . . a)where offence committed . . . directly or indirectly in benefit of foreign power—shall be punishable with death or with imprisonment which may extend to fourteen years.; b)in any other case, with imprisonment for a term which may extend to two years, or fine, . . . both.	

Which of the following legislation, procedures, measures, agencies exist to control border crossings, export/import and other transfers of BW and Related Materials? Can violators be penalized?	National legal framework		Enforcement: civil/criminal penalties, and measures of implementation, etc		Remarks
	YES	If YES, indicate source document	YES	If YES, indicate source document	
		Section 5 1. Wrongful communication, etc., of information: (1) If any person having in his possession or control any secret official code or pass word or any sketch, plan, model, article, note, document or information which relate to or is used in a prohibited place or relates to anything in such a place, or which has been made or obtained in contravention of this Act, or which has been entrusted in confidence to him by any person holding office under Government, . . . (a) willfully communicates the code or pass word (b) uses information in his possession (c) retain the sketch . . . (d) fail to take reasonable care. . .shall be guilty of the offence under this section			

		(2) If a person voluntarily receive any secret official code. . .shall be guilty of the offence under this section.			
Transit Control	X	• Export Control on Goods, Technology, Material Equipment related to Nuclear and Biological Weapons and their • Delivery Systems Act 2004 • Customs Act 1969	X	Section 4 ibid	Page 4 and 5 of the report.
Trans-shipment control	X		X	Section 4 ibid	
Re-export control	X		X	Section 4 ibid	
Control of providing of funds	X	• Export Control on goods, technologies, material and equipment related to nuclear and biological weapons and their delivery system Act 2004 **Section 8 (2)** Any person who attempts to commits or abets to commission of an offense under this Act shall be proceeded against in the Same manners as if he has committed such offence • Anti Treeorism Act 1997 **Section 11-J and 11-N** 11-J Funding Arrangements.—person commits an offence if (a) enters into or becomes concerned in an arrangement as a result of which money	X	11-N **Punishment under section 11-H to 11-K**. . .shall be punishable on conviction with imprisonment for a term not less than six months and not exceeding five years and with fine. **213.Taking gift, etc., to screen an offender from punishment:** Whoever accept or attempts to obtain, or agrees to accept, any gratification for himself or any other person, or any restitution of property to himself or any other person, in consideration of his concealing an offence or of his screening any person from legal punishment for any offence, or of his not proceeding against any person for the purpose of bring him to legal punishment.	

Which of the following legislation, procedures, measures, agencies exist to control border crossings, export/import and other transfers of BW and Related Materials? Can violators be penalized?	National legal framework		Enforcement: civil/criminal penalties, and measures of implementation, etc		Remarks
	YES	**If YES, indicate source document**	**YES**	**if YES, indicate source document**	
		or other property is made available or is to be made available to another, and (b) has reasonable cause to suspect that it will or may be used for the purposes of terrorism. • Pakistan Penal Code 1860		**if a capital offence:** shall, if the offence is punishable with death, be punished with imprisonment of either description for a term which may extend to seven years, and shall also be liable to fine: **if punishable with imprisonment for life, or with imprisonment**: and if the offence is punishable with imprisonment for life or with imprisonment which may extend to ten years, shall be punished with imprisonment of either description for a term which may extend to three years, shall also be liable to fine: and if the offence is punishable with imprisonment not extending to ten years, shall be punished with description provided for the offence for a term which may extend to one-fourth part of the longest term of imprisonment	

				provided for the offence, or with fine, or with both. **214 Offering gift or restoration of property in consideration of screening offender**: Whoever gives or causes or offers or agrees to give or cause, any gratification to any person, or to restore or cause to restoration of any property to any person, in consideration of that person's concealing an offence, or of his screening any person form legal punishment for any offence, or his not proceeding against any person for the purpose of bringing him to legal punishment; **if the a capital offence:** shall, if the offence is punishable with death, be punished with imprisonment of either description for a term which may extend to seven years and shall also be liable to fine **if punishable with imprisonment for life or with imprisonment**: and the offence is punishable with imprisonment for life, or with imprisonment which may extend to three years, shall be punished with imprisonment	

Which of the following legislation, procedures, measures, agencies exist to control border crossings, export/import and other transfers of BW and Related Materials? Can violators be penalized?	**National legal framework**		**Enforcement: civil/criminal penalties, and measures of implementation, etc**		**Remarks**
	YES	**If YES, indicate source document**	**YES**	**If YES, indicate source document**	
				of either description for a term may extend to three years, and shall also be liable to fine; and if the offence is punishable with imprisonment not extending to ten years, shall be punishable with imprisonment of the description provided for the offence for a term which may extend to one-fourth part of the longest term of imprisonment provided for the offence, or with fine, or with or with both.	
Control of providing transport services	X	• Export Control on goods, technologies, material and equipment related to nuclear and biological weapons and their delivery system Act 2004 **Section 4 (4) Ibid** • Pakistan Penal Code 1860	X	**Section 8 ibid** **Section 407** **Criminal breach of trust by the carrier, etc**. Whoever, being entrusted with such property as a carrier, wharfinger or ware house-keeper, commits criminal breach of trust in respect of such property, shall be	Offender can be prosecuted under abetment provision as well.

				punished with imprisonment of either description which may extend to seven years, and shall also be liable to fine.	
Control of importation	X	• Import Policy Order 2004 • The Pakistan Animal Quarantine (Import and Export Animal and Animal Products) Ordinance 1979 • The Pakistan Biosafety Rules 2005			Page 3 of the report.
Extraterritorial applicability	X	• Export Control on goods, technologies, material and equipment related to nuclear and biological weapons and their delivery system Act 2004 **Section 1** **It applies to** (a)every citizen of Pakistan or a person in service of Pakistan within and beyond Pakistan or any Pakistani visiting or working abroad (b) any Foreign national . . . in Pakistan . . . (c) any ground transport ship or air craft register in Pakistan			Page 4 of the report.

Which of the following legislation, procedures, measures, agencies exist to control border crossings, export/import and other transfers of BW and Related Materials? Can violators be penalized?	National legal framework		Enforcement: civil/criminal penalties, and measures of implementation, etc		Remarks
	YES	If YES, indicate source document	YES	If YES, indicate source document	
		• Pakistan Penal Code 1860 **Section 4 read with 108 A 104. Extension** of Code of extraterritorial offences: The provisions of this Code apply also to any offence committed by—(1) any citizen of Pakistan or any person in the service of Pakistan in any place without and beyond Pakistan (2) and (3) omitted (4) any person on any ship or aircraft registered in Pakistan wherever may be. Explanation.. . . In this section the word "offence" includes every act committed outside Pakistan which, if committed in Pakistan would be punishable under this Code.			

		108A **Abetment in Pakistan, of offences outside it**. A person abets an offence within the meaning of this Code who, in Pakistan, abets the commission of any act without and beyond Pakistan which would constitute an offence committed in Pakistan.			
Other					

OP 3 (c) and (d) and related matters from OP 6 and OP 10—Controls of CW including Related Materials

State: **Pakistan**
Date of Report: 27 October 2004

Which of the following legislation, procedures, measures, agencies exist to control border crossings, export/import and other transfers of CW and Related Materials? Can violators be penalized?	**National legal framework**		**Enforcement: civil/criminal penalties, and measures of implementation, etc**		**Remarks**
	YES	**If YES, indicate source document**	**YES**	**If YES, indicate source document**	
Border control	X	• Chemical Weapon Convention Implementation Ordinance, 2000 • Imports and Exports (Control) Act 1950 • SRO 482(I)/2000	X		Page 7 of the report.

Which of the following legislation, procedures, measures, agencies exist to control border crossings, export/import and other transfers of CW and Related Materials? Can violators be penalized?	National legal framework		Enforcement: civil/criminal penalties, and measures of implementation, etc		Remarks
	YES	If YES, indicate source document	YES	If YES, indicate source document	
		• Customs Act 1969 • West Pakistan Rangers Ordinance 1959 **Section 13 read with 6** 6.The Force shall perform the following functions:- a. protection of persons and property in the border areas; b. Apprehension of persons unlawfully entering into or going out of Pakistan territory c. Organization of village Defence in the border areas; d. Prevention of smuggling e. Collection of intelligence in the border areas f. Coordinate of activities of Police and other civil agencies in the prevention and detection of smuggling 13(g)(vi) quits his guard, piquet, party or patrol, without being regularly relieved or without leave, shall be punished with rigorous imprisonment for a term which may extend to fourteen years . . .			

		• Airport Security Force Ordinance 1975 **Section 7 read with 6(e)(f)(g)** **6. Powers** and duties of officers and members.— (e) take effective measures for prevention hijacking, sabotage, placement of car bombs, letter bombs and dangerous articles, smuggling of precious metals, stones, arms, ammunition, narcotics and any other goods the brining into, or taking out of, Pakistan of which is prohibited by or under nay law for the time being in face; (f) use such arms and ammunition of equipment as may be; authorized by the Force Commander for the purpose of this Ordinance; (g) search and arrest without warrant any person who he suspects of endangering, or attempting to endanger, or having endangered, the safety of an aerodrome or airport or an aircraft or a civil aviation installation and may use such force as may be necessary in the discharge of his duties aforesaid; and (h) perform such other functions as the competent authority may require him to perform.			

Which of the following legislation, procedures, measures, agencies exist to control border crossings, export/import and other transfers of CW and Related Materials? Can violators be penalized?	National legal framework		Enforcement: civil/criminal penalties, and measures of implementation, etc		Remarks
	YES	If YES, indicate source document	YES	If YES, indicate source document	
		(2) An officer, for the purpose of this Ordinance, shall exercise, within the areas in which this Ordinance applies, all the powers Station under the Police Act, 1861 (V of 1861), and the Code of Criminal Procedure, 1898 (Act V of 1898). **7. Liabilities of officers and members.—(1)** it shall be the duty of every officer and member promptly to obey and to obey and to execute all orders and instructions issued to him by any competent authority. (2) Every officer and member shall be liable to serve wherever he is required to serve by the competent authority. • Pakistan Coast Guards Act 1973 **Section 3** 3. Powers to constitute and maintain the force and its functions.—The Federal Government may constitute and maintain a Force to be called the			

		Pakistan Coast Guards for performing the following functions, namely:- (a) prevention of smuggling; (b) prevention of illegal immigration to and migration from the country; (c) stopping enemy agents or saboteurs from Infiltrating into the country along the coastal areas: and (d) supplementing defense in war. • The Pakistan Railway Police Act 1977 **Section 11 read with 3** **3. (1)** Notwithstanding anything contained in any other law for the time being in force, the Federal Government may constitute, control and maintain a force to be called the Pakistan Railways Police for performing, within such territorial limits as the Federal Government may, by notification in the official Gazette, specify the following functions, namely:- a) preventing loss to Railway property and property consigned to the Railways and prevention of offences in respect thereof; b) ensuring proper conduct of persons on the Railways;			

Which of the following legislation, procedures, measures, agencies exist to control border crossings, export/import and other transfers of CW and Related Materials? Can violators be penalized?	National legal framework		Enforcement: civil/criminal penalties, and measures of implementation, etc		Remarks
	YES	If YES, indicate source document	YES	If YES, indicate source document	
		c) general maintenance of law and order on the Railways and taking cognizance of offences committed on them; d) to render all possible assistance to passengers and railway servants; e) to protect travelers from injury to person or property; f) to keep Railway platforms and other Railway premises clear of idlers and beggars and to keep a lookout for suspicious persons, smugglers and persons traveling with arms without a license or in contravention of rules, regulations or orders for the time being in force **11.**—(1) It shall be the duty of every officer and member promptly to obey and to execute all orders and instructions issued to him by the competent authority. • Police Order 2002			

		Section 5 Emergency duties of police with regard to essential services.__(1) The Government may, in an emergency, by notification in the Official Gazette, declare any specified services to be an essential service to the community. (2) upon a declaration being made under clause (1) and so long as it remains in force, it shall be the duty of every police officer to obey any lawful order given by a senior police officer in relation to the declaration. • Maritime Security Act 1994 **Section 9 read with 10, 11, 12** 9. Application of the Pakistan Navy ordinance, 1961, etc.—(1) Subject to the provisions of this Act, every officer and member of the staff shall, whether appointed through initial recruitment or otherwise, unless he is already so subject, be subject to the Pakistan Navy Ordinance, 1961 (XXXV of 1961), hereinafter referred to as the said Ordinance. 10. Powers and functions of the Agency.—(1) The Agency shall be responsible for the regulation and protection of the maritime interests of Pakistan and to assert and enforce national jurisdiction and jurisdiction and sovereignty in the Maritime Zones.			

Which of the following legislation, procedures, measures, agencies exist to control border crossings, export/import and other transfers of CW and Related Materials? Can violators be penalized?	National legal framework		Enforcement: civil/criminal penalties, and measures of implementation, etc		Remarks
	YES	If YES, indicate source document	YES	If YES, indicate source document	
		2) Without prejudice to the generality of the provisions of sub-section (1), the functions of the Agency shall be to . . . (c) enforce the national and international laws agreements and conventions on and under the water in the Maritime Zones; . . . (j) cooperate with, and provide assistance to Customs, Coast Guards and other departments, agencies and authorities in Maritime Zones in the discharge of their duties and functions; (k) provide an effective secondary maritime force for deployment in any emergency, war or conflict; and (l) perform such other functions as may be assigned to it by the Federal Government, from time to time, to protect maritime interests of Pakistan. 11. Other functions of the officers of Agency, etc.—(1) In addition to the powers and functions as			

		officers of the Agency, such officers may perform functions of . . . (i) Officers of customs as may be entrusted to them and exercise such powers under the Customs Act, 1969 (IV of 1969), as may be delegated to them under Section 6 of that Act; and (iii) Police Officer, and exercise all the powers conferred on an officer in charge of a Police Station under the Police Act, 1861(V of 1861), and under the Code of Criminal Procedure, 1898 (Act V of 1898). (2) The Government may, at any time, assign or delegate any other functions or powers upon any officer of the Agency under any law for the time being in force in the Maritime Zones. 12. Power of searches, arrest, etc.—In exercise of the powers and performance of their functions under this Act, the officers and members of the staff may make inquiries, examinations, inspections, investigations, searches, seizures, and arrests for prevention, detection suppression of contravention of any law for the time being in force within the Maritime Zones and for that purpose the officers and members of the staff may board any vessel except ships,			

Which of the following legislation, procedures, measures, agencies exist to control border crossings, export/import and other transfers of CW and Related Materials? Can violators be penalized?	National legal framework		Enforcement: civil/criminal penalties, and measures of implementation, etc		Remarks
	YES	If YES, indicate source document	YES	If YES, indicate source document	
		vessel or crafts of Pakistan Armed Forces. • Karachi Port Trust Security Force Ordinance 2002 **Section 3** **Establishment, constitution and maintenance of the force, its powers and functions.**—(1) The chairman with the approval of the Federal Government shall establish, constitute and maintain a force to be called the Karachi Port Security Force to maintain security and safety of the Karachi Port Area for performing of the following functions, namely:- (a) maintain law and order in the Port Area and take cognizance of offences committed therein or connected thereto; (k) prevent pollution; spillage, waste fire hazards, chemical hazards, water hazards, biological hazards, hazardous waste and hazardous substances and			

		also prevent the generation, collection transport treatment, disposal, storage, handling import, export of the same may be prescribed; and • Frontier Corp Ordinance 1959 **3. Powers** to maintain Frontier Corps.—There shall continue to be maintained by the Central Government the Frontier Corps forces or units as listed in the First Schedule, primarily for the better protection and administration of the external frontiers of Pakistan within the limits of or adjoining the Special Areas of West Pakistan • Civil/ Armed Forces Entrustment of Power Through Custom Rules, Notifications & SRO' s SRO 29 (I)/73 **ENTRUSTMENT OF THE FUNCTIONS OF CUSTOMS OFFICERS TO OFFICERS OF WEST PAKISTAN RANGERS** Notification No.SRO 29(I)/73 dated 3rd January, 1973.—In exercise of the powers conferred by section 6 of the Customs Act, 1969 (IV of 1969), and in suppression of its Notifications No. SRO 314 and 315, dated the 11th July, 1959, the Central Board of			

Which of the following legislation, procedures, measures, agencies exist to control border crossings, export/import and other transfers of CW and Related Materials? Can violators be penalized?	National legal framework		Enforcement: civil/criminal penalties, and measures of implementation, etc		Remarks
	YES	If YES, indicate source document	YES	If YES, indicate source document	
		Revenue is pleased to entrust; the functions of officers of customers under sections 157, 158, 159, 160, 161, 162, 163, 164, 165, 166, 167,m sub-sections (1), (3) and (4) of section 168, sections 169 and 171 of the said Act to all officers of the West Pakistan Rangers not below the rank of Sub-Inspector (and all officers of the West Pakistan Rangers not below the rank of Havildar only the Powers under sections 158, 159, 161 and 164 of the said act). SRO 524(I)/74 **ENTRUSTMENT OF POWERS TO THE OFFICERS OF THE FRONTIER CONSTABULARY** Notification No.SRO 524(I)/74, dated 23rd April, 1974.—In exercise of the powers conferred by section 6 of the Customs Act, 1969 (IV of 1969), the Central Board of Revenue is pleased to entrust, subject to such limitations and restrictions as are laid down in the			

		Rules made under the said Act, to the officers of the Frontier Constabulary specified in the first column of the Table below, the functions of officers of Customs under the provisions of the said Act............ SRO 1017(I)/74 **ENTRUSTMENT TO POWERS OF THE OFFICERS OF CUSTOMS TO THE OFFICERS OF THE FRONTIER CORP** Notification No.SRO 1017(I)/74, dated 26th July, 1974.—In exercise of the powers conferred by section 6 of the Customs Act, 1969 (IV of 1969), the Central Board of revenue is pleased to entrust to the officers of the Frontier Corps, operating within 2(sixty kilometers) along the international borders adjoining the Province of Baluchistan 3(and North Western Frontier Province), as specified in the first column of the Table below the functions of officers of customs under the provisions of the said Act specified . . . Customs or other law enforcement agencies keep tight vigil. • Custom Authority			

Which of the following legislation, procedures, measures, agencies exist to control border crossings, export/import and other transfers of CW and Related Materials? Can violators be penalized?	National legal framework		Enforcement: civil/criminal penalties, and measures of implementation, etc		Remarks
	YES	If YES, indicate source document	YES	If YES, indicate source document	
Technical support of border control measures	X	• Bilateral, technical cooperation with different countries. • Capacity building technical courses. • Special training to detect sensitive materials • Deployment of scanners, etc • Collaboration/cooperation with international organizations. • Custom General Order 2005 **Chapter –IX STORAGE, DISPOSAL & SAMPLING OF SEIZED AND CONFISCATION GOODS—INSTRUCTIONS REGARDING** 32. Storage by law enforcing agencies.—For Law Enforcement agencies hereinafter referred to as Agencies, including the Civil Armed Forces of Pakistan who have delegated anti- smuggling powers under the Custom act, 1969.	X		Page 7 of the report.

		The following directions are issued for strict compliance:- VIII. Appointment of State-warehouses IX. Appointment of custodians X. Working of the State-warehouses XI. . . . XII. . . . XIII. Inspection of seized goods and sampling thereof. XIV. . . . • Pakistan Council of Scientific and Industrial Research Act 1973 **Section 6** **The functions of the Council shall be. . .** *d) undertake such special scientific and technological surveys and investigations as* may be referred to it by the Federal Government/from time to time.			PCSIR provides technical assistance in investigating the material found during Border Control operations that can facilitate prosecution
Control of brokering, trading in, negotiating, otherwise assisting in sale of goods and technology	**X**	• Chemical Weapons Convention Implementation Ordinance 2000 **Section 3 read with 21** **Prohibition on development, etc of chemical weapons.**—(1) No person shall-(a) develop, produce, otherwise, acquire, or stockpile or retain in chemical weapon, or transfer, directly or indirectly, a chemical weapon to anyone;			

Which of the following legislation, procedures, measures, agencies exist to control border crossings, export/import and other transfers of CW and Related Materials? Can violators be penalized?	National legal framework		Enforcement: civil/criminal penalties, and measures of implementation, etc		Remarks
	YES	If YES, indicate source document	YES	If YES, indicate source document	
		(b) use a chemical weapon; (c) engage in any military preparation to use chemical weapon; (d) assist, encourage or induce, in any way, any other person to engage in any activity prohibited to a State party under the Convention; Convention; (e) use a riot control agent as a method of warfare **21. Disclosure of information**. **(1)** Any person who produces, possesses, consumes, transfers, exports or imports any schedule chemical or produces discrete organic chemical not being the scheduled chemical or a chemical containing the elements phosphorous, sulphur or fluorine or who hold a riot control . . . a)provide the prescribed information, at the prescribed time and in the prescribed form, to the National Authority; and			

		b)keeps and maintain the prescribed documents in Pakistan, at his place of business or such other place as may be specified by the National Authority, in he prescribed manner and for the prescribed period; and)on request, provide documents to the National Authority • Officials Secrets Act 1923 **Section 5** 1. Wrongful communication, etc., of information: (1) If any person having in his possession or control any secret official code or pass word or any sketch, plan, model, article, note, document or information which relate to or is used in a prohibited place or relates to anything in such a place, or which has been made or obtained in contravention of this Act, or which has been entrusted in confidence to him by any person holding office under Government, . . . (a) willfully communicates the code or pass word (b) uses information in his possession (c) retain the sketch . . . (d) fail to take reasonable care . . . shall be guilty of the offence under this section		(3)A person guilty of an offence under this section shall be punishable,____ a)where offence committed. . .directly or indirectly in benefit of foreign power. . .shall be punishable with death or with imprisonment which may extend to fourteen years.; b)in any other case, with imprisonment for a term which may extend to two years, or fine,—both.	

Which of the following legislation, procedures, measures, agencies exist to control border crossings, export/import and other transfers of CW and Related Materials? Can violators be penalized?	National legal framework		Enforcement: civil/criminal penalties, and measures of implementation, etc		Remarks
	YES	If YES, indicate source document	YES	If YES, indicate source document	
		(2) If a person voluntarily receive any secret official code . . . shall be guilty of the offence under this section. • The Defence of Pakistan Ordinance 1965 **Section 3(2)** 3(2)(xxv)prohibiting or regulating the possession, use or disposal of— a) explosives, inflammable substances, *corrosive* and other dangerous substances or articles, arms and ammunitions of war; b) vessels, c) wireless telegraphic apparatus, or any other apparatus capable of transmitting messages, d) aircraft, and e) photographic and signaling apparatus and any means of recording information • Imports and Exports (Control) Act 1950		imprisonment for a term which may extend to five years and also be liable to fine. . . .	

		Section 4A, 4B read with 5 4-A No person shall sell, purchase or otherwise deal in any import licence other than an import licence issued. . . . 4-B Except with pervious permission in writing. . .no person shall sell or otherwise transfer such goods, use the goods for a purpose other than the purpose or purposes for which the licence is issued. . . .		5.If any person contravenes any provision of this Act be punishable with imprisonment for a term which may extend to one year, or with fine, or with both.	
Enforcement agencies/ authorities	X	• Federal Investigation Agencies Act 1974 • West Pakistan Rangers Ordinance 1959 • The Pakistan Railway Police Act 1977 • Pakistan Coast Guards Act 1973 • Airport Security Force Ordinance 1975 • Police Order 2002 • Maritime Security Act 1994 • Karachi Port Trust Security Force Ordinance 2002 • Frontier Corp Ordinance 1959			Page 5 of the report.
Export contrat legislation in place	X	• The Imports and Exports (Control) Act, 1950 • Export Policy Order 2004 • Chemical Weapons Convention Implementation Ordinance – 2000, • Passenger Non- Tourist Baggage Rules 1998	X		Page 3 of the report.

Which of the following legislation, procedures, measures, agencies exist to control border crossings, export/import and other transfers of CW and Related Materials? Can violators be penalized?	National legal framework		Enforcement: civil/criminal penalties, and measures of implementation, etc		Remarks
	YES	If YES, indicate source document	YES	If YES, indicate source document	
		Section 4 Prohibition on import of arms, ammunition, etc.—Arms, ammunition, . . . shall not be imported under these rules.			
Licensing provisions	X	• SRO 482(1)/2000 • Chemical Weapons Convention Implementation Ordinance 2000 **Section 23** **Registration**.—(1) The National Authority may, directly or through notice, require an individual or organization involved in production, processing, consumption, transfer, import or export of any schedule chemical or any discrete organic chemical not being a schedule chemical, or a chemical containing elements of phosphorous, sulfur, or fluorine, to register themselves with the National Authority or any other office as may be prescribed within a specified time period.	X	(2) Whoever contravenes the provisions of this section shall be guilty of an offence punishable with imprisonment for a term, which may extent to two years, or with fine, or with both.	

Individual licensing	X	• Chemical Weapons Convention Implementation Ordinance 2000 **Section 23 ibid** • SRO 482(I)/2000		**Section 12 (2)(b)**	
General licensing	X	• Chemical Weapons Convention Implementation Ordinance 2000 **Section 23 ibid** • SRO 482 (I)/2000			
Exceptions from licensing					
Licensing of deemed export/ visa	X	• SRO 482 (I)/2000 • Chemical Weapons Convention Implementation Ordinance 2000 **Section 23 ibid**			
National licensing authority	X	• Ministry of Foreign Affairs.			Page 4 of the report.
Interagency review for license	X	• Ministry of Commerce • SRO 482 (I)/2000			Page 6 of the report.
Control lists	X	• Chemical Weapons Convention Implementation Ordinance–2000, • The Imports and Exports (Control) Act, 1950 • SRO 482(I)/2000			Page 8 of the report.
Updating of lists	X	• Federal Government Notifications • Custom SRO & CGO			
Inclusion of technologies	X	• Chemical Weapons Convention Implementation Ordinance–2000,	X		Page 7 of the report.

Which of the following legislation, procedures, measures, agencies exist to control border crossings, export/import and other transfers of CW and Related Materials? Can violators be penalized?	National legal framework		Enforcement: civil/criminal penalties, and measures of implementation, etc		Remarks
	YES	If YES, indicate source document	YES	If YES, indicate source document	
		Section 3 **Prohibition on development, etc of chemical weapons**—(1) No person shall- (a) develop, produce, otherwise, acquire, or stockpile or retain in chemical weapon, or transfer, directly or indirectly, a chemical weapon to anyone; (b) use a chemical weapon; (c) engage in any military preparation to use chemical weapon; (d) assist, encourage or induce, in any way, any other person to engage in any activity prohibited to a State party under the Convention;		(3) Whoever contravenes the provisions of this section shall be guilty of an offence punishable with imprisonment for a term which may extend to twenty five years.	
Inclusion of means of delivery	X	• Chemical Weapons Convention Implementation Ordinance–2000 **Section 2(c)** (ii) a munition or device specifically design to cause death . . .			

		(iii) any equipment specifically designed for use directly in connection with the employment of a munition or device— • SRO 482 (I)/2000			
End-user controls	X	• SRO 482 (I)/2000			Page 7 of the report.
Catch all clause	X	• Chemical Weapons Convention Implementation Ordinance–2000 • SRO 482 (I)/2000			Page 7 of the report.
Intangible transfers	X	• Officials Secrets Act 1923 **Section 5** 1. Wrongful communication, etc., of information: (1) If any person having in his possession or control any secret official code or pass word or any sketch, plan, model, article, note, document or information which relate to or is used in a prohibited place or relates to anything in such a place, or which has been made or obtained in contravention of this Act, or which has been entrusted in confidence to him by any person holding office under Government, . . . (e) willfully communicates the code or pass word (f) uses information in his possession (g) retain the sketch . . .	X	(3) A person guilty of an offence under this section shall be punishable,____ a) where offence committed, . . . directly or indirectly in benefit of foreign power . . . shall be punishable with death or with imprisonment which may extend to fourteen years.; b) in any other case, with imprisonment for a term which may extend to two years, or fine, . . .both.	

Which of the following legislation, procedures, measures, agencies exist to control border crossings, export/import and other transfers of CW and Related Materials? Can violators be penalized?	National legal framework		Enforcement: civil/criminal penalties, and measures of implementation, etc		Remarks
	YES	If YES, indicate source document	YES	If YES, indicate source document	
		(h) fail to take reasonable care. . . shall be guilty of the offence under this section (2) If a person voluntarily receive any secret official code . . . shall be guilty of the offence under this section. • The Defence of Pakistan Ordinance 1965 **Section 3(2)** 3(2)(xxv)prohibiting or regulating the possession, use or disposal of— a) explosives, inflammable substances, *corrosive* and other dangerous substances or articles, arms and ammunitions of war: b) vessels, c) wireless telegraphic apparatus, or any other apparatus capable of transmitting messages, d)aircraft, and e) photographic and signaling apparatus and any means of recording information		imprisonment for a term which may extend to five years and also be liable to fine. . . .	

Transit control	X	• Custom Act 1969 **Section 129** 129. Transit of goods across Pakistan to a foreign territory.– Where any goods are entered for transit across Pakistan to a destination outside Pakistan, the appropriate officer may, subject to the provisions of the rules, allow the goods to be so transited without payment of the duties which would otherwise be chargeable on such goods: Provided that the Federal Government may, by notification in the official Gazette, prohibit the bringing into Pakistan by sea, land or air in transit to a foreign territory any goods or class of goods. • SRO 482 (I)/2000			
Trans-shipment control	X	• Chemical Weapons Convention Implementation Ordinance–2000 • Custom Notification SRO. 7 (I)/2001 **Rule 333** Goods not permitted for transshipment.—The following goods shall not be allowed transshipment to up-country customs port or stations— a. . . . b. . . . c. . . .			Page 7 of the report.

Which of the following legislation, procedures, measures, agencies exist to control border crossings, export/import and other transfers of CW and Related Materials? Can violators be penalized?	National legal framework		Enforcement: civil/criminal penalties, and measures of implementation, etc		Remarks
	YES	If YES, indicate source document	YES	If YES, indicate source document	
		d. explosive, as defined in the Explosive Act, 1884 e. arms and ammunition. . . . *(as defined in Arms Act 1878 and its successor Act. Pakistan Arms Ordinance 1965.)*			
Re-export control	X	• Custom Notification SRO. 7 (I)/2001 **Rule 253 & 357** **253. Re-export** of imported inputs goods.—(1) The licensee may be allowed to re-export input goods imported for manufacture of export goods under these rules in their original and unprocessed form within three years of their import *subject to the limitations and restrictions of Import Policy Order and Export Trade Control Order for the time being in force.* **357. Re-export** of ware-housed goods.—(1) The Licensee of a warehouse may be allowed by the officer not below the rank of an Additional Collector of Customs to			

		re-export the warehouse goods in their original and unprocessed form within three years of their import *subject to the conditions, limitations and restrictions of the Acts, Import Policy Order and Export Trade Control Order for the time being in force.* • SRO 482 (I)/2000			
Control of providing funds	**X**	• Chemical Weapons Convention Implementation Ordinance–2000 **Section 3** 3. **Prohibition on development, etc of chemical weapons**— (1) No person shall- (a) develop, produce, otherwise, acquire, or stockpile or retain in chemical weapon, or transfer, directly or indirectly, a chemical weapon to anyone; (b) use a chemical weapon; (c) engage in any military preparation to use chemical weapon; (d) assist, encourage or induce, in any way, any other person to engage in any activity prohibited to a State party under the Convention; (e) use a riot control agent as a method of warfare.. . . • Anti-Terrorism Act 1997 **Section 11-J and 11-N** 11-J **Funding Arrangements**.—A person commits an offence if he-	**X**	(3) Whoever contravenes the provisions of this section shall be guilty of an offence punishable with imprisonment for a term which may extend to twenty five years. 11-N **Punishment under section 11-H to 11-K**. . .shall be punishable on conviction with imprisonment for a term not less than six months and not exceeding five years and with fine. **Section 213 & 214** **Taking gift, etc., to screen an offender from punishment**: Whoever accept or attempts to obtain, or agrees to accept, any gratification for himself or any other person, or any restitution of property to himself or any other person, in consideration of his concealing an offence or of his screening any person from legal punishment for any offence, or of his not proceeding against any person for	

Which of the following legislation, procedures, measures, agencies exist to control border crossings, export/import and other transfers of CW and Related Materials? Can violators be penalized?	National legal framework		Enforcement: civil/criminal penalties, and measures of implementation, etc		Remarks
	YES	If YES, indicate source document	YES	If YES, indicate source document	
		(a) enters into or becomes concerned in an arrangement as a result of which money or other property is made available or is to be made available to another, and (b) has reasonable cause to suspect that it will or may be used for the purposes of terrorism. • Pakistan Penal Code 1860		the purpose of bring him to legal punishment. **if a capital offence:** shall, if the offence is punishable with death, be punished with imprisonment of either description for a term which may extend to seven years, and shall also be liable to fine: **if punishable with imprisonment for life, or with imprisonment**: and if the offence is punishable with imprisonment for life or with imprisonment which may extend to ten years, shall be punished with imprisonment of either description for a term which may extend to three years, shall also be liable to fine: and if the offence is punishable with imprisonment not extending to ten years, shall be punished with description provided for the offence for a term which may extend to one-fourth part of the longest term of imprisonment provided for the offence, or with fine, or with both.	

				Offering gift or restoration of property in consideration of screening offender: Whoever gives or causes or offers or agrees to give or cause, any gratification to any person, or to restore or cause to restoration of any property to any person, in consideration of that person's concealing an offence, or of his screening any person form legal punishment for any offence, or his not proceeding against any person for the purpose of bringing him to legal punishment; **if the a capital offence:** shall, if the offence is punishable with death, be punished with imprisonment of either description for a term which may extend to seven years and shall also be liable to fine; **if punishable with imprisonment for life or with imprisonment**: and the offence is punishable with imprisonment for life, or with imprisonment which may extend to three years, shall be punished with imprisonment of either description for a term may extend to three years, and shall also be liable to fine; and if the offence is punishable with imprisonment not extending to ten years, shall be punishable with imprisonment of the description provided for	

Which of the following legislation, procedures, measures, agencies exist to control border crossings, export/import and other transfers of CW and Related Materials? Can violators be penalized?	National legal framework		Enforcement: civil/criminal penalties, and measures of implementation, etc		Remarks
	YES	If YES, indicate source document	YES	If YES, indicate source document	
				the offence for a term which may extend to one-fourth part of the longest term of imprisonment provided for the offence, or with fine, or with or with both.	
Control of providing transport services	X	• National Highway Safety Ordinance 1997 **Section 65 (f)(h)(i)** Establishment of a police for National Highway (f) under take initial action in respect of offences committed on National Highways and then transfer the cases to the concerned Police Station for Investigation. (h) to keep Highways clear from any encroachment and keep a look out for suspicious persons and criminals. (i) take into possession any abandoned property for its disposal under the law • Railway Act 1890			Offender can be prosecuted under abetment provision as well.

		Section 59 (1) No person shall be entitled to take with him, or to require a railway administration to carry, any dangerous or offensive goods upon a railway.			
Control of importation	X	• Import Policy Order 2004 • The Explosives Rule 1940 **Chapter III Part III** **Importation by Land**. No explosive shall be imported by land save with the previous sanction in each case of the Central Government and under such conditions and restriction as it may impose.			Page 3 of the report.
Extraterritorial applicability	X	• Chemical Weapon Convention Implementation Ordinance 2000 **Section 25** The provision of this ordinance apply to any offence committed by (a) any citizen of Pakistan or any person in service of Pakistan in any place without and beyond Pakistan b) any person on any ship or aircraft registered in Pakistan wherever it may be • Pakistan Penal Code 1860 **Section 4 read with 108 A** **4. Extension of** Code of extra-territorial offences: The provisions			

Which of the following legislation, procedures, measures, agencies exist to control border crossings, export/import and other transfers of CW and Related Materials? Can violators be penalized?	National legal framework		Enforcement: civil/criminal penalties, and measures of implementation, etc		Remarks
	YES	If YES, indicate source document	YES	If YES, indicate source document	
		of this Code apply also to any offence committed by—(1) any citizen of Pakistan or any person in the service of Pakistan in any place without and beyond Pakistan (2) and (3) omitted (4) any person on any ship or aircraft registered in Pakistan wherever may be. Explanation.—In this section the word "offence" includes every act committed outside Pakistan which, if committed in Pakistan would be punishable under this Code. **108 A.** **Abetment in Pakistan, of offences outside it**. A person abets an offence within the meaning of this Code who, in Pakistan, abets the commission of any act without and beyond Pakistan which would constitute an offence committed in Pakistan.			
Other					

OP 3 (c) and (d) and related matters from OP 6 and OP 10 - Controls of NW including Related Materials

State: Pakistan
Date of Report: 27 October 2004

Which of the following legislation, procedures, measures, agencies exist to control border crossings, export/import and other transfers of NW and Related Materials? Can violators be penalized?	National legal framework		Enforcement: civil/criminal penalties, and measures of implementation, etc		Remarks
	YES	If YES, indicate source document	YES	If YES, indicate source document	
Border control	X	• Pakistan Nuclear Regulatory Ordinance 2001 **Section 19** Power to issue licence.__(1) No person shall, unless he is exempted as may prescribed by the regulations, or unless he is the holder of a licence issued by the Authority. . . (2) Subject to sub-section (1),the Authority may, on application made to it accompanied by such fee, information and documents, as may be prescribed by the regulations, issued a licence for carrying out of such activities as are specified in the licence for such period as may. . . . • Export Control on goods, technologies, material and equipment related to nuclear and biological weapons	X		Page 7 of the report.

Which of the following legislation, procedures, measures, agencies exist to control border crossings, export/import and other transfers of NW and Related Materials? Can violators be penalized?	National legal framework		Enforcement: civil/criminal penalties, and measures of implementation, etc		Remarks
	YES	If YES, indicate source document	YES	If YES, indicate source document	
		and their delivery system Act 2004 **Section 4(4)** (4) The Federal Govt shall control export, re export, *transshipment, transit of goods,* technologies material and equipment. . . which may contribute to designing, development, production, stockpiling, . . . use of nuclear and biological weapons and the delivery systems • Customs Act 1969 • Imports and Exports (Control) Act 1950 • SRO 111(I)/2004			
		• West Pakistan Rangers Ordinance 1959 **Section 13 read with 6** 6. The Force shall perform the following functions:- a. protection of persons and property in the border areas;			

		b. Apprehension of persons unlawfully entering into or going out of Pakistan territory c. Organization of village Defence in the border areas; d. Prevention of smuggling e. Collection of intelligence in the border areas f. Coordinate of activities of Police and other civil agencies in the prevention and detection of smuggling 13(g)(vi) quits his guard, piquet, party or patrol, without being regularly relieved or without leave, shall be punished with rigorous imprisonment for a term which may extend to fourteen years . . . • Airport Security Force Ordinance 1975 **Section 7 read with 6(e)(f)(g) members**. (e) take effective measures for prevention hijacking, sabotage, placement of car bombs, letter bombs and dangerous articles, smuggling of precious articles, smuggling of precious metals, stones, arms, ammunition, narcotics and any other goods the brining into, or taking out of,			

Which of the following legislation, procedures, measures, agencies exist to control border crossings, export/import and other transfers of NW and Related Materials? Can violators be penalized?	National legal framework		Enforcement: civil/criminal penalties, and measures of implementation, etc		Remarks
	YES	If YES, indicate source document	YES	If YES, indicate source document	
		Pakistan of which is prohibited by or under nay law for the time being in face; (f) use such arms and ammunition of equipment as may be; authorized by the Force Commander for the purpose of this Ordinance; (g) search and arrest without warrant any person who he suspects of endangering, or attempting to endanger, or having endangered, the safety of an aerodrome or airport or an aircraft or a civil aviation installation and may use such force as may be necessary in the discharge of his duties aforesaid; and (h) perform such other functions as the competent authority may require the him to perform. (2) An officer, for the purpose of this Ordinance, shall exercise, within the areas in which this Ordinance applies,			

		all the powers conferred on an officer in-charge of a Police Station under the Police Act, 1861 (V of 1861), and the Code of Criminal Procedure, 1898 (Act V of 1898). **7. Liabilities of officers and members.—(1)** it shall be the duty of every officer and member promptly to obey and to obey and to execute all orders and instructions issued to him by any competent authority. (2) Every officer and member shall be liable to serve wherever he is required to serve by the competent authority. • Pakistan Coast Guards Act 1973 **Section 3** 3. Powers to constitute and maintain the force and its functions.—The Federal Government may constitute and maintain a Force to be called the Pakistan Coast Guards for performing the following functions, namely:- (a)prevention of smuggling; (b)prevention of illegal immigration to and migration from the country;			

Which of the following legislation, procedures, measures, agencies exist to control border crossings, export/import and other transfers of NW and Related Materials? Can violators be penalized?	National legal framework		Enforcement: civil/criminal penalties, and measures of implementation, etc		Remarks
	YES	If YES, indicate source document	YES	If YES, indicate source document	
		(c) stopping enemy agents or saboteurs from Infiltrating into the country along the coastal areas; and (d) supplementing defense in war. • The Pakistan Railway Police Act 1977 **Section 11 read with 3** 3.(1) Notwithstanding anything contained in any other law for the time being in force, the Federal Government may constitute, control and maintain a force to be called the Pakistan Railways Police for performing, within such territorial limits as the Federal Government may, by notification in the official Gazette, specify the following functions, namely:- a) preventing loss to Railway property and property consigned to the Railways and prevention of offences in respect thereof;			

		b) ensuring proper conduct of persons on the Railways; c) general maintenance of law and order on the Railways and taking cognizance of offences committed on them; d) to render all possible assistance to passengers and railway servants e) to protect travelers from injury to person or property; f) to keep Railway platforms and other Railway premises clear of idlers and beggars and to keep a lookout for suspicious persons, smugglers and persons traveling with arms without a license or in contravention of rules, regulations or orders for the time being in force 11.—(1) It shall be the duty of every officer and member promptly to obey and to execute all orders and instructions issued to him by the competent authority. • Police Order 2002 **Section 5** Emergency duties of police with regard to essential services.__(1) The Government may, in an			

Which of the following legislation, procedures, measures, agencies exist to control border crossings, export/import and other transfers of NW and Related Materials? Can violators be penalized?	National legal framework		Enforcement: civil/criminal penalties, and measures of implementation, etc		Remarks
	YES	If YES, indicate source document	YES	If YES, indicate source document	
		emergency, by notification in the Official Gazette, declare any specified services to be an essential service to the community. (2) upon a declaration being made under clause (1) and so long as it remains in force, it shall be the duty of every police officer to obey any lawful order given by a senior police officer in relation to the declaration. • Maritime Security Act 1994 **Section 9 read with 10, 11, 12** 9. Application of the Pakistan Navy ordinance, 1961, etc.—(1) Subject to the provisions of this Act, every officer and member of the staff shall, whether appointed through initial recruitment or otherwise, unless he is already so subject, be subject to the Pakistan Navy Ordinance, 1961			

		(XXXV of 1961), hereinafter referred to as the said Ordinance. 10. Powers and functions of the Agency.—(1) The Agency shall be responsible for the regulation and protection of the maritime interests of Pakistan and to assert and enforce national jurisdiction and jurisdiction and sovereignty in the Maritime Zones. 2) Without prejudice to the generality of the provisions of sub-section (1), the functions of the Agency shall be to. . . c) enforce the national and international laws agreements and conventions on and under the water in the Maritime Zones; . . . (j) cooperate with, and provide assistance to Customs, Coast Guards and other departments, agencies and authorities in Maritime Zones in the discharge of their duties and functions; (k) provide an effective secondary maritime force for deployment in any emergency, war or conflict; and (l) perform such other functions as may be assigned to it by the Federal Government,			

Which of the following legislation, procedures, measures, agencies exist to control border crossings, export/import and other transfers of NW and Related Materials? Can violators be penalized?	National legal framework		Enforcement: civil/criminal penalties, and measures of implementation, etc		Remarks
	YES	If YES, indicate source document	YES	If YES, indicate source document	
		from time to time, to protect maritime interests of Pakistan. 11. Other functions of the officers of Agency, etc.—(1) In addition to the powers and functions as officers of the Agency, such officers may perform functions of. . . (i) Officers of customs as may be entrusted to them and exercise such powers under the Customs Act, 1969 (IV of 1969), as may be delegated to them under Section 6 of that Act; and (iii) Police Officer, and exercise all the powers conferred on an officer in charge of a Police Station under the Police Act, 1861(V of 1861), and under the Code of Criminal Procedure, 1898 (Act V of 1898). (2) The Government may, at any time, assign or delegate any other functions or powers			

		upon any officer of the Agency under any law for the time being in force in the Maritime Zones. 12.Power of searches, arrest, etc.—In exercise of the powers and performance of their functions under this Act, the officers and members of the staff may make inquiries, examinations, inspections, investigations, searches, seizures, and arrests for prevention, detection suppression of contravention of any law for the time being in force within the Maritime Zones and for that purpose the officers and members of the staff may board any vessel except ships, vessel or crafts of Pakistan Armed Forces • Karachi Port Trust Security Force Ordinance 2002 **Section 3** **Establishment, constitution and maintenance of the force, its powers and functions**.. . .(1) The chairman with the approval of the Federal Government shall establish, constitute and maintain a force to be called the Karachi Port Security Force to maintain			

Which of the following legislation, procedures, measures, agencies exist to control border crossings, export/import and other transfers of NW and Related Materials? Can violators be penalized?	National legal framework		Enforcement: civil/criminal penalties, and measures of implementation, etc		Remarks
	YES	If YES, indicate source document	YES	If YES, indicate source document	
		security and safety of the Karachi Port Area for performing of the following functions, namely:- (a) maintain law and order in the Port Area and take cognizance of offences committed therein or connected thereto; (k) prevent pollution; spillage, waste fire hazards, chemical hazards, water hazards, biological hazards, hazardous waste and hazardous substances and also prevent the generation, collection transport treatment, disposal, storage, handling import, export of the same may be prescribed; and • Frontier Corp Ordinance 1959 **3. Powers** to maintain Frontier Corps.—There shall continue to be maintained by the			

		Central Government the Frontier Corps forces or units as listed in the First Schedule, primarily for the better protection and administration of the external frontiers of Pakistan within the limits of or adjoining the Special Areas of West Pakistan • Civil/ Armed Forces Entrustment of Power Through Custom Rules, Notifications & SRO's SRO 29 (I)/73 **ENTRUSTMENT OF THE FUNCTIONS OF CUSTOMS OFFICERS TO OFFICERS OF WEST PAKISTAN RANGERS** Notification No.SRO 29(I)/73 dated 3rd January, 1973.—In exercise of the powers conferred by section 6 of the Customs Act, 1969 (IV of 1969), and in suppression of its Notifications No.SRO 314 and 315, dated the 11th July, 1959, the Central Board of Revenue is pleased to entrust; the functions of officers of customers under sections 157, 158, 159, 160, 161, 162, 163, 164, 165, 166, 167,m sub-sections (1), (3) and (4) of section 168, sections 169 and 171 of the said Act to all officers of the West			

Which of the following legislation, procedures, measures, agencies exist to control border crossings, export/import and other transfers of NW and Related Materials? Can violators be penalized?	National legal framework		Enforcement: civil/criminal penalties, and measures of implementation, etc		Remarks
	YES	If YES, indicate source document	YES	If YES, indicate source document	
		Pakistan Rangers not below the rank of Sub-Inspector (and all officers of the West Pakistan Rangers not below the rank of Havildar only the Powers under sections 158, 159, 161 and 164 of the said act). SRO 524(I)/74 **ENTRUSTMENT OF POWERS TO THE OFFICERS OF THE FRONTIER CONSTABULARY** Notification No.SRO 524(I)/74, dated 23rd April, 1974.—In exercise of the powers conferred by section 6 of the Customs Act, 1969 (IV of 1969), the Central Board of Revenue is pleased to entrust, subject to such limitations and restrictions as are laid down in the Rules made under the said Act, to the officers of the Frontier Constabulary specified in the first column of the Table below, the functions			

		of officers of Customs under the provisions of the said Act . . . SRO 1017(I)/74 **ENTRUSTMENT TO POWERS OF THE OFFICERS OF CUSTOMS TO THE OFFICERS OF THE FRONTIER CORP** Notification No.SRO 1017(I)/74, dated 26th July, 1974.—In exercise of the powers conferred by section 6 of the Customs Act, 1969 (IV of 1969),the Central Board of revenue is pleased to entrust to the officers of the Frontier Corps, operating within 2(sixty kilometers) along the international borders adjoining the Province of Baluchistan 3(and North Western Frontier Province), as specified in the first column of the Table below the functions of officers of customs under the provisions of the said Act specified . . . Customs or other law enforcement agencies keep tight vigil.			
Technical support of border control measures	X	• Bilateral, technical cooperation with different countries. • Capacity building technical courses.	X		

Which of the following legislation, procedures, measures, agencies exist to control border crossings, export/import and other transfers of NW and Related Materials? Can violators be penalized?	National legal framework		Enforcement: civil/criminal penalties, and measures of implementation, etc		Remarks
	YES	If YES, indicate source document	YES	If YES, indicate source document	
		• Special training to detect sensitive materials • Deployment of scanners, etc • Collaboration/cooperation with international organizations. • Custom General Order 2005 **Chapter –IX STORAGE, DISPOSAL & SAMPLING OF SEIZED AND CONFISCATION GOODS ____ INSTRUCTIONS REGARDING** 32. Storage by law enforcing agencies.—For Law Enforcement agencies hereinafter referred to as Agencies, including the Civil Armed Forces of Pakistan who have delegated anti-smuggling powers under the Custom act, 1969. The following directions are issued for strict compliance:-			Page 7 of the report.

		XV. Appointment of State-warehouses XVI. Appointment of custodians XVII. Working of the State-warehouses XVIII. . . . XIX. . . . XX. Inspection of seized goods and sampling thereof. XXI. . . . • Pakistan Council of Scientific and Industrial Research Act 1973 **Section 6** **The functions of the Council shall be**. . . *d) undertake such special scientific and technological surveys and investigations as* may be referred to it by the Federal Government / from time to time			PCSIR provides technical assistance in investigating the material found during Border Control operations that can facilitate prosecution
Control of brokering, trading in, negotiating, otherwise assisting in sale of good and technology	**X**	• Pakistan Nuclear Regulatory Authority Ordinance 2001. **Section 19 (c)** **Section 19**. Power to issue Licence.—(1)No person shall, unless he is exempted as may prescribed by the regulations, or unless he is the holder of a licence issued by the Authority. . .	**X**	(3)A person guilty of an offence under this section shall be punishable,— a)where offence committed. . .directly or indirectly in benefit of foreign power. . .shall be punishable with death or with imprisonment which may extend to fourteen years.;	

Which of the following legislation, procedures, measures, agencies exist to control border crossings, export/import and other transfers of NW and Related Materials? Can violators be penalized?	National legal framework		Enforcement: civil/criminal penalties, and measures of implementation, etc		Remarks
	YES	**If YES, indicate source document**	**YES**	**If YES, indicate source document**	
		(c) explore for mines and mill, extract acquire handle use,. . ., sell, lease lend by transfer import export convert enrich, produce, store, process, reprocess, fabricate, transport, dispose of any radioactive ore, radio active material, nuclear substance or any other substance as the authority may by notification. . .specify • Export Control on goods, technologies, material and equipment related to nuclear and biological weapons and their delivery system Act 2004 • Officials Secrets Act 1923 **Section 5** 1. Wrongful communication, etc., of information: (1) If any person having in his possession or control any secret official code or pass word or any sketch, plan, model, article, note, document or information which relate to		b)in any other case, with imprisonment for a term which may extend to two years, or fine,. . .both.	

		or is used in a prohibited place or relates to anything in such a place, or which has been made or obtained in contravention of this Act, or which has been entrusted in confidence to him by any person holding office under Government,. . . (a) willfully communicates the code or pass word (b) uses information in his possession (c) retain the sketch . . . (d) fail to take reasonable care . . . shall be guilty of the offence under this section (2) If a person voluntarily receive any secret official code. . .shall be guilty of the offence under this section. • Defence of Pakistan Ordinance 1965 **Section 3(2)** 3(2)(xxv prohibiting or regulating the possession, use or disposal of— a) explosives, inflammable substances, corrosive and other dangerous substances or articles, arms and ammunitions of war; b) vessels, c) wireless telegraphic apparatus, or any other			

Which of the following legislation, procedures, measures, agencies exist to control border crossings, export/import and other transfers of NW and Related Materials? Can violators be penalized?	National legal framework		Enforcement: civil/criminal penalties, and measures of implementation, etc		Remarks
	YES	**If YES, indicate source document**	**YES**	**If YES, indicate source document**	
		apparatus capable of transmitting messages, d) aircraft, and e) photographic and signaling apparatus and any means of recording information • Imports and Exports (Control)Act 1950 **Section 4A, 4B read with 5** 4-A No person shall sell, purchase or otherwise deal in any import licence other than an import licence issued . . . 4-B Except with pervious permission in writing . . . no person shall sell or otherwise transfer such goods, use the goods for a purpose other than the purpose or purposes for which the licence is issued . . .		imprisonment for a term which may extend to five years and also be liable to fine . . . 5.If any person contravenes any provision of this Act be punishable with imprisonment for a term which may extend to one year, or with fine, or with both.	
Enforcement agencies/ authorities	X	• Pakistan Customs. • Federal Investigation Agencies Act 1974 • West Pakistan Rangers Ordinance 1959			Page 5 of the report.

		• The Pakistan Railway Police Act 1977 • Pakistan Coast Guards Act 1973 • Airport Security Force Ordinance 1975 • Police Order 2002 • Maritime Security Act 1994 • Karachi Port Trust Security Force Ordinance 2002 • Frontier Corp Ordinance 1959			
Export control legislation in place	X	• Export Control on Goods, Technology, Material and Equipment related to Nuclear and Biological Weapons and their Delivery Systems Act, of 23 September 2004. • Pakistan Nuclear Regulatory Authority Ordinance (PNRA), of 2001 Ordinance No. III of 2001 • The Imports and Exports (Control) Act, 1950 • Pakistan Nuclear Safety and Radiation Protection (PNSRP) Regulation of 1990: Nuclear substances and radioactive materials	X	**Section 8** 8(1) Any person who contravenes. . . shall be guilty for an offence punishable on conviction by imprisonment for a term which may extend to 14 years and with fine not exceeding 5 million rupees or both and—. Property and assets where ever they may be shall be forfeited to Federal Government. **Section 44 (1)** 44(1) Any person who contravenes . . . shall be punished - for a term . . .extend to 7 years or with fine which may extend to 1 million or with both	Page 3 and 4 of the report.

Which of the following legislation, procedures, measures, agencies exist to control border crossings, export/import and other transfers of NW and Related Materials? Can violators be penalized?	National legal framework		Enforcement: civil/criminal penalties, and measures of implementation, etc		Remarks
	YES	If YES, indicate source document	YES	If YES, indicate source document	
		• Export Policy Order 2004 (EPO) • Customs Act 1969		**Section 156 (Provide punishments for offences under this Act)**	
Licensing provisions	X	• Pakistan Nuclear Regulatory Authority Ordinance (PNRA), 2001 Ordinance No. III of 2001., **Sections 19 to 23** **19.Power to issue license.**— (1) No person shall, unless he is exempted as may prescribed by the regulations, or unless he is the holder of a licence issued by the Authority. . . (2) Subject to sub-section (1), the Authority may, on application made to it accompanied by such fee, information and documents, as may be prescribed by the regulations, issued a licence for carrying out of such activities as are specified in the licence for such period as may . . .	X		Page 4 of the report.

		20. Power to grant authorization.___ (1) The Authority may, on application made to it accompanied by such fee, information and documents, as may be prescribed by the regulations, grant an authorization for carrying out such activities as are specified in the authorization for such period as it may specify . . . **21. Authorization prior to licensing**. ___No person shall commence construction of any nuclear installation without first obtaining an authorization . . .from the Authority as may be prescribed by regulation. **22. Authorization prior to radioactive** waste discharge and disposal.___No person shall discharge, or dispose of, radioactive waste to environment without first obtaining an authorization . . . from the Authority. . . **23. Authorization for nuclear powered vehicle, vessel or aircraft, and any vehicle, vessel or aircraft carrying nuclear material** . . . No person shall cause a nuclear powered vehicle, vessel or aircraft, and			

Which of the following legislation, procedures, measures, agencies exist to control border crossings, export/import and other transfers of NW and Related Materials? Can violators be penalized?	National legal framework		Enforcement: civil/criminal penalties, and measures of implementation, etc		Remarks
	YES	If YES, indicate source document	YES	If YES, indicate source document	
		vehicle, vessel or aircraft carrying nuclear material to enter in Pakistan without first obtaining an authorization for this purpose from the Authority as may be prescribed by regulation.			
Individual licensing	X	• Export Control on Goods, Technology, Material and Equipment related to Nuclear and Biological Weapons and their Delivery Systems Act, of 23 September 2004 **Section 5** **5. The Federal Govt shall control export, re-export, transshipment**, transit of goods, technologies, material and equipment, subject to the provisions of this Act, which may contribute to the designing, development, production, stockpiling, maintenance or use of nuclear			

		and biological weapons and their delivery systems • Pakistan Nuclear Regulatory Authority Ordinance (PNRA), 2001 Ordinance No. III of 2001, **Sections 19 to 23 ibid**			
General licensing	X	• Export Control on Goods, Technology, Material and Equipment related to Nuclear and Biological Weapons and their Delivery Systems Act, of 23 September 2004 **Section 5 Ibid** • Pakistan Nuclear Regulatory Authority Ordinance (PNRA), 2001 Ordinance No. III of 2001., **Sections 19 to 23 ibid**			
Exceptions from licensing					
Licensing of deemed export/visa	X	• Pakistan Nuclear Safety and Radiation Protection (PNSRP). 1990 **Rule 20** **20. No Objection Certificate** (1)Any Person desirous of importing and exporting, radioactive material, or radiation apparatus, shall apply			

Which of the following legislation, procedures, measures, agencies exist to control border crossings, export/import and other transfers of NW and Related Materials? Can violators be penalized?	National legal framework		Enforcement: civil/criminal penalties, and measures of implementation, etc		Remarks
	YES	**If YES, indicate source document**	**YES**	**If YES, indicate source document**	
		to the Director for No Objection Certificate. (2) The Director may require the applicant to produce invoices or other documents which may show the origin, technical specifications and other details as the Director may deem necessary. (3) The Director may defer the consideration of the application and may require the applicant to do such other acts which he deems necessary and under the safety standards laid down in these			
National licensing authority	X	• Pakistan Nuclear Regulatory Authority Act 2001 **Section 19 ibid**			Page 4 of the report.
Interagency review for licenses	X	• SRO 111(I)/2004 • Pakistan Nuclear Regulatory Authority Act 2001			Custom Department and PNRA liaison and an NOC is required from Ministry of Foreign Affairs.

		Section 24 **24. Cancellation or Suspension of an authorization or a License** (1) Where any person has been found to have contravened any of the provisions of this Ordinance, the rules regulations, or has consistently failed to comply with terms and conditions of an authorization or as the case may be, a licence, the Authority may subject to sub-section (2), cancel or suspend the authorization or, as the case may be, the licence. (2) Before taking any action taken under sub- section (1),the Authority shall issue a notice to such person to show cause and give him an opportunity of being heard or an opportunity to rectify the ommisinon subject such conditions as the Authority may specify. • Pakistan Nuclear Safety and Radiation Protection (PNSRP). 1990 **Rule 16, 17** **16. Suspension of License** If at any time on receiving the information or otherwise the Director is of the opinion that			

Which of the following legislation, procedures, measures, agencies exist to control border crossings, export/import and other transfers of NW and Related Materials? Can violators be penalized?	National legal framework		Enforcement: civil/criminal penalties, and measures of implementation, etc		Remarks
	YES	If YES, indicate source document	YES	If YES, indicate source document	
		the licensee is violating any provision of the ordinance or these regulation or any of the terms and condition of the license,he may order immediate stoppage of the work or order such other action as may be necessary to stop, minimize or check the increase in the level of radiation,or any nuclear damage, provided that if the licensee fails to comply with such orders the Director may carry out the same at the cost of the licensee. **17. Revocation /surrender of Licence** (1) After giving an opportunity of showing cause, and on being satisfied that the licensee has violated the provisions of the ordinance or of these regulations or the terms and condition of licence, the Director may revoke the licence			

		(2)The Licensee shall have a right to surrender his licence by giving three months prior notice to the Director			
Control list	X	• Export Control on Goods, Technology, Material and Equipment related to Nuclear and Biological Weapons and their Delivery Systems Act 2004 **Section 4** (1) The Federal Government shall maintain a Control Lists, to be notified separately, of goods and Technologies subject to licensing requirements under this Act. (2) The control lists shall be reviewed periodically, and revised or updated, as required by the Federal Government and notified accordingly. (3) The Federal Government shall notify all licensing requirements and procedures			The existing PNRA Ordinance provides for controls over export and other transfer of radioactive material and nuclear substances section 16, 19 and 23. Ministry of Commerce has notified this in its Export Policy and Procedure Order 2000 as amended by SRO No.III (I)/2004
Update of list	X	• Federal Government Notifications • Custom SRO & CGO • Export Control on Goods, Technology, Material and Equipment related to Nuclear and Biological Weapons and their Delivery Systems Act 2004			Page 4 and 5 of the report.

Which of the following legislation, procedures, measures, agencies exist to control border crossings, export/import and other transfers of NW and Related Materials? Can violators be penalized?	**National legal framework**		**Enforcement: civil/criminal penalties, and measures of implementation, etc**		**Remarks**
	YES	**If YES, indicate source document**	**YES**	**If YES, indicate source document**	
		Section 4 ibid Customs Act 1969 **Section 16.**			
Inclusion of technologies	X	• Export Control on Goods, Technology, Material and Equipment related to Nuclear and Biological Weapons and their Delivery Systems Act, of 2004 **Section 2 (I)** technology means any documents including blue prints, plans, diagram, models, formulae, tables, engineering, design or specifications, manuals or instructions, necessary for development and production of nuclear or biological weapons and their delivery system. **Section 4(4) ibid** • Custom General Order 2005 **Restrictions - section 95 Industrial policy-recognized industry.**—The Government has liberalized its		**Section 8 ibid**	Page 4 and 5 of the report.

		industrialized policy and sanctioning procedure have been deregulated. According to this policy, the sanction of the Government is required only in the following cases:- (i) . . . (ii) Arms and ammunition (iii) . . . (iv) High explosives. (v) . . .			
Inclusion of means of delivery	X	Export Control on Goods, Technology, Material and Equipment related to Nuclear and Biological Weapons and their Delivery Systems Act 2004 **Section 4 ibid**			Page 4 and 5 of the report.
End-user controls	X	• The Explosive Act 1884 • The Explosives Substance act 1908 • The Pakistan Arms Ordinance 1965 • Surrender of Illicit Arms Act 1991 • The Anti terrorism Act 1997			Page 4 and 5 of the report.
Catch all clause	X	Export Control on Goods, Technology, Material and Equipment related to Nuclear and Biological Weapons and their Delivery Systems Act, of **Section 4,5**			Page 4 and 5 of the report. The provision of various laws have option of "catch all offences " which include Anti Terrorism Act 1997

Which of the following legislation, procedures, measures, agencies exist to control border crossings, export/import and other transfers of NW and Related Materials? Can violators be penalized?	National legal framework		Enforcement: civil/criminal penalties, and measures of implementation, etc		Remarks
	YES	If YES, indicate source document	YES	If YES, indicate source document	
		4(1) The Federal Govt shall maintain a Control Lists, to be notified separately, of goods and Technologies subject to licensing requirements under this Act. (2) The control lists shall be reviewed periodically, and revised or updated, as required by the Federal Govt and notified accordingly. (3) The Federal Govt shall notify all licensing requirements and procedures **5. The Federal Govt shall control export, re-export, transshipment**, transit of goods, technologies, material and equipment, subject to the provisions of this Act, which may contribute to the designing, development, production, stockpiling, maintenance or use of nuclear and biological weapons and their delivery systems.	X		

		• Anti Terrorism Act 1997 **6. Terrorism**. (1) In this Act, "terrorism" means the use or threat of action where: (3) The use or threat of use of any action failing within sub-section (2) which involves the use of firearms, explosives or any weapon, is terrorism, whether or not subsection 1(c) is satisfied. (6) A person who commits an offence under this section or any other provision of this Act, shall be guilty of an act of terrorism • The Pakistan Arms Ordinance 1965		**Section 7 read with 6(3)(4)(5)(6)** **7 Punishment** for acts of terrorism. Whoever commits an act of terrorism under section 6, whereby:- (h) the act of terrorism committed under clause (h) to (n) of sub-section (2) of section 6, shall be punishable, on conviction, to imprisonment of not less than one year and not more than ten years and with fine; and (i) any other act of terrorism not falling under clauses (a) to (h) above or under any other provision of this Act, shall be punishable, on conviction, to imprisonment of not les than six months and not less than five years or with fine or with both. **Section 5, 8 read with 13** **5. Power to prohibit transport.**—Government may, from time to time, by notification in the official Gazette, regulate or prohibit the transport of any description of arms, ammunition or military stores over the whole of the Province or any part thereof	

Which of the following legislation, procedures, measures, agencies exist to control border crossings, export/import and other transfers of NW and Related Materials? Can violators be penalized?	National legal framework		Enforcement: civil/criminal penalties, and measures of implementation, etc		Remarks
	YES	If YES, indicate source document	YES	If YES, indicate source document	
				either altogether or except under a licence and to the extent and in the manner permitted by such licence. Explanation.—Arms, ammunition or military stores transshipped at a port in the Province within the meaning of this section. **7. Prohibition of going armed without licence**.—(1) No persons shall go armed with any arms except under and to the extend and in the manner permitted thereby.(2) Any person so going armed without a licence or in contravention of its provisions may be disarmed by any Magistrate, Police Officer or other person empowered by the Government in this behalf . . . **13. Penalty for breach of Section 4, 5, 8, 11**. Subject to Section 13-A whoever	

				commits any of the following offence namely d. sells, or keeps, offers or exposes for sale, any arms, ammunition or military stores, or undertakes. . . e.. . . f. Transport any arms, ammunition or military stores in contravention of a regulation or prohibition issued under sections5. . . (d). . .(e). . .(f). . .(i). . .(g). . .(h) Shall be punished with imprisonment for a term which may extend to seven years or with fine, or with both: Provided that the punishment for an offence committed in respect of any; a) *Cannon*, grenades, bomb or rocket; —Shall be imprisonment for a term which may not be less than three years. . . .	
Intangible transfers	X	• Export Control on Goods, Technology, Material and Equipment related to Nuclear and Biological Weapons and their Delivery Systems Act of 2004 **Section 2 (I)(i)** Any document or information	X	**Section 8 ibid**	

Which of the following legislation, procedures, measures, agencies exist to control border crossings, export/import and other transfers of NW and Related Materials? Can violators be penalized?	National legal framework		Enforcement: civil/criminal penalties, and measures of implementation, etc		Remarks
	YES	If YES, indicate source document	YES	If YES, indicate source document	
		that is in public domain or is related to basic scientific research. . . **Section 4(4) ibid** • Pakistan Nuclear Regulatory Authority Ordinance 2001 **Section 51 and 52** 51. Declaration of fidelity and secrecy.___ the chairman, every member, advisor, consultant, officer or any other employee of the Authority shall, before entering upon his duties, shall make declaration of fidelity and secrecy as may be prescribed by the rules. 52. Chairman, members, etc., to public servants.___ The Chairman, members, officers and employees of the authority shall, when acting or purporting to act in pursuance of any of the provisions of this Ordinance, be deemed to be			

		public servants within the meaning of section 21 of the Pakistan Penal Code (Act XLV of 1860) • Officials Secrets Act 1923 **Section 5 ibid** • Pakistan Atomic Energy Commission Ordinance 1965 Rule 18. • The Defence of Pakistan Ordinance 1965 **Section 3(2)(xxv)** prohibiting or regulating the possession, use or disposal of— (a) explosives, inflammable substances, corrosive and other dangerous substances or articles, arms and ammunitions of war; (b) vessels, (c) wireless telegraphic apparatus, or any other apparatus capable of transmitting messages, (d) aircraft, and (e) photographic and signaling apparatus and any means of recording information:			
Transit control	X	• Export Control on Goods, Technology, Material and Equipment related to Nuclear and Biological Weapons and their Delivery Systems Act, of 23 September 2004			Page 4 of the report.

Which of the following legislation, procedures, measures, agencies exist to control border crossings, export/import and other transfers of NW and Related Materials? Can violators be penalized?	National legal framework		Enforcement: civil/criminal penalties, and measures of implementation, etc		Remarks
	YES	If YES, indicate source document	YES	If YES, indicate source document	
		Section 4 ibid • Custom Act 1969 **Section 129** Transit of goods across Pakistan to a foreign territory.- Where any goods are entered for transit across Pakistan to a destination outside Pakistan, the appropriate officer may, subject to the provisions of the rules, allow the goods to be so transited without payment of the duties which would otherwise be chargeable on such goods: Provided that the Federal Government may, by notification in the official Gazette, prohibit the bringing into Pakistan by sea, land or air in transit to a foreign territory any goods or class of goods.			
Trans-shipment control	X	• Export Control on Goods, Technology, Material and Equipment related to Nuclear and Biological			Page 4 of the report.

		Weapons and their Delivery Systems Act, of 23 September 2004 **Section 4 ibid** • The Pakistan Arms Ordinance 1965 **Section 5** **Power to prohibit transport.—** Government may, from time to time, by notification in the official Gazette, regulate or prohibit the transport of any description of arms, ammunition or military stores over the whole of the Province or any part thereof either altogether or except under a licence and to the extent and in the manner permitted by such licence. explanation.—Arms, ammunition or military stores transshipped at a port in the Province within the meaning of this section. • Custom Notification SRO 7(I)2001 **Rule 333** Goods not permitted for transshipment.—The following goods shall not be allowed transshipment to up-country customs port or stations. . .			

Which of the following legislation, procedures, measures, agencies exist to control border crossings, export/import and other transfers of NW and Related Materials? Can violators be penalized?	**National legal framework**		**Enforcement: civil/criminal penalties, and measures of implementation, etc**		**Remarks**
	YES	**If YES, indicate source document**	**YES**	**If YES, indicate source document**	
		a.. . . b.. . . c.. . . d. explosive, as defined in the Explosive Act, 1884 e. arms and ammunition . . .			
Re-export control	X	• Export Control on Goods, Technology, Material and Equipment related to Nuclear and Biological Weapons and their Delivery Systems Act, of 23 September 2004 **Section 4 ibid** • Custom Notification SRO 7(I)/2001 **Rule 253 & 357** 253. Re-export of imported inputs goods.—(1) The licensee may be allowed to re-export input goods imported for manufacture of export goods under these rules in their original and unprocessed form within three years of their			Page 4 of the report.

		import *subject to the limitations and restrictions of Import Policv Order and Export Trade Control Order for the time being in force.357* Re-export of ware-housed goods.___ (1) The Licensee of a warehouse may be allowed by the officer not below the rank of an Additional Collector of Customs to re-export the warehouse goods in their original and unprocessed form within three years of their import *subject to the conditions, limitations and restrictions of the Acts. Import Policy Order and Export Trade Control Order for the time being in force.*			
Control of providing funds	X	• Export Control on Goods, Technology, Material and Equipment related to Nuclear and Biological Weapons and their Delivery Systems Act, of 23 September 2004 • The Pakistan Penal Code 1860	X	**Section 8(2)** **Section 213 & 214** **Taking gift, etc., to screen an offender from punishment:** Whoever accept or attempts to obtain, or agrees to accept, any gratification for himself or any other person, or any restitution of property to himself or any other person, in consideration of his concealing an offence or of his screening any person from legal punishment for	

Which of the following legislation, procedures, measures, agencies exist to control border crossings, export/import and other transfers of NW and Related Materials? Can violators be penalized?	National legal framework		Enforcement: civil/criminal penalties, and measures of implementation, etc		Remarks
	YES	If YES, indicate source document	YES	If YES, indicate source document	
				any offence, or of his not proceeding against any person for the purpose of bring him to legal punishment. **if a capital offence:** shall, if the offence is punishable with death, be punished with imprisonment of either description for a term which may extend to seven years, and shall also be liable to fine: **if punishable with imprisonment for life, or with imprisonment:** and if the offence is punishable with imprisonment for life or with imprisonment which may extend to ten years, shall be punished with imprisonment of either description for a term which may extend to three years, shall also be liable to fine: and if the offence is	

				punishable with imprisonment not extending to ten years, shall be punished with description provided for the offence for a term which may extend to one-fourth part of the longest term of imprisonment provided for the offence, or with fine, or with both. **Offering gift or restoration of property in consideration of screening offender:** Whoever gives or causes or offers or agrees to give or cause, any gratification to any person, or to restore or cause to restoration of any property to any person, in consideration of that person's concealing an offence, or of his screening any person form legal punishment for any offence, or his not proceeding against any person for the purpose of bringing him to legal punishment; **if the a capital offence:** shall, if the offence is punishable with death, be punished with imprisonment of either description for a term which may extend to seven years and shall also be liable to fine;	

Which of the following legislation, procedures, measures, agencies exist to control border crossings, export/import and other transfers of NW and Related Materials? Can violators be penalized?	National legal framework		Enforcement: civil/criminal penalties, and measures of implementation, etc		Remarks
	YES	If YES, indicate source document	YES	If YES, indicate source document	
		• The Anti terrorism Act 1997 **11-J Funding Arrangements.—** A person commits an offence if he- (a) enters into or becomes concerned in an arrangement as a result of which money or other property is made available or is to be made available to another, and (b) has reasonable cause to suspect that it will or may be used for the purposes of terrorism.		**if punishable with imprisonment for life or with imprisonment**: and the offence is punishable with imprisonment for life, or with imprisonment which may extend to three years, shall be punished with imprisonment of either description for a term may extend to three years, and shall also be liable to fine; and if the offence is punishable with imprisonment not extending to ten years, shall be punishable with imprisonment of the description provided for the offence for a term which may extend to one-fourth part of the longest term of imprisonment provided for the offence, or with fine, or with or with both	

		• The Explosive Substances Act 1908		**11-N Punishment under section 11-H to 11-K**. . .shall be punishable on conviction with imprisonment for a term not less than six months and not exceeding five years and with fine. **6.Punishment of abettors:** Any person who by the supply of or solicitation for money, the providing of premises, the supply of material, or in any manner whatsoever, procures counsels, aids, abets, or is accessory to, the commission of any offence under this Act shall be punished with the punishment provided for the offence.	
Control of providing transport services	X	• Export Control on goods, technologies, material and equipment related to nuclear and biological weapons and their delivery system Act 2004 **Section 4(4) read with 8 ibid** • National Highway Safety Ordinance 1997 **Section 65 (f)(h)(i)** Establishment of a police for National Highway (f)under take initial action in respect of			Offender can be prosecuted under abetment provision as well.

Which of the following legislation, procedures, measures, agencies exist to control border crossings, export/import and other transfers of NW and Related Materials? Can violators be penalized?	National legal framework		Enforcement: civil/criminal penalties, and measures of implementation, etc		Remarks
	YES	If YES, indicate source document	YES	If YES, indicate source document	
		offences committed on National Highways and then transfer the cases to the concerned Police Station for Investigation. (h) to keep Highways clear from any encroachment and keep a look out for suspicious persons and criminals. (i) take into possession any abandoned property for its disposal under the law Railway Act 1890 **Section 59 (1)** No person shall be entitled to take with him, or to require a railway administration to carry, any dangerous or offensive goods upon a railway			
Control of importation	X	• Import Policy Order 2004 • The Explosives Rule 1940 **Chapter III Part III Importation by Land**. No explosive shall be imported by			Page 3 of the report.

		land save with the previous sanction in each case of the Central Government and under such conditions and restriction as it may impose.			
Extraterritorial applicability	X	• Pakistan Penal Code 1860 **Section 4 read with 108 A** **4. Extension of Code of extraterritorial offences:** The provisions of this Code apply also to any offence committed by—(1) any citizen of Pakistan or any person in the service of Pakistan in any place without and beyond Pakistan (2) and (3) omitted (4) any person on any ship or aircraft registered in Pakistan wherever may be. Explanation.—In this section the word "offence" includes every act committed outside Pakistan which, if committed in Pakistan would be punishable under this Code.	X	**108A. Abetment in Pakistan, of offences outside it**. A person abets an offence within the meaning of this Code who, in Pakistan, abets the commission of any act without and beyond Pakistan which would constitute an offence committed in Pakistan.	Page 4 of the report.
Other					

OP 6,7 and 8 (d)—Control lists Assistance, Information

State: **Pakistan**
Date of Report: 27 October 2004

Can information be provided on the following issues?	Yes		Remarks
Control lists – items (goods/ equipment/materials/technology)	X	1. CWC Schedule I, II and III chemicals 2. Control list of goods and technologies subject to licensing under the Export Control on Goods, Technology, Material and Equipment related to Nuclear and Biological Weapons and their Delivery Systems Act, 2004	Page 8 of the report
Control lists – other	X	Being developed	
Assistance offered	X	Pakistan is in a position to provide assistance in response to requests which should be sent through the Permanent Mission of Pakistan to the United Nations	Page 9 of the report
Assistance requested			
Assistance in place (bilateral/ plurilateral/multilateral)	X	U.S bilateral assistance under EXBS arrangement.	
Information for industry	X	Government maintains close working relationship with industry, particularly with chemical industry and with chambers of commerce	Page 10 of the report
Information for the public			

DOCUMENT NO. 15

UN RESOLUTIONS ON KASHMIR

United Nations Resolutions on Kashmir

- Resolution of the Security Council of April 21, 1948
- Resolution of the Commission of August 13, 1948
- Resolution of the Commission of January 5, 1949
- Resolution of the Security Council of March 14, 1950
- Resolution of the Security Council of March 30, 1951
- Resolution adopted by the Security Council at its 765th meeting on 24 January 1957, concerning the India–Pakistan Question
- Resolution adopted by the Security Council at its meeting on 20 September 1965

Resolution of the Security Council of April 21, 1948

The Security Council,

Having considered the complaint of the Government of India concerning the dispute over the State of Jammu and Kashmir;

Having heard the representation of India in support of that complaint and the reply and counter-complaints of the representative of Pakistan;

Being strongly of the opinion that the early restoration of peace and order in Jammu and Kashmir is essential and that India and Pakistan should do their utmost to bring about a cessation of all fighting;

Noting with satisfaction that both India and Pakistan desire that the question of the accession of Jammu and Kashmir to India or Pakistan should be decided through the democratic method of a free and impartial plebiscite;

Considering that the continuation of the dispute is likely to endanger international peace and security,

Reaffirms the Council's resolution of 17 January;

Resolves that the membership of the Commission established by the resolution of the Council of 20 January 1948, shall be increased to five and shall include in addition to the membership mentioned in that resolution, representatives of . . . and . . . and that if the membership of the Commission has not been completed within ten days from the date of the adoption of this resolution the President of the Council may designate such other Member of Members of the United Nations as are required to complete the membership of five;

Instructs the Commission to proceed at once to the Indian Subcontinent and there place its good offices and mediation at the disposal of the Governments of India and Pakistan with a view to facilitating the taking of the necessary measures, both with respect to the restoration of peace and order and to the holding of a plebiscite, by the two Governments, acting in co-operation with one another and with the Commission, and further instructs the Commission to keep the Council informed of the action taken under the resolution, and to this end,

Recommends to the Governments of India and Pakistan the following measures as those which in the opinion of the Council are appropriate to bring about a cessation of the fighting and to create proper conditions for a free and impartial plebiscite to decide whether the State of Jammu and Kashmir is to accede to India or Pakistan.

A. Restoration of Peace and Order

1. The Government of Pakistan should undertake to use its best endeavors:

   (a) to secure the withdrawal from the State of Jammu and Kashmir of tribesmen and Pakistani nationals not normally resident therein who have entered the State for the purpose of fighting and to prevent any intrusion into the State of such elements and any furnishing of material aid to those fighting in the State;

   (b) To make known to all concerned that the measures indicated in this and the following paragraphs provide full freedom to all subjects of the State, regardless of creed, caste, or party, to express their views and to vote on the question of the accession of the State, and that therefore they should co-operate in the maintenance of peace and order.

2. The Government of India should:

   (a) When it is established to the satisfaction of the Commission set up in accordance with the Council's resolution of 20 January that the tribesmen are withdrawing and that arrangements for the cessation of the fighting have become effective, put into operation in consultation with the Commission a plan for withdrawing their own forces from

Jammu and Kashmir and reducing them progressively to the minimum strength required for the support of the civil power in the maintenance of law and order:

(b) Make known that the withdrawal is taking place in stages and announces the completion of each stage;

(c) When the Indian forces shall have been reduced to the minimum strength mentioned in (a) above, arrange in consultation with the commission for the stationing of the remaining forces to be carried out in accordance with the following principles:

(i) That the presence of troops should not afford any intimidation or appearance of intimidation to the inhabitants of the States;

(ii) That as small a number as possible should be retained in forward areas;

(iii) That any reserve of troops which may be included in the total strength should be located within their present base area.

3. The Government of India should agree that until such time as the Plebiscite Administration referred to below finds it necessary to exercise the powers of direction and supervision over the State forces and police provided for in paragraph 8, they will be held in areas to be agreed upon with the Plebiscite Administrator.

4. After the plan referred to in paragraph 2(a) above has been put into operation, personnel recruited locally in each district should so far as possible be utilized for the re-establishment and maintenance of law and order with due regard to protection of minorities, subject to such additional requirements as may be specified by the Plebiscite Administration referred to in paragraph 7.

5. If these local forces should be found to be inadequate, the Commission, subject to the agreement of both the Government of India and the Government of Pakistan, should arrange for the use of such forces of either Dominion as it deems effective for the purpose of pacification.

B. Plebiscite

6. The Government of India should undertake to ensure that the Government of the State invite the major political groups to designate responsible representatives to share equitably and fully in the conduct of the administration at the Ministerial level, while the plebiscite is being prepared and carried out.

7. The Government of India should undertake that there will be established in Jammu and Kashmir a Plebiscite Administra-tion to hold a plebiscite as soon as possible on the question of the accession of the State to India or Pakistan.

8. The Government of India should undertake that there will be delegated by the State to the Plebiscite Administration such powers as the latter considers necessary for holding a fair and impartial plebiscite including, for that purpose only, the direction and supervision of the State forces and police.

9. The Government of India should, at the request of the Plebiscite Administration, make available from the Indian forces such assistance as the Plebiscite Administration may require for the performance of its functions.

10. (a) The Government of India should agree that a nominee of the Secretary-General of the United Nations will be appointed to be the Plebiscite Administrator;

(b) The Plebiscite Administrator, acting as an officer of the State of Jammu and Kashmir, should have authority to nominate his assistants and other subordinates and to draft regulations governing the plebiscite. Such nominees should be formally appointed and such draft regulations should be formally promulgated by the State of Jammu and Kashmir;

(c) The Government of India should undertake that the Government of Jammu and Kashmir will appoint fully qualified persons nominated by the Plebiscite Administrator to act as special magistrates within the State judicial system to hear cases which in the opinion of the Plebiscite Administrator have a serious bearing on the preparation for and the conduct of a free and impartial plebiscite;

(d) The terms of service of the Administrator should form the subject of a separate negotiation between the Secretary-General of the United Nations and the Government of India. The Administrator should fix the terms of service for his assistants and subordinates;

(e) The Administrator should have the right to communicate directly with the Government of the State and with the Commission of the Security Council and, through the Commission, with the Security Council, with the Governments of India and Pakistan and with their representatives with the Commission. It would be his duty to bring to the notice of any or all of the foregoing (as he in his discretion may decide) any circumstances arising which may tend, in his opinion, to interfere with the freedom of the plebiscite.

11. The Government of India should undertake to prevent, and to give full support to the Administrator and his staff in preventing, any threat, coercion or intimidation, bribery or other undue influence on the voters in the plebiscite, and the Government of India should publicly announce and should cause the Government of the State to announce this undertaking as an international obligation binding on all public authorities and officials in Jammu and Kashmir.

12. The Government of India should themselves and through the Government of the State declare and make known that all subjects of the State of Jammu and Kashmir, regardless of creed, caste or party, will be safe and free in expressing their views and in voting on the question of the accession of the State and that there will be freedom of the press, speech and assembly and freedom of travel in the State, including freedom of lawful entry and exit.

13. The Government of India should use and should ensure that the Government of the State also use their best endeavors to effect the withdrawal from the State of all Indian nationals other than those who are normally resident therein or who on or since 15 August 1947 have entered it for a lawful purpose.

14. The Government of India should ensure that the Government of the State release all political prisoners and take all possible steps so that:

(a) All citizens of the State who have left it on account of disturbances are invited, and are free, to return to their homes and to exercise their rights as such citizens;

(b) There is no victimization;

(c) Minorities in all parts of the State are accorded adequate protection.

15. The Commission of the Security Council should at the end of the plebiscite certify to the Council whether the plebiscite has or has not been really free and impartial.

C. General Provisions

16. The Governments of India and Pakistan should each be invited to nominate a representative to be attached to the Commission for such assistance as it may require in the performance of its task.

17. The commission should establish in Jammu and Kashmir such observers as it may require of any of the proceedings in pursuance of the measures indicated in the foregoing paragraphs.

18. The Security Council Commission should carry out the tasks assigned to it herein.

Resolution of the Commission of August 13, 1948

The United Nations Commission for India and Pakistan, having given careful consideration to the points of view expressed by the representatives of India and Pakistan regarding the situation in the State of Jammu and Kashmir, and

Being of the opinion that the prompt cessation of hostilities and the correction of conditions the continuance of which is likely to endanger international peace and security are essential to implementation of its endeavors to assist the Governments of India and Pakistan in effecting a final settlement of the situation,

Resolves to submit simultaneously to the Governments of India and Pakistan the following proposal:

Part I

Cease-fire Order

A. The Governments of India and Pakistan agree that their respective High Commands will issue separately and simultaneously a cease-fire order to apply to all forces under their control in the State of Jammu and Kashmir as of the earliest practicable date or dates to be mutually agreed upon within four days after these proposals have been accepted by both Governments.

B. The High Commands of the Indian and Pakistani forces agree to refrain from taking any measures that might augment the military potential of the forces under their control in the State of Jammu and Kashmir.(For the purpose of these proposals forces under their control shall be considered to include all forces, organized and unorganized, fighting or participating in hostilities on their respective sides.)

C. The Commanders-in-Chief of the forces of India and Pakistan shall promptly confer regarding any necessary local changes in present dispositions which may facilitate the cease-fire.

D. In its discretion and as the Commission may find practicable, the Commission will appoint military observers who, under the authority of the Commission and with the co-operation of both Commands, will supervise the observance of the cease-fire order.

E. The Government of India and the Government of Pakistan agree to appeal to their respective peoples to assist in creating and maintaining an atmosphere favourable to the promotion of further negotiations.

Part II

Truce Agreement

Simultaneously with the acceptance of the proposal for the immediate cessation of hostilities as outlined in Part I, both Governments accept the following principles as a basis for the formulation of a truce agreement, the details of which shall be worked out in discussion between their representatives and the Commission.

A

1. As the presence of troops of Pakistan in the territory of the State of Jammu and Kashmir constitutes a material change in the situation since it was represented by the Government of Pakistan before the Security Council, the Government of Pakistan agrees to withdraw its troops from that State.

2. The Government of Pakistan will use its best endeavour to secure the withdrawal from the State of Jammu and Kashmir of tribesmen and Pakistani nationals not normally resident therein who have entered the State for the purpose of fighting.

3. Pending a final solution, the territory evacuated by the Pakistani troops will be administered by the local authorities under the surveillance of the Commission.

B

1. When the Commission shall have notified the Government of India that the tribesmen and Pakistani nationals referred to in Part II, A, 2 hereof have withdrawn, thereby terminating the situation which was represented by the Government of India to the Security Council as having occasioned the presence of Indian forces in the State of Jammu and Kashmir, and further, that the Pakistani forces are being withdrawn from the State of Jammu and Kashmir, the Government of India agrees to begin to withdraw the bulk of its forces from that State in stages to be agreed upon with the Commission.

2. Pending the acceptance of the conditions for a final settlement of the situation in the State of Jammu and Kashmir, the Indian Government will maintain within the lines existing at the moment of the cease-fire the minimum strength of its forces which in agreement with the Commission are considered necessary to assist local authorities in the observance of law and order. The Commission will have observers stationed where it deems necessary.

3. The Government of India will undertake to ensure that the Government of the State of Jammu and Kashmir will take all measures within its power to make it publicly known that peace, law and order will be safeguarded and that all human and political rights will be guaranteed.

C

1. Upon signature, the full text of the truce agreement or a communiqué containing the principles thereof as agreed upon between the two Governments and the Commission will be made public.

Part III

The Government of India and the Government of Pakistan reaffirm their wish that the future status of the State of Jammu and Kashmir shall be determined in accordance with the will of the people and to that end, upon acceptance of the truce agreement, both Governments agree to enter into consultations with the Commission to determine fair and equitable conditions whereby such free expression will be assured.

Resolution of the Commission of January 5, 1949

The United Nations Commission for India and Pakistan,

Having received from the Governments of India and Pakistan, in communications dated 23 December and 25 December 1948, respectively, their acceptance of the following principles which are supplementary to the Commission's Resolution of 13 August 1948:

1. The question of the accession of the State of Jammu and Kashmir to India or Pakistan will be decided through the democratic method of a free and impartial plebiscite;

2. A plebiscite will be held when it shall be found by the Commission that the cease-fire and truce arrangements set forth in Parts I and II of the Commission's resolution of 13 August 1948 have been carried out and arrangements for the plebiscite have been completed;

3. (a) The Secretary-General of the United Nations will, in agreement with the Commission, nominate a Plebiscite Administrator who shall be a personality of high international standing and commanding general confidence. He will be formally appointed to office by the Government of Jammu and Kashmir.

(b) The Plebiscite Administrator shall derive from the State of Jammu and Kashmir the powers he considers necessary for organizing and conducting the plebiscite and for ensuring the freedom and impartiality of the plebiscite.

(c) The Plebiscite Administrator shall have authority to appoint such staff of assistants and observes as he may require.

4. (a) After implementation of Parts I and II of the Commission's resolution of 13 August 1948, and when the Commission is satisfied that peaceful conditions have been restored in the State, the Commission and the Plebiscite Administrator will determine, in consultation with the Government of India, the final disposal of Indian and State armed forces, such disposal to be with due regard to the security of the State and the freedom of the plebiscite.

(b) As regards the territory referred to in A.2 of Part II of the resolution of 13 August, final disposal of the armed forces in that territory will be determined by the Commission and the Plebiscite Administrator in consultation with the local authorities.

5. All civil and military authorities within the State and the principal political elements of the State will be required to co-operate with the Plebiscite Administrator in the preparation for the holding of the plebiscite.

6. (a) All citizens of the State who have left it on account of the disturbances will be invited and be free to return and to exercise all their rights as such citizens. For the purpose of facilitating repatriation there shall be appointed two Commissions, one composed of nominees of India and the other of nominees of Pakistan. The Commission shall operate under the direction of the Plebiscite Administrator. The Governments of India and Pakistan and all authorities within the State of Jammu and Kashmir will collaborate with the Plebiscite Administrator in putting this provision into effect.

(b) All person (other than citizens of the State) who on or since 15 August 1947 have entered it for other than lawful purpose, shall be required to leave the State.

7. All authorities within the State of Jammu and Kashmir will undertake to ensure, in collaboration with the Plebiscite Administrator, that:

(a) There is no threat, coercion or intimidation, bribery or other undue influence on the voters in the plebiscite;

(b) No restrictions are placed on legitimate political activity throughout the State. All subjects of the State, regardless of creed, caste or party, shall be safe and free in expressing their views and in voting on the question of the accession of the State to India or Pakistan. There shall be freedom of the press, speech and assembly and freedom of travel in the State, including freedom of lawful entry and exit;

(c) All political prisoners are released;

(d) Minorities in all parts of the State are accorded adequate protection; and

(e) There is no victimization.

8. The Plebiscite Administrator may refer to the United Nations Commission for India and Pakistan problems on which he may require assistance, and the Commission may in its discretion call upon the Plebiscite Administrator to carry out on its behalf any of the responsibilities with which it has been entrusted;

9. At the conclusion of the plebiscite, the Plebiscite Administrator shall report the result thereof to the Commission and to the Government of

Jammu and Kashmir. The Commission shall then certify to the Security Council whether the plebiscite has or has not been free and impartial;

10. Upon the signature of the truce agreement the details of the foregoing proposals will be elaborated in the consultations envisaged in Part III of the Commission's resolution of 13 August 1948. The Plebiscite Administrator will be fully associated in these consultations;

Commends the Governments of India and Pakistan for their prompt action in ordering a cease-fire to take effect from one minute before midnight of 1 January 1949, pursuant to the agreement arrived at as provided for by the Commission's Resolution of 13 August 1948; and

Resolves to return in the immediate future to the Sub-continent to discharge the responsibilities imposed upon it by the Resolution of 13 August 1948 and by the foregoing principles.

Resolution of the Security Council of March 14, 1950

The Security Council,

Having received and noted the reports of the United Nations Commission for India and Pakistan, established by the resolutions of 20 January and 21 April 1948

Having also received and noted the report of General A. G. L. McNaughton on the outcome of his discussion with the representatives of India and Pakistan which were initiated in pursuance of the decision taken by the Security Council on 17 December 1949

Commending the Governments of India and Pakistan for their statesman-like action in reaching the agreements embodied in the United Nations Commission's resolutions of 13 August 1948 and 5 January 1949 for a cease-fire, for the demilitarization of the State of Jammu and Kashmir and for the determination of its final disposition in accordance with the will of the people through the democratic method of a free and impartial plebiscite and commending the parties in particular for their action in partially implementing these resolutions by

- The Cessation of hostilities affected 1 January 1949;
- The establishment of a cease-fire line on 27 July, and
- The agreement that Fleet Admiral Chester W. Nimitz shall be Plebiscite Administrator,

Considering that the resolution of the outstanding difficulties should be based upon the substantial measure of agreement on fundamental principles already reached, and that steps should be taken forthwith for the demilitarization of the State and for the expeditious determination of its future in accordance with the freely expressed will of the inhabitants,

1. Calls upon the Governments of India and Pakistan to make immediate arrangements without prejudice to their rights or claims and with due regard to the requirements of law and order, to prepare and execute within a period of five months from the date of this resolution a programmer of demilitarization on the basis of the principles of paragraph 2 of General McNaughton's proposal or of such modifications of those principles as may be mutually agreed;

2. Decides to appoint a United Nations Representative for the following purposes who shall have authority to perform his functions in such place or places as he may deem appropriate:

(a) To assist in the preparation and to supervise the implementation of the programme of demilitarization referred to above and to interpret the agreements reached by the parties for demilitarization,

(b) To place himself at the disposal of the Governments of India and Pakistan and to place before these Governments or the Security Council any suggestions which, in his opinion, are likely to contribute to the expeditious and enduring solution of the dispute which has arisen between the two Governments in regard to the State of Jammu and Kashmir?

(c) To exercise all of the powers and responsibilities devolving upon the United Nations Commission by reason of existing resolutions of the Security Council and by reason of the agreement of the parties embodied in the resolutions of the United Nations Commission of 13 August 1948 and 5 January 1949,

(d) To arrange at the appropriate stage of demilitarization for the assumption by the Plebiscite Administrator of the functions assigned to the latter under agreements made between the parties,

(e) To report to the Security Council as he may consider necessary submitting his conclusions and any recommendations which he may desire to make;

3. Requests the two Governments to take all necessary precautions to ensure that their agreements regarding the cease-fire shall continue to be faithfully observed, and calls upon them to take all possible measures to ensure the creation and maintenance of an atmosphere favorable to the promotion of further negotiations;

4. Extends its best thanks to the members of the United Nations Commission for India and Pakistan and to General A. G. L. McNaughton for their arduous and fruitful labours;

5. Agrees that the United Nations Commission for India and Pakistan shall be terminated, and decides that this shall take place one month after both parties have informed the United Nations Representative of their acceptance of the transfer to him of the powers and responsibilities of the United Nations Commission referred to in paragraph 2 (c) above.

Resolution of the Security Council of March 30, 1951

Having received and noted the report of Sir Owen Dixon, the United Nations Representative for India and Pakistan, on his mission initiated by the Security Council resolution of 14 March 1950;

Observing that the Governments of India and Pakistan have accepted the provisions of the United Nations Commission for India and Pakistan resolutions of 13 August 1948 and 5 January 1949 and of the Security Council resolution of 14 March 1950, and have re-affirmed their desire that the future of the State of Jammu and Kashmir shall be decided through the democratic method of a free and impartial plebiscite conducted under the auspices of the United Nations;

Observing that on 27 October 1950 the General Council of the "All Jammu and Kashmir National Conference" adopted a resolution recommending the convening of a Constituent Assembly for the purpose of determining the "future shape and affiliations of the State of Jammu and Kashmir"; observing further from statements of responsible authorities that action is proposed to convene such a Constituent Assembly and that the area from which such a Constituent Assembly would be elected is only a part of the whole territory of Jammu and Kashmir;

Reminding the Governments and Authorities concerned of the principle embodied in the Security Council resolutions of 21 April 1948, 3 June 1948 and 14 March 1950 and the United Nations Commission for India and Pakistan resolutions of 13 August 1948 and 5 January 1949, that the final disposition of the State of Jammu and Kashmir will be made in accordance with the will of the people expressed through the democratic method of a free and impartial plebiscite conducted under the auspices of the United Nations; Affirming that the convening of a Constituent Assembly as recommended by the General Council of the "All Jammu and Kashmir National Conference," and any action that Assembly might attempt to take to determine the future shape and affiliation of the entire State or any part thereof would not constitute a disposition of the State in accordance with the above principle;

Declaring its belief that it is the duty of the Security Council in carrying out its primary responsibility for the maintenance of international peace and security to aid the parties to reach an amicable solution of the Kashmir dispute and that a prompt settlement of this dispute is of vital importance to the maintenance of international peace and security;

Observing from Sir Owen Dixon's report that the main points of difference preventing agreement between the parties were:

(a) The procedure for and the extent of demilitarization of the State preparatory to the holding of a plebiscite, and

(b) The degree of control over the exercise of the functions of government in the State necessary to ensure a free and fair plebiscite;

The Security Council,

1. Accepts, in compliance with his request, Sir Owen Dixon's resignation and expresses its gratitude to Sir Owen for the great ability and devotion with which he carried out his mission;

2. Decides to appoint a United Nations Representative for India and Pakistan in succession to Sir Owen Dixon;

3. Instructs the United Nations Representative to proceed to the Sub-continent and , after consulation with the Governments of India and Pakistan, to effect the demilitarization of the State of Jammu and Kashmir on the basis of the United Nations Commission for India and Pakistan resolutions of 13 August 1948 and 5 January 1949;

4. Calls upon the parties to co-operate with the United Nations Representative to the fullest degree in effecting the demilitarization of the State of Jammu and Kashmir;

5. Instructs the United Nations Representative to report to the Security Council within three months from the date of his arrival on the Sub-continent. If, at the time of this report, he has not effected demilitarization in accordance with paragraph 3 above, or obtained the agreement of the parties to a plan for effecting such demilitarization, the United Nations Representative shall report to the Security Council those points of difference between the parties in regard to the interpretation and execution of the agreed resolutions of 13 August 1948 and 5 January 1949 which he considers must be resolved to enable such demilitarization to be carried out;

6. Calls upon the parties, in the event of their discussions with the United Nations Representative failing in his opinion to result in full agreement, to accept arbitration upon all outstanding points of difference reported by the United Nations Representative in accordance with paragraph 5 above; such arbitration to be carried out by an Arbitrator, or a panel of Arbitrators, to be appointed by the President of the International Court of Justice after consultation with the parties;

7. Decides that the Military Observer group shall continue to supervise the cease-fire in the State;

8. Requests the Governments of India and Pakistan to ensure that their agreement regarding the cease-fire shall continue to be faithfully observed and calls upon them to take all possible measures to ensure the creation and maintenance of an atmosphere favourable to the promotion of further negotiations and to refrain from any action likely to prejudice a just and peaceful settlement;

9. Requests the Secretary-General to provide the United Nations Representative for India and Pakistan with such services and facilities as may be necessary in carrying out the terms of this resolution.

Resolution Adopted by the Security Council at its 765th Meeting on 24 January 1957, Concerning the India–Pakistan Question:

The resolution is a reaffirmation of the Security Council resolution of 30 March 1951 that the convening of a Constituent Assembly and any action taken by it would not constitute disposition of the State in accordance with the will of the people of Kashmir expressed through the democratic method of a free and impartial plebiscite conducted under the auspices of the United Nations. It was introduced by Australia, Colombia, Cuba, the United Kingdom and the U.S.A., and supported by 10 members of the Council, the Soviet Union abstaining.

The Security Council,

Having heard statements from representatives of the Governments of India and Pakistan concerning the dispute over the State of Jammu and Kashmir,

Reminding the Governments and authorities concerned of the principle embodied in its resolutions of 21 April 1948 (S/726), 3 June 1948 , 14 March 1950 (S/1469) and 30 March 1951 (S/2017/Rev. 1), and the United Nations Commission for India and Pakistan resolutions of 13 August 1948 (S/1100, para. 75) and 5 January 1949 (S/1196, para. 15), that the final disposition of that State of Jammu and Kashmir will be made in accordance with the will of the people expressed through the democratic method of a free and impartial plebiscite conducted under the auspices of the United Nations,

1. Reaffirms the affirmation in its resolution of 30 March 1951 and declares that the convening of a Constituent Assembly as recommended by the General Council of the 'All Jammu and Kashmir National Conference' and any action that Assembly may have taken or might attempt to take to determine the future shape and affiliation of the entire State or any part thereof, or action by the parties concerned in support of any such action by the Assembly, would not constitute a disposition of the State in accordance with the above principles;

2. Decides to continue its consideration of the dispute.

24 January 1957

Resolution adopted by the Security Council at its meeting on 20 September 1965 :

The Security Council;

1. demands that a cease-fire should take effect on Wednesday, Sept. 22, 1965, at 0700 hours GMT, and calls upon both Governments to issue orders for a cease-fire at that moment and a subsequent withdrawal of all armed personnel back to the positions held by them before Aug. 5, 1965;

2. Requests the Secretary-General to provide the necessary assistance to ensure supervision of the cease-fire and withdrawal of all armed personnel;

3. calls on all States to refrain from any action which might aggravate the situation in the area;

4. Decides to consider, as soon as operative paragraph 1 of the Council's resolution of Sept. 6 has been implemented, what steps could be taken to assist towards a settlement of the political problem underlying the present conflict, and in the meantime calls on the two Governments to utilize all peaceful means, including those listed in Article 33 of the Charter, to this end;

5. Requests the Secretary-General to exert every possible effort to give effect to this resolution, to seek a peaceful solution, and to report to the Security Council thereon.

DOCUMENT NO. 16

PAKISTAN-U.S. RELATIONS

CRS Reports
IB94041

September 5, 2002

K. Alan Kronstadt
Foreign Affairs, Defense, and Trade Division

Summary

The major areas of U.S. concern in Pakistan include nuclear nonproliferation; counterterrorism; regional stability; democratization and human rights; and economic reform and development. A potential Pakistan-India nuclear arms race, fueled by rivalry over Kashmir, continues to be the focus of U.S. nonproliferation efforts in South Asia and a major issue in U.S. relations with both countries. This attention intensified following nuclear tests by both India and Pakistan in May 1998. South Asia is viewed by some observers as a likely prospect for use of such weapons. India has developed short- and intermediate-range missiles, and Pakistan has acquired short-range missiles from China and medium-range missiles from North Korea. India and Pakistan have fought three wars since 1947.

U.S.-Pakistan cooperation began in the mid-1950s as a security arrangement based on U.S. concern over Soviet expansion and Pakistan's fear of neighboring India. Cooperation peaked during the 1979–89 Soviet occupation of Afghanistan. U.S.-Pakistan ties weakened following the October 1990 cutoff of U.S. aid and arms sales, which were suspended by President Bush under Section 620E(e) of the Foreign Assistance Act (FAA) (the so-called "Pressler amendment"). Further U.S. sanctions were imposed on Pakistan (and India) as a result of their 1998 nuclear tests. The seesaw Pakistan-U.S. relationship has been on the upswing following Pakistan's enlistment as a frontline state in the U.S.-led war on terrorism resulting from the September 2001 attacks on New York and Washington. Nuclear sanctions on Pakistan and India have been waived; Congress also has given the President authority to waive, for 2 years, sanctions imposed on Pakistan following its 1999 military coup.

Both Congress and the Administration consider a stable, democratic, economically thriving Pakistan as key to U.S. interests in South, Central, and West Asia. Although ruled by military regimes for half of its existence, between 1988 and 1999 Pakistan had democratic governments as a result of national elections in 1988, 1990, 1993, and 1997. During that time, Benazir Bhutto, leader of the Pakistan People's Party, and Nawaz Sharif, leader of the Pakistan Muslim League, each served twice as prime minister. Neither leader served a full term, being dismissed by the president under constitutional provisions that have been used to dismiss four governments since 1985.

In October 1999, the government of Prime Minister Nawaz Sharif was ousted in a bloodless coup led by Chief of Army Staff Gen. Pervez Musharraf, who suspended the parliament and declared himself chief executive. In June 2001, General Musharraf assumed the title of President, a move ostensibly legitimized by an April 2002 referendum. The United States has strongly urged the Pakistan military government to restore the country to civilian democratic rule. President Musharraf has scheduled national elections for October 10, 2002. The Musharraf government has begun to address Pakistan's many pressing and longstanding problems, including the beleaguered economy, corruption, terrorism, and poor governance. Pakistan will receive well over one billion dollars in U.S. assistance and several billion dollars from international organizations to help strengthen the country as a key member of the U.S.-led anti-terrorism coalition.

Most Recent Developments

Pakistani President Musharraf will travel to New York September 7–13 where he will meet with President Bush and address the UN General Assembly. There are reports that Musharraf may use the opportunity to introduce a significantly new Pakistani approach to interstate relations with India and the dispute over Kashmir.

Tensions between Pakistan and India have stabilized at moderate, but still dangerous levels over the summer, as both the U.S. and Indian governments acknowledged that Musharraf has been partly successful in curtailing the cross-border movement of militants in the Kashmir region. However, insistent that infiltration is ongoing, the Indian government has maintained its military mobilization along the shared border, and a virulent war of words between the two countries has continued since the current crisis began some 9 months ago.

U.S. military commanders have suggested that as many as 1,000 Al Qaeda fighters may be active within the borders of Pakistan, and that expanding anti-terror operations to states neighboring Afghanistan may be necessary.

Anti-Christian violence in Pakistan surged during August, with grenade and machine gun attacks on two Christian schools causing many civilian casualties. The attacks are widely viewed as expressions of anti-Western sentiment in the face of President Musharraf's participation in the U.S.-led anti-terror coalition.

On August 21, President Musharraf announced major changes to the country's constitution. Many of these unilaterally imposed changes are meant to greatly augment Musharraf's already considerable powers and institutionalize a permanent governing role for the military. The United States has expressed concern that such changes will make the path to restore democracy in Pakistan more difficult, and has urged Musharraf to ensure that upcoming October elections are free and fair.

Background and Analysis

Historical Background

The long and checkered U.S.-Pakistan relationship has its roots in the Cold War and South Asia regional politics of the 1950s. U.S. concern about Soviet expansion and Pakistan's desire for security assistance against a perceived threat from India prompted the two countries to negotiate a mutual defense assistance agreement in May 1954. By late 1955, Pakistan had further aligned itself with the West by joining two regional defense pacts, the South East Asia Treaty Organization (SEATO) and the Central Treaty Organization (CENTO). As a result of these alliances and a 1959 U.S.-Pakistan cooperation agreement, Pakistan received more than $700 million in military grant aid from 1955 to 1965. U.S. economic aid to Pakistan between 1951 and 1982 totaled more than $5 billion.

Differing expectations of the security relationship have long bedeviled bilateral ties. During the Indo-Pakistani wars of 1965 and 1971, the United States suspended military assistance to both sides, resulting in a cooling of the U.S.-Pakistan relationship. In the mid-1970s, new strains arose over Pakistan's apparent efforts to respond to India's 1974 underground test of a nuclear device by seeking its own capability to build a nuclear bomb. Limited U.S. military aid was resumed in 1975, but it was suspended again by the Carter Administration in April 1979 in response to Pakistan's covert construction of a uranium enrichment facility.

Following the Soviet invasion of Afghanistan in December 1979, Pakistan was again viewed as a frontline state in the effort to block Soviet expansionism. In September 1981, the Reagan Administration negotiated a $3.2 billion, 5-year economic and military aid package with Islamabad. Pakistan became a funnel for arms supplies to the Afghan resistance, as well as a camp for three million Afghan refugees.

Despite the renewal of U.S. aid and close security ties, many in Congress remained concerned about Pakistan's nuclear program. Concern was based in part on evidence of U.S. export control violations that suggested a crash Pakistani program to acquire a nuclear weapons capability. In 1985, Section 620E(e) (the "Pressler amendment") was added to the FAA, requiring the President to certify to Congress that Pakistan does not possess a nuclear explosive device during the fiscal year for which aid is to be provided. This amendment represented a compromise between those in Congress who thought that aid to Pakistan should be cut off because of evidence that it was continuing to develop its nuclear option and those who favored continued support for Pakistan's role in opposing Soviet occupation of Afghanistan. A $4 billion, 6-year aid package for Pakistan was signed in 1986.

With Soviet withdrawal from Afghanistan beginning in May 1988, Pakistan's nuclear activities again came under closer U.S. scrutiny. In October 1990, President Bush suspended aid to Pakistan. Under the provisions of the Pressler amendment, most economic and all military aid to Pakistan was stopped and deliveries of major military equipment suspended. Narcotics assistance of $3–5 million annually was exempted from the aid cutoff. In 1992, Congress partially relaxed the scope of the aid cutoff to allow for P.L. 480 food assistance and continuing support for nongovernmental organizations (NGOs).

One of the most serious results of the aid cutoff for Pakistan was the nondelivery of some 71 F-16 fighter aircraft ordered in 1989. In December 1998, the United States agreed to pay Pakistan $324.6 million from the Judgment Fund of the U.S. Treasury—a fund used to settle legal disputes that involve the U.S. government—as well as provide Pakistan with $140 million in goods, including agricultural commodities.

Pakistan-India Rivalry

Three wars—in 1947–48, 1965, and 1971—and a constant state of military preparedness on both sides of the border have marked the half-century of bitter rivalry between India and Pakistan. The acrimonious nature of the partition of British India into two successor states in 1947 and the continuing dispute over Kashmir have been major sources of tension. Both Pakistan and India have built large defense establishments at the cost of economic and social development. The Kashmir problem is rooted in claims by both countries to the former princely state, divided since 1948 by a military line of control into the Indian state of Jammu and Kashmir and Pakistan-controlled (Free) Kashmir. India blames Pakistan for supporting a separatist rebellion raging in the Muslim-dominated Kashmir Valley that has claimed 30,000 lives since 1990. Pakistan admits only to lending moral and political support to the rebellion, while accusing India of creating dissension in Pakistan's Sindh province. (For further discussion see below.)

The China Factor

India and China fought a brief border war in 1962, and an oftentimes tense border dispute remains unresolved. A strategic rivalry also exists between these two large nations. Pakistan and China, on the other hand, have enjoyed a generally close and mutually beneficial relationship over recent decades. Pakistan served as a link between Beijing and Washington in 1971, as well as a bridge to the Muslim world for China during the 1980s. China's continuing role as a major arms supplier for Pakistan began in the 1960s, and included helping to build a number of arms factories in Pakistan, as well as supplying complete weapons systems. In September 1990, China agreed to supply Pakistan with components for M-11 surface-to-surface missiles, which brought warnings from the United States. Although it is not a member of the Missile Technology Control Regime (MTCR), China agreed to abide by the restrictions of the regime. In August 1993, the United States determined that China had transferred to Pakistan prohibited missile technology and imposed trade sanctions on one Pakistan and 11 Chinese entities (government ministries and aerospace companies) for 2 years. The U.S. intelligence community reportedly has evidence of PRC provision of complete M-11 ballistic missiles to Pakistan. In February 1996, leaked U.S. intelligence reports alleged that China in 1995 sold ring magnets to Pakistan that could be used in enriching uranium for nuclear weapons. Pakistan denied the reports.

On November 21, 2000, the United States imposed 2-year sanctions on the Pakistan Ministry of Defense and Pakistan's Space and Upper Atmosphere Research Organization, as well as on Iranian entities, as a result of past Chinese assistance to Pakistani and Iranian missile programs. In September 2001, the U.S. State Department again imposed 2-year sanctions on a PRC company and Pakistan's National Development Complex. The PRC company reportedly delivered 12 shipments of components for Pakistan's Shaheen missiles in early 2001. (For background and updates on China-Pakistan technology transfer, see CRS Issue Brief IB92056, *Chinese Proliferation of Weapons of Mass Destruction: Current Policy Issues*.)

Pakistan Political Setting

On August 21, 2002, President Musharraf's government announced sweeping changes in the Pakistani constitution, changes that would provide the office of President with amounts of power previously unseen in the country's constitutional history. These amendments would include provisions for Presidential dissolution of the National Assembly, and appointment of the Army Chief and provincial governors, among others. The Supreme Court recently upheld a provision requiring all candidates for National Assembly seats to be college graduates. This amendment disqualifies more than 98% of all Pakistanis (and more than half of the politicians who served in the last parliament) from holding national office, and will make it difficult for opposition parties to field candidates for the scheduled October elections.

While the Musharraf government states that such changes will "lay the foundation for real democracy in Pakistan," critics contend that such amendments will make a "near puppet" of the Prime Minister and almost certainly "ring the death knell of democracy in Pakistan." All major political parties, including those of a pro-government bent, have registered their opposition to the amendments. The country's two main political parties have recently called on Musharraf to resign and allow a caretaker government to oversee parliamentary elections scheduled for next October.

On April 30, 2002, Pakistanis went to the polls in a national referendum to extend President Musharraf's term by 5 years. The referendum question was, "For the survival of the local government system, establishment of democracy, continuity of reforms . . . would you like to elect President General Pervez Musharraf as president of Pakistan for five years?" The president won 98% of the vote from an officially reported 50% voter turnout. The Alliance for the Restoration of Democracy, a coalition of political parties that are opposed to the election, claimed that turnout was closer to 5%. These parties denounced the referendum as fraudulent and urged Pakistanis to boycott the poll. Post-referendum protestations were such that within weeks President Musharraf publically acknowledged and apologized for irregularities in the voting.

In a post-October governmental structure likely to be instituted by Musharraf, the Prime Minister is not to have control over Pakistan's National Security Council—an institution that is to be dominated by the President and the military. As envisaged, the Prime Minister would not cast a binding vote. The current National Security Council has a wide range of authority and advises the president on issues relating to national security, sovereignty, Islamic ideology, and the integrity and solidarity of the country.

There is also concern about the legitimacy of the scheduled October 2002 elections. President Musharraf has refused to allow former prime ministers and leading politicians Benazir Bhutto and Nawaz Sharif to participate in the elections, issuing decrees that make illegal their candidacy and threatening both with imprisonment should either return to Pakistan. Senior government sources have also stated that Pakistan's political parties will face crucial reforms under the Political Parties Act, which could see a purge of their senior leaders. To replace them, President Musharraf apparently plans to groom a new generation of political leaders under his patronage.

At the same time, there has there has been an easing of pressure on Islamic fundamentalist groups in Pakistan. The leader of the pro-Taliban

Jamiat-e-Ulema Islam was released from prison, while the head of the banned terrorist organization Jaish-e-Mohammad was released from prison and placed under house arrest. On Pakistan's national day, the Jamaat-i-Islami was allowed to hold a public gathering in Rawalpindi, seat of the army's General Headquarters. Leaders and activists of the moderate and secular Alliance for the Restoration of Democracy were arrested in Lahore when they tried to exercise their right of association.

Changes have also taken place in Pakistan's Kashmir policy. In an effort to assuage international concerns, President Musharraf has moved away from direct support of the banned Jaish-e-Mohammed and Lashkar-e-Taiba groups. Instead, it is expected that he will call for the people of Kashmir to determine their own future without the support of the Pakistan-based Islamic jihadi network. A recent meeting in Azad Kashmir reflects Pakistan's changing Kashmir policy: the meeting was attended by the All-Parties Hurriyat Conference (an umbrella organization of 23 separatist groups), leading Kashmiri intellectuals, and three Pakistani brigadiers. Participants concluded that the policies of Kashmir fighters should represent Kashmiri interests rather than those of Pakistan.

Background. Military regimes have ruled Pakistan for half of its 55 years, interspersed with periods of generally weak civilian governance. After 1988, Pakistan had democratically elected governments, and the army appeared to have moved from its traditional role of power wielder or king-maker to one of power broker or referee. During the past decade, Benazir Bhutto and Nawaz Sharif each served twice as prime minister. Bhutto was elected prime minister in October 1988, following the death of military ruler Mohammad Zia-ul Haq in a plane crash. General Zia had led a coup in 1977 deposing Bhutto's father, Prime Minister Zulfiqar Ali Bhutto, who was later executed. Despite the restoration of democratic process to Pakistan in 1988, the succeeding years were marred by political instability, economic problems, and ethnic and sectarian violence. In August 1990, President Ishaq Khan dismissed Bhutto for alleged corruption and inability to maintain law and order. The president's power to dismiss the prime minister derived from Eighth Amendment provisions of the Pakistan constitution, which dated from the era of Zia's presidency.

Elections held in October 1990 brought to power Nawaz Sharif, who himself was ousted in 1993 under the Eighth Amendment provisions. The 1993 elections returned Bhutto and the PPP to power. The new Bhutto government faced serious economic problems and, according to some observers, performance also was hampered by the reemergence of Bhutto's husband, Asif Ali Zardari, in a decisionmaking role. In November 1996, President Farooq Leghari dismissed the Bhutto government for "corruption, nepotism, and violation of rules in the administration of the affairs of the Government," and scheduled new elections for February 1997.

Nawaz Sharif's PML won a landslide victory in the February 1997 parliamentary elections, which, despite low voter turnout, were judged by international observers to be generally free and fair. Sharif moved quickly to consolidate his power by curtailing the powers of the President and the judiciary. In April 1997, the Parliament passed the Thirteenth Amendment to the constitution, deleting the President's former Eighth Amendment powers to dismiss the government and to appoint armed forces chiefs and provincial governors. The new amendment was passed unanimously by both houses of parliament and signed by President Leghari. As the result of a power struggle, Sharif replaced the Supreme Court Chief Justice in November; Leghari resigned; and Sharif chose Mohammad Rafiq Tarar as president. As a result of these developments and the PML control of the Parliament, Nawaz Sharif emerged as one of Pakistan's strongest elected leaders since independence. Critics accused him of further consolidating his power by intimidating the opposition and the press. In April 1999, a two-judge Bench of the Lahore High Court convicted former Prime Minister Benazir Bhutto and her husband of corruption and sentenced them each to 5 years in prison, fined them $8.6 million, and disqualified them from holding public office. Bhutto was out of the country at the time. Some analysts believe that Sharif acted out "political vindictiveness." In April 2001, the Pakistan Supreme Court ruled that former Prime Minister Benazir Bhutto's 1999 conviction for corruption was biased and ordered a retrial.

Pakistan-U.S. Relations and Bilateral Issues

U.S. policy interests in Pakistan encompass a wide range of issues, including nuclear weapons and missile proliferation; South Asian regional stability; democratization and human rights; economic reform and market opening; and efforts to counter terrorism and narcotics. These concerns have been affected by several developments in recent years, including: 1) the cutoff of U.S. aid to Pakistan in 1990, 1998, and 1999 over nuclear and democracy issues; 2) India and Pakistan's worsening relationship over Kashmir since 1990, and their continuing nuclear standoff; 3) Pakistan's see-saw attempts to develop a stable democratic government and strong economy in the post-Cold War era; and, most recently, 4) the terrorist attacks of September 11, 2001 on New York and Washington.

The Bush Administration has identified exiled Saudi dissident Osama bin Laden, who had long been harbored by the Taliban government in Afghanistan, as the prime suspect in the terrorist attacks on the United States. On September 13, President Musharraf—under strong U.S. diplomatic pressure—offered President Bush Pakistan's "unstinted cooperation in the fight against terrorism." Because of its shared border with Afghanistan and former close ties with the Taliban, Pakistan is considered key to U.S.-led efforts to combat terrorism in the region. The Taliban and bin Laden enjoy strong support among a substantial percentage of the Pakistan population, who share not only conservative Islamic views but also ethnic and cultural ties with Afghanistan. A major issue facing the Administration is how to make use of Pakistan's support—including for military operations in Afghanistan—without seriously destabilizing an already fragile state that has nuclear weapons and ballistic missiles.

In an effort to shore up the Musharraf government, most sanctions relating to Pakistan's (and India's) 1998 nuclear tests and Pakistan's 1999 military coup were waived in September and October of last year. On October 29, 2001, a State Department spokesman pledged well over one billion dollars in U.S. assistance for Pakistan and several billion dollars from international organizations to help strengthen it as a key member of the U.S.-led anti-terrorism coalition. Direct assistance programs will include aid for health, education, food, democracy promotion, child labor elimination, counter-narcotics, border security and law enforcement, as well as trade preference benefits. The United States also will support grant, loan, and debt rescheduling programs for Pakistan by the various international financial institutions, including the World Bank, International Monetary Fund, and Asian Development Bank. In addition, Pakistan has received promises of substantial aid, debt relief, and trade concessions from Japan and the European Union in recognition of its support for the international anti-terrorism coalition. Japan, Pakistan's largest bilateral aid donor, announced on October 26, 2001, that it was suspending sanctions imposed on Pakistan and India following their 1998 nuclear tests.

On November 10, 2001, President Bush met with President Musharraf in New York, where both addressed the U.N. General Assembly. According to the White House, the two leaders discussed the anti-terrorism campaign, regional security issues, economic cooperation, human rights, the October 2002 Pakistani elections, and ways to strengthen the U.S.-Pakistan relationship.

Security

Nuclear Weapons and Missile Proliferation. Since the September 2001 terrorist attacks on the United States, U.S. and Pakistan officials have held talks on improving security and installing new safeguards on Pakistan's nuclear weapons and nuclear power plants. Fears that Pakistan could become destabilized by the U.S. anti-terrorism war efforts in Afghanistan have heightened U.S. nuclear proliferation concerns in South Asia. On May 11 and 13, 1998, India conducted a total of five underground nuclear tests, breaking a 24-year, self-imposed moratorium on nuclear testing. Despite U.S. and world efforts to dissuade it, Pakistan followed, claiming five tests on May 28, 1998, and an additional test on May 30. The unannounced tests created a global storm of criticism, as well as a serious setback for two decades of U.S. nuclear nonproliferation efforts in South Asia. (See also CRS Report 98–570, *India-Pakistan Nuclear Tests and U.S. Response* and CRS Report RL30623, *Nuclear Weapons and Ballistic Missile Proliferation in India and Pakistan: Issues for Congress.*)

On May 13, 1998, President Clinton imposed economic and military sanctions on India, mandated by section 102 of the Arms Export Control Act (AECA), and applied the same sanctions to Pakistan on May 30. Humanitarian assistance, food, or other agricultural commodities are excepted from sanctions under the law. In November1998, the U.S. Department of Commerce published a list of more than 300 Indian and Pakistani government agencies and companies suspected of working on nuclear, missile, and other weapons programs. Any U.S. exports to these entities required a Commerce Department license, and most license requests reportedly were denied. On the one hand, Pakistan was less affected than India by the sanctions, since most U.S. assistance to Pakistan had been cut off since 1990. On the other hand, Pakistan's much smaller—and currently weaker—economy was more vulnerable to the effects of the sanctions.

U.S. policy analysts consider the apparent arms race between India and Pakistan as posing perhaps the most likely prospect for the future use of nuclear weapons. India conducted its first, and only, previous nuclear test in May 1974, following which it maintained ambiguity about the status of its nuclear program. Pakistan probably gained a nuclear weapons capability sometime in the 1980s. India is believed to have enough plutonium for 75 or more nuclear weapons. Pakistan may have enough enriched uranium for 25 nuclear weapons. Both countries have aircraft capable of delivering weapons. India has short-range missiles (Prithvi) and is reported to have inducted an intermediate-range ballistic missile (Agni) with enough payload to carry a nuclear warhead. Pakistan reportedly has acquired technology for short-range missiles (Shaheen) from China and medium-range missiles (Ghauri) from North Korea, both capable of carrying small nuclear warheads.

Proliferation in South Asia may be part of a chain of rivalries—India seeking to achieve deterrence against China, and Pakistan seeking to gain an "equalizer" against a larger and conventionally stronger India. India began its nuclear program in the mid-1960s, after its 1962 defeat in a short border war with China and China's first nuclear test in 1964. Despite a 1993 Sino-Indian troop reduction agreement and some easing of tensions, both nations continue to deploy forces along their border. Pakistan's nuclear program was prompted by India's 1974 nuclear test and by Pakistan's defeat by India in the 1971 war and consequent loss of East Pakistan, now independent Bangladesh.

U.S. Nonproliferation Efforts. Neither India nor Pakistan are signatories to the Nuclear Nonproliferation Treaty (NPT) or the Comprehensive Test Ban Treaty (CTBT). India has consistently rejected both treaties as discriminatory, calling instead for a global nuclear disarmament regime. Pakistan traditionally has maintained that it will sign the NPT and CTBT only when India does so. Aside from security concerns, the governments of both countries are faced with the prestige factor attached to their nuclear programs and the domestic unpopularity of giving them up. Following the 1998 tests, the United States set forth five nonproliferation "benchmarks" for India and Pakistan. They include the following: halt further nuclear testing and sign and ratify the Comprehensive Test Ban Treaty; halt fissile material production and pursue Fissile Material Control Treaty negotiations; refrain from deploying nuclear weapons and testing ballistic missiles; restrict totally the exportation of any nuclear materials or technologies; and take steps to reduce bilateral tensions, especially on the issue of Kashmir.

The prospects for India-Pakistan detente suffered a severe setback in May-July 1999, when the two countries teetered on the brink of their fourth war, once again in Kashmir. In the worst fighting since 1971, Indian soldiers sought to dislodge some 700 Pakistan-supported infiltrators who were occupying fortified positions along mountain ridges overlooking a supply route on the Indian side of the line of control (LOC) near Kargil. Following a meeting between then Pakistan Prime Minister Nawaz Sharif and President Clinton in Washington on July 4, the infiltrators withdrew across the LOC. (See CRS Report RS20277, *Recent Developments in Kashmir and U.S. Concerns.*)

Tensions between India and Pakistan remained extremely high in the wake of the Kargil conflict, which cost more than 1,100 lives. Throughout 2000, cross-border firing and shelling continued at high levels. India accused Pakistan of sending a flood of militants into Kashmir and increasingly targeting isolated police posts and civilians. Pakistan also accused India of human rights violations in Kashmir. The United States strongly urged India and Pakistan to create the proper climate for peace, respect the LOC, reject violence, and return to the Lahore peace process. In November 2000, India announced a unilateral halt to its military operations in Kashmir during the Muslim holy month of Ramadan. In December, the Pakistan government announced that its forces deployed along the LOC in Kashmir would observe maximum restraint and that some of its troops would be pulled back from the LOC. Indian army officials noted that clashes between Indian and Pakistani forces along the LOC had virtually stopped since the cease-fire began and that there had been a definite reduction of infiltration of militants from Pakistan. In February, Prime Minister Vajpayee extended the cease-fire until the end of May 2001. Kashmir's main militant groups, however, rejected the cease-fire as a fraud and continued to carry out attacks on military personnel and government installations. As security forces conducted counter-operations, deaths of Kashmiri civilians, militants, and Indian security forces continued to rise.

In May 2001, the Indian government announced that it was ending its unilateral ceasefire in Kashmir but that Prime Minister Vajpayee would invite President Musharraf to India for talks. The July summit talks in Agra between Musharraf and Vajpayee failed to produce a joint communique, reportedly as a result of pressure from hardliners on both sides. Major stumbling blocks were India's refusal to acknowledge the "centrality of Kashmir" to future talks and Pakistan's objection to references to "cross-border terrorism." Since the Agra talks, tensions have continued to rise. According to Indian government reports, more than 2,000 people have died since January 2001 as a result of the fighting in Jammu and Kashmir state, including 618 civilians, 1,133 militants, and 228 security forces. According to Amnesty International, more than 1,100 people have disappeared in Kashmir since the revolt began in 1990.

On October 16–17, 2001, U.S. Secretary of State Colin Powell visited Pakistan and India in an effort partly aimed at easing the seriously escalating tensions over Kashmir. India responded to an October 1 terrorist attack by the Pakistan-based Jaish-e-Muhammad, which killed 38 people in Kashmir, by resuming heavy firing across the line of control that divides the disputed territory. Cross-border firing between India and Pakistan had been largely suspended since November 2000. Powell urged both countries to seek a peaceful resolution of the Kashmir dispute. On October 29, the chief of the U.N. Military Observers Group in India and Pakistan (UNMOGIP) accused both countries of playing "political games" on the issue of Kashmir. In reportedly the first instance of a public statement by the UNMOGIP in 50 years, Maj. Gen. Hermann K. Loidolt stated further: "My assessment is that the situation will become more tense in the time coming, not only along the LOC [Line of Control] but also in the whole of Jammu and Kashmir state."

An attack against the Indian parliament on December 13, 2001, thought to have been carried out by Pakistan-based Islamic militants, left 14 dead and brought India and Pakistan to the brink of war. India blamed the suicide attack on two militant groups that Indian leaders believe were sponsored by Pakistan: Jaish-e-Muhammad and Lashkar-e-Taiba. These two groups allegedly have been fighting from bases in Pakistan to end Indian rule in part of the disputed Himalayan region of Kashmir. Following the attack, Indian Prime Minister Vajpayee stated "We do not want war, but war is being thrust on us, and we will have to face it." Pakistani leaders, in turn, accused India of ratcheting up tensions between the two countries and said that Pakistan would make India pay "a heavy price for any misadventure."

In the weeks following the attack on the Indian parliament, both India and Pakistan have, in a "tit-for-tat" fashion, issued threats, conducted military maneuvers and repositioned missile batteries along their border, and levied sanctions against each other.

The events of May seemed to be pushing India and Pakistan to escalate the standoff on their border to a full-scale military conflict. The attack by Kashmiri militants on the army base in Kaluchak, Jammu was viewed as a serious provocation by the Indian government and it intensified war plans. In response, the Pakistani government began to reassign troops from the Afghanistan border to the eastern border with India. It also recalled all Pakistani troops engaged in international peacekeeping operations.

Pakistan tested three ballistic missiles, the intermediate range Ghauri and the short-range Ghaznavi and Abdali, from May 25–28, 2002, sending a message to India that it would not hesitate to use nuclear weapons in a forthcoming conflict. Pakistan's representative to the United Nations also made it clear that in the event of a conflict the country had not ruled out the first use of nuclear weapons. President Musharraf added that Pakistan would not start a war, but it would respond forcefully to aggression and carry out "offensive defense"—take the war into Indian territory. The thinking in Pakistan, reportedly, is that should a conflict take place, India's Muslim minority would rise in rebellion—particularly in the state of Kashmir. This would complicate Indian warfighting efforts.

Congressional Action. Through a series of legislative measures, Congress has incrementally lifted sanctions on Pakistan and India resulting from their 1998 nuclear tests. In October 1999, Congress passed H.R. 2561, the Department of Defense Appropriations Act, 2000, and it was signed by the President as P.L. 106-79 on October 29. Title IX of the act gives the President authority to waive sanctions applied against Pakistan and India in response to the nuclear tests. In a presidential determination on Pakistan and India issued on October 27, 1999, the President waived economic sanctions on India. Pakistan, however, remained under sanctions triggered under Section 508 of the annual foreign assistance appropriations act as a result of the October 1999 coup. The Foreign Operations Export Financing and Related Appropriations Agencies Act, 2001, provided an exception under which Pakistan could be provided U.S. foreign assistance funding for basic education programs (P.L. 106-429; Section 597). The U.S. Agency for International Development request for FY2002 includes $7 million for programs to strengthen civil society and reform public education in Pakistan.

After the terrorist attack on the United States on September 11, 2001, and in recognition of Pakistan's cooperation with the U.S.-led coalition being assembled, policymakers searched for new means of providing assistance to Pakistan. President Bush's issuance of a final determination on September 22, 2001, removed remaining sanctions on Pakistan and India resulting from their 1998 nuclear test, finding that denying export licences and assistance was not in the national security interests of the United States. Also, on October 27, President Bush signed into law S. 1465 (P.L. 107-57), which gives the President 2-year waiver authority to lift sanctions on foreign assistance imposed on Pakistan following the 1999 military coup if he determines that such a waiver would facilitate the transition to democratic rule in Pakistan and is important to U.S. efforts to combat international terrorism. The law not only gives the president authority to waive sanctions related to democracy but to waive sanctions imposed on Pakistan for its debt servicing arrearage to the United States under the terms of the Foreign Operations Appropriations Act. At the end of 2000, Pakistan's international debt was estimated at $38 billion. P.L. 107-57 allowed for an agreement of Pakistan to reschedule $379 million of its debt to the United States thereby enabling it to cancel its arrearage. After President Musharraf's visit to Washington D.C. in February 2002, President Bush wrote a letter to Congress stating that he had ordered $220 million in emergency funds that had been given to the Defense Department for warfighting and to the State Department for security upgrades, be reallocated to Pakistan "for costs incurred in aiding U.S. military forces in Operation Enduring Freedom."

For FY2003, the Bush Administration has proposed increased funding for Pakistan that includes $50 million for development assistance (up from an estimated $15 million in 2001), $200 million in the Economic Support Fund (up from $9.5 million in 2001), $1 million for International Military Education and Training (same as 2001), $50 million for Foreign Military Financing (up from zero in 2001), and $4 million for International Narcotics Control (up from $2.5 million in 2001). (For details, see CRS Report RS20995, *India and Pakistan: Current U.S. Economic Sanctions*, by Dianne E. Rennack.)

Pakistan-U.S. Military Cooperation. The close U.S.-Pakistan military ties of the Cold War era—which had dwindled since the 1990 aid cutoff—are in the process of being restored as a result of Pakistan's role in the U.S. anti-terrorism operations in Afghanistan. Pakistan also has been a leading country in supporting U.N. peacekeeping efforts with troops and observers. Some 5,000 Pakistani troops were stationed in Saudi Arabia and the United Arab Emirates as part of the U.S.-led Persian Gulf War efforts in 1990. Pakistani troops played an important role in the U.S.-led humanitarian operations in Somalia from 1992 to 1994. In November 2001, there were 5,500 Pakistani troops and observers participating in U.N. peacekeeping efforts in Sierra Leone, East Timor, Kosovo, Congo, and other countries. In the wake of the September 11 attacks and President Musharraf's participation in the anti-terror coalition, U.S. law enforcement agents have assisted in tracking and capturing Al Qaeda and Taliban fugitives that have sought refuge in Pakistani border areas and cities.

Democratization and Human Rights

Democratization Efforts. The United States considers the October 1999 Pakistan military coup to be a serious setback to the country's efforts to return to the democratic election process beginning in 1988. National elections, judged by domestic and international observers to be generally free and fair, were held in 1988, 1990, 1993, and 1997. Pakistan democracy between 1988 and 1999, however, was marred by wide-scale corruption, volatile mass-based politics, and a continuing lack of symmetry between the development of the military and civilian bureaucracies and political institutions. The politics of confrontation between parties and leaders flourished at the expense of effective government; frequent walkouts and boycotts of the national and provincial assemblies often led to paralysis and instability. The major political parties lacked grassroots organization and failed to be responsive to the electorate.

There had been hopes that upcoming national elections in October 2002 would reverse the trend and set Pakistan back on the path toward democratic governance. Such hopes have been eroded by the passage of a number of highly restrictive election laws—including those that likely will prevent the country's two leading civilian politicians from participating—as well as President Musharraf's unilateral imposition of major constitutional amendments in August, 2002. The United States has expressed concern that these developments may make the ultimate realization of true democracy in Pakistan more elusive.

Human Rights Problems. The U.S. State Department, in its *Pakistan Country Report on Human Rights Practices for 2001* (issued March 4, 2002), noted that, although Pakistan's human rights record remained poor under the military government, there were improvements in some areas, including freedom of the press. The government bureaucracy continued to function but was "monitored" by the military. The judiciary continued to be subject to the executive branch but in May 2000, President Musharraf promised to abide by a Supreme Court ruling that national elections will be held no later than 90 days after October 12, 2002. The State Department report cited continuing problems of police abuse, religious discrimination, and child labor. Security forces were cited for committing extrajudicial killings and for using arbitrary arrest and detention, torturing and abusing prisoners and detainees, and raping women. Political and religious groups also engaged in killings and persecution of their rivals and ethnic and religious minorities. Politically motivated violence and a deteriorating law and order situation reportedly continued to be a serious problem.

In recent years, the Human Rights Commission of Pakistan and Amnesty International have issued reports critical of abuses of the rights of women and minorities. According to the reports, rape is a serious problem, particularly rape of minors and gang rape. The State Department human rights report also noted a high rate of abuse of female prisoners—including rape and torture—by male police officers. Women also suffer discrimination in education, employment, and legal rights. Discrimination against women is widespread, and traditional constraints—cultural, legal, and spousal—have kept women in a subordinate position in society. The adult literacy rate for men in Pakistan is about 50% and for women about 24%. Religious minorities—mainly Christians, Hindus, and Ahmadi Muslims—reportedly are subjected to discriminatory laws and social intolerance. A 1974 amendment to the Pakistan constitution declared Ahmadis to be a non-Muslim minority because they do not accept Muhammad as the last prophet. The Zia government, in 1984, made it illegal for an Ahmadi to call himself a Muslim or use Muslim terminology. Blasphemy laws, instituted under the Zia regime and strengthened in 1991, carry a mandatory death penalty for blaspheming the Prophet or his family. Blasphemy charges reportedly are usually brought as a result of personal or religious vendettas.

Economic Issues

Pakistan's current military government inherited an economy in recession. The period from July 2000-June 2001 saw the economy grow by only 2.7%, a significant decline from the previous year. A decade of political instability left a legacy of soaring foreign debt, declining production and growth rates, failed economic reform policies, and pervasive corruption. Foreign debt totals more than $32 billion; foreign reserves are less than $1.5 billion (about 6 weeks of imports); and both agricultural and industrial growth have dropped since 1998.

Over the long term, analysts believe Pakistan's resources and comparatively well-developed entrepreneurial skills hold promise for more rapid economic growth and development. This is particularly true for Pakistan's textile industry, which accounts for 60% of Pakistan's exports. Analysts point to the pressing need to broaden the country's tax base in order to provide increased revenue for investment in improved infrastructure, health, and education, all prerequisites for economic development. Less than 1% of Pakistanis currently pay income taxes. Agricultural income has not been taxed in the past, largely because of the domination of parliament and the provincial assemblies by wealthy landlords.

Successive Bhutto and Sharif governments made agreements with the International Monetary Fund (IMF), promising austerity, deficit reduction, and improved tax collection in return for loans and credits. The promised reforms, however, fell victim to political instability and a host of other problems, including floods, drought, crop viruses, strikes, a bloated and inefficient bureaucracy, widespread tax evasion, weak infrastructure, and a swollen defense budget. The Musharraf government has had some success in putting economic reforms back on track, including expanding collection of income and sales taxes, trade liberalization, and improving transparency. In January 2001, the Paris Club of creditor nations agreed to reschedule $1.7 billion in repayments on Pakistan's foreign debt of $32 billion. On August 29, an International Monetary Fund team cleared release of the final installment of a $596 million standby loan to Pakistan and confirmed "Pakistan's solid macroeconomic performance, including lower inflation, a strengthening of the balance of payments, and reduction of fiscal imbalances."

Meetings between Pakistani government officials and representatives of the IMF, the World Bank, and the Asian Development Bank have been successful, as the financial institutions reportedly have been pleased with the progress made in stabilizing and reforming the Pakistani economy. The Pakistani government has stabilized the country's external debt at $38 billion and the country's hard currency reserves grew to $6.41 billion by July 2002—an increase of more than $4 billion since October 1999. At the same time, the IMF and the World Bank urged the Pakistani government to cut defense expenditures from the current 3.5% GDP to 3.3% of GDP by 2003–2004. The World Bank said that if regional tensions subsided and the Kashmir dispute was resolved, this would provide a further fiscal cushion for a peace dividend. Most recently, a "structural adjustment credit" of $500 million and four projects totaling $237 million were approved to support Pakistan's ongoing reform program. A new arms race with India, however, could be fiscally disastrous.

On the positive side, Pakistan's economic reforms and a more prudent fiscal policy have reduced the fiscal deficit from 7% of GDP to about 5.2% of GDP. Foreign remittances have exceeded $1.6 billion—$772 million more than in 2000. Exports exceeded $9 billion for the first time in 7 years, and inflation, at 3%, was the lowest in three decades. Interest on public debt together with defense spending, however, consume 70% of total revenues, thus squeezing out development expenditure, including social spending. A July country report from the IMF indicates that progress toward macroeconomic and structural goals is meeting program standards as of March 2002.

In the view of the International Financial Institutions—the World Bank, the IMF, and the Asian Development Bank—the major risk to economic reforms and to future investment was the possibility that there might be a break in the continuity of policy after the October 2002 elections for the national and provincial assemblies. President Pervez Musharraf's victory in the April 30, 2002 referendum has had some effect of boosting investor and international financial institution confidence that the economic and political reforms will stay the course.

Trade and Trade Issues. In 2001, U.S. exports to Pakistan totaled $542 million, an increase of 17.3% over 2000. Imports from Pakistan totaled $2.2 billion for 2001, up nearly 4% over the previous year. The resulting trade deficit of $1.7 billion has remained static. The United States has been strongly supportive of Pakistan's economic reform efforts, begun under the first Nawaz Sharif government in 1991. According to the report of the U.S. Trade Representative (USTR) for 2001, however, a number of trade barriers remain. Some items are either restricted or banned from importation for reasons related to religion, national security, luxury consumption, or protection of local industries. U.S. companies have complained repeatedly about violations of their intellectual property rights in the areas of patents and copyrights. Pakistan's patent law currently protects only processes, not products, from infringement. A 1992 Pakistan copyright law that provides coverage for such works as computer software and videos is being enforced but has resulted in a backlog of cases in the court system. The International Intellectual Property Alliance estimated trade losses of $143.3 million in 2001—a result of pirated films, sound recordings, computer programs, and books—and recommends that Pakistan be placed on the Priority Watch List.

Narcotics

In recent years, the Pakistan-Afghanistan border region has supplied a reported 20%–40% of heroin consumed in the United States and 70% of that consumed in Europe. The region is second only to Southeast Asia's Golden Triangle as a source of the world's heroin. Opium grown in Afghanistan and Pakistan is processed into heroin in more than 100 illegal laboratories in the border region. Although much of the heroin is smuggled by land and sea routes to Europe and the United States, a substantial portion is consumed by Pakistan's rapidly growing domestic market. The Pakistan government estimates the 4 million drug addicts in the country include 1.5 million addicted to heroin. According to some experts, Pakistan's drug economy amounts to as much as $20 billion. Drug money reportedly is used to buy influence throughout Pakistan's economic and political systems.

Pakistan's counter-narcotics efforts are hampered by a number of factors, including lack of government commitment; scarcity of funds; poor infrastructure in drug-producing regions; government wariness of provoking unrest in tribal areas; and corruption among police, government officials, and local politicians. U.S. counter-narcotics aid to Pakistan, administered by the State Department's Bureau of International Narcotics and Law

Enforcement Affairs, totaled $3.5 million in FY2001, with $3.5 million requested for FY2002. The major counter-narcotics efforts engaged in by the Pakistan government, some of which receive U.S. or U.N. support, include: improved law enforcement; reduction of demand; opium crop destruction and crop substitution; and outreach programs that include supplying roads, irrigation, drinking water, and schools to remote tribal areas.

In March 2001, President Bush submitted to Congress his annual list of major illicit drug producing and transiting countries eligible to receive U.S. foreign aid and other economic and trade benefits. Pakistan was among the countries certified as having cooperated fully with the United States in counter-narcotics efforts, or to have taken adequate steps on their own. According to the report, Pakistan almost achieved its goal of eliminating opium production by reducing the poppy crop to a record low of 500 hectares, down from 8,000 hectares in 1992. A more recent State Department report shows Pakistan's poppy production dropping by 59% from 2000 to 2001. Pakistan, however, faces major challenges as a transit country, despite reduced production of opium in Afghanistan. Cooperation with the United States on counter-narcotics efforts was described as excellent, including arrests, extradition, and poppy eradication.

Terrorism

After the September 11 attacks on the United States, Pakistan pledged and has provided support for the anti-terror coalition effort. According to the U.S. State Department report on global terrorism for 2001, Pakistan has afforded the United States unprecedented levels of cooperation by allowing the U.S. military to use bases within the country, helping to identify and detain extremists, and tightening the border between Pakistan and Afghanistan.

In December 2001, President Musharraf announced a proposal to bring Pakistan's madrassas (religious schools)—some of which have served as breeding grounds for extremists—into the mainstream educational system. Pakistan also began sweeping police reforms, upgraded its immigration control system, and began work on new anti-terrorist finance laws. Musharraf also began cracking down on "anti-Pakistan" extremists and, by January 2002, authorities had arrested more than 2,000, although many have subsequently been released.

In May 2002, a bomb blast in Karachi killed 14 people (including 12 French military contractors) and raised fears that terrorist groups would complicate the law and order situation within the country. The blast was attributed to various groups including Indian intelligence and members of the Al Qaeda. In the war on terror, Pakistani troops, for the first time since independence, operated in tribal areas of the country—an area that they traditionally stayed out of for fear of antagonizing the local population. By late May, however, President Musharraf was beginning to pull some troops from the region to help strengthen the eastern border with India.

At the same time, the Pakistani government has been under pressure from various nations to terminate the infiltration of insurgents from Pakistani Kashmir into Indian Kashmir. As India increased its preparations for war—following the attack in the Kaluchak region of Jammu—the United States, Britain, and Russia called upon Pakistan to stop militants from crossing into Indian Kashmir. President Bush challenged President Musharraf to show results in stopping militants from carrying out terrorist acts in Indian Kashmir. While expressing concern about Pakistan's missile tests the president made it clear that preventing terrorism was a higher priority. He said, "I am more concerned about making sure . . . that President Musharraf show results in terms of stopping people from crossing the border." He added, "Stopping terrorism—that is more important than the missile testing." President Musharraf, in an interview with the *Washington Post,* countered, "[T]here is nothing happening across the Line of Control. And I've also said that Pakistan is a part of the coalition to fight terrorism. And we will ensure that terrorism does not go from Pakistan anywhere outside into the world." Critics have charged, however, that President Musharraf has eased up on militants in the country by releasing some of the people he had jailed after September 11 in his promised crackdown on Islamic militants.

President Musharraf asked the international community to credit Pakistan for having the courage to send troops into the tribal areas to capture suspected Al Qaeda operatives. He pointed out that Pakistani troops were the first troops to have moved into the area in more than a century. The President continued that there were three elements of terror that the world was concerned with: Al Qaeda, Kashmiri militants, and the growing Sunni sectarian terrorism in Pakistan. He also pointed out that the Indian goal was to destabilize Pakistan: "[T]heir aim is to destabilize me, my government, and Pakistan. Destabilize us economically, and politically, and diplomatically. That is what they want to achieve."

DOCUMENT NO. 17

PAKISTAN-U.S. ANTI-TERRORISM COOPERATION

CRS Report
RL31624

March 28, 2003

K. Alan Kronstadt
Analyst in Asian Affairs
Foreign Affairs, Defense, and Trade Division

Summary

Pakistan is a key front-line ally in the U.S.-led anti-terrorism coalition. After September 2001, Pakistani President Musharraf ended his government's ties with the Taliban regime of Afghanistan and has since cooperated with and contributed to U.S. efforts to track and capture remnants of Al Qaeda and Taliban forces that have sought refuge inside Pakistani territory. Pakistan's cooperation has been called "crucial" to past and ongoing U.S. successes in the region, but there is growing concern that the bilateral relationship is fragile and may be undermined by potentially disruptive developments in the areas of weapons proliferation, democracy-building, and Pakistan-India relations.

Remaining proliferation- and democracy-related aid restrictions on Pakistan were removed in the final months of 2001, and the United States continues to make large aid donations to Pakistan and to support that country's interests in negotiations with international financial institutions. There are concerns that October 2002 national elections in Pakistan were not sufficiently free and open by Western standards and that the military-dominated government in Islamabad intends to remain in power through manipulation of constitutional and democratic processes. This possibility led some Members of the 107th Congress to seek the renewal of aid restrictions or a modification of the President's waiver authority until such time that a more robust democratic process is sustained and a civilian-led government effectively is in place. There also is concern that possibly growing anti-American sentiment in Pakistan and the potential "re-Talibanization" of that country's western provinces bordering Afghanistan could adversely affect U.S. interests in the region.

During 2002, the United States took an increasingly direct, if low-profile, role in both law enforcement and military operations being conducted on Pakistani territory. These operations have led to favorable results in tracking and apprehending dangerous Islamic militants, but the activities of U.S. personnel in the country have led to increasing signs of anti-American backlash and Pakistani sovereignty concerns. Recent electoral gains by a coalition of Pakistani Islamist political parties are viewed as an expression of such sentiments that may lead to reduced Pakistan-U.S. cooperation in counterterrorism operations in the future. The civilian Parliament and Prime Minister that were seated in Islamabad in November 2002 may powerfully influence the course and scope of future U.S. presence in the region.

This report reviews the status of Pakistan-U.S. anti-terrorism cooperation in the areas of law enforcement, intelligence, and military operations. U.S. arms transfers to and security cooperation with Pakistan are also discussed. A following section addresses the major domestic repercussions of Pakistan-U.S. counterterrorism efforts, the ways in which such efforts are perceived by newly-empowered Pakistan Islamists and their followers, and the possible effects these dynamics may have on future Pakistan-U.S. cooperation in this realm. The final section assesses the overall status of Pakistan-U.S. anti-terrorism cooperation and key points of U.S. concern. Broader discussion of bilateral relations and relevant legislation is found in IB94041, *Pakistan-U.S. Relations*. This report will be updated periodically.

Congressional Interest

Pakistan is a key front-line ally in the U.S.-led anti-terrorism coalition, and the Bush Administration has expressed satisfaction with ongoing Pakistan-U.S. cooperation in this area.[1] Top U.S. government officials regularly praise Pakistan and its leadership for their "fine efforts" in joint counterterrorism operations, most recently with the capture of suspected Al Qaeda leader Khalid Mohammed in the Pakistani city of Rawalpindi on March 1, 2003. Yet the bilateral relationship has come under significant strain in recent months due to signs of growing U.S. frustration with the continued existence of Islamic militants both along the Afghan-Pakistani border and

[1] Ari Fleischer, "Transcript: White House Daily Briefing," USIS Washington File, March 3, 2003; Richard Boucher, "Transcript: State Department Noon Briefing," USIS Washington File, March 3, 2003; Assistant Secretary of State for South Asia Rocca, "Transcript: Hearing of the Subcommittee on Asia and the Pacific of the House International Relations Committee," Federal News Service, March 20, 2003.

infiltrating into Indian-held Kashmir; doubts about the commitment of Pakistan's intelligence service to Islamabad's stated anti-terrorism policies; widespread anti-American sentiment in Pakistan; reports of alleged Pakistani nuclear proliferation activities; continued perceived anti-democratic practices in Islamabad; new U.S. immigration regulations; and continued antagonistic relations between Islamabad and New Delhi.

One senior observer reports that U.S. frustration with Islamabad grew alarmingly high in the latter months of 2002.[2] At the same time, suspicion of and resentment toward the United States is reported to be spreading rapidly throughout Pakistani society.[3] A sense of the difficulties faced in pursuing U.S. policies in Pakistan's conservative Muslim western regions can be found in the March 2003 assertion by the spokesman for Pakistan's largest Islamist party that captured alleged Al Qaeda leader Khalid Mohammed is a "hero of Islam" and that there is "no reason to believe that Al Qaeda really exists." Many Pakistanis reportedly believe that September 2001 terrorist attacks on the United States were a ploy by Israel designed to cause anti-Muslim backlash.[4] For several years, analysts have discussed the potential dangers to Pakistan and its people's civil liberties represented by increased Islamization there.[5] There are newer concerns that U.S. military action in Iraq may fuel Islamic radicalism in Pakistan; March 2003 witnessed anti-U.S./anti-war marches in Karachi, Lahore, and other cities organized by Islamist political parties and involving as many as 250,000 demonstrators at a time.[6]

107th Congress

After the September 2001 terrorist attacks on the United States, a previously poor bilateral relationship with Pakistan was quickly improved. On September 22, 2001, President Bush lifted all remaining nuclear proliferation-related sanctions on Pakistan (and India). The Congress then passed, and the President signed into law, S. 1465 (P.L. 107-57) in October 2001.

[2] Ahmed Rashid, "U.S. Grows Frustrated With Pakistan Coalition," *Wall Street Journal*, December 2, 2002. A February 2003 editorial in the *Washington Post* decried the "steady unraveling of commitments by Pakistan's president . . . to support the United States in the war on terrorism," and ended by asserting that "the Bush Administration must reconsider whether its attenuated alliance with the general is worth the growing cost" ("Out of Pakistan," *Washington Post*, February 25, 2003).

[3] David Rohde, "Anti-American Feeling Rises in Pakistan as U.S. Confronts Iraq," *New York Times*, December 22, 2002. A public opinion poll released in December 2002 indicates that only 10% of Pakistanis hold a "favorable view" of the United States (Pew Center for Research, "What the World Thinks In 2002," December 4, 2002. Online at [http://people-press.org/reports/files/report165.pdf]).

[4] Erik Eckholm, "Qaeda Operative is 'Hero' to Some in Pakistan," *New York Times*, March 5, 2003.

[5] See, for example, Jessica Stern, "Pakistan's Jihad Culture," *Foreign Affairs*, November 2000; "Pakistan: The Mullahs and the Military," International Crisis Group Asia Report 49, March 20, 2003.

[6] Edward Luce and Farhan Bokhari, "US Invasion Pushes Pakistanis Toward Islam," *Financial Times* (London), March 27, 2003; "Pakistan Heads Anti-War Protests," BBC News, March 2, 2003; Jalilur Rehman, "200,000 Gather in Anti-US March in Pakistan," Agence France-Presse, March 23, 2003.

With this law, Congress exempted Pakistan from all sanctions related to democracy and debt-arrearage for FY2002, and granted the President authority to waive such sanctions through FY2003. Presidential Determination 2003–16 exercised this authority for FY2003 on March 14, 2003.

Members of the 107th Congress introduced several Pakistan-related bills that were not voted upon, including one that would authorize the President to reduce or suspend duties on Pakistani textiles (S. 1675); one that would repeal the President's authority to waive economic sanctions and end assistance to Pakistan as a country whose elected head of government was deposed by military coup (H.R. 5150); and one that would require Presidential certification of Pakistan's successful efforts to halt cross-border terrorism into India, that the country's national elections are conducted freely and fairly, and that waivers on aid restrictions would facilitate both U.S. anti-terror efforts and the transition to democratic rule in Pakistan (H.R. 5267).

During the final months of 2002, in response to reports alleging Pakistani assistance to North Korea's covert nuclear weapons program, a Member of Congress urged reinstatement of proliferation-related aid restrictions pursuant to P.L. 106-79, Title IX. A similar call was taken up in another Member's February 2003 request that the Bush Administration take "immediate steps" to ban all military sales to Pakistan and reimpose proliferation-related sanctions under §669 of the Foreign Assistance Act of 1961 (the Symington Amendment). However, in March 2003, the Bush Administration announced that it had "carefully reviewed the facts relating to the possible transfer of nuclear technology from Pakistan to North Korea and decided that they do not warrant the imposition of sanctions under applicable U.S. laws."[7]

108th Congress

Members of the 108th Congress may confront more proliferation- and democracy-related aid issues with regard to Pakistan, as questions about Islamabad's possible nuclear technology transfers and about levels of democratic governance in Pakistan continue to surface.[8] Pakistan's enthusiastic desire to purchase U.S.-made weapons is likely to be an area of continuing congressional interest. Trade-related legislation may again arise, especially

---

[7] House International Relations Committee member Rep. Gary Ackerman, "Letter to President Bush," November 7, 2002; House International Relations Committee member Rep. Frank Pallone, Jr., "Letter to Secretary of State Powell," February 11, 2003; Assistant Secretary of State for Legislative Affairs Paul Kelly, "Letter to Sen. Daschle," March 12, 2003.

[8] On March 20, 2003, Rep. Frank Pallone introduced H.R. 1403 to remove the democracy-related sanctions exemption with respect to Pakistan (i.e., to repeal the President's waiver authority that was exercised in early March). In February 2003 testimony before the House International Relations Committee, Secretary of State Powell indicated that the Administration has been "reviewing all of the various sanctions legislation that has been in existence for a number of years" and would seek to extend the President's waiver authority on democracy-related and other aid restrictions for FY2003 and FY2004.

in the area of textile duties.[9] U.S. assistance to Pakistan rose steeply after September 2001, from about $10 million in FY2001 to more than $1 billion in FY2002. P.L. 108-7 includes authorization for Pakistan to use $188 million in FY2003 Economic Support Funds to cancel approximately $1 billion in concessional debt to the U.S. government. The Bush Administration is requesting bilateral assistance to Pakistan in the amounts of $305 million for FY2003 and $395 million for FY2004.[10]

Background

Prior to the September 2001 terror attacks on the United States, and especially after Islamabad's 1998 nuclear tests and 1999 military coup, U.S. relations with Pakistan had become marked by discord and distance. After the attacks, and under intense diplomatic pressure, Pakistani President Gen. Pervez Musharraf made a swift decision to end his government's support for the Taliban regime in Afghanistan and join the U.S.-led anti-terrorism coalition. The United States and Pakistan now share pressing interests in the region. These chiefly are related to ending Islamic militancy that continues to wreak terror and destruction in South Asia and elsewhere, and that poses a threat to the continued existence of moderate government in a nuclear-armed Pakistan.

The policy reversal by Musharraf took place without the full support of the country's Islamic citizens or its military and intelligence organizations. Islamabad subsequently has asked the United States for military equipment, aid, and other forms of security cooperation to both assist in the anti-terror campaign and in an effort to maintain balance with India's conventional forces. Within Pakistan, however, a negative political reaction is fueling anti-government and anti-American sentiment that may jeopardize longer-term U.S. interests in the region.

A further complication is that the massive U.S. bombardment of Afghanistan's Tora Bora region in late-2001 and Operation Anaconda in Afghanistan's eastern Shah-i-Kot mountains in March 2002 apparently prompted two waves of up to 5,000 Al Qaeda fighters fleeing into Pakistan.[11]

---

[9] During a February 2003 visit to the United States, the Pakistani Foreign Minister Kasuri requested greater access to U.S. markets as a means of reducing poverty and thus also the forces of extremism in Pakistan. He made a direct link between poverty and the continued existence of Islamic schools (madrassas) that are implicated in teaching militant anti-American values ("Pakistan: 'A Front-Line Ally' on Terrorism," *Los Angeles Times*, February 2, 2003).

[10] These amounts include $49.5 million in Foreign Military Financing (FMF) already allocated for FY2003 and $75 million in FMF requested for FY2004.

[11] Tim McGirk, "Al Qaeda's New Hideouts," *Time*, July 29, 2002. At least one subsequent report claimed that most or all of these Al Qaeda fighters were evacuated from the area by Pakistani military aircraft and in the company of "dozens of senior Pakistani military, including two generals" (Seymour Hersh, "Transcript: Jane Wallace Talks With Seymour Hersh," Now With Bill Moyers, Public Broadcasting Service, February 21, 2003, available at [http://www.pbs.org/now/transcript/transcript_hersh.html].

Press reports indicate that Pakistan has been allowing the United States to conduct low-level military or military support operations in Pakistan's western border regions since April 2002.[12] U.S. efforts to pursue counter-terror operations in Pakistan are complicated by alleged assistance given to the Taliban, Al Qaeda, and indigenous Pakistani terrorist groups by elements of Pakistan's powerful Inter-Services Intelligence agency (ISI).[13] Anti-terrorism operations may meet further obstacles if recently bolstered Pakistani Islamist political parties succeed in exerting their anti-American influences on the country's foreign policy orientation.

The United States continues to make large aid donations to Pakistan and to support that country's interests in negotiations with international financial institutions. President Bush and Secretary of State Powell commonly refer to the Islamabad regime as a "crucial ally." Yet there are concerns that 2002 national elections in Pakistan were not sufficiently free and open by Western standards and that the military-dominated government in Islamabad intends to remain in power through manipulation of constitutional and democratic processes. This possibility has led some Members of Congress to seek the renewal of aid restrictions until such time that a more robust democratic process is sustained and a civilian-led government is effectively in place.[14]

At the same time, the very democratic process encouraged by the United States may bring to power Islamist political groups that do not share some key U.S. interests and concerns. There is also possibly growing anti-American sentiment in Pakistan, and the potential "re-Talibanization" of that country's western provinces bordering Afghanistan could lead to a reduction of Pakistan-U.S. cooperation in counterterrorism efforts, thereby harming U.S. interests in the region.[15] Some Islamist members of Pakistan's national assembly have warned U.S. forces to stay out of areas near the border with Afghanistan, and the provincial government of one such region recently dropped the criminal charges that had been brought against hundreds of Pakistani citizens for taking part in anti-U.S. demonstrations last year.[16]

---

[12] See, for example, Dexter Filkins, "F.B.I. and Military Unite in Pakistan to Hunt Al Qaeda," *New York Times*, July 14, 2002; Erik Eckholm, "F.B.I. Active in Pakistan, But Profile is Low," *New York Times*, March 4, 2003.

[13] See, for example, David Sands, "India Says Pakistan Aids Ousted Extremists," *Washington Times*, January 4, 2002; Gretchen Peters, "Al Qaeda-Pakistani Ties Deepen," *Christian Science Monitor*, March 6, 2003. The Indian government accuses the ISI of fomenting terrorism in Kashmir, as well as in Bangladesh, Nepal, and Indian urban centers (Sayantan Chakravarty, "Terror's Hidden Face," *India Today* (New Delhi), November 11, 2002).

[14] For a review of sanctions issues, see CRS Report RS20995, *India and Pakistan: Current U.S. Sanctions*, by Dianne Rennack.

[15] See also CRS Issue Brief IB94041, Pakistan-U.S. Relations, and CRS Report RS21299, *Pakistan's Domestic Political Developments: Issues for Congress*, by Alan Kronstadt.

[16] "Pakistan Tribal Belt MPs Denounce US-Led Al Qaeda Hunt," Agence France-Presse, December 3, 2002; Riaz Khan, "Charges Dropped for Activists in Pakistan," *Washington Post*, December 4, 2002.

It was reported that, following Pakistan's October 2002 elections and the ascension of an Islamist coalition there, U.S. officials presented to the Islamabad government three policy priorities: 1) a preference that the Islamists not be included in the ruling national coalition; 2) that provincial governments being run by Islamist politicians not be allowed to interfere with ongoing anti-terror operations involving U.S. personnel; and 3) that the basic understanding between the United States and Pakistan—agreed to between Secretary of State Powell and President Musharraf on September 14, 2001, and guaranteeing full Pakistani cooperation with the U.S.-led anti-terror campaign—"must continue unhindered."[17]

This report reviews the current status of Pakistan-U.S. anti-terrorism cooperation in the areas of law enforcement, intelligence, and military operations. U.S. arms transfers to and security cooperation with Pakistan are also discussed. A following section addresses the major domestic repercussions of Pakistan-U.S. counterterrorism efforts, the ways in which such efforts are perceived by newly-empowered Pakistan Islamists and their followers, and the possible effects these dynamics may have on future Pakistan-U.S. cooperation in this realm. The final section assesses the overall status of Pakistan-U.S. anti-terrorism cooperation and key points of U.S. concern.

Law Enforcement and Intelligence Cooperation

Pakistan historically has demonstrated inconsistency in its efforts to reign in Islamic militants operating inside its borders. The United States has long been aware of the existence of outlawed groups both in Pakistan-held Kashmir and within Pakistani cities. The government of neighboring India continues to call Pakistan the "epicenter of global terrorism." In July 2000 testimony before the House International Relations Committee, a senior U.S. counterterrorism official called Pakistan's record on combating terrorism "mixed," noting that "Pakistan has tolerated terrorists living and moving freely within its territory" and is believed to have provided "material support for some of these militants, including the Harakat ul-Mujahidin, a group that [the United States] has designated as an FTO [Foreign Terrorist Organization]." The official pointed to the role played by Islamic religious schools, or madrassas, some of which "inculcate extremism and a violent anti-Americanism in their students."[18]

---

[17] "Pakistan's Islamists Raise US Fears," *Jane's Intelligence Digest*, December 13, 2002.

[18] Ambassador Michael Sheehan, "Testimony on Counterterrorism and South Asia," USIS Public Diplomacy Query, July 12, 2000. Pakistan continues to be plagued with domestic terrorism. The February 2002 kidnaping and murder of *Wall Street Journal* reporter Daniel Pearl is believed to have spurred an increased U.S. effort to track and assist in apprehending indigenous Pakistani terrorists. Each of the following terrorist attacks took place in the sprawling port city of Karachi: In May, a car bomb killed 14 people, including 11 French defense technicians. A June car bombing outside the U.S. consulate killed 12 Pakistani nationals. Two lethal terror attacks on Christian schools in Pakistan

Pakistan's tolerance of and support for hardline Islamists in both the country and the region has been rooted in ethnic Pashtun ties that cross the Afghani-Pakistani border and in former President Gen. Zia ul-Haq's moves to strengthen Islamists during the 1980s. President Musharraf's sweeping policy shift away from Islamic extremism began with the severing of all official ties to the Taliban in September 2001 and culminated in a landmark January 2002 speech in which he vowed to end Pakistan's use as a base for terrorism of any kind, criticized religious extremism and intolerance in the country, and banned numerous militant groups, including Lashkar-e-Taiba and Jaish-e-Muhammad (both blamed for terrorist violence in Kashmir and India).[19] The Islamabad government also instituted sweeping police reforms, upgraded its immigration control system, and began work on new anti-terrorist finance laws. In the wake of the speech, about 3,300 extremists were arrested and detained, though at least one-third of these have since been released, including the founders of both Lashkar-e-Taiba and Jaish-e-Muhammad.[20]

American military successes in Afghanistan in the final months of 2001 apparently ended the existence of Al Qaeda as a coherent entity in that country. Yet the first half of 2002 saw increasing indications that the group—along with its Taliban cohorts—was making progress in regrouping, first in the tribal western regions of Pakistan and later in major urban centers. By late-2002, intelligence analysts believed that Al Qaeda had established a new base of operations in the sprawling city of Karachi, Pakistan's most populous. In early-2003, President Musharraf shifted his previous stance and opined that Osama bin Laden himself may be in Pakistan.[21]

---

in August increased concerns that anti-Western violence would escalate. In September, 7 Pakistani Christians were murdered execution-style at a charity office. In October and November, parcel bombs sent to police stations severely injured 10. In December, a bomb at the Macedonian consulate killed three. In February 2003, a bomb killed one man outside the offices of Pakistan's state oil company and a barrage of automatic weapons fire at a Shiite mosque left 9 worshipers dead and another 9 wounded. Later in the month, gunmen shot and killed two Pakistani police officers outside the U.S. consulate; another five officers and a bystander were wounded. In a move praised by the U.S. government, Pakistan in January 2003 assigned 650 police officers to a new Diplomatic Protection Department created to reassure foreign nationals in the wake of terrorist attacks in 2002 (Munir Ahmad, "Pakistan Deploys Diplomatic Security Unit," *Washington Post*, January 14, 2003).

[19] Shortly after the December 2001 terrorist attack on the Indian Parliament, Secretary of State Powell designated the Pakistan-based Lashkar-e-Taiba and Jaish-e-Mohammed groups as Foreign Terrorist Organizations under U.S. law. Both the U.S. and Indian governments repeatedly have indicated that these groups have been involved in numerous terrorist attacks in an effort to "undermine peace and stability in South Asia and destroy relations between India and Pakistan" ("Designation of Foreign Terrorist Organizations," U.S. Department of State Press Release, December 26, 2001). In January 2003, the United States added to the FTO list the Pakistan-based Lashkar-i-Jhangvi—a group held responsible for "numerous deadly attacks in Pakistan," including the January 2002 kidnaping and murder of *Wall Street Journal* reporter Daniel Pearl.

[20] Paul Watson, "Revolving Doors for Pakistan's Militants," *Los Angeles Times*, November 17, 2002; "Musharraf Says Heads of Two Extremist Groups Did Nothing Illegal," Agence France-Presse, March 2, 2003; "Militant Suspects Freed in Pakistan," BBC News, January 31, 2003.

[21] David Rohde, "Qaeda Uses Teeming Karachi as New Base, Pakistanis Say," *New York Times*, November 1, 2002; Steve LeVine, "Musharraf Now Says Bin Laden may Be in Pakistan," *Wall Street Journal*, March 24, 2003.

In response, U.S. law enforcement agencies, led by the F.B.I., began in early 2002 to provide active assistance to Pakistan in its effort to hunt terrorists and their allies. The number of U.S. counterterrorism agents in Pakistan has been reported at between "several dozen" and "the low hundreds."[22] While U.S. officials claim that the involvement of American agents in field operations and raids has been quite limited, senior Pakistani officials have indicated that F.B.I. agents participated in numerous raids, where they "carry guns" and "help us break down doors."[23] Yet a spokesman for the Pakistan Foreign Office stated in April 2002 that there exist "no independent F.B.I. offices in Pakistan," and Pakistan's interior minister repeatedly has claimed that F.B.I. operatives are not involved in hunting Al Qaeda supporters in Pakistan.[24]

Director of Central Intelligence Tenet is reported to have made at least one trip to Pakistan after September 2001, and the Islamabad government is said to be cooperating with the C.I.A. in the ongoing hunt for Osama bin Laden, Mullah Omar, and other top-level Islamic militant fugitives.[25] There have been some concerns raised that U.S. counterterrorism agents, by working in tandem with Pakistani security organizations that have been accused of human rights abuses including extralegal deportation and torture, may share responsibility for any such abuses that may be occurring.[26] December 2002 press reports suggest that "stress and duress" techniques used by the C.I.A. to interrogate suspected Al Qaeda and Taliban members may be abusing human rights. New York-based Human Rights Watch has written a letter to President Bush calling for an investigation into what the rights group alleges may be the use of torture by U.S. officials.[27]

The February 2002 kidnaping and subsequent murder of *Wall Street Journal* reporter Daniel Pearl is believed to have spurred an intensified U.S. focus on law enforcement in Pakistan and efforts to assist local security forces in tracking and capturing Islamic militants in that country's urban centers. Al Qaeda is believed by U.S. officials to have assisted Pakistani militants in carrying out two deadly car bombings in the spring of 2002: a May attack that killed 14, including 11 French military technicians, and a June explosion that killed 12 Pakistani nationals outside the American consulate

---

22 Paul Watson and Josh Meyer, "Pakistanis See FBI in Shadows," *Los Angeles Times*, August 25, 2002.

23 Dexter Filkins, "F.B.I. and Military Unite in Pakistan to Hunt Al Qaeda," *New York Times*, July 14, 2002.

24 "Pakistan Denies Osama's Presence in Faisalabad," Pakistan Press International, April 8, 2002; "FBI Not Involved in Raids: Faisal," *Dawn* (Karachi), December 31, 2002.

25 Peter Baker and Kamran Khan, "Pakistan to Forgo Charges Against 2 Nuclear Scientists; Ties to Bin Laden Suspected," *Washington Post*, January 30, 2002.

26 Paul Watson and Josh Meyer, "Pakistanis See FBI in Shadows," *Los Angeles Times*, August 25, 2002.

27 Alan Cooperman, "CIA Interrogation Under Fire; Human Rights Groups Say Techniques Could Be Torture," *Washington Post*, December 28, 2002.

in Karachi. Al Qaeda links also are suspected in numerous other violent anti-Western and anti-Christian attacks in Pakistan.[28]

On May 8, 2002, senior U.S. government officials from several executive-branch agencies hosted the first meeting of the U.S.-Pakistan Joint Working Group on Counterterrorism and Law Enforcement. Pakistan's Minister of Interior, Moin Haider, led the Pakistani delegation. The two governments discussed a broad range of bilateral law enforcement issues, including counternarcotics, counterterrorism, extradition, money laundering, trafficking in persons, demand reduction and drug abuse control, alternative development and poppy eradication, police and legal system reform, and issues related to the repatriation of Pakistani nationals detained in the United States in connection with immigration proceedings.[29] The two governments agreed to strengthen their cooperation in each of these areas, and ensuing trips to Pakistan by Deputy Secretary of State Armitage and Coordinator for Counterterrorism Taylor marked a continuation of this process. Officials from the U.S. Departments of State and Justice met with Pakistani counterparts in Islamabad in September 2002, and another full meeting of the U.S.-Pakistan Joint Working Group on Counterterrorism and Law Enforcement is slated to take place in Washington in April 2003.[30]

In November 2002, then-U.S. Treasury Secretary O'Neill met with top officials in Islamabad to discuss Pakistan's ongoing efforts to halt terrorist financing. He stated that Pakistan was "leading the world" in the fight to eradicate money-laundering, but some officials are more pessimistic.[31] Islamabad has taken action against at least 185 of the 247 U.S.-designated entities operating on Pakistani territory, and has taken its own initiative to detain operatives and designate active groups suspected of financing terrorist activities. Yet Pakistan's legal and regulatory structures remain insufficient for a fully effective anti-terrorism financing regime, especially with an inability to monitor the activities of foreign charities, and the newly seated Assembly has yet to enact a proposed money laundering bill. U.S. officials continue to encourage stricter oversight and regulation, and the United States has agreed to provide technical assistance and training to Pakistani customs and finance officials as part of this effort.[32]

---

[28] See, for example, "Militants' Lair Raided, 12 Arrested in Pakistan," *Chicago Tribune*, August 29, 2002.

[29] U.S. Department of State Press Release, "U.S.-Pakistan Joint Working Group on Counterterrorism and Law Enforcement," May 8, 2002.

[30] Telephonic interview with U.S. State Department official, March 24, 2003.

[31] "Pakistan Leading the World in Tackling Money-Laundering: US Treasury Chief," Agence France-Presse, November 19, 2002; telephonic interview with U.S. Treasury Department official, March 21, 2003.

[32] Carlotta Gall, "U.S. to Train Pakistanis to Help Bar Terrorist Funds," *New York Times*, November 20, 2002.

Notable Projects Underway

Supplemental FY2002 U.S. aid to Pakistan included $73 million in International Narcotics and Law Enforcement (INCLE) Emergency Response Funds that continue to be used in FY2003 for border security and related law enforcement efforts.[33] The United States reportedly has supplied numerous instruments to bolster Pakistani security forces, including five used transport helicopters, 750 short- and long-range radios, and 434 vehicles (trucks, tractors, SUVs, and motorcycles) to increase mobility. During her December 2002 visit to Islamabad, Assistant Secretary of State for South Asia Rocca announced the provision to Pakistan of some 8,000 pieces of sophisticated communication and surveillance equipment worth more than $4 million. The equipment is to be used in efforts to track down suspected terrorists and those involved in drug trafficking. Also, the United States is undertaking to train Pakistani police investigators and is helping to establish a national fingerprint database modeled on that of the F.B.I. In March 2003, the United States disbursed to Pakistan $10 million for the Criminal Information Database, along with nearly $20 million more for road-building projects in the Federally Administered Tribal Areas. The roads are expected to improve access for law enforcement and security personnel, as well as bolster the region's economy.[34]

In what may become the most ambitious integrated national identification system ever installed, the United States reportedly is supplying to Pakistan the Personnel Identification Secure Comparison Evaluation System (PISCES). This computer software is said to make real-time comparisons of photographs and other personal details with the F.B.I. database in order to track the movements of Islamic militants. The ultimate aim is to monitor travelers entering or leaving Pakistan at all 18 major transit points. The system is reported to be in place at Karachi, Islamabad, and Lahore airports, and is expected to soon be operational at airports in Quetta and Peshawar, as well.[35]

Key Arrests

It is through the provision of intelligence that American agents are reported to be making their greatest contributions to such operations as those

[33] The Bush Administration is requesting another $38 million in INCLE funds for FY2004 to further improve the effectiveness of Pakistan's law enforcement efforts in the areas of border security and counternarcotics. Planned projects include a new forward operating location in Peshawar that will access the North West Frontier Province (NWFP), infrastructure enhancements such as road building, provision of forensic laboratory equipment, and myriad other support and assistance programs (see U.S. Department of State, "FY2004 Congressional Budget Justification for Foreign Operations," February 13, 2003, available at [http://www.state.gov/m/rm/rls/cbj/2004]).

[34] Zaffar Abbas, "US Help for Pakistan Terror Fight," BBC News, December 17, 2002; "Pakistan to Get $30 Million From United States for Fighting Crime," *Daily Times* (Lahore), March 13, 2003; telephonic interview with U.S. State Department official, March 25, 2003.

[35] "Passengers' Identity System Installed," *Dawn* (Karachi), November 11, 2002.

noted below.[36] The interception and tracing of satellite telephone transmissions has been a key tool in joint U.S.-Pakistani efforts to capture fugitive Taliban and Al Qaeda forces in Pakistan. American agents also closely monitor email and other Internet traffic for signs of terrorist communications. The F.B.I. is reported to have trained and equipped a number of former Pakistani army officers and others in what is known as the "Spider Group," an informal intelligence-gathering unit that is especially focused on monitoring the activities of Pakistani Islamist groups.[37]

U.S. government efforts to assist Pakistan with counterterrorism and law enforcement have produced many positive results. U.S. law enforcement personnel are reported to have played vital and direct, if low-profile roles in each of the following operations:[38]

- In March 2002, Abu Zubaydah, believed to be Al Qaeda's field commander, was shot and captured while trying to flee a raid in the Pakistani city of Faisalabad. He is said to have provided abundant intelligence to American authorities. Also that month, an F.B.I. agent was asked by the Pakistan government to provide sworn testimony to help in the prosecution of Daniel Pearl's kidnappers. Finally, in the eastern cities of Faisalabad and Lahore, a major raid netted 26 suspected Al Qaeda and Taliban fugitives.
- In June, 8 suspected members of banned extremist organizations were captured in Lahore.
- In July, 10 "Arab mujahideen"—alleged escapees from Kohat—were arrested in Hyderabad.
- In August, an office used by Harakat-ul-Mujahideen, a group linked to Al Qaeda, was raided, resulting in the arrest of 12 suspected militants and the seizure of explosives and other incriminating evidence.
- In September, Ramzi bin al-Shibh, said to be a key figure in the planning of the September 2001 terror attacks on the United States, and Sharib Ahmad, the most-wanted militant in Pakistan and alleged organizer of the June 2002 car bomb attack on the U.S. consulate in Karachi, were both apprehended. Later in the month, two Algerian nationals believed to be Al Qaeda members were arrested in Karachi, bringing to 10 the number of Algerians apprehended over a two-day period.
- In October, a raid on a refugee camp near Peshawar netted four suspected Al Qaeda operatives. Days later, a pre-dawn raid on another

[36] See, for example, Aamir Ashraf, "Pakistan Caught Key Sept 11 Figure on Anniversary," Reuters News, September 14, 2002; "Top Al Qaeda Agent's Trail Heated Up After Routine Arrest," *New York Times*, March 2, 2003.

[37] Aamir Latif, "FBI Puts 'Spiders' to Work in Pakistan," *Washington Times*, November 27, 2002.

[38] Reports of captured Al Qaeda suspects and others are culled from numerous open sources.

refugee camp led to the capture of five suspected militants wanted in connection with a spate of terror attacks on Pakistani Christians, as well as Khan Mohammad, said to be security chief for renegade Afghani warlord Gulbuddin Hekmatyar. Later in the month, FBI agents interrogated a physician who admitted to treating Osama bin Laden and collaborating with Al Qaeda in Afghanistan.

- In December, two tribesmen from Pakistan's South Waziristan Agency were handed over to U.S. agents for interrogation for their alleged involvement in an attack on a U.S. military camp in Afghanistan. Later in the month, a joint raid by Pakistani police and F.B.I. agents netted 9 suspected Al Qaeda operatives, including two naturalized American citizens.
- In January 2003, Pakistani police and F.B.I. agents arrested three suspected Al Qaeda operatives after a gunfight on the outskirts of Karachi. Computers, grenades, and $30,000 in U.S. currency were recovered. Among the nine suspects arrested in December was a Pakistani doctor, Ahmed Khawaja, who is named in January, and then charged along with his brother in February, as having provided material assistance to numerous Al Qaeda figures.
- On March 1, Khalid Mohammed, alleged mastermind of the September 2001 terrorist attacks and close associate of bin Laden, was arrested along with two cohorts in a pre-dawn raid in Rawalpindi. The efforts of U.S. communications specialists reportedly were key to locating the suspects. Seized at the scene were computer and communications equipment that are said to provide a "trove" of valuable data on Al Qaeda's methods of operations, support networks, and finances. One week after, 10 Al Qaeda suspects were arrested in Peshawar, including one believed to have had recent contact with Osama bin Laden. Later in March, police arrested alleged Al Qaeda financier and communications operative Yassir al-Jaziri in Lahore. This arrest appears to have provided leads resulting in the arrest of 6 more suspected Al Qaeda militants near Lahore and two in Peshawar on March 17.

The arrest of Khalid Mohammed in early March spurred heightened speculation that Osama bin Laden's capture was imminent. The White House called Mohammed's capture a "joint operation" between Pakistani and U.S. authorities and President Bush expressed his "deep appreciation and gratitude to President Musharraf and to the government of Pakistan" for their "fine efforts" in combating terrorism.[39] In the wake of the announced capture, rumors abounded that the ISI had known of Mohammed's

[39] "Text: U.S. Commends Detention of Mastermind Behind Sept. 11 Attacks," USIS Washington File, March 1, 2003; "Transcript: White House Daily Press Briefing," USIS Washington File, March 3, 2003.

whereabouts for weeks or even months before and that they may have staged the videotaped seizure that was shown to reporters.[40] In mid-March, Pakistan's intelligence agency claimed to have captured 442 foreign nationals suspected of terrorist activities and to have remanded 346 of these to U.S. custody (at least 36 have been transferred to other countries and more than 50 released without charge) since September 2001.[41]

Cooperation in Military Operations

Pakistan has served as a vital basing and transit point for Operation Enduring Freedom, the U.S.-led anti-terror mission in Afghanistan. According to the U.S. Department of Defense, Pakistan is providing basing and overflight permission for all United States and coalition forces engaged in Afghanistan. The airbase near Jacobabad has been vital to U.S. military operations in the region, and the airport of Dalbandin, near the Afghan border, is a key forward operational base. More than 57,000 U.S. military sorties have originated on Pakistani territory. U.S. military personnel reportedly have installed extensive radar facilities at three Pakistani airfields, allowing for coverage of the entire Pakistani airspace. Pakistan also deployed more than 115,000 regular and paramilitary troops along the tribal belt bordering Afghanistan and Iran in support of U.S.-led efforts to capture Taliban and Al Qaeda fugitives (many of the regular army troops were redeployed to the Pakistan-India border during a 10-month period of heightened tensions between Islamabad and New Delhi from December 2001–October 2002). Some 45,000 Pakistani troops were reported to be actively supporting Operation Enduring Freedom as of October 2002.[42]

Reports indicate that U.S. special operations soldiers and C.I.A. paramilitary agents participate in operations on Pakistani territory at the company-level (small teams of American specialists accompany much larger Pakistani units).[43] These reports are not confirmed by either Washington or Islamabad, as both governments make no official statements about such joint operations. The presence and activities of U.S. military personnel in Pakistan is a subject of great sensitivity in both capitals. Officially, there is only a handful of U.S. troops operating on Pakistani territory. In order to blend in with Pakistani military units, American special forces personnel are said

---

[40] Farhan Bokhari and Mark Huband, "Warning Over Pakistan Extradition," *Financial Times* (London), March 4, 2003; Simon Denyer, "Pakistan Accused of Staging Bin Laden Aide Arrest," Reuters News, March 11, 2003.

[41] Erik Eckholm, "Pakistan Reports on Leads From Qaeda Aide's Arrest," *New York Times*, March 11, 2003; "Pakistan Arrests More Suspects in Qaeda Hunt," Reuters News, March 17, 2003.

[42] U.S. Central Command, "International Contributions to the War on Terrorism: Pakistan." Online at [http://www.centcom.mil/Operations/Coalition/Coalition_pages/pakistan.htm].

[43] See, for example, Susan Schmidt and Thomas Ricks, "Pentagon Plans Shift in War on Terror," *Washington Post*, September 18, 2002; Douglas Waller, "The CIA's Secret Army," *Time*, February 3, 2003.

to all be of medium-height, Pashto-speaking, and wearing Pakistani Army uniforms.[44]

A July 2002 press report stated that more than 3,500 Al Qaeda operatives crossed into Pakistan while fleeing U.S. military operations in neighboring Afghanistan. There is continuing concern that these militants intend to establish a permanent presence in Pakistani cities.[45] In August, a U.S. military assessment estimated the presence of up to 1,000 Al Qaeda fighters in Pakistan, spurring the top officer of the U.S. Central Command, Gen. Tommy Franks, and Secretary of Defense Rumsfeld to suggest that the successful continuation of his Afghanistan mission would require expanding U.S. military operations into "neighboring countries."[46] His statement was met with adamant Pakistani assertions that any U.S. troop presence on their territory is "out of the question" given the professed sufficiency of ongoing Pakistani security operations.[47] U.S. military operations in Afghanistan extremely close to the Pakistan border and employing thousands of troops have been ongoing.[48] In this mountainous region, the location of the international border is not always clear, but there remain no confirmed open-source reports of large-scale American troop movements or aerial sorties in Pakistani territory.[49]

Pakistani government officials have issued contradictory statements on the issue of Al Qaeda's presence in their country, but many have flatly denied that Al Qaeda forces have entered Pakistan in any but the smallest numbers. In September 2002, a senior Pakistani security official claimed that his forces had "broken the back" of Al Qaeda in the country,[50] but more recent

---

44 Zahid Hussain, "Pakistan, U.S. Improve Ties in Antiterror Fight," *Asian Wall Street Journal* (Hong Kong), September 23, 2002.

45 Tim McGirk, "Al Qaeda's New Hideouts," *Time*, July 29, 2002.

46 Chris Otton, "More Al Qaeda May Now Be in Pakistan Than Afghanistan," Agence France-Presse, August 18, 2002; Secretary of Defense Donald Rumsfeld, "DoD News Brief—Secretary Rumsfeld and Gen. Franks," August 15, 2002. Online at [http://www.defenselink.mil/news/Aug2002/t08152002_t0815sd.html].

47 Hasan Akhtar, "Pakistan Rules Out US Troop Operation," *Dawn* (Karachi), August 27, 2002.

48 "US Combs Southeast Afghanistan; May Use Up To 2,000 Troops," Dow Jones Newswire, October 2, 2002; "US Launches Major Al Qaeda Hunt," BBC News, March 20, 2003.

49 In the first reported incident of its kind, a December 2002 statement by the U.S. Department of Defense indicated that a 500-pound bomb was dropped on a Pakistani border patrol position after U.S. troops came under fire. The incident led to a brief, but fiery debate over the alleged right of U.S. forces to engage in "hot pursuit" of adversaries who flee across the border from Afghanistan into Pakistan. Multiple reports indicated that the United States and Pakistan agreed to limited, low-profile pursuits, though Islamabad publically denied that U.S. forces are allowed to operate in Pakistan. One report claimed that a senior U.S. military commander held "secret talks" in Islamabad in a bid to avoid the repetition of any similar incidents in the future ("US Soldier Shot, Wounded by Pakistani Border Guard," Reuters News, December 31, 2002; Marc Kaufman, "U.S. Asserts Right to Enter Pakistan," *Washington Post*, January 4, 2003; Scott Baldauf, "US 'Hot Pursuit' Roils Pakistanis," *Christian Science Monitor*, January 6, 2003; Naqveed Ahmad, "US Not Assured of Quiet Hot Pursuit," *News International* (Karachi), January 7, 2003; "Foreign Troops Can't Operate in Pakistan: Kasuri," *Daily Times* (Lahore), January 17, 2003; "Pentagon Mends Fences in Pakistan," *Far Eastern Economic Review* (Hong Kong), January 23, 2003).

50 Shamim-ur-Rahman, "422 Osama Men Handed Over to US," *Dawn* (Karachi), September 23, 2002.

pronouncements have been less assured: after acknowledging that Al Qaeda members are in hiding throughout the country, the chief of Karachi's police investigation department stated in December 2002 that Al Qaeda is "down, but not out" in Pakistan. It is estimated that up to 5,000 Al Qaeda and Taliban fighters are still on the loose in the North West Frontier Province (NWFP) alone.[51]

Press reports in early 2003 suggested that Al Qaeda and Taliban forces have regrouped on Pakistani territory near the Afghani border in preparation for spring offensive operations against U.S.-led coalition units in Afghanistan.[52] More recently, however, the chairman of the Senate Intelligence Committee claimed that the March arrest of Khalid Mohammed likely would preclude any planned Al Qaeda offensive, and a U.S. military spokesman was quoted as saying he does not expect a spring offensive by Al Qaeda because he does not think there is "that much spring in them."[53]

Arms Sales and Security Cooperation

Arms Sales

Almost immediately upon joining the U.S.-led anti-terrorism coalition in September 2001, the Pakistani government sought compensation for its support, primarily through economic aid, debt forgiveness, and renewed access to sophisticated U.S. weaponry. The transfer to Pakistan of U.S. military equipment was ended in 1990 when then-President Bush could no longer certify that Pakistan was not pursuing a nuclear weapons program. U.S. economic sanctions triggered by Pakistan's May 1998 nuclear tests and October 1999 military coup were waived by President George W. Bush and new legislation in October 2001,[54] spurring Islamabad to present Washington with a "wish list" that was reported to have included a variety of missiles, artillery and rocket launching systems, unmanned aerial vehicles, and the release of previously purchased F-16 jets. An unnamed Pakistani defense ministry source was quoted as saying, "We want the kind of relationship the United States has with Egypt in terms of weapons sales."[55] In the lead-up to his January 2003 visit to the

---

[51] Scott Baldauf, "Pakistan's Release of Islamic Militants Rattles India," *Christian Science Monitor*, December 16, 2002.

[52] See, for example, Scott Baldauf, "Portrait of an Al Qaeda Camp," *Christian Science Monitor*, January 17, 2003.

[53] Don Van Natta, Jr., "Al Qaeda Hobbled by Latest Arrest," *New York Times*, March 3, 2003; "US Says Al Qaeda Failing to Regroup," *Daily Times* (Lahore), March 18, 2003.

[54] See CRS Report RS20995, *India and Pakistan: Current U.S. Sanctions* by Dianne Rennack. In October 2001, a State Department official pledged well over one billion dollars in U.S. assistance for Pakistan and several billion dollars from international organizations to help strengthen it as a key member of the U.S.-led anti-terrorism coalition.

[55] Quoted in Mohammed Abdullah, "Pakistan Seeks U.S. Weapons for Anti-Terror Partnership," *Defense Week*, October 22, 2001.

United States, Pakistani Foreign Minister Kasuri urged the United States to "take steps to reduce the conventional weapons disparity" between Pakistan and India as a means of halting a nuclear arms race in South Asia.[56]

There have been numerous foreign press reports, along with Pakistani and Indian government officials' claims, that Islamabad has secured deals for the purchase of major U.S. weapons platforms, including F-16s fighter jets, P-3 maritime surveillance aircraft, and Harpoon anti-ship missiles. Yet, as of late March 2003, the Bush Administration has notified Congress of only two pending transfers: the first, dated July 16, 2002, involves seven used C-130E transport aircraft (one being for spare parts); the second, dated July 26, 2002, is for six Aerostats—sophisticated, balloon-mounted surveillance radars. These mark the first noteworthy arms sales to Pakistan in more than a decade and reportedly are intended to support Islamabad's ability both to move troops quickly and to detect infiltration (thus aiding in counterterror operations).

Pakistan lately has emphasized a perceived need to bolster its air forces, if not through acquisition of new F-16s then at least through the receipt of spare parts and weaponry for its existing fleet of 1970s-era F-16A fighters (many of which are grounded for want of maintenance and munitions).[57] While most of Pakistan's arsenal is of Chinese origin, major U.S.-made weapons systems include P-3 Orion and C-130 Hercules aircraft, Harpoon and Stinger missiles, and 155mm howitzers. Past U.S.-imposed sanctions have caused many of these systems to become inoperable.[58]

Security Cooperation

The long-moribund Pakistan-U.S. Defense Cooperation Group (DCG)—created to oversee a bilateral defense relationship that has existed since the 1950s—met in Pakistan in late September 2002. This was the first such meeting since 1997. The two-day session included discussions among working groups on military cooperation, security assistance, and anti-terrorism. A joint statement issued by the DCG reports that the meetings "served the purpose of providing a forum to exchange views on security matters and, in Pakistan's case, share with the United States its views of its security environment."[59]

---

[56] Shaukat Piracha, "End Indo-Pak Arms Disparity, US Told," *Daily Times* (Lahore), January 15, 2003.

[57] In February 2003, U.S. Assistant Secretary of State for South Asia Rocca stated that the issue of F-16 sales to Pakistan is "not on the table now" (Nathan Hodge, "F-16s 'Not On the Table' For Pakistan," *Defense Week*, February 4, 2003).

[58] Nathan Hodge, "Talks Solidify U.S.-Pakistan Military Cooperation," *Defense Week*, September 30, 2002.

[59] "Joint Statement: Pakistan-US Defense Cooperation Group (DCG) Meeting, September 25–27, 2002, Rawalpindi, Pakistan," Defense Security Cooperation Agency, U.S. Department of Defense.

October 2002 saw the first joint U.S.-Pakistan military exercises in nearly five years, with approximately 120 soldiers from each country coming together in Pakistan for "Inspired Gambit III." U.S. Central Commander Gen. Tommy Franks witnessed the event. As with recent joint U.S.-Indian military exercises, an emphasis was placed upon increasing interoperability in weapon systems and tactics.[60] Numerous Pakistani press reports in early 2003 claimed that further joint exercises were being planned, but these reports are not confirmed by the U.S. government. U.S. assistance to Pakistan under security-related programs includes $396.5 million distributed in FY2002, $56.5 million allocated for FY2003, and $120 million requested for FY2004.[61]

As a current rotating member of the UN Security Council (UNSC), the Pakistani government faced a dilemma in addressing early-2003 discussions related to Iraq. Islamabad's external role as a key U.S. ally and member of the U.S.-led counterterrorism effort came up against powerful domestic opposition to Pakistan's participation in or condoning of a war against another Muslim country. So great were the countervailing pressures that most analysts foresaw a Pakistani abstention on a potential UNSC Res. 1442, but the vote never came. Upon the initiation of U.S.-led military operations against Iraq in March 2003, Islamabad called the war "unjustified" and vowed to oppose it in all fora, while nearly all Pakistani opposition parties—religious and secular, alike—were harshly critical of U.S. policy.[62]

Domestic Repercussions in Pakistan

November 2002 saw the formation of a fragile, pro-Musharraf ruling coalition in Islamabad, and President Musharraf ostensibly has turned day-to-day governance of the country over to civilian politicians.[63] The composition and actual level of influence exerted by the National Assembly and Prime Minister Zafarullah Jamali may have significant impact on

[60] "US General Watches Pakistan-US Military Exercise," Reuters News, October 20, 2002. Gen. Franks returned to Islamabad in January 2003 for a series of "routine consultations" with Pakistani leaders ("Top US General Holds Talks With Pakistan's Musharraf," Agence France-Presse, January 27, 2003).

[61] "Security-related programs" are Foreign Military Financing (FMF), International Military Training and Education (IMET), International Narcotics and Law Enforcement (INCLE), Nonproliferation, Anti-Terrorism, Demining, and Related Programs (NADR), and Peacekeeping Operations (PKO). FY2002 assistance included $220 million in PKO funds.

[62] Khalid Piracha, "Pakistan to Oppose War at All Fora," *Daily Times* (Lahore), March 20, 2003; "Pakistani Lawmakers Slam US as Parliament Opens Debate on Iraq," Agence France-Presse, March 18, 2003.

[63] Numerous analysts portray Pakistan's newly revived democratic institutions as being extremely fragile and largely cosmetic covers for the Pakistani military's continued rule (see, for example, "Jean-Herve Deiller, "Behind Civilian Rule, Pakistan's Army Looms Stronger Than Ever," Agence France-Presse, March 2, 2003).

future Pakistan-U.S. security relations in general and on U.S. counterterrorism efforts in South and Southwest Asia in particular. Thus far, the new civilian government in Islamabad has stated that it will "fulfill all its commitments to the international community in the fight against terrorism" and that "the policies initiated by President Pervez Musharraf will be continued."[64] A rough estimate indicates that regional anti-terrorism efforts have caused the Pakistani economy losses in excess of $10 billion since October 2001.[65]

President Musharraf's cooperation with U.S.-led anti-terrorism efforts is widely recognized as placing him in a precarious circumstance between external pressures to uphold pledges to eliminate Al Qaeda, Taliban, and Kashmiri separatist militants operating from Pakistani soil on the one hand, and internal pressures to maintain foreign policy independence, support for Kashmiri freedom, and even Islamic cohesion on the other. A February 2003 report indicates that Musharraf survived at least 6 assassination attempts during 2002, and notes that the risk of a coup staged by "senior-ranking" Pakistani military officials who disapprove of his relationship with the West cannot be ruled out.[66] The latter development could place Pakistan's nuclear arsenal of up to 75 warheads in the hands of Islamic extremists. In March 2003, large-scale street demonstrations organized by Islamist parties, combined with persistent calls by opposition political figures that Musharraf drop his "illegal" package of constitutional amendments and resign his post as Army Chief, are said by many to be making the Pakistani government "extremely uncomfortable."[67]

Sovereignty Concerns

The escalation of U.S. military involvement in anti-terrorism operations in western Pakistan apparently has brought some positive results and probably keeps Al Qaeda and Taliban remnants off-balance, but a negative political reaction within Pakistan is fueling anti-government and anti-American sentiments that may jeopardize longer-term U.S. interests in the region. An apparent breakdown of the long-standing autonomy of Pakistan's tribal zone along the border with Afghanistan, combined with an unprecedented U.S. military presence in the country, is reported to be causing increased anger and resentment among the ethnic Pashtun majority there. Likewise, the presence of American law enforcement agents in

64 "U.S. Secretary of State Colin Powell Gets Assurances of Continued Cooperation from Pakistan," Associated Press Newswires, December 13, 2002.

65 U.S. Central Command, "International Contributions to the War on Terrorism: Pakistan." Online at [http://www.centcom.mil/Operations/Coalition/Coalition_pages/pakistan.htm].

66 "Pakistan's Unseen Conflict," *Jane's Intelligence Digest*, February 7, 2003.

67 Zaffar Abbas, "Pakistan Senate in an Uproar," BBC News, March 12, 2003; Muddassir Rizvi, "Pakistan: Regime Squirms as Religious Parties Protest War on Iraq," Inter Press Service, March 3, 2003.

Pakistani cities is seen to be having similar effects among middle- and upper-class urban Pakistanis.

The Islamabad government has attempted to assuage this negative political response. Pakistani ballistic missile tests in early October 2002 were viewed as both a pre-election message of continued hawkishness vis-a-vis Kashmir and India, and a demonstration of foreign policy independence from the United States, given Washington's expressed displeasure at any signs of arms race dynamics in the region. The presence in Pakistan of U.S. law enforcement and military personnel, and the arrest and extradition of several Pakistani nationals, have spurred frequent expressions of sovereignty concerns, especially by leaders of the Muttahida Majlis-e-Amal (MMA), a coalition of six leading Islamist parties. In late-2002 and early-2003:

- the president of the Peshawar Bar Association described Pakistan as having become "a U.S. colony;"
- senior legal figures in Baluchistan have complained that F.B.I. operations in that region are "clear violations of the Pakistani constitution;"
- MMA Secretary-General Maulana Rehman made a declaration of "jihad against America that has stationed its forces in Pakistan to do away with our sovereignty;"
- top MMA chief Liaquat Baloch demanded that all Americans living in Pakistan should be fingerprinted and tested for AIDS;
- the MMA vice president stated that police forces in the NWFP and Baluchistan had been instructed to comply only with the orders of their provincial governments and not with those given by any U.S. agencies;
- and reports that F.B.I. agents had raided several mosques and madrassas in the Pakistani capital elicited complaints and warnings from Islamic clerics that such raids would lead to a "direct clash."[68]

The Pakistani government also has been critical of the newly-instituted U.S. policy of fingerprinting and photographing all Pakistani men who enter the United States, considering the policy unwarranted and "discriminatory" against the citizens of a U.S. ally. Islamabad formally requested that the United States remove Pakistan from the list of 20 nations subject to such immigration restrictions, with Pakistani Foreign Minister Kasuri

[68] "Pakistani Lawyers Slam FBI Presence Amid Further Protests," Agence France-Presse, December 23, 2002; Mohammad Ejaz Khan, "FBI Raids in Pakistan Unconstitutional," News International (Karachi), January 9, 2003; "MMA Declares Jihad Against US," *Dawn* (Karachi), January 4, 2003; "MMA Demands New Foreign Policy," Dawn (Karachi), February 1, 2003; "MMA to Resist FBI in NWFP, Baluchistan," *Dawn* (Karachi), January 7, 2003; Tahir Ikram, "Pakistani Clerics Demand Action Against FBI Agents," Reuters News, January 16, 2003; "MNA Warns Against FBI Raids," *Dawn* (Karachi), January 18, 2003.

warning that his country's presence on the new U.S. registration list could destabilize the Islamabad government and bolster the cause of radicals in Pakistan. Secretary of State Powell responded by assuring Kasuri that the United States is "very sensitive" to Pakistani concerns on this issue and emphasizing that the registration program "is not something directed at Pakistan or directed at Muslims or directed at Pakistanis in America"[69] The issue reflects a growing perception in Pakistan that the United States maintains a double-standard of friendly relations with the Islamabad government and "adversarial" relations with the Pakistani people.

Islamist Sentiments

Negative repercussions also were manifest in Pakistan's October 2002 national elections. The polls resulted in unexpectedly strong showings for candidates of the United Action Forum (known as MMA in its Urdu-language acronym), a coalition of six Islamic parties that ran on what largely was an anti-American platform and that won 68 seats—about 20% of the total—in the national assembly. The MMA also controls the provincial assembly in the North West Frontier Province and leads the coalition running that in Baluchistan (the two Pashtun-majority regions which border Afghanistan). This circumstance has led to concerns that a major shift in Pakistan's foreign policy may be in the offing, most especially with renewed indications of the "Talibanization" of western border regions. Yet anti-Americanism as expressed through support for Islamic parties is not limited to the rural western regions; religious candidates won parliamentary seats in Islamabad, Lahore, and Karachi, and resentment of perceived U.S. support for what are called President Musharraf's anti-democratic practices and military dictatorship has arisen even among Pakistan's monied elite.[70]

Leading Islamist politicians in Pakistan reportedly have made numerous provocative comments since coming to power. One senior MMA leader stated that "Taliban and Al Qaeda members are our brothers." MMA parliamentary leader Qazi Hussain Ahmed has threatened that, if Musharraf supported any U.S. military action against Iraq, "the MMA will make the government unmanageable." During prayers on the floor of the Pakistani Parliament for a Pakistani national recently executed in Virginia for two murders outside the CIA headquarters in 1993, a senior MMA member stated that, "America is the biggest terrorist state." In the first days of

[69] Anwar Iqbal, "Pakistan Seeks Deletion From INS List,"*Dawn* (Karachi), December 27, 2002; Dan Eggen, "Pakistan Seeks Exemption From New U.S. Registration," *Washington Post*, January 28, 2003; "Transcript: Powell Says U.S. 'Very Sensitive' to Pakistani Concerns Over NSEERS," USIS Washington File, January 29, 2003.

[70] David Rohde, "Pakistan's Elite Show Anti-Americanism in Elections," *New York Times*, October 13, 2002.

January 2003, the chief of Jamat al-Daawa—one of 6 MMA coalition parties—asserted his belief that "all anti-Muslim forces including the United States are trying to paralyze the Muslims economically, socially, and politically all over the world." MMA leader Maulana Mahmood stated later in the month that Pakistan's opposition groups will "break America into pieces like Russia" and "erase America from the world."[71] Anti-American sentiment is notably more virulent in Pakistan's Urdu-language press, where references to an alleged Christian-Jewish assault on Islam and the "traitorous" status of Pakistan's Western-allied leadership are more explicit.[72]

Along with Islamist expressions of anger at the United States and the Musharraf-Jamali government's current alliance with it, there are plentiful signs of efforts underway to "re-Talibanize" Pashtun-majority areas near the Afghani-Pakistani border. In 2003, MMA lawmakers in the NWFP have pledged to accelerate the process of Islamization in the region, and have made requests that the federal government grant them the authority to impose harsh penalties under *Sharia*, such as amputating the hands of thieves and stoning adulterers, as well as severely limiting women's freedoms. The seizure and burning of books and videotapes deemed "pornographic" has become common; numerous carnivals and theaters have been shut down. Even a leading Muslim separatist group in India's Jammu and Kashmir state has criticized Pakistan for the "Talibanization" of Indian Kashmir by sending jihadis across the Line of Control.[73]

Although the MMA did enjoy a strong showing in October 2002 elections, Pakistani government officials repeatedly have stated that Islamabad's foreign policy will remain unchanged. Moreover, Pakistan does have a small, but politically active middle-class, as well as a notable camp of moderate political figures who seek to establish a firm middle ground between the perceived poles of secular military dictatorship and the institution of Islamic rule. These figures often root their ideas in the writings of

---

[71] David Rohde, "Muslim Parties' Election Strength Weakens Musharraf," *New York Times*, October 12, 2002; "Pakistan's Position if US Attacks Iraq," *Daily Times* (Lahore), December 10, 2002; Zahid Hussain, "Pakistani MP Brands America a 'Terrorist'," *Times* (London), November 20, 2002; "US Trying to Destroy Muslims: Saeed," Dawn (Karachi), January 9, 2003; Zaffar Abbas, "Pakistanis Rally Against Iraq War," BBC News, January 31, 2003.

[72] See, for example, Shamin Akhtar, "Still Unashamed, Pakistan is Fighting a U.S. War," *Jasarat* (Karachi in Urdu), August 2, 2002 via Foreign Broadcast Information Service (FBIS), August 9, 2002; "Plea to Undertake Operation Against Pakistan," *Ummat* (Karachi in Urdu), August 20, 2002 via FBIS, August 20, 2002; "Social Boycott of an Imam in Southern Waziristan Over Loyalty with the United States," *Ummat* (Karachi in Urdu), July 2, 2002, via FBIS, July 9, 2002.

[73] Riaz Khan, "Lawmakers in Northwestern Pakistan Vow to Accelerate Islamization Process," Associated Press Newswire, January 4, 2003; Mohammed Shehzad, "One Step Forward, Two Centuries Back," *Friday Times* (Lahore), February 21, 2003; Munir Ahmad, "Pakistani Region Seeks Harsher Penalties," Associated Press Newswire, January 7, 2003; "Officials Destroy Tapes and CDs in Pakistani Province," *New York Times*, January 19, 2003; "Pakistan 'Talibanizing' Kashmir: JKLF," *Times of India* (Delhi), January 17, 2003.

Mohammed Ali Jinnah, Pakistan's founding father and proponent of a moderate and democratic Islamic republic. To date, such moderate views usually have been outweighed by militarist influences and/or the perception of widespread corruption among Pakistan's civilian politicians, which have fostered political polarization.

Assessment and U.S. Concerns

In March 2003, a top U.S. diplomat stated that U.S.-Pakistan relations are both "significantly broadened" and "solid." She called Pakistan-U.S. anti-terrorism cooperation "excellent" and "100 percent solid," and noted that "Pakistan has apprehended close to 500 suspected Al Qaeda operatives and affiliates."[74] However, while the U.S. State Department and White House continue to be almost wholly positive in their pronouncements relevant to Pakistani cooperation, the first months of 2003 have seen increasing expressions of U.S. doubts and concerns, emanating especially from top military and congressional leaders. Specific issues most commonly raised regard the continuation of Islamist militant infiltration into Indian Kashmir, the continued presence in Pakistan of wanted terrorists and illegal terrorist groups, and the extent to which Pakistan's government and its intelligence apparatus are committed to Islamabad's stated anti-terrorism policies.

In an unusually strong rebuke, U.S. Ambassador to Islamabad Nancy Powell stated in January that Pakistan is being used as a "platform for terrorism" and that this must stop. Later in the month, an unnamed U.S. State Department official was quoted as saying that the amount of infiltration of Islamic militants across the Line of Control into Indian Kashmir was increasing and that Pakistan was not doing enough to halt it.[75] Leading U.S. military commanders overseeing Operation Enduring Freedom have complained that renegade Al Qaeda and Taliban fighters are able to attack coalition troops in Afghanistan then escape across the Pakistani frontier. They have expressed dismay at the "slow pace of progress" in capturing wanted fugitives, especially Taliban leaders, in Pakistan and have urged Pakistan to "do more" to secure its rugged western border area.[76] The U.S. Special Envoy to Afghanistan Khalilzad stated in February that, "There are some key Taliban figures in Pakistan . . . some Al Qaeda people in the

[74] Assistant Secretary of State for South Asia Rocca, "Transcript: Hearing of the Subcommittee on Asia and the Pacific of the House International Relations Committee," Federal News Service, March 20, 2003.

[75] "U.S. Asks Pakistan to Insure Pledges on Kashmir," Reuters News, January 23, 2003; "Pakistan Not Doing Enough to Stop Kashmir Incursions: US," Agence France-Presse, January 30, 2003.

[76] "US Seeks Greater Military Cooperation," *Dawn* (Karachi), January 29, 2003; Marc Kaufman, "U.S. Seeks Joint Military Action With Pakistan, *Washington Post*, March 16, 2003 David Brunnstrom, "U.S. Coalition General Says Pakistan Could Do More," Reuters News, December 27, 2002.

border areas" and that the U.S. government "will not accept" these individuals being allowed to "find refuge" in Pakistan.[77] In the same month, the two senior members of the Senate Foreign Relations Committee—Sen. Lugar and Sen. Biden—expressed "deep concern" that "elements of Pakistan's powerful Inter-Services Intelligence agency might be helping members of the Taliban and Al Qaeda operate along the border and infiltrate into Afghanistan."[78]

In a security-related matter that may affect future Pakistan-U.S. anti-terrorism cooperation, late-2002 and early-2003 press reports citing U.S. intelligence officials indicated that Pakistan appears to have provided nuclear weapons-related technologies to North Korea beginning in the late-1990s and possibly continuing through July 2002.[79] Subsequent reports suggest that Iran's nuclear program may also have benefitted from Pakistani assistance in the past.[80] Islamabad adamantly denies that any such transfers have occurred. In October 2002, Musharraf gave Secretary of State Powell a "400% assurance" that such transfers to North Korea are "not taking place now." When asked about past transfers, Secretary Powell said, "The past is the past and there isn't a whole lot I can do about it." In March 2003, the Bush Administration declared that it had "carefully reviewed the facts relating to the possible transfer of nuclear technology from Pakistan to North Korea, and decided that they do not warrant the imposition of sanctions under applicable U.S. laws."[81]

Congressional oversight of U.S.-Pakistan relations in a March 2003 hearing of the Subcommittee on Asia and the Pacific of the House International Relations Committee included Member expressions of concern about possible links between Al Qaeda and Pakistan's largest Islamic party; about

[77] Carlotta Gall, "U.S. Won't Accept Refuge in Pakistan for Al Qaeda and Taliban," *New York Times*, February 10, 2003. On the same day, in testimony before the Senate Intelligence Committee, C.I.A. Director Tenet stated that "lawless zones" like those along the Afghan-Pakistani border are places where "extremist movements find shelter and can find the breathing space to grow," while D.I.A. Director Jacoby noted the "continued cross-border infiltration from Pakistan" into Indian-held Kashmir, and that "Pakistan does not completely control areas in the northwest where concentrations of Taliban and Al Qaeda remain," and warned that a "coup or assassination [of Musharraf] could result in an extremist Pakistan" (George Tenet, "DCI's Worldwide Threat Briefing,"February 10, 2003; Lowell Jacoby, "Current and Projected National Security Threats to the United States," February 11, 2003).

[78] James Dao, "Terror Aid From Pakistan Concerns Senators," *New York Times*, February 13, 2003.

[79] See David Sanger and James Dao, "U.S. Says Pakistan Gave Technology to North Korea," *New York Times*, October 18, 2002; Glenn Kessler, "Pakistan's N. Korea Deals Stir Scrutiny," *Washington Post*, November 13, 2002; David Sanger, "In North Korea and Pakistan, Deep Roots of Nuclear Barter, *New York Times*, November 24, 2002; Seymour Hersh, "The Cold Test," *New Yorker*, January 21, 2003; "Pakistan's Nuclear Activities," Jane's Intelligence Digest, January 22, 2003.

[80] Michael Gordon, "Inspectors View Nuclear Work at Iranian Site," *New York Times*, February 23, 2003.

[81] "Secretary of State Powell Delivers Remarks, Los Cabos, Mexico," Federal Document Clearing House, October 26, 2002; "Transcript: Secretary of State Colin Powell Interviewed on ABC's This Week," USIS Washington File, October 20, 2002; Assistant Secretary of State for Legislative Affairs Paul Kelly, "Letter to Sen. Daschle," March 12, 2003.

Musharraf's possibly continuing support for "Kashmiri terrorists;" about the possibility that "lower-level operatives within the ISI" may be assisting Al Qaeda and Taliban fugitives; about possible ISI involvement in regional heroin trafficking; about Pakistan's possible nuclear weapons proliferation activities and "contradictions" in U.S. nonproliferation policy toward the region; about the role madrassas play in raising levels of Islamic radicalism in Pakistan; and about problems with Pakistani democratization and the danger of the United States "giving full recognition to a military coup" through continuous waivers of democracy-related aid restrictions.[82]

Pakistan-U.S. anti-terrorism cooperation has been broad in both scale and scope, and has realized tangible successes since October 2001. Yet the wide range of U.S. concerns about relations with Pakistan indicate that such partnership between the two countries may be undermined. A reduction of U.S. cooperative efforts could result from increased indications of sub-optimal levels of Pakistani commitment or from exacerbated Pakistan-India tensions that are linked to infiltration in Kashmir. Differences over weapons proliferation and human rights violations could trigger far-reaching restrictions on future U.S. aid to Pakistan. The Islamabad government, for its part, may come under increasing pressure to adjust its foreign policy to more accurately reflect the sentiments of Pakistan's opposition parties, especially the virulently anti-Western Islamists. This could erode Pakistani cooperative efforts and is made even more likely as domestic violence and public disturbances in Pakistan continue. Given such numerous and substantial potential disruptions to present levels of Pakistan-U.S. anti-terrorism cooperation, it may be unwise to assume that such cooperation is sustainable in the middle- and long-term.

[82] "Transcript: Hearing of the Subcommittee on Asia and the Pacific of the House International Relations Committee," Federal News Service, March 20, 2003.

Figure 1: Map of Pakistan

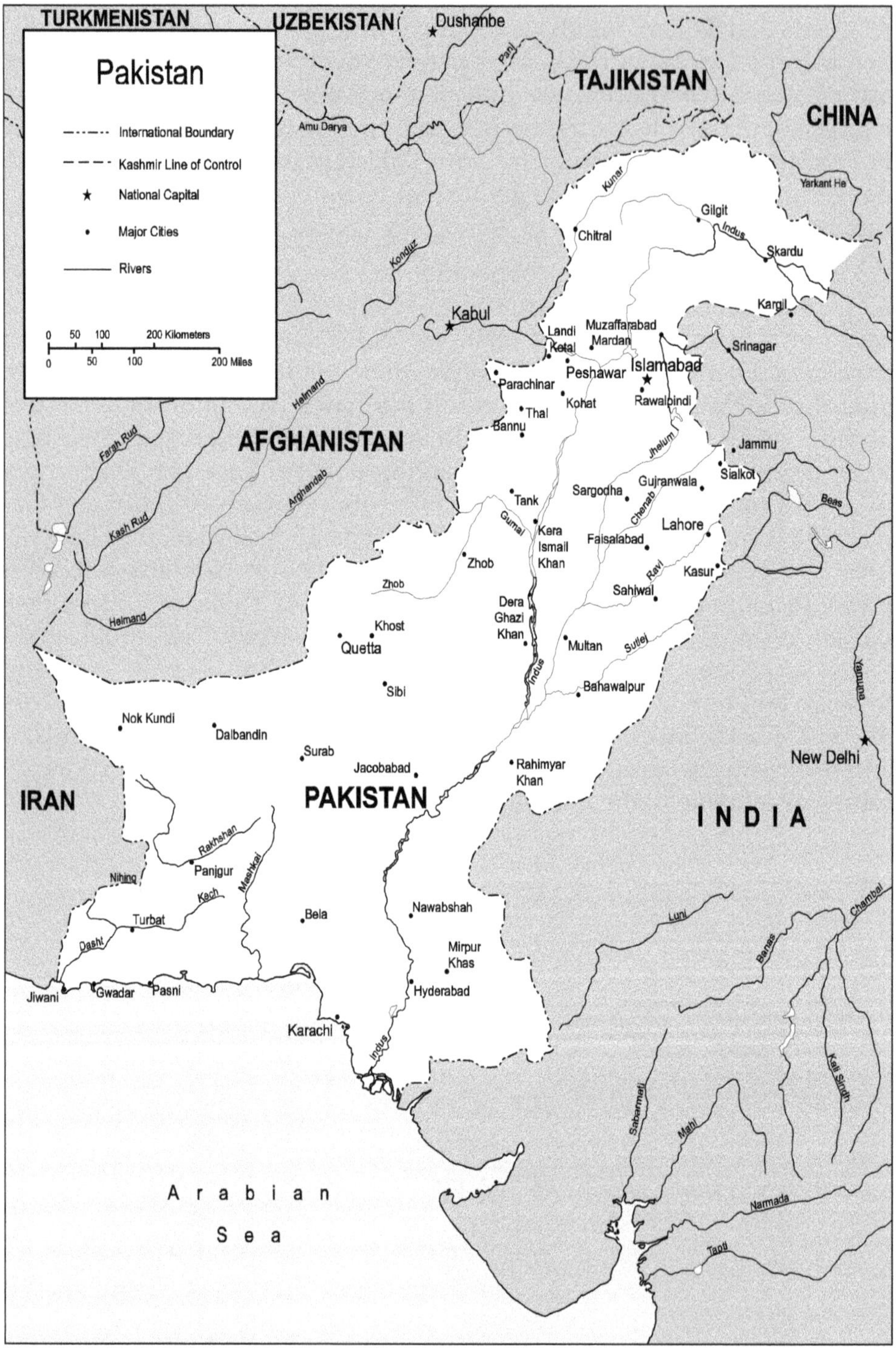

Source: Map Resources. Adapted by CRS. (M.Chin 03/03)
Note: Boundary representations not necessarily authoritative.

DOCUMENT NO. 18

TERRORISM IN SOUTH ASIA

CRS Report
RL32259

August 31, 2005

K. Alan Kronstadt
Coordinator
Analyst in Asian Affairs
Foreign Affairs, Defense, and Trade Division
Bruce Vaughn
Analyst in Southeast and South Asian Affairs
Foreign Affairs, Defense, and Trade Division

Summary

This report reviews the recent incidence of terrorism in South Asia, concentrating on Pakistan and India, but also including Afghanistan, Bangladesh, Sri Lanka, and Nepal. The existence of international terrorist groups and their supporters in South Asia is identified as a threat to both regional stability and to the attainment of central U.S. policy goals. Al Qaeda forces that fled from Afghanistan with their Taliban supporters remain active on Pakistani territory, and Al Qaeda is believed to have links with indigenous Pakistani terrorist groups that have conducted anti-Western attacks and that support separatist militancy in Indian Kashmir. Al Qaeda founder Osama bin Laden and his lieutenant, Ayman al-Zawahiri, are widely believed to be in Pakistan. A significant portion of Pakistan's ethnic Pashtun population is reported to sympathize with the Taliban and even Al Qaeda. The United States maintains close counterterrorism cooperation with Pakistan aimed especially at bolstering security and stability in neighboring Afghanistan. In the latter half of 2003, the Islamabad government began limited military operations in the traditionally autonomous tribal areas of western Pakistan. Such operations have since intensified in coordination with U.S. and Afghan forces just across the international frontier.

The relationships between international terrorists, indigenous Pakistani extremist groups, and some elements of Pakistan's political-military structure are complex and murky, but may represent a serious threat to the attainment of key U.S. policy goals. There are past indications that elements of Pakistan's intelligence service and Pakistani Islamist political parties provided assistance to U.S.-designated Foreign Terrorist Organizations (FTOs). A pair of December 2003 attempts to assassinate Pakistan's President Musharraf reportedly were linked to Al Qaeda. Lethal, but failed attempts to assassinate other top Pakistani officials in summer 2004 also were linked to Al Qaeda-allied groups. Security officers in Pakistan have enjoyed notable successes in breaking up significant Al Qaeda and related networks operating in Pakistani cities, although numerous wanted militants remain at large.

The 9/11 Commission Report contains recommendations for U.S. policy toward Pakistan, emphasizing the importance of eliminating terrorist sanctuaries in western Pakistan and near the Afghanistan-Pakistan border and calling for provision of long-term and comprehensive support to the government of President Musharraf so long as that government remains committed to combating extremism and to a policy of "enlightened moderation." Legislation passed by the 108th Congress (S. 2845) seeks to implement this and other Commission recommendations.

The United States remains concerned by the continued "cross-border infiltration" of Islamic militants who traverse the Kashmiri Line of Control to engage in terrorist acts in India and Indian Kashmir. India also is home to several indigenous separatist and Maoist-oriented terrorist groups. Moreover, it is thought that some Al Qaeda elements fled to Bangladesh. The Liberation Tigers of Tamil Eelam (LTTE) of Sri Lanka have been designated as an FTO under U.S. law, while Harakat ul-Jihad-I-Islami/ Bangladesh, and the Communist Party of Nepal (Maoist)/United Peoples Front, appear on the State Department's list of "other terrorist groups."

Terrorism in South Asia

This report reviews the recent incidence of terrorism in South Asia, concentrating on Pakistan and India, but also including Afghanistan, Bangladesh, Sri Lanka, and Nepal.[1] In the wake of the September 2001 terrorist attacks on the United States, President Bush launched major military operations in South and Southwest Asia as part of the global U.S.-led antiterrorism effort. Operation Enduring Freedom in Afghanistan has seen

[1] "Terrorism" here is understood as being "premeditated, politically motivated violence perpetrated against noncombatant targets by subnational groups or clandestine agents, usually intended to influence an audience" (see Title 22, Section 2656f(d) of the United States Code).

substantive success with the vital assistance of neighboring Pakistan. Yet the United States remains concerned that members of Al Qaeda and its Taliban supporters have found haven and been able, at least partially, to regroup in Pakistani cities and in the rugged Pakistan-Afghanistan border region. This latter area is inhabited by ethnic Pashtuns who express solidarity with anti-U.S. forces. Al Qaeda also reportedly has made alliances with indigenous Pakistani terrorist groups that have been implicated in both anti-Western attacks in Pakistan and terrorism in Indian Kashmir. These groups seek to oust the government of President Gen. Pervez Musharraf and have been named as being behind two December 2003 assassination attempts that were only narrowly survived by the Pakistani leader. In fact, Pakistan's struggle with militant Islamic extremism appears for some to have become an matter of survival for that country.[2] Along with these concerns, the United States expresses an interest in the cessation of "cross-border infiltration" by separatist militants based in Pakistani-controlled areas who traverse the Kashmiri Line of Control (LOC) to engage in terrorist activities both in Indian Kashmir and in Indian cities. U.S.-designated terrorist groups also remain active in Bangladesh, Nepal, and Sri Lanka.

In March 2004, the Assistant Secretary of State for South Asia, Christina Rocca, told the Senate Foreign Relations Committee that the top U.S. policy goal in the region is "combating terror and the conditions that breed terror in the frontline states of Afghanistan and Pakistan."[3] *The 9/11 Commission Report*, released in July 2004, emphasizes that the mounting of large-scale international terrorist attacks appears to require sanctuaries in which terrorist groups can plan and operate with impunity. It also notes that Al Qaeda benefitted greatly from its former sanctuary in Afghanistan that was in part made possible by logistical networks that ran through Pakistan. The report further notes that Pakistan's vast unpoliced regions remain attractive to extremist groups and that almost all of the 9/11 attackers traveled the north-south nexus from Kandahar in Afghanistan through Quetta and Karachi in Pakistan. The Commission identifies the government of President Musharraf as the best hope for stability in Pakistan and Afghanistan, and recommends that the United States make a long-term commitment to provide comprehensive support for Islamabad so long as Pakistan itself is committed to combating extremism and to a policy of "enlightened moderation."[4]

---

[2] See, for example, Syed Rifaat Hussain, "War Against Terrorism: Pakistani Perspective," *IPRI Journal* (Islamabad), Winter 2004, p. 42.

[3] "State's Rocca Outlines Assistance Plans for South Asia," U.S. Department of State Washington File, Mar. 2, 2004.

[4] See Sections 12.1 and 12.2 of *The 9/11 Commission Report*, available at [http://www.gpoaccess.gov/911/]; Pervez Musharraf, "A Plea for Enlightened Moderation," *Washington Post*, June 1, 2004.

Legislation passed by the 108th Congress seeks to implement this and other Commission recommendations, in part through the provision of comprehensive and long-term assistance to Pakistan.[5] The National Intelligence Reform Act of 2004 (P.L. 108-458) calls for U.S. aid to Pakistan to be sustained at a minimum of FY2005 levels, with particular attention given to improving Pakistan's education system, and extended the President's authority to waive coup-related sanctions through FY2006. It further required the President to report to Congress by June 15, 2005, a description of a long-term U.S. strategy to engage with and support Pakistan. In passing the Foreign Operations FY2005 Appropriations bill (P.L. 108-447), Congress approved the President's $700 million aid request for Pakistan, half of which is to fund security-related programs.[6] Pending legislation in the 109th Congress includes the Targeting Terrorists More Effectively Act of 2005 (S. 12). Sec. 232 of the bill identifies "a number of critical issues that threaten to disrupt" U.S.-Pakistan relations, calls for "dramatically increasing" USAID funding for Pakistan-related projects, would require the President to report to Congress a long-term strategy for U.S. engagement with Pakistan, would set nuclear proliferation-related conditions on assistance to Pakistan, and would earmark $797 million in economic and military assistance to Pakistan for FY2006.

Most Recent Developments

In early 2005, the United States began advertizing in mass-circulation Urdu-language newspapers and on radio and television stations in Pakistan's Northwest Frontier Province to promote a rewards program for wanted **Al Qaeda** suspects. In May, Al Qaeda fugitive Abu Faraj al-Libbi, a Libyan native wanted in connection with lethal December 2003 attempts to assassinate President Musharraf, was captured in the northwestern Pakistani city of Mardan. Information provided by Libbi reportedly led to the arrest of six suspected Al Qaeda members, including two Arabs and four Pakistanis, and the targeted killing of an alleged Al Qaeda bomb expert near the Afghan border. Musharraf claimed that Pakistan had "broken their [Al Qaeda's] back" with recent arrests. Two months later, in the wake of deadly July bombings in Britain and Egypt, Musharraf again declared that Al Qaeda's ability to operate in Pakistan had been destroyed.[7]

---

[5] See CRS Report RL32518, *Removing Terrorist Sanctuaries: The 9/11 Commission Recommendations and U.S. Policy*.

[6] The Emergency Supplemental Appropriations Act, 2005 (P.L. 109-13) funding of $150 million in FMF and $4 million in additional counter-drug funding brought total estimated FY2005 U.S. assistance to about $692 million.

[7] "Six Al Qaeda Suspects Arrested," *Dawn* (Karachi), May 9, 2005; Dana Priest, "Surveillance Operation in Pakistan Located and Killed Al Qaeda Official," *Washington Post*, May 15, 2005; Jo Johnson and Farhan Bokhari, "Al Qaeda's Back Has Been Broken, Says Musharraf," *Financial Times* (London), May 15, 2005; Farhan Bokhari, "Pakistan Claims Al Qaeda Command Destroyed," *Financial Times* (London), July 25, 2005.

Debate over the whereabouts of fugitive Al Qaeda founder Osama bin Laden continues to focus on the rugged Afghan-Pakistani border region: Pakistani officials generally insist there is no evidence that bin Laden is hiding there, but numerous U.S. officials have suggested otherwise. In June, Director of Central Intelligence Goss claimed to have "an excellent idea of where [bin Laden] is" and suggested that "sanctuaries in sovereign states" and "our sense of international obligation" present obstacles to his capture.[8] The Pakistani president has issued contradictory statements on the topic.

Efforts to kill or capture Al Qaeda and Taliban militants near **the Afghanistan-Pakistan border** continue to bring mixed results. An apparently resurgent Taliban has suffered major battlefield losses in eastern and southern Afghanistan during the spring and summer of 2005, but U.S. and Afghan officials continue to claim that insurgents are able to cross into Afghanistan to attack U.S.-led forces before returning to Pakistan and, in June, Afghan officials were complaining of a "steady stream of terrorists" entering their country from Pakistan. The Afghan-Pakistani rift deepened, spurring President Bush to make a personal call to Musharraf in an effort to smooth relations between two key U.S. allies in the region. In July, Pakistan reported moving 4,000 additional troops to the border region, bringing the total to some 80,000, and Prime Minister Aziz visited Kabul, where he vowed "seamless cooperation" with the Afghan government in fighting terrorism and Islamic extremism. Still, U.S. officials continue to urge Islamabad (and Kabul) to "do more" to end insurgent operations in the region and some reports indicate that Taliban recruiting and training continues to take place on Pakistani territory without government interference.[9]

Pakistan's western tribal regions continue to be the site of tensions and sporadic Islamic militant-related violence. Pakistani military operations in South Waziristan wound down in 2004. Late in that year, the regional Pakistani corps commander declared that "peace has been restored in Wana," the area where the bulk of combat had taken place. Attention has become focused on the North Waziristan district, where scores and possibly hundreds of "unwanted foreigners" have found refuge. The Islamabad government is using a carrot-and-stick approach, offering economic and infrastructure development incentives to encourage cooperation from tribal chieftains while threatening use of force in those areas where militants are given haven. Yet cooperative tribal leaders have come under lethal attack by militants and resistance to Islamabad's cooperation with

[8] "10 Questions for Porter Goss," *Time*, June 27, 2005.

[9] Robert Birsel, "Afghan Rebels Attack From Pakistan," Reuters, May 16, 2005; "Afghan Violence Shatters Pakistan Alliance," *New York Times*, June 22, 2005; "Extra Troops for Afghan Border," BBC News, July 6, 2005; "Pakistan to Help Afghans Contain Election Strife," *New York Times*, July 25, 2005; "US Says Wants More Pressure on Afghan Insurgents," Reuters, July 14, 2005; Jay Solomon, et. al., "Despite U.S. Effort, Pakistan Remains Key Terror Hub," *Wall Street Journal*, July 22, 2005; Paul Watson, "Pakistan Connection Seen in Taliban's New Tactics," *Los Angeles Times*, July 28, 2005.

U.S.-led efforts in Afghanistan remains widespread. On July 15, U.S. forces based in Afghanistan exchanged heavy weapons fire with militants just across the border in Pakistan, killing 24 of them. Thousands of Pakistani tribesmen later denounced the U.S. action and Pakistan told the United States that border violations would not be tolerated.[10]

Pakistan continues to struggle with a virulent strain of belligerent Islamism that some analysts say threatens the survival of the country. In December 2004, President Musharraf called his "biggest fear" the extremism, terrorism, and militancy that has "really polluted society in Pakistan." He also conceded that some of Pakistan's religious schools are part of the problem: "There are many [madrassas] which are involved in militancy and extremism."[11] Major sectarian bomb attacks in May again raised questions about the ability of Pakistan's security forces to maintain order in the country's urban centers (where, not incidentally, the great majority of top Al Qaeda fugitives have been found). Positive news did come with July announcements that the Islamabad government would reinvigorate its efforts to curtail indigenous terrorism by detaining suspected militants, shuttering the offices of extremist groups, and regulating the activities of the country's thousands of religious schools, some of which are involved in the teaching of militancy.

Pakistan-U.S. counterterrorism cooperation continues apace. In November 2004, the Pentagon notified Congress of three possible major Foreign Military Sales to Pakistan involving eight P-3C maritime reconnaissance aircraft, 2,000 TOW anti-armor missiles, and six Phalanx naval guns. The deals could be worth up to $1.2 billion for Lockheed Martin and Raytheon, the prime contractors. The Department of Defense characterized the P-3Cs and TOW missiles as having significant anti-terrorism applications (a claim that elicited skepticism from some analysts), and it asserted that the proposed sales would not affect the military balance in the region. India's external affairs minister later "cautioned the United States" against any decision to sell F-16 fighter jets to Pakistan, adding that the "U.S. arms supply to Pakistan would have a negative impact on the goodwill the United States enjoys with India, particularly as a sister democracy."[12] Yet, in March 2005, the Bush Administration announced that the United States would resume sales of F-16 fighters to Pakistan after a 16-year hiatus (see CRS Report RS22148, *Combat Aircraft Sales to South Asia*).

Separatist-related violence and terrorism in **Kashmir** has increased in the summer of 2005. The India-Pakistan peace initiative begun in April 2003

[10] Haji Mujataba, "Pakistani Tribesmen Vent Anger Over US Counter-Attack," Reuters, July 16, 2005; "Border Violations Will Not Be Tolerated, Abizaid Told," *Daily Times* (Lahore), July 20, 2005.

[11] "Transcript: Interview With Pervez Musharraf," CNN Late Edition, Dec. 5, 2004.

[12] "India Cautioned US Against Selling F-16s to Pakistan: Foreign Minister," Agence France Presse, Dec. 8, 2004; "Pranab Sticks to His Guns," *Telegraph* (Calcutta), Dec. 12, 2004.

continues, most concretely with a formal cease-fire agreement along the Kashmiri Line of Control (LOC) and the entire international border (the cease-fire has held for nearly two years). In April 2005, a new bus service was launched in the disputed Kashmir region and the Indian and Pakistan leaders called the bilateral peace process "irreversible." However, while New Delhi indicates that rates of militant infiltration across the LOC are down significantly as compared to past years, ongoing separatist-related violence in India's Jammu and Kashmir state has claimed scores of lives and Indian officials have renewed criticisms that Pakistan has not acted to eliminate the "terrorist infrastructure" on Pakistani territory.

In **India's northeastern states**, decades-old separatist movements continue. After two Assamese separatist leaders reportedly surrendered in February, United Liberation Front of Assam terrorists conducted a series of coordinated bomb attacks in March, spurring Indian security forces to launch a 2,000-man operation against militants there in April. In May, New Delhi signed a truce with the National Democratic Front of Bodoland, a leading Assamese separatist group designated as terrorists by the Indian government. Moreover, rebels continue to make deadly assaults on government forces in Manipur.[13] Meanwhile, attacks perpetrated by **Maoist "Naxalites"** operating in India (the two largest organizations being U.S.-designated terrorist groups) became more numerous and have cost scores of lives 2005. Maoist militants are said to have expanded their operations into more than half of India's 28 states, spurring some observers to issue dire warnings about India's deteriorating internal security circumstances. New Delhi vows to bolster the capabilities of security forces battling the militants.[14] Other recent terrorist violence in India included a July incident in which six militants, including a suicide bomber, were killed in the midst of an unsuccessful attack on the site of a controversial temple that is claimed by both Hindus and Muslims in the Uttar Pradesh city of Ayodhya. Ensuing protests by Hindu activists led to thousands of arrests. The culprits reportedly were linked to the Pakistan-based Lashkar-e-Taiba terrorist group.[15]

India-U.S. counterterrorism cooperation appears set to further expand. In June, the United States and India signed a ten-year defense framework agreement which lists "defeating terrorism and violent religious extremism" as one of four key shared security interests, and which calls for a bolstering of mutual defense capabilities required for such a goal.[16]

---

[13] "Assam Separatist Chiefs Surrender," BBC News, Feb. 28, 2005; "India: United Liberation Front of Assam," *Jane's Terrorism & Security Monitor*, Mar. 16, 2005; "India Moves Against Assam Rebels," BBC News, Apr. 1, 2004; "India Truce With Bodo Rebels," BBC News, May 24, 2005.

[14] Josy Joseph, "Naxalism: Biggest Threat to India," *Times of India* (Delhi), May 10, 2005; "Naxalites on Patil Radar," *Telegraph* (Calcutta), July 11, 2005.

[15] "Hindu Groups Rage Against India Holy Site Attack," Reuters, July 6, 2005; Atiq Khan and Arun Sharma, "Lashkar's Terror Track to Ayodhya Traced," *Indian Express* (Bombay), July 15, 2005.

[16] "Statements Made by U.S. Secretary of Defense Donald Rumsfeld and Indian Defense Minister Pranab Mukherjee," U.S. Department of Defense News Transcript, Dec. 9, 2004; "New Framework

On August 17, about 350 small bombs exploded almost simultaneously across **Bangladesh**, killing at least two people and injuring more than 125 others. No one claimed responsibility for the attacks, but leaflets produced by the banned militant Jamatul Mujahideen and calling for Islamic law in Bangladesh were found at most sites. Numerous suspects subsequently were arrested, including many suspected members of the Jamatul Mujahideen. The United States offered law enforcement assistance to Dhaka in its ongoing investigation of the blasts.[17] After meeting with U.S. Assistant Secretary of State Christina Rocca, on May 12, 2005, in Dhaka, Bangladesh Foreign Minister M. Morshed Khan reportedly stated that he was optimistic that Bangladesh would receive American assistance for capacity building to improve the law and order situation in Bangladesh.[18] It was also reported that the two discussed the need to better protect the coastal zone from piracy and to build up Bangladesh's capacity to face any terrorist challenges.[19] During her visit, Rocca reportedly urged Bangladesh to "go after those who would undermine its long tradition of tolerance, moderation and peace." Rocca welcomed Bangladesh's ban on the Jamatul Mujahideen and the Jagrata Muslim Janata Bangladesh for their alleged role in recent bombings.[20] Foreign Minister Morshed Khan met with Secretary of State Rice during his visit to Washington later in May 2005. At that time, he reiterated Bangladesh's commitment to work with the United States in the war against terror. Rice described Bangladesh as "a democratic force and a voice of moderation."[21] Foreign Minister Khan reportedly described the U.S. view of Bangladesh as "an unavoidable partner" in bridging religious divides across the world."[22] Bangladesh recently assumed the Chair of the BIMSTEC grouping comprised of Bangladesh, Bhutan, India, Nepal, Burma, Sri Lanka, and Thailand. The June 1, 2005 BIMSTEC meeting in Dhaka reportedly reviewed progress of a joint working group on terrorism which met in Delhi in December 2004.[23]

Assistant Secretary Rocca also traveled to **Nepal** during her May 2005 trip to South Asia. There is rising concern among some analysts that King Gyanendra's February 1, 2005 takeover has broadened the divide between the king and democratic elements in the country and thereby weakened the government's ability to fight the Maoists. Such a situation favors the

for the U.S.-India Defense Relationship," June 28, 2005, available at [http://www.indianembassy.org/press_release/2005/June/31.htm].

17 "Concerted Bombs Hit 100 Bangladesh Sites," Associated Press, Aug. 18, 2005; "US Offers FBI Support for Probe Into Blasts," *New Nation* (Dhaka), Aug. 29, 2005.

18 "Dhaka Hopeful of U.S. Help for Capacity Building," *Asia-Pacific News Agencies*, May 12, 2005.

19 "Dhaka, Washington Discuss Roadmap for Bilateral Relations," *Asia Pulse*, May 13, 2005.

20 "Top US Diplomat Ends S Asian Tour Urging Action on Terrorism," *Agence France Presse*, May 14, 2005.

21 "Morshed-Condoleezza Talks," *United News of Bangladesh Limited*, May 20, 2005.

22 "Bangladesh Unavoidable Partner of America," *United News of Bangladesh*, May 29, 2005.

23 "Bangladesh Assumes BIMSTEC Chair," *United News of Bangladesh*, June 3, 2005.

Maoists as it appears to preclude a unified front against them. Violence has increased in recent months and the death toll of the conflict with the Maoists is now thought to exceed 11,500. India may be increasingly concerned that the conflict in Nepal could spill over into neighboring areas. Maoist tactics are reportedly changing with increased daytime attacks and increased use of roadblocks and blockades. In August, Kathmandu accused Maoist rebels of "executing" 40 captured soldiers in the deadliest incident since the king's February power seizure, spurring analysts to again conclude that the government's counterinsurgency efforts are making little headway.[24]

The **Sri Lanka** peace process has come under new threat after the August 12 assassination of Foreign Minister Lakshman Kadirgamar, an ethnic Tamil known for his vehement anti-rebel stance. Kadirgamar also was one of President Kumaratunga's closest allies. The Liberation Tigers of Tamil Eelam (LTTE) denied playing any role in the murder, but the cease-fire may not hold.[25] The peace process had already been stalled with growing instability as divisions within the LTTE ranks has devolved into internecine warfare and targeted assassinations amongst the Northern and Eastern factions. The LTTE leadership has also attempted to apply pressure on both the Sri Lankan Government and the Norwegian-backed Sri Lanka Monitoring Mission (SLMM) by staging isolated attacks on Sri Lankan units accompanied by monitors. The LTTE also announced in May 2005 that it is looking at acquiring an air capability, which is in violation of the cease-fire and could be destabilizing due to the possibility that such capabilities could be used in terrorist suicide-bombings. Divisions within the Sri Lankan government have hampered talks as well, as there are internal disagreements over negotiating strategies and possible concessions to the LTTE in any eventual peace agreement. The U.S. Administration has voiced continuing support for negotiations and the possibility of peace in Sri Lanka and continues to call on the LTTE to disarm and disavow violence.

Al Qaeda, the Taliban, and Pakistani Extremism[26]

The Al Qaeda-Taliban Nexus

Among the central goals of Operation Enduring Freedom are the destruction of terrorist training camps and infrastructure within Afghanistan, the capture of Al Qaeda and Taliban leaders, and the cessation of terrorist

[24] Removing Terrorist Sanctuaries: The 9/11 Commission Recommendations and U.S. Policy; "Nepal Country Report," *Economist Intelligence Unit*, Feb. 2005; "At Least 66 Killed as Nepal Battles Maoist Rebels in Western District," *New York Times*, Aug. 10, 2005.

[25] Somini Sengupta, "Assassination Threatens to End Cease-Fire in Sri Lanka," *New York Times*, Aug. 14, 2005.

[26] This section written by K. Alan Kronstadt, Analyst in Asian Affairs. See also CRS Report RL30588, *Afghanistan: Post-War Governance, Security, and U.S. Policy*, by Kenneth Katzman; and CRS Report RS21973, *Al Qaeda: Statements and Evolving Ideology*, by Christopher Blanchard.

activities in Afghanistan.[27] Most, but not all, of these goals have been achieved. However, since the Taliban's ouster from power in Kabul and subsequent retreat to the rugged mountain region near the Afghanistan-Pakistan border, what the U.S. military calls its "remnant forces" have been able to regroup and to conduct "hit-and-run" attacks against U.S.-led coalition units, often in tandem with suspected Al Qaeda fugitives. These forces are then able to find haven on the Pakistani side of the border.[28] One senior Pakistani official was quoted as saying that South Waziristan, a district of the traditionally autonomous Federally Administered Tribal Areas (FATA), had by mid-2002 become "the hub of Al Qaeda operations in the whole world." Three years later, some analysts continue to call Pakistan "the global center for terrorism and for the remnants of Al Qaeda."[29] Al Qaeda founder Osama bin Laden and his lieutenant, Egyptian Islamic radical leader Ayman al-Zawahiri, are believed by many to be in Pakistan's North West Frontier Province, an area roughly the size of Virginia. Pakistani officials generally insist there is no evidence that bin Laden is hiding in the border region,[30] but numerous U.S. officials have suggested otherwise.[31] In June 2005, Director of Central Intelligence Goss claimed to have "an excellent idea of where [bin Laden] is" and suggested that "sanctuaries in sovereign states" and "our sense of international obligation" present obstacles to his capture.[32] The Pakistani president has issued contradictory statements on the topic of bin Laden's whereabouts.[33] Some analysts speculate

---

[27] Al Qaeda members are most readily identified as being Arabs or other non-Afghans who primarily are fighting an international jihad; Taliban members are ethnic Pashtun Afghans and Pakistanis who primarily are fighting for Islamic rule in Kabul and/or Islamabad. Al Qaeda is designated as a Foreign Terrorist Organization under U.S. law; the Taliban are Specially-Designated Global Terrorists (see the U.S. Treasury Department's master list at [http://www.ustreas.gov/offices/eotffc/ofac/sdn/index.html]).

[28] Director of Central Intelligence George Tenet, Testimony Before the Senate Select Intelligence Committee, Feb. 24, 2004; Robert Birsel, "Afghan Rebels Attack From Pakistan," Reuters, May 16, 2005. Pakistan's western regions are populated by conservative ethnic Pashtuns who share intimate religious and tribal linkages with their counterparts in Afghanistan and who are seen to sympathize with Taliban and sometimes Al Qaeda forces while holding vehement anti-Western and anti-American sentiments (see, for example, Eliza Griswold, "In the Hiding Zone," *New Yorker*, July 26, 2004).

[29] James Risen and David Rohde, "A Hostile Land Foils the Quest for Bin Laden," *New York Times*, Dec. 13, 2004; "Interview With Pakistani Scholar Ahmed Rashid," *Spiegel* (Hamburg), July 22, 2005.

[30] In January 2005, a recently retired Pakistani general who had led the hunt for Al Qaeda fugitives in western tribal areas said the hunt for bin Laden on Pakistani territory was "pointless," as he had seen "not a single indication" that the Al Qaeda founder was in Pakistan (Christina Lamb, "Bin Laden Hunt is 'Pointless,'" *London Sunday Times*, January 23, 2005).

[31] In late-2004, then-Secretary of State Powell, a top U.S. military commander in Afghanistan, and a member of the 9/11 Commission issued separate suggestions that the Al Qaeda founder is in that area (Secretary Colin Powell, "Interview by Clarence Page of the Chicago Tribune," U.S. Department of State Washington File, Oct. 14, 2004; Mike Collett-White, "Osama Probably Alive, in Pakistan, Top Officials Say," Reuters, Sep. 27, 2004; Jim Mohr, "Osama Hiding in Pakistan," *San Bernardino Sun*, Oct. 21, 2004).

[32] "10 Questions for Porter Goss," *Time*, June 27, 2005.

[33] In December 2004, President Musharraf claimed that bin Laden's trail had gone cold, with no recent intelligence on where he and his top lieutenants were hiding. He suggested that the United States was partly responsible because a shortage of U.S.-led forces on the Afghan side of the border had left "voids." However, in June 2005, Musharraf called it likely that bin Laden was still alive and living

that bin Laden's capture in Pakistan could create a backlash among his sympathizers there and some reports suggest growing U.S. frustration with the lack of progress in finding "high value targets" in the region.[34]

Pakistan-Afghanistan Relations. The frequency of attacks on U.S.-led coalition forces in southern and eastern Afghanistan increased throughout 2003 and, in October of that year, then-U.S. Special Envoy and Ambassador to Afghanistan Zalmay Khalilzad warned that resurgent Taliban and Al Qaeda forces presented a serious threat to Afghan reconstruction efforts. In the wake of spring 2004 military operations by Pakistan near the Afghan border, the Afghan foreign minister praised Pakistan for its role in fighting terrorism, but Afghan President Karzai expressed concern that militants trained on Pakistani territory continue to cross into Afghanistan to mount anti-government attacks there.[35] Karzai paid a visit to Islamabad in August 2004, where President Musharraf assured him that Pakistan would not allow extremists to use Pakistani territory to disrupt upcoming Afghan elections. Just days before those October 2004 elections, Islamabad announced having moved extra troops and "quick reaction forces" near the Afghan border to prevent militant infiltrations. Although the top U.S. general in Afghanistan had earlier expressed concerns that Al Qaeda-linked operatives were actively encouraging militants to disrupt the elections, the successful and mostly peaceful polling led him to later declare that the Taliban were no longer a meaningful threat to Afghan stability.[36]

However, the influence of Pashtun tribal animosities and lingering pro-Taliban sentiments—combined with reports that some elements of Pakistan's security apparatus and Islamist religious parties remain sympathetic to anti-U.S. forces —have some analysts concerned that the Musharraf government is insufficiently committed to pacifying the border.[37] Political tensions related to Afghan instability and Pakistan's role again rose in 2005, reaching alarming levels in mid-year. In January, a "misunderstanding" led to a cross-border exchange of artillery and machinegun fire between

near the Afghan border where "it's very easy for a person to hide" (Robin Wright and Peter Baker, "Musharraf: Bin Laden's Location is Unknown," *Washington Post*, Dec. 5, 2004; "Pakistan's Musharraf Says Osama Bin Laden Still Alive," Agence France Presse, June 14, 2005).

[34] See, for example, the comments of former Central Intelligence Agency official Gary Schroen in "Search for Osama at an Apparent Stalemate," National Public Radio (transcript), May 3, 2005; Gordon Corera, "US 'Impatience' in Bin Laden Hunt," BBC News, June 20, 2005; "Bin Laden Search Hampered by Musharraf's Dilemma," *Jane's Foreign Report*, July 7, 2005.

[35] Carlotta Gall, "Taliban May Be Planning Larger Attacks, U.S. Envoy Says," *New York Times*, Oct. 7, 2003; Sayed Salahuddin, "Kabul Asks Pakistan to Do More on Terrorism," Reuters, July 12, 2004.

[36] "'Pakistan Will Not Allow Militants to Disrupt Afghan Polls,'" *News* (Karachi), Aug. 24, 2004; "More Troops Moved to Western Border," *Daily Times* (Lahore), Oct. 6, 2004; Carlotta Gall, "Al Qaeda Tries to Upset Afghan Vote," *New York Times*, Sep. 26, 2004; "Coalition General Says Afghan Election Major Defeat for Taliban," U.S. Department of State Washington File, Oct. 20, 2004.

[37] Joshua Kucera, "Counter-Insurgency in Afghanistan," *Jane's Defense Weekly*, Dec. 15, 2004; Carlotta Gall, "Despite Years of Pressure, Taliban Fight On in Jagged Hills," *New York Times*, June 4, 2005; Ahmed Rashid, "Rival Aims Hinder War on Terror," BBC News, July 5, 2005.

Afghan and Pakistani troops.[38] In April, a top U.S. military commander in Afghanistan claimed that Pakistan was preparing to launch military operations in North Waziristan near the Afghan border. A Pakistani general later denied the claim and called the comments "highly irresponsible."[39] A May *Newsweek* magazine report claimed that a Koran had been desecrated at the U.S. facility at Guantanamo Bay, allegedly spurring violent anti-U.S. protests in both Afghanistan and Pakistan (senior U.S. and Afghan officials later disputed the connection).[40] Subsequent questions were raised about a possible role of Pakistan's intelligence service in sparking the riots; some Pakistani strategists may oppose a long-term U.S. presence in Afghanistan, viewing it as inimical to Islamabad's interests in the region.[41]

Revived Taliban insurgent activity killed many hundreds in Afghanistan during the spring of 2005. In May, a U.S. Army colonel in Kabul commended Pakistan's "considerable" military efforts in Waziristan, but said insurgents continue to cross into Afghanistan to attack U.S.-led forces before returning to Pakistan.[42] By June, Afghan officials were complaining of a "steady stream of terrorists" entering their country from Pakistan, and the Afghan president made a personal appeal to his Pakistani counterpart to halt the exfiltration. President Musharraf issued assurances of full support for the Kabul government, but Afghan authorities reported arresting three Pakistani nationals minutes before they planned to kill the outgoing U.S. Ambassador to Afghanistan, Zalmay Khalilzad, in Kabul. The Afghan-Pakistani rift deepened, spurring President Bush to make a personal call to Musharraf in an effort to smooth relations between two key U.S. allies in the region.[43] In July 2005, Pakistan reported moving 4,000 additional troops to the border region, bringing the total to some 80,000, and Prime Minister Aziz visited Kabul, where he vowed "seamless cooperation" with the Afghan government in fighting terrorism and Islamic extremism. Still, U.S. officials continue to urge Islamabad (and Kabul) to "do more" to end insurgent operations in the region and some reports indicate that Taliban recruiting and training continues to take place on Pakistani territory without government interference.[44]

---

[38] "Pak, Afghan Troops Trade Heavy Fire," *News* (Karachi), January 5, 2005.

[39] "US Military Claim Angers Pakistan," BBC News, Apr. 20, 2005.

[40] May 9, 2005; "Riots Over US Koran 'Desecration,'" BBC News, May 11, 2005; "Anti-U.S. Protests Spread to Pakistan," *Washington Post*, May 13, 2005; "Afghan Riots Not Tied to Report on Quran Handling, General Says," U.S. Department of State Washington File, May 12, 2005.

[41] "Pakistan Intelligence and Afghan Unrest," *Jane's Intelligence Digest*, May 27, 2005; Sarah Chayes, "With a Little Help From Our Friends," *New York Times*, May 26, 2005; Imtiaz Gul, "US-Afghan Strategic Partnership Worries Neighbors," *Friday Times* (Lahore), May 27, 2005.

[42] Robert Birsel, "Afghan Rebels Attack From Pakistan," Reuters, May 16, 2005.

[43] N.C. Aizenman, "Karzai Asks Musharraf for Border Help," *Washington Post*, June 22, 2005; Carlotta Gall, "Afghans Arrest 3 Pakistanis Accused of Plot to Kill U.S. Envoy," *New York Times*, June 20, 2005; "Afghan Violence Shatters Pakistan Alliance," *New York Times*, June 22, 2005; "Bush Intervenes in Terror Dispute," BBC News, June 22, 2005.

[44] "Extra Troops for Afghan Border," BBC News, July 6, 2005; "Pakistan to Help Afghans Contain Election Strife," *New York Times*, July 25, 2005; "US Says Wants More Pressure on Afghan Insurgents,"

Al Qaeda and Related Groups in Pakistan. Links between Al Qaeda and Pakistani Islamic militant groups, while possibly extensive, are believed to be mostly informal, with existing Pakistani religious extremists facilitating Al Qaeda activities in that country without being considered "members."[45] Al Qaeda reportedly was linked to several anti-U.S. and anti-Western terrorist attacks in Pakistan during 2002, although the primary suspects in most attacks were members of indigenous Pakistani groups.[46] With the post-9/11 capture of numerous Arab Al Qaeda leaders (most of them in Pakistani cities), there are indications that a new wave of ringleaders is made up of Pakistani nationals.[47] President Musharraf's further efforts to crack down on outlawed groups—along with his suggestions that Pakistan may soften its long-held Kashmir policies—may have fueled even greater outrage among radical Islamists already angered by Pakistan's September 2001 policy reversal, when Musharraf cut ties with the Afghan Taliban regime and began facilitating U.S.-led anti-terrorism operations in the region.[48] Musharraf and his top lieutenants themselves became targets of Al Qaeda and Al Qaeda-linked violent extremism:[49]

- On December 13, 2003, a remote-controlled bomb destroyed a Rawalpindi bridge less than one minute after Musharraf's motorcade had passed over it. A U.S.-supplied electronic jamming device is believed to have delayed detonation.
- On December 25, 2003, dual suicide car bomb attacks on Musharraf's motorcade in Rawalpindi failed to harm the Pakistani president, but killed 15 people, including the attackers.[50]

Reuters, July 14, 2005; Jay Solomon, et. al., "Despite U.S. Effort, Pakistan Remains Key Terror Hub," *Wall Street Journal*, July 22, 2005; Paul Watson, "Pakistan Connection Seen in Taliban's New Tactics," *Los Angeles Times*, July 28, 2005.

45 C. Christine Fair, "Militant Recruitment in Pakistan," *Studies in Conflict and Terrorism*, May 2004.

46 Among these incidents was the January 2002 kidnaping and ensuing murder of *Wall Street Journal* reporter Daniel Pearl. Also occurring in 2002 were a March grenade attack on a Protestant church in Islamabad that killed five, including a U.S. Embassy employee and her daughter, likely the work of LeT; a May car bombing that killed 14 outside a Karachi hotel, including 11 French defense technicians, was linked to Al Qaeda; and a June car bombing outside the U.S. consulate in Karachi that killed 12 Pakistani nationals also was linked to Al Qaeda. There have been arrests and some convictions in each of these cases. See U.S. Department of State, *Patterns of Global Terrorism 2002*, Apr. 2003.

47 Victoria Burnett, "Pakistan Cites Growing Extremist Network," *Boston Globe*, Sep. 11, 2004; Owais Tohid, "Next Wave of Al Qaeda Leadership," *Christian Science Monitor*, Oct. 5, 2004.

48 Bryan Bender and Farah Stockman, "Extremist Influence Growing in Pakistan, US Officials Fear," *Boston Globe*, January 11, 2004.

49 In March 2004, an audio tape believed to have been made by Al Qaeda leader Ayman al-Zawahri urged "every Muslim in Pakistan" to overthrow the Musharraf regime for its "surrender to the Americans" ("'Uncover the Truth of Musharraf, the Traitor and the Killer of Muslims,'" *Outlook India* (Delhi), Mar. 27, 2004).

50 Both December 2003 assassination attempts were blamed mainly on operatives of the indigenous Jaish-e-Mohammed terrorist group. Numerous Pakistanis and foreign nationals—including Afghans, Chechens, and Kashmiris—were arrested in connection with the attacks, with officials suggesting a possible Al Qaeda link (Salman Masood, "Link to Qaeda Cited in Effort to Assassinate Pakistan Chief," *New York Times*, Mar. 16, 2004). Some also suggested a possible ISI role, noting a long history

- On June 10, 2004, militants attacked the motorcade of a top Pakistan Army commander and Musharraf ally in Karachi, killing ten, but leaving the general unharmed.
- On July 30, 2004, a suicide bomber killed eight other people in a failed attempt to assassinate the Prime Minister-designate, Shaukat Aziz, who was unharmed.

The F.B.I. played a role in the investigations into attempts on President Musharraf's life and the United States has undertaken to provide improved training to Musharraf's bodyguards. Nonetheless, it is considered likely that future assassination attempts on Musharraf will occur.[51] Low-level Pakistani security officers and soldiers were convicted for involvement in the attacks on Pakistani leaders, heightening concerns that the Musharraf government is finding it difficult to control domestic extremism, especially among some elements of Pakistan's security apparatus.[52] As more evidence arises exposing Al Qaeda's deadly new alliance with indigenous Pakistani militants—and military operations continue to cause death and disruption in Pakistan's western regions—concern about Pakistan's fundamental political and social stability has increased.[53]

The United States also notes past indications of links between Al Qaeda and Pakistani army officers, intelligence agents, weapons experts, and militant leaders. There also have been reports that Pakistan allows Taliban militants to train in Pakistan for combat in Afghanistan and that Al Qaeda camps near the Afghan Pakistani border remain active.[54] Signs of collusion between some elements of Al Qaeda, Lashkar-e-Taiba, and influential Pakistanis fuel skepticism among those who doubt the sincerity of Pakistan's commitment to moderation. For example, of three major Al Qaeda figures captured in Pakistan, one (Abu Zubaydah) was found at a Lashkar-e-Taiba safehouse in Faisalabad, suggesting that some LeT members have facilitated the movement of Al Qaeda members in Pakistan.[55]

---

of ties between Pakistan's intelligence service and JeM leader Masood Azhar (John Lancaster and Kamran Khan, "Investigation of Attacks on Musharraf Points to Pakistani Group," *Washington Post*, January 14, 2004).

[51] Mubashir Zaidi, "FBI Joins Inquiry Into Blasts Aimed at Pakistani Leader," *Los Angeles Times*, Dec. 27, 2003; Dana Priest, "U.S. Aids Security of Musharraf," *Washington Post*, January 3, 2004; Mazhar Abbas, "Agencies Fear More Suicide Attempts on Musharraf," *Friday Times* (Lahore), Feb. 13, 2004.

[52] Salman Masood, "A Top Pakistani General Escapes Assassination Attempt that Kills Ten People," *New York Times*, June 11, 2004; "Al Qaeda Group Claims Bombing," *Los Angeles Times*, Aug. 1, 2004; "Junior Officers Tried to Kill Me: Musharraf," *Daily Times* (Lahore), May 27, 2004.

[53] John Lancaster and Kamran Khan, "Pakistan Losing Grip on Extremists," *Washington Post*, Aug. 29, 2004; "Pakistan Sliding Towards Lawlessness: Human Rights Body," Press Trust of India, Aug. 30, 2004; Mazhar Abbas, "Terrorist Attacks Leave Government Helpless," *Friday Times* (Lahore), Oct. 15, 2004; "How Al Qaeda Bankrolls Terror in Pakistan," *Jane's Islamic Affairs Analyst*, May 1, 2005.

[54] Carlotta Gall, "Pakistan Allows Taliban to Train, a Detained Fighter Says," *New York Times*, Aug. 4, 2004; "Intelligence Indicates Activity at Al Qaeda Camps," CNN.com. Aug. 5, 2004; Munir Ahmed, "PM Denies Terrorist Camps Exist in Pakistan After Men Arrested in California," Associated Press, June 11, 2005.

[55] U.S. Department of State, *Country Reports on Terrorism 2004*, Apr. 2005.

Another (Khalid Sheikh Mohammed) was seized at the Rawalpindi home of a member of the Jamaat-i-Islami (JI), one of Pakistan's leading religious Islamist political parties. In fact, at least four top captured Al Qaeda suspects had ties to JI. In August 2004, Pakistan's interior minister asked the JI leadership to explain why several important Al Qaeda fugitives were captured in the homes of party workers, and a leader of the ruling Muslim League party acknowledged that terrorists were linked to "individual" JI leaders. JI chief Qazi Hussain Ahmed responded by denying that the party had any ties to Al Qaeda. When asked about the issue, President Musharraf expressed "the greatest disappointment . . . that there are some political elements" in Pakistan that "keep on instigating" foreign terrorists. He denied implicating any specific religious parties as a whole while conceding that individual terrorist suspects have been JI members.[56]

During the time that Islamabad was actively supporting the Afghan Taliban regime it had helped to create, Pakistan's powerful Inter-Services Intelligence (ISI) agency is believed to have had direct contacts with Al Qaeda figures.[57] Sympathetic ISI officials may even have provided shelter to Al Qaeda members in both Pakistan and Kashmir.[58] At least one source suggests the ISI collaborated with Al Qaeda's shift into South Waziristan in 2002.[59] Two senior Pakistani nuclear scientists reportedly met with Osama bin Laden in 2001 to conduct "long discussions about nuclear, chemical and biological weapons."[60] In July 2005, six Pakistan army officers, including two colonels, were convicted on charges of plotting with Al Qaeda members.[61] Moreover, known Islamic extremists with ties to Al Qaeda appear to have remained active on Pakistani territory. For example, longtime Pakistani terrorist chief Fazlur Rehman Khalil, who co-signed Osama bin Laden's 1998 edict declaring it a Muslim's duty to kill Americans and Jews, has lived openly in Rawalpindi, not far

[56] "Pakistan Asked to Explain Islamic Party Link to Al Qaeda Suspects," Agence France-Presse, Mar. 3, 2003; Muhammad Anis, "Faisal Asks JI to Explain Activists' Al Qaeda Links," *Dawn* (Karachi), Aug. 17, 2004; "Terrorists Have Individual Links With Some JI Leaders: Shujaat," *Daily Times* (Lahore), Aug. 18, 2004; "No Links With Al Qaeda: Qazi," *Daily Times* (Lahore), Aug. 18, 2004; "Pakistan President Gives TV Interview on Security, India Ties, Iraq Troops," BBC Monitoring South Asia, Aug. 17, 2004.

[57] James Risen and Judith Miller, "Pakistani Intelligence Had Links to Al Qaeda, U.S. Officials Say," *New York Times*, Oct. 29, 2001. Declassified U.S. Defense Intelligence Agency documents from October 2001 indicate that the Al Qaeda camp targeted by American cruise missiles in 1998 was funded and maintained by the ISI, and that Pakistani agents "encouraged, facilitated and often escorted Arabs from the Middle East into Afghanistan" (National Security Archive Electronic Briefing Book 97, available at [http://www.gwu.edu/~nsarchiv/NSAEBB/NSAEBB97/index.htm]). See also Steve Coll, *Ghost Wars* (Penguin Press, 2004).

[58] Bob Drogin, et. al., "Al Qaeda Gathering Strength in Pakistan," *Los Angeles Times*, June 16, 2002; Philip Smucker, "Al Qaeda Thriving in Kashmir," *Christian Science Monitor*, July 2, 2002.

[59] Mariam Abou Zahab and Olivier Roy, *Islamist Networks* (Columbia University Press, 2004).

[60] Kamran Khan and Molly Moore, "2 Nuclear Experts Briefed Bin Laden, Pakistanis Say," *Washington Post*, Dec. 12, 2001.

[61] "Contact With Al Qaeda," *Pakistan* (Islamabad in Urdu), Aug. 2, 2005.

from Pakistan's Army General Headquarters.[62] Khalil is the leader of Harakat ul-Mujahideen, one of the many Pakistan-based terrorist groups opposed to both the continued rule of President Musharraf and to U.S. policy in the region.

Mid-2004 saw significant developments in the fight against Al Qaeda-linked militants in Pakistan, including the capture or killing of several allegedly senior Al Qaeda operatives and other wanted fugitives (Al Qaeda suspects Masrab Arochi, Ahmed Khalfan Ghailani, and Mohammed Naeem Noor Khan were captured in Pakistani cities in June and July; see "Notable Al Qaeda Figures Captured or Killed in Pakistan," below). Pakistan's interior minister said that security agencies had captured 12 foreign and 51 Pakistani "terrorists" between mid-July and mid-August 2004. As many as ten of these were suspected Al Qaeda members whom the Pakistani government said were planning attacks on Pakistan government and Western targets, including the U.S. Embassy, to coincide with Pakistani Independence Day.[63] In mid-August 2004, Pakistan published pictures of six "most-wanted terrorists" along with offers of major monetary rewards for information leading to their capture.[64] In September, Pakistan reported having killed one of these fugitives, suspected top Al Qaeda operative Amjad Farooqi, and two other militants during a 4-hour gunbattle in the southern city of Nawabshah. Farooqi was described as having been the chief Al Qaeda contact in Pakistan and a longtime associate of Khalid Sheik Mohammed.[65] Within days, Pakistan said 11 more militants had been captured, including members of Jaish-e-Mohammed wanted in connection with a May 2002 car bombing in Karachi that killed 11 French military technicians. Pakistan's interior minister declared that the arrests had "broken the back of Al Qaeda in Pakistan," a claim identical to that made by another top Pakistani official two years earlier. In September 2004, then-Deputy Secretary of State Armitage called the activities of Pakistani security forces "very noteworthy" and "extraordinarily appreciated."[66]

---

62 Paul Watson and Mubashir Zaidi, "Militant Flourishes in Plain Sight," *Los Angeles Times*, January 25, 2004; Mike Collet-White and Amir Zia, "Pakistan Crack Down on Militants," Reuters, Aug. 8, 2004.

63 Munir Ahmad, "Monthlong Anti-Terror Raids in Pakistan Net 63 Terror Suspects," Associated Press, Aug. 16, 2004; "Pakistan Arrests Al Qaeda Suspects," *Washington Post*, Aug. 22, 2004.

64 Five of the suspects were Pakistani and one a Libyan. A reward of 20 million rupees (about $340,000) each was offered for information leading to the arrest of Amjad Hussain Farooqi and Libyan Abu Faraj, both wanted in connection with attempts to assassinate President Musharraf in December 2003 ("Pakistan Publishes 'Most-Wanted Terrorists' List," Reuters, Aug. 18, 2004).

65 Farooqi also was identified as a member of the Lashkar-i-Janghvi terrorist group and one of the hijackers of an Indian passenger jet in 1999 (Kamran Khan, "Pakistani Forces Kill Top Fugitive," *Washington Post*, Sep. 27, 2004).

66 Paul Haven, "Arrests Damage Al Qaeda Network," Associated Pres, Aug. 7, 2004; Mike Collet-White and Amir Zia, "Pakistan Crack Down on Militants," Reuters, Aug. 8, 2004; Kamran Khan, "Al Qaeda Arrest in June Opened Valuable Leads," *Washington Post*, Aug. 3, 2004; "Pakistanis Tell of More Arrests," *New York Times*, Aug. 4, 2004; "State's Armitage Calls for Syrian Troops Withdrawal From Lebanon," "U.S. Hails Pakistan's Efforts to Fight Terror, Build Democracy," U.S. Department of State Washington File, Oct. 1, 2004. The United States was criticized by intelligence experts for releasing

While developments in 2004 marked notable strides in Pakistani and multilateral efforts to eliminate Al Qaeda and other Islamic extremist elements in the region, the problem for Pakistan is far from resolved. Reports indicate that Pakistan's western border regions—especially the traditionally autonomous Wazir districts of the FATA—remain a sanctuary for scores or even hundreds of non-Pakistani militants with Al Qaeda links or sympathies.[67] Pakistani forces continue to hunt suspected Al Qaeda members in both urban areas and western border regions.[68] In a controversial turn, the Islamabad government has made large cash payments to Pashtun tribal commanders in an effort to sever Wazir ties to Al Qaeda (see "Pakistani Military Operations" section below).[69]

In 2005, the United States has bolstered efforts to capture wanted Al Qaeda fugitives in part with local-language television, radio, and newspaper advertising offering large monetary rewards for information leading to the arrest of 14 most wanted terrorists.[70] An apparent rift between Arab Al Qaeda members and their Central Asia (primarily Uzbek) allies reportedly has been exploited by U.S. and Pakistani intelligence services; such internal Al Qaeda conflict may have allowed for the capture of Abu Faraj al-Liby in May 2005.[71] The arrest spurred President Musharraf and Pakistan's interior minister to (again) insist that their security forces had "broken the back" of Al Qaeda in Pakistan.[72] Yet, in June 2005, a senior fugitive Taliban leader appeared on Pakistani television to claim that Osama bin Laden and Taliban chief Mullah Omar were both alive and in good health, spurring the outgoing U.S. Ambassador to Afghanistan to claim that the two fugitives were not in Afghanistan.[73]

Following deadly July 7, 2005 bombings in London, and subsequent confirmation that at least two of the culprits had made recent visits to Pakistan, Islamabad was faced with renewed international scrutiny of the country's links to Islamic extremism. President Musharraf launched a new nationwide

Khan's name to the press even as Khan was said to be covertly cooperating with investigators (Peter Graff, "Unmasking of Qaeda Mole a Security Blunder - Experts," Reuters, Aug. 7, 2004).

67 See, for example, Shiv Malik, "Where Bin Laden Can Still Roam Free," *New Statesman* (London), Feb. 21, 2005; Declan Walsh, "Most Wanted," *Guardian* (Manchester), Aug. 1, 2005.

68 "Pakistan Kills Two Al Qaeda Suspects, Arrests 11," Reuters, Mar. 5, 2005; "Pakistan Nabs Ten Terror Suspects," CNN.com, Mar. 13, 2005; Nadeem Saeed, "Three AL Qaeda 'Suspects' Held," *Dawn* (Karachi), May 21, 2005; Iqbal Khattak, "Two Local Qaeda Suspects Arrested in North Waziristan," *Daily Times* (Lahore), June 2, 2005.

69 Owais Tohid, "Cash Weans Tribes From Al Qaeda," *Christian Science Monitor*, Feb. 16, 2005.

70 "U.S. Posts 'Most Wanted' in Pakistan Paper," Reuters, Jan. 7, 2005; Richard Boucher, State Department Daily Briefing, Feb. 15, 2005;

71 Paul Haven and Katherine Shrader, "Ethnic Rifts Tearing at Al Qaeda," Associated Press, May 10, 2005.

72 Jo Johnson and Farhan Bokhari, "Al Qaeda's Back Has Been Broken, Says Musharraf," *Financial Times* (London), May 15, 2005; "Al Qaeda Badly Hurt, Pakistani Official Says," *Miami Herald*, May 16, 2005.

73 "Bin Laden, Omar Are Well, Taliban Commander Says," Reuters, June 155, 2005; "Bin Laden 'is not in Afghanistan,"BBC News, June 16, 2005.

crackdown on suspected militants and officials began investigating possible ties between the London attack and Pakistan-based terrorist groups with known links to Al Qaeda. By month's end, Musharraf was again declaring that Al Qaeda's operational structure in Pakistan had been destroyed and he excluded the possibility that the terrorist network could have carried out recent attacks in Britain or Egypt.[74]

Notable Al Qaeda Figures Captured or Killed in Pakistan

- **Abu Zubaydah** (March 2002), a Saudi-born Palestinian captured in the east-central city of Faisalabad. Zubaydah was Al Qaeda's chief recruiter during the 1990s and was alleged to have directed Al Qaeda's reorganization in Pakistan after 2001.
- **Ramzi bin al-Shibh** (September 2002), a Yemeni captured in the southern city of Karachi. Bin al-Shibh had been a member of the "Hamburg cell" and allegedly was a key figure in the 9/11 plot.
- **Khalid Sheikh Mohammed** (March 2003), a Pakistani captured in the northeastern city of Rawalpindi. Sheikh Mohammed was the alleged "mastermind" of the 9/11 plot.
- **Mustafa al-Hawsawi** (March 2003), a Saudi captured along with Sheikh Mohammed, has been called Al Qaeda's "chief financial officer" and was said to have been key to funding the 9/11 plot.
- **Walid bin Attash** (April 2003), a Yemeni captured in the southern city of Karachi. Bin Attash was called the "mastermind" of the 2000 attack on the USS Cole.
- **Masrab Arochi** (June 2004), a Pakistani relative of Sheikh Mohammed captured in the southern city of Karachi. Arochi was implicated in a failed but bloody May 2004 attempt to assassinate a Pakistani Corps Commander.
- **Nek Mohammed** (June 2004), a leading Pashtun militant and former Taliban commander reported killed by a missile (likely fired from a pilotless U.S. drone) in a tribal area near the Afghan border. Mohammed was accused of providing sanctuary to Al Qaeda members.
- **Ahmed Khalfan Ghailani** (July 2004), a Tanzanian captured in the east-central city of Gujrat. Ghailani had appeared on the FBI's most-wanted list after his indictment for murder in connection with the 1998 Al Qaeda bombings of two U.S. Embassies in East Africa.

[74] "Pakistanis Check Al Qaeda Link to Bombings," Associated Press, July 15, 2005; Farhan Bokhari et. al., "Pakistan Claims Al Qaeda Command Destroyed," *Financial Times* (London), July 25, 2005.

- **Mohammed Naeem Noor Khan** (July 2004), a Pakistani captured in the east-central city of Lahore. Khan was an alleged Al Qaeda computer expert wanted in connection with a plot to bomb London's Heathrow airport.
- **Amjad Farooqi** (September 2004), a Pakistani killed in a gunbattle in the southern city of Nawabshah. Farooqi had been sought in connection with the 2002 kidnaping and murder of reporter Daniel Pearl and two lethal December 2003 attempts to assassinate President Musharraf.
- **Abu Faraj al-Libbi** (May 2005), a Libyan captured in the northwestern city of Mardan. Libbi, called the third-most senior Al Qaeda operative by some analysts, was wanted in connection with lethal attempts to assassinate President Musharraf in December 2003.
- **Haithem al-Yemeni** (May 2005), a Yemeni killed by what was reported to be a missile fired from a pilotless U.S. drone in the North West Frontier Province near the Afghan border. Al-Yemeni was a suspected Al Qaeda explosives expert.

Source: U.S. Department of State terrorism reports and various news agencies.

Narcotics. Compounding the difficulty of battling regional extremists has been a major spike in Afghan opium production, spurring acute concerns that Afghanistan may become or already is a "narco-state," and that terrorist groups and their supporters in both Afghanistan and Pakistan are reaping huge profits from the processing and trafficking of heroin.[75] A bumper opium crop in 2004 was two-thirds larger than the previous year's, with Afghan opium now said to comprise up to 90% of the world's supply and the opium trade accounting for about half of Afghanistan's gross domestic product. The director of Pakistan's Anti-Narcotics Force has estimated that 70% of narcotics produced in Afghanistan is trafficked through Pakistan. Some analysts express worry that Pakistan is forced to divert scarce security resources to counternarcotics efforts.[76] There is congressional concern that heroin trafficking has become a major source of funding for Al Qaeda.[77]

[75] "Afghanistan as a Narco State," *Christian Science Monitor*, Mar. 8, 2005; A. Brownfeld, "Al Qaeda's Drug-Running Network," *Jane's Terrorism & Security Monitor*, Feb. 1, 2004; Hugh Williamson and Victoria Burnett, "Afghan Militants Linked to Drugs Trade," *Financial Times* (London), Apr. 2, 2004; Thom Shanker, "Pentagon Sees Anti-Drug Effort in Afghanistan," *New York Times*, Mar. 25, 2005; Paul Watson, "Afghanistan: A Harvest of Despair," *Los Angeles Times*, May 29, 2005.

[76] "Fight Against Opium in Afghanistan Moving at Glacial Pace," Agence France Presse, May 23, 2005; "'70% Afghan Narcotics Move Through Pakistan,'" *Daily Times* (Lahore), Mar. 21, 2005; Peter Chalk and Christine Fair, "Pakistan Tackles Impact of Afghan Opium Trade," *Jane's Intelligence Review*, Mar. 1, 2005.

[77] See CRS Report RL32686, *Afghanistan: Narcotics and U.S. Policy*, by Christopher Blanchard.

Indigenous Pakistani Terrorism

Pakistan is known to be a base for numerous indigenous terrorist organizations. Many analysts locate the genesis of this now serious problem in the Islamization process initiated by Z.A. Bhutto after 1971 and greatly accelerated by Gen. Zia-ul-Haq in the 1980s. Some also hold the United States complicit, given its overt support for Zia, an authoritarian military leader who represented a "frontline ally" against Soviet expansionism. Zia sought greater domestic political legitimacy in part by strengthening the country's conservative religious elements which would later play a major role in Pakistan's Afghan and Kashmir policies.[78]

Pakistan has in the past demonstrated inconsistency in its efforts to rein in Islamic militants operating inside its borders. The United States has for many years been aware of the existence of outlawed groups both in Pakistan-held Kashmir and within Pakistani cities. In July 2000 testimony before the House International Relations Committee, a senior U.S. counterterrorism official called Pakistan's record on combating terrorism "mixed," noting that "Pakistan has tolerated terrorists living and moving freely within its territory" and is believed to have provided "material support for some of these militants, including the Harakat ul-Mujahidin, a group that [the United States] has designated as an FTO [Foreign Terrorist Organization]."[79]

In the past, sectarian and Kashmir-oriented militant groups in Pakistan generally operated within their own distinct geographic and functional spheres, separate from one another and also from mostly non-Pakistani militants who came to the region intent on fighting an international jihad. These distinctions have become less clear in the post-9/11 period.[80] In January 2002, Pakistan banned five extremist groups, including Lashkar-e-Taiba (LeT), Jaish-e-Mohammed (JeM), and Sipah-e-Sahaba Pakistan (SSP). The United States officially designates LeT and JeM as terrorist groups; SSP appears on the State Department's list of "other selected terrorist organizations."[81] Following Al Qaeda's 2001–2002 expulsion from

---

78 See Stephen Cohen, "The Jihadist Threat to Pakistan," *Washington Quarterly* 26, 3 (Summer 2003), p. 15, and Dennis Kux, *The United States and Pakistan 1947–2000: Disenchanted Allies* (Washington: Woodrow Wilson Center Press, 2001), p. 240–241. Pakistani leaders continued to manipulate radical Islamic groups during the 1990s as part of a strategy to "fuel the jihad in Kashmir and Afghanistan" (Ashley Tellis, "U.S. Strategy: Assisting Pakistan's Transformation," *Washington Quarterly* 28, 1 (Winter 2004–05), p. 106). The issue of past U.S. complicity in the radicalization of Pakistan's religious politics has been raised with the author by Pakistani government officials and scholars.

79 Ambassador Michael Sheehan, "Testimony on Counterterrorism and South Asia," USIS Public Diplomacy Query, July 12, 2000.

80 See C. Christine Fair, "Militant Recruitment in Pakistan," *Studies in Conflict and Terrorism*, May 2004.

81 See CRS Report RL32223, *Foreign Terrorist Organizations*, and CRS Report RL32120, *The 'FTO List' and Congress*, both by Audrey Kurth Cronin. LeT appears to be expanding its jihadi efforts well beyond their Pakistani-Kashmiri origins to places such as Iraq, Indonesia, and Australia ("Pakistani Militants Arrested in Iraq," Agence France Presse, Apr. 1, 2004; E. Blanche, "Lashkar-e-Taiba Spreads Its Tentacles," *Jane's Terrorism & Security Monitor*, Sep. 1, 2004).

Afghanistan and ensuing relocation of some core elements to Pakistani cities such as Karachi and Peshawar, some Al Qaeda activists are known to have joined forces with indigenous Pakistani Sunni militant groups, including LeT, JeM, SSP, and Lashkar-i-Jhangvi (LJ), an FTO-designated offshoot of the SSP that has close ties to Al Qaeda.[82] The United Nations lists JeM and LJ as "entities belonging to or associated with the Taliban and Al Qaeda organization."[83]

In his landmark January 2002 speech, President Musharraf vowed to end Pakistan's use as a base for terrorism, and he criticized religious extremism and intolerance in the country. In the wake of the speech, about 3,300 extremists were detained, though most of these were soon released (including one man who later tried to assassinate Musharraf).[84] Among those released were the founders of both Lashkar-e-Taiba and Jaish-e-Muhammad. Although officially banned, these groups continued to operate under new names: LeT became Jamaat al-Dawat; JeM became Khudam-ul Islam.[85] In November 2003, just two days after the U.S. Ambassador expressed particular concern over the continuing activities of banned organizations, Musharraf moved to arrest members of these groups and shutter their offices. Six groups were formally banned, including offshoots of both the JeM and SSP, and more than 100 offices were raided. Musharraf vowed to permanently prevent banned groups from resurfacing, and his government moved to seize their financial assets.[86] Some analysts called the efforts cosmetic, ineffective, and the result of external pressure rather than a genuine recognition of the threat posed.[87]

Nearly two years later, and in the wake of deadly July 2005 bombings in London that had a possible Pakistan connection, both President Musharraf

---

[82] U.S. Department of State, *Patterns of Global Terrorism 2002*, Apr. 2003; Howard French, "Officials Warn of Links Between Al Qaeda, Pakistanis," *New York Times*, May 29, 2002; Hasan Mansoor, "Karachi Killings Reveal Sectarian-Jihadi Nexus," *Friday Times* (Lahore), Oct. 10, 2003; Kamran Khan and John Lancaster, "Suspect Predicts Attack on U.S. Forces," *Washington Post*, Mar. 7, 2003.

[83] See [http://www.un.org/Docs/sc/committees/1267/1267ListEng.htm].

[84] Paul Watson, "A Delicate Balance of Rule for Pakistan's Musharraf," *Los Angeles Times*, Mar. 5, 2004.

[85] Paul Watson, "Revolving Doors for Pakistan's Militants," *Los Angeles Times*, Nov. 17, 2002; "Musharraf Says Heads of Two Extremist Groups Did Nothing Illegal," Agence France-Presse, Mar. 2, 2003; "Militant Suspects Freed in Pakistan," BBC News, Jan. 31, 2003.

[86] "U.S. Committed to Strong Relationship With Pakistan," U.S. Department of State Washington File, Nov. 13, 2003; "Owais Tohid, "Pakistan Tries Again to Shutter Terror Groups," *Christian Science Monitor*, Nov. 26, 2003; Rafaqat Ali, "Musharraf Vows to Root Out Extremism," *Dawn* (Karachi), Dec. 5, 2003; "Pakistan Freezes Accounts of Three More Banned Islamic Groups," Associated Press, Dec. 12, 2003. The United States had signaled increased pressure on Islamabad in October 2003 when the Treasury Department designated the Pakistan-based Al Akhtar Trust as a terrorist support organization under Executive Order 13224 and identified Indian crime figure Dawood Ibrahim as a "global terrorist" with links to both Al Qaeda and Lashkar-e-Taiba. Ibrahim is believed to be in Pakistan ("U.S. Designates Al Akhtar," U.S. Treasury Department Press Release, Oct. 14, 2003; "U.S. Designates Dawood Ibrahim," U.S. Treasury Department Press Release, Oct. 16, 2003).

[87] Husain Haqqani, "Skepticism Over Crackdown," *Nation* (Lahore), Nov. 19, 2003; Najam Sethi, "Writing On the Wall," *Friday Times* (Lahore), Nov. 21, 2003.

and Prime Minister Aziz restated their strident intention to combat religious extremism. From 800 to as many as 3,000 arrests were made in nationwide sweeps when security forces raided numerous mosques and religious seminaries. However, there is widespread scepticism among analysts that Musharraf's most recent initiatives will lead to more effective action; many contend that such assurances have been given by the Pakistani leader numerous times in the past without meaningful result.[88] Moreover, reports that militant training facilities remain operative on Pakistani-controlled territory have become more common in mid-2005 and emanate from such disparate quarters as government officials in Kabul and New Delhi, as well as from local and Western media.[89]

Since 2003, Pakistan's domestic terrorism mostly has involved Sunni-Shia conflict. Sectarian violence has plagued Pakistan for decades.[90] According to one report, Pakistan's sectarian conflict is "the direct consequence of state policies of Islamization and marginalization of secular democratic forces" wherein Sunni orthodoxy and militancy have been bolstered and manipulated by successive military-dominated governments in Islamabad.[91] Repression of religious minorities in Pakistan is noted by the United States.[92] Major suicide bombings in Islamabad and Karachi left

---

[88] See, for example, Farhan Bokhari, "Musharraf's Tough Talking in Doubt," *Financial Times* (London), July 22, 2005; Stephen Cohen, "Musharraf's Great Failure, *Globe and Mail* (Toronto), July 27, 2005; Amir Mir, "New Commitments, New Betrayals," *Outlook India* (Delhi), Aug. 1, 2005; N.C. Aizenman, "Musharraf's Contradictory Crackdown on Radicals," *Washington Post*, Aug. 5, 2005.

[89] See, for example, James Rupert, "Terrorist Camps Thriving," *Newsday*, July 22, 2005; Jay Solomon, et. al., "Despite U.S. Effort, Pakistan Remains Key Terror Hub," *Wall Street Journal*, July 22, 2005; Amir Mir, "Open For Admission," *Outlook India* (Delhi), July 25, 2005; Paul Watson, "Pakistan Connection Seen in Taliban's New Tactics," *Los Angeles Times*, July 28, 2005; David Rohde and Carlotta Gall, "In a Corner of Pakistan a Debate Rages: Are Terrorist Camps Still Functioning?," *New York Times*, Aug. 28, 2005.

[90] About three-quarters of Pakistan's Muslims are Sunnis. Major sectarian violence in 2003 included a July strike on a Quetta mosque that killed more than 50 Shiite worshipers (blamed on the militant Sunni SSP), and the October assassination of Maulana Azam Tariq, leader of the SSP and member of the Pakistani parliament, who was gunned down with four others in Islamabad. A March 2004 machine gun and bomb attack on a Shia procession in Quetta killed at least 44 and injured more than 150 others. A pair of bombings in early October 2004 left at least 72 people dead in the cities of Sialkot and Multan. In March 2005, at least 40 people were killed and scores injured when a bomb exploded at a Shiite shrine in remote part of the southwestern Baluchistan province. In May 2005, a suicide bomber killed 20 people and injured up to 100 more in an apparent sectarian attack on a Muslim shrine in Islamabad. Days later, suicide bombers killed themselves and at least two other people, and injured 20 more, in an attack on a Shiite mosque in Karachi. An enraged crowd of some 1,000 Shias rioted, killing at least six more people.

[91] The roots of this dynamic are most readily found in the policies of Gen. Zia from 1977–1988, but Pakistan's security organizations pursued foreign policy goals in part through continued co-optation of religious extremist elements even under the civilian governments of the 1990s. According to the report, President Musharraf has continued the military's tradition of making alliances with mullahs at the expense of moderate political forces ("The State of Sectarianism in Pakistan," International Crisis Group Asia Report 95, Apr. 18, 2005). See also Husain Haqqani, *Pakistan: Between Mosque and Military* (Carnegie Endowment for International Peace), 2005.

[92] The United States has for six consecutive years singled out Pakistan for "state hostility toward minority or non-approved religions," indicating that the Pakistani government continues to impose limits on freedom of religion, to fail in many respects to protect the rights of religious minorities, and to fail at times to intervene in cases of sectarian violence. President Musharraf rejects the claims as

dozens dead in May 2005, and again raised concerns about Pakistan's sectarian violence and domestic stability. Some analysts believe that, by redirecting Pakistan's internal security resources, an increase in such violence may ease pressure on Al Qaeda and affiliated groups and so allow them to operate more freely there.[93]

Madrassas and Pakistan Islamists

The Taliban movement itself began among students attending Pakistani religious schools (madrassas). Among the 10,000–20,000 or more madrassas training up to two million children in Pakistan are a small percentage that have been implicated in teaching militant anti-Western, anti-American, anti-Hindu, and even anti-Shia values. Secretary of State Powell identified these as "programs that do nothing but prepare youngsters to be fundamentalists and to be terrorists." There is, however, little evidence that madrassas are producing known anti-Western terrorists.[94] Many of these madrassas are financed and operated by Pakistani Islamist political parties such as Jamaat-e-Ulema Islam (JUI, closely linked to the Taliban), as well as by multiple unknown foreign entities, many in Saudi Arabia.[95] As many as two-thirds of Pakistan's seminaries are run by the Deobandi sect, known in part for a traditionally anti-Shia sentiment and at times linked to the Sipah-e-Sahaba terrorist group.[96] Some senior members of JUI reportedly have been linked to several U.S.-designated Foreign Terrorist Organizations.[97] The JUI chief, Fazlur Rehman, is a vocal critic of Pakistan's cooperation with the United States. In May 2004, he was named Leader of the Opposition in Pakistan's Parliament. In September 2004, Musharraf reportedly assured an audience of leading Pakistani religious seminarians that his government would not interfere in the affairs of madrassas and was under no foreign pressure to do so. He did, however, acknowledge

"absolutely incorrect" and "contrary to the real situation" in Pakistan (U.S. State Department, *International Religious Freedom Report 2004* at [http://www.state.gov/g/drl/rls/irf/2004/35519.html]; "Pakistan President Rejects US Report on Human Rights," BBC Monitoring South Asia, Sep. 29, 2004).

93 "Pakistan: A New Wave of Sunni-Shiite Violence?," Stratfor.com, Oct. 7, 2003.

94 "House Appropriations Subcommittee on Foreign Operations, Export Financing, and Related Programs Holds Hearing on FY2005 Appropriations," FDCH Transcripts, Mar. 10, 2004; Peter Bergen and Swati Pandney, "The Madrassa Myth," New York Times, June 14, 2005. See also CRS Report RS32009, *Education Reform in Pakistan*, by K. Alan Kronstadt; and CRS Report RS21654, *Islamic Religious Schools, Madrasas*, by Christopher Blanchard.

95 In June 2004, the Co-Director of the Independent Task Force on Terrorism Financing told a Senate panel that, "Saudi financing is contributing to the radicalization of millions of Muslims" in places such as Pakistan and, "Foreign funding for extremist madrassas in Pakistan alone . . . is estimated to be in the tens of millions, much of it historically from Saudi Arabia" (Testimony of Lee Wolosky Before the Senate Governmental Affairs Committee, "An Assessment of Current Efforts to Combat Terrorism Financing," June 15, 2004). See also CRS Report RL32499, *Saudi Arabia: Terrorist Financing Issues*, by Alfred Prados and Christopher Blanchard.

96 Khaled Ahmed, "Our Madrassas and Our World View," *Friday Times* (Lahore), Mar. 7, 2003.

97 Praveen Swami, "A Peacemaker From Pakistan,"*Frontline* (Madras), Aug. 15, 2003.

that a small number of seminaries are "harboring terrorists" and he asked religious leaders to help isolate these by openly condemning them.[98]

In July 2005, international attention to Pakistan's religious schools intensified after Pakistani officials acknowledged that three of the four suspects in the 7/7 London bombings visited Pakistan during the previous year and two may have spent time at a madrassa near Lahore.[99] An ensuing crackdown on Pakistani religious extremists included a (new) government deadline for madrassa registration, the expulsion of 1,400 foreign nationals from Pakistani religious schools, and police raids on some suspect seminaries. Pakistani Islamist leaders criticized the government's moves as human rights abuses and vowed to take action to block them. Moreover, a small percentage of seminaries have refused to participate in the registration program and the country's leading madrassa grouping—the Wafaq-ul-Madaris—has been critical of certain requirements, including an obligation to report funding sources.[100]

Since 2002, the U.S. Congress has allocated tens of millions of dollars to assist Pakistan in efforts to reform its education system, including changes that would make madrassa curriculum closer in substance to that provided in non-religious schools. The *9/11 Commission Report* recommends U.S. support for better Pakistani education and legislation passed by the 108th Congress (P.L. 108-458) calls for the devotion of increased U.S. government attention and resources to this issue.[101] While President Musharraf has in the past pledged to crack down on the more extremist madrassas in his country, there is little concrete evidence that he has done so. According to two observers, Musharraf's promises "came to nothing. His military government never implemented any program to register madrassas, follow their financing or control their curricula."[102] Many speculate that Musharraf's reluctance to enforce reform efforts is rooted in his desire to

98 "No Interference in the Affairs of Madrassas," *Dawn* (Karachi), Sep. 8, 2004; "Some Madrassas Bad: Musharraf," *Daily Times* (Lahore), Sep. 8, 2004.

99 Somini Sengupta, "Three London Bombing Suspects Visited Pakistan Last Year," *New York Times*, July 18, 2005; Alastair Lawson, "Pakistan's Islamic Schools in the Spotlight,"BBC News, July 14, 2005; "London Bombings Reverberate in Pakistani Madrassahs," *New York Times*, July 18, 2005.

100 "President's Address to the Nation" (transcript), Pakistan Ministry of Foreign Affairs, July 21, 2005; "Madrassa Foreigners 'Must Leave,'" BBC News, July 29, 2005; "Pakistan Soldiers Raid Madrassa," BBC News, July 29, 2005; "Fazl Slams Crackdown on Seminaries," *News* (Karachi), July 23, 2005; "'We Will Start a Movement If the Crackdown on Madrassas Does Not Stop,'" *Khabrain* (Lahore in Urdu), July 27, 2005; "Madrassas Resist Registration," BBC News, Aug. 24, 2005.

101 In August 2004, 9/11 Commission Co-Chair Lee Hamilton told a House panel that the current five-year, $100 million USAID program for Pakistan education reform was a "drop in the bucket" ("House International Relations Committee Holds Hearing on September 11 Commission Report," FDCH Transcripts, Aug. 24, 2004).

102 Samina Ahmed and Andrew Stroehlein, "Pakistan: Still Schooling Extremists," *Washington Post*, July 17, 2005. See also "Pakistan: Reforming the Education Sector," International Crisis Group Report 84, Oct. 7, 2004. Author interviews with Pakistani government officials and scholars have tended to confirm that movement on madrassa reform is slow, at best.

remain on good terms with Pakistan's Islamist political parties, which are seen to be an important part of his political base.[103]

The Muttahida Majlis-e-Amal (MMA)—a coalition of six Islamist opposition parties—holds about 20% of Pakistan's National Assembly seats, while also controlling the provincial assembly in the North West Frontier Province (NWFP) and leading a coalition in the provincial assembly of Baluchistan. Pakistan's Islamists denounce Pakistani military operations in western tribal areas, resist governmental attempts to reform religious schools that teach militancy, and harshly criticize Islamabad's cooperation with the U.S. government and movement toward rapprochement with India. The leadership of the MMA's two main constituents—the Jamaat-i-Islami and the Jamiat-Ulema-Islami-Fazlur—are notable for their rancorous anti-American rhetoric; they have at times called for "jihad" against what they view as the grave threat to Pakistani sovereignty that alliance with Washington entails.[104] One senior MMA leader went so far as to suggest that Western governments may have "engineered" the 7/7 London bombings.[105] In addition to decrying and seeking to end President Musharraf's cooperation with the United States, many also are viewed as opposing the U.S.-supported Kabul government. In September 2003, Afghan President Karzai called on Pakistani clerics to stop supporting Taliban members who seek to destabilize Afghanistan. Two months later, the Afghan foreign minister complained that Taliban leaders were operating openly in Quetta and other cities in western Pakistan. In the wake of a March 2004 battle between the Pakistan Army and Islamic militants in the traditionally autonomous western Federally Administered Tribal Areas (FATA), Pakistan's interior minister accused MMA politicians of giving a "free hand" to terrorists.[106] Musharraf repeatedly has called on Pakistan's Muslim clerics to assist in fighting extremism and improving Pakistan's image as a moderate and progressive state, but there continues to be evidence that Pakistan's religious parties are becoming even more brazen in challenging these efforts.[107]

---

[103] John Lancaster and Kamran Khan, "At an Islamic School, Hints of Extremist Ties," *Washington Post*, June 13, 2004; Vali Nasr, "Military Rule, Islamism, and Democracy in Pakistan," *Middle East Journal* 58, 2, Spring 2004.

[104] See "Enlightened Moderation Threat to Country: Qazi," *Dawn* (Karachi), Mar. 23, 2005; Owais Tohid, "'Talibanization' Fears in Pakistan," *Christian Science Monitor*, Apr. 13, 2005. JUI leader Maulana Fazlur Rehman reportedly said he considers Americans to be "criminals" and the Taliban "innocent" ("MMA Opposes Pak-US Military Drive," *News* (Karachi), June 24, 2003).

[105] Sadaqat Jan, "Radical Pakistani Lawmaker Says London Attacks May Have Been 'Engineered' by West," Associated Press Newswires, July 8, 2005.

[106] "Karzai Tells Pakistan Clerics-Don't Back Taliban," Reuters, Sep. 12, 2003; Shaun Waterman and Anwar Iqbal, "Taliban Leaders Plotting in Cities," *Washington Times*, Nov. 14, 2003; "MMA Accused of Patronizing Terrorists," *Dawn* (Karachi), Apr. 1, 2004.

[107] Rana Qaisar, "Clerics Asked to Help Fight Terror," *Daily Times* (Lahore), Feb. 18, 2004; Owais Tohid, "'Talibanization' Fears in Pakistan," *Christian Science Monitor*, Apr. 13, 2005.

Pakistan-U.S. Counterterrorism Cooperation[108]

According to the U.S. Departments of State and Defense, Pakistan has afforded the United States unprecedented levels of cooperation by allowing the U.S. military to use bases within the country, helping to identify and detain extremists, and deploying tens of thousands of its own security forces to secure the Pakistan-Afghanistan border. The State Department's *Country Reports on Terrorism 2004* characterized Pakistan as one of the most important U.S. partners in the war on terrorism. A revived high-level U.S.-Pakistan Defense Consultative Group—moribund since 1997—has meet three times since 2001. Pakistan was designated as a Major Non-NATO Ally of the United States in June 2004, and top U.S. officials regularly praise Pakistan's anti-terrorism efforts.[109] The State Department indicates that Islamabad has captured more than 600 alleged terrorists and their supporters. Several hundred of these have been transferred to U.S. custody, including some top suspected Al Qaeda leaders.[110] Pakistan also has been ranked third in the world in seizing terrorists' financial assets.[111] In July 2005, President Bush said Pakistani President Musharraf "has been a good partner in the global war on terrorism and in the ideological struggle that we're now engaged in."[112]

In August 2004, then-State Department Coordinator for Counterterrorism Cofer Black was in Pakistan for a meeting of the U.S.-Pakistan Joint Working Group on Counterterrorism and Law Enforcement, the first since April 2003. In September 2004, President Bush met with President Musharraf in New York, where the two leaders reaffirmed their commitment to broaden and deepen the U.S.-Pakistan relationship, and Musharraf also visited Washington to inaugurate a new Congressional Pakistan Caucus at present comprised of 65 U.S. Representatives. In December 2004, Musharraf made a brief stopover in Washington, where President Bush praised the Pakistani leader for working to combat terrorism, saying that the Pakistani army "has been incredibly active and very brave in southern Waziristan."

108 This section written by K. Alan Kronstadt, Analyst in Asian Affairs. See also CRS Report RL31624, *Pakistan-U.S. Anti-Terrorism Cooperation*, by K. Alan Kronstadt; and CRS Report RS22148, *Combat Aircraft Sales to South Asia*, by Christopher Bolkcom, Richard Grimmett, and K. Alan Kronstadt.

109 Ally designation was made on June 16, 2004, by President Bush under Section 517 of the Foreign Assistance Act of 1961, as amended. In January 2004, the Commander of the U.S. Central Command, Gen. Abizaid, said, "Pakistan has done more for the United States in the direct fight against Al Qaeda than any other country" (Ron Laurenzo, "Abizaid: Pakistan Best Ally in War on Terror," *Defense Week*, Feb. 2, 2004).

110 U.S. Department of State, *Country Reports on Terrorism 2004*, Apr. 2005.

111 U.S. Department of State, *Patterns of Global Terrorism 2002*, Apr. 2003. The United States has welcomed Pakistan's response to relevant U.N. Security Council Resolutions, including seizure of more than $10 million of Al Qaeda assets, and has provided assistance on drafting a new Pakistani Anti-Money Laundering/Terrorist Financing law (Statement of Paul Simons, Deputy Assistant Secretary of State for Economic and Business Affairs, before the House International Relations Committee, May 4, 2005).

112 "White House Report," U.S. Department of State Washington File, July 28, 2005.

Four months later, President Bush said that the United States is more secure "because Pakistani forces captured more than 100 extremists across the country [in 2004], including operatives who were plotting attacks against the United States." Top U.S. government and military officials regularly meet with Musharraf in Islamabad to discuss counterterrorism and for consultations on regional security.[113]

Obstacles

Many experts aver that, beginning most substantively with the policies of President Gen. Zia in the early 1980s, Islamabad's leaders have for decades supported and manipulated Islamic extremism as a means of forwarding their perceived strategic interests in the region. Thus, despite Pakistan's "crucial" cooperation, there continue to be doubts about Islamabad's full commitment to core U.S. concerns in the vast "lawless zones" of the Afghan-Pakistani border region where Islamic extremists find shelter.[114] Until September 2001, Islamabad's was one of only three world governments to recognize the Afghan Taliban regime, and Pakistan had been providing material support to the Taliban movement throughout the 1990s. Especially worrisome are indications that members of the Taliban continue to receive logistical and other support inside Pakistan. Senior U.S. Senators reportedly have voiced such worries, including concern that elements of Pakistan's intelligence agencies might be helping members of the Taliban and other Islamic militants.[115] In August 2003, at least three Pakistani army officers, including two colonels, were arrested on suspicion of having ties to Al Qaeda. Soon after, then-Deputy Secretary of State Armitage was quoted as saying he does "not think that affection for working with us extends up and down the rank and file of the Pakistani security community."[116]

In October 2003 testimony before the Senate Foreign Relations Committee, Assistant Secretary of Defense Peter Rodman said, "There are elements in the Pakistani government who we suspect are sympathetic to the old policy of before 9/11," adding that there still existed in northwestern Pakistan a radical Islamic infrastructure that "spews out fighters that go into Kashmir

---

113 "President and President Musharraf Discuss International Relations, Commerce," White House Press Release, Dec. 4, 2004; "President Discusses War on Terror," White House Press Release, Mar. 8, 2005; "Rumsfeld Meets US Ally Musharraf in Pakistan," Agence France Presse, Apr. 13, 2005; Sadaqat Jan, "Chief of U.S. Central Command in Pakistan," *Washington Post*, May 2, 2005; "U.S. Central Command Chief Meets With Pakistani President, Top Military Official," Associated Press, July 19, 2005.

114 Statement of George Tenet Before the Senate Select Committee on Intelligence, "Worldwide Threats to National Security," Feb. 6, 2002.

115 James Dao, "Terror Aid From Pakistan Concerns Senators," *New York Times*, Feb. 13, 2003. See also Testimony of Timothy Hoyt Before the Joint Hearing of the Subcommittees on Asia and the Pacific and International Terrorism, Nonproliferation, and Human Rights, Oct. 29, 2003.

116 Owen Bennett-Jones, "The Threat of Pakistan's Suicide Bombers," BBC News, Nov. 19, 2004; "Armitage: Some Pakistanis Reluctant to Work With US," Reuters, Sep. 30, 2003.

as well as into Afghanistan." In July 2004, a senior Pakistan expert told the same Senate panel that, "in the absence of greater U.S. guarantees regarding Pakistan's long-run security interests, it is dangerous [for the Pakistani military] to completely remove the threat of extremism to Kabul and Delhi." He went on to characterize a full and sincere decision by Islamabad to eradicate extremism as "tantamount to dismantling a weapons system."[117] Until mid-2004, the number of Al Qaeda figures arrested in Pakistan had been fairly static for more than one year, causing some U.S. military officials to question the extent of Islamabad's commitment to this aspect of U.S.-led counterterrorism efforts.[118]

A July 2004 hearing of the Senate Foreign Relations Committee focused specifically on Pakistan and counterterrorism. One area in which there appeared to be consensus among the three-person panel of veteran Pakistan watchers was the potential problems inherent in a U.S. over-reliance on President Gen. Pervez Musharraf as an individual at the potential cost of more positive development of Pakistan's democratic institutions and civil society. Many analysts believe such development is key to the long-term success of stated U.S. policy in the region. According to one expert, the United States is attempting to deal with Pakistan through "policy triage and by focusing on the personal leadership of President Musharraf," both of which are "flawed concepts." Another provided similar analysis, asserting that Musharraf is best seen as a "marginal satisfier" who will do only the minimum expected of him. This analyst recommended that, "The United States must alter the impression our support for Pakistan is essentially support for Musharraf," a sentiment echoed by many Pakistani commentators, as well. These perspectives suggest that many observers reject the specific conclusion of the *9/11 Commission Report* that Musharraf's government is the "best hope for stability in Pakistan and Afghanistan."[119]

Pakistani Military Operations

Background. In an effort to block infiltration along the Pakistan-Afghanistan border, Islamabad had by the end of 2002 deployed some 70,000 troops to the region. In April 2003, the United States, Pakistan, and Afghanistan formed a Tripartite Commission to coordinate their efforts to stabilize the border areas. In June 2003, in what may have been a response to increased U.S. pressure, Islamabad for the first time sent its armed forces into the

[117] "Senate Foreign Relations Committee Holds Hearing on Security and Democracy in Afghanistan," FDCH Transcripts, Oct. 16, 2003; Testimony of Professor Vali Nasr, "Senate Foreign Relations Committee Holds Hearing on Pakistan and Counterterrorism," FDCH Transcripts, July 14, 2004.

[118] Author interviews with U.S. military officials, Islamabad, Jan. 2004.

[119] See the testimony of Ambassador Teresita Schaffer and Professor Marvin Weinbaum, "Senate Foreign Relations Committee Holds Hearing on Pakistan and Counterterrorism," FDCH Transcripts, July 14, 2004; Ahmed Quraishi, "Assassination: The Message," *News* (Karachi), Aug. 3, 2004; Section 12.2 of *The 9/11 Commission Report*, available at [http://www.gpoaccess.gov/911/].

Federally Administered Tribal Areas (FATA) in search of Al Qaeda and Taliban fighters who have eluded the U.S.-led campaign in Afghanistan. By September 2003, Islamabad had up to 25,000 troops in the tribal areas, and a major operation—the first ever of its kind—took place in coordination with U.S.-led forces on the Afghan side of the border. A firefight in early October saw Pakistani security forces engage suspected Al Qaeda fugitives in South Waziristan, the southernmost of the FATA's seven districts which borders Afghanistan's Paktika province.[120] The operations encouraged U.S. officials, who saw in them a positive trend in Islamabad's commitment to tracking and capturing wanted extremists on Pakistani territory. Still, these officials admitted that the Pakistani government was finding it more difficult politically to pursue Taliban members who enjoy ethnic and familial ties with Pakistani Pashtuns.[121]

After the two December 2003 attempts on President Musharraf's life, the Pakistan military increased its efforts in the FATA. Many analysts speculated that the harrowing experiences brought a significant shift in Musharraf's attitude and caused him to recognize the dire threat posed by radical groups based in his country. In February 2004, Musharraf made his most explicit admission to date that Muslim militants were crossing from Pakistan into Afghanistan to battle coalition troops there. In the same month, the Vice Chairman of the U.S. Joint Chiefs of Staff told a Congressional panel that the Islamabad government had "taken some initiatives to increase their military presence on the border, such as manned outposts, regular patrols, and security barriers." By August 2004, 75,000 Pakistani troops were in the western border areas. Islamabad's more energetic operations in the western tribal regions brought vocal criticism from Musharraf's detractors among Islamist groups, many of whom accuse him of taking orders from the United States.[122]

Operations in 2004. In March 2004, up to 6,000 Pakistani soldiers took part in a pitched, 12-day battle with Islamic militants in South Waziristan. More than 130 people were killed in the fighting, including 46 Pakistani soldiers, but no "high-value" Al Qaeda or Taliban fugitives were killed or captured. Pakistani officials called the operation a victory, but the apparent escape of militant leaders, coupled with the vehement and lethal

---

[120] John Lancaster, "Pakistan Touts Control of Border," *Washington Post*, Sep. 2, 2003; "Pakistan Army Launches Border Operation," BBC News, Sep. 4, 2003.

[121] See the testimony of both William Taylor and Brig. Gen. Gary North in "Transcript: Senate Foreign Relations Committee Holds Hearing on Security and Democracy in Afghanistan," FDCH Transcripts, Oct. 16, 2003.

[122] David Rohde and Carlotta Gall, "Pakistani Offensive Aims to Drive Out Taliban and Al Qaeda," *New York Times*, Feb. 23, 2004; "Pakistan Says That Afghan Rebels May Be Using Its Soil," Reuters, Feb. 12, 2004; Statement of Gen. Peter Pace Before the House Committee on Armed Services, Feb. 4, 2004; "Pakistan rejects Border Criticism," BBC News, Aug. 26, 2004; "Fazl Accuses Govt for Taking Dictation From US for Tribal Operation," Pakistan Press International, Jan. 14, 2004; "US Provoking Tribesmen Against Army, Says Qazi," *Dawn* (Karachi), Feb. 24, 2004.

resistance put up by their well-armed cadre (believed to be remnants of the Islamic Movement of Uzbekistan), led many observers to call the operation a failure marked by poor intelligence and hasty planning.[123] During the course of the battle, Pakistani troops began bulldozing the homes of Wazirs who were suspected of providing shelter to "foreign terrorists," and the United States made a short-notice delivery of 2,500 surplus protective vests to the Pakistani military.[124]

Concurrent with these developments, the Islamabad government made progress in persuading Pashtun tribal leaders to undertake their own efforts by organizing tribal "lashkars," or militias, for the purpose of detaining (or at least expelling) wanted fugitives.[125] Political administrators in the district, impatient with the slow pace of progress, issued an "ultimatum" that included threats of steep monetary fines for the entire tribe, as well as for any individuals who provide shelter to "unwanted foreigners."[126] After March's military setback, a deadline was set for foreigners living in the tribal areas to register with the government and surrender their weapons with the understanding that they would be allowed to remain in Pakistan if they forswore terrorism. The original date passed without a single registrant coming forward and the government extended the deadline on several occasions.

On April 24, 2004, the five most-wanted Pashtun tribesmen "surrendered" to government authorities and were immediately granted amnesty in return for promises that they would not provide shelter to Al Qaeda members or their supporters. All five were reported to be supporter's of Maulana Fazlur Rehman's JUI Islamist party. Islamabad insisted that this "Shakai agreement" would mark no diminution of its counterterrorism efforts, but the top U.S. military officer in Afghanistan at the time, Lt. Gen. David Barno, expressed concern that Pakistan's strategy of seeking reconciliation with militants in western tribal areas "could go in the wrong direction." Almost immediately upon making the deal, the most outspoken of the tribal militants, 27-year-old Nek Mohammed, who had fought with the Taliban in Afghanistan, issued threats against Islamabad and pledged his fealty to fugitive Taliban chief Mohammed Omar. During the following weeks, a series of what some analysts called "spurious" deals were struck

---

[123] Pamela Constable, "Conflict Ends in Pakistani Tribal Lands," *Washington Post*, Mar. 29, 2004; Owais Tohid, "Mixed Results for Pakistan's Tribal Offensive," *Christian Science Monitor*, Mar. 31, 2004.

[124] Owais Tohid, "Pakistan Marks Pro-Al Qaeda Clan," *Christian Science Monitor*, Mar. 23, 2004; U.S. Embassy Islamabad Press Release, Mar. 24, 2004.

[125] There are indications that such progress came through outright coercion. The top U.S. commander in Afghanistan at the time, Lt. Gen. Barno, said that Pakistani government and military officials threatened tribal leaders with "destruction of homes and things of that nature" unless they cooperated ("U.S. Says Pakistan is Confronting Tribal Leaders," *New York Times*, Feb. 17, 2004).

[126] David Rohde and Ismail Khan, "Pakistan Adopting a Tough Old Tactic to Flush Out Qaeda," *New York Times*, Jan. 31, 2004; Ismail Khan, "Operation in S. Waziristan," *Dawn* (Karachi), Feb. 18, 2004; Iqbal Khattak, "Army Ready to Search South Waziristan," *Daily Times* (Lahore), Feb. 18, 2004.

between the government and foreign militants, but these proved unsuccessful after the foreigners failed to register, and numerous tribal militias sought but failed to capture any of them.[127]

In response to this apparent failure of its conciliatory approach, Islamabad ordered authorities in South Waziristan to shutter more than 6,000 merchant shops in an effort to use economic pressure against uncooperative tribesmen, and a "massive mobilization" of federal troops was reported. Then, in June, the government rescinded its amnesty offer to the five key militants noted above and issued a "kill or capture" order against them. The next day, fixed-wing Pakistani warplanes bombed three compounds being used by militants in South Waziristan, including one that was described as a terrorist training camp. More than 20,000 troops were said to be involved in a sweep operation that left about 72 people dead, including 17 soldiers, after three days of fighting.[128] On June 18, Nek Mohammed was located, apparently through signals intelligence, and was killed along with seven others by a missile that may have come from an American Predator drone.[129]

In early September 2004, some 55 suspected Islamic militants were killed when Pakistan warplanes attacked an alleged Al Qaeda training camp in South Waziristan. The military claimed that 90% of the dead were foreigners (mostly Uzbeks and Chechens), but other reports said half were locals, and eyewitnesses told of numerous civilian casualties. Intense fighting continued throughout the month, bringing renewed criticism of the government by both human rights groups and Islamist leaders. The Islamabad government is said to be paying reparations for property damage, and for the death or injury of innocents.[130]

In mid-September 2004, Abdullah Mahsud—a Pakistani Pashtun militant who lost a leg fighting for the Taliban in Afghanistan and who was held for more than two years at the U.S. facility at Guantanamo Bay before

[127] "Rebel Tribesmen Agree to Surrender," *Gulf News* (Dubai), Apr. 24, 2004; M. Ilyas Khan, "Who Are These People," *Herald* (Karachi), Apr. 2004; "US 'Concern' at Pakistan Strategy," BBC News, May 3, 2004; Zeeshan Haider, "Pakistani Militant Says Taliban Boss His Leader," Reuters, May 6, 2004; "Pakistan Dealing With Both Hands," Stratfor.com, May 13, 2004; "Pakistan Amnesty Deal Hit By Setback," BBC News, May 124, 2004; "Lashkar Completes Hunt in Azam Warsak," *News* (Karachi), May 19, 2004.

[128] Ismail, Khan, "Wana Amnesty for Militants Revoked," *Dawn* (Karachi), June 10, 2004; Salman Masood, "Pakistan Bombs Compounds Used by Foreign Militants," *New York Times*, June 11, 2004; Munir Ahmad, "Pakistan Ends Operation Against Al Qaeda suspects," *Washington Post*, June 14, 2004.

[129] "Pakistan Army Kills Tribal Leader," BBC News, June 18, 2004; Ismail Khan and Dilawar Khan Wazir, "Night Raid Kills Nek, Four Other Militants," *Dawn* (Karachi), June 19, 2004.

[130] "Raid on Al Qaeda Camp Kills 55," CNN.com, Sep. 9, 2004; Dilawar Khan Wazir, "Wana Dead Included 25 Local Militants," *Dawn* (Karachi), Sep. 12, 2004; "Pakistan Opposition, Rights Leaders Condemn Military Attack on Tribal Areas," BBC Monitoring South Asia, Sep. 11, 2004; "Qazi Terms Wana Action State Terrorism," *Dawn* (Karachi), Sep. 12, 2004; Imtiaz Gul, "Wana Turning Into a War Zone," *Friday Times* (Lahore), Oct. 1, 2004; Amir Mohammed Khan, "Army Operation in S Waziristan to End Soon: IPSR," *News* (Karachi), Dec. 8, 2004.

being released in 2004—reportedly refused to allow Pakistan security forces to use a key road connecting North and South Waziristan. Mahsud was believed to be trying to fill the shoes of Nek Mohammed, a leading tribal militant killed in June. In October, two Chinese engineers traveling through South Waziristan along with two Pakistani security officers were kidnaped by Mahsud and his followers, who threatened to kill their hostages. Pakistani commandos stormed the militants' hideout and killed five kidnappers inside, but Mahsud was not found (one Chinese national was freed, but the other was killed in the shootout). Later in the month, a group of tribal leaders who had been trying to broker Mahsud's surrender came under attack from what the military called rockets fired by "miscreants." Fourteen were killed in a sign of growing intra-tribal conflict over government policy in the FATA.[131]

In the midst of ongoing and lethal military operations, the five most-wanted Pashtun tribal militant leaders in South Waziristan "surrendered" to government authorities in November 2004 by promising to remain peaceful and provide no shelter to foreign militants. In return, the government reportedly vowed to pay reparations for property damage and to release tribal prisoners. Soon after, the regional corps commander declared that "peace has been restored in Wana," the area where the bulk of combat took place in 2004. The general also announced that all but 3,000 troops and nine check posts would be withdrawn from the Wana region, where less than one hundred militants were said to remain. A U.S. State Department spokesman later said the United States was assured that Pakistani forces were not withdrawing from Waziristan and that Pakistan remained "fully committed to continuing the campaign against Al Qaeda and Al Qaeda supporters."[132] The Peshawar Corps Commander reported that 35 military operations in Waziristan left 250 militants (and 175 Pakistani soldiers) dead and 600 captured in 2004, but no "high-value targets" are known to have been among these, and the militants swept out of South Waziristan were believed to have found refuge in other areas where Pakistani troops are not active.[133]

Operations in 2005. During 2005, attention shifted to the North Waziristan district where Pakistani security forces made sporadic raids in which scores of suspected militants—local Pashtun tribals, Afghans, and other

131 Dilawar Khan Wazir, "Waziristan Clashes Leave 13 Dead," *Dawn* (Karachi), Sep. 13, 2004; "14 Pakistani Tribesmen Killed While Trying to Broker Militant Surrender," Agence France Presse, Oct. 27, 2004.

132 "Pakistan Troops Launch New Attack," BBC News, Nov. 12, 2005; Iqbal Khattak and Mujeebur Rehman, "Wazir Militants Agree to Peace Pact," *Daily Times* (Lahore), Nov. 11, 2004; Mohamed Khan and David Rohde, "Pakistan to Scale Back Force Around Town Near Afghan Border," *New York Times*, Nov. 28, 2004; State Department Noon Briefing, Nov. 29, 2004.

133 Aamer Ahmed Khan, "Musharraf Thrives on US Support," BBC News, Dec. 8, 2004; Qudissa Akhlaque, "Militants Find New Sanctuaries," *Dawn* (Karachi), Dec. 11, 2004.

foreigners such as Uzbeks and Arabs—were killed or captured.[134] In early spring, Pakistani commanders issued warnings to Wazir tribal leaders that failure to expel foreign militants from the region would result in large-scale military operations and, in April, hundreds of Pakistani troops reportedly launched search operations for foreign militants in North Waziristan near the Afghan border.[135] A top U.S. military commander in Afghanistan claimed Pakistan was launching new major operations in the region, eliciting strong denials from a Pakistani commander who called the claim "highly irresponsible."[136] Reports suggest that tensions in North Waziristan remain high.[137]

The Islamabad government's "peace deals" with South Waziristan militants appear to have largely ended overt conflict there in 2005.[138] However, there are indications that underlying tensions remain significant and could bring future unrest.[139] In March, Islamic militants in the Wana area warned the peace there could unravel if the government reneged on promises to remove checkpoints and pay compensation for damage to local homes and, in May, a bomb exploded at the home of a tribal leader in South Waziristan, killing two women and four children. On the first anniversary of Nek Mohammed's June 2004 death, Muslim clerics and "thousands" of Taliban in South Waziristan reportedly marked occasion by vowing to continue their jihad against America. One month later, gunmen killed nine tribesmen, including five pro-government tribal elders, in three separate attacks in South Waziristan. The elders had been assisting army efforts to capture or kill fugitive Islamic militants in the region.[140] Despite this violence, Pakistani officials insist that Al Qaeda-linked militants have been completely eradicated from South Waziristan.[141]

---

[134] See, for example, "20 Suspects Held in N Waziristan Raid," *News* (Karachi), Jan. 16, 2005; "Pakistan Army Raids Village in Hunt for Al Qaeda," Reuters, Mar. 13, 2005; "18 Killed in Clashes Near Afghan Border," Associated Press, July 17, 2005.

[135] "N. Waziristan Elders Warned of Action," *Dawn* (Karachi), Mar. 12, 2005; Iqbal Khattak, "Military Warns Tribes of Action," *Daily Times* (Lahore), Apr. 20, 2005; "Troops Launch Search Operation in N Waziristan," *News* (Karachi), Apr. 22, 2005.

[136] "US Military Claim Angers Pakistan," BBC News, Apr. 20, 2005.

[137] Zulfiqar Ali, "Perpetual Siege," *Herald* (Karachi), May 2005.

[138] In early 2005, a Pakistan Army spokesman confirmed that a November 2004 deal included giving Baitullah Mehsud and three other tribal leaders about $540,000 to repay loans they had taken from Al Qaeda. Abdullah Mehsud vowed to continue his "jihad" despite the pact between the Pakistan government and several of his former allies. ("Pakistan Pays Tribe Al Qaeda Loan," BBC News, Feb. 9, 2005; "Abdullah Mehsud Says He Will Continue 'Jihad,'" *Daily Times* (Lahore), Feb. 10, 2005).

[139] "Waziristan Set for Uncertain Future," *Jane's Terrorism and Security Monitor*," Mar. 16, 2005; Imtiaz Gul, "South Waziristan: A Case of Fudging the Facts," *Friday Times* (Lahore), June 3, 2005; Rahimullah Yusufzai, "Threats by Tribal Commanders Fuels Concern in S Waziristan," *News* (Karachi), July 29, 2005.

[140] Rahimullah Yusufzai, "Situation Could Worsen If Pact Ignored, Warn Militants," *News* (Karachi), Mar. 10, 2005; "Waziristan House Bomb Kills Six," BBC News, May 25, 2005; Iqbal Khattak, "Wana Clerics Vow to Continue Jihad," *Daily Times* (Lahore), June 20, 2005; "Assailants Kill Tribal Elders in Pakistan," *New York Times*, July 22, 2005.

[141] "Pakistan 'Clears Al Qaeda Haven,'" BBC News, May 28, 2005.

Fallout. As was noted above, President Musharraf's post-September 2001 policy reversals and his efforts to crack down on Islamic extremist groups likely motivated the two deadly December 2003 attempts to assassinate the Pakistani leader. As Pakistan's coercive counterterrorism policies became more vigorous, numerous observers warned that increased government pressure on tribal communities and military operations in the FATA were creating a backlash, sparking unrest and strengthening pro-Al Qaeda sentiments both there and in Pakistan's southern and eastern cities.[142] Developments in 2004 appeared to have borne out these analyses. As his army battled militants in South Waziristan in June of that year, President Musharraf told an interviewer that he was concerned about "fallout" from the recent military operations, and a Pakistan Army spokesman drew direct links between a six-week-long spate of mostly sectarian bombings and killings in Karachi and government efforts to root out militants in South Waziristan. A leading pro-Taliban militant in the tribal areas accused Islamabad of "conniving" with the U.S. government to kill Nek Mohammed, and he warned that military operations in South Waziristan would lead to further violence across Pakistan. Several international aid organizations suspended their operations in the Baluchistan province after receiving threats of suicide attacks.[143]

Islamic militant outrage appeared to again peak in mid-summer 2004: During the week spanning July and August, a suicide bomber killed a senior Pakistani intelligence officer in Kohat near the tribal areas; another suicide bomber murdered nine people in a failed attempt to assassinate Pakistan's Prime Minister-designate (an Al Qaeda-affiliated group claimed responsibility for the attack); and gunmen killed a police officer in a failed effort to assassinate the Baluchistan Chief Minister. As conflict and bloodshed in Pakistan increased, analysts again expressed acute concerns about the country's fundamental political stability.[144]

U.S. Military Presence

The issue of small-scale and sporadic U.S. military presence on Pakistani soil is a sensitive one, and reports of even brief incursions from neighboring

---

[142] See, for example, Iqbal Khattak, "Military Operation in Waziristan May Backfire," *Friday Times* (Lahore), Feb. 20, 2004; Simon Denyer and Zeeshan Haider, "Pakistan Risks Enraging Tribes in Bin Laden Hunt," Reuters, Mar. 21, 2004; Mazhar Abbas, "Wana to Karachi: Militants Take on the Army," *Friday Times* (Lahore), June 18, 2004.

[143] "Musharraf Worried About Wana Operation Fallout," *Dawn* (Karachi), June 21, 2004; Hafiz Wazir, "Pakistan Kills Pro-Al Qaeda Tribal Fighter," Reuters, June 18, 2004; Rahimullah Yusufzai, "Militants' Commander Warns of Wana Fallout," *News* (Karachi), Aug. 1, 2004; "Agencies Halt Pakistan Operations," BBC News, June 6, 2004.

[144] "Bomb Kills Pakistan Intelligence Chief," CNN.com, July 28, 2004; "Several Arrests Made in Pakistan Attack," *New York Times*, Aug. 1, 2004; "Pakistan Politician Survives Raid," BBC News, Aug. 2, 2004. On political stability, see, for example, expert testimony before the Senate Foreign Relations Committee on "Pakistan and Counterterrorism," July 14, 2004; "Musharraf's Tightrope Act," *Jane's Intelligence Digest*, Aug. 6, 2004.

Afghanistan have caused tensions between Islamabad and Washington.[145] In March 2004, U.S. and Afghan forces conducted Operation Mountain Storm southern and eastern Afghanistan, employing new tactics and in coordination with Pakistani troops across the international border.[146] A press report earlier in the year had suggested that the U.S. military in Afghanistan had plans for a spring offensive that would "go into Pakistan with Musharraf's help" to neutralize Al Qaeda forces, a suggestion that President Musharraf's said was "not a possibility at all." The Commander of U.S. Central Command, Gen. Abizaid, stated that he had no plans to put U.S. troops in Pakistan against Islamabad's wishes, and a senior U.S. diplomat and senior U.S. military officer later told a House Armed Services Committee panel that it is "absolutely" the policy of the United States to keep its troops on the Afghan side of the Afghan-Pakistani border. In April 2004, the U.S. Ambassador to Afghanistan caused some further annoyance in Islamabad when he said that the Pakistani leadership must solve the ongoing problem of militant infiltration into Afghanistan or "we will have to do it for ourselves." American artillery reportedly can be fired onto militant forces with Islamabad's permission.[147] U.S. military officials in Kabul say that Pakistan has agreed to allow "hot pursuit" up to ten kilometers into Pakistani territory, although this is officially denied by the Islamabad government.[148]

Since the spring of 2002, U.S. military and law enforcement personnel reportedly have been engaging in direct, low-profile efforts to assist Pakistani security forces in tracking and apprehending fugitive Al Qaeda and Taliban fighters on Pakistani territory, especially with signals and other intelligence. U.S. forces in Afghanistan reportedly provide significant support to Pakistani forces operating near the Afghan border—including spy satellites, electronic surveillance planes, armed aerial drones, and sophisticated ground sensors—and law enforcement efforts within Pakistan reportedly benefit from CIA- and FBI-supplied surveillance equipment and other backing. There also have been reports that the United States is assisting Pakistan in the creation of a 700-man "Counter-Terrorism Cell,"

---

145 "Pakistan Protests at US Incursion," BBC News, May 5, 2004.

146 "US Launches Major Al Qaeda Hunt," BBC News, Mar. 20, 2004; David Sanger and Eric Schmitt, "New U.S. Effort Steps Up Hunt for Bin Laden," *New York Times*, Feb. 29, 2004.

147 Christine Spolar, "U.S. Plans Al Qaeda Offensive That Would Reach Inside Pakistan," *Chicago Tribune*, Jan. 27, 2004; Stephan Graham, "U.S. Military 'Sure' to Catch Bin Laden," *Chicago Tribune*, Jan. 29, 2004; "House Armed Services Committee Holds Hearing on Afghanistan Security and Reconstruction," FDCH Transcripts, Apr. 29, 2004; "Envoy Warns Pakistan Over Havens," CNN.com, Apr. 5, 2004; Thomas Coghlan, "Up Close in al Qaeda Hunt," BBC News, Oct. 13, 2004.

148 Author interviews with U.S. military officials, Kabul, Jan. 2004. Pakistan also denied a March 2004 report that the it had agreed to allow U.S. Special Forces soldiers on its territory in return for a softened U.S. policy toward Pakistan's apparent role in nuclear proliferation activities, and a December 2004 report that the C.I.A. had established a series of small, covert bases in northwestern Pakistan in late 2003 where U.S. agents work under strict Pakistani supervision in the hunt for Osama bin Laden (Seymour Hersh, "The Deal," *New Yorker*, Mar. 8, 2004; James Risen and David Rohde, "A Hostile Land Foils the Quest for Bin Laden," *New York Times*, Dec. 13, 2004).

and Pakistan's air force chief said in September 2004 that U.S. forces continued to make use of several air bases near the Afghan border.[149]

U.S. Government Assistance

Security-related U.S. assistance programs for Pakistan are said to be aimed at bolstering Islamabad's counterterrorism and border security efforts, and have included U.S.-funded road-building projects in the Northwest Frontier Province and Federally Administered Tribal Areas, the provision of night-vision equipment, communications gear, protective vests, 26 transport helicopters, and, currently in the pipeline, six used C-130 transport aircraft. The United States also has undertaken to train and equip new Pakistan Army Air Assault units that can move quickly to find and target terrorist elements.[150] The Chairman of the U.S. Joint Chiefs of Staff reports that the Pakistani Army has "significantly improved their counterterrorism capabilities, thanks in part to equipment we are providing them, and has played a vital role in enhancing security in this region."[151]

In September 2004, the Pentagon notified Congress of the possible Foreign Military Sale to Pakistan of $78 million worth of military radio systems meant to improve Pakistani communication capabilities and to increase interoperability between Pakistani and U.S.-led counterterrorist forces. In November, potential sales to Pakistan of eight P-3C maritime reconnaissance aircraft, six Phalanx naval guns, and 2,000 TOW anti-armor missiles were announced. The deals could be worth up to $1.2 billion for Lockheed Martin and Raytheon, the prime contractors. The Department of Defense characterizes the P-3Cs and TOW missiles as having significant anti-terrorism applications (a claim that has elicited skepticism from some analysts), and it asserted that the proposed sales would not affect the military balance in the region. India's external affairs minister has "cautioned the United States" against any decision to sell F-16 fighter jets to Pakistan, adding that the "U.S. arms supply to Pakistan would have a negative impact on the goodwill the United States enjoys with India, particularly as a sister democracy." The Pentagon reports Foreign Military Sales agreements with

[149] Josh Meyer and Greg Miller, "Terror Plotter May Be Trapped," *Los Angeles Times*, Mar. 19, 2004; Howard LaFranchi, "Arrests Bolster Bush's Embrace of Pakistan," *Christian Science Monitor*, Aug. 9, 2004; Imtiaz Gul, "In the Clutches of the CIA-FBI Combine," *Friday Times* (Lahore), Aug. 13, 2004; Mubasher Bukhari, "US Will Help Pakistan Set Up Anti-Terror Cell," *Daily Times* (Lahore), Sep. 3, 2004; A.H. Khanzada, "US Forces Operating From PAF Forward Bases: CAS," *News* (Karachi), Sep. 15, 2004.

[150] Statement of Lt. Gen. Walter Sharp Before the House Committee on Armed Services, Apr. 29, 2004; Mubasher Bukhari, "US Choppers Given to Army Aviation Wing," *Daily Times* (Lahore), July 25, 2004; U.S. Department of State, *Congressional Budget Justification for Foreign Operations, FY2005*, released Feb. 10, 2004.

[151] Statement of Gen. Richard Myers before the Senate Armed Services Committee, Feb. 17, 2005.

Figure 1: U.S. Assistance to Pakistan, FY2001–FY2005 and 2006 Administration Request

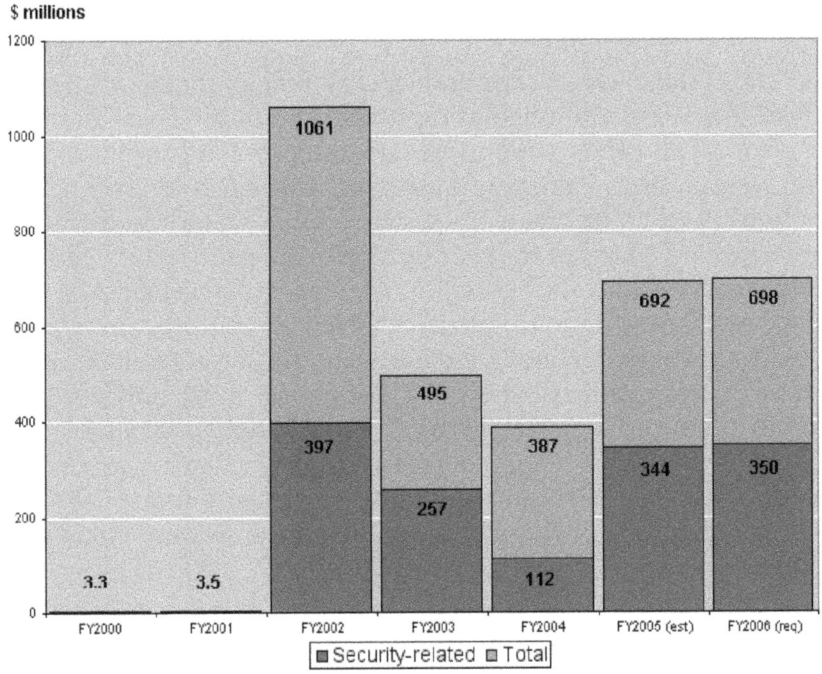

Sources: U.S. Department of State and U.S. Agency for International Development
Notes: FY2005 amounts are estimates, FY2006 amounts are requested. FY2005 amounts include Emergency Supplemental Appropriations Act, 2005 (P.L. 10-13) funding of $150 million in FMF and $4 million in additional counter-drug funding for Pakistan.

Pakistan worth $27 million in FY2002, $167 million in FY2003, and $176 million in FY2004.[152]

With FY2005 appropriations included, Pakistan will have received $1.1 billion in direct U.S. security-related assistance since September 2001 (Foreign Military Financing totaling nearly $675 million plus about $437 million for other programs, see Figure 1).[153] Congress also has allocated billions of dollars in additional defense spending to reimburse Pakistan and other cooperating nations for their support of U.S. counterterrorism operations. Pentagon documents indicate that Pakistan received coalition support funding of more than $1.3 billion for the period January 2003-September 2004,

[152] "India Cautioned US Against Selling F-16s to Pakistan: Foreign Minister," Agence France Presse, Dec. 8, 2004; on sales figures, see Defense Security Cooperation Agency Facts Books 2003, available at [http://www.dsca.osd.mil]. See also see also CRS Report RS22148, *Combat Aircraft Sales to South Asia*, by Christopher Bolkcom, Richard Grimmett, and K. Alan Kronstadt.

[153] "Security-related assistance" here includes Foreign Military Financing; International Military Education and Training; International Narcotics Control and Law Enforcement; Nonproliferation, Anti-Terrorism, Demining, and Related; and Peacekeeping Operations.

an amount roughly equal to one-third of Pakistan's total defense expenditures during that period. A report of the House Armed Services Committee (H.Rept. 109–89) said the Secretary of Defense expects to disburse another $1.2 billion to Pakistan in FY2005.

During 2004, there were clear indications that both the United States and Pakistan were re-invigorating their efforts to find and capture those terrorists and their supporters remaining in Pashtun-majority areas of Afghanistan and Pakistan. Moreover, during mid-2005, President Musharraf has taken further steps to crack down on indigenous Pakistani extremist groups. Many of these groups have links not only to individuals and organizations actively fighting in Afghanistan and Pakistan, but also with groups that continue to pursue a violent separatist campaign in the disputed Kashmir region along Pakistan's northeast frontier. A November 2003 cease-fire agreement between Pakistan and India holds at the time of this writing, and appears to have contributed to what New Delhi officials acknowledge is a major decrease in the number of "terrorist" infiltrations.[154] However, separatist militants vowed in January 2004 to continue their struggle regardless of the status of the nascent Pakistan-India dialogue.

Terrorism in Kashmir and India[155]

As a vast mosaic of ethnicities, languages, cultures, and religions, India can be difficult to govern. Internal instability resulting from diversity is further complicated by colonial legacies such as international borders that separate members of the same ethnic groups, creating flashpoints for regional dissidence and separatism. Separatist movements in the northwestern Jammu and Kashmir state, and in remote and underdeveloped northeast regions, confound New Delhi and create international tensions by operating out of neighboring Pakistan, Bangladesh, Burma, Bhutan, and Nepal. Moreover, indigenous Maoist rebels continue to operate in eastern states, possibly in collusion with Nepali Maoists at war with the Kathmandu government. The Indian Home Ministry reported to Parliament that a total of 7,458 people were killed in 10,788 incidents of separatist and Maoist "Naxalite" violence in India during the year ending October 31, 2004. More than half of these deaths and incidents occurred in Kashmir.[156]

[154] In January 2005, India's army chief said that the number of infiltration attempts at the Kashmiri Line of Control were down 90 percent in 2004 ("Infiltration on LoC Down 90 Percent: Army Chief," Indo-Asian News Service, Jan. 15, 2005).

[155] This section written by K. Alan Kronstadt, Analyst in Asian Affairs.

[156] "7,458 Persons Killed in Kashmir, North-East, and Naxal Violence," Press Trust of India, Dec. 15, 2004.

Kashmiri Separatism

Separatist violence in India's Jammu and Kashmir state has continued unabated since 1989. New Delhi has long blamed Pakistan-based militant groups for lethal attacks on Indian civilians, as well as on government security forces, in both Kashmir and in major Indian cities.[157] India holds Pakistan responsible for providing material support and training facilities to Kashmiri militants. Pakistan denies rendering anything more than diplomatic and moral support to separatists, and it remains critical of India's allegedly severe human rights violations in Jammu and Kashmir.[158] Disagreement over the meaning of the word "terrorism" has been a sticking point in India-Pakistan relations.[159] According to the U.S. government, several anti-India militant groups fighting in Kashmir are based in Pakistan and are closely linked to Islamist groups there. Many also are said to maintain ties with international jihadi organizations, including Al Qaeda:

- Harakat ul-Mujahideen (an FTO-designate), based in Muzaffarabad (Azad Kashmir) and Rawalpindi, is aligned with the Jamiat Ulema-i-Islam Fazlur Rehman party (JUI-F), itself a main constituent of the MMA Islamist coalition in Pakistan's National Assembly;
- Hizbul Mujahideen (on the State Department's list of "other selected terrorist organizations"), believed to have bases in Pakistan, is the militant wing of Pakistan's largest Islamic political party and leading MMA member, the Jamaat-i-Islami;
- Jaish-e-Mohammed (JeM) (an FTO-designate), based in both Peshawar and Muzaffarabad, also is aligned with JUI-F; and
- Lashkar-e-Taiba (LeT) (an FTO-designate), based in Muzaffarabad and near Lahore, is the armed wing of a Pakistan-based, anti-U.S. Sunni religious organization formed in 1989.[160]

---

157 Grenade and bomb attacks against civilians have been a regular occurrence in India and Indian Kashmir for many years. Among the notable terrorist incidents in recent times were a May 2002 attack on an Indian army base in Kaluchak, Kashmir that killed 37, many of them women and children (New Delhi identified the attackers as Pakistani nationals); a July 2002 attack on a Jammu village that killed 27; an August 2002 grenade attack in Kashmir that killed nine Hindu pilgrims and injured 32 others; a September 2002 attack on a Gujarat temple that left 32 dead; a March 2003 massacre of 24 Hindu villagers in Nadimarg, Jammu; a July 2003 attack on a Jammu village that killed seven and injured more than 20; a July 2003 bus bombing in a Bombay suburb that left four dead and 42 injured; and a pair of August 2003 car bombings in a crowded Bombay district that killed 52 and injured some 150 more. Indian authorities linked each of these attacks to the LeT, although the last may have been planned by indigenous elements (John Lancaster, "India Shocked by Bombay Bombings, and Suspects," *Washington Post*, Sep. 12, 2003).

158 For example, Pakistan's state television network reported that Indian troops had "martyred 1,675 innocent Kashmiris" in 2004, including 104 women and children ("Kashmir Deaths by Indian Troops in 2004 Put at 1,675 - Pakistan TV," BBC Monitoring South Asia, Jan. 1, 2005). The U.S. Department of State and international human rights groups have issued reports critical of human rights abuses in Indian-controlled Kashmir.

159 India-Pakistan Talks on 'Terror,'" BBC News, Aug. 11, 2004.

160 U.S. Department of State, *Country Reports on Terrorism 2004*, Apr. 2005. Among the State Department's "other selected terrorist organizations" active in Kashmir are the Al Badhr Mujahideen, the Harakat

JeM claimed responsibility for an October 2001 suicide bomb attack on the Jammu and Kashmir state assembly building in Srinagar that killed 31 (it later denied the claim). In December 2001, the United States designated both LeT and JeM as Foreign Terrorist Organizations shortly after they were publically implicated by New Delhi for an attack on the Indian Parliament complex that killed nine and injured 18. This assault spurred India to fully mobilize its military along the India-Pakistan frontier. An ensuing 10-month-long standoff in 2002 involved one million Indian and Pakistani soldiers and was viewed as the closest the two countries had come to full-scale war since 1971, causing the U.S. government to become "deeply concerned . . . that a conventional war . . . could escalate into a nuclear confrontation."[161]

Pakistan's powerful and largely autonomous ISI is widely believed to have provided significant support for militant Kashmiri separatists over the past decade and a half in what is perceived as a proxy war against India.[162] In March 2003, the chief of India's Defense Intelligence Agency reported providing the United States with "solid documentary proof" that 70 Islamic militant camps were operating in Pakistani Kashmir. In May 2003, the Indian defense minister claimed that about 3,000 "terrorists" were being trained in camps on the Pakistani side of the Line of Control (LOC). Some Indian officials have suggested that Al Qaeda may be active in Kashmir.[163] Then-U.S. Deputy Secretary of State Armitage reportedly received a June 2002 pledge from Pakistani President Musharraf that all "cross-border terrorism" would cease, followed by a May 2003 pledge that any terrorist training camps in Pakistani-controlled areas would be closed. Yet, in September 2003, Indian PM Vajpayee reportedly told President Bush that continued cross-border terrorism from Pakistan was making it difficult for

---

ul-Jihad-e-Islami (linked to both Al Qaeda and to the JUI-F, a major Pakistani Islamist political party), and the Jamiat ul-Mujahideen. All are said to have bases in Pakistan, and all are designated as terrorist organizations by the Indian government (Indian Ministry of Home Affairs, "The Prevention of Terrorism Act, 2002," available at [http://mha.nic.in/poto-02.htm#schdule]).

161 Statement of Director of Central Intelligence George Tenet Before the Senate Armed Services Committee, "Worldwide Threat: Converging Dangers in a Post-9/11 World," Mar. 19, 2002.

162 "Although Pakistan did not begin the [1989] uprising in Kashmir, the temptation to fan the flames was too great for Islamabad to resist. Using guerrilla warfare expertise gained during the Afghan war, Pakistan's ISI began to provide active backing for Kashmiri Muslim insurgents" (Dennis Kux, *The United States and Pakistan 1947–2000: Disenchanted Allies*, Woodrow Wilson Center Press, 2001, p. 305). Many Indian analysts emphasize evidence of a direct link between Pakistan-sponsored militancy in Kashmir and the wider assortment of radical Islamic groups active in Pakistan after 2001, with one going so far as to call Lashkar-e-Taiba a "wholly owned subsidiary of the ISI" (Indrani Bagchi, "Beyond Control," *India Today* (New Delhi), Dec. 8, 2003). In June 2005, several credible Kashmiri and Pakistani parties accused current Pakistani Information Minister Rashid of operating a training camp for Kashmiri separatist militants during the 1980s (B. Muralidhar Reddy, "Troublesome Links," *Frontline* (Madras), July 15, 2005).

163 "India Says It Has Given Proof of 70 Islamic Militant Camps in Pakistan-Controlled Kashmir," Associated Press, Mar. 14, 2003; "3,000 'Terrorists' Being Trained in Pakistani Kashmir: India," Agence France Presse, July 30, 2003. In October 2003, the Indian Chief of Army Staff raised the possibility of an Al Qaeda presence, as "most of the terrorists killed in [Jammu and Kashmir] are foreign nationals these days" ("Al Qaeda Presence Not Ruled Out in J&K," *Hindu* (Madras), Oct. 12, 2003).

India to maintain its peace initiative, and a series of bloody attacks seemed to indicate that infiltration rates were on the rise.[164]

President Musharraf adamantly insists that his government is doing all it can to stem infiltration at the LOC and he has called for a joint Pakistan-India monitoring effort there. Positive signs have come with a November 2003 cease-fire agreement between Pakistan and India along the entire LOC and their shared international border (holding at the time of this writing) and a January 2004 pledge by Musharraf reassuring the Indian Prime Minister that no territory under Pakistan's control could be used to support terrorism. Ensuing statements from Indian government officials confirmed that infiltration rates were down significantly. However, separatist-related violence spiked in Indian Kashmir in the summer of 2004, with shootouts and bombings causing scores of deaths. While on a July 2004 visit to New Delhi to meet with top Indian leaders, then-Deputy Secretary of State Armitage told reporters that "the infrastructure [in Pakistan] that supports cross-border activities [in Kashmir] has not been dismantled." Still, by year's end, the Indian government acknowledged that infiltration rates were at their lowest ebb in many years, perhaps partly due to the completion of fence structures along the entire LOC.[165] New Delhi has confirmed that "the level of violence and tension in Jammu and Kashmir in 2004 was significantly lower as compared to 2003."[166]

Despite waning rates of infiltration, the issue continues to rankle leaders in New Delhi and remains a serious potential impediment to progress in the current India-Pakistan peace initiative. In August 2004, India's ruling Congress Party claimed that Pakistan continues to support ongoing "cross-border terrorism" in Kashmir (Pakistan's outgoing prime minister rejected the claims). In September, former Indian Prime Minister Vajpayee said that President Musharraf was not fulfilling his January 2004 pledge to end the use of Pakistani territory by terrorist groups and, just before meeting Musharraf in New York, current Indian Prime Minister Singh said that India would continue talks with Pakistan "provided that the threat by terrorist elements can be kept under control." India's foreign minister issued an even stronger statement of the same demand in October. In May 2005, in a somewhat anomalous departure from the milder rhetoric associated with improved India-Pakistan relations, the Indian prime minister again

[164] Chidanand Rajghatta, "Cross-Border Terror Continues, Vajpayee Tells Bush," *Times of India* (Delhi), Sep. 25, 2003; Scott Baldauf, "Insurgents Push Into Kashmir," *Christian Science Monitor*, Oct. 7, 2003.

[165] "Armitage Finds Pakistan-India Relations Improving," U.S. Department of State Washington File, July 15, 2004; "Infiltration on LoC Down 90 Percent: Army Chief," Indo-Asian News Service, Jan. 15, 2005; "LOC Fencing Complete: Mukherjee," *Times of India* (Delhi), Dec. 16, 2004: "Infiltration Has Come Down, Says Pranab," *Hindu* (Madras), Feb. 8, 2005.

[166] The Home Ministry reported only 707 "incidents" in 2004, as compared to 3,041 in 2003. The numbers of civilians killed in 2004 (707), however, was nearly the great as in 2003 (795) (Government of India, *Ministry of Home Affairs Annual Report 2004–05*).

chided Pakistan for doing too little to dismantle the "terrorist infrastructure" on Pakistani-controlled territory.[167] Even as the normalization of India-Pakistan relations continues—and to some extent in reaction to their apparent marginalization in the face of such developments—separatist militants continue their attacks on both civilians and Indian security forces, and some in India believe that active support for Kashmiri militants remains Pakistani policy. In August 2005, India's national security advisor expressed concern that terrorist attacks by or on behalf of Kashmiri separatists were showing a "much higher level of sophistication" and were taking place in many areas of India beyond Kashmir.[168]

Indigenous Indian-Designated Terrorist Groups

Northeastern Separatism. Since the time of India's foundation, numerous separatist groups have fought for ethnic autonomy or independence in the country's northeast region. Some of the tribal struggles in the small states known as the Seven Sisters are centuries old. The United States does not designate as terrorist organizations most of those groups that continue violent separatist struggles in India's northeastern states. Many of these groups have, however, been implicated in lethal attacks on civilians and have been designated as terrorist organizations by New Delhi under the 2002 Prevention of Terrorism Act (POTA).[169] More than 6,000 people, one-third of them insurgents, are estimated to have been killed since 1992 in related violence in the states of Nagaland, Assam, Manipur, and Tripura.[170] Among the dozens of insurgent groups active in the northeast are:

- the United Liberation Front of Assam (ULFA);[171]
- the Nationalist Social Council of Nagaland;
- the National Liberation Front of Tripura;

[167] "Pakistan Hasn't Ended Cross-Border Terror: Congress," *Hindustan Times* (Delhi), Aug. 22, 2004; "Vajpayee Says Musharraf Backtracking on Promise," Press Trust of India, Sep. 8, 2004; "India to Pursue Talks With Pakistan If Terrorism 'Under Control,'" Agence France Presse, Sep. 20, 2004; "India Says Peace Talks 'Dependent' On Pakistan Reining In Kashmir Rebels," Agence France Presse, Oct. 9, 2004; "Indian Leader Says Pakistan Must Do More to Rein in Extremists," *Washington Post*, May 31, 2005.

[168] "Militants Defy India-Pakistan Detente," *Jane's Security & Terrorism Monitor*, May 18, 2005; Saurabh Shukla, "Back on the Terror Trail," *India Today* (Delhi), Feb. 7, 2005; Raj Chengappa, "'Our Bomb Program is Untouched'" (interview), *India Today* (Delhi), Aug. 15, 2005.

[169] See Indian Ministry of Home Affairs, "The Prevention of Terrorism Act, 2002," available at [http://mha.nic.in/poto-02.htm#schdule]. In September 2004, New Delhi's new Congress-led government repealed the controversial POTA in response to widespread allegations of human rights abuses, although the status of designated organizations was unchanged. Another controversial law, the Armed Forces Special Powers Act, has come under fire for facilitating "grave human rights violations" ("POTA Repealed, Law Amended to Fight Terrorism," *Hindustan Times* (Delhi), Sep. 18, 2004; Amnesty International, "India: Briefing on the Armed Forces Special Powers Act, 1958," May 9, 2005).

[170] "Conflict Rages in India's Northeast," *Jane's Terrorism & Security Monitor*, Apr. 13, 2005.

[171] In April 2005, ULFA appeared on the U.S. Department of State's list of "other selected terrorist organizations," the first time an Indian separatist group outside of Kashmir was so designated.

- the National Democratic Front of Bodoland (NDFB); and
- the United National Liberation Front (seeking an independent Manipur).

The Indian government has at times blamed Bangladesh, Burma, Nepal, and Bhutan for "sheltering" one or more of these groups beyond the reach of Indian security forces, and it has accused Pakistan's intelligence agency of training members and providing them with material support.[172] In December 2003, after considerable prodding by New Delhi, Bhutan launched military operations against ULFA and NDFB rebels based in border areas near India's Assam state. The leader and founder of ULFA was captured and, two months later, India's army chief declared that nearly 1,000 militants in Bhutan had been "neutralized"—killed or captured.[173] Yet the rebels appeared to regroup and attacks on civilians did not end: in August 2004, a bomb exploded at an Independence Day parade in Assam, killing 18 people, many of them children. Police blamed ULFA for the blast. Six weeks later, a spate of bombings and shootings in Assam and Nagaland left at least 83 people dead in what was called a joint operation by ULFA and NDFB. Although two senior ULFA leaders surrendered in February 2005, the rebels later launched a series of coordinated bomb attacks across the Assam state. In a further sign that Assamese rebels remain a serious problem, 2,000 Indian security forces moved against ULFA positions in April 2005.[174] Both Burma and Bangladesh may increase pressure on Indian rebels based on their territory; New Delhi has suggested coordinated military operations in the border areas and has increased its counterterrorism cooperation with Kathmandu and Thimphu.[175]

Maoist Militancy. Also operating in India are "Naxalites"—communist insurgents ostensibly engaged in violent struggle on behalf of landless laborers and tribals. These groups, most active in inland areas of east-central India, claim to be battling oppression and exploitation in order to create a classless society. Their opponents call them terrorists and extortionists. According to the U.S. Department of State, major Naxalite groups are enlarging the

---

172 "Northeast Carnage Blamed on Terror Bases Across Borders," *Hindustan Times* (Delhi), Oct. 6, 2004; "ISI Has Shifted Militant Camps to Bangladesh: BSF DG," Press Trust of India, Sep. 14, 2004; Mahendra Ved, "Center Suspects ISI Hand in N-E Blasts," *Times of India* (Delhi), Oct. 8, 2004; "Buddhadeb Alleges ISI Activities on Eastern Border," *Hindu* (Madras), Dec. 24, 2004.

173 Wasbir Hussain, "Going for the Kill," *Outlook India* (Delhi), Dec. 22, 2003; Nirmal Banerjee, "N-Proliferation From Pak Dangerous: Vij," *Times of India* (Delhi), Feb. 5, 2004; "Screws Tighten on Indian Rebels," BBC News, Jan. 2, 2004.

174 Robert Karinol, "Rebels Look to Re-Establish Base in Bhutan," *Jane's Security & Terrorism Monitor*, Sep. 15, 2004; "Bomb Kills Many Indians at Parade," BBC News, Aug. 15, 2004; "Ten Killed in Fresh Assam Attack," BBC News, Oct. 5, 2004; "Assam Separatist Chiefs Surrender," BBC News, Feb. 28, 2005; "United Liberation Front of Assam Rebels," *Jane's Terrorism & Security Monitor*, Mar. 16, 2005; "India Moves Against Assam Rebels," BBC News, Apr. 2005.

175 "India Ready for Joint Operations: Manmohan," *Hindu* (Madras), Oct. 27, 2004; "India, Nepal Agree to Step Up Anti-Terror Cooperation," BBC Monitoring South Asia, Sep. 12, 2004; "India Offers Bhutan Security Assistance," Press Trust of India, Oct. 12, 2004; "India's Counterinsurgent Policy," *Jane's Foreign Report*, Apr. 28, 2005.

scope of their influence, and analysts contend that the abilities of Indian Maoist militants to conduct insurgency has spread to nearly half of India's 28 states, in part through the forging of cross-border links with Nepali insurgents.[176] As the Naxalites' range of operations has increased, so too has related bloodshed. Most notable of India's Maoist groups are the People's War Group (PWG), mainly active in the southern Andhra Pradesh state, and the Maoist Communist Center of West Bengal and Bihar. In September 2004, the two merged to form the Communist Party of India - Maoist. In 2004, for the first time and without public explanation, these groups appeared on the U.S. State Department's list of "other terrorist groups" (it is likely that the move was spurred by a U.S. interest in assisting both New Delhi and Kathmandu in efforts to combat Maoist insurgents in Nepal[177]). Both also are designated as terrorist groups by New Delhi; each is believed to have about 2,000 cadres. PWG fighters were behind an October 2003 landmine attack that nearly killed the Chief Minster of Andhra Pradesh.[178]

In July 2004, the government of Andhra Pradesh lifted an 11-year-old ban on the PWG in preparation for planned peace talks. A September 2004 rally in Hyderabad, the PWG's first since 1990, attracted tens of thousands of supporters. Yet the concord was short-lived: in January 2005, the Maoists accused the state government of breaking a cease-fire by "staging" several encounters that left 15 people dead and they withdrew from negotiations.[179] The U.S. Ambassador to India later expressed concerns about Naxalite violence in Andhra Pradesh and the impact it might have on foreign investors in the state, and at least one Indian commentator has opined that the scale and growth of Naxalite violence "is a direct challenge to [India's] vaunting pretensions to superpower status, and its ambitious quest for dramatic economic growth and inclusion in the elite club of the world's 'developed countries.'" In August, just days after suspected Maoist rebels shot dead ten civilians, the Andhra Pradesh government formally banned the Communist Party of India - Maoist.[180]

---

176 U.S. Department of State, *Country Reports on Terrorism 2004*, Apr. 2005, p. 115; Rahul Bedi, "Cross-Border Links Strengthen India's Insurgent Groups," *Jane's Intelligence Review*, Nov. 1, 2004. See also Sanjay Jha, "The Grassroots Terror," *Outlook India* (Delhi), Jan. 17, 2005.

177 Interview with U.S. State Department official, May 2004.

178 See "The 14 Spokes of a Revolution," *Outlook India* (Delhi), Oct. 20, 2003; "India: Terrorist Groups," South Asia Terrorism Portal, available at [http://www.satp.org/satporgtp/countries/india/terroristoutfits/index.html].

179 Omer Farooq, "Indian State Lifts Bans on Rebel Group," Associated Press, July 21, 2004; "Huge Turnout for Indian Maoists," BBC News, Sep. 29, 2004; "India Rebels Abandon Peace Talks," BBC News, Jan. 17, 2005.

180 "Indo-US Ties at All-Time High: David Mulford," *Economic Times* (Delhi), Jan. 29, 2005; Ajai Sahni, "Red Alert," *Outlook India* (Delhi), Feb. 1, 2005. See also Prafulla Das, "A Naxalite Corridor," *Frontline* (Madras), July 15, 2005; "Indian State Ban on Maoist Group," BBC News, Aug. 18, 2005.

India-U.S. Counterterrorism Cooperation

One facet of the emerging "strategic partnership" between the United States and India is increased counterterrorism cooperation. The U.S.-India Joint Working Group on Counterterrorism was established in January 2000 to intensify bilateral cooperation; this body met for the sixth time in August 2004. In November 2001, President Bush and then-Indian Prime Minster Vajpayee agreed that "terrorism threatens not only the security of the United States and India, but also our efforts to build freedom, democracy and international security and stability around the world."[181] In May 2002, India and the United States launched the Indo-US Cyber Security Forum to safeguard critical infrastructures from cyber attack. The State Department believes that continued engagement with New Delhi will lead to India's playing a constructive role in resolving terrorist insurgencies in Nepal and Sri Lanka. Calling New Delhi a "close ally of the United States in the global war on terrorism," the Bush Administration has undertaken to provide India with better border security systems and training, and better intelligence in an effort to prevent future terrorist attacks. Moreover, the two countries' militaries have continued to work together to enhance their capabilities to combat terrorism and increase interoperability.[182] U.S. military sales to India are to include $29 million worth of equipment meant to enhance the counterterrorism capabilities of India's special forces, and India may also purchase chemical and biological protection equipment.[183]

The seating of a new left-leaning national government in New Delhi in May 2004 had no significant effect on continued U.S.-India security ties. A sixth meeting of the bilateral Defense Policy Group in June ended with a joint statement that recognized "growing areas of convergence on fundamental values," including combating terrorism. Shortly after, while on a visit to New Delhi to meet with top Indian leaders, then-U.S. Deputy Secretary of State Armitage told reporters that the new Indian government appeared to be just as desirous of enhanced U.S.-India relations as the previous one and that the United States has "absolute confidence that the U.S.-India relationship is going to grow in all its aspects."[184] President Bush met with new Indian Prime Minister Manmohan Singh in New York in

[181] "Joint Statement of U.S., India on Terrorism, Bilateral Ties," U.S. Department of State Washington File, Nov. 9, 2001.

[182] U.S. Department of State, Bureau of Resource Management, "FY2004 Performance Plan," Mar. 2003. Assistant Secretary of State Christina Rocca, "U.S., Regional Governments Cooperating Against South Asian Terrorism," U.S. Department of State Washington File, Oct. 29, 2003; U.S. Department of Defense, Office of the Press Secretary, "Joint Statement on U.S.-India Defense Policy Group," Aug. 8, 2003.

[183] "U.S. Recognizes India as a 'Natural Trading Partner,'" U.S. Department of State Washington File, Aug. 24, 2004.

[184] "Indo-US Defense Policy Group Meeting Concludes," Indian Ministry of Defense Press Release, June 3, 2004; "U.S.-India Ties Remain Strong with Congress Party Government," U.S. Department of State Washington File," July 14, 2004.

September 2004 and noted the U.S.-India relations are as close as they have ever been. Secretary of State Rice and the Indian external affairs minister separately have echoed the sentiment in 2005.[185] In June 2005, the United States and India signed a ten-year defense framework agreement which lists "defeating terrorism and violent religious extremism" as one of four key shared security interests, and which calls for a bolstering of mutual defense capabilities required for such a goal.[186]

Other South Asian Countries

Bangladesh[187]

Bangladesh's political and economic development continues to be hampered by the forces of corruption, radicalism, and partisan fighting. Rivalry between the leaders of the nation's two largest political parties has led to an ongoing series of demonstrations, strikes, and increasingly to politically motivated violence. The frustration caused by the combination of poverty, corruption, and the lack of good governance due to a stalemated political process is thought by some to contribute to increasing radicalization of society and thereby to the recruitment of Islamist radicals to the cause of terrorism.

Bangladesh's form of moderate Islam is increasingly under threat by radical elements. In early 2005 there was increased concern over the rise of Islamic extremism in Bangladesh. Khaleda Zia's Bangladesh National Party (BNP) has coalition partners in government that are thought to have ties to radical Islamist elements that give cause for concern. Some view the government's coalition with hardline Islamist coalition members as promoting the spread of violence.[188] The radical Harkat-ul-Jihad-al-Islami (HuJI) is thought to have ties to both Al Qaeda and the Islamic Oikya Jote, which is a coalition partner in the government. HuJI is on the United States State Department list of other terrorist organizations and is thought to have been behind an assassination attempt on then Prime Minister Sheikh Hasina in July 2000.[189] HuJI also signed the 1998 fatwa by Usama bin Laden which declared American civilians to be legitimate targets.[190]

---

[185] "Bush, Indian Prime Minister Singh Hold First Meeting," U.S. Department of State Washington File, Sep. 21, 2004; Secretary of State Condoleezza Rice, "Remarks En Route to India," U.S. Department of State Washington File, Mar. 15, 2005; "Press Conference by External Affairs Minister Natwar Singh," Embassy of India Press Release, Apr. 15, 2005.

[186] "New Framework for the U.S.-India Defense Relationship," June 28, 2005, available at [http://www.indianembassy.org/press_release/2005/June/31.htm].

[187] This section written by Bruce Vaughn, Analyst in Southeast and South Asian Affairs.

[188] Testimony by Dr. Christine Fair, Human Rights Watch, Congressional Human Rights Caucus Hearing on Bangladesh, May 24, 2005.

[189] State Department, *Patterns of Global Terrorism 2002*, Apr. 2003, p. 133.

[190] United States Department of State, *Country Reports on Terrorism, 2004*, Apr. 2005.

Fundamentalist leader Bangla Bhai, who promotes Islamic revolution in Bangladesh, has been accused of having ties to the Jamaat-e-Islami (JI) which is another coalition partner with the BNP government. Bangla Bhai fought in Afghanistan and is thought to seek to install a Taliban-style government in Bangladesh particularly in areas bordering India. His supporters have reportedly terrorized communists, leftists, liberal intellectuals, Hindus, Christians, members of the Islamic Ahmadiyya sect and Buddhists in the cause of promoting Islamic extremism.[191] The government of Bangladesh was criticized by the Awami league for denying the existence of fundamentalist organizations in Bangladesh. The Bangladesh government banned Bangla Bhai's organization in 2005.[192]

Political infighting is debilitating to Bangladesh. Former Prime Minister Sheik Hasina of the Awami League survived an assassination attempt in August 2004 when a grenade was thrown at her which killed 20 others. Hasina has accused the BNP-Jamaat alliance of being involved in the assassination attempt.[193] Prime Minister Khaleda Zia has reportedly stated that there are no Islamic fundamentalists in Bangladesh.[194] Such attacks have undermined political stability in Bangladesh. A recent government of India report has found an "alarming rise" in political assassinations in Bangladesh and is also concerned with the smuggling of arms to insurgents in India's northeast as well as the rise of Islamic fundamentalism in Bangladesh.[195]

Former State Department Coordinator for Counterterrorism Cofer Black reportedly stated that he was concerned over "the potential utilization of Bangladesh as a platform for international terrorism" when visiting Dhaka in September 2004.[196] Media reports in India increasingly are concerned that Bangladesh has the potential to become a "center of extremist Wahhabi-oriented terrorism."[197] Harkat-ul-Jihad-al-Islami (HuJI) reportedly sent a letter to the Indian High Commission to Bangladesh in December 2004 threatening to kill the Indian cricket team if they entered Bangladesh. The team planned to play a series of test matches in Bangladesh in December including in the Chittagong region.[198] One source reported in September that the number of radical mosques and madrassas in the Chittagong Hill Tracts (CHT) region of Bangladesh had grown considerably and that HuJI continued to maintain several terrorist training camps in the CHT region.[199]

---

191 Eliza Griswold, "The Next Islamist Revolution?," *The New York Times Magazine*, Jan. 23, 2005.

192 "Jalil-OPM," *United News of Bangladesh*, Feb. 25, 2005.

193 "Hasina-Departure," *United News of Bangladesh*, Mar. 7, 2005.

194 "Khleda Denies Existence of Islamic Fundamentalists in Bangladesh," *Press Trust of India*, Mar. 16, 2005.

195 "Alarming Rise in Assassinations in Bangladesh," *Agence France Presse*, May 13, 2005.

196 Dan Morrison, "Terror on the Rise in Bangladesh," *Newsday*, Nov. 23, 2004.

197 G. Parthasarathy, "In a Disturbed Neighborhood," *Business Line* (The Hindu), Sep. 24, 2004.

198 "Terror Threat Delays Indian Tour Opener," *The Daily Telegraph*, Dec. 9, 2004.

199 Anirban Roy, "Qaeda Fuels HuJI Run in Bangladesh," *Hindustan Times*, Dec. 9, 2004.

Another source also linked the camps to Harkat and indicated that they receive funding from Islamic charities with ties to Al-Qaeda.[200] HuJI is thought to remain active in the area south from Chittagong to Cox's Bazar and the border with Burma. A report sourced to a former senior Indian intelligence official alleges that HuJI is training Burmese Rohingya, as well as small groups from Thailand, Cambodia, Indonesia and Brunei.[201]

There is concern among analysts that Bangladesh might serve as a base from which both South and Southeast Asian terrorists could regroup. There have been reports that up to 150 Taliban and Al Qaeda fighters fled to Bangladesh from Afghanistan in December 2001 aboard the *MV Mecca*, which reportedly sailed from Karachi to Chittagong.[202] This was evidently not the beginning of Al Qaeda connections with Bangladesh. Al Qaeda had reportedly recruited Burmese Muslims, known as the Rohingya, from refugee camps in southeastern Bangladesh to fight in Afghanistan, Kashmir and Chechnya.[203] An Al Qaeda affiliate, Harkat-ul-Jihad-al-Islami (HuJI) was founded by Osama bin Laden associate Fazlul Rahman.[204] HuJI is also on the State Department's list of other terrorist organizations.[205] Rahman joined bin Laden's World Islamic Front for the Jihad Against the Jews and the Crusaders in 1998.[206] It has the objective of establishing Islamic rule in Bangladesh. HuJI has recruited its members, thought to number from several thousand to 15,000, from the tens of thousands of madrassas in Bangladesh, many of which are led by veterans of the "jihad" against the Soviets in Afghanistan. The organization is thought to have at least six camps in Bangladesh as well as ties to militants in Pakistan.[207] The Bangladesh National Party coalition government includes the small Islamic Oikya Jote party which has connections to HuJI. [208]It was reported that French intelligence prompted the arrest of 16 Bangladeshis on December 4, 2003, in Bolivia for allegedly planning to hijack a plane to attack the United States. According to reports, they were later released for lack of evidence. Eleven Bangladeshis were arrested in Saudi Arabia on August 14, 2003, on suspicion of planning a terrorist act.[209]

---

200 Dan Morrison, "Terror on the Rise in Bangladesh," *Newsday*, Nov. 23, 2004.

201 Shefali Rekhi, "Clerics' Call to Terror," *The Straits Times*, Oct. 21, 2004.

202 Alex Perry, "Deadly Cargo, "*Time Asia*, Oct. 21, 2003.

203 Zachary Abuza, *Militant Islam in Southeast Asia*, (Boulder: Lynne Rienner Publishers, 2003), p. 174.

204 Zachary Abuza, *Militant Islam in Southeast Asia*, (Boulder: Lynne Rienner Publishers, 2003), p. 174.

205 *Patterns of Global Terrorism 2002*, United States Department of State, Office of the Coordinator of Counter-terrorism, Apr. 2003.

206 Rohan Gunaratna, *Inside Al Qaeda* (New York: Berkeley Books, 2003), p. 60.

207 *Patterns of Global Terrorism, 2002*, United States Department of State, Office of the Coordinator of Counter-terrorism, Apr. 2003, p. 133–4.

208 Bertil Lintner, "Bangladesh: Breeding Ground for Muslim Terror," [http://www.atimes.com]. See also Bertil Lintner, "Religious Extremism and Nationalism in Bangladesh," Paper presented at the Center for Security Studies, Honolulu, Aug. 19, 2002.

209 Anand Kumar, "Bangladesh Weak Link in War on Terror," *The Straits Times*, Dec. 16, 2003.

The Rohingya Solidarity Organization (RSO) is the largest organization representing the over 120,000 Rohingyas in Bangladesh.[210] The number of Rohingyas varies depending on the level of pressure they are under in their homelands in Burma. The Rohingya also speak the same language as Bangladeshis from the Chittagong area. These "destitute and stateless people" have proved to be a "fertile ground" for recruitment to various militant Islamist groups.[211] The RSO has reportedly received support from the Jamaat-e-Islami in Bangladesh. Afghan instructors are reported to have been seen in RSO camps.

There are also reports, based on information derived from the interrogation of Jemaah Islamiya (JI) leader Hambali, who was arrested in Thailand in August 2003, that indicate that he had made a decision to shift JI elements to Bangladesh in response to recent counter-terrorist activity in Southeast Asia. The decision to move operations west may also be evident in the arrest of 13 Malaysians and six Indonesians, including Hambali's brother Rusman Gunawan, in Pakistan in September 2003. Bangladeshis have been among those arrested in Pakistan on suspicion of being linked to terrorist organizations.[212] Some have speculated that JI militants, thought to be from Malaysia and Singapore, would not have made it to southeastern Bangladesh without some degree of tacit agreement from the Directorate General of Forces Intelligence of Bangladesh which is thought, by some, to have close ties with ISI.[213] It is also thought that Fazlul Rahman's Rohingya Solidarity Organization, which is based in southeast Bangladesh, has also established ties with JI.[214] These reports are difficult to confirm.

The Government of Bangladesh has denied that Bangladesh has become a haven for Islamic militants, such as the Taliban or Al Qaeda.[215] The Bangladesh government has also denied allegations made by former Indian Deputy Prime Minister Advani that Bangladesh had aided Pakistan's Inter-Services Intelligence and Al Qaeda elements.[216] It has also been reported that the Bangladesh Rifles and police have captured weapons during anti-terrorist operations in the southeastern border region with Burma in August and September 2003.[217] (For further information on Bangladesh, see CR S R ep o rt RS20489, *Bangladesh: Background and U.S. Relations*, by Bruce Vaughn.)

---

210 Bertil Lintner, "Bangladesh: Breeding Ground for Muslim Terror," [http://www.atimes.com]

211 *Ibid.*

212 "Pakistan Nabs Six More Terror Suspects," *Xinhua News Agency*, Sep. 26, 2003.

213 Bertil Lintner, "Bangladesh: Celebrations and Bombs," [http://www.atimes.com]

214 Statement of Dr. Zachary Abuza, House International Relations Subcommittee on International Terrorism, Non-proliferation and Human Rights, Oct. 29, 2003.

215 "Bangladesh Calls Time Article on Militant Fictitious," *Associated Press*, Oct. 16, 2002.

216 "India's Remarks on Bangladesh Aiding Terrorists Rejected," *Xinhua News Agency*, Nov. 8, 2002.

217 "Bangladesh Country Report," *Economist Intelligence Unit*, Oct., 2003.

Nepal[218]

The Communist Party of Nepal (Maoist)/ United Peoples Front has been identified as an Other Terrorist Group by the U.S. Department of State.[219] On October 31, 2003, the United States Government went further and announced that for national security reasons it was freezing Maoist terrorist assets. The security situation in Nepal has deteriorated since the collapse of the cease fire between the Maoists and the government on August 27, 2003. The numbers of Nepalese killed since August has risen significantly. This brings the total number killed since 1996 to 11,500 by some estimates. India remains concerned over linkages between the Maoists and leftist extremists in India.[220]

The Maoists' message frequently calls for the end of "American imperialism" and for the "dirty Yankee" to "go home." The Maoists' Chief Negotiator and Chairman of the "People's Government," Baburam Bhattarai, reportedly threatened the United States with "another Vietnam" if the United States expands its aid to Nepal.[221] In September, Bhattarai sent a letter to the U.S. Ambassador in Kathmandu which called on the United States to stop "interfering" in the internal affairs of Nepal.[222] Maoists claimed responsibility for killing two off-duty Nepalese security guards at the American Embassy in 2002,[223] and the Maoists have made it known that American trekkers are not welcome in Maoist-controlled Nepal.[224] Further, the Maoists stated on October 22nd that American-backed organizations would be targeted. Rebel leader Prachanda is reported to have stated that groups funded by "American imperialists" would not be allowed to operate in Nepal.[225]

After the cease fire, the Maoists appeared to be shifting from large-scale attacks on police and army headquarters to adopting new tactics that focused on attacks by smaller cells conducting widespread assassinations of military, police and party officials.[226] The unpopularity of this policy appears to have led the Maoists to shift policy again and declare that they would not carry out further political killings or further destroy government infrastructure. Despite this guarantee, attacks continue. In May 2005,

218 This section written by Bruce Vaughn, Analyst in Southeast and South Asian Affairs.

219 *Patterns of Global Terrorism*, United States Department of State, Office of the Coordinator of Counter-Terrorism, Apr. 2003.

220 "New CRPF Unit to Fight Naxals Likely," *Business Standard*, Nov. 5, 2003.

221 Thomas Bell, "Maoist Army Wins Hearts and Minds in West Nepal," *The Globe and Mail*, Sep. 18, 2003.

222 Binaj Gurubacharya, "Maoist Rebel Leader Asks U.S., China, India to Stop Interfering in Nepal," *Associated Press*, Sep. 25, 2003.

223 Binaj Gurubacharya, "Nepal Rebels Threaten U.S.-Funded Groups," *Associated Press*, Oct., 22, 2003.

224 Amy Waldman, "Chance for Peace Fades in Nepal as Deaths Rise," *The New York Times*, Oct. 13, 2003.

225 Binaj Gurubacharya, "Nepal Rebels Threaten U.S.-Funded Groups," *Associated Press*, Oct. 22, 2003.

226 "Nepal: Back to the Gun," *International Crisis Group*, Oct. 22, 2003.

Maoist commander in the Parsa District threatened attacks against Americans and American interests.[227] The Maoists' guarantee against terrorist attacks did not extend to projects "run directly by the United States."[228] The United States Agency for International Development and Save the Children both operate in Nepal. On October 27, Maoist leader Prachanda stated that "we will ensure that no American citizens—tourists or officials—except those who come to the battlefield with the Nepal Army would be caused any harm by the Maoist militia."[229] (For further details on the Maoists and Nepal, see CRS Report RL31599, *Nepal: Background and U.S. Relations*, by Bruce Vaughn.)

Sri Lanka[230]

The United States Department of State continues to designate the Liberation Tigers of Tamil Eelam (LTTE) as a Foreign Terrorist Organization in 2005. More than 64,000 people are thought to have died during this conflict over the last 20 years and the LTTE has consistently been one of the most effective and active users of suicide-bomber tactics in the world. In addition, some analysts claim to have observed or heard of efforts by the LTTE recently to establish an air capability by the acquisition of two Cessna-class light aircraft. If true, this represents a worrisome event, as the LTTE's past history shows a penchant for adapting other means of transportation such as cars, motorbikes, and naval craft for suicide bomb attacks and it is not far-fetched to assume that the same could be done with these aircraft. The Black Tigers unit, the elite special-operations cadre of the LTTE, are those charged with carrying out such terrorist operations and it could be appropriate to watch for signs that these cadre members are receiving flight training to further verify any new air capabilities.

A Norwegian-brokered peace process has produced notable successes, though it was suspended by the LTTE in the spring of 2003 due to differences over interim administration arrangements. In February 2002, a permanent cease-fire was reached and generally has been observed by both sides. In September 2002, the government in Colombo and the LTTE held their first peace talks in seven years, with the LTTE indicating that it was willing to accept autonomy rather than independence for Tamil-majority regions. The two sides agreed in principle to seek a solution through a federal structure. However, LTTE leader Prabakaran has stated that there may be a return to fighting. The period from 2004 to early 2005 has

[227] "Maoist Commander Threatening Attacks Against Americans," Warden Message, *Overseas Security Advisory Council*, May 25, 2005.

[228] Kedar Man Singh, "Nepal's Maoist Rebels Say They Will Not Carry Out Political Killings," *Agence France Presse*, Oct. 22, 2003.

[229] Kedar Man Singh, "Nepal Maoists Say Americans Safe," *Agence France Presse*, Oct. 27, 2003.

[230] This section written by Severn Anderson, Analyst in Asian Affairs.

witnessed increasing instability within the ranks of both the Sinhalese government and the LTTE which has led to increasing concern over the future of the peace process. In June of 2005, Christina Rocca, the Assistant Secretary for South Asian Affairs, told a House International Relations Committee panel that

> the United States continues to support Norway's facilitation of a peace settlement in Sri Lanka. The cease-fire of 2002 is holding, although violence is ongoing and the peace process has stalled. This is due in part to divisions within the Sri Lankan government and the absence of trust between the government and the LTTE, which continues to use assassinations and suicide bombers, underscoring their character as an organization wedded to terrorism and justifying their designation as a Foreign Terrorist Organization.[231]

The LTTE has also, of late, experienced instability and intra-factional disagreements. In March 2004 there was a major rupture within the LTTE ranks. Vinayagamoorthi Muralitharan, alias Col. Karuna (who, as Special Commander, Batticaloa-Amparai District, was in over-all charge of the LTTE's military operations in the Eastern Province) split with the Northern command of the LTTE headed by the supreme commander of the LTTE (Veluppillai Prabhakaran) and took an estimated 6,000 soldiers with him. Col. Karuna then called for a separate truce with the government. Factional fighting ensued between Karuna's splinter group and the Northern faction of the LTTE and resulted in Prabhakaran's reassertion of control over the eastern areas which Karuna had previously operated.

Since that time there have been numerous instances of political and military operatives being killed by each side as they jockey for power in the East. The LTTE has accused Col. Karuna and those loyal to him of cooperating with Sri Lankan Army (SLA) paramilitaries and special forces in raids and targeted killings of forces under their command, which the SLA denies. Karuna has since withdrawn to a fortified base in the jungles of eastern Sri Lanka where they have repelled several LTTE attacks.[232] Between February and April 2005 there were several recorded instances of serious violations of the ceasefire. First was the death of a high level LTTE political officer, E. Kousalyane, in early February which was followed by an increase in politically motivated killings of individuals throughout the eastern provinces.[233] In early April there was also a much publicized incident when a Sea Tiger unit attacked a Sri Lankan Navy vessel carrying a peace monitor, slightly wounding him. This led to a formal censure of the LTTE by the ceasefire monitoring group, the Sri Lanka Monitoring Mission (SLMM),

[231] "House International Relations Subcommittee on Asia and the Pacific Holds Hearing on United States and South Asia," FDCH Transcripts, June 14, 2005.

[232] *PTI News Agency*, New Delhi, Mar. 21, 2005.

[233] V.S. Sambandan, "Batticaloa LTTE Leader Killed," *Hindu* (Madras), Feb. 7, 2005.

and marked a particularly brazen attack as the Sri Lankan Navy vessel was flying the SLMM flag indicating that monitors were abroad.[234]

Figure 2: Map of South Asia

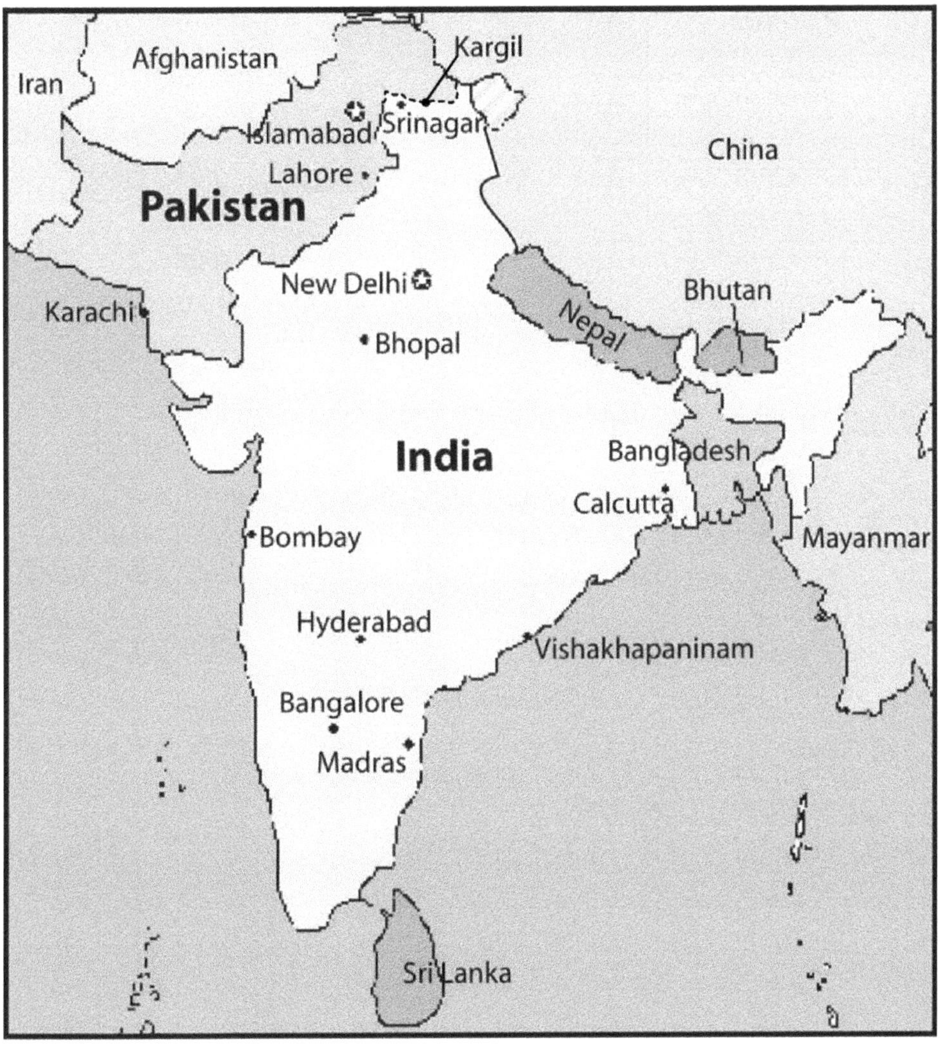

Adapted by CRS from Magellan Geographix. Boundary representations not authoritative.

234 "Tamil Tiger 'Breached Ceasefire'," *BBC News*, Apr. 8, 2005

Figure 3: Map of Pakistan

Source: Map Resouces. Adapted by CRS. (K. Yancey 11/12/04)

DOCUMENT NO. 19

U.S.-PAKISTAN ENGAGEMENT: THE WAR ON TERRORISM AND BEYOND

United States Institute of Peace Special Report

August 2005

Touqir Hussain

About the Report

While the war on terrorism may have provided the rationale for the latest U.S. engagement with Pakistan, the present relationship between the United States and Pakistan is at the crossroads of many other issues, such as Pakistan's own reform efforts, America's evolving strategic relationship with South Asia, democracy in the Muslim world, and the dual problems of religious extremism and nuclear proliferation. As a result, the two countries have a complex relationship that presents a unique challenge to their respective policymaking communities.

This report examines the history and present state of U.S.-Pakistan relations, addresses the key challenges the two countries face, and concludes with specific policy recommendations for ensuring the relationship meets the needs of both the United States and Pakistan. It was written by Touqir Hussain, a senior fellow at the United States Institute of Peace and a former senior diplomat from Pakistan, who served as ambassador to Japan, Spain, and Brazil.

The views expressed in this report do not necessarily reflect the views of the United States Institute of Peace, which does not advocate specific policy positions.

About the Institute

The United States Institute of Peace is an independent, nonpartisan federal institution created by Congress to promote the prevention, management, and peaceful resolution of international conflicts. Established in 1984, the Institute meets its congressional mandate through an array of programs, including research grants, fellowships, professional training, education programs from high school through graduate school, conferences and workshops, library services, and publications. The Institute's Board of Directors is appointed by the President of the United States and confirmed by the Senate.

Summary

- The current U.S. engagement with Pakistan may be focused on the war on terrorism, but it is not confined to it. It also addresses several other issues of concern to the United States: national and global security, terrorism, nuclear proliferation, economic and strategic opportunities in South Asia, democracy, and anti-Americanism in the Muslim world.
- The current U.S. engagement with Pakistan offers certain lessons for U.S. policymakers. These are related to the risks involved in basing policy on principles without having a strategy, isolating a country that has the capacity to harm, and nation-building in a country ambivalent or resistant to the United States' embrace.
- The United States must help Pakistan pursue a path that meets its people's democratic aspirations and socioeconomic needs and is resilient

enough to accommodate ethnolinguistic, regional, religious, and sectarian differences. Only such a course can help Pakistan become a stable and responsible member of the international community, at peace with itself and with its neighbors.

- Sanctions toward Pakistan should not be a policy option. However, the United States should put some pressure on Pakistan to keep the country's reform effort on track and to induce it to act as a responsible nuclear power. For this purpose, the United States should not allow Pakistan to feel that the United States needs Pakistan more than Pakistan needs the United States.
- An assured and secure Pakistan is more likely to define its future in economic terms, wage peace with India, and be a natural ally of the United States. Therefore, Pakistan's peace process with India must be supported by the United States. The benefits to Pakistan must counterbalance the effects of a renunciation of Kashmir and the attendant loss of national honor this will cause.
- Anti-Americanism exists in Pakistan but it can be toned down if the United States reaches out to liberal forces, the business community, and the female population. The United States should also reach out to the younger generation in Pakistan, which may resent U.S. power but not its ideals. Indeed, youth in Pakistan support a U.S.-backed normalization of relations with India, the fight against religious extremism, and educational and institutional reforms.
- U.S.-Pakistan relations will stand or fall based on whether they benefit the Pakistani nation. And in their success or failure lies the future of Islamic extremism in the country.

Introduction

Why is it that Pakistan has rarely disappeared for any length of time from the United States' strategic radar screen? For more than five decades, it has loomed large in one form or another, as either a staunch ally, a troublesome friend, or even a threat. Now, for the first time, it is all of these things.

The war on terrorism may have provided the rationale for the current U.S. reengagement with Pakistan, but this war neither limits the relationship's scope nor exhausts the challenges it faces. The reengagement has merged with Pakistan's own reform effort, America's evolving strategic relationship with South Asia, and the broader issue of democracy in the Muslim world. And in Pakistan and beyond, this new relationship collides with the crosscurrents of religious extremism.

But U.S. policy choices toward Pakistan are complex and imperfect. Though Pakistan is not a failed state nor a failing or a rogue state, it has had, to varying degrees, tendencies of all three. On top of that, it is a nuclear power. So how should the U.S. relate to Pakistan? Pakistan is now not only a challenge but also a crucial partner in the war on terrorism. How does the United States keep Pakistan on its side when it may also target Pakistan? And if Pakistan is to be an object of reforms, how does the United States help the country, especially its democratization process?

The United States faces a great balancing act in its relations with Pakistan. It must work with President Pervez Musharraf but not identify with his personal ambitions, nudge him to democratize but not discourage his strong hand, and advance U.S. nonproliferation objectives but not lose Pakistan's support in the war on terrorism.

Critical U.S. policy choices toward Pakistan must also be integrated with broader regional policies. South Asia has changed and so has the basis of U.S. relations with it. The currents of change, spawned by the post–Cold War world and globalization and gestated by the war on terrorism, have been flowing in varying directions. This presents new threats and opportunities for U.S. foreign policy. For example, India offers the United States great economic and strategic opportunities, but it is Pakistan's internal dynamics and relationship with India that have been at the root of challenges to U.S. foreign policy in South Asia.

This report will examine these and other questions by looking at the U.S.-Pakistan relationship in multiple contexts and will conclude with policy recommendations for both Pakistan and the United States, suggesting ways of broadening the relationship to make it long-term, stable, and mutually beneficial, as envisioned in the *9/11 Commission Report*.

Historical Perspective

What has been unusual about the relationship between the United States and Pakistan is that their spells of close ties have been, and may continue to be, single-issue engagements of limited or uncertain duration, which enjoyed, at best, limited or qualified support among their respective public and strategic communities. During each engagement there has been either a military or military-dominated government in Pakistan, while in Washington, the policy direction on Pakistan has largely been in the hands of the White House, Pentagon, and the CIA.

The relationship has also shared problems typical of U.S. ties with a small country. Pakistan has traditionally responded to regional impulses, while the United States tends to consider global dynamics in its relationships. The United States has historically made light of Pakistan's security concerns and underestimated the strength of Pakistan's commitment to its nuclear program, and Pakistan has failed to see that an inflated U.S.-Pakistan engagement had no staying power. Pakistan particularly has not understood the enormous challenges of running U.S. foreign policy and the need of U.S. policymakers to weigh foreign policy concerns against domestic political considerations, the dynamics of the media, America's sense of exceptionalism and moral purpose, the country's historical experience, and cold-blooded power politics. All this made it neither compelling nor easy for the United States to harmonize its strategic and tactical goals, short- and long-term agenda, and global and regional interests.

As a consequence, the U.S.-Pakistan relationship, for much of its history, has lacked continuity, a larger conceptual framework, and a shared vision beyond the narrowly based and vaguely defined. It is no wonder, then, that as soon as the United States achieved its objectives vis-à-vis Pakistan in past engagements, U.S.-Pakistan policy consensus would break down. Pakistan was either consigned to benign neglect or hit with a succession of punitive sanctions that left in their trail resentment and a sense of betrayal. In a strange irony, this led the engagements between the two countries to alternate with periods of estrangements. Consequently, the United States did not have the influence or leverage to address issues of concern, including those born of its own close cooperation with Pakistan. Such highs and lows turned into a love-hate relationship between the two.

Yet, U.S.-Pakistan cooperation has served some important mutual interests in the past and is doing so again in the present. As with previous periods of engagement, the current relationship may yet leave in its wake serious problems that may have to be addressed in the future at a much higher cost. Historically, the issues marking the U.S.-Pakistan relationship, whether they united or divided the two countries, have had a critical bearing on their respective national goals and priorities.

The first of the three major U.S. engagements with Pakistan occurred during the height of the Cold War, from the mid-1950s to mid-1960s; the second was during the Afghan Jihad in the 1980s, again lasting about a decade; and the third engagement dates to September 11, 2001, and relates to the war on terrorism.

The First Engagement

The U.S.-Pakistan relationship began during the Cold War. Pakistan was deeply conscious of the power disparity in the Subcontinent and was actively looking for ways to redress it. The heightened security concerns and need for economic development compelled Pakistan to reach out to the United States, which was then trying to promote a strategic alliance of Asian states to check the expanding lines of Soviet influence. With the viability of the state at issue, Pakistan opted to become "the most allied ally" of the United States in the region.

The United States strengthened Pakistan's defense capabilities and potential for economic development. But in doing so the United States also helped encourage undemocratic tendencies in the country, as U.S. patronage of the Pakistan army raised the military's national profile. The military came to dominate the country's politics through a pro-Western alliance of conservative forces, including Islamists. At the time, Pakistan's religious profile caused little concern to the United States; in fact, it suited the United States as the religion provided for both a measure of internal stability and a defense against communism.

But, as became evident, U.S.-Pakistan relations were not based on shared perspectives. There was nothing, for example, in Pakistan's national experience to lend substance to the U.S. view that communism was inherently expansionist or destabilizing and posed a threat to Pakistan. And for its part, the United States did not consider the Indian threat to Pakistan to be credible or real. There was another variable, too. As the regional and international situation evolved, the two countries responded to emerging trends with policy adjustments that generated their own tensions. For example, Pakistan's opening to China in the early 1960s and the shift in U.S. interest toward India to balance China's growing power are cases in point. Eventually, the United States lost strategic interest in Pakistan—and would not become reengaged with the country until the Soviet invasion of Afghanistan in 1979.

The Second Engagement

Pakistan's help was so critical to the success of U.S.-led efforts to expel the Soviets that it preempted any other concerns that the United States had toward Pakistan, such as those related to democracy and nuclear proliferation. The United States found in Pakistan an eager ally as the country's isolated military regime was willing to forswear some of its own larger interests in exchange for international legitimacy. The regime allowed Pakistan to be used as a sanctuary, training ground, and staging area during the war. The CIA and the ISI, Pakistan's intelligence agency, collaborated in mounting an insurgency against the Soviet military. Calls for jihad added substance to this struggle.

Though the engagement between the United States and Pakistan in this period made a historic contribution to the end of the Cold War, it prospered in the darkening shadow of looming forces that would later come to threaten not only the security of Pakistan and the United States, but also the world. The radicalism spawned by the Afghan jihad and co-opted by Pakistan would not only rock the region but radiate far beyond. Yet the United States walked away from the region as soon as the Soviets withdrew from Afghanistan in 1989. In fact, the United States suddenly hit the country, its close ally of ten years in the struggle for Afghanistan's freedom, with sanctions.

The Problem of Sanctions

During the 1990s, three sets of sanctions were placed on Pakistan. The first came in 1990 under the provisions of the Pressler Amendment; the second came in 1998 after Pakistan conducted a series of nuclear tests; and the third came in 1999 after the military takeover of the country. Enacted in 1985, the Pressler Amendment stipulated that most military and economic assistance to Pakistan could only be authorized after an annual certification by the U.S. president that Pakistan did not possess a nuclear device. Certification was not offered in 1990, and the resulting punitive measures did the most damage to U.S.-Pakistan relations of all the 1990s sanctions.

Collectively, however, these sanctions would come to affect more than this relationship. In particular, the sanctions alienated the army, propelling it into a binge of willful strategic thinking that was neither rooted in an enlightened calculation of larger national interests nor shared by civilian institutions. Indeed, during the 1990s, weak civilian leadership overly solicitous of army support submitted to the military's flawed priorities without thought. Pakistan, increasingly isolated from the world, was seized by dangerous trends in strategic thought that were unrelieved by any outside moderating influence. This period witnessed the rise of the Taliban, the Kashmir jihad, the Kargil operation, and the AQ Khan affair. But the United States did not have the influence to restrain Pakistan's behavior. Sanctions were too weak to be an effective lever against Pakistan yet strong enough to be seen as an affront. Further, the United States offered Pakistan no incentive to change.

When it finally did come, the incentive for change in Pakistan came internally. General Musharraf realized not long after he took control of the country in October 1999 that Pakistan was in a much worse condition than it had been during previous army takeovers, both in terms of its international standing and internal stability. The country's very foundation was being undermined by religious extremism and strained by ethnic conflicts and poor governance. This put not only the country's future at risk but also, by extension, the army's. In such a fragile national environment, it was not easy for the army to pursue a forward policy, especially toward Kashmir and Afghanistan.

But the problem was how to mobilize the army's support for any strategic reorientation. The Pakistan army's self-image was formed not only by its parochial conception of national security but also by its instinct to compete with the Indian army as an institution. This drive to compete almost became an end in itself, often preceding or subsuming national interest. Further, the success of the Afghan jihad under army patronage had fostered two illusions: one was an exaggerated perception of Pakistan's national strength and its strategic reach in the region, and the other was the army's vain

U.S. Legislation on Pakistan (1900–2004)	
August 1990: Pressler Amendment Sanctions	The 1985 Pressler Amendment authorized banning most military and economic assistance to Pakistan if an annual presidential determination that Pakistan did not possess a nuclear device was not given. In 1990, President George H.W. Bush was the first to withhold such a determination.
May 1998: Pakistani Nuclear Test Sanctions	After Pakistan's May 1998 nuclear tests, President Bill Clinton imposed additional sanctions on Pakistan, invoking the 1994 Glenn Amendment, which authorizes sanctions on nonnuclear weapon states that detonate nuclear explosions, and the Symington Amendment, which prohibits military and economic assistance to any country that delivers and/or receives nuclear assistance.
October 1999: "Democracy Sanctions"	After Musharraf's October 12, 1999, coup, Congress invoked Section 508 of the Foreign Assistance Act, prohibiting all U.S. economic and military aid toward Pakistan.
Sep./Oct 2001: Sanctions lifted after 9/11	The Glenn, Symington, and Pressler sanctions were waived by President George W. Bush under the authority given him by an earlier piece of legislation known as Brownback II. Congress voted to allow President Bush to waive the "democracy sanctions" imposed on Pakistan through September 30, 2003. These democracy sanctions have since been waived annually.
December 2004: Ackerman Amendment	This amendment to the Intelligence Authorization Act requires the CIA, over a five-year period, to make annual reports to Congress about Pakistan's nuclear activities, democratic development, and counterterror efforts.

hopes for recapturing the glory of Islam without the strength of faith or the power of the state. September 11 firmed Musharraf's hand in deflating these notions.

Pakistan and the War on Terrorism

After September 11, the Pakistan army knew its strategic overextension in the region, especially its support for the Taliban and, by implication, al-Qaida, was untenable. But nearly bankrupt, the country had neither the political will nor the resources to take on these forces. The United States would provide Musharraf with both and, in turn, receive critical support from Pakistan in the war on terrorism.

Pakistan has cooperated with the United States in a number of ways, by granting logistics facilities, sharing intelligence, and capturing and handing over al-Qaida terrorists. Says Christine Fair in her book, *The Counterterror Coalitions: Cooperation with Pakistan and India*, U.S. officials acknowledge that "Pakistan has provided more support, captured more terrorists, and committed more troops than any other nation in the GCTF (Global Counterterrorism Force)." Additionally, Pakistan has sealed off its western border and has made two naval bases, three air force bases, and its airspace available to the U.S. military.

According to Pakistan Embassy officials in Washington, D.C., Pakistan has deployed more than seventy thousand of its troops to the Afghan border and has launched more than thirty-eight major successful operations to flush out foreign terrorists. More than three hundred Pakistan army and paramilitary troops have been killed, and an even larger number have been injured, accounting for more casualties than any other U.S. ally in the war on terrorism. Pakistan is the only regional country to participate in the Coalition Maritime Interdiction Operations, the maritime component of Operation Enduring Freedom. Additionally, the intelligence provided by Pakistan has led to successes against terrorism around the world. For example, all of the top al-Qaida leaders captured to date have been apprehended in Pakistan with the government's help, while Pakistan itself has arrested more than seven hundred terror suspects. The country has also banned or placed on watch lists a large number of sectarian and militant organizations and has enacted numerous antiterrorism laws, freezing thirty-two bank accounts suspected of belonging to terrorist organizations. Finally, Pakistan is currently creating a national criminal database and is the first country to successfully install PISCES, a terrorist-interdiction program set up at seven Pakistani airports and at border crossings with India.

For its part, in the three years after September 11, the United States extended grants to Pakistan equaling $1 billion and wrote off $1 billion in debt. In June 2003, the U.S. announced a $3 billion assistance package for Pakistan to start in October 2004 and to be distributed over five years, with roughly equal amounts going to economic aid and security assistance. Additionally, a framework agreement on trade and investment (TIFA) has been signed, and the two countries have begun negotiating a bilateral investment treaty. On the security front, the U.S. approved a $1.2 billion arms-sale package that includes roughly $950 million for the purchase of P3C Orion aircraft. In March 2005, President Bush authorized the sale of a yet-to-be-specified number of F-16 fighter jets to Pakistan. The United States has also reinstated a military-training program through which some three hundred officers have received instruction at U.S. military institutions since 2001.

The current U.S.-Pakistan engagement may be focused on cooperation in the war on terrorism, especially on building the military-intelligence partnership between the two countries, but it is not limited to it. Pakistan's domestic order, especially its weak institutional architecture, stillborn political process, underdeveloped economy, poor educational system, unsure civil society, and simmering internal tensions, enhances the potential for extremism and instability and has been of serious concern to the United States. Musharraf, too, realizes the dangers and is trying to lead the country in a new direction.

He recognizes that there is a need for institution building, economic development, improvement in relations between the center and provinces, and bringing an end to extremism and sectarianism. He has the support of the United States, not only because broader reforms in Pakistan are central to combating religious extremism and succeeding in the war on terrorism, but also because regional peace and stability are requisite to the realization of America's economic and strategic interests in the region. Nonetheless, both Pakistan and the United States face difficult challenges.

Challenges for Musharraf's Pakistan

Understanding the complexity of the challenges that both Musharraf and Pakistan face may help answer questions in the United States not only about Musharraf's commitment to reforms and sincerity in fully cooperating with the United States on the war on terrorism, but also questions about Pakistan's post-Musharraf future.

Regional Security Environment

Pakistan's geopolitical environment remains a threat to its external and internal security and may explain Musharraf's wariness to take bold steps, especially in dealing with the jihadists. Relations with India are a case in point. India and Pakistan may have come a long way from their posture of confrontation, but peace between them is still far off. Only time will tell if there has been an enduring change in India's strategic stance toward Pakistan or the Kashmir dispute. Musharraf, therefore, has to watch India's moves carefully.

India's hope is that in time the so-called "CBMs" (confidence building measures) between the two countries will become their own reward, and that perhaps with increased economic and commercial exchanges, cultural interplay, and trends toward moderation in Pakistan, Pakistanis will develop a different perception of India and Kashmir. India also hopes that other critical issues, such as energy, sharing of water resources, security, and good neighborly relations, may eventually take precedence over Kashmir in defining the countries' relationship, freeing India to find an internal solution to the dispute, facilitated by Pakistan's diminished leverage and unforced concessions. There might be gains for Pakistan in the relationship with India, but not in Kashmir, whose centrality to India-Pakistan relations will have gradually eroded.

There is no guarantee the Indian ploy will work unless the Pakistan leadership itself has made a strategic decision to acquiesce to such a fait accompli. There is no firm indication that this decision has been made. Nor is there a national consensus about India in Pakistan, as the public does not have a clear idea about what will come of the peace initiative. Indeed, in both countries domestic constituencies against normalization have yet to be conciliated, so the potential for renewed tensions between India and Pakistan remains.

On the Western front, Iran, with its regional ambitions, emerging nuclear capability, strategic rivalry with Pakistan, and suspicions of a U.S.-Pakistan axis, has the motive and capability, if not the intention, to leverage Pakistan's policies. Iran is also a rival influence in Afghanistan and an economic competitor for access to Central Asia, which itself remains unstable. Furthermore, an unsettled Afghanistan, especially where the Taliban rump—which has affinities with and support from Pakistan's tribal areas—still remains, can be a source of potential instability on the Pakistan-Afghan border and an irritant in the relations between the two countries.

The regional security environment thus compels Musharraf to have some semblance of leverage in dealing with both India and Afghanistan. That is why he is leaving the jihadi outfits unscathed and has also not turned on the Taliban with full force. Even if Musharraf had no future use for the jihadists, he would not want a showdown with them. He might find this confrontation a dangerous and unnecessary provocation as, in light of a possible resolution of the Kashmir dispute and normalization of relations with India, these outfits may become rebels without a cause and thus die their own deaths.

Domestic Order

The no less precarious domestic order in Pakistan reinforces Musharraf's caution. The country has serious problems relating to social change, governance, and democratization. One can debate endlessly as to whether the army or politicians are to blame for Pakistan's problems. Seen from a historical perspective, both have failed. Each has done enough damage to fully account for Pakistan's troubled history. They have both been united in common pursuit of strengthening their class and institutional interests. Indeed, their identities fluctuate and often merge imperceptibly. The army relied on the politicians for its legitimacy, while, in turn, the politicians have relied on the army's support to keep themselves in power and shield themselves from accountability. Both have pandered to the Islamists, who have provided the ideological underpinnings of a security-denominated nationalism in Pakistan that has guaranteed the military's dominant political profile. As a result, by creating political space for the Islamists, the military has helped foster religious extremism in the country.

Thus, in a broad context, religion, politics, social order, national security, and foreign policy have all been rolled into one in Pakistan and—suffused with illusions and emotions—have come to both reflect and affect Pakistan's national priorities. Any sense of pursuing genuine national aims and moving in a positive direction has yielded to passions and empty slogans. Politics has become suffused with cant, hypocrisy, and fraud.

Pakistan's multiple problems are now seamlessly linked and need to be attacked simultaneously. Above all, Pakistan needs to change its external behavior to strengthen its internal order, rather than pursue external goals at the expense of its internal stability. But because of his lack of legitimacy, Musharraf is dependent on forces resistant to change. These include the mullahs, whose extremism, ironically, he is fighting against, and the traditionally pro-establishment politicians who, like Musharraf, themselves have legitimacy problems and are fighting shy of reforms for fear of the mullahs and of social change that may erode the feudal and social structure they represent. Further, the support of the army, Musharraf's main constituency, imposes its own cost. By offering the military civilian jobs and economic and commercial incentives, the army's stake in its domination of political power only grows further and comes at the expense of democracy. Musharraf has disparate allies with discordant agendas, none of whom can offer him unqualified support. While each may support him on one issue, they may oppose him on another. Thus, with each reform that is made another must be sacrificed.

Criticism provoked by his alignment with the United States and suspicions that his reforms are at the behest of the United States have also weakened Musharraf. Indeed, the strongest resistance to him comes from the Islamists, whose tolerance toward him has already been stretched to the limit by his cooperation in the war on terrorism. He is afraid to test it any further, as he is expending most of his political capital on complying with the U.S. war on terrorism and securing his own survival, both personal and political. As a consequence, Musharraf's reforms—except for his opening to India and the vastly improved financial sector under the direction of Prime Minister Shaukat Aziz—have been fitful and insufficient. However, Musharraf's commitment and resolve to reform do not appear to have waned.

Challenges for the United States

The United States is currently engaged in an internal and external struggle to find a new mission and sense of purpose in a rapidly changing world. Scarred by the September 11 trauma, inspired by a religious outlook, and driven by a supreme consciousness of power, this struggle simplifies and distorts the emerging global challenges and devolution of power. These far-reaching changes may have made the United States the sole superpower, but they ironically have also raised the status of other powers with competing interests and policies. This makes it hard for the United States to lead, tempting it to dominate and resort to unilateralism, as in Iraq, which, in turn, provokes strong reactions and resistance. American power, therefore, is not absolute. And, on many issues, the United States is walking alone, making its power even less absolute.

While the United States has the power to dismantle, it may not necessarily have the power to rebuild. Military interventions, as a high-risk instrument of U.S. foreign policy, are costly and provocative, lacking sustained public support at home and arousing anxiety abroad. They also raise questions of legality under international law and legitimacy in the court of international public opinion. The United States also has the added challenge of confronting contrary and incompatible objectives in the Islamic world, as the war on terrorism often conflicts with calls for democracy and nonproliferation. For example, giving support to authoritarian regimes in the Middle East that align with U.S. policies and oil interests there comes at the expense of democracy. Further, the use of force to prevent a nuclear Iran would hurt the United States' standing in the Islamic world. It is thus almost impossible to have a policy that can harmonize all objectives; some policy changes and compromises will be necessary—the crucial question then becomes where and to what extent should these tradeoffs be made.

Though Musharraf's own vision of Pakistan—one which rests on modern and liberal values, what he calls "enlightened moderation"—is compatible with U.S. objectives and allows for the current U.S.-Pakistan reengagement, both he and the United States face dilemmas in the implementation of this reengagement. At the center of the challenges the U.S. faces in Pakistan is, of course, securing Pakistan's cooperation in the war on terrorism. However, in this regard, concerns about the future of Pakistan after Musharraf are misplaced and may be limiting U.S. policy directions there.

Questions over what would happen if Musharraf were eliminated reflect how much the United States has staked its relationship with Pakistan on a single individual. These concerns are relevant only in the context in which he were to be eliminated—that is, whether he is a target of assassination in a stable political environment, such as now, or whether he is violently removed during civil unrest, political turmoil, or an army coup. In the former scenario, he would be replaced by another general, probably with a similar mind-set, who could either institute military rule or, as General Baig did in 1988, order elections. Both cases would have negligible impact on U.S.-Pakistan relations. Rather than being preoccupied with the personal fate of Musharraf, the United States should focus on preventing the latter scenario. This is where the question of Pakistan's democratization comes to the fore.

The essential truth is that after years of living dangerously, Pakistan has been in a mess that can only be sorted out now by some measure of strong government, a "soft authoritarianism." But Musharraf's strategy seems to focus on giving Pakistan a new sense of purpose—peace and economic development—and on setting new national priorities that reinvent the army's rationale for appropriating political power. The United States faces a delicate balancing act between supporting him in his reform efforts and being critical of his army-dominated rule that preempts democratization efforts.

It is not just in Pakistan that the United States faces the dilemma of reconciling its geopolitical interests with its calls for democracy. Yes, there is a lot of talk in Washington about freedom and democracy, but in large measure it may be driven by the need to redefine the Iraq invasion for the sake of history and to sustain domestic consensus for the war effort. This talk may also be meant to give a moral veneer to the hard-line approach the Bush administration has taken toward authoritarian regimes that threaten U.S. interests or its friends in the Middle East.

U.S. intentions to democratize Iraq and the rest of the Islamic world may be genuine from Washington's perspective, but given its past and existing record of supporting undemocratic regimes, Muslims do not take these intentions seriously. They feel that interventions in Afghanistan and Iraq were not about democracy. They were about removing certain threats to the United States and to global security. Indeed, the United States has hurt its cause by its treatment of prisoners suspected of terrorism. Not only the Islamic world but also the United States' European allies have questioned the legal and moral basis of U.S. actions. Allegations that guards desecrated the Quran at Guantanamo Bay have also damaged the image of the United States.

What is required for the United States in most Islamic countries, including Pakistan, is to create and support pressures for social change and mental and cultural habits that sustain an open political process and democratic way of life. To do so, the United States needs influence and for that, in most Islamic countries, the United States may have to face the challenge of navigating between illiberal but friendly regimes on one hand, and liberal but unfriendly forces on the other. This is not an easy task. There is also a powerful force of reactionary elements in the Islamic world that must be contended with, a force resisting not only U.S. influence but also social change and liberal habits of thought. In meeting these challenges, the United States will have to contend with anti-Americanism.

Anti-Americanism

Anti-Americanism in Pakistan has a complex dynamic. It is framed by four concentric circles: general reaction to U.S. might and power, America's current international conduct, relations between Islam and the West, and the history of U.S.-Pakistan relations. Indeed, as the most powerful nation on earth, the United States provokes envy and resentment around the world. As for America's international conduct, its legitimacy and self-centeredness have been under challenge, especially after September 11. Regarding Islam and the West, the picture is even more complex.

September 11 did not change history so much as it signaled the arrival in history of new struggles and conflicts and a dissolution of traditional patterns of power relationships. Well before, the relations between big powers were becoming at once cooperative, tense, and competitive: globalization was inciting serious discontent, the Islamic world was looking disordered, and regional disputes were beginning to radiate much violence and instability. There was a new wave of predominantly religion-based revisionism against the vestiges of the colonial and imperialist era and the domestic and international orders, which appealed to moderates and radicals alike in the Muslim world.

Pakistan and the rest of the Islamic world are in ferment. Islamic societies that have invariably experienced colonialism or varied forms of Western domination have been experiencing conflict in their search for national identities, political stability, and effective ways of absorbing modern liberal values. They have also been coming to terms with anti-Western feelings that have interloped into their culture. Across the Islamic world, the West, especially the United States, is believed to have historically complicated this search by becoming a party to this conflict. There is also a class antipathy to the ethically intolerable value system of the ruling classes, which themselves are invariably Western oriented.

The war on terrorism has sharpened the tensions between Islam and the West. The United States seems to be fighting terrorism with traditional instruments of power, whose bluntness obscures the subtlety and complexity of the issues involved, and with a crusading zeal that speaks of an ideological struggle and clash of civilizations. Elements on both sides see their basic value system as under siege and have exaggerated their mutual fears and are busy defaming and demonizing each other. Moral issues have been undifferentiated or confused, or sacrificed to self-righteousness. Each side is judging the other with its own ideals, ideals from which it has fallen short itself. The Islamic world especially rationalizes its own errant behavior by accusing the West of double standards. No wonder, in Pakistan, liberals and conservatives alike are outraged by the mistreatment of their "national hero" AQ Khan.

Within this larger framework, the history of U.S.-Pakistan relations has generated its own anti-Americanism, which is triggered by a perception that the United States has not been a reliable ally and has not helped Pakistan much in its conflict with India. September 11 and U.S. reengagement added new issues to the debate. For instance, liberal aspirations for democracy have been heightened but tend to flow into anti-American channels because of Musharraf's association with the United States. These aspirations both merge with and deviate from the religious wave, as democracy and religion use the same jargon of social protest but advocate different means of empowerment. Nationalism, too, has come to the fore and is expressed, on one level, through anti-Americanism provoked by the war on terrorism and, on another, through the assertion of the will of smaller provinces.

Liberals in the Islamic world have their own reasons to be disaffected with the United States, particularly those aspects of the war on terrorism that are seen as repressive. There is a sense that the United States has fallen short of its ideals and its foreign policy has abandoned soft power, losing its moral superiority. Most liberals also feel that the United States is closing its doors on them with some of the more heavy-handed visa policies of the Department of Homeland Security. Besides, the United States has provoked anger all around by denigrating Muslim societies as backward and failed and by patronizing them with offers to help them modernize.

Anti-Americanism has one additional dimension in Pakistan. For decades, governments in Pakistan that often lacked popular support acquiesced to public resentment of America, using the United States as a lightning rod to divert dangerous currents of socioeconomic discontent within Pakistan. Now this same anti-Americanism is being exploited by the Islamists to gain popular support.

Nonetheless, there is also a muted appreciation of what America has done for Pakistan, especially in the nation's early history, when it was struggling for survival. And all the main political parties, including the Islamists, have channels of communication open with the United States and are prepared to work with it.

Policy Recommendations for Pakistan

Musharraf has provided the dynamic for change by boldly articulating some of the critical challenges confronting Pakistan, including economic development and Islamic extremism, and by boldly calling for a modern, liberal Islamic state that is nationally cohesive, at peace with itself and its neighbors, and a responsible member of the international community. But to meet these strategic objectives, Pakistan must develop policies that contest regressive socioeconomic structures; promote education; encourage moderation, tolerance, and accommodation; seek an end to poverty and corruption; and address ethnolinguistic, religious, and sectarian prejudices. Above all, peace with India and a strategic reorientation in the army's core beliefs are critical to Pakistan's economic survival and national security. Stakes are high. Failure to reform will only give strength to the Islamists and their competing vision for the future of Pakistan.

Musharraf should realize that enlightened moderation is more than cultural liberalization. Only political liberalization will help strengthen liberal and secular forces that can be his allies in defeating religious extremism. Otherwise, cultural openness could backfire and give further ammunition to the fundamentalists, provoking a cultural war that could get entangled with class conflicts. Musharraf should also bear in mind that economic development is neither a substitute for democracy nor a guarantee of his own survival or of Pakistan's political stability. One need only look to what happened in Iran—where despite economic gains people rose up against the Shah—as evidence of this.

Its rhetoric may be revolutionary, but Pakistan's political system is quasi-reactionary—that is, it is the same civil-military bureaucratic complex that continues to work under the cover of a flawed democracy dominated by feudal tribal interests. Even working at its most efficient, the system will only be able to change Pakistan modestly before it itself becomes a road-block to change. Thanks to the economic policies and management of Prime Minister Aziz, Pakistan has registered an impressive growth rate, but prospects of a major economic transformation remain uncertain.

Pakistan's economic development will remain limited if the country does not come to terms with problems of poor public services, corruption, inequities in land and income distribution, social exclusion of the marginalized and vulnerable, particularly women, and high illiteracy rates. Above all, as Steve Cohen has said in his book *The Idea of Pakistan*, Pakistan needs a new organizing idea and an improved relationship between its provinces and center. For example, the province of Baluchistan is significant for Pakistan's future economic prospects. It is rich in mineral resources that are strategically located near vital sea lanes and two oil-bearing regions, the Persian Gulf and Central Asia. But the development of Baluchistan is resisted by tribal chiefs who fear their traditional authority will be undermined there. (Similarly, the sharing and harnessing of water resources for irrigation and hydroelectric power are also contentious issues between the central government and the provinces.) The problem is political, not economic. Only through better management of relations between the central and provincial governments—which may even require constitutional adjustments—can Pakistan realize its full economic potential.

Political stability and peaceful internal order are essential for attracting critically needed foreign investment for economic development. The ability to provide such security depends upon the integrity and effectiveness of Pakistan's political process. In other words, economic development and democracy are interdependent. Economic change will foster a middle class that may help lead the balance of economic and political power away from the feudal stranglehold. Musharraf should work toward this end and prepare the country for a full restoration of parliamentary and civilianized democracy in 2007.

Beyond 2007, the army should have only a watch-dog role in the government. This should be for a designated period of time, provided there is a national consensus and constitutional support for the idea. Pakistan will not become a perfect democracy overnight, but such a move may be necessary to carry the reforms further; otherwise, the country will become depoliticized and may accelerate toward extremism and internal disorder.

If there is a broad spectrum of political and economic change empowering a new civilian leadership, the military will have no rationale to dominate Pakistan's political life. This may be the only way to resolve the complexity of having to deal with two imperfect choices—immediate democratization in a social context that hosts forces resistant to reforms, and open-ended reliance on army rule that is committed to reforms but is resistant to democracy.

Pakistan has to make the best possible use of the current U.S. engagement but also keep in mind two facts. First, Pakistan has to change and reform on its own. (Thus far, the United States' principal interest has only been in stabilizing Pakistan.) Second, while in the past Pakistan criticized the United States for lack of commitment to the relationship, Pakistan itself showed little regard for Washington by pursuing policies that defied U.S. concerns, such as those related to terrorism and the export of nuclear technology. Pursuing these policies served no conceivable national interest of Pakistan.

On proliferation, Pakistan needs to come clean about the past and assure the United States about the future. It is best to discuss the past now while the relationship is strong enough to absorb any further shocking disclosures.

Pakistan also has to recognize that opposition to some of America's core concerns, especially as it relates to nuclear proliferation, democracy, and peace with India, may be tolerated by Washington in the near term for the sake of expediency, but that such opposition will have no lasting place in a long-term relationship with the United States.

Policy Recommendations for the United States

Eventually terrorism will be reduced to one of the regular threats that can be addressed with a range of normal military, intelligence, and foreign policy options, but the rationale for United States' reengagement with Pakistan may live on. To meet challenges beyond the war on terrorism, the U.S.-Pakistan relationship must be broadened to include a strong economic partnership, educational and cultural linkages, and a shared perspective on democracy, nonproliferation, and peace in South Asia. Only then will the relationship enjoy strong domestic support in both countries.

India and Pakistan

Critical U.S. policy choices in the region require an integrated approach to the issues of concern as they are all inextricably linked. Militancy and extremism, for instance, are linked as much to Pakistan's sense of insecurity as to the army's ambitions. Some of the core U.S. foreign policy concerns are thus rooted in India-Pakistan tensions. U.S. relations with India and Pakistan, therefore, should be designed to advance the prospects of regional peace and stability. Preoccupied by Iraq and relieved by the apparent success of the India-Pakistan dialogue, the United States may be tempted by a laissez-faire approach to the peace process. But the fact is, favorable and reciprocal changes in multiple contexts—domestic, bilateral, and international—are requisite to the resolution of long-standing conflicts. In that sense, enhanced U.S. stakes in South Asia are a stimulus to the peace process. However, this strategic pressure point will be eroded by any U.S. indifference to the India-Pakistan dialogue. Indeed, if the peace process fails, the United States will be blamed by the people of Pakistan on one hand for seemingly "pressuring" Pakistan to normalize relations with India and on the other for weakening Pakistan's leverage in Kashmir with the war on terrorism. The United States must therefore be engaged in the peace process to insure against its failure, as dissatisfaction among Pakistanis from an adverse outcome will ignite agitation against Musharraf.

Additionally, a successful normalization of relations between Pakistan and India benefits the United States in more ways than one. It could, for instance, ease Pakistan's security fears and help lower the army's political profile, opening the way for democratization, and advance the prospects of an integrated South Asia market linked to energy-rich Central Asia, increasing opportunities for U.S. investment there.

Peace between India and Pakistan will also ease fears of a nuclear war, may open up the possibility of their incorporation into the international nuclear community, and will help strengthen their command and control structure, which will encourage nonproliferation. Though the United States will not let India and Pakistan be accepted into the Nuclear Non-Proliferation Treaty regime as nuclear powers, the United States is keen to sign on both Pakistan and India to the Proliferation Security Initiative (PSI), the Bush administration's latest strategy to contain the proliferation of nuclear weapons. But Pakistan is not likely to join the PSI without India's participation. To get Pakistan and India on board, China's help should also be solicited. As a nuclear power with complex relations with both South Asian states, China can be an important contributor to strategic stabilization in South Asia.

Institution Building and Democracy

The U.S. strategic community has emphasized institution building and reform. Pakistan's problems are not lack of institutions but the trivialization of the institutions. If institutions are not working, especially the police, judiciary, and administrative services, it is because they have been undermined by their subservience to the dominant centers of power. They can only be reformed if social and political structures are first reformed. Education and social sectors, however, are in a dysfunctional state and in need of urgent help.

As for democracy, the United States must encourage Musharraf to make the political process more inclusive, open, and legitimate. To this end, the scheduled 2007 elections should be free, fair, and open to all political parties. The present political system is neither strong nor stable enough to withstand any mass resistance to the army's political power, civil unrest due to economic discontent, conservative backlash over a "sellout" to India, or agitation over the fairness or legitimacy of the upcoming elections.

The United States must also put pressure on Musharraf to take off the uniform after 2007, and it should work behind the scenes with the army high command to support him even as a civilian president. The United States has to make clear that its support for the army-dominated political dispensation cannot last beyond 2007. By then the war on terrorism will have achieved many of its core objectives, reducing the U.S. dependence on Musharraf, and Pakistan will have achieved minimum stabilization, enabling the United States to switch its priorities toward addressing issues such as democracy and proliferation.

Educational Reforms

USAID considers educational reform to be the most important current development project in Pakistan. In July 2002, more than $100 million was dedicated to a five-year education reform plan. USAID and Pakistan's Ministry of Education are working together to improve (1) policy and planning, (2) teacher and administrator training, (3) adult and youth literacy programs, and (4) partnership development and community building between the public and private spheres. USAID also has projects dedicated to improving teacher training and developing teaching materials; to building and furnishing schools in the Federally Administered Tribal Areas; to training Pakistani educators in the United States; and to promoting democratic values in teachers and students. These extensive efforts will only succeed if they are implemented countrywide and emphasize local solutions for meeting educational goals rather than impose unworkable or culturally insensitive solutions from the outside. Besides, the current levels of

U.S. aid allocation for educational reforms do not appear to be adequate to the task and may have to be doubled, at least.

Given the problems already identified with Pakistan's bureaucracy, the United States has an understandable distrust of the government machinery for channeling U.S. aid to education reforms. The United States has turned to nongovernmental organizations (NGOs) as an alternative mechanism for implementing change in the education sector. An uncritical trust of NGOs is also a risk, however—many are themselves a product of an elitist and self-serving system. Pakistan should be encouraged to emulate the example of Bangladesh, where grass-roots-based NGOs have a stronger sense of public service. Indeed, the United States should help Pakistan build civil society, the most important institution-building challenge in the country after education.

According to Pakistan's minister of education, the government has vastly enhanced his ministry's budget to carry out wide-ranging reforms in the education system, including increasing teacher salaries, opening new schools, especially in villages, and modernizing the curriculum. The government has given him a budget allocation of 5.5 billion rupees to reform madrassahs by introducing science subjects and the teaching of English to their curricula, provide computers for classroom use, and upgrade their physical infrastructure. To date, madrassahs have been hesitant to accept such government intervention for reform.

However, there is a high risk that such policies will end up strengthening the madrassahs without actually reforming them. Their funding is already drying up, and reform will only give them a shot in the arm. Over the long run, with an expanded and reformed public educational system, the madrassahs will wither on the vine. Instead of bailing them out, they should be gradually absorbed into the mainstream educational system.

Political Islam

The U.S. relationship with Pakistan must show some immediate results to demonstrate that there is an alternative vision for Pakistan and that it is working. The engagement must not fail because the alternative, an extremist Pakistan that itself becomes a U.S. target, will be a policy nightmare.

To be successful, the engagement must be geared toward benefiting the people, not just the regime. This will raise the people's confidence in the country's relationship with the United States. Additionally, the United States must not appear to be in conflict with Islam. Political Islam is not something out there on the fringes that the United States can combat and conquer. To varying degrees, it has been ingrained in the social ethos of the Muslim world because of the emotional appeal of the causes it espouses. To this end, leaders of Muslim countries may have to make some compromises with the religion. The United States has to respect not only these concessions but also some minimum nationalist and democratic aspirations in the Islamic world.

Economic and Security Assistance and Sanctions Policy

The United States needs to find a new paradigm for its relationship with Pakistan. The weak sanctions of the 1990s that offered Pakistan no incentive for change did not work. In the future, sanctions should not be a policy option as long as there are strong reasons for the United States to be engaged with Pakistan and to help its reform efforts. Reform should be an end in itself, as a reformed Pakistan is in the interest of the United States whether or not there is a quid pro quo. Additionally, the United States needs to build a broader coalition of countries to support Pakistan's reform efforts, including highly visible donors such as Japan.

The United States must also help Pakistan create a dynamic economy that generates employment. To this end, the bilateral investment agreement between the two countries should be expedited. It will be seen by the international business community as an affirmation of Pakistan's economic stability, and thus raise investor confidence in the country. Indeed, U.S. and Japanese companies should be offered special incentives to invest in Pakistan. Pakistan considers the free-trade agreement with the United States an essential component of its economic development program. In the meantime, both the United States and Japan should provide greater market access for Pakistani textiles as an effective interim measure for relief.

The U.S. aid program toward Pakistan should focus heavily on supporting poverty-reduction strategies. There is already a perception among Pakistanis of increased poverty in the country, concerns about rising inflation, and discontent over the army's growing domination of the civilian institutions, not to mention a host of other internal tensions in the country. In the absence of a charismatic secular leader, the entire range of opposition could coalesce under an Islamic banner, such as happened in the Iranian revolution. The U.S. would be well-advised to avoid such a scenario.

A minimum level of security assistance should also be immune from any future sanctions or political pressure by the United States. Pakistan has genuine defense and foreign policy concerns. Even if the country has overplayed these threats, they are real. Nor should Pakistan be any less deserving of the international community's sympathy and understanding just because of its past errant behavior. A reformed Pakistan, headed toward moderation, strongly committed against militancy, and at peace with India, is unlikely to go against America's core interests. Indeed, a strong Pakistan may be helpful in moderating India's ambitions.

The ability of the United States to help reform Pakistan will be strengthened if the United States appears to be less in need of Pakistan than Pakistan is in need of the United States. U.S. interests go well beyond the war against terrorism. By expending all of its political capital in securing Pakistan's cooperation in that war, the United States risks diminishing its leverage with Pakistan and neglecting other important strategic goals, such as promoting democracy in Pakistan and the Muslim world and containing nuclear proliferation. Any increase in the existing levels of security assistance, or any further sale of major defense equipment beyond the F-16s, should be linked to Pakistan's cooperation on these issues, as well as on the war on terrorism. What is needed is a broader framework for its relationship with Pakistan, one in which the war against terrorism is at the center of the agenda but does not crowd out other interests.

Conclusion

Fulfilling conflicting objectives without sacrificing any of them is a central policy dilemma for the United States. Both Musharraf and the United States need each other to address the complexity of this challenge.

There are stirrings of change in Pakistan under Musharraf, but if they are not perceptible, it is because a massive amount of work needs to be done. This is why even a significant achievement seems so little in proportion to the magnitude of the challenge. It might be said that only rhetoric has changed in Pakistan, not the reality on the ground. The fact is, in a society long entrenched in an unchanging self-image and worldview, rhetoric and substance merge indistinguishably. So if the rhetoric changes, changes in substance may not be far behind. For that to happen, the United States must remain engaged with Pakistan, not only to meet its current challenges, but its future challenges as well.

Future U.S. interests in the region may be defined, not just by the looming strategic shadow of a resurgent China, but also of India and possibly of Russia. There is also the risk of a possible surge in radical Islam in the region fostered by the inevitable crumbling of some of the conservative or repressive Arab regimes. This would be compounded by a nuclear Iran. China is already positioning itself to fill any future power vacuum caused by any receding U.S. standing in the region and has begun building bridges with Iran and India. As a result, the U.S.-Pakistan relationship will increasingly intersect with issues that go far beyond the war on terrorism.

There is therefore a compelling rationale for the United States to remain engaged in the region. And given its geopolitical environment and dependence on borrowed power, as well as its chronic domestic weaknesses that may take time to heal, Pakistan could remain a friend and possibly even an ally.

An online edition of this and related reports can be found at our website (www.usip.org), together with additional information on the subject.

United States Institute of Peace
1200 17th Street NW
Washington, DC 20036
www.usip.org

DOCUMENT NO. 20

EXPERT TESTIMONY IN UNITED STATES V. HAMID HAYAT, BY EVAN F. KOHLMANN

Evan F. Kohlmann

February 2006

Adapted from an expert report submitted on behalf of federal prosecutors in *United States v. Hamid Hayat* (U.S. District Court for the Eastern District of California, CR#05-240GB) - February 2006

I. Introduction to the Jihad Movement in Pakistan

To fully understand the current "holy war" of Pakistani terrorist groups such as Jaish-e-Muhammad (JEM), Harakat ul-Mujahideen (HUM), and Anjuman Sipah-e-Sahaba (SSP), one must first appreciate the significance of the Soviet-Afghan war of the 1980s through the eyes of Sunni Muslim extremists from around the world—including in Pakistan. At first glance, no one could have imagined the lasting significance of the Soviet invasion of Afghanistan in December 1979. Afghanistan was not an American Cold War ally; in fact, the United States had more or less ignored opportunities during the 1960s and 70s to draw Afghanistan into the Western fold. With most attention focused on the importance of neighboring Pakistan, Afghanistan was largely left to its own devices.

However, internal power struggles and public discontent with the communist regime threatened to topple the political status quo that the Soviets had carefully constructed. Fearing the collapse of Marxism in Afghanistan, the Soviets invaded under the pretext of restoring order and replaced the ruling government with one more beholden to the interests of Moscow. The sporadic rebellion in the tribal hinterlands against the reformed Afghan communist regime in early 1979 was not predicted to have much of a future. In the face of thousands of arriving Soviet troops, one former

U.S. Ambassador to Afghanistan even estimated that "the Russians would wipe out the resistance in months."[1]

But rather than achieving a quick victory, the Soviets found themselves surrounded by a relentless guerilla adversary. Countless numbers of Afghanis joined the Islamic resistance, which was organized into several native mujahideen organizations with headquarters in Peshawar, Pakistan. Though these Afghan parties were theoretically structured along Islamic ideological lines, there is good reason to believe that many local guerillas that fought in the war against the Soviets had motivations outside of religion, including jealousy and greed. Mujahideen units in Afghanistan often switched party allegiances, and even entered into alliances with the supposedly "infidel" Soviets against their own indigenous Afghan Muslim rivals.

Nevertheless, the flurry of activity in Peshawar caught the imagination of the entire Islamic world, far beyond the borders of battered Afghanistan. In certain fanatic circles, the indignity and injustice of the Soviet invasion had aroused a much more enraged response. According to these Islamic extremists, the jihad in Afghanistan should be treated as a critical turning point in modern world history and is a basic military blueprint for the larger struggle to ultimately "re-create" an omnipotent Muslim theocratic empire stretching from Morocco to the Philippines. The young foreign fighters who came from Saudi Arabia, Egypt, Algeria, Pakistan, and elsewhere to sacrifice their blood and souls in the battle to "save" Afghanistan from the infidel communists are revered to this day as heroes of the highest order. Their faces and their names are legendary, even beyond the traditional Muslim world. These inexperienced but unusually persistent fighters simply referred to themselves as mujahideen, or "Islamic holy warriors." In the Western discourse, they have become collectively known during the years since as the "Arab-Afghans."

The Afghan cauldron provided unprecedented opportunities to disparate groups of global Islamists for unification of thought, purpose, and infrastructure. When Soviet forces were finally forced to withdraw, those who had fought alongside the Afghan mujahideen were exhilarated. In 1988, Shaykh Tamim al-Adnani—a senior Palestinian leader and recruiter of Arab mujahideen in Afghanistan—explained to a group of American Muslims in Kansas that "the best thing is [to] continue Jihad. Nothing but Jihad . . . Even after liberation of Afghanistan, even after the Islamic government, [the mujahideen] will not stop. They will go up to the Muslim countries of Russia, Islamic republics. They will go down to Palestine, to [Jerusalem]." Moreover, Al-Adnani offered this chilling addendum: "[if]

[1] Eliot, Theodore L., Jr. *Gorbachev's Afghan Gambit*. Institute for Foreign Policy Analysis; Cambridge, MA. ©1988. *Page 1.*

Anybody stops in their way, Oh my God! Smash them! Any ruler, [if] he will not let us go, we will go by force! Jihad!"[2] Speaking at another Islamic conference in the United States, a representative of Afghan fundamentalist warlord Gulbuddin Hekmatyar proclaimed:

> "You have seen in your own life one of the biggest superpowers—Soviet Union—is gone. God is the greatest. One of the biggest superpowers—USA was afraiding from the Soviet Union. Where right now is the Soviet Union? As you say, Allahu Akhbar. It means, just Allah is the superpower . . . this year, praise be to God, Soviet Union is gone! Soviet Union divided by 15 states. Soviet Union wanted to eliminate an Islamic country from the world—Afghanistan. Allah created five more Islamic states from the Soviet Union. God is the greatest . . . We don't say that everything is finished, no. Still we have some problems. But we hope, if God wills it, finally we will not just liberate Afghanistan, God-willing, we will liberate the whole area. God is the greatest. Besides Afghanistan, in Central Asian countries . . . God-willing, in the very near future, we will liberate all human beings from these devils."[3]

II. The Emergence of the Jihad Movements in Pakistan

As the Soviet occupation of Afghanistan began to fade, a group of Pakistani Muslim militants decided to "take[] a leaf from the book of [the] Afghans . . . [and] lit the torch of Jihad movement."[4] By 1991, the celebrated Afghan jihad had devolved into chaos as communism crumbled and the power-hungry Afghan mujahideen turned on one another. The glorious days of the Afghan jihad were left behind and replaced with scenes of Muslims killing other innocent Muslims. During an interview with mujahideen recruiter Abu Hamza al-Masri in London, he tried to explain to me the mindset of Arab and Pakistani mujahideen volunteers at this time: "People are dedicated to the [religion] . . . They went to Afghanistan to defend their brothers and sisters. So, they find Afghanistan now, the destruction of war and Muslims fighting against each other." As a result, in the aftermath of the disaster in Afghanistan, "they want[ed] to [struggle against] something that is indisputable, which is non-Muslims raping, killing, and maiming Muslims."[5] It would not be long before Pakistani "Afghans" would turn their attention to a conflict much closer to home: the fight to control the contested Kashmir region straddling Muslim Pakistan and neighboring Hindu-dominated India.

---

[2] Emerson, Steven. *Jihad in America*. SAE Productions (for PBS); Washington, DC. Originally aired November 21, 1994. Running time: 1 hour.

[3] Videotape of 17th Annual Conference of the Islamic Circle of North America (ICNA); July 17–19, 1992. Session: "Freedom and Struggle in the Ummah." Speaker: Sair ur Rehman Halimi (Hezb-i-Islami Afghanistan). Topic: "Afghanistan: the Challenge Today."

[4] Taiba Bulletin (nadqpk@yahoo.com). "Subject: Eleven Years of Lashker-e-Taiba." April 22, 2001. http://groups.yahoo.com/group/muslimworldnews.

[5] Interview with Shaykh Abu Hamza al-Masri at the Finsbury Park Mosque; June 28, 2002.

Since their independence in August 1947, Pakistan and India have fought at least two major wars over the disputed Kashmir zone; the United Nations has drawn a temporary dividing line of control in an attempt to reduce regional tensions. Both nations are armed with nuclear weapons and have indicated a willingness to use them if necessary. Hundreds of thousands of Pakistani and Indian troops face off along the line of control and regularly trade rifle and artillery fire during small skirmishes. In approximately 1989, a major insurgent rebellion began in the Kashmir region led primarily by Muslim militants opposed to Hindu rule. Within a brief period of time, virtually every Pakistani mujahideen faction that had fought during the Soviet-Afghan jihad mobilized for a new holy war against India. An English-language mujahideen guidebook to the Pakistani militant organizations active in Kashmir published in 1999 explained, "There are various groups fighting in the cause of Allah under a variety of slogans and titles at least numbering in excess of ten at the time of writing." Despite occasional episodes of antagonism and internecine conflict among the Pakistani jihadis, the guidebook assured readers that "co-operation is widespread, this being the best and obvious way to function."[6]

Several loosely-allied Afghan-trained Pakistani mujahideen groups, in particular, gained notoriety for their ruthless tactics and fanatic ideologies—to the point of being named by the U.S. State Department as Designated Foreign Terrorist Organizations (FTOs).

- **Harakat ul-Mujahideen (HUM)**

On October 8, 1997, HUM was first designated by the U.S. Secretary of State as a Foreign Terrorist Organization (FTO) pursuant to Section 219 of the Immigration and Nationality Act. According to the U.S. State Department's *Patterns of Global Terrorism: 2003*:

> "The HUM is an Islamic militant group based in Pakistan that operates primarily in Kashmir. It is politically aligned with the radical political party, Jamiat Ulema-i-Islam Fazlur Rehman faction (JUI-F). Longtime leader of the group, Fazlur Rehman Khalil, in mid-February 2000 stepped down as HUM emir, turning the reins over to the popular Kashmiri commander and his second in command, Farooq Kashmiri. Khalil, who has been linked to Usama Bin Ladin and signed his fatwa in February 1998 calling for attacks on US and Western interests, assumed the position of HUM Secretary General. HUM operated terrorist training camps in eastern Afghanistan until Coalition airstrikes destroyed them during fall 2001. In 2003, HUM began using the name Jamiat ul-Ansar (JUA), and Pakistan banned the successor JUA in November 2003 . . . [HUM] [h]as conducted a number of operations against Indian troops and civilian targets in Kashmir . . .

[6] Al-Hindi, `Esa. *The Army of Madinah in Kashmir*. Maktabah Al Ansaar Publications; Birmingham, UK. ©1999. Page 18.

> The HUM is responsible for the hijacking of an Indian airliner on 24 December 1999, which resulted in the release of Masood Azhar—an important leader in the former Harakat ul-Ansar imprisoned by the Indians in 1994—and Ahmed Omar Sheik, who was convicted of the abduction/murder in January-February 2002 of US journalist Daniel Pearl. The HUM trained its militants in Afghanistan and Pakistan . . . In anticipation of asset seizures in 2001 by the Pakistani Government, the HUM withdrew funds from bank accounts and invested in legal businesses, such as commodity trading, real estate, and production of consumer goods."[7]

According to the former English-language website of HUM, the group was founded by five people in 1985 and "in a very short span of time HUM became a very strong & effective Mujahid Force. During Soviet intervention in Afghanistan, HUM was one of the front liners and stood like a rock besides the rest of the Mujahideen groups. HUM's Mujahids shed their blood on every corner of Afghanistan during Jihad and also rendered valuable contribution against international conspiracies and to neutralize propaganda against Afghanistan, especially the Jew's Geneva conference." In its propaganda materials, HUM boasted of "very cordial relations with all Afghan leaders from the day of interception", including "the Islamic Revolution . . . in the form of Taliban . . . [which] was not to the liking of the western satanic groups, of which the Zionists are at the top."[8]

HUM responded bitterly to being one of the first organizations named by the U.S. government as a Designated Foreign Terrorist Organization. On its website, it moaned of being referred to as "terrorist, idealists, fundamentalists etc." The website continued on to criticize "Jewish Lobby controlled countries" for placing punitive sanctions on HUM and further vowed, "HUM stood like a rock against all odds and will remain so, Insha Allah, in the future."[9] Indeed, negative attention in Europe and North America did little to dampen the HUM's interest in carrying out terrorist operations. The 1999 hijacking of an Indian Airliner in order to gain the freedom of Maulana Masood Azhar (among others) was admittedly one of HUM's proudest achievements. According to the English-language *Army of Madinah in Kashmir* mujahideen guidebook, "In a daring fete that seemed to be a throw back to the heydays of the sixties and seventies when professional revolutionaries such as Illich Ramirez Navas, a.k.a. Carlos the Jackal, had waged war on the Capitalist world, the HuM members rewound the tape and pulled off the seemingly impossible in a day and age of a new world which considers itself to be fully conversant in handling hostage situations."[10]

---

7 "Appendix B: Background Information on Designated Foreign Terrorist Organizations." *Patterns of Global Terrorism: 2003*. U.S. State Department; Office of the Coordinator for Counterterrorism. April 29, 2004. http://www.state.gov/s/ct/rls/pgtrpt/2003/31711.htm.

8 http://www.harkatulmujahideen.org/history.html. December 2000.

9 http://www.harkatulmujahideen.org/history.html. December 2000.

10 Al-Hindi, `Esa. *The Army of Madinah in Kashmir*. Maktabah Al Ansaar Publications; Birmingham, UK. ©1999. Page 150.

- **Jaish-e-Muhammad (JEM)**

On October 12, 2001, Jaish-e-Muhammad (JEM) was first designated by the State Department under Executive Order 13224. According to the annual publication Patterns of Global Terrorism 2001:

> "The Jaish-e-Mohammed (JEM) is an Islamic extremist group based in Pakistan that was formed by Masood Azhar upon his release from prison in India in early 2000. The group's aim is to unite Kashmir with Pakistan. It is politically aligned with the radical political party, Jamiat-i Ulema-i Islam Fazlur Rehman faction (JUI-F) . . . The group was banned and its assets were frozen by the Pakistani Government in January 2002 . . . Supporters are mostly Pakistanis and Kashmiris and also include Afghans and Arab veterans of the Afghan war. [JEM] [u]ses light and heavy machineguns, assault rifles, mortars, improvised explosive devices, and rocket grenades . . . The JEM maintained training camps in Afghanistan until the fall of 2001. Most of the JEM's cadre and material resources have been drawn from the militant groups Harakat ul-Jihad al-Islami (HUJI) and the Harakat ul-Mujahedin (HUM). The JEM had close ties to Afghan Arabs and the Taliban. Usama Bin Ladin is suspected of giving funding to the JEM. The JEM also collects funds through donation requests in magazines and pamphlets. In anticipation of asset seizures by the Pakistani Government, the JEM withdrew funds from bank accounts and invested in legal businesses, such as commodity trading, real estate, and production of consumer goods."[11]

The U.S. Treasury Department has also taken several actions against alleged JEM charitable front groups, including the Al-Rashid Trust and the Al-Akhtar Trust. According to "information available to the U.S. government", Jaish-e-Muhammad members set up these two organizations, among others, "hop[ing] to give the impression that the . . . new organizations were separate entities and sought to use them as a way to deliver arms and ammunition to their members under the guise of providing humanitarian aid to refugees and other needy groups."[12] The U.S. Treasury Department specifically accused JEM of establishing Al-Akhtar Trust "for the purpose of providing financial assistance for mujahideen, financial support to the Taliban and food, clothes, and education to orphans of martyrs.[13] During a "custodial interview" in early 2003, a senior Al Qaida detainee related that Al Akhtar Trust and Al-Rashid Trust were the "primary relief

[11] "Appendix B: Background Information on Designated Foreign Terrorist Organizations." *Patterns of Global Terrorism: 2001*. U.S. State Department; Office of the Coordinator for Counterterrorism May 21, 2002. http://www.state.gov/s/ct/rls/pgtrpt/2001/html/10252.htm#jem.

[12] "JS-899: U.S. Designates Al Akhtar Trust: Pakistani Based Charity is Suspected of Raising Money for Terrorists in Iraq." U.S. Treasury Office of Public Affairs. October 14, 2003. http://www.treas.gov/press/releases/js899.htm.

[13] "JS-899: U.S. Designates Al Akhtar Trust: Pakistani Based Charity is Suspected of Raising Money for Terrorists in Iraq." U.S. Treasury Office of Public Affairs. October 14, 2003. http://www.treas.gov/press/releases/js899.htm.

agencies that Al Qaida used to move supplies into Qandahar, Afghanistan."[14] Additionally, during a second "custodial interview" in mid-April 2003, a senior Al Qaida detainee stated that Al-Rashid Trust and Al Akhtar Trust "provided donations to Al Qaida . . . Al-Akhtar Trust was providing a wide range of support to Al-Qaida and Pakistani based sectarian and jihadi groups, specifically Lashkar-e-Tayyiba, Lashkar-i-Jhangvi, and Jaish-e-Mohammed."[15]

JEM's top leader, Maulana Masood Azhar—freed from Indian custody during a December 1999 airline hijacking engineered by Harakat ul-Mujahideen (HUM)—has made no secret of his violent anti-Indian and anti-Western military agenda. He has published at least two books which have been translated into English and he contributed regular articles to various English-language jihad publications such as the Taliban's Dharb-i-Mumin (also linked to the JEM). In late July 2001, Azhar urged his followers to "take the advantages of the spring":

> "From where do all the mujahideen get all these weapons, wondered the Kuffar of the world in amazement. Waves of terror then started striking against their minds . . . In conditions such as these, Jaish-i-Muhammad sallallahu `alaihe wassalaam rose on the horizon of Kashmir with the shining splendour of emaan [faith]. The fidayee [commando] attack of Afaq Shaheed terrified India out of its wits while the fidayee attack of Bilal Shaheed sent shock waves across the whole world of Kufr [disbelief]. Lines of anxiety became visible, on the black and white faces of the Kuffar [infidels] and India's nerves became jittery . . . Behind the lofty mountains, the lions who are sacrificing their lives day and night for the glory of Islam continue on their way down the road of Jihad, unconcerned and indifferent with the talks. They are following, with all their strength and vigor, the blood covered path of their shuhada [martyrs]."[16]

In his book, *Virtues of Jihad*, Azhar openly endorses international terrorism as an essential requirement of his followers:

> "The Kafirs [infidels] only fear the blasts of those bombs which are detonated in the Israeli army's installations and barracks. They are scared of those mines which blast the Indian army's vehicles . . . They fear a blind holy man like Umar Abdul-Rahmaan (a distinguished Aalim, presently in a US jail on trumped up charges) who dared to speak about the greatness of Islam. They are afraid of those Muslim youths of Europe who openly stroll

[14] "JS-899: U.S. Designates Al Akhtar Trust: Pakistani Based Charity is Suspected of Raising Money for Terrorists in Iraq." U.S. Treasury Office of Public Affairs. October 14, 2003. http://www.treas.gov/press/releases/js899.htm.

[15] "JS-899: U.S. Designates Al Akhtar Trust: Pakistani Based Charity is Suspected of Raising Money for Terrorists in Iraq." U.S. Treasury Office of Public Affairs. October 14, 2003. http://www.treas.gov/press/releases/js899.htm.

[16] Azhar, Maulana Masood (Amir, JEM). "Take the advantages of the spring." *Dharb-i-Mumin*. Vol. 3; Issue 8. July 20–26, 2001. http://www.dharb-i-mumin.com.

> the streets of London and Paris wearing military clothing . . . They are scared of Shamil Basayev (leader of the Mujahideen, who successfully carried out the Jihad inside Russia) who with a handful of Mujahideen had forced the whole of Russia to their knees . . . Their minds are disturbed with the thought of those unknown Mujahideen who forced the Americans to pack their bags from Somalia. They are frightened of those Muslim daughters who somehow transport weapons to the Mujahideen in Kashmir, Palestine, and Bosnia. All Kafirs [infidels] fear the word of Jihad. It is our duty and responsibility to revive this forgotten obligation of JIHAD."[17]

Similarly, at a July 2001 conference in Karachi organized "under the auspices of Jaish-e-Muhammad", the chief of JEM's "Fostering Virtue and Repressing Vice Bureau" Maulana Qari Mansoor Ahmad admonished over 450 other JEM leaders and clerics that "Jihad was the only source which provided a powerful centre in the face of Islamic Emirate of Afghanistan . . . the most powerful ruler on earth is Ameer-ul-Mu'mineen, [Taliban leader] Mulla `Umar Mujahid, who is not afraid of anyone but Allah."[18] Another speaker at the conference, Sheikh Mufti Atiq-ur-Rahman further acknowledged that everyone "who has confronted imperialism has met with immense difficulties and obstacles, so the Ulema and the mujahideen must fight back imperialism's propaganda, conspiracies, and baseless allegations leveled against Islam."[19] In April 2001, JEM leader Masood Azhar told a gathering of JEM supporters in Mardan, "I want to warn Vajpayee and Advani that if burning the copies of Quran and desecration of mosques was not stopped then the fire burning in Kashmir will reach their halls; from Bombay to Delhi, self-sacrificing attacks will play havoc with India."[20]

As one might surmise, the JEM has a fanatically anti-American agenda and is rigidly hostile in its dealings with the U.S. In a editorial published in the weeks following 9/11, JEM defiantly brushed aside Western accusations of terrorism: "Definitely, this is a matter of delight and a medal for us that Almightly Allah's enemies are troubled by us and they are giving the testimony of our Jihad . . . In this battle the winners are the Muslims only if they are faithful to their religion. Today the Taliban movement has reached the infidel annoying stage and is busy in the war . . . Jaish-e-Muhammad (Sallalahu alaihi wasallam) has also reached the infidel annoying stage in a short period." The newsletter reportedly continued on to denounce America as "the global terrorist, the murderer of millions, Aids-stricken . . . [run by]

---

17 Azhar, Maulana Masood. *Virtues of Jihad*. Ahle Sunnah Wal Jama'at Publications. ©1996.

18 "Jihad will continue for Islam's sanctity." *Dharb-i-Mumin*. Vol. 3, Issue 5. June 29-July 5, 2001. http://www.dharb-i-mumin.com.

19 "Jihad will continue for Islam's sanctity." *Dharb-i-Mumin*. Vol. 3, Issue 5. June 29-July 5, 2001. http://www.dharb-i-mumin.com.

20 "Ameer-i-Jaish flays silence on sacrilege of mosques, Quran in India." April 7, 2001. Internet newsgroups: soc.culture.malaysia.

crusading monsters."[21] When interviewed by Reuters in October 2001, JEM's then-regional commander in Pakistan's Baluchistan province Abdul Jabbar declared, "Wherever Muslims are under attack, we are ready to fight. We are international. Our goal, when Muslims are in trouble, is to free them, to fight with them against our common enemies, wherever that may be."[22]

- **Anjuman Sipah e-Sahaba Pakistan (SSP)**

Though Sipah-e-Sahaba Pakistan (SSP) has never been specifically designated as a Foreign Terrorist Organization by the United States, the U.S. State Department does officially categorize SSP as a "terrorist organization." According to *Patterns of Global Terrorism: 2003*:

> "The Sipah-I-Sahaba/Pakistan (SSP) is a Sunni sectarian group that follows the Deobandi school. Violently anti-Shia, the SSP emerged in central Punjab in the mid-1980s as a response to the Iranian Revolution. Pakistani President Musharraf banned the SSP in January 2002. In August 2002, the SSP renamed itself Millat-i-Islami, and Musharraf re-banned the group in November 2003. The group's activities range from organizing political rallies calling for Shia to be declared non-Muslims to assassinating prominent Shia leaders."[23]

III. Mujahideen Training Camps in Pakistan: 1998–2002

Since the early days of the Soviet-Afghan war, Pakistani territory has served as a major base for fundamentalist madrassas and militant training camps, including for Al-Qaida. In 1988, one such facility inside Pakistan known as "Al-Sadda" was described in the founding documents of Al-Qaida as an "open camp" from which the best "brothers" would be selected to join the new terrorist organization.[24] As native Pakistani mujahideen organizations began to flourish with the opening of a second frontline in Kashmir during the 1990s, a host of new indoctrination and training camps sprang up across both Afghanistan and Pakistan—in such places as Peshawar, Akora Khattak, Mansehra, Muzaffarabad, Balakot, and beyond. For many years, militant groups like HUM, Lashkar-e-Taiba, and JEM also maintained public offices and recruitment venues in major Pakistani cities, including Lahore and Islamabad.

---

[21] Syed Ali, Naziha. "A Call to Arms." *Newsline* (Pakistan). December 2001. http://www.newsline.com.pk/NewsDec2001/cover5.htm.

[22] Fullerton, John. "Muslim charities treading fine line on politics." *Reuters*. October 3, 2001.

[23] "Appendix C—Background Information on Other Terrorist Groups." *Patterns of Global Terrorism: 2003*. U.S. State Department; Office of the Coordinator for Counterterrorism. April 29, 2004. http://www.state.gov/s/ct/rls/pgtrpt/2003/31759.htm.

[24] Government's Response to Defendant's Position Paper as to Sentencing Factors." *United States of America v. Enaam M. Arnaout*. United States District Court Northern District of Illinois Eastern Division. Case #: 02 CR 892. *Page 38*.

In an article published in the Taliban's *Dharb-i-Mumin* in February 2001, JEM chief Masood Azhar announced an "important . . . re-organization of [JEM's] central office." Azhar explained that the main office was being temporarily re-located from its previous home in Islamabad to Bahawalpur in order to expand its operations and accommodate "the monumental load of work" and "the public who wanted to contact Jaish." According to Azhar, JEM traded its Islamabad office for space in a local Bahawalpur mosque because "a mosque is the real centre of jihad." Azhar also thanked "sincere friends" who had ensured the "continued progress of jihad" by "gift[ing] large tracts of land to Jaish while some others had promised new pieces of land."[25] JEM maintained two physical mailing addresses for its Central Office while in Bahawalpur: Post Box no. 7. G.P.O Bahawalpur, and House No. F-16, Ehsaan Colony, Bahawalpur.[26]

On Pakistani soil alone, JEM operated at least four major military training camps located in Balakot, Muzzaffarabad, Hajeera, and Mansehra.[27] According to Pakistani researchers, the JEM facility in Balakot is "the largest military training centre of Jaish-e-Mohammed . . . directly under the supervision of Maulana Masood Azhar and run by Qari Shah Mansur."[28] Indeed, in February 2001, JEM chief Masood Azhar claimed in *Dharb-i-Mumin* to be expanding JEM's activities in Balakot. He noted, "recently, a most excellent system of education and training has been announced in Madrasah Sayyed Ahmad Shaheed rahimahullah. The students who are acquiring jihad training there will now be able to benefit from deeni and contemporary education too . . . I spend the first five days of every month in Madrasah Sayyed Ahmed Shaheed, Balakot punctually."[29] In a separate appeal for donations to help support the new mujahideen camps, Maulana Masood Azhar announced:

> "A training centre of Jaish-i-Muhammad (Sallallahu 'Alaihe wasallam) is being built in Balakot. The name of this training centre is Madrasah Sayyed Ahmad Shaheed Rahimahullahu Ta'ala. A masjid, large water tanks, a ground for physical training, and rooms for the mujahideen are being constructed on its premises. Some women have sent their jewellery for the construction of the mosque and the other buildings. Just think, what felicity

[25] Azhar, Maulana Masood. "Organizing Central Office of Jaish-i-Muhammad (sallallahu `alaihe wa sallam)." *Dharb-i-Mumin*. Vol. 2; Issue 36. January 26-February 2, 2001. http://www.dharb-i-mumin.com.

[26] Azhar, Maulana Masood. "Organizing Central Office of Jaish-i-Muhammad (sallallahu `alaihe wa sallam)." *Dharb-i-Mumin*. Vol. 2; Issue 36. January 26-February 2, 2001. http://www.dharb-i-mumin.com.

[27] Rana, Muhammad Amir. *A to Z of Jehadi Organizations in Pakistan*. Mashal Publishing; Lahore, Pakistan. ©2005. Pages 225–226.

[28] Rana, Muhammad Amir. *A to Z of Jehadi Organizations in Pakistan*. Mashal Publishing; Lahore, Pakistan. ©2005. Page 226.

[29] Azhar, Maulana Masood. "Organizing Central Office of Jaish-i-Muhammad (sallallahu `alaihe wa sallam)." *Dharb-i-Mumin*. Vol. 2; Issue 36. January 26-February 2, 2001. http://www.dharb-i-mumin.com.

> and good fortune, what blessings these women have acquired in exchange for their lifeless gold! How many will be the mujahideen, the future [martyrs] offering [prayers] in this masjid, how countless will be the Ibn-e-Qasim and Salahuddin produced, how numerous Afaq Shaheeds [referring to the past example of a JEM suicide commando] will acquire training in this ground—in the 'ajr' of all of them these Muslim women will have a share."[30]

Allegedly, according to JEM internal records, as many as 7,000 "students" were enrolled at JEM's Balakot camp in the year 2000 alone.[31] Moreover—according to sources in Pakistan—in November 2001, former JEM spokesman Abdul Jabbar convened a meeting at the same Balakot camp, where participants swore "to resist the increasing US influence in Pakistan through any means possible, including suicide bombings."[32] Dissident members of JEM have subsequently admitted that a number of their former colleagues "were adamant to carry out suicide missions against the US interests in Pakistan to avenge the fall of the Taliban regime in Afghanistan."[33] Unfortunately, it appears that those who have advocated anti-American suicide bombings "largely control the dominant faction of Jaish."[34]

Consonant with its self-declared "internationalist" mission, JEM has helped recruit Muslim converts and Pakistani Muslims living in the West, often connecting them directly with Al-Qaida in Afghanistan. In this sense, JEM and other Pakistani mujahideen organizations acted as a virtual breeding ground for other designated foreign terrorist organizations. After arriving in Pakistan in June 2001, Australian Muslim convert Shane Kent reportedly attended an orientation session at a mujahideen training camp near the Chinese border run by Jaish-e-Muhammad. After receiving his initial indoctrination from JEM, Kent graduated up the ranks and was later transferred to Al-Qaida's Al-Farooq Camp near Kandahar, Afghanistan. At least seven Saudi nationals who later served as suicide hijackers in the September 11, 2001 terrorist attacks received "basic training" at the Al-Farooq camp. According to the Congressional 9/11 Commission final report, "[t]his particular camp appears to have been the preferred location for vetting and training the potential muscle hijackers because of its proximity to Bin Ladin and senior al Qaeda leadership."[35] JEM recruit Shane Kent was finally

30 "The Fortunate Woman." *Dharb-i-Mumin*. Vol. 2; Issue 8. November 8, 2000. As reprinted at http://www.jamiat.org.za/isinfo/fwoman.html.

31 Rana, Muhammad Amir. *A to Z of Jehadi Organizations in Pakistan*. Mashal Publishing; Lahore, Pakistan. ©2005. Page 226.

32 Rana, Muhammad Amir. *A to Z of Jehadi Organizations in Pakistan*. Mashal Publishing; Lahore, Pakistan. ©2005. Page 20.

33 Rana, Muhammad Amir. *A to Z of Jehadi Organizations in Pakistan*. Mashal Publishing; Lahore, Pakistan. ©2005. Page 25.

34 Rana, Muhammad Amir. *A to Z of Jehadi Organizations in Pakistan*. Mashal Publishing; Lahore, Pakistan. ©2005. Page 27.

35 *The 9/11 Commission Report*. Final Report of the National Commission on Terrorist Attacks Upon the United States. July 22, 2004. Page 234.

arrested by police in Melbourne in November 2005 and accused of conspiring to wage "violent jihad" in Australia.[36]

In August 2004, the U.S. Bureau of Immigrations and Customs Enforcement (ICE) deported Denver, Colorado resident Sajjad Nassar to his homeland in Pakistan. Nassar—who became enraged when his brother died fighting U.S. military forces in Afghanistan—was indicted by a federal grand jury for immigration fraud and "showed deception" when given polygraph exams about his possible involvement in terrorist activities. Nasser admitted attending a JEM militant training camp during a trip to Pakistan in 2001 at the urging of a high school friend who had become a recruiter for the group. At the camp, Nasser allegedly received training in "rocket launchers, shooting from a pickup bed and other paramilitary tactics, all the while being watched over by machine gun-toting guards." Nassar claimed that after a week it became "too much running and too many push-ups" and he left the camp.[37] Despite his protestations, ICE insisted that Nassar's "participation in a training camp sponsored by Jaish-e-Mohammed . . . [which] amounted to providing material support to a designated terrorist organization."[38]

Indeed, many of those who trained with JEM ostensibly to fight Indian forces in Kashmir were tasked with missions of a much greater scope. On March 17, 2002, Sarfaraz Ahmed—a member of a JEM splinter group—carried out a suicide bombing inside the Protestant International Church in Islamabad. According to Pakistani media, Ahmed was furious at alleged atrocities committed by U.S. forces in Afghanistan against Muslims and he was said "to be close" to former JEM spokesman Maulana Abdul Jabbar. On August 5, 2002, three JEM activists blew themselves up in order to evade capture after killing six people in a brutal attack on a Christian school near Muree.[39] Jameel Suddhan and Khalique Ahmed—the two suicide bombers who rammed their explosives-laden vehicles into Pervez Musharraf's convoy on December 25, 2003—were both reportedly active members of JEM and "staunch followers" of JEM chief Maulana Masood Azhar.[40] Such incidents made it abundantly clear that the U.S. military campaign in Afghanistan had failed to dislodge a host of jihad bases and training camps inside neighboring Pakistan. In his January 2002 State of

36 Neighbour, Sally. "Aussies schooled by al-Qa`ida—Terror Hits Home." *The Australian*. November 9, 2005. Page 3.

37 Pankratz, Howard and John Ingold. "Pakistani case creates gap of opinion; Feds, 3 indicted men differ widely on facts." *The Denver Post*. April 6, 2003 Pg. B01.

38 "ICE Deports Two Linked to Terror Activity." *Inside ICE*. Vol. 1, Issue 11; September 13, 2004. http://www.ice.gov/graphics/news/insideice/articles/insideice_091304_Web4.htm.

39 Mir, Amir. "Manufacturing Martyrs." *Newsline* (Pakistan). September 2005. http://www.newsline.com.pk/NewsSep2005/sprepsep2005.htm.

40 Mir, Amir. "Manufacturing Martyrs." *Newsline* (Pakistan). September 2005. http://www.newsline.com.pk/NewsSep2005/sprepsep2005.htm.

the Union address, President George W. Bush vowed, "we will shut down terrorist camps, disrupt terrorist plans and bring terrorists to justice . . . Our military has put the terror training camps of Afghanistan out of business, yet camps still exist in at least a dozen countries. A terrorist underworld—including groups like . . . Jaish-i-Mohammed—operates in remote jungles and deserts, and hides in the centers of large cities."[41]

JEM was not the only local mujahideen organization to maintain offices and training camps inside Pakistani territory after 9/11. Harakat ul-Mujahideen boasted more than 24 different recruitment and administration offices spread across Pakistan in 2002, including the cities of Islamabad and Karachi.[42] HUM's most prominent military training camp inside Pakistan, Moaskar Shah Ismail Shaheed, is located near the town of Mansehra. According to Pakistani sources:

> "[Moaskar Shah Ismail Shaheed] is the largest training camp of Harakatul Mujahideen in Pakistan and has the capacity of training 700 mujahideen at a time. Mufti Mohammed Asghar has been in charge of this camp. Iqbal, a mujahid from Multan who used to be part of the camp management, is now working at the Kotli office [of the HUM]. He told us that the camp had been closed in March [2002], but as soon as things return to normal it will be reopened."[43]

IV. Training Camps Under the "Regime of Controlled Freedom"

In the years that have followed 9/11, Pakistani mujahideen organizations associated with the Kashmir conflict have come under increasing pressure from the Pakistani government to restrain their activities. Needless to say, the involvement of JEM and HUM activists in sectarian terror attacks and assassination attempts on Pervez Musharraf have not improved their regional standing. In 2003, following two failed bombing attacks on Musharraf, Pakistani Interior Minister Shaykh Rashid Ahmed admitted, "Kashmiri and Afghan militant groups were behind the latest assassination attempt on General Musharraf . . . It's a huge network of terrorists having tentacles from Kashmir to Afghanistan, [with] international ties."[44] Between 2002-2003, the Pakistani government officially banned several

[41] President George W. Bush's 2002 State of the Union Address. January 29, 2002. http://www.pbs.org/newshour/bb/white_house/sotu2002/sotu_text.html.

[42] Rana, Muhammad Amir. *A to Z of Jehadi Organizations in Pakistan*. Mashal Publishing; Lahore, Pakistan. ©2005. Page 250.

[43] Rana, Muhammad Amir. *A to Z of Jehadi Organizations in Pakistan*. Mashal Publishing; Lahore, Pakistan. ©2005. Page 251.

[44] Rana, Muhammad Amir. *A to Z of Jehadi Organizations in Pakistan*. Mashal Publishing; Lahore, Pakistan. ©2005. Page 20.

prominent jihad factions active in Kashmir, including JEM, HUM, and Lashkar-e-Taiba.[45]

Yet, despite a series of highly-publicized Pakistani government crackdowns, as one militant leader puts it, the militant organizations (many of which have simply been renamed) are once again up to their "old habits" and are still able to actively function under a "regime of controlled freedom."[46] Pakistani mujahideen analyst Amir Mir has commented, "At the moment, it seems that the Musharraf-establishment does not want to take any extreme measures against the militant groups . . . a complete dismantling of the militant network in Jammu and Kashmir is highly unlikely . . . those who most want Musharraf dead have traditionally been the closest allies of the Musharraf-led military establishment."[47] This odd predicament was clearly well understood by Pakistani militant organizations facing off against the Musharraf government. In 2002, a Pakistani researcher interviewed HUM member Mohammed Saleh at HUM's local office in the town of Kotli. Saleh was asked, "Jehadi camps have been shut down, how are you going to get your training now?" In response, Saleh insisted, "There is no need to worry, the camp in Mansehra will [stay] open and if it doesn't I'll just train here [at the HUM office in Kotli]."[48]

Recent developments strongly indicate that any would-be interruption in the activities of Pakistani mujahideen training camps was quite brief and only temporary. In July 2004, *New York Times* reporters were given access to Muhammad Sohail, a young Pakistani from the city of Karachi who was captured by Afghan forces only three months earlier during combat with Taliban guerillas in southern Afghanistan. Afghan officials claimed to have seized Sohail's membership card in Jamiat ul-Ansar—a post-9/11 pseudonym for HUM—and a list of phone numbers of high-level party officials. In 2002, Sohail reportedly traveled with a group of 15 others to a Jamiat/HUM training camp near Mansehra, where he received a one month training course in explosives and weapons. Following their training in Mansehra, Sohail claimed that his group was sent to Islamabad, where he met with leaders of Jamiat-ul-Ansar. Three months later, Sohail and his friends were mobilized to "fight the Americans" and were subsequently dispatched to the Afghan city of Kandahar. Other Afghan militants captured alongside Sohail described receiving military training in large, walled residential

---

[45] Rana, Muhammad Amir. *A to Z of Jehadi Organizations in Pakistan*. Mashal Publishing; Lahore, Pakistan. ©2005. Page 23.

[46] Ali, Zulfiqar. "Back to Camp." Pakistan Herald. July 11, 2005. http://www.dawn.com/herald. *See also*: Rana, Muhammad Amir. *A to Z of Jehadi Organizations in Pakistan*. Mashal Publishing; Lahore, Pakistan. ©2005. Page 23.

[47] Rana, Muhammad Amir. *A to Z of Jehadi Organizations in Pakistan*. Mashal Publishing; Lahore, Pakistan. ©2005. Pages 9–10.

[48] Rana, Muhammad Amir. *A to Z of Jehadi Organizations in Pakistan*. Mashal Publishing; Lahore, Pakistan. ©2005. Pages 106–107.

compounds in and around the Pakistani border city of Quetta, according to the governor of Afghanistan's Helmand Province.[49]

In response to reports printed in the *New York Times* and elsewhere, Pakistani journalists traveled personally to Mansehra in an attempt to confirm what Sohail and other captured Pakistani fighters had claimed during their interrogations. Though some of the camps in Mansehra were briefly abandoned in 2004, a local mujahideen guide triumphantly declared, "now we can start again."[50] According to a "top manager" of the training camp in Mansehra, all the major militant organizations—including HUM and others—had begun renovating and re-activating facilities that were briefly deserted under pressure from the Pakistani government. The manager explained, "Our transport fleet is back, electricity has been restored and the communications system is in place."[51] Pakistani media alleged that at least 13 major military camps in the Mansehra region were restored to near full operation, including in Pano Dheri, Jallo, Sufaida, Ogi, Khewari, Jabba, Batrasi, Naradoga, Akherilla, Hisari, Boi, Tanglaee and Achherian.[52]

Despite heavy scrutiny by Pakistani intelligence services, the training camps in Pakistan continued to draw foreign extremists seeking a stepladder to "greater glory." In late 2004, Shahzad Tanweer—one of the July 7, 2005 suicide bombers in London—reportedly spent time taking courses at an HUM training camp in Mansehra, where he was schooled in handling arms and explosives.[53] In the wake of the London bombings, two mujahideen confirmed to a Pakistani journalist working on contract for the *New York Times* that they had personally met Tanweer while he was training at the HUM camp in Mansehra.[54]

Meanwhile in 2005, Afghan authorities continued to intercept Pakistani nationals fighting alongside the Taliban who claimed to have received recent military training at jihad camps near Mansehra. A Pakistani militant captured in Afghanistan told a private Afghan television channel in June 2005 that he had been trained at a camp based in Mansehra.[55] According to an Afghan intelligence official quoted by the *Times*, three Pakistanis recently sentenced to prison terms for trying to assassinate the U.S. ambassador

[49] Gail, Carlotta. "Journey to Jihad: Pakistan Allows Taliban to Train, a Detained Fighter Says." *New York Times*. August 4, 2004.

[50] Ali, Zulfiqar. "Back to Camp." *Pakistan Herald*. July 11, 2005. http://www.dawn.com/herald.

[51] Ali, Zulfiqar. "Back to Camp." *Pakistan Herald*. July 11, 2005. http://www.dawn.com/herald.

[52] Ali, Zulfiqar. "Back to Camp." *Pakistan Herald*. July 11, 2005. http://www.dawn.com/herald.

[53] Herbert, Ian. "Terror Investigation: 'Khaka' and 'Sid', the committed jihadists who turned to murder." *The Independent* (London). December 17, 2005. Page 2.

[54] Rohde, David and Carlotta Gall. "In a Corner of Pakistan a Debate Rages: Are Terrorist Camps Still Functioning?" *New York Times*. August 28, 2005. Page 11.

[55] Rohde, David and Carlotta Gall. "In a Corner of Pakistan a Debate Rages: Are Terrorist Camps Still Functioning?" *New York Times*. August 28, 2005. Page 11.

in Kabul admitted they had been trained in the Mansehra region.[56] Sher Ali, yet another 28-year-old Pakistani captured en route to join the mujahideen, explained, "Nowadays they don't have legal camps [in Pakistan]. I got the feeling it was a very secret place."[57] In southern Afghanistan, Mullah Sayed Mir—a Taliban commander who defected to the Afghan government—claimed that similar training programs were also being conducted near the Pakistani town of Quetta: "The Taliban have rented houses in Pakistan, they live there and also get training there. Then, they are sent to Afghanistan."[58]

The continued proliferation of mujahideen organizations and training camps inside Pakistan was particularly highlighted during last fall's devastating South Asia earthquake. In October 2005, an Australian journalist interviewed 29-year old Tabark Hussein in the notorious region of Balakot. Hussein acknowledged that he was a member of HUM and that the organization was still quite active in the region: "We were at the Harkat ul-Mujahideen office [in Balakot] when the earthquake hit. Our commanders told us, go to the affected areas and help. We have fanned out across the region, we are in lots of affected towns."[59] Other Western journalists in the town of Parian came across a group of 14 JEM mujahideen who had mobilized to help with local relief efforts. One bearded member of the group who identified himself only as "Muaz" explained, "We're short of colleagues in this particular area because we have dispatched others to different quake-stricken areas."[60]

Besides assisting in earthquake relief, organizations like HUM and JEM nevertheless continued their operations in 2005 supporting international terrorist activity. In November, Pakistan counterterrorism forces reportedly raided the offices of an Islamic charity in Quetta known as "Madina Trust"—a JEM-linked financial front group. During the raid, one suspect was killed and two others were allegedly captured: an Pakistani member of JEM and Syrian Abu Musab al-Suri (a.k.a. Mustafa Setmariam Nasar).[61] According to the FBI:

> "Mustafa Setmariam Nasar, also known as Abu Musab al-Suri, is an al-Qa'ida member and former trainer at the Derunta and al-Ghuraba terrorist camps in Afghanistan . . . He attempted to organize his own extremist

[56] Rohde, David and Carlotta Gall. "In a Corner of Pakistan a Debate Rages: Are Terrorist Camps Still Functioning?" *New York Times*. August 28, 2005. Page 11.
[57] Rohde, David and Carlotta Gall. "In a Corner of Pakistan a Debate Rages: Are Terrorist Camps Still Functioning?" *New York Times*. August 28, 2005. Page 11.
[58] Rohde, David and Carlotta Gall. "In a Corner of Pakistan a Debate Rages: Are Terrorist Camps Still Functioning?" *New York Times*. August 28, 2005. Page 11.
[59] "The South Asian catastrophe." *Canberra Times* (Australia). October 15, 2005. Page B03.
[60] Watson, Paul. "Kashmir Militants Lend a Hand." *Los Angeles Times*. October 24, 2005. Page 3.
[61] "One terror suspect killed, another held in Pakistani raid." *Associated Press*. November 5, 2005.

group prior to September 11, 2001 - but in the wake of the attacks he pledged loyalty to Usama Bin Ladin as a member of al-Qa'ida. While in Afghanistan, Nasar worked closely with Midhat Mursi al-Sayid `Umar AKA Abu Khabab al-Masri to train extremists in poisons and chemicals. Nasar also conducted training at the al-Ghuraba camp in Afghanistan."[62]

[62] http://www.rewardsforjustice.net/english/wanted_captured/index.cfm?page=Nasar. January 2006.

DOCUMENT NO. 21

RESOLVING THE PAKISTAN-AFGHANISTAN STALEMATE

United States Institute of Peace Special Report

October 2006

Barnett R. Rubin and Abubakar Siddique

About the Report

The United States Institute of Peace has been working on the stabilization and reconstruction of Afghanistan since 2002. Institute initiatives focus on security, the rule of law, conflict resolution, building civil society, and education in Afghanistan and Afghanistan's relations with its neighbors. The Institute's Afghanistan Working Group, chaired by Dr. Barnett R. Rubin, is composed of government officials and nongovernmental organizations that discuss critical issues facing Afghanistan with top experts and policymakers and work directly to help the Afghan people build a peaceful and prosperous society.

The idea for this report started with discussions by Barnett Rubin with delegates to the Afghan constitutional *Loya Jirga*, President Hamid Karzai, and journalist Ahmed Rashid in December 2003. In spring and summer 2004 Abubakar Siddique conducted field work on the current positions of the diverse stakeholders in this complex region. During subsequent trips the coauthors carried out additional research, most recently in July–August 2006, when Rubin visited Afghanistan and Siddique visited Pakistan.

Grants from the Rockefeller Foundation, the Open Society Institute, the Royal Government of Norway, and the Government of the United Kingdom supported the research. The authors gratefully acknowledge the assistance of Afrasiab Khattak and Ahmed Rashid in Pakistan and Omar Zakhilwal, Rasul Amin, Hamed Wardak, and Humayun Hamidzada in Afghanistan. They also thank many anonymous informants and commentators from Pakistan, Afghanistan, and the United States. Ahmed Rashid, Marvin Weinbaum, and Sebastien Trives reviewed earlier drafts.

Dr. Barnett R. Rubin is chair of the Institute's Afghanistan Working Group and director of studies at the Center on International Cooperation at New York University. Abubakar Siddique is a journalist and Fulbright scholar who has covered Afghanistan, Pakistan, and Central Asia for many years.

The views expressed in this report do not necessarily reflect the views of the United States institute of Peace, which does not advocate specific policy positions.

About the Institute

The United States Institute of Peace is an independent, nonpartisan institution established and funded by Congress. Its goals are to help prevent and resolve violent conflicts, promote post-conflict peacebuilding, and increase conflict-management tools, capacity, and intellectual capital worldwide. The Institute does this by empowering others with knowledge, skills, and resources, as well as by its direct involvement in conflict zones around the globe.

Board of Directors

Members Ex Officio

Summary

- The Taliban and al Qaeda insurgencies today are equally active in Afghanistan and Pakistan. The nationalist insurgency in Pakistani Baluchistan, which Pakistani leaders assert receives support from Indian agents in Afghanistan, also aggravates relations between the two countries. The challenges of violent insurgency require both countries to address their relationship, particularly as it affects the border areas. Formation of such a policy is essential to the vital interests of the United States, NATO, and the international community, which has committed itself to the effort in Afghanistan through UN Security Council resolutions and other measures.

- Afghanistan and Pakistan have had largely antagonistic relations under all governments but the Taliban since Pakistan was created as part of the partition of India in 1947. Some elements of friction were also inherited from conflicts between Afghanistan and India when it was under British imperial rule. Afghanistan's governments, including that of the Taliban, have never recognized the Durand Line between the two countries as an international border and have made claims on the Pashtun and Baluch regions of Pakistan. Today's cross-border insurgencies, with their sanctuaries and support networks in Pakistan, are nurtured by the same sources as previous conflicts, as well as global Islamist movements.
- Arrangements to secure the frontier of the British Empire in the nineteenth century by isolating Afghanistan as a buffer state do not work for a twenty-first-century borderland integrated into networks of global conflict. The United States and other external powers that seek to support the new order in Afghanistan and stabilize both Pakistan and Afghanistan should encourage a multidimensional process of dialogue and peacebuilding focused on the problems of the border region. Pressure may also be needed to convince some actors to engage seriously in such a process, but pressure alone will not succeed.
- A process should work toward reforms in the Federally Administered Tribal Areas (FATA) of Pakistan, leading to their integration into Pakistani national politics and administration; the recognition by Afghanistan of the international border; assured access by Afghanistan to Pakistani ports and transit facilities; the maintenance by both countries of open borders for trade, investment, and cultural relations; agreement by both countries and by India to keep the India-Pakistan dispute out of Afghanistan's bilateral relations with both; and agreements on both sides to cease supporting or harboring violent opposition movements against the other.
- The United States, NATO, and the UN must agree to send a common message to Islamabad: that the persistence of Taliban havens in Pakistan is a threat to international peace and security that Pakistan must address immediately. They also must agree to urge Afghanistan and India to do all in their power to encourage Pakistan to make difficult decisions by addressing sources of Pakistani insecurity, including issues relating to the border region and Kashmir. They should actively promote this process and act as guarantors and funders of any agreements that result from it.

Introduction

On January 13, 2006, the sleepy village of Damadola in the Bajaur tribal district of Pakistan on the Afghan frontier became the focus of global attention. With the American news networks in the lead, global media broadcast coverage of the Central Intelligence Agency's attempt to kill al Qaeda's number two, Ayman al-Zawahiri, who had reportedly attended a dinner in the village to commemorate the Muslim holiday *`Id-ul-Adha*. Pictures of tribal members digging dead bodies from the debris of their bombed-out mud houses were beamed around the globe. Pakistan's Islamist political parties called for severing all ties with the United States for this attack on the country's sovereignty (Reuters 2006). President Pervez Musharraf, who initially minimized the attack 's importance, later announced that at least five top al Qaeda figures had been killed, although al-Zawahiri himself had escaped (Khan 2006).

Three days later, in what appeared to be a reprisal, a suicide bomber riding a motorcycle blew himself up among spectators of a wrestling match in the southern Afghan town of Spin Boldak, across from the Pakistani border town of Chaman. It was Afghanistan's worst suicide attack, killing twenty-two civilians and leaving dozens more injured (Synovitz 2006).

This was the largest in a rash of suicide attacks in Afghanistan, some of which have taken place even in the relatively secure northern and western provinces (Qureshi and Sarwaryar 2006). With 1,500 violent deaths, more members of the Afghan security forces and the U.S.-led international coalition were killed in combat in 2005 than in any year since the overthrow of the Taliban regime in late 2001. In the first six months of 2006, Afghanistan faced thirty-two suicide attacks, unprecedented in the country's three decades of violence (Karzai and Jones 2006). Since May 2006 violence has reached new levels. Some 800 insurgents, civilians, and soldiers died in the four southwestern provinces. The reorganized Taliban, operating in Afghanistan from bases in Pakistan, form the bulk of the insurgency, which also includes elements led by Afghan Islamist Gulbuddin Hikmatyar's *Hizb-i-Islami* and foreign jihadi forces, including the leadership of al Qaeda.

The violence, which has spread to both sides of the frontier, escalated in the run-up to President Bush's mid-March 2006 visit to South Asia—especially in Waziristan, a craggy region of 5,000 square miles divided into the South and North Agencies, or tribal districts. Some 300 Islamist militants, civilians, and Pakistani soldiers died in the fighting, which forced tens of thousands of people to flee the Pakistani town of Miran Shah, administrative headquarters of the North Waziristan tribal district. In neighboring South Waziristan, skirmishes, rocketing, assassinations, and land-mine blasts continue (*Economist* 2006). Since al Qaeda's retreat from Afghanistan in winter 2001, some tribal areas have become a small-scale copy of Taliban-controlled Afghanistan, where Islamist militants can recover and plan fresh operations while gradually imposing their will on the secluded region. Violence also has spread into the adjacent districts of the Northwest Frontier Province (Hussain 2006).

Hot Wars on the Borders

Despite the presence of some 80,000 Pakistani soldiers, Islamist militias have grown along the border. Before the fighting in Miran Shah in spring 2006, the violence in Waziristan had claimed the lives of some 250 members of the security forces and 300 civilians. Unofficial casualty counts place the figure much higher.

The Pakistan military also claimed to have killed 194 foreign militants and 552 of their local supporters in periodic operations since mid-2002. The majority of these fighters were Uzbeks, Chechens, and Arabs led by Qari Tahir Yuldashev, erstwhile leader of the Islamic Movement of Uzbekistan, who survived American bombing in the northern Afghan town of Kunduz in 2001. Two senior al Qaeda figures, Haitham al-Yamani and Abu Hamza Rabia, were killed in North Waziristan in 2005. International media attributed their deaths to Hellfire missiles fired from CIA drones (ABC News 2005; Peters 2005). In April 2006 Pakistani forces killed Muhsin Matwalli Atwah, an Egyptian known as Abdul Rahman, in an air raid north of Miran Shah. Charged with being a bomb maker who had participated in the 1998 bombing of the U.S. embassies in Kenya and Tanzania, Rahman had a $5 million price on his head (Gall and Khan 2006). A week later a Saudi national, Abu Marwan al-Suri, was killed at a checkpoint in Khar, the administrative headquarters of the Bajaur tribal district. Known for his expertise with explosives, he had been one of the targets of the January 13 strike in Damadola (*Dawn* 2006).

Another insurgency along the border, in resource-rich southwestern Baluchistan province, also remains a major headache for Islamabad. Desolate but rich in mineral resources and hydrocarbons, Baluchistan is important to Pakistan's future development. This province provides Pakistan with most of its gas. With $150 million in Chinese assistance, Pakistan is building a major deepwater seaport in the small fishing town of Gwadar. Elsewhere it wants to dig oil and gas wells and excavate gold and other minerals. Today's Baluch nationalist rebels view these projects as exploitation of their province's wealth for the exclusive benefit of the Pakistani state, dominated by military officers and bureaucrats from Punjab and Urdu-speaking migrants from India who often call themselves *mohajir* (immigrants). The Baluch nationalists call for maximum provincial autonomy and control over their resources before they will agree to mega-development projects such as the Gwadar port.

Since the 1947 creation of Pakistan, autonomy-minded Baluch nationalists have carried out five insurgencies, in 1948, 1958–59, 1962–63, 1973–77, and 2004–06. The military suppressed all of these revolts. During the 1970s insurgency 6,000 Baluch tribesmen and 3,000 Pakistani soldiers died. Some 30,000 Baluch tribesmen went into exile in southern Afghanistan for more than a decade (Hussain 2006).

A dormant insurgency in the region escalated in December 2005, when Baluch nationalist guerillas fired rockets at a gathering presided over by Pakistani President Gen. Pervez Musharraf while he was visiting Baluchistan. By June 2006, hundreds of Baluch militants, civilians, paramilitary fighters, and soldiers had died in the skirmishes and as a result of insurgent sabotage. The killing of Nawab Akbar Bugti, a respected politician and former governor of Baluchistan, made the insurgency both a major national crisis and a critical factor in Pakistan's relations with Afghanistan and India, where governments, parliamentarians, and the press condemned the killing.

The Islamist militancy and ethnic revolt on both sides of the Durand Line, the 2,400-kilometer frontier between Afghanistan and Pakistan, are linked to many complex global and regional problems. Policymakers and journalists say Osama bin Laden and his deputy Zawahiri are hiding somewhere in the northeastern part of this rugged region. In December 2001, under intense U.S. pressure, Pakistan deployed regular military units in the Kurram and Khyber agencies to block al Qaeda's exodus from Tora Bora, but a delay in their arrival and the U.S. decision not to deploy available U.S. Marines to the area allowed bin Laden and his followers to escape. The number of Pakistani troops steadily grew to 80,000 and drastically changed the region, which had been under "indirect rule" for more than a century.

Afghanistan never has recognized the Durand Line as an international border. The administration of President Hamid Karzai, charging Pakistan with supporting the Taliban, has leaned toward India. Further antagonized, Pakistan blames rising Indian influence in Afghanistan for the violent nationalist insurgency in Baluchistan. This dispute presents a problem for the United States, which has been trying to dislodge al Qaeda and the Taliban from the region since early 2002. U.S. policies, however, have not addressed the long-standing conflicts over the frontier region.

Pakistan and Afghanistan inherited their multilayered border and its complex governance mechanisms from the British Empire. In the late nineteenth century the British tried to make Afghanistan an isolated buffer state between their empire and Russia, but nineteenth-century border arrangements on the margins of an empire do not work in an area at the heart of twenty-first-century global strategy.

The neighbors now need to resolve the myriad problems of the border region. They have to overcome past differences and circumvent the violence unleashed by nonstate actors, sometimes with official support, to reach a comprehensive settlement. The international community in general and the United States in particular have to facilitate such a process through diplomacy and help pay for the long overdue reforms and economic development on the rugged frontier. They also may have to press reluctant actors to explore alternatives to deeply entrenched policies. Kabul and Islamabad must formulate policies to promote a peaceful and prosperous future rather than remaining hostages to the bitter disputes of the past.

Old Conflict and New Bitterness

The Durand Line is named after the British foreign secretary, Sir Henry Mortimer Durand, who demarcated the boundary with agents of the Afghan Amir Abdul Rahman Khan in 1893. The Pakistan side of the border area includes the provinces of Baluchistan, the North West Frontier Province (NWFP), and the adjacent FATA. On the Afghan side the frontier stretches from Nuristan province in the northeast to Nimruz in the southwest. The border region is predominantly inhabited by ethnic Pashtuns, who were divided by the Durand Line. The 30 million to 35 million Pashtuns in Pakistan represent 15 to 20 percent of the country's population. In Afghanistan they are the largest ethnic group, comprising about half its estimated 30 million people. The Baluch also live on both sides of the Durand Line in the southwest border region, as well as in neighboring Iran.

This region's passes and trading routes have connected South Asia to Central and West Asia for millennia. The political and legal structure of the region is a product of centuries of empire building and resistance, but it started to assume its contemporary form in the early nineteenth century, when the British East India Company was expanding toward northwest India. About 25 years after taking Delhi in 1804, the British became concerned about czarist expansion toward Central Asia. During the first Anglo-Afghan war (1840–42), the British invaded Afghanistan but were defeated by an uprising in Kabul that turned into a rout.

By 1876 Russian advances in Central Asia reached the Amu Darya, the river that now constitutes Afghanistan's northern border. The Afghan amir's efforts to establish friendly relations with his northern neighbor led the British to launch the second Anglo-Afghan war in 1879, deposing the amir and occupying Kabul. This was the peak of the "Great Game," when the European powers vied for control of Central Asia, with Afghanistan as the central arena.

The British forced Amir Yaqub Khan to sign the Treaty of Gandamak in 1879, while their army was occupying Kabul. Successive Afghan governments have repudiated this treaty, claiming it was signed under duress. Afghanistan agreed to let the British open an embassy and gave up control of several frontier districts, including most of today's FATA and parts of Baluchistan. The treaty guaranteed British support to Kabul against external aggression and provided an annual subsidy of money and arms with which the Afghan ruler was to subdue his own territory. Anglo-Russian commissions demarcated Afghanistan's northern and western borders with Central Asia, Iran, and China between 1870 and 1896.

Following the second Anglo-Afghan war, the British set about developing what they hoped would be a durable border regime, involving separate statuses and mechanisms for Afghanistan, the border tribes, and the Pashtun and Baluch territories under the administration of British India. They invited Abdul Rahman Khan, a nephew of Amir Sher Ali Khan living in exile in Russian Turkistan, to assume the throne in 1880. During a brutal twenty-year reign, the "Iron Amir" laid the foundation of modern Afghanistan. He gave the country its administrative institutions and agreed to the formal demarcation of its borders, including the Durand Line. The amir always contended that excluding the tribal territories from Afghanistan was a mistake, as he could control the tribes better than the British could.

The demarcation of the Durand Line required the British to establish a regime to deal with the tribal borderlands. Five tribal regions were placed under the direct control of the central government in Delhi. After the creation of Pakistan in 1947, three new agencies were carved out of other tribal districts. The British devised a special legal structure called the Frontier Crimes Regulations (FCR). Evolving through the late nineteenth century, the regulations were finally promulgated as statutory law under Viceroy Lord Curzon in 1901 and are still the legal regime in FATA.

After the failure of the British "forward policy" in the first Anglo-Afghan war, Delhi settled on a "close border" policy to make the frontier into a buffer. To British administrators, frontier meant a "wide tract of border country, hinterland or a buffer state." The most important feature of this arrangement was its transformation into a "frontier of separation," in contrast to a "frontier of contact." The result was the "threefold frontier." The first frontier was the outer edge of the directly administered territory (the river Indus in the nineteenth century and the settled districts of NWFP in the mid-twentieth century); the second was the Pashtun tribal area between Afghanistan and the settled districts of NWFP, which was placed under indirect rule; and the third comprised the protectorates of Nepal and Afghanistan on the outer edge of the sphere of influence.

In recent times Pakistan has used its support for the anti-Soviet *mujahidin* and then the Taliban to ensure that in the event of conflict with India, Afghanistan would provide Pakistan with support and use of its land and air space if needed. Pakistani military planners referred to this as the quest for "strategic depth." The similarity of the threefold frontier to this quest in Afghanistan illustrates the continuity of strategic policy in this region.

The 1907 Anglo-Russian convention formally ended the Great Game. It divided Persia into zones of influence of the two great powers, protecting Afghanistan's western borders from Russian penetration. Both powers agreed to recognize Chinese control over Tibet. Russia conceded Afghanistan to the British sphere of influence, but Britain was not to occupy or annex any part of the country or interfere in its internal affairs. Amir Habibullah of Afghanistan declared the convention illegal because Afghanistan was not a party to the agreement, but his protest went unheeded.

Popular resistance movements throughout the century of British rule also shaped the border region. At times these were local affairs, as when a clan or a tribe resisted the British; but on other occasions the tribes launched wider movements, sometimes coordinating with the larger Afghan and Indian struggles against European colonialism. Charismatic tribal leaders or clerics led many such rebellions. These leaders fought small-scale battles and larger wars, such as the one in Waziristan, where the British kept 50,000 soldiers, more troops than on the rest of the subcontinent, as late as the 1930s. On other occasions the British used more indirect counterinsurgency methods. Seventy thousand tribal members serving as scouts under British officers suppressed the Great Tribal Uprising of 1897, in which most Pashtun tribes east of the Durand Line joined in an uncoordinated war against the British.

As Afghanistan lacked a modern army, the rulers of Kabul often mobilized the tribes to fight in the early twentieth century. The modernist and nationalist King Amanullah declared jihad for full independence from the British in 1919. Pashtun tribal *lashkars*, or posses, from both sides of the Durand Line fought the month-long war. Afghanistan subsequently obtained full sovereignty from a weakened British Empire in the 1919 Treaty of Rawalpindi.

In 1929, King Amanullah lost his throne in a revolt led by a Tajik guerrilla leader, Habibullah Kalakani, who was supported by conservative clergy. A tribal posse headed by the king's distant cousin, Nadir Khan, and composed of Pashtuns from both sides of the Durand Line, put an end to the rule of Amir Habibullah II, commonly known as *Bacha-yi Saqao* (son of the water carrier) in admiration or mockery of his humble origins.

In return for their military services, Nadir Shah gave the tribes of the *Loya*, or Greater Paktia region of southeastern Afghanistan, maximum tribal autonomy. He exempted them from taxation and conscription on the assumption that they could mobilize lashkars if needed. Throughout the twentieth century Afghanistan also maintained a sizable number of tribal sympathizers east of the Durand Line through honorary and material rewards, including recruitment into the officer corps (Trives 2006).

Members of the tribes that had fought for Nadir Shah from both sides of the Durand Line predominated among the military officers trained in the Soviet Union, who joined or sympathized with the Afghan communist groups.

Modern Pashtun nationalism emerged in NWFP in 1930, when British troops killed unarmed protestors in Peshawar. Khan Abdul Ghaffar Khan headed the Afghan *jirga,* which was later called the *Khudai Khidmatgars* (servants of God). Ghaffar Khan allied with the Indian National Congress to win the 1937 and 1946 elections in NWFP, after which his movement formed the provincial governments. The Khudai Khidmatgars parted ways with Congress in 1946, when the latter accepted the British partition plan providing for a plebiscite in the province on joining India or the new state of Pakistan. This movement demanded inclusion of an option to establish an independent state of Pashtunistan.

In August 1947 two states, India and Pakistan, emerged from the British Indian empire. The Afghan government voted against Pakistan's admission to the United Nations in 1947, arguing that Pakistan should not be recognized as long as the "Pashtunistan" problem remained unresolved. Afghanistan withdrew this objection after only a month, however, and in February 1948 it became one of the first nations to establish diplomatic relations with Pakistan. The Pashtun nationalist Khudai Khidmatgars moderated their stand soon after partition and declared their loyalty to the new country. Some tribal leaders in FATA maintained militias in the name of Pashtunistan. Successive governments in Pakistan tried to handle the Pashtun nationalist claims by suppressing their advocates.

Pakistan then ended the British policy of military control of tribal areas by withdrawing army units from the agencies. Soon Pakistan was able to mobilize a sizable Pashtun tribal posse from both sides of the Durand Line to fight for control of Kashmir, a Muslim majority state, when its maharaja declared accession to India in 1947. Although the tribal members made a spectacular march, they failed to capture Srinagar, the capital of Kashmir. Since 1947 Pakistan and India each have occupied parts of Kashmir, divided by the line of control. Today Kashmir remains divided between India and Pakistan. India claims that the state of Jammu and Kashmir is now an integral part of the Republic of India, while Pakistan still demands implementation of UN Security Council resolutions calling for a plebiscite on whether Kashmir should join India or Pakistan. Some Kashmiri movements have demanded independence.

The Durand Line border dispute soon brought the Cold War to the Khyber Pass. In July 1949, after a Pakistani bombing raid on an Afghan border village, the Afghan government convened a *loya jirga,* or grand tribal assembly, in Kabul. This supreme national decision-making body declared support for the Pashtunistan demand. The jirga affirmed the Afghan government's position that Pakistan was a new state rather than a successor state to British India, and all past treaties with the British pertaining to the status of the border were therefore null and void. Such agreements included the 1893 Durand Agreement, the Anglo-Afghan Pact of 1905, the Treaty of Rawalpindi of 1919, and the Anglo-Afghan Treaty of 1921. It reaffirmed Afghanistan's rejection of the 1879 Treaty of Gandamak. Afghanistan eventually turned to the Soviet Union for military aid, because its position on Pashtunistan made it impossible to receive aid from the United States, which was allied with Pakistan.

For Pashtun nationalists in Pakistan and Afghanistan, Pashtunistan meant different things, ranging from an independent country to an autonomous province of Pakistan to an integral part of Afghanistan. The Soviet Union and India paid lip service to Pashtuni-stan for decades. The Soviets wanted to prevent Afghanistan from joining any Western military alliance and to pressure Pakistan; India wanted to divert Pakistan's military resources by cultivating the fear of an unstable western border.

The Pashtunistan demand served domestic Afghan political purposes as well. In the twentieth century successive Afghan rulers used the issue to strengthen Pashtun ethnic support for the state. By harnessing the state to the Pashtun ethnic cause, however, the government intensified ethnolinguistic rivalry between Pashtuns and non-Pashtuns.

In 1961 relations between the neighbors hit rock bottom when Pakistan closed the border and the countries broke off diplomatic relations. With Afghanistan's principal trade route cut off, the Afghan economy was pressed to the breaking point. Differences within the royal family led to the resignation of Prime Minister Daud Khan in 1963. After ten years of constitutional monarchy with a contentious but ineffective parliament that dissolved the government three times, Daud launched a bloodless coup against his cousin, Zahir Shah. He justified it in part by claiming that Zahir's government had neglected Pashtunistan to improve relations with the United States and Pakistan.

Zahir's government was accused of not responding forcefully to the firing of the National Awami Party provincial governments in NWFP and Baluchistan by Pakistani Premier Zulfiqar Ali Bhutto in 1973. These governments were composed mainly of Pashtun and Baluch nationalists. After the dismissals, Nawab Bugti was appointed governor of Baluchistan. Eventually he became the political leader of the 2005–06 Baluch insurgency and was killed by the Pakistan military on August 26, 2006.

After the creation of Bangladesh in 1971, the Pashtun and Baluch nationalist movements along the western borders posed the most active secessionist threats to the remainder of Pakistan. Thus the 1972–77 government of

Zulfiqar Ali Bhutto both cracked down on nationalists and sought to extend Pakistani state authority by bringing economic development to the border region and FATA. It built some roads and hospitals and a few factories.

This meager development effort, however, was not matched by any political reforms. On the contrary, Bhutto's administration strengthened the colonial system by incorporating the border regime into the 1973 constitution. Pakistan also started supporting Afghan Islamists who opposed Daud's secular ethno-nationalism. The Islamists had publicly opposed the partition of Pakistan to create Bangladesh in 1971 and protested against foreign influence in Afghanistan by both the Soviet Union and the West.

The long history of each state offering sanctuary to the other's opponents has built bitterness and mistrust between the two neighbors. This intensified in the 1970s, when Kabul extended shelter to some 30,000 Marri Baluch tribesmen who had escaped a Pakistani military crackdown after the nationalist insurgency in Baluchistan. Islamabad then extended refuge and military training to Afghan Islamists such as Ahmed Shah Massoud and Gulbuddin Hikmatyar, who staged an abortive uprising with Pakistani support in 1975. Pakistan hosted the Afghan mujahidin in the 1980s, while Afghanistan's pro-Soviet regime provided safe haven to *al-Zulfiqar*, a militant offshoot of the Pakistan Peoples Party. Headed by Murtaza Bhutto, the group intended to destabilize Gen. Muhammad Zia-ul-Haq's military regime, which had overthrown and hanged Murtaza's father, Zulfiqar Ali Bhutto. The current claims and counterclaims of sheltering each other's opponents indicate that the same strategies may be continuing.

Globalization of the Conflict around the Borderlands

The final collapse of the Afghan Durrani ruling dynasty with the overthrow of President Daud by communist factions in April 1978 shattered cooperative relations in the borderlands, precipitating the rounds of war that continue. The Christmas Eve 1979 Soviet invasion was the first major step toward globalizing the conflict in the border region.

The Soviet invasion made Pakistan a frontline ally of the United States. The country's ruling military virtually had a free hand to shape the Afghan resistance based in the refugee camps along the Durand Line. Pakistan wanted to prevent the establishment of Afghan nationalist guerillas on its soil and thus refused to recognize parties and exiles associated with the old regime. It guided the supplies from the United States, Saudi Arabia, Western Europe, and China toward the Islamists, who were also generously funded by wealthy private donors in the Gulf. The regime of Gen. Muhammad Zia-ul-Haq promoted the jihad in neighboring Afghanistan as part of its overriding priority: using the "Islamization" of Pakistan to legitimize military rule. In the process it militarized and radicalized the border region.

From the funding of thousands of Islamic *madrassahs*, or seminaries, to the arming of domestic Islamist organizations, Pakistan experienced a major transformation. Pakistan engaged in the successive wars in and around Afghanistan—the Cold War struggle, the post–Cold War civil conflict, and the war on terror—as a way of dealing with its basic national security threat: India, a country with more than eight times its population and economic resources. India's elites, at least in Pakistani perceptions, do not fully accept the legitimacy of Pakistan's existence. Pakistan's support for Islamist parties (especially for the Islamic Party of Gulbuddin Hikmatyar) and then for the Taliban constituted attempts to impose on Afghanistan a government that would never allow an Indian presence on its territory, giving the Pakistani military a secure border and strategic depth. In other words, Pakistan sought to support a client regime in Afghanistan that was supposed to provide a space for the retreat and recuperation of the Pakistani military in case of a confrontation with India. This policy was a continuation under different conditions of the British policy of treating Afghanistan as part of the security buffer zone of South Asia.

After the Soviet withdrawal under the Geneva Accords of April 14, 1988, completed in February 1989, a U.S.-Soviet dialogue tried to prepare the ground for a transitional government to preside over elections. Had they been implemented, the Geneva Accords would have resulted in a weak Afghan government, still close to the Soviet Union but without a Soviet troop deployment. In effect, Afghanistan would have become a de facto buffer within the Soviet sphere of influence. The war continued, however, in the absence of great-power agreement over the political settlement in the borderlands, eventually resulting in state collapse in Afghanistan. The United States and Pakistan pursued an anti-Soviet "rollback" policy (equivalent to the British "forward policy") to wipe out Soviet influence in Afghanistan by continuing to aid and arm the anti-Soviet Afghan guerrillas, the mujahidin. During this period, when many Afghans considered the jihad ended with the departure of Soviet troops, the rollback policy increasingly relied on Salafi Arab fighters who joined the jihad for very different reasons than Afghans had.

Representative rule in Pakistan was restored following Zia-ul-Haq's death in an air crash in August 1988. The Pashtun nationalist political parties with seats in the Pakistani national and provincial legislatures moderated their demands, replacing the name Pashtunistan with "Pashtunkhwa," denoting a province for all Pashtuns living east of the Durand Line. Such a province would include NWFP, some districts of Baluchistan, and the tribal agencies. The change to superficially civilian government between 1988 and 1999 hardly affected Pakistan's Afghan policy, which remained in the hands of the military.

In October 1994, the Taliban, a previously unknown group of clerics from the puritanical Sunni Deobandi sect, initiated a military movement to overpower the mujahidin factions. The Taliban originated in Kandahar province of Afghanistan and the neighboring Baluchistan province of Pakistan. They showed to what extent the mass violence, migrations, and ideological mobilization of the past three decades had transformed the border region. They are a phenomenon of the borderland, a joint Afghan-Pakistan network and organization. Afghan refugees, their children, and their grandchildren have coped with and interpreted their experiences in the refugee camps, tribal territories, and urban slums of Pakistan through the lens of the Islamist education that Pakistan's military regime and its Saudi and U.S. patrons offered them alongside their classmates from Pakistan, including FATA.

The unmonitored border and the ungoverned frontier between the two countries provided the space in which Pakistan could use the resulting social networks for asymmetrical warfare that served its strategic purpose on the Afghan and Kashmiri fronts, while sheltering itself through nuclear deterrence from conventional reprisal. The instability of this arrangement twice has precipitated the threat of nuclear escalation, once over the 1999 Pakistani intrusion in Kargil, in Indian-occupied Kashmir, and then over the 2002 attack on the Indian parliament by a Pakistan-based terrorist group (Coll 2006).

Pakistan's attempt to stabilize Afghanistan and gain strategic depth through control by the Taliban constituted a reprise with variations on the theme of a forward policy composed by the British Empire. This policy was to place Afghanistan under a nonhostile regime, harsh enough to control opposition with some military and financial assistance, and guarantee that hostile forces (mainly India, but also Russia and Iran) would not gain a foothold in the adjacent territory. Under the British, however, the Afghan ruler was an autocrat who used Islam to strengthen the central state while bringing the clergy under control. Founded as a state for Indian Muslims and basing its power on an alliance of the military and the mosque, Pakistan used Afghan clerics. Their Islamic allegiances would ensure their cooperation against secular Hindu India, Pashtun nationalists, and tribal leaders on both sides of the Durand Line.

The Taliban captured Kabul in September 1996. They moved north of the capital in a failed offensive in May–June 1997 but captured most of the north and center of Afghanistan by August 1998, only a few days after the bombing of U.S. embassies in Kenya and Tanzania. These bombings revealed to high-level policymakers and the general public a new dimension of globalization of the Afghan conflict—the consolidation of Osama bin Laden's international network of anti-Western Islamist militants now known as al Qaeda.

In the 1980s thousands of Islamist radicals from the Arab world and a lesser number from Southeast Asia flocked to Pakistan to fight and assist the anti-Soviet jihad in Afghanistan. They established support networks in NWFP and bases along the Afghan side of the Durand Line in areas such as the Jaji district of Khost (the al-Masada or "lion's den" camp) and Khugiani district of Nangarhar (Tora Bora). The concept of al Qaeda formed in Peshawar, Pakistan, in the late 1980s. A decade later it had a somewhat formal organizational structure whose aims and objectives bin Laden and Zawahiri announced to the world from Khost, Afghanistan, in 1998.

Al Qaeda was founded in the borderlands, but none of its leaders was Pakistani or Afghan. The war in the borderlands produced the leaders and ideologues of modern global jihad such as bin Laden, Zawahiri, and the Palestinian scholar Abdullah Azzam, who was killed in Peshawar in November 1989. After the Soviet withdrawal in 1989, many Arabs remained, and a second wave of jihadis gathered in the borderlands. During the 1990s additional waves of Islamists from Chechnya, Central Asia, Chinese Turkistan, Southeast Asia, and Europe joined the Arabs to form a truly global conglomerate.

This globalization of the Afghan conflict also introduced structural changes to Pashtun society and politics on both sides of the Durand Line. The fragmented tribal nature of this polity provided fertile ground for ideological penetration. Pashtun nationalism was modernist and secular, associated with the royalist elite, tribal leaders, and intellectuals. The Islamic conservatives joined the nationalists to oppose foreign domination during British colonialism, but they opposed the adoption of Western or liberal social or political institutions or values. The radical Islamists who began to organize in the 1960s opposed liberal institutions with at least equal fervor, but they tried to Islamize rather than reject institutions or concepts such as the nation-state, political ideology, political party, revolution, and development.

Pashtuns are no more or less prone to extremism than members of any other ethnic group in the region, but intelligence agencies and radical movements have used their cross-border ties and strategic location to spread extremism. The war in Afghanistan provided Pakistan with a golden opportunity to act on its long-standing desire to weaken Pashtun nationalism. It actively supported pan-Islamism among the Afghan refugees while bankrolling Pakistani Islamist parties in the border region. This resulted in a newer brand of Pashtun Islamism, some of whose characteristics were manifested and reinforced during the Taliban's ascent to power in Afghanistan, where pan-Islamist solidarity surpassed tribalism and ethnic cohesion.

While decades of Pakistani investment in Pashtun Islamism turned it into a formidable political force and reduced the nationalist threat, it also created its own transborder ethnic realities, which are backfiring against its original sponsors, whose primary allegiance is to the state of Pakistan. The operational and strategic vision of a Pakistani nation-state directly clashes with the pan-Islamism of Talibanization, which demands a complete overhaul of the state and society in Pakistan, Afghanistan, and beyond. This new reality, however, corresponds to the goals of some in Pakistan who envisage a broader Islamist union of Pakistan, Afghanistan, and Central Asia.

During the early 1990s, Afghanistan became an international pariah as the United States walked away from the Cold War's last battleground. Successive U.S. administrations did not consider the collapse of Afghanistan as a threat to the United States or a global strategic issue. Not until the attacks of September 11, 2001, did they heed warnings that in the absence of legitimate order in the borderlands, a global terrorist opposition was consolidating its links and building its skills, using the human and physical capital they had supplied to these networks through Pakistan in pursuit of the Cold War strategic agenda.

The hurried negotiations between the United States and Pakistan immediately after 9/11 changed Pakistan's behavior, but not its interests. Pakistan first asked for a pause to allow it to install a "moderate Taliban" government in Afghanistan that would break with al Qaeda. When that failed, Pakistan demanded that the Northern Alliance, backed by Russia, Iran, and, most importantly, India, not be allowed to enter Kabul or form the government. The U.S. agreement to support UN efforts to dilute Northern Alliance control with remnants of Afghanistan's royal regime and some technocrats did little to mollify the generals in Islamabad. Nonetheless, to save its nuclear deterrent and military supply relationship with the United States, Islamabad acquiesced in reining in its use of asymmetrical warfare, while keeping the capacity in reserve.

The presence of the United States, the UN, and the International Security Assistance Force (ISAF, the UN-mandated, multinational force in Afghanistan, under NATO command since August 2003) initially acted as a deterrent to both overt external subversion and open warfare among the power-holders the United States had re-armed in the war to oust the Taliban. This deterrent created an opportunity to build an Afghan state that could be reintegrated into the regions it borders. Given the cross-border movements of capital, trade, population, arms, ideologies, and identities, however, it was no longer possible for Afghanistan to play the role of a buffer or insulator state separating South Asia, Central Asia, and the Gulf. Instead, Afghanistan would have to become what its government calls a "land bridge" linking these areas.

The prerequisite for the stabilization of Afghanistan under these conditions has been the formation of an Afghan state with sufficient resources and legitimacy to control and develop its territory while posing no threat to any of its neighbors, especially Pakistan. Its deep interpenetration of Afghan society and politics enables Pakistan to play the role of spoiler whenever it chooses. For the United States, such a project would have required additional troops, whether from the coalition or ISAF, especially in border provinces; rapid investment in the infrastructure and development of the country; and an active program of diplomacy and regional cooperation. The Bush administration's opposition to U.S. investment in "nation-building," which it did not relax until 2003, led to delays in all such projects. Nor did the United States or others address the long-standing conflicts over the frontier.

In this context, especially given the new U.S. doctrine of preventive war, Pakistan and other neighbors of Afghanistan see the consolidation of a state dependent on the United States as a long-term threat. Pakistan sees the United States increasingly favoring India, particularly in the area of nuclear cooperation, and faces an Afghan government whose rhetoric has become more confrontational. As a result, Pakistan sees no strategic advantage in eliminating the Taliban, who have established themselves in parts of southwestern and southeastern Afghanistan, control parts of FATA, and have their main headquarters and support networks in Baluchistan. The ability of this Pakistan-based group to destabilize Afghanistan sends a message that Islamabad, not Delhi or Kabul, is the key to stability in the region.

These transborder political and military networks are reinforced by the economic components of "network war," which relies on transnational links of communications, funding, recruitment, and armament, rather than a territorial base. Trafficking in drugs, arms, and other items, including people, is an important element of network war, and smuggling is the classic livelihood of the borderlands; both of the major frontier ethnic groups—Pashtuns and Baluch—gain much of their income from it. The borderlands already have become a land bridge for the criminal (drugs) and criminalized (transit trade) economies of the region. The transnational economic actors exploit the weakness and illegitimacy of statehood in the region to pursue profit, part of which pays for protection provided by transnational and parallel military and political forces. The fight to protect these transnational economic activities is increasingly inseparable from the armed conflicts around the borderlands.

The Anomaly of FATA

With an area of 27,000 square kilometers, slightly larger than Luxembourg, and a 600-kilometer border with Afghanistan, FATA is the real administrative, political, and economic anomaly in the border region. FATA is divided into seven agencies, or administrative units, which from north to south are

Bajaur, Momand, Khyber, Orakzai, Kurram, and North and South Waziristan. A few more frontier regions adjacent to the settled districts of Peshawar, Kohat, Dera Ismail Khan, Bannu, and Tank are also part of FATA. The area had a population of some 3.1 million people at the time of the 1998 census, and current unofficial estimates range up to 7 million, mostly ethnic Pashtuns whose tribes straddle the Durand Line (Siddique and Khattak 2004).

Pakistan's 1973 constitution gives the president executive authority over the region. But he does not exercise this authority in Islamabad, where the people of FATA have representatives in the national assembly. The area is largely ruled from Peshawar, where the governor of NWFP, a presidential appointee, exercises enormous authority with no legislative check. The provincial government controls all the agencies that deliver services such as health care, education, support for agriculture, and communications in the tribal areas, but the people of FATA have no representation in the NWFP provincial assembly to which the government is accountable.

The real authority in a tribal agency is the political agent. He combines legislative, law enforcement, and economic management functions. Apart from being the top civilian official in the territory, the political agent is the judge, jury, police chief, jail warden, district magistrate, and public prosecutor. He collects and disburses revenue with virtually no accountability. He also oversees all development schemes and public service departments.

The political agent governs through the Frontier Crimes Regulations (FCR). For more than a century these regulations have been used as a whip to control the border tribes. Under them a political agent may impose an economic blockade or siege of "hostile" or "unfriendly" tribes or inflict fines on whole communities where certain "crimes" have been committed. He can prohibit the construction of houses and raze houses of tribal members as punishment for not meeting the agent's demands. Some of the harshest clauses establish collective responsibility, under which an entire tribe can be held responsible for crimes committed by a single member or occurring anywhere within that tribe's territory. The law empowers the political agent to deliver multiyear jail sentences without due process or right of appeal to any superior court. The political agent also can appoint and refer civil and criminal cases to a handpicked jirga, or tribal council. During the 2003–06 crises in Waziristan, political agents invoked all of these clauses.

The administration also manipulates local politics through its exploitation of the *lungi* or *malaki* system of appointed tribal leadership. Hand-picked tribal leaders are showered with government allowances and other economic incentives in return for loyalty. Every tribal administrator controls millions of dollars in secret funds to buy loyalty, leading to widespread corruption in the administration.

The British and their Pakistani successors have claimed that the FCR are rooted in tribal customs and traditions, but they contradict the egalitarian Pashtun ethos. The regulations also contradict the Pakistani constitution, which guarantees fundamental rights for all its citizens, and respect for international human rights conventions. The administrative arrangements of FATA deprive tribal members of political participation and economic development. All political parties, aid agencies, and civil society organizations are banned from working in the tribal areas, although radical extremist clerics are free to preach and campaign. Such clerics consequently won most of the elections held on a nonparty basis after adult franchise was introduced in 1996 (Human Rights Commission of Pakistan 2005).

The economic situation in the borderlands is equally dire. The wars in and over Afghanistan during the past three decades have transformed the economy of these tribal territories from one based on subsistence agriculture and nomadic pastoralism to dependence on the unregulated, cross-border trade of goods, including contraband such as drugs and arms. The area depends on smuggling routes that exploit the Afghan Transit Trade Agreement, under which goods may be imported duty-free into Pakistan for re-export to Afghanistan; many are illegally re-exported to or simply sold in Pakistan. In 2001 the World Bank estimated the value of such trade, as well as other transit trade through Afghanistan, at nearly $1 billion per year.

The deployment of military forces along Pakistan's western border, however, has threatened this cross-border trade. Pakistan and Afghanistan have set some of their respective tariff levels at par, eliminating most of the profit for smugglers. As both countries approach admission to the World Trade Organization, the cross-border trade may dry up. The unavailability of alternative livelihoods for FATA is likely to add a new dimension of economic resistance to the struggles in the region, as does the lack of alternative livelihoods for opium poppy farmers and opiate traders in Afghanistan.

Human development indicators in FATA are no better than in neighboring Afghanistan. Poverty levels are as high as 60 percent, twice those in the rest of Pakistan (*Dawn* 2005). Official statistics estimate the literacy rate in the tribal territories at 17.4 percent: 29.5 percent for men and less than 3 percent for women. The primary school enrollment rate is 68 percent for boys and 19 percent for girls. Only 102 colleges (equivalent to Western high schools) exist in the tribal areas, and only two or three of them are for women. On the other hand, madrassahs have mushroomed, and today up to 300 operate in the region. Only 524 medical doctors practice in FATA, one for every 6,307 people, and there is no healthcare infrastructure in some remote regions. Only two or three hospitals in all of FATA have rudimentary facilities for complex surgical procedures (Siddique and Khattak 2004).

With 2.4 percent of the national population, FATA receives only about 1 percent of the national budget. The per capita development allocation is one-third of the national average. No aid agencies or NGOs can work in the tribal belt, while in the other regions of the country they run substantial development projects. The per capita income in FATA is half that of Pakistan's national average. The region had the country's highest emigration ratio even before the advent of Islamist militancy, which, along with army offensives, has further displaced tens of thousands of people. The unemployment rate is 60 to 80 percent, or even close to 100 percent seasonally, if remittances and migrant labor are not counted (Awami National Party 2006).

Toward a Border Settlement

Pakistan enunciated its position on the border in 1947:

> [The] Durand Line delineated in the 1893 treaty is a valid international boundary subsequently recognized and confirmed by Afghanistan on several occasions. The drawing of this international border terminated any Afghan sovereignty over the territory or influence over the people east of [the] Durand Line. Pakistan as a successor state to British India derived full sovereignty over this region and its people and has all the rights and obligation of a successor state. In addition, the question of self-determination for Pashtuns was foreclosed by the British supervised plebiscite held in 1947 in NWFP in which 99 percent of votes cast were in favor of joining Pakistan. The Tribal Areas too expressed their assent through special Jirgas (Embree 1979: 134).

No Afghan government has accepted these claims. Despite Afghanistan's formal position, however, no government has made any serious effort to advance territorial claims either bilaterally or in international forums. Instead, its governments have used these claims as bargaining chips or to address domestic political concerns.[1]

In practice, Pakistan has done more than Afghanistan to undermine the status of the Durand Line as an international border. Successive governments in Islamabad have exploited the porosity of the threefold frontier to use covert asymmetrical warfare as a tool of national security policy. While the Pakistani military's deliberate fashioning of the Afghan resistance on an Islamist model gave Pakistan strategic depth and neutralized Afghan nationalism, it also relied on transnational networks that ignored the Durand Line as consistently as any border tribe. Pakistan is now paying the price for this policy by losing control of much of the frontier area to

[1] Interviews with experts and politicians in Islamabad in March–April 2004 and an undated, internal Pakistan Foreign Office document shared by a Foreign Office spokesperson.

groups it has supported, groups that exploit their ties in Afghanistan just as the Taliban exploit their ties in Pakistan.

The Pakistan military's relationship with cross-border Islamist groups also affected the domestic situation in Pakistan. It strengthened and spread beyond an alliance vis-à-vis Afghanistan and Kashmir to cooperation in domestic politics, including elections. In the words of Husain Haqqani, Pakistani author and former adviser to the country's government, "[The] Islamists staunchly adopted the Pakistani state's national security agenda and, in return, increasing number of officers accepted the Islamist view of a more religious state" (Haqqani 2005: 197). Increasingly, however, Islamist transnational goals have triumphed over the state's strategic objectives, as the Islamists have established a strategic presence in Pakistani state institutions, military, civil society, and campuses.

Since 9/11, a clear tension has developed between these visions. Pakistan's stated position as a frontline ally in the "war on terrorism" has led to tensions within the Islamist-military alliance over arresting al Qaeda leaders, cooperating with the United States, and cracking down on the Taliban and local militants. Islamist militancy, however, remains Pakistan's most successful strategic weapon against Indian regional hegemony, including its penetration into Afghanistan. However, by providing $650 million in economic and military assistance to the Karzai government, India is consolidating its position in Afghanistan. The semi-military Indian Border Roads Organization is building a major highway on the Pakistan border in the southwestern province of Nimruz, bordering on Baluchistan.

Pakistan is increasingly wary of this growing Indian influence and also accuses Indian consulates in the border cities of Jalalabad and Kandahar of fueling the Baluch nationalist insurgency. Pakistan sees the Indian presence as a major strategic defeat and a loss of years of investments that established an Islamist regime that kept all things Indian away from Pakistan's western borders.

Pakistani Pashtun nationalists, now organized in two major political parties, the Awami National Party and the Pashtunkhwa Milli Awami Party, view their relations with the Pakistani state and Afghanistan differently than do Pakistan's civil and military establishment and the Islamist political parties. Since 1947, the Pashtuns have been integrated to varying degrees into Pakistan's economy and state institutions such as the army and bureaucracy, weakening separatist sentiments. They have relied mostly on parliamentary politics to demand democratization, provincial autonomy, and friendly relations with Afghanistan.

Although it still lacks internal communications, the remote border region has been linked more closely to the rest of Pakistan through the extension of roads and communication networks. The lack of economic development in the borderlands has motivated Pashtuns to use this transport infrastructure to migrate for employment to Punjab and Sindh, particularly the southern seaport city of Karachi, which after Peshawar contains the largest urban concentration of Pashtuns—some 12 percent of its estimated population of 12 million.

Pashtun nationalists now propose restructuring the Pakistani state to unite all Pashtun regions in FATA, NWFP, and northern Baluchistan into a new province of Pashtunkhwa. This new province would form part of a revitalized federal structure in which provinces would enjoy enhanced powers within a genuinely democratic Pakistan. Once such restructuring occurred, the Awami National Party would support the recognition of the Durand Line as an international border between Pakistan and Afghanistan and encourage Afghanistan to move in that direction. As long as Pashtun nationalists conclude that Pakistan is still essentially a centralized military dictatorship, however, they say they will maintain their present position.

In the interim, Pashtun nationalists are calling for fast-paced economic development and reforms in FATA. They maintain that the border between Pakistan and Afghanistan can be pacified only if Pashtuns in both countries have unhindered, cross-border movement through formal recognition of open borders. As Pashtuns dominate regional trade and transport, regional peace and open borders will bring major improvements to the economy of the borderlands.[2]

Unlike the Pashtuns, the Baluch are divided among three states: Pakistan, Afghanistan, and Iran. The Baluch nationalists hold that the colonial boundaries weakened them economically and culturally, resulting in their impoverished life as minorities in all three states. They have viewed Afghanistan in a relatively favorable light, however, because Afghanistan's demand for Pashtunistan led Kabul to extend moral and material support to the Baluch nationalists as well.

As the fifth Baluch nationalist insurgency rages and expands into a nationwide political crisis with the killing of Bugti, many members of the ethnic group feel marginalized in the Pakistani state. With a population of nearly 5 million, Baluch nationalists feel extremely vulnerable to demographic extinction if mega-development projects such as Gwadar port are implemented in their province without guarantees of provincial autonomy within a federal Pakistan. Thus the Durand Line is not the foremost concern of the Baluch. But like Pashtun nationalists, they demand federal arrangements in Pakistan with enhanced provincial autonomy as a precursor to the settlement of the border and abandonment of secessionism.

[2] Interviews with Pashtun politicians in Islamabad and Peshawar, March–April 2004 and July–August 2006.

In contrast to Pashtun nationalists, the Baluch have used military means to protest and bargain politically with Islamabad.[3]

Afghanistan's current government has not issued a formal policy on the Durand Line. In April 2006, however, Afghanistan's minister for border and tribal affairs, Abdul Karim Brahui, told the lower house of the Afghan parliament that Afghanistan does not recognize the Durand Line as an international border. Brahui, a member of a small ethnic group closely linked to the Baluch, stated that his government does not have the mandate to negotiate this old dispute. Only a loya jirga could settle the issue permanently, he claimed, just as a loya jirga first ratified Afghanistan's policies on the post-partition frontier.

Since 2002, Kabul has feared a regrouping of the Taliban and al Qaeda in the border region. Although the Pakistani military buildup in the tribal areas is ostensibly to support the U.S.-led coalition's effort to eliminate the Taliban and al Qaeda, Kabul has charged that these forces have occupied territory on the Afghan side of the Durand Line. It suspects that the deployment might provide a platform for further interference. Such fears, coupled with uncertainty over western commitment, have pushed Karzai to align with India, seen as a more dependable, long-term, regional ally.

As post-Taliban Afghanistan has grappled with a plethora of domestic issues, Pashtunistan and the border region have not figured prominently in the national political discourse. Although some Pashtun publications play up the issue from time to time, the Afghan Mellat political party and other Pashtun nationalists are concentrating on domestic issues. Some non-Pashtun intellectuals and political activists, on the other hand, advocate agreement on a final border settlement in return for access to the sea and assurances of noninterference from Pakistan. Some argued for the inclusion of such an agreement in the 2004 constitution.[4]

Afghan politicians of all ethnic groups, including nationalists, Islamists, and former communists, oppose reviving the conflict and heightening tensions with Pakistan. This is an issue of such political sensitivity that every Afghan leader we interviewed on the subject reemphasized that all comments were off the record before proceeding. Many call for confidence-building measures, such as open borders, enhanced bilateral trade, and more people-to-people contact, including direct interaction between the two countries' parliaments. Some argue that the time is ripe to seek a settlement. "If we cannot solve this now, with the support of the entire

[3] Interviews with Baluch nationalist parliamentarians in Islamabad, March 2004.

[4] Abdul Hafiz Mansur, "*Nazari piramun-i Qanun-i Asasi*" (a look at the constitution), Kabul, December 2003, lists as its first point that "the lack of defined borders on the south and southeast frontiers of Afghanistan has created all kinds of security and other problems, and the constitution should recognize these borders."

international community, we will never resolve it," said a leader of the parliamentary opposition.

Paktia Governor Hakim Taniwal, assassinated September 10 by a suicide bomber, noted how much this dispute had cost Afghanistan: "The reason that Afghanistan adopted friendship with the Soviets was for Pashtunistan . . . and the result was, we did not gain Pashtunistan, but we almost lost Afghanistan. It would be good if we recognized the Durand Line—good for FATA, NWFP, Pakistan-Afghanistan relations. But we have to get something in return, such as a corridor to Karachi or Gwadar."

Others echo the traditional view that Pakistan, an "artificial state," is destined to dissolve, and that Afghanistan should not make any concessions while it is weak. Local leaders are discussing the issue as well. At a meeting of elders from eastern Afghanistan, one volunteered that this unresolved issue gave the neighbors an opportunity to meddle in internal Afghan affairs. Just as Afghanistan no longer claimed territory it once ruled in today's Iran or Uzbekistan, "we should accept this border as a border." This proposal, however, prompted loud protests from others, who insisted that the Durand Line Treaty under which Afghanistan ceded control of the areas across the Durand Line, expired after 100 years (in 1993), and Pakistan was obligated to return the territory. Among the leaders we interviewed, the myth of the expiration of the Durand Line Treaty was almost universally accepted.[5]

Given the political sensitivity of the issue and opposition to Pakistan's Afghan policy, which people across all factions and ethnic groups see as a major threat to Afghanistan, no major leader has publicly supported rapid settlement of the border issue. Although the Karzai government has not aggressively raised the Pashtunistan issue, it has begun to follow the path of previous Afghan governments in using border issues and Pashtun cross-border ethnic solidarity as political tools. It has revived relations with Pashtun nationalists in Pakistan and fallen back on Afghan nationalism to wage a war of words with the neighbor.

Recommendations and Conclusion

Afghanistan, Pakistan, and the neighboring regions would all benefit from a recognized open border between the two countries. Such a border would clarify that all Pashtuns have rights as citizens of one or another state and would enable them to communicate, trade, and develop both their economy and their culture in cooperation with one another. Such a settlement would strengthen democracy in both states and facilitate both Pakistan's access to Central Asia and Afghanistan's access to the sea. It would lessen

[5] Interviews in Kabul, Gardez, and Peshawar, March–April 2004 and August 2006.

domestic ethnic tensions and strengthen national unity in both states. It would, however, require difficult internal changes in both countries, a reversal of the hostility that has predominated in relations between the two governments for sixty years, and credible international guarantees.

A major challenge to such objectives is the Islamist insurgency on both sides of the border. In 2005 Musharraf responded to charges that the Taliban were engaging in cross-border activity by proposing to fence and mine the Durand Line, a solution reminiscent of the policies of Israel and Uzbekistan. As in Central Asia and the Middle East, such a solution will not work for many reasons. International political and military officials in Afghanistan, as well as counterinsurgency experts, agree that the key to strategic success is disrupting the Taliban's command and control, mainly in Quetta and Waziristan, not wasting resources on the impossible task of blocking infiltration by easily replaceable foot soldiers across snow-capped mountains and trackless deserts.[6] Fencing would further isolate the border region and create an additional obstacle to its economic development.

Crafting a twenty-first-century border settlement will require ending the nineteenth-century regime in FATA. Since 9/11, Pakistan has ended FATA's autonomy by deploying 80,000 troops in the mountainous region, but these operations have not been matched by political and economic reforms. Stabilizing the border region must include the political integration of FATA into Pakistan. Almost all Pakistani political parties have urged reform packages. The extension to FATA of the Political Parties Act of 2002 would allow mainstream political parties to organize there and counter extremist propaganda. These parties would provide an opportunity for tribal members to campaign for their rights in national institutions.

The Awami National Party, one of the most vocal proponents of reforms in FATA, wants to overhaul the administrative and judicial system. It supports tribal representation in the legislature of an NWFP that would include FATA. The Awami National Party emphasizes the fact that in the 1960s and early 1970s FATA was represented in the provincial assembly of a united West Pakistan. Over the past decades, many tribal members have acquired farmland and businesses in the settled areas. They also obtain health care and education in NWFP's urban centers (Awami National Party 2006).

The Frontier Crimes Regulations have remained virtually unchanged since Lord Curzon promulgated their final version in 1901. Today human rights advocates and tribal intellectuals call for an overhaul of the law. They demand

- Conformity of the law to contemporary human rights standards;
- Transfer to parliament of all legislative and administrative powers over FATA now resting with the president;

[6] Interviews in Kabul, July–August 2006.

- Extension of the jurisdiction of higher Pakistani courts to FATA and separation of the region's judiciary from the executive;
- Abolition of collective punishment and territorial responsibility;
- Extension of political and civic freedoms to FATA; and
- Implementation of a comprehensive disarmament and demobilization program in the region (Human Rights Commission of Pakistan 2005).

No reform program would be successful without a complementary strategy for economic development. It is crucial to reinforce reconstruction in Afghanistan with a compatible model across the border in FATA. The Awami National Party has asked for a detailed baseline survey by the World Bank or another international agency to assess the economic situation and help Pakistan and the people of FATA devise a comprehensive strategy. Linking FATA to Afghan reconstruction and creating special opportunity zones along the Durand Line will be first steps in this direction. Work is under way to establish such zones on the Afghan side. In May 2006 Musharraf hinted at establishing them with the help of the U.S. government. Such development would also open U.S. markets to products produced in FATA (Raza 2006).

FATA's isolation can be broken only by improving its infrastructure. A major highway spanning FATA, from Bajaur in the north to Waziristan and Zhob in the south, is needed to encourage contact. Pakistan's bilateral trade with Afghanistan now surpasses $2 billion a year (with Pakistani exports to Afghanistan totaling $1.2 billion, and Afghanistan's exports to Pakistan totaling $700 million).[7] But so far there are only two official border crossings, Torkham in the north and Chaman in the south. At least a dozen more border crossings could be opened to facilitate trade.

More than seventy FM radio stations broadcast illegally in FATA, often inciting sectarian violence and hatred, but the region has not joined the telecommunication revolution in the rest of Pakistan. The area needs mobile telephony and Internet access. Trade and commerce also should be modernized by establishing tribal chambers of commerce and accounting and financial information systems. Since most of the land in the region is communal, there is a need for a baseline study of land rights and a strategy for reform. To accomplish this, the government should extend the municipal laws of land settlement to FATA. Proper utilization of several known mineral deposits in FATA will result in the growth of labor-intensive mining and manufacturing industries in marble and precious stones. Agriculture in general, and fruit in particular, can be made profitable by introducing

[7] These figures do not include the Afghan transit trade.

new techniques to tribal farmers and helping them gain access to markets (Awami National Party 2006).

Such a transformation requires complementary measures by Afghanistan, the United States, the UN, and NATO. The persistence of a safe haven for the Taliban insurgency in Pakistan threatens the objectives of the international community in Afghanistan. Success in Afghanistan is fundamental to the U.S. "war on terror," the UN's credibility, and NATO's viability. Forces whose command and control and networks of recruitment, funding, training, and equipment are located in Pakistan are killing Afghan, American, British, and Canadian troops and civilians. The United States, the UN, and NATO must agree quickly to send a message to Islamabad that the persistence of Taliban havens in Pakistan is, in the words of the UN Charter, a threat to international peace and security that Pakistan must address immediately.

The United States, UN, and NATO also must agree on sending a message to Afghanistan and India that they must do all in their power to encourage Pakistan to make such difficult decisions by addressing sources of Pakistani insecurity, including issues related to the border region and Kashmir. The international community must offer generous aid and support to Pakistan if it undertakes needed reforms in the governance of FATA and creates a development area along the border in coordination with the reconstruction effort in Afghanistan.

The United States should use its influence to impress on Pakistan the gravity of the risks it is taking by not disrupting the Taliban command and to persuade all governments in the region to lower the tone of confrontation. Only the United States is likely to be able to persuade Pakistan and Afghanistan to keep India out of their bilateral relationship by agreeing to a set of ground rules and to press India to abide by them. India's contribution to Afghanistan is welcome and mostly constructive, but it should reduce its staff and activities in the border regions for the sake of regional stability. The size of the Indian consulates should be limited and their roles strictly defined.

U.S. diplomacy prevented nuclear confrontations between India and Pakistan in 1999 and 2002 and helped these arch-rivals begin talking. It also should facilitate a political process between Pakistan and Afghanistan. The United States helped set up the tripartite commission composed of senior Afghan, Pakistani, and U.S. military officials in 2003; it now includes NATO but still deals only with military coordination. Until now, Pakistan has delayed responding to a proposal to expand the consultations to the political level. As part of their joint initiative, the United States and NATO need to press Pakistan for a positive response.

Afghanistan has more international backing and support than ever. A growing segment of opinion privately holds that now is the time to address these issues; but only leadership can encourage those harboring such ideas to propose them in public. The Karzai administration should take advantage of this situation to begin a national dialogue to develop a consensus on resolving the conflicts with Pakistan that have caused so much damage to both countries. Afghanistan needs to show good will to Pakistan regarding the border issue and make a historic compromise.

Both countries should facilitate and encourage people-to-people contact as well as contact between officials at all levels across the border. If the wars in Afghanistan had any positive impact it was to expose Afghans to the outside world. Nearly half of today's Afghan population has visited Pakistan at some point, making it the country that Afghans are most familiar with outside their homeland. About 60,000 Pakistanis currently work in Afghanistan, and 10,000 of them cross the border daily. Pakistan's exports to Afghanistan grew from $221 million in 2001 to $1.2 billion in 2006, but the economy in the border region faces a sharp decline. Despite the intimate contact of the two peoples, however, the governments remain isolated from each other. The governors and chief ministers of NWFP and Baluchistan should meet with counterparts in the Afghan border provinces regularly, as should police chiefs, customs officers, and other officials.

In 2006, no secessionist nationalist movement operates among the Pashtuns in Pakistan, and Afghanistan has not revived its irredentist claims. Tribes on both sides of the border are clamoring for development. Economic pressures have forced Pashtuns to migrate to Karachi and the Gulf region in huge numbers. Only policy changes in both Kabul and Islamabad can involve their Pashtun populations in mutual confidence building, which could lead to an amicable resolution of the border issue.

Three contending visions of relations between Pakistan and Afghanistan emerged in spring 2006. One was the launch of the friendship bus service between the eastern Afghan city of Jalalabad and the western Pakistani city of Peshawar. People in both countries celebrated the occasion and greeted the arriving delegations by showering them with rose petals, playing music, and dancing in joy (Agence France-Presse 2006). Another vision of cross-border relations was expressed in the rather implausible proposal of fencing the Durand Line (Pajhwok Afghan News 2006). A third and worrying trend is Talibanization and escalating violence in the areas around the Durand Line. People in both countries have chosen the peaceful alternative; now their governments and leaders should follow suit.

Sources

ABC News. "Senior al-Qaida Operative Struck by Predator Missile," May 13, 2005.

Agence France-Presse. "First Pakistan-Afghanistan bus service runs," March 15, 2006.

Awami National Party. "Federally Administered Tribal Area, A Development Framework," unpublished paper, April 2006.

Bangash, Mumtaz A. *Political and Administrative Development of Tribal Areas, A Focus on Khyber and Kurram*, unpublished Ph.D dissertation, University of Peshawar, 1996.

Benjamin, Daniel, and Steven Simon. *The Age of Sacred Terror*. New York: Random House, 2003.

Coll, Steve. "The stand-off," *The New Yorker*, February 13, 2006.

Dawn. "Development backlog in FATA," November 22, 2005.

—. "Wanted Al-Qaida militant killed," April 21, 2006.

Dupree, Louis. *Afghanistan*. Princeton: Princeton University Press 1980.

Economist. "The other Taliban," March 16, 2006.

Embree, Ainslie, ed. *Pakistan's Western Borderlands, the Transformation of a Political Order*. Karachi: Royal Book Company, 1979.

Gall, Carlotta, and Muhammad Khan. "Qaida bomber is reported killed," *New York Times*, April 13, 2006.

Haqqani, Husain. *Pakistan between Mosque and Military*. Washington, D.C.: Carnegie Endowment for International Peace, 2005.

Human Rights Commission of Pakistan. "FCR—a bad law nobody can defend," 2005.

Hussain, Zahid. "Musharrafs Other War," *Newsline Magazine* (Karachi), January 2006.

—. "Terror in Miran Shah," *Newsline Magazine*, April 2006.

Kakar, Hassan. "Afghanistan; a Political and Diplomatic History, 1863–1901," unpublished manuscript.

Karzai, Hekmat, and Seth Jones. "How to curb suicide terrorism in Afghanistan," *Christian Science Monitor*, July 18, 2006.

Khan, Gulzar Ahmed. "Bajaur raid killed five foreigners: Musharraf," *Dawn*, February 12, 2006.

Magnus, Ralph, and Eden Naby *Afghanistan Mullah, Marx and Mujahid*. Boulder: Westview Press, 1998.

Pajhwok Afghan News. "Islamabad's border-fencing idea irks Pashtun leaders," March 8, 2006.

Peters, Gretchen. "Violence grows in Pakistan's tribal zone, despite Army presence," *Christian Science Monitor*, December 12, 2005.

Qureshi, Ahmad, and Ihsan Sarwaryar. "Suicide attack at Herat PRT kills two, injures nine," Pajhwok Afghan News, April 8, 2006. www.pajhwak.com/views toryasp?lng=eng&id=16242.

Raza, Shahzad. "Civil, military man to be political agents," *Daily Times* (Lahore), May 10, 2006.

Reuters. "Pakistan opposition barred from US air-strike village," January 23, 2006.

Roy, Olivier. *Islam and Resistance in Afghanistan*. Cambridge: Cambridge University Press, 1986.

Rubin, Barnett R. *The Fragmentation of Afghanistan: State Formation and Collapse in the International System*. New Haven: Yale University Press, 2002.

Siddique, Abubakar, and Iqbal Khattak. "War on terror highlights development needs in FATA," *The Friday Times* (Lahore), January 23, 2004.

Synovitz, Ron. "Afghanistan: Are militants copying Iraqi insurgents' suicide tactics?" Radio Free Europe/Radio Liberty. www.rferl.org/featuresarticle/2006/01/71de933c-eb38-4c16-a7aa-a42f46a74250.html.

Trives, Sebastien. "Afghanistan: Tackling the insurgency, the case of the Southeast," *Politique étrangère*, January 2006.

World Bank. "Afghanistan's international trade relations with neighboring countries." http://lnweb18.worldbank.org/SAR/sa.nsf/Attachments/8/$File/intltrade.pdf.

An online edition of this and related reports can be found on our Web site (www.usip.org), together with additional information on the subject.

United States Institute of Peace
1200 17th Street NW
Washington, DC 20036
www.usip.org

DOCUMENT NO. 22

INDICTMENT OF SABRI BENKAHLA

February 9, 2006

IN THE UNITED STATES DISTRICT COURT FOR THE
EASTERN DISTRICT OF VIRGINIA
Alexandria Division

UNITED STATES OF AMERICA	)	CRIMINAL NO.1:06Cr9
v.	)	Counts 1 & 2: False Declarations
	)	(18 USC § 1623)
SABRI BENKAHLA	)	Count 3: Obstruction of Justice
	)	(18 USC § 1503)

Indictment

February 2006 Term—At Alexandria

General Allegations

THE GRAND JURY CHARGES THAT:

1. As used in this superseding Indictment:

   a. "Jihad" describes a religious obligation of Muslims to struggle or strive for the defense of and advancement of Islam.

   b. "Mujahideen" describes warriors engaged in violent jihad.

2. The Taliban, at all times relevant to this Indictment until early 2002, was the political/military entity headquartered in Kandahar, Afghanistan, that exercised de facto control over the territory of Afghanistan until its defeat in late 2001 and early 2002 by a multi-national coalition that included the United States.

3. Lashkar-e-Taiba—translated as "the Army of the Pure" or "the Army of the Righteous"—claims to have trained thousands of mujahideen to fight

in areas including Afghanistan, Kashmir, Bosnia, Chechnya, Kosovo, and the Philippines. Lashkar-e-Taiba claims to have four camps for training mujahideen from around the world, including camps known as Taiba, Aqsa, Um-al-Qur'a, and Abdullah bin Masud.

4. On July 4, 1999, President Clinton declared a national emergency to deal with the threat posed by Al-Qaeda and the Taliban. In Executive Order 13129, President Clinton prohibited, among other things, United States persons from making or receiving any contribution of funds, goods, or services to or for the benefit of the Taliban.

Count 1

1. The Grand Jury realleges and incorporates by reference the General Allegations listed in this Indictment.

2. On or about August 26, 2004, in the Eastern District of Virginia, defendant SABRI BENKAHLA, while testifying under affirmation and penalty of perjury in a proceeding before Grand Jury No. 04-2, a Grand Jury of the United States in the Eastern District of Virginia, did unlawfully and knowingly make a false material declaration, that is to say:

3. At the time and place aforesaid the grand jury was conducting an investigation to determine whether violations of Title 50, United States Code, Section 1705, or Title 18, United States Code, Sections 924, 960, 2339A, or 2339B had been committed, and to identify the persons who had committed, caused the commission of, and conspired to commit such violations. It was material to that investigation that the grand jury ascertain if SABRI BENKAHLA and/or others had participated in a jihad training camp and/or combat in July 1999 and fired automatic weapons and rocket propelled grenades in the territory of Afghanistan controlled by the Taliban and/or across the border in Pakistan, and who had helped BENKAHLA arrange to participate in such combat and/or camp and use such weapons, and who else known to BENKAHLA was interested in participating in such combat and/or a jihad training camp and using such weapons in such areas and/or with such organizations.

4. At the time and place alleged, SABRI BENKAHLA, appearing as a witness under affirmation and under penalty of perjury at a proceeding before the grand jury did knowingly, willfully, and intentionally make one or more false material declarations, to wit, he was asked the following questions and gave the following answers, the false answers being underlined below:

A.

Q: . . . And the next email we'll take a look at . . . dated July 9th, 1999. Do you have that before you?

A: Yes.

Q: Okay. Now, this is an email to Allison . . . correct?

A: Right.

Q: Now, in this email, Mr. Benkahla, you, you said that you will "leave tomorrow on my trip to Britain, then Ireland, then a place far, far away, sorry, it's top secret info, can't tell you where it is over the Internet." Now, in that e-mail when you talked about this secret destination, were you referring to Afghanistan or any place in Afghanistan?

A: *No.*

(Transcript of Grand Jury Testimony, page 14)

* * *

Q: Did you participate in any training relevant to combat at any time during your trip to Pakistan or Afghanistan in the summer of 1999?

A: *No, I did not.*

Q: Did you see any training relevant to violent jihad at any time during your trip to Pakistan or Afghanistan—

A: *No, I did not.*

Q: —in the summer of 1999? Let me finish the question. Is the answer to that question no?

A: Yes, it is.

Q: Did you see any training relevant to combat at any time during your trip to Pakistan or Afghanistan in the summer of 1999?

A: You just asked that question.

Q: I asked you if you saw any training relevant to violent jihad.

A: Uh-huh. The next question—

Q: Was any training relevant to combat.

A: *No.*

Q: Did you handle a firearm at any time during your trip to Pakistan or Afghanistan in the summer of 1999?

A: *No, I did not.*

Q: Did you handle an explosive device at any time during your trip to Pakistan or Afghanistan in the summer of 1999?

A: *No.*

Q: Did you fire a firearm at any time during your trip to Pakistan or Afghanistan in the summer of 1999?

A: *No, I did not.*

Q: Did you fire an explosive device at any time during your trip to Pakistan or Afghanistan in the summer of 1999?

A: *No, I did not.* Fire an explosive device?

Q: Correct.

A: Explosives—*no, I haven't.*

Q: Do you understand the question?

A: I understand the question, but I don't know if it's correct English.

Q: Well, did you fire—

A: *I didn't fire anything whatsoever when I was in Pakistan and I've never been in Afghanistan, to my knowledge,* just to cut it short.

Q: Did you see anyone—all right, Mr. Benkahla, did you see anyone fire a firearm at any time during your trip to Pakistan or Afghanistan in the summer of 1999?

A: *Not to my recollection, no.* And I answered that.

Q: Could—is the answer to that question no?

A: *To my recollection. I never saw anybody fire any firearms.* I saw people maybe carrying arms, but I never saw them firing arms.

Q: Okay. During the entire trip of the summer of 1999?

A: *That's what I recall.*

Q: All right. Did you see anyone fire an explosive device at any time during your trip to Pakistan or Afghanistan in the summer of 1999?

A: *No.*

(Transcript of Grand Jury Testimony, pages 28–30)

B.

Q: All right. Now, Mr. Benkahla, have you yourself ever fired at any time, not just in the summer of 1999, but at any time, an AK-47 style rifle?

A: I fired an M-16 once when I was in ROTC training at George Mason. *I never fired an AK-47.*

Q: Have you yourself ever fired a rocket propelled grenade?

A: *No, I did not.*

(Transcript of Grand Jury Testimony, page 30–31)

C.

Q: Mr. Benkahla, you have before you . . . an e-mail dated April 6th, 2000. It's to *hamka55@hotmail.com*. It's from *sabribk@yahoo.com*. Is that you?

A: yes.

Q: All right. Why did you send this e-mail to hamka55?

A: I was asking advice about jihad training, I guess you can say.

* * *

Q: Now, about halfway into the e-mail you—there's the line that says "I have done some studying in Afghan for only a short period, and while I was at GMU was involved with the Army ROTC." What did you mean when you said that you had done some studying in Afghan?

A: *I just meant like cultural studies.* I studied about the country and—a little bit, and like, tried to give him the impression that I had been there to him, so he would give me like permission or something like that to come in, or to suggest for me to train.

Q: Now, had you actually been to Afghanistan?

A: *No, not to my knowledge.* Like I said last time, when I—I wasn't sure of that area, that I was in Afghanistan or not, when I told—

Q: All right. We'll get to that, but why did you want to leave this person with the impression that you had been to Afghanistan?

A: Because usually like—the thing I was thinking about at the time was to go to Chechnya to try to help there, and they won't let like any, you, person just go in that never had any training or anything like that. So, I thought, you know, to give the impression I kind of trained—

Q: All right. So, were you attempting to indicate to this person that you had actually been to jihad training in Afghanistan with this e-mail?

A: Indirectly, yeah, something like that.

Q: And had you in fact been to jihad training in Afghanistan?

A: *No, I never went to jihad training in Afghanistan.*

* * *

Q: Well, you were trying to convince this person that you had had training but you're saying now that you did not have training, correct?

A: *Right.*

* * *

Q: Well, when you say you wanted to leave him with the impression you had been in Afghanistan, do you mean that you wanted to leave him the impression that you had done some jihad training in Afghanistan or that you had been studying doing cultural studying in Afghanistan?

A: I was trying to give the impression that I had some jihad training, *but the reality was I only did cultural studies. Like I kind of worded it that way so I won't be lying but I won't be telling him, like, that I don't have any training whatsoever.*

Q: So, so, to be clear on this, is it your testimony that what you wanted hamka55 to understand—to believe was that you had undergone jihad training in Afghanistan?

A: Yeah, something like that. . . . I mean, in like weapons training or something like, just, you know, like jihad type training, whatever.

Q: In Afghanistan?

A: Yes.

(Transcript of Grand Jury Testimony, page 7–12)

D.

Q: [Y]ou have before you a, a e-mail. . . . dated June 10th, 2000. . . . . And you received and saved this e-mail. It's from *myunus@talk21.com.* Who is that person?

A: I'm not sure.

Q: Now, in this e-mail, it also mentions at the bottom "salaams to Haroon". Who was the Haroon that's mentioned by you and *myunus@talk21.com.* in this e-mail?

A: This is my writing, or is he writing it to me?

* * *

Q: Whether you sent it or whether you received it, do you know who the Haroon is in this e-mail?

A: *No.*

Grand Juror: Okay. And who did you say ["]myunus["] was?

A: *I wasn't sure who he was.*

Grand Juror: You sent him this email, right?

A: Yes.

Grand Juror: Okay. On the next page, right before you close, where it says ["]your brother Sabri["]—

A: Yes.

Grand Juror: —could you please read the last sentence of your paragraph?

A: "Please stay in touch and please give my salem to Haroon.

* * *

Grand Juror: —what is this "salem"? Is it a prayer or thoughts—greetings?

A: It's a greeting. Like say, say hi, hi to Haroon. *But I'm not sure who this "yunis" is and which Haroon this is.* So, maybe you can write or they can write to the—this person and find out who he is, and tell me his full name, who he is.

(Transcript of Grand Jury Testimony, pages 13–44, 50–51)

5. The questions and underlined answers in Paragraph 4 were material to the grand jury's investigation in that the grand jury was attempting to ascertain who had participated in combat and/or a jihad training camp in July 1999, who had fired automatic weapons and rocket propelled grenades in the area of Afghanistan under the control of the Taliban, and/or in Pakistan under the control of the Lashkar-e-Taiba or other jihad organizations espousing hatred and violence for the United States and countries with whom the United States was at peace; who had helped BENKAHLA arrange to participate in such combat and/or camp and use such weapons; and who else known to BENKAHLA was interested in participating in such combat and/or a jihad training camp and using such weapons in such areas and/or with such organizations.

6. The aforesaid underscored testimony of defendant SABRI BENKAHLA in Paragraph 4 was false in that, as SABRI BENKAHLA then well knew and believed:

A. In his email to Allison from July 9, 1999, when he stated that he would "leave tomorrow on my trip to Britain, then Ireland, then a place far, far away, sorry, it's top secret info, can't tell you where it is over the Internet," he was referring to his plans to travel to Pakistan and Afghanistan to participate in a jihad training camp.

B. He participated in a jihad training camp in the summer of 1999, and in doing so, fired weapons including AK-47-style rifles and destructive devices including a rocket-propelled grenade, and saw others doing the same.

C. In his email of April 6th, 2000, to *hamka55@hotmail.com.* soliciting advice regarding whether he should go to fight in Chechnya or continue with his studies, his statement that he had "trained in Afghan"—meaning that he had obtained jihad training at a jihad training camp in Afghanistan—was true.

D. *BENKHALA* knew who were Myunus and Haroon, the individuals referenced in *BENKHALA*'s email of June 7, 2000, to *myunus@talk21.com* advising that *BENKHALA* planned to "travel to Pakistan" but might "finish up" his studies in Saudi Arabia first

(In violation of Title 18, United States Code, Section 1623)

Count 2

THE GRAND JURY FURTHER CHARGES THAT;

1. The Grand Jury realleges and incorporates by reference the General Allegations listed in this Indictment.

2. On or about November 16, 2004, in the Eastern District of Virginia, defendant SABRI BENKAHLA, while testifying under affirmation and penalty of perjury in a proceeding before Grand Jury No. 04-1, a Grand Jury of the United States in the Eastern District of Virginia, did unlawfully and knowingly make a false material declaration, that is to say:

3. At the time and place aforesaid the grand jury was conducting an investigation to determine whether violations of Title 50, United States Code, Section 1705, or Title 18, United States Code, Sections 924, 960, 2339A, or 2339B had been committed, and to identify the persons who had committed, caused the commission of, and conspired to commit such violations. It was material to that investigation that the grand jury ascertain if SABRI BENKAHLA and/or others had participated in a jihad training camp and/or combat in July 1999 and fired automatic weapons and rocket propelled grenades in the territory of Afghanistan controlled by the Taliban and/or across the border in Pakistan, and who had helped BENKAHLA arrange to participate in such combat and/or camp and use such weapons, and who else known to BENKAHLA was interested in participating in such combat and/or a jihad training camp and using such weapons in such areas and/or with such organizations.

4. At the time and place alleged, SABRI BENKAHLA, appearing as a witness under affirmation and under penalty of perjury at a proceeding before the grand jury did knowingly, willfully, and intentionally make one or more false material declarations, to wit, he was asked the following

questions and gave the following answers, the false answers being underlined below:

A.

Q: Right, So aside from Pakistani Army soldiers, did you see anybody carrying arms besides people walking along in the village carrying arms?

A:*I don't recall, no.*

(Transcript of Grand Jury Testimony, pages 4–5)

B.

Q: Okay. Have yon ever fired a rifle that may not have been an AK-47 rifle but was an AK-47 style rifle, besides the M-16 you talked about?

A: During ROTC training?

Q: At any time.

A: *I don't recall ever firing anything like an AK-47.*

Q: Okay, have you ever fired an automatic weapon of any kind?

A: I don't know if you'd classify as an automatic or semiautomatic. Just the gun that I told you that I fired, that's it.

Q: One bullet, one—one pull of the trigger shoots one bullet, that's a semiautomatic. One pull of the trigger, more than one bullet is automatic.

A: No, I did semiautomatic handgun.

Q: Okay. Ever an automatic weapon?

A: *No.*

(Transcript of Grand Jury Testimony, pages 7–8)

C.

Q: Have you ever handled a rocket-propelled grenade?

A: *No.*

(Transcript of Grand Jury Testimony, page 8)

D.

Q: Well, if you were telling Allison you were going to go someplace secret, meaning Pakistan, why didn't you buy a ticket to Pakistan from the U.S. instead of going to London and buying another ticket, London to Pakistan from London?

A: *Like I said, I wasn't sure if I was going to go to Pakistan or not.* I just had it in my mind that I wanted to visit Pakistan. I knew a lot of friends in Britain that were from Pakistan. This e-mail, in general, I was trying to be funny and I wasn't you know, a lot of it's in joking context.

(Transcript of Grand Jury Testimony, page 15)

E.

Q: How was it that the person you ended up going with was somebody you'd never met before, this Abdellah?

A: Because he was going there. The other ones weren't leaving. My friends that I did know weren't going there. I mean, he spent the night at the mosque with me for a couple of days, so—

Q: And he just agreed to show you around Pakistan?

A: Well, he told—*I said, like, I was thinking about going to Pakistan. He said, "Well, I'm leaving to Pakistan," I forget, in a week or whatever, "if you want to come with me, you know. I'll show you around." I said okay.*

(Transcript of Grand Jury Testimony, pages 17–18)

5. The aforesaid underscored testimony was material to the grand jury's investigation, and was false as the defendant well knew when he gave such testimony, for the reasons outlined in Paragraphs 5 and 6 of Count 1 of this Indictment, which are incorporated by reference herein.

(In violation of Title 18, United States Code, Section 1623)

Count 3

THE GRAND JURY FURTHER CHARGES THAT:

1. The Grand Jury realleges and incorporates by reference the General Allegations listed in this Indictment.

2. Between on or about August 26, 2004, and on or about November 16, 2004, in the Eastern District of Virginia, defendant SABRI BENKAHLA unlawfully, willfully, and knowingly did corruptly influence, obstruct and impede, and endeavor to corruptly influence, obstruct and impede the due administration of justice by knowingly and willfully testifying falsely and evasively before Grand Jury No. 04-1 and Grand Jury No. 04-2 of the Alexandria Division of the United States District Court for the Eastern District of Virginia with the intent to impede and obstruct that grand jury, as set forth in Paragraph 4 of Count 1 and Paragraph 4 of Count 2 of this Indictment, which are here realleged and incorporated by reference.

3. The false and evasive testimony realleged and incorporated by reference in the preceding paragraph was false, and evasive, for the reasons set forth in Paragraphs 5 and 6 of Count 1 of this Indictment, which are here realleged and incorporated by reference.

4. The false and evasive testimony realleged and incorporated by reference in Paragraph 2 of this Count obstructed and impeded the grand jury's ability to ascertain who had participated in a jihad training camp or combat in July 1999 with BENKAHLA, in the area of Afghanistan under the control of the Taliban, or in Pakistan under the control of the Lashkar-e-Taiba or other jihad organizations espousing hatred and violence for the United States and countries with whom the United States was at peace, and who had fired automatic weapons and rocket propelled grenades in the course of such participation in such combat or camp. It obstructed and impeded the grand jury's ability to ascertain who had helped arrange BENKAHLA'S participation in such a jihad training camp and/or combat, and who else known to BENKAHLA was interested in participating in such a jihad training camp or combat. The identity of the individuals who had helped arrange BENKAHLA'S participation in the jihad training and/or combat, and other individuals who wanted to participate in such jihad training and/or combat was a matter of interest to the grand jury in the course of carrying out its duties, as BENKAHLA then and there well knew.

(In violation of Title 18, United States Code, Section 1503)

A TRUE BILL:

Pursuant to the E-Government Act,
the original of this page has been filed
under seal in the Clerk's Office.

____

FOREPERSON

Paul J. McNulty
United States Attorney

By: ______________________

Robert Spencer
Assistant United States Attorney
Chief, Criminal Division

____

Gordon D. Kromberg
Assistant United States Attorney

____

John T. Gibbs
Department of Justice Trial Attorney

DOCUMENT NO. 23

UNITED STATES OF AMERICA
V.
SABRI BENKAHLA

4th cir. June 23, 2008

Before WILKINSON, MOTZ, and DUNCAN, Circuit Judges.

Affirmed by published opinion. Judge Wilkinson wrote the opinion, in which Judge Motz and Judge Duncan joined.

Counsel

ARGUED: William Benjamin Moffitt, MOFFITT & BROADNAX, Reston, Virginia, for Appellant. Gordon Dean Kromberg, OFFICE OF THE UNITED STATES ATTORNEY, Alexandria, Virginia, for Appellee. **ON BRIEF:** Andrew L. Hurst, REED SMITH, L.L.P., Washington, D.C., for Appellant. Chuck Rosenberg, United States Attorney, Alexandria, Virginia, for Appellee. Mara Verheyden-Hilliard, PARTNERSHIP FOR CIVIL JUSTICE, Washington, D.C., for Muslim American Society Freedom Foundation; John Kenneth Zwerling, ZWERLING, LEIBIG & MOSELEY, P.C., Alexandria, Virginia, Nadhira F. Al-Khalili, Washington, D.C., for Council on American-Islamic Relations, Amici Supporting Appellant.

Opinion

WILKINSON, Circuit Judge:

Sabri Benkahla was part of a network of people the government was investigating for crimes connected to radical Islamic terrorism and violent jihad. The FBI questioned him and prosecutors twice called him before grand juries. Then he was prosecuted himself for false declarations, false statements, and obstructing justice. He raises three main issues on appeal. First, he claims his prosecution violated the collateral estoppel component of the Double Jeopardy Clause, as he had already been prosecuted and acquitted for some of the activities he was questioned about. Second, he claims the trial court admitted irrelevant and unduly prejudicial evidence about terrorism and violent jihad. Third, he claims the trial court erred in determining his sentence by applying the Sentencing Guidelines' terrorism enhancement. For the reasons below, we reject all three claims and affirm the judgment of the district court.

I.

An organization in Falls Church, Virginia, known as the Dar al-Arqam Islamic Center, has figured in no fewer than fourteen terrorism prosecutions so far. *See, e.g., United States v. Chandia*, 514 F.3d 365 (4th Cir. 2008); *United States v. Khan*, 461 F.3d 477 (4th Cir. 2006). Some of those prosecutions centered on a group of young men who assembled at Dar al-Arqam and, in early 2000, started training together for violent jihad. The group escalated stepwise from an ideological attraction to religious violence to actually taking up arms against nations they saw as enemies of Islam: Russia in Chechnya, India in Kashmir, and the United States. They began by talking with some of the more militant leaders at Dar al-Arqam. Then they started conducting quasi-military exercises with paintball guns in the Virginia woods and practicing marksmanship with AK-47 style rifles on Virginia shooting ranges. A few members traveled to Pakistan or Afghanistan to train at jihadist camps run by Lashkar-e-Taiba (a designated terrorist organization since December 2001).

Then came the attacks of September 11th and a schism at Dar al-Arqam between those who condemned and those who condoned the attacks. Within a few days, the leader of the violent wing, a Dar al-Arqam founder named Ali Al-Timimi (later convicted of solicitation to levy war against the United States), held a secret meeting at which the core of the paintball group formally dedicated itself to violence. More members went abroad to the jihadist camps. Some who went, upon returning to the United States, purchased sophisticated aerial surveillance technology to send to Lashkar-e-Taiba overseas. Then, in 2003, the group was arrested and eleven men indicted together. Six of the men pled guilty. Three were convicted. One was acquitted. The instant case concerns the eleventh man: Sabri Benkahla.

Benkahla's case was severed from the other ten defendants. The indictment charged the other members of the group chiefly with a conspiracy, beginning in 2000, to engage in armed hostilities against the United States, take part in military expeditions against nations with which the United States was at peace, and provide material support to terrorists. *See* 18 U.S.C. §§ 960, 2339A, 2390 (2000). But Benkahla was not charged with that conspiracy. He had taken a trip to England in the summer of 1999, and, from there, had bought a ticket to Pakistan, where he traveled with a man called "Abdullah." According to the government, in August 1999 he crossed from Pakistan into Afghanistan and there attended a Lashkar-e-Taiba jihadist training camp, where he fired an AK-47 and a rocket-propelled grenade launcher—conduct charged (since attending a Lashkar-e-Taiba jihadist training camp was not necessarily illegal at the time) as supplying services to the Taliban and using a firearm in furtherance of a crime of violence. *See* 50 U.S.C. § 1705 (2000); Exec. Order No. 13, 129 (July 4, 1999), 31 C.F.R. § 545.204 (prohibiting transactions with the Taliban); 18 U.S.C. §§ 924(c)(1)(B)(ii), 3238 (2000). Benkahla was arrested in Saudi Arabia in 2003, where he had been studying Islamic law and traveling with Ahmed Omar Abu Ali, a friend from Dar al-Arqam and a member of al Qaeda (eventually convicted of conspiracy to assassinate the President of the United States, among other crimes). Ultimately, having waived his right to a jury trial, Benkahla appeared before the U.S. District Court for the Eastern District of Virginia for a bench trial in March 2004.

It was clear in the trial that Benkahla was drawn to violent jihad, had traveled to Pakistan in August 1999, and had cultivated relationships with various individuals connected to terrorist organizations and jihadist training. In its decision, the trial court indicated that it thought he had attended a jihadist camp somewhere, either in Pakistan or Afghanistan, and fired an AK-47 and rocket-propelled grenade launcher while there. The court stated that "[i]f the standard of proof for the government were by a preponderance of the evidence, I would be able to find this defendant guilty." But the nature of the charges required that the camp be located in Afghanistan and that Benkahla have provided some meaningful form of support to the Taliban while there. In the court's judgment, there simply was not enough evidence on those points to convict beyond a reasonable doubt.

Within a few weeks of his March 2004 acquittal, Benkahla was subpoenaed. The government had been unable to prove that he had attended a jihadist training camp in Afghanistan, but it was by no means convinced that he hadn't attended a jihadist training camp at all. Indeed, it was still investigating such camps, the individuals who facilitated training at them, and several militants associated with Dar al-Arqam. Specifically, the government had convened two grand juries to investigate violations of 18 U.S.C. §§ 2339A and 2339B, which concern the provision of material support to terrorists and terrorist organizations. Thus over the next few months, the government compelled Benkahla to testify before each of the grand juries and to meet with the FBI several times in ancillary proceedings, with immunity from criminal prosecution for truthful testimony.

The questions throughout the proceedings focused anew on whether Benkahla had attended a jihadist training camp during that August 1999 trip. But they no longer centered on the camp's location, and the government took the approach of asking about the camp in the disjunctive (as in

"Did you participate in any training . . . during your trip to Pakistan *or* Afghanistan in the summer of 1999?"). The questions also concerned the individuals with whom Benkahla had communicated in the course of exploring violent jihad and planning the 1999 trip abroad. For his part, Benkahla consistently denied attending any such camp anywhere, or knowing anything substantial about the individuals.

The proceedings ended in November 2004. A little over a year later, in 2006, the government indicted Benkahla for making false material declarations to the two grand juries, 18 U.S.C. § 1623 (2000), obstructing justice on account of the false declarations, 18 U.S.C. § 1503 (2000), and making false material statements to the FBI, 18 U.S.C. § 1001(a) (2000). Specifically, Benkahla stood accused of a set of false denials: that he had participated in a jihadist training camp somewhere in August 1999; that he had handled weapons while there and observed others doing the same; and that he knew about the various people he had communicated with about training for jihad (such as "Abdullah," Ali Al-Timimi, and other persons of interest to the FBI in terrorism-related investigations). Benkahla moved to dismiss on collateral estoppel grounds and lost, and the case went to a jury in January and February 2007.

The jury trial lasted four days and included a good deal of background testimony on terrorism and violent jihad worldwide from the government's expert witness, Evan Kohlmann, as well as further testimony on the subject from an FBI agent working on Benkahla's case, Sarah Linden. After a day-and-a-half of deliberation, the jury convicted Benkahla on all counts, though it acquitted him of certain particular allegations in its special verdict form (each count alleged multiple falsehoods). Post-trial motions also led the court to strike Count II (concerning whether Benkahla handled weapons at the camp) for being based on uncorroborated admissions. Benkahla's convictions under Counts I, III, and IV—false declarations to the grand jury, obstruction of justice by virtue of the false declarations, and false statements to the FBI—stood.

At Benkahla's sentencing, the pivotal issue was whether to apply the terrorism enhancement of U.S. Sentencing Guidelines Manual § 3A1.4 (2007): "If the offense is a felony that involved, or was intended to promote, a federal crime of terrorism," increase the offense level to at least a 32 (and by no less than 12 levels) and the criminal history category to a Category VI (the maximum). According to Application Note 2, "[f]or purposes of this guideline, an offense that involved . . . obstructing an investigation of a federal crime of terrorism, shall be considered to have involved, or to have been intended to promote, that federal crime of terrorism." In Benkahla's case, applying the enhancement meant a Guidelines sentence over six times longer than he otherwise would get—jumping from a range of 33 to 41 months to a range of 210 to 262 months.

The court held that Benkahla qualified for the enhancement. *See United States v. Benkahla*, 501 F. Supp. 2d 748, 751-57 (E.D. Va. 2007). First, the investigations Benkahla obstructed concerned "federal crimes of terrorism" under the statutory definition of the term. *See* 18 U.S.C. § 2332b(g)(5) (2006). The investigations concerned offenses enumerated in § 2332b(g)(5), namely the provision of material support to terrorists and terrorist groups. And the investigations were sufficiently particular to satisfy § 2332b(g)(5), being oriented to a set of people (particularly Abu Ali and Al-Timimi) who would ultimately be prosecuted. Furthermore, the court thought Benkahla's false statements had genuinely impeded the government's investigation, preventing it from finding out about Lashkar-e-Taiba training camps or uncovering the true identities of Benkahla's correspondents.

Benkahla's Guidelines range was thus 210 to 262 months. But the court thought the case called for a downward departure under § 4A1.3 or (in the alternative) a variance under 18 U.S.C. § 3553(a). "Sabri Benkahla is not a terrorist," the court stated. *Benkahla*, 501 F. Supp. 2d at 759. He "has not committed any other criminal acts" and his likelihood of doing so upon release is "infinitesimal." *Id.* Also, Benkahla's former co-defendants, the other ten members of the Dar al-Arqam paintball group, had received lesser sentences for what were more dangerous and more violent offenses, a disparity the court found "staggering." *Id.* at 762. The court thus treated Benkahla as having a Category I criminal history and sentenced him to 121 months.

Benkahla has appealed chiefly three issues: whether his second prosecution violated principles of collateral estoppel; whether the trial court admitted irrelevant or unduly prejudicial evidence concerning radical Islamic terrorism; and whether the court improperly applied the terrorism enhancement of Sentencing Guideline § 3A1.4. A fourth issue—Benkahla's claim that the government's evidence was insufficient as a matter of law—received only passing attention in the briefs and argument, and we find it unpersuasive.[1] For its part, the government takes issue with the district court's characterization of Benkahla and calls its calculation of his criminal history category "baseless" and "mystifying," but, on the grounds that the sentence imposed "does not constitute an abuse of discretion" when treated as a variance, filed no cross-appeal. *Appellee's Br.* 62.

II.

We begin with Benkahla's collateral estoppel claim. Collateral estoppel, in the criminal context, is one part of the Fifth Amendment's guarantee

[1] Only one part of Benkahla's insufficiency of evidence argument is substantive: the claim that the uncorroborated admissions that led the trial court to strike Count 2 were repeated in Counts 1 and 4. In our judgment, however, the admissions were corroborated, and, in any case, Counts 1 and 4 rest mainly on other, unrelated false denials and false statements.

against double jeopardy. The guarantee as a whole prohibits twice prosecuting or punishing a person for the same offense. *See United States v. Dixon*, 509 U.S. 688, 695-96 (1993). Its collateral estoppel strand "means simply that when an issue of ultimate fact has once been determined by a valid and final judgment, that issue cannot again be litigated between the same parties in any future lawsuit." *Ashe v. Swenson*, 397 U.S. 436, 443 (1970). Benkahla argues that, since he was acquitted of attending a jihadist training camp in Afghanistan, he could not afterwards be prosecuted for falsely denying that he attended such a camp in (as the government framed it) "Pakistan *or* Afghanistan."

Benkahla's claim arises in an area of legal tension. On the one hand, there is some potential for abuse in the government's procedure of acquittal, questioning on matters related to the acquittal, and second prosecution for some form of perjury. Accusing someone of a false denial does indeed assume the truth of the matter denied, and prosecutors frustrated at an acquittal should not lightly be able to take a second bite at the apple by bringing perjury charges afterwards. Nor may the device of the "or" be used to create a spurious appearance of dissimilarity between prosecutions with a common core.

On the other hand, a defendant does not win with acquittal a license to commit perjury. *Cf. United States v. Dunnigan*, 507 U.S. 87, 96 (1993) ("[A] defendant's right to testify does not include a right to commit perjury."); *Bryson v. United States*, 396 U.S. 64, 72 (1969) ("Our legal system provides methods for challenging the Government's right to ask questions—lying is not one of them."). Law enforcement is entitled to keep investigating a criminal enterprise even after one defendant is acquitted, and if that defendant is presented with a subpoena and cloaked with the dual protections of court-ordered immunity and the guarantee against double jeopardy, he may well be required to admit the very conduct he successfully denied at trial.

Given this tension, a mechanical approach to the collateral estoppel rule will not do—and the law has never required one. "[T]he rule of collateral estoppel in criminal cases is not to be applied with the hypertechnical and archaic approach of a 19th century pleading book, but with realism and rationality. . . . The inquiry must be set in a practical frame and viewed with an eye to all the circumstances of the proceedings." *Ashe*, 397 U.S. at 444 (quotation omitted). A practical approach means closely examining the record of both trials to discern whether an "issue of ultimate fact" resolved in the first was indeed reopened in the second. *Id.* at 443. Thus our circuit has asked whether the two trials involved an "identical" issue "necessarily adjudicated" in the first, *United States v. Nash*, 447 F.2d 1382, 1386 (4th Cir. 1971); or whether an "identical" issue was "actually" and "necessarily decided" in the first trial, after "a full and fair opportunity to litigate" and a "final and valid" judgment, *United States v. Fiel*, 35 F.3d 997, 1006 (1994); or again whether "certain facts were necessarily determined in the first trial" that "constituted ultimate issues" in the second, *United States v. Yearwood*, 518 F.3d 220, 229 (4th Cir. 2008) (quotation omitted). Consistent throughout these cases over nearly forty years is the detailed, trial-specific look at the factual issues asked and answered at each prosecution.

Benkahla's first prosecution was a bench trial that concluded with a full judicial explanation of the verdict—a welcome thing, for a good deal of the law in this area stems from the mysteries of the general jury verdict. *See, e.g., United States v. Ruhbayan*, 325 F.3d 197, 203 (4th Cir. 2003) ("[D]oubt as to what was decided by a prior judgment should be resolved against using it as an estoppel." (quotation omitted)). There is no mystery as to why the court acquitted in the first proceedings. What disturbed it was a lack of evidence showing that the jihadist training camp was in Afghanistan rather than Pakistan, and, if it was in Afghanistan, that Benkahla provided any serious form of support to the Taliban while there. "I would find . . . that at some point, Mr. Benkahla has fired an automatic AK-47 and RPG" while abroad, the court said. But much of the evidence "is equally consistent in my view with going to a training camp in Pakistan as it would be to go to Afghanistan." The question was nonetheless close; the court stated that it "would be able to find this defendant guilty" on a preponderance of the evidence standard. But the charges brought required a high degree of certainty that the camp was located in Afghanistan and that by attending Benkahla was actually fighting or preparing to fight for the Taliban. At the factual heart of Benkahla's acquittal was a measure of uncertainty about those matters. In no way did the court's decision turn on doubt about whether Benkahla attended a jihadist training camp somewhere.

The second prosecution, Benkahla argues, once again put whether he attended a jihadist training camp in Afghanistan at issue. Asking the second jury whether he falsely denied attending a camp in "Pakistan *or* Afghanistan," he claims, invited conviction on a thinly veiled forbidden ground. But this argument mistakes the factual issues at stake in both trials. An analogy helps: One may be quite uncertain whether a man who always wears a blue or grey suit to work wore the blue one on Monday—but quite certain that he wore one or the other. In the same sense, the charges in the first trial required that the court determine with some certainty whether Benkahla attended a camp in Afghanistan and fought for the Taliban while there (the equivalent of the "blue suit on Monday" question). It could not. But the court was confident that Benkahla had attended a camp somewhere in the "Pakistan or Afghanistan" collective—and what mattered factually in the second trial, given the new charges, was that collective. Indeed, the form the government's questioning took, asking about "Pakistan *or* Afghanistan," was not in this context a device with which to evade a matter already decided. It was exactly the question suggested by the first acquittal, a question to which both the first court and the second jury were prepared to answer "Yes."

On that note, it is worth observing that the investigations in which Benkahla was interviewed and the questions he was asked show no sign of having been manufactured for the sake of a second prosecution. Given the character of the first court's acquittal, the government had every right to think Benkahla had attended a jihadist training camp somewhere (it would have been anomalous for it to have thought otherwise), and, for the best of reasons, the government was still investigating those camps and the people involved in them. Indeed, the two grand juries to which Benkahla testified were convened to investigate violations of 18 U.S.C. §§ 2339A and 2339B, which concern the provision of support to terrorists and terrorist organizations. And those investigations or connected ones eventuated in indictments—including ones for serious terrorists like Al-Timimi (whom Benkahla had been questioned about, leading to one of the grounds for Benkahla's false statements conviction), Abu Ali, and Chandia. It was legitimate to ask Benkahla, even post-acquittal, about his jihadist training in Pakistan or Afghanistan, and it was legitimate to prosecute him when he spoke falsely about it.

Thus the issue of ultimate fact in Benkahla's two prosecutions was distinct, and collateral estoppel presents no bar to the second.

III.

Benkahla next claims that the trial court admitted irrelevant and unduly prejudicial testimony and exhibits. He takes special exception to the government's terrorism expert, Evan Kohlmann, who runs a consulting company on Islamic terrorism and regularly testifies in terrorism-related prosecutions. Kohlmann's testimony was proffered mainly under Federal Rule of Evidence 702 to "assist the trier of fact to understand the evidence or to determine a fact in issue," and he gave background information on radical Islam and jihad generally rather than discussing Benkahla individually. As to that background, he spoke at length, beginning with the nature and history of the Taliban government in Afghanistan but ultimately touching on many of the individuals, ideologies, and organizations underlying the current conflict. Benkahla takes special note of a passage in which Kohlmann remarked that, for Osama bin Laden and al Qaeda, "Americans, no matter where they are on earth, whether they're civilian or military, are considered to be a target. There are no innocent civilians." Benkahla argues that this sort of testimony inflamed the jury and condemned him by association. It was too far afield from the issues in his case to be relevant under Rules 401, 402, and 702, he claims, and to the extent it was relevant, its probative value was substantially outweighed "by the danger of unfair prejudice, confusion of the issues, . . . or needless presentation of cumulative evidence" under Rule 403.[2]

Benkahla makes a similar argument against the testimony and exhibits admitted to prove that his false statements were material to the government's investigation—materiality being an element of both the false declarations and false statements charges. *See* 18 U.S.C. §§ 1001(a), 1623 (2000); *United States v. Sarihifard*, 155 F.3d 301, 306 (4th Cir. 1998) ("An essential element in both grand jury perjury and the crime of making false statements is materiality."). This testimony came mainly from Sarah Linden, an FBI agent working on Benkahla's case, who spoke at length about the set of investigations connected to Dar al-Arqam and the network of terrorists and terrorist organizations facilitating jihadist training abroad. The exhibits included several dozen videos, photographs, and documents (how many exactly is in dispute) in support of Linden's testimony. Benkahla argues that this evidence went well beyond what was necessary to establish materiality and became "a vehicle for placing irrelevant and prejudicial statements and events before the jury." *Appellant's Br.* 41. He particularly objects to a taped confession from Abu Ali that was played for the jury.

Judgments of evidentiary relevance and prejudice are fundamentally a matter of trial management, for "[t]rial judges are much closer to the pulse of a trial than we can ever be and broad discretion is necessarily accorded them." *United States v. Simpson*, 910 F.2d 154, 157 (4th Cir. 1990) (quotation omitted). The standard of review therefore counsels deference to the discretion of trial courts: "In a criminal appeal, we will not vacate a conviction unless we find that the district court judge acted arbitrarily or irrationally" in admitting evidence. *United States v. Ham*, 998 F.2d 1247, 1252 (4th Cir. 1993); *see also United States v. Udeozor*, 515 F.3d 260, 265 (4th Cir. 2008) (requiring "extraordinary circumstances" where discretion was "plainly abused") (quotation omitted).

For Kohlmann, the relevance inquiry turns on Rule 702: His testimony had to "assist the trier of fact to understand the evidence or to determine a fact in issue." *See Daubert v. Merrell Dow Pharm., Inc.*, 509 U.S. 579, 591 (1993). The trial court could fairly conclude that it did. The evidence in this case was complicated, touching by necessity on a wide variety of ideas, terms, people, and organizations connected to radical Islam. The indictment alone refers to "jihad"; "jihad training camp[s]" and the "organizations" participating in them; "Lashkar-e-Taiba"; "other jihad organizations" espousing violence toward "the United States and countries with whom

[2] Benkahla also attacks Kohlmann's qualifications as an expert, but those qualifications were obviously substantial and the district court acted well within its discretion in determining that they were sufficient.

the United States was at peace"; "the Taliban"; "the territory of Afghanistan controlled by the Taliban"; "the territory . . . across the border in Pakistan"; "the area north of Peshawar in Pakistan"; "lectures at Dar Al-Arqam"; the Arabic word "salaam"; and men named (or identified as) "Haroon," "Myunus," "Abdullah," "Ibrahim Buisir," "Muhammad Siddique," "Abdel Atti Al Bakai," "Emara Al Bashir Binkaid," and "Ali Al-Timimi." Of course, the evidence required to evaluate the indictment involved a broader frame of reference still. In these circumstances, the trial judge could well conclude that lengthy testimony about various aspects of radical Islam was appropriate, and indeed necessary, for the jury "to understand the evidence" and "determine [the] fact[s]."

For Linden and the exhibits that supported her testimony, the relevance inquiry turns on materiality under 18 U.S.C. §§ 1001(a) and 1623. A statement is "material," the Supreme Court has held, "if it has a natural tendency to influence, or was capable of influencing, the decision of the decisionmaking body to which it was addressed." *Kungys v. United States*, 485 U.S. 759, 770 (1988). Thus it was Linden's task, with the help of the exhibits, to "show[] a nexus between the false statements and the scope of the grand jury's [and FBI's] investigation," and she had some leeway in doing so: "Given the wide-ranging investigative function of the grand jury, the materiality of any line of inquiry pursued by a grand jury must be broadly construed." *United States v. Farnham*, 791 F.2d 331, 333-34 (4th Cir. 1986) (citation omitted). Here, Linden essentially testified to the FBI's and grand juries' investigations of jihadist camps abroad, the people who facilitate training at them, and the militants associated with Dar al-Arqam. These are exactly the subjects of Benkahla's alleged false denials and false statements. The relevance is clear.

Thus we come to the Rule 403 heart of Benkahla's argument against the witnesses and exhibits. At base, his contention is that the subject of terrorism arouses so much passion these days that its prominent presence at his trial put him at risk of a jury "excited to irrational behavior." *Udeozor*, 515 F.3d at 264 (quotation omitted). He cites as analogy *United States v. Ham*, where we reversed a trial judge under Rule 403 for admitting evidence of child molestation in a fraud case. 998 F.2d at 1251-54.

Undoubtedly, some of what Kohlmann and Linden had to say, and some of what the exhibits showed, was alarming. Undoubtedly the evidence's scope was wide. But the jury in this case *acquitted* Benkahla of several alleged falsehoods—not exactly the mark of irrational fervor. *Cf. United States v. Chandia*, 514 F.3d 365, 375 (4th Cir. 2008) (finding the claim that evidence of terrorism spurred an emotional conviction "discredited to a significant extent by the jury's rejection of one of the four counts charged"). And more importantly, Rule 403 is not an injunction to exclude prejudicial evidence but a mandate, entrusted mainly to the trial court, to weigh prejudice against probative value. *See United States v. Hammoud*, 381 F.3d 316, 341 (4th Cir. 2004) ("The mere fact that the evidence will damage the defendant's case is not enough—the evidence must be *unfairly* prejudicial, and the unfair prejudice must *substantially* outweigh the probative value of the evidence." (quotation omitted, emphasis in original)), *vacated on unrelated grounds*, 543 U.S. 1097 (2005). In this case, the relevance of the challenged evidence cannot be doubted, and the same qualities that made it relevant gave it a probative value that the trial judge could fairly think outweighed its prejudicial risk. To reverse that judge for an abuse of discretion would betray too much distrust of the ability of the adversary process to reach just results when the evidence on both sides is in.

The trial judge managed the proceedings in this case with care and skill, and we see no abuse of discretion in the testimony and exhibits admitted.

IV.

Finally, Benkahla claims that the district court should not in his case have applied the terrorism enhancement of U.S. Sentencing Guidelines Manual § 3A1.4 (2007). Under *Gall v. United States*, "a district court should begin all sentencing proceedings by correctly calculating the applicable Guidelines range" and then decide whether "an outside-Guidelines sentence is warranted." 552 U.S. _, 128 S. Ct. 586, 596-97 (2007). The appellate court must then "review the sentence under an abuse-of-discretion standard" with an eye toward both "procedural" and "substantive reasonableness." *Id.* at 597. Here, Benkahla argues that the terrorism enhancement led the district court to the wrong starting point.

The Guideline, adopted November 1, 1995, states:

> § 3A1.4. Terrorism
>
> (a) If the offense is a felony that involved, or was intended to promote, a federal crime of terrorism, increase by 12 levels; but if the resulting offense level is less than level 32, increase to level 32.
>
> (b) In each such case, the defendant's criminal history category from Chapter Four (Criminal History and Criminal Livelihood) shall be Category VI.

Two relevant application notes follow:

> 1. "Federal Crime of Terrorism" Defined.—For purposes of this guideline, "federal crime of terrorism" has the meaning given that term in 18 U.S.C. § 2332b(g)(5).
>
> 2. Harboring, Concealing, and Obstruction Offenses.—For purposes of this guideline, an offense that involved . . . obstructing an investigation of a federal crime of terrorism, shall be considered to have involved, or to have been intended to promote, that federal crime of terrorism.

Application Note 1 took shape in response to the Antiterrorism and Effective Death Penalty Act of 1996. *See* U.S. Sentencing Guidelines Manual app. C, amend. 539 (2007). The statute it refers to, 18 U.S.C. § 2332b(g)(5) (2006), states:

> [T]he term "Federal crime of terrorism" means an offense that—
>
> (A) is calculated to influence or affect the conduct of government by intimidation or coercion, or to retaliate against government conduct; and
>
> (B) is a violation of . . . 2339A (relating to providing material support to terrorists), 2339B (relating to providing material support to terrorist organizations). . . .

Application Note 2 was passed in response to the USA Patriot Act of 2001 "to clarify that § 3A1.4 may apply in the case of offenses that occurred after the commission of the federal crime of terrorism." U.S. Sentencing Guidelines Manual app. C, amdt. 637 (2007).

In light of these provisions, applying § 3A1.4 in Benkahla's case seems straightforward. He was convicted of obstruction offenses. Application Note 2 says that obstruction offenses qualify for the enhancement so long as the thing obstructed qualifies as an investigation into a "federal crime of terrorism." Application Note 1 tells us that the term "federal crime of terrorism" has a statutory definition. The statute, 18 U.S.C. § 2332b(g)(5), defines it in two parts. Benkahla obstructed a grand jury investigation into violations of §§ 2339A and 2339B, which satisfies the second part. And the violations involved jihadist camps training people to fight the governments of India, Russia, and the United States, which satisfies the first.

Nonetheless, Benkahla presents several arguments against applying the enhancement to him. First, with reference to the *United States v. Booker* line of cases, Benkahla contends that applying the enhancement depended on finding as a matter of fact that he "actually obstructed an investigation of a federal crime of terrorism." *Appellant's Br.* 22. The trial court, not the jury, found that fact. His sentence plainly would not survive reasonableness review, he argues, but for that fact. And therein lies the problem, for if a sentence *depends* on judge-found facts to survive reasonableness review, he contends, it violates the Sixth Amendment.

This argument is too creative for the law as it stands. Sentencing judges may find facts relevant to determining a Guidelines range by a preponderance of the evidence, so long as that Guidelines sentence is treated as advisory and falls within the statutory maximum authorized by the jury's verdict. Indeed, "many individual Guidelines apply higher sentences in the presence of special facts" and "[i]n many cases, the sentencing judge, not the jury, will determine the existence of those facts." *Rita v. United States*, 551 U.S. _, 127 S. Ct. 2456, 2465 (2007). That "does not violate the Sixth Amendment," however, because "[a]s far as the law is concerned, the judge could disregard the Guidelines and apply the same sentence . . . in the absence of the special facts." *Id.* at 2465-66; *see also United States v. Battle*, 499 F.3d 315, 322-23 (4th Cir. 2007) ("When applying the Guidelines in an advisory manner, the district court can make factual findings using the preponderance of the evidence standard."). The point is thus that the Guidelines must be advisory, not that judges may find no facts. Here, in a case in which the district court slashed the defendant's Guidelines sentence in half, no one could doubt that the Guidelines were advisory. There is no Sixth Amendment violation.

Benkahla next argues that Application Note 2 contradicts Guideline § 3A1.4, and we should therefore hold Application Note 2 invalid. *See Stinson v. United States*, 508 U.S. 36, 43 (1993) ("[If] commentary and the guideline it interprets are inconsistent in that following one will result in violating the dictates of the other, the Sentencing Reform Act itself commands compliance with the guideline."). The two must contradict, he claims, because a person can obstruct an investigation into a federal crime of terrorism without necessarily committing, in § 3A1.4's words, "a felony that involved, or was intended to promote, a federal crime of terrorism."

In general, we have a duty to harmonize Guidelines and commentary. *See Stinson*, 508 U.S. at 44-46; *United States v. Pedragh*, 225 F.3d 240, 244-45 (2d Cir. 2000). One might wonder, in the abstract, whether obstructing an investigation into a federal crime of terrorism necessarily "involve[s]" a federal crime of terrorism, but plainly one could think that it does, and Application Note 2 decides the matter. Indeed, the language of Application Note 2 is identical in all material respects to the language of § 3A1.4 itself. There is no inconsistency of any kind.

Finally, Benkahla claims that Application Note 2, even if constitutional and consistent with § 3A1.4, does not apply to him. The argument rests less on Application Note 2 itself than on two conclusions of law the district court came to in the course of its sentencing decision. The court reasoned that to qualify for the enhancement, Benkahla had to *actually* obstruct a terrorism investigation (not just attempt to obstruct one), and that the investigation itself had to be specific and targeted, oriented to particular terrorism offenses rather than to general intelligence-gathering. *See United States v. Benkahla*, 501 F. Supp. 2d 748, 751-54, 756 (E.D. Va. 2007). Benkahla echoes these conclusions of law, but contrary to the district court, insists that the investigation in his case was too general, and his obstruction too ineffectual, for the enhancement to apply.

There is no need to review the district court's legal conclusions. Whether those conclusions are correct or incorrect, the court's factual findings clearly support applying the enhancement. *See Gall*, 128 S. Ct. at 597 (holding that appellate courts review district courts' sentencing facts for clear error).

All the evidence indicates that Benkahla attended a jihadist training camp abroad, was acquainted with a network of people involved in violent jihad and terrorism, and lied about both. Moreover, the sentencing judge, after a meticulous review of the evidence, concluded that "[i]n the same investigation in which Defendant was questioned, eight individuals to whom he was connected went to foreign jihad training camps and one was convicted of soliciting treason to fight against the United States." *Benkahla*, 501 F. Supp. 2d at 755. Testimony secured from some of those individuals led to "convictions for specific terrorist acts in Australia, France, and England." *Id.* And "[m]ost notable . . . at the time Defendant was questioned, Ali Al-Timimi and Ahmed Abu-Ali were yet to be indicted." *Id.* Benkahla "had relationships with both." *Id.* The district court also found that Benkahla's falsehoods not only delayed some parts of the investigation, but wholly frustrated others. When Benkahla was questioned, "the Government did not know the details about Lashkar-e-Taiba training camps, training techniques, curriculum, and locations," the court wrote. *Id.* at 757. In addition, "because of Defendant's false or intentionally misleading answers, the Government still does not know the identity or whereabouts of the persons about whom Defendant was questioned, their involvement with Lashkar-e-Taiba, and their role in aiding persons to obtain jihad training." *Id.*

This factual amplitude stands in contrast to the situation in *United States v. Chandia*, 514 F.3d 365 (4th Cir. 2008), on which Benkahla relies. There we vacated and remanded an application of the terrorism enhancement because the district court "appeared to assume (erroneously) that the enhancement automatically applies to a material support conviction" and so "did not make any factual findings related to the intent element." *Id.* at 376. Here, the district court made extensive factual findings and the terrorism enhancement is doing just what it ought to do: Punishing more harshly than other criminals those whose wrongs served an end more terrible than other crimes.

We therefore approve the application of the terrorism enhancement to Benkahla. As the government has not appealed the district's court's downward departure or variance, we do not address it.

V.

For the foregoing reasons, the judgment is in all respects

AFFIRMED.

DOCUMENT NO. 24

PAKISTAN AND TERRORISM: A SUMMARY

CRS Report
RS22632

March 27, 2007

K. Alan Kronstadt Specialist in Asian Affairs
Foreign Affairs, Defense, and Trade Division

Summary

This report provides a summary review of issues related to Pakistan and terrorism, especially in the context of U.S. interests, policy goals, and relevant assistance.[1] The outcomes of U.S. policies toward Pakistan since 9/11, while not devoid of meaningful successes, have neither neutralized anti-Western militants and reduced religious extremism in that country, nor have they contributed sufficiently to the stabilization of neighboring Afghanistan. Many observers thus urge a broad re-evaluation of such policies. For a substantive review, see a forthcoming CRS Report entitled *Pakistan and Terrorism*. This report will be updated periodically.

In the wake of the September 2001 terrorist attacks on the United States, President George W. Bush launched major military operations as part of a global U.S.-led anti-terrorism effort. *Operation Enduring Freedom* in Afghanistan has realized major successes with the vital assistance of neighboring Pakistan. Yet a resurgent Taliban today operates in southern and eastern Afghanistan with the benefit of apparent sanctuary in parts of

[1] Sources for this report include, *inter alia*, the U.S. Departments of State and Defense, congressional transcripts, intergovernmental and nongovernmental organizations, regional press reports, and major newswires.

western Pakistan. The United States is increasingly concerned that members of Al Qaeda, its Taliban supporters, and other Islamist militants find safe haven in Pakistani cities such as Quetta and Peshawar, as well as in the rugged Pakistan-Afghanistan border region. This latter area is inhabited by ethnic Pashtuns who express solidarity with anti-U.S. forces. Al Qaeda militants also reportedly have made alliances with indigenous Pakistani terrorist groups that have been implicated in both anti-Western attacks in Pakistan and terrorism in India. These groups seek to oust the Islamabad government of President Gen. Pervez Musharraf and have been implicated in assassination attempts that were only narrowly survived by the Pakistani leader and other top officials. In fact, Pakistan's struggle with militant Islamist extremism appears for some to have become a matter of survival for that country. As more evidence arises exposing Al Qaeda's deadly new alliance with indigenous Pakistani militants—and related conflict continues to cause death and disruption in Pakistan's western regions—concern about Pakistan's fundamental political and social stability has increased. In his January 2007 State of the Union Address, President Bush said, "We didn't drive Al Qaeda out of their safe haven in Afghanistan only to let them set up a new safe haven in a free Iraq." Yet many observers warn that an American preoccupation with Iraq has contributed to allowing the emergence of new Al Qaeda safe havens in western Pakistan.

U.S. Policy and Concerns

South Asia is viewed as a key arena in the fight against militant religious extremism, most especially in Pakistan and as related to Afghan stability. In November 2006, the State Department's Under Secretary for Political Affairs, Nicholas Burns, said, "It is in South Asia where our future success in the struggle against global terrorism will likely be decided—in Afghanistan and Pakistan."[2] *The 9/11 Commission Report* emphasized that mounting large-scale international terrorist attacks appears to require sanctuaries in which terrorist groups can plan and operate with impunity. It further claimed that Pakistan's "vast unpoliced regions" remained attractive to extremist groups. The Commission identified the government of President Musharraf as the best hope for stability in Pakistan and Afghanistan, and recommended that the United States make a long-term commitment to provide comprehensive support for Islamabad so long as Pakistan itself is committed to combating extremism and to a policy of "enlightened moderation."[3]

---

[2] "U.S. Policy in South Asia," Nov. 27, 2006, at [http://www.state.gov/p/us/rm/2006/76984.htm].

[3] *The 9/11 Commission Report*, at [http://www.gpoaccess.gov/911/]; Pervez Musharraf, "A Plea for Enlightened Moderation," *Washington Post*, June 1, 2004.

In January 2007 Senate testimony assessing global threats, the outgoing Director of National Intelligence, John Negroponte, captured in two sentences the dilemma Pakistan now poses for U.S. policy makers: "Pakistan is a frontline partner in the war on terror. Nevertheless, it remains a major source of Islamic extremism and the home for some top terrorist leaders." In what were surely well-calculated remarks, he went on to identify Al Qaeda as posing the single greatest terrorist threat to the United States and its interests, and warned that the organization's "core elements . . . maintain active connections and relationships that radiate outward from their leaders' secure hideouts in Pakistan."[4] This latter reference was considered the strongest such statement to date by a high-ranking Bush Administration official. Throughout the opening months of 2007, Administration officials, U.S. military commanders, and senior U.S. Senators issued further incriminating statements about Pakistan's assumed status as a terrorist base and the allegedly insufficient response of the Islamabad government.

The United States also remains concerned with indigenous extremist groups in Pakistan, and with the ongoing "cross-border infiltration" of Islamist militants who traverse the Kashmiri Line of Control and other borders to engage in terrorist acts in India and Indian Kashmir. Many analysts consider such activities conceptually inseparable from the problem of Islamist militancy in western Pakistan and in Afghanistan. Domestic terrorism in Pakistan, much of it associated with Islamist sectarianism, has become an increasingly serious problem affecting major Pakistani cities. Separatist violence in India's Muslim-majority Jammu and Kashmir state has continued unabated since 1989, with some notable relative decline in recent years. Many experts reject efforts by the Pakistani government and others to draw significant distinctions between U.S.- and Indian-designated terrorist groups fighting in Kashmir and those fighting in western Pakistan and Afghanistan, and in Pakistan's interior. India blames Pakistan for the infiltration of Islamist militants into Indian Kashmir, a charge Islamabad denies. The United States reportedly has received pledges from Islamabad that all "cross-border terrorism" would cease and that any terrorist facilities in Pakistani-controlled areas would be closed. Similar pledges have been made to India.

Numerous experts raise questions about the determination, sincerity, and effectiveness of Pakistani government efforts to combat religious extremists. Doubts are widely held by Western experts, many of whom express concerns about the implications of maintaining present U.S. policies toward the region, and about the efficacy of Islamabad's latest strategy,

[4] Statement before the Senate Select Committee on Intelligence, Jan. 11, 2007, at [http://intelligence.senate.gov/hearings.cfm?hearingId=2467].

which appears to seek reconciliation with pro-Taliban militants.[5] Islamabad is adamant in asserting that it serves its own self-interests through closer relations with the United States since 2001, that there should be no doubts about the sincerity of its anti-terrorism policies (with a corollary that any failings in this area are rooted in Pakistan's capabilities rather than in its intentions), and that solely military efforts to combat religious militancy are bound to fail. Instead, Pakistani officials aver, the so-called "war on terrorism" must emphasize socioeconomic uplift and resolution of outstanding disputes in the Muslim world, including in Kashmir, Palestine, and Iraq.[6]

The outcomes of U.S. policies toward Pakistan since 9/11, while not devoid of meaningful successes, have neither neutralized anti-Western militants and reduced religious extremism in that country, nor have they contributed sufficiently to the stabilization of neighboring Afghanistan. Many observers thus urge a broad re-evaluation of such policies, including a questioning of a seeming U.S. reliance on the institution of the Pakistani military and on the person of President Musharraf, along with a shifting of considerable U.S. assistance funds toward programs that might better engender long-term stability in Pakistan.[7]

Congressional Action

In June 2003, President Bush hosted President Musharraf at Camp David, Maryland, where he vowed to work with Congress on establishing a five-year, $3 billion aid package for Pakistan. Annual installments of $600 million each, split evenly between military and economic aid, began in FY2005. In the Intelligence Reform and Terrorism Prevention Act of 2004 (P.L. 108-458), the 108th Congress broadly endorsed the recommendations of *The 9/11 Commission Report* by calling for U.S. aid to Pakistan to be sustained at a minimum of FY2005 levels and requiring the President to report to Congress a description of long-term U.S. strategy to engage with and support Pakistan. The premiere House resolution of the 110th Congress (H.R. 1, the Implementing the 9/11 Commission Recommendations Act of 2007) was passed in January 2007. Section 1442 of the act contains discussion of U.S. policy toward Pakistan, including a requirement that the President report to Congress a long-term U.S. strategy for engaging Pakistan and making a statement of policy that further waivers of coup-related aid

---

[5] See Paul Wiseman, "Is Pakistan Doing Its Part in the War on Terrorism?," *USA Today*, Sep. 20, 2005; Pamela Constable, "Pakistan's Awkward Balancing Act On Islamic Militant Groups," *Washington Post*, Aug. 26, 2006 .

[6] Author interview with Pakistani government officials, Embassy of Pakistan, Washington, DC, Mar. 14, 2007.

[7] See, for example, statements by three expert witnesses at a House International Relations Subcommittee on the Middle East and South Asia hearing on Pakistan, Mar. 21, 2007.

sanctions "should be informed by the pace of democratic reform, extension of the rule of law, and the conduct of the parliamentary elections" scheduled to take place in late 2007. Perhaps most notably, the section includes a provision that would end U.S. military assistance and arms sales licensing to that country in FY2008 unless the President certifies that the Islamabad government is "making all possible efforts" to end Taliban activities on Pakistani soil.

Many analysts view Section 1442 as a signal that a Democratic-controlled Congress may pressure the Bush Administration to review its Pakistan policy, although many also warn that such overt conditionality is counterproductive to the goal of closer U.S.-Pakistan relations. The Bush Administration explicitly opposes the certification provision on such grounds and it instead urges that the certification be replaced with a reporting requirement.[8] A Senate version of the House bill (S. 4) was passed in March, but contains no Pakistan-specific language. In response to U.S. congressional signals of a possible shift in U.S. policy toward Islamabad, the Pakistani National Assembly's Defense Committee unanimously passed a resolution threatening to end or reduce Islamabad's cooperation on counterterrorism if U.S. aid to Pakistan were to be made conditional.

U.S. Government Assistance and Policy Options

Direct U.S. Foreign Assistance and Coalition Support Funding. In the years since September 2001, Pakistan has received nearly $1.5 billion in direct U.S. security-related assistance (Foreign Military Financing totaling $970 million plus about $516 million for other programs). Congress also has appropriated billions of dollars to reimburse Pakistan for its support of U.S.-led counterterrorism operations. Some 80% of Defense Department spending for coalition support payments to "Pakistan, Jordan, and other key cooperating nations" has gone to Islamabad. At $4.75 billion to date, averaging more than $80 million per month, the amount is equal to more than one-quarter of Pakistan's total military expenditures. The Bush Administration requested another $1 billion in emergency supplemental coalition support funds for FY2007, however, H.R. 1591, passed by the full House on March 23, 2007, called for only $300 million in such funds. The Administration also has requested another $1.7 billion in coalition support for FY2008. In justifying these requests, the Administration claims that coalition support payments to Pakistan have led to "a more stable [Pakistan-Afghanistan] border area."

---

[8] David Montero, "Pakistan Faces a Less-Friendly US Congress," *Christian Science Monitor*, Jan 29, 2007; Statement of Administration Policy at [http://www.whitehouse.gov/omb/legislative/sap/110-1/hr1sap-h.pdf].

Arms Transfers. Major U.S. defense sales and grants in recent years have included advanced aircraft and missiles. The Pentagon reports Foreign Military Sales (FMS) agreements with Pakistan worth $836 million in FY2003-FY2005. In-process sales of F-16 combat aircraft raised the FY2006 value to nearly $3.5 billion. (In June 2006, the Pentagon notified Congress of a planned FMS for Pakistan worth up to $5.1 billion. The deal involves up to 36 advanced F-16s, along with related refurbishments, munitions, and equipment, and would represent the largest-ever weapons sale to Pakistan.) The Pentagon has characterized F-16 fighters, P-3C maritime patrol aircraft, and anti-armor missiles as having significant anti-terrorism applications, a claim that elicits skepticism from some analysts.

Security Assistance. Security-related U.S. assistance programs for Pakistan are said to be aimed especially at bolstering Islamabad's counterterrorism and border security efforts, and have included U.S.-funded road-building projects in western Pakistan and the provision of night-vision equipment, communications gear, protective vests, and transport helicopters and aircraft. The United States also has undertaken to train and equip new Pakistan Army Air Assault units that can move quickly to find and target terrorist elements. U.S. security assistance to Pakistan's civilian sector is aimed at strengthening the country's law enforcement capabilities through basic police training, provision of advanced identification systems, and establishment of a new Counterterrorism Special Investigation Group. U.S. efforts may be hindered by Pakistani shortcomings that include poorly trained and poorly equipped personnel who generally are underpaid by ineffectively coordinated and overburdened government agencies.

Possible Adjustments to U.S. Assistance Programs. Many commentators on U.S. assistance programs for Pakistan have recommended making adjustments to the proportion of funds devoted to military versus economic aid and/or to the objectives of such programs. Currently, funds are split roughly evenly between economic and security-related aid programs, with the great bulk of the former going to a general economic (budget) support fund and most of the latter financing "big ticket" defense articles such as airborne early warning aircraft, and anti-ship and anti-armor missiles. It may be useful to better target U.S. assistance programs in such a way that they more effectively benefit the country's citizens. One former senior Senate staffer has called for improving America's image in Pakistan by making U.S. aid more visible to ordinary Pakistanis.[9]

An idea commonly floated by analysts is the "conditioning" of aid to Pakistan, perhaps through the creation of "benchmarks." For example,

---

[9] Lisa Curtis, "Denying Terrorists Safe Haven in Pakistan," Heritage Foundation Backgrounder No. 1981, Oct. 26, 2006, at [http://www.heritage.org/Research/AsiaandthePacific/upload/bg_1981.pdf].

in 2003, a task force of senior American South Asia watchers issued a report on U.S. policy in the region which included a recommendation that the extent of U.S. support for Islamabad should be linked to that government's own performance in making Pakistan a more "modern, progressive, and democratic state" as promised by President Musharraf in January 2002. Specifically, the task force urged directing two-thirds of U.S. aid to economic programs and one-third to security assistance, and conditioning increases in aid amounts to progress in Pakistan's reform agenda.[10] A more recent perspective is representative of ongoing concerns about the emphases of U.S. aid programs:

> [T]he United States has given Musharraf considerable slack in meeting his commitments to deal with domestic extremism or his promises to restore authentic democracy. The U.S. partnership with Pakistan would probably be on firmer footing through conditioned programs more dedicated to building the country's political and social institutions than rewarding its leadership.[11]

Other analysts, however, including those making policy for the Bush Administration, believe that conditioning U.S. aid to Pakistan has a past record failure and likely would be counterproductive. Some add that putting additional pressure on an already besieged Musharraf government might lead to significant political instability in Islamabad.

The Bush Administration has come under fire from some quarters for over-emphasizing its relationship with the person of Pervez Musharraf—an army general who came to power through extra-constitutional means—at the expense of democratization processes in Pakistan and, further, for maintaining a single-minded focus on anti-terrorism that has "given a pass" to Musharraf and the Pakistani military in the areas of nuclear proliferation, rule of law, and human rights. For several years, veteran Pakistan watchers have been calling attention to the potential problems inherent in a U.S. over-reliance on President Musharraf as an individual at alleged cost to more positive development of Pakistan's democratic institutions and civil society.[12] In 2006, two former senior U.S. diplomats jointly urged the Bush Administration to move beyond its fairly limited focus on the person of Pervez Musharraf by creating better links with a wider array of pro-democracy civil society elements there.[13]

---

[10] [http://www.asiasociety.org/policy_business/india-southasia10-30-03.pdf].

[11] Marvin Weinbaum, "Afghanistan and Its Neighbors," U.S. Institute of Peace Special Report 162, June 2006, p. 18, at [http://www.usip.org/pubs/specialreports/sr162.pdf].

[12] See the statements of Ambassador Teresita Schaffer and Dr. Marvin Weinbaum before the Senate Foreign Relations Committee, July 14, 2004.

[13] Teresita Schaffer and Karl Inderfurth, "A US Itinerary for Action in Pakistan," *Christian Science Monitor*, Mar. 1, 2006, at [http://www.csmonitor.com/2006/0301/p09s02-coop.html].

More substantive military-to-military relations could be of significant benefit to overall U.S.-Pakistan relations and the attainment of U.S. goals in South Asia. Related sanctions imposed on Pakistan in 1990 were in some respects harmful to subsequent U.S. interests in the region. For example, the suspension of military training (IMET) programs meant that for more than a decade there was no exchange between the Pakistani and U.S. militaries. A Washington-based expert on the Pakistani military has insisted that such exchanges are crucial in encouraging a liberal, secular outlook among Pakistan's officer corps, and provide the United States unique access to that country's leading institution.[14]

In apparent response to growing concerns about the course of events in Pakistan and in U.S.-Pakistan relations, Assistant Secretary of State for South and Central Asian Affairs Richard Boucher met with top Pakistani leaders in Islamabad in mid-March, where he lauded Pakistan's role as a vital U.S. ally and announced a new five-year, $750 million aid initiative for development programs in Pakistan's western tribal regions. The Administration also will seek Pentagon authority to spend $75 million in FY2007 funds to improve the capacity of Pakistan's paramilitary Frontier Corps.

[14] Stephen P. Cohen, *The Idea of Pakistan* (Brookings Institution, 2004), p. 318.

DOCUMENT NO. 25

TESTIMONY OF C. CHRISTINE FAIR ON U.S.-PAKISTAN RELATIONS

CT-297

January 16, 2008

C. Christine Fair[1]
The RAND Corporation

U.S.-Pakistan Relations Assassination, Instability, and the Future of U.S. Policy[2]

Before the Foreign Affairs Committee
Subcommittee on the Middle East and South Asia
United States House of Representatives

January 16, 2008

Thank you, Mr. Chairman, for inviting me to participate in today's hearing about Pakistan.[3] Pakistan is perhaps the most important U.S. partner in the war on terrorism. Not only has Pakistan lost more personnel in this conflict than any other ally, critical fuel for vehicles and aircraft used in the war effort in Afghanistan moves through Pakistan without problem. Without this logistical support, both Operation Enduring Freedom and NATO operations in Afghanistan would prove very difficult to sustain without

---

1 The opinions and conclusions expressed in this testimony are the author's alone and should not be interpreted as representing those of RAND or any of the sponsors of its research. This product is part of the RAND Corporation testimony series. RAND testimonies record testimony presented by RAND associates to federal, state, or local legislative committees; government-appointed commissions and panels; and private review and oversight bodies. The RAND Corporation is a nonprofit research organization providing objective analysis and effective solutions that address the challenges facing the public and private sectors around the world. RAND's publications do not necessarily reflect the opinions of its research clients and sponsors.

2 This testimony is available for free download at http://www.rand.org/pubs/testimonies/CT297/.

3 This testimony is based on my expertise on Pakistan and while I have recently rejoined RAND, most of this discussion today is derived from my research at the United States Institute of Peace. I would like to thank Husain Haqqani and Polly Nayak who provided feedback on earlier drafts of this statement.

interruption. While there is no doubt that Pakistan is a crucial ally of the United States, it is a state mired in instability and uncertainty. This raises questions about the will and capacity of Pakistan's leadership to remain engaged in the war on terrorism.

Both Washington and Islamabad have made decisions that have precipitated this current crisis. For Washington's part, by focusing upon President and former Chief of Army Staff Pervez Musharraf and by acquiescing to his various extra-constitutional moves, it has alienated further the Pakistani polity who harbor various suspicions about the United States and its intentions.[4] As is well known, the bulk of $10 billion in U.S. monies to Pakistan since 9/11 has been comprised of coalition support funds and other forms of military assistance. Indeed, there is an implicit assumption that President Musharraf and his purportedly secular army can help secure Pakistan's future as a moderate Islamic state as encapsulated in President Musharraf's much-lauded notion of Enlightened Moderation.[5] Relatively little of this assistance has been enjoyed by ordinary Pakistanis who increasingly doubt the U.S. commitment to Pakistan and Pakistanis and perilously few resources have been devoted to strengthening Pakistan's emaciated civilian institutions.[6]

For Islamabad's part, President Musharraf has increasingly sought to secure his political position and has imposed excessive constraints upon an ever-more mobilized civil society, who should be important partners in fighting extremism in Pakistan. At the same time, Musharraf has shown his incapacity to both control the Islamist violence that is roiling his country and to lead his country to fight it. Inept, ill-prepared and heavy-handed military operations in the tribal areas and adjacent Pashtun localities have spawned seething resentment towards the Pakistani state and animated a wider Islamist cum Pashtun militancy which has been exacerbated by infrequent but deadly U.S. unilateral military strikes. It is worth mentioning that the Pakistani armed forces undertook these operations under immense U.S. pressure. U.S. expectations about the timing of the operations and their potential outcome relied upon a number of erroneous assumptions about Pakistan's capabilities. This should occasion reflection about U.S. expectations and how well it understands the capacities of this important partner.

---

[4] For survey results about Pakistani views of U.S. policies and intentions, see C. Christine Fair, Clay Ramsay and Steven Kull. "Pakistani Public Opinion on Democracy, Islamist Militancy, and Relations with the U.S." (Washington D.C.: PIPA, USIP, January 7, 2008).

[5] Pervez Musharraf, "Time for Enlightened Moderation," June 2, 2004. http://www.presidentofpakistan.gov.pk/EnlightenedModeration.aspx.

[6] For various discussions of U.S. assistance, see Craig Cohen, "When $10 Billion is Not Enough: Rethinking U.S. Strategy Towards Pakistan," *The Washington Quarterly*, Vol. 30, No. 2 (Spring 2007), C. Christine Fair and Peter Chalk, *Fortifying Pakistan: The Role of U.S. Security Assistance* (Washington: USIP, 2006); Craig Cohen, *A Perilous Course: U.S. Strategy ad Assistance to Pakistan* (Washington: CSIS, 2007).

In recent years the chasm between American interests and those of President Musharraf has dramatically expanded. Specifically, the United States would like to see stability, consistent action against al Qaeda and Taliban forces operating in and from Pakistan, greater efforts to curb a wide array of Islamist militant groups in the country and most recently greater moves towards at the least the procedures of democracy if not the substance. It has become clear in recent years that President Musharraf, while he may share some of these concerns, has increasingly become focused upon securing his personal future—not that of Pakistan. This has compelled him to pursue policies of appeasement towards Islamists and militants alike while marginally satisfying the United States with respect to war on terrorism. By late 2004, Musharraf's ability to crackdown upon Islamist militants operating throughout the country seemed suspect and remains so. In recent years, journalists, military and intelligence officials and some analysts have increasingly noted with dismay the sanctuary that al Qaeda, Taliban and Kashmir-focused militant organizations enjoy and some analysts have even accused the state of active support of the of these organizations.[7]

With Bhutto's assassination, the clarion need for a stable Pakistan is ever more apparent as is the realization that President Musharraf is increasingly unable to bring such stability to Pakistan on his own. Moreover, even if Pakistan's security elites were to recognize that Pakistan's future is imperiled by the militant groups menacing Pakistan and embrace the war on terror as its own and take decisive action against *all* militant groups active in the country, the current government enjoys little legitimacy among Pakistanis. Without popular legitimacy and support, Musharraf will be unable to convince his country that Pakistan is struggling for its own survival-not his.

Thus there is urgent need to reconsider the lineaments of the U.S-Pakistan relationship and the reciprocal expectations that each state holds of the other. I concede that it is difficult to re-imagine the terms of the relationship given the tendency to assume that stasis is tantamount to stability. However, pursuit of the status quo will likely put the United States and Pakistan on a course of greater conflict *not less* and will undermine, *not buttress*, the prospects for a stable and prosperous Pakistan which is in the supreme interest of Pakistanis and Americans.

With this important background firmly in mind, I would like to address some of the immediate concerns expressed by this committee, including: the likelihood of free and fair elections; potential for civil unrest and stability should the elections appear to be fraudulent; and the likelihood that the new prime minister's government will vigorously pursue counter-terrorism

7 Seth G. Jones, "Pakistan's Dangerous Game," *Survival*, Vol. 49, No. 1, 2007, pp. 15–32.

objectives. I have also been asked to discuss developments in the Federally Administered Tribal Areas (FATA)[8], including the planned investments of $750 million as well as to comment upon the risk that the current situation poses for Pakistan's nuclear assets. However, in addition, I would also like to offer some near-term and long-term suggestions about how the United States should move forward in forging a relationship with Pakistan and its peoples rather than a relationship with President Pervez Musharraf and the Pakistan army.

Maximally Free and Fair Elections Required for Near-term Stability

While President Musharraf always sought to undermine and eviscerate his political nemeses and their parties (Benazir Bhutto and her Pakistan People's Party and Nawaz Sharif and his Pakistan Muslim League-N), 2007 witnessed a dramatic escalation of efforts to secure his personal support base at the expense of Pakistan's civilian institutions. His March 2007 ousting of Supreme Court Justice Iftikhar Mohammad Chaudhry sparked a surprising mobilization of civil society and concomitant crackdown upon the same. Mounting concerns about Musharraf's ever-eroding power base galvanized U.S. efforts to broker a rapprochement between Benazir Bhutto and President Musharraf in hopes that Musharraf could drape himself in her electoral legitimacy. The confrontation between the state and civil society persisted throughout the summer increasing demands for Musharraf to step down at least as army chief if not as president. Despite opposition from widening corners, Musharraf pushed through his extra-legal re-election in October through Pakistan's electoral college.

Fearing that the Supreme Court would vacate that victory, on November 3, Musharraf declared a state of emergency through a Provisional Constitutional Order (PCO). Thousands of lawyers, political party activists, reporters and human rights activists were detained while high-value Taliban activists were exchanged for Pakistani military and paramilitary personnel taken hostage in August. Moreover, 17 Supreme Court and more than 40 High Court judges refused to take an oath to the PCO

[8] Pakistanis make the distinction between the "tribal areas" and "settled areas." The former is comprised of seven "Tribal Agencies" (e.g. Khyber, Kurram, Bajaur, Mohmand, Orakzai, North and South areas of Waziristan) and six Frontier Regions (FR) (FR Peshawar, FR Kohat, FR Tank, FR Banuu, FR Lakki and FR Dera Ismail Khan). The Tribal Areas are governed by a colonial-era legal framework called the Frontier Crimes Regulation (FCR) and reside outside of Pakistan's constitutional legal framework. This system persists despite 60 years of independence and despite rulings in Pakistan's high courts that the FCR is unconstitutional. In contrast, the "settled areas" are those areas in which Pakistan's legal system applies. While Pakistanis may tolerate some kinds of destabilizing behavior in the "tribal belt" owing to cultural perceptions about Pashtuns in those areas, Pakistanis are alarmed when militancy and obscurantism reaches the settled areas as exemplified by the Red Mosque affair.

and were fired. This left the courts stacked with judges who would acquiesce to if not support Musharraf and his loyalists.[9]

On November 19, he announced the elections would be held on January 8 and on November 28th, he stepped down as Army Chief. On December 15, he lifted the emergency and restored the constitution. However, before doing so, he promulgated six Constitutional amendments using executive power.[10]

These extra-constitutional and other policies of the Musharraf government rendered free and fair elections in January 2008 improbable. All of these impediments are in place today, but after Bhutto's death, their import is even more salient for the proposed February elections. As these issues have been covered elsewhere, I will note the most prominent here only briefly. This list is not meant to be exhaustive.

- **Compromised Judiciary**. The judiciary will ultimately be called upon to inveigh upon allegations of vote rigging, fraud or other violations of electoral law. Without the reinstatement of those judges who were ousted for upholding the constitution against the PCO, transparent and equitable adjudication of disputes is unlikely.
- **Politicized Election Commission (EC)**. The EC is comprised of retired Supreme Court and serving High Court judges from the four provinces. As such, the proper functioning of the EC is hampered by Musharraf's manipulations of the judiciary. The Chief Election Commissioner is charged with appointing Election Tribunals to adjudicate disputes, which in turn are comprised of High Court judges. When their decisions are challenged, the case moves before provincial High Courts and ultimately the Supreme Court. An impartial (EC) is impossible with the current judiciary. Many criticized the EC's rejections of Nawaz Sharif's papers as indicative of its loyalties to Musharraf rather than the electoral process.
- **Dubious voters' registration list**. Millions of voters have been variously missing and/or added without verification. So far, the EC has denied review of the list. (N.B.: The electoral registration process was funded by the United States).

[9] The "emergency" declared by Musharraf differed substantially from the emergency provision authorized in article 232 of Pakistan's 1973 constitution. The constitutionally permitted emergency provides for Pakistan's institutions to remain intact and requires review by Pakistan's Supreme Court. Musharraf s PCO, in contrast, vitiated the judiciary by forcing all judges to swear an oath to it and prohibited any court or judgment from challenging the PCO, the Proclamation of Emergency, the President or his designated functionaries. See Testimony of Mark L. Schneider (Vice President of the International Crisis Group) to the House Committee on Oversight and Government Reform on "Pakistani Elections: Will they be fair and free or fundamentally flawed?", December 20, 2007.

[10] Carlotta Gall, "Musharraf Lifts State of Emergency in Pakistan," *The New York Times*, December 16, 2007; Muhammad Saleh Zaafir, "Musharraf to amend Constitution before lifting emergency,' *The News*, December 11, 2007.

- **Constraints upon the political parties.** Parties' efforts to hold rallies or meetings are highly regulated by the new Code of Conduct for political parties as are their statements about the government, its leaders and its institutions among other issues. This silences debate about the state's problems, which are core issues for politicians everywhere.[11] Political parties are not permitted to operate in the Federally Administered Tribal Areas (FATA), ceding political space to Islamist parties who have access to mosques and madrassahs.
- **Partisan Caretaker Government.** The current caretaker government with its firm Musharraf alignment does not foster confidence in free and fair elections, remains unacceptable to the opposition parties and thus remains a spark for controversy.
- **Restrictive curbs upon the media.** The government has retained prohibitions on media coverage that criticizes the state, its leaders or its institutions. While most major outlets have been permitted to operate, important private media like Geo can only be accessed by the internet or satellite. Pakistani interlocutors contend that Geo will not be restored until after the elections because it has a unique capacity to monitor grass roots developments and to conduct basic exit polling. Popular talk shows on major media have also been suspended as they frequently inveigh upon the political and leadership crisis in the country.
- **Unreasonable restraints on election monitoring missions.** Massive and unprecedented curbs were placed on electoral monitoring missions, compelling both the International Republican Institute and the National Democratic Institute to abandon plans for monitoring the elections. Equally damning: several long term observers returned with the conviction that the election was already being "cooked," with some noting the intrusive role played by the intelligence agencies and other government functionaries.[12]
- **Inadequate security.** Inadequate security and electoral violence present daunting challenges to free and fair elections.

It is imperative that a credible government emerge from the elections and there is only one way forward: The Musharraf government must

[11] Election Commission of Pakistan, "Notification [of the new Code of Conduct for the General Elections 2007-08], November 20, 2007. http://ecp.gov.pk/COCFinal.pdf.

[12] See among others International Republican Institute, "IRI Pakistan Pre-Election Observation Mission Statement," November 13, 2007. http://www.iri.org/mena/pakistan/2007-11-12-Pakistan.asp; National Democratic Institute, "Press Release: Daschle Sees Little Action Thus Far To Ensure Free And Fair Elections In Pakistan," November 20, 2007. http://www.accessdemocracy.org/library/2241_pk_release_daschle_122007.pdf; Testimony of Former Senate Majority Leader Tom Daschle before the House Oversight and Government Reform Subcommittee on National Security and Foreign Affairs, December 20, 2007. http://www.accessdemocracy.org/library/2242_pk_testimony_daschle_122007.pdf.

immediately address all of these issues, something that it is very unlikely to do without concerted and consistent persuasion from the United States and other international actors.

While maximally free and fair elections are a necessary precondition for stabilizing Pakistan in the near term, the elections alone are insufficient. In the wake of Bhutto's death, there is a surprising solidarity among most of the opposition political parties. If sustained, this alliance could secure a majority of seats in the national assembly. Unless President Musharraf and the emergent prime minister quickly establish a modus vivendi, more instability awaits. In free and fair elections, Musharraf's "King's Party"—the PML-Q—is unlikely to prevail as Musharraf and his party are widely (if unfairly) held accountable for Benazir Bhutto's death. The future prime minister and Musharraf will likely have a hostile and dysfunctional relationship, which may prompt Musharraf to exercise his right to dissolve the national assembly, throwing the country into further political chaos. To pre-empt such moves, the assembly may quickly act to strip the president of his expropriated powers if they have two-thirds majority in the assembly to do so.[13] (They can even strip the constitutional provision permitting his tenure of President as a punitive measure.) Any of these developments could again make the chief of the army, now Gen. Ashfaq Parvez Kayani, as the arbiter between Musharraf and the political parties. This is a role the army is long accustomed to playing. Should maximally free and fair elections produce a Musharraf-friendly candidate, these tensions may be less likely to emerge. However such an outcome is unlikely in the absence of extreme electoral irregularities.

To pre-empt further post-election crises, it is urgent that President Musharraf seek political rapprochement with the major parties, the judiciary, human rights groups and other civil society organizations. Such a process may afford an opportunity for Musharraf to embrace a greater symbolic role and recede from politics without further diminishing his legacy. In contrast, an activist Musharraf is likely to remain a flashpoint in Pakistan's fragile political terrain. Such a process of reconciliation may also afford an opportunity for the political parties and the army to come to an understanding that permits the army to confidently re-focus on its primary task of securing the country while the politicians assume responsibility for the domestic affairs of the state. It should be stressed that a retreat by the army (while perhaps desired) and by Musharraf are unlikely events even if the United States and its allies move swiftly to persuade Musharraf and the army chief to do so.

[13] It will require a two-thirds majority to overturn the amendments or to impeach him. However, with a simple majority, they could send the question of the legality of his election back to the courts.

The Elections Implications for Pakistan's Contributions to the War on Terrorism

To assess whether or not the elections will favorably affect Pakistan's ability to contribute to the war on terrorism requires an assessment of Musharraf's contributions in recent years. Many analysts believe that he has been a declining asset, deeply compromised by his efforts to simultaneously satisfy numerous persons and entities to secure his political position. His army is demoralized by years of fighting a war against its own citizens which it does not seem capable of winning. Defections have been reported within the paramilitary organizations and within the army itself. The army and other armed forces have been infiltrated as attested to by the various attacks against military targets, including the attempts upon Musharraf's life, the suicide attack against commandos in a mess hall in Tarbela among numerous other incidents. More worrisome is the fact that few Pakistanis embrace this war as their own. Indeed Pakistanis increasingly oppose military operations in the Pashtun belt even though they perceive the groups in question to be threats to their national security.[14]

Instead, Pakistan's effort to counter insurgents in the Pashtun belt and beyond requires political legitimacy, which Musharraf lacks. I am optimistic than an elected prime minister can be motivated to continue the fight. With a new army chief who is not seen as Washington's protégé, General Kiyani may be able to rally his armed forces *more* effectively than Musharraf.

However, it is critical that the United States communicate the message broadly that it will work with whoever emerges from this process. Thus discussions of aid cut-offs and conditionality are fraught with dangers. Pakistanis note that in the past, the U.S. has been most generous with military leaders while cutting off aid when civilian leadership returns. This has fostered cynicism among Pakistanis that the United States prefers a democratic Pakistan to one that is dominated by the military. Similarly, it fosters concerns within the Pakistan army that civilian leaders are unable to secure resources for Pakistan's national defense. The need to support whoever may emerge also underscores the danger of supporting particular persons and parties. The return of Nawaz Sharif surprised the administration which had written off Sharif and thrown its weight behind Ms. Bhutto. Thus the United States must engage a broad swathe of political actors to ensure that it has the beginnings of a working relationship with Pakistan's future Prime Minister and other elected officials. These *elected* officials should comprise the focal point of U.S. political engagement while the army continues to enjoy support through military-to-military engagements.

[14] C. Christine Fair, Clay Ramsay and Steven Kull. "Pakistani Public Opinion on Democracy, Islamist Militancy, and Relations with the U.S." (Washington D.C.: PIPA, USIP, January 7, 2008).

Thus the heroic task before the United States is how it can selectively use aid and military funding to encourage the likelihood of a free and fair election, a military retreat from politics and a gradual evolution of competent and effective politics and politicians in Pakistan. Pakistan's *civilian* leadership must been as important American partners in forging a secure and prosperous Pakistan.

The Federally Administered Tribal Areas (FATA)

Since 2004, Pakistan witnessed the development of the so-called Pakistani Taliban and an increasing "Pakistanization" of al Qaeda. While "Talibanization" of the tribal areas was limited to North and South Waziristan in 2004, the phenomenon next spread to Bajaur. Pakistan Taliban have emerged in areas that had previously been peaceful, such as Mohmand, Orakzai, and Kurram agencies. They have also emerged in the so-called settled frontier areas of Bannu, Tank, Kohat, Lakki Marwar, Dera Ismil Khan, and Swat. Some analysts have also raised concerns about Chitral.[15]

To win the confidence of FATA residents, the Pakistan government has been requesting development funds for this area for several years. At long last, the United States has agreed to spend some $750 million in FATA. At this juncture, it is difficult to be optimistic about the impact of these funds. (Perhaps had this funding been available *before* the onset of the wider insurgency such pessimism would be unwarranted.) Unfortunately, the security environment will render such projects very difficult particularly if the United States seeks to "brand" those developments in effort to garner good will. The United States will have very little ability to monitor the programs' implementation and Pakistani interlocutors are doubtful about the implementing partners of Islamabad's choosing.

Due to the lack of political liberalization in the tribal areas, moving forward with particular projects will involve negotiating with religious and possibly even militant leadership who will benefit financially, politically and socially should they choose to play this role. However, without these interlocutors, projects may be funded that do not serve local needs or preferences (e.g. roads that connect military posts to villages rather than roads that connect villages to markets; girls' schools instead of electricity and

[15] There is very little scholarly literature on this phenomenon with most coverage taking place in the popular press or security publications. See inter alia Rahimullah Yusufzai, "The Emergence of the Pakistani Taliban," Janes Information Group, December 11, 2007 available at http://www8.janes.com. See also C. Christine Fair, "Pakistan Loses Swat to Local Taliban," *Terrorism Focus*, Vol. 4, No. 37 (2007); Hassan Abbas, "Is the NWFP Slipping out of Pakistan's Control?" *Terrorism Monitor*, Vol. 5, No. 22 (2007); Hassan Abbas, "Increasing Talibanization in Pakistan's Seven Tribal Agencies," *Terrorism Monitor*, Vol. 5, No. 18 (2007); Idrees Bakhtiar, "Between the Lines," *The Herald*, (July 2007); Ghafar AN Khan, "The Lost Frontier," The Herald, (July 2007), Owais Tohid, "The New Frontier," *Newsline* (April 2004); Owais Tohid, "The Warrior Tribes," *Newsline* (April 2004); Zahid Hussain, "Al-Qaeda's New Face," *Newsline* (August 2004).

water facilities). Some critics of the deal note the paucity of groups that can function in FATA and suggest that the most likely entity to execute large infrastructure projects will be the Frontier Works Organization, an arm of the Pakistan military. Given the expanding insurgency in large swathes of FATA, it may make better sense to move quickly to fund projects in relatively secure areas within FATA as well as the adjacent settled areas. The settled Pashtun areas provide greater visibility because some civil society groups and media can operate there and there is greater security. However, as noted above, the insurgency is quickly moving into these areas and "safe zones" are constricting rapidly.

There is no doubt that development of FATA is critical as it remains the most under-developed region in Pakistan. However, one must understand that successive governments in Pakistan made choices to under-invest there and to ensure that FATA exists outside of the Pakistani legal, social and political mainstream in large part because doing so served the state's interests in various ways. Thus this problem is not simply one of resources, but one of will and sustained state preference.

While there is a rush to allocate funds for development in FATA, neither Washington nor Islamabad has embraced much-needed legal and political reform in FATA. Notably, the colonial-era Frontier Crimes Regulation (FCR), which Pakistan's own high courts have deemed unconstitutional, continues to govern the area with its draconian and illiberal provisions.[16] Recent survey work shows that there is widespread support among urban Pakistanis to reform or abolish the FCR.[17]

Similarly, political parties are not allowed to operate in FATA as the problematic Political Parties Act has not been extended there. Failure to extend the act has denied regional and non-Islamist parties the ability to cultivate and mobilize supporters in FATA, while permitting Islamist parties unfettered access to the public through Friday sermons at mosques and through access to FATA's numerous madrassah.[18] Thus, when adult franchise was

[16] International Crisis Group, *Pakistan's Tribal Areas: Appeasing the Militants* (Brussels, Islamabad: International Crisis Group, 2006); Seth G. Jones, Olga Oliker, Peter Chalk, C. Christine Fair, Rollie Lal, and James Dobbins, *Securing Tyrants or Fostering Reform? Evaluating U.S. Internal Security Assistance to Selected Repressive and Transitioning Regimes* (Washington D.C.: OSI/RAND, 2006).

[17] C. Christine Fair, Clay Ramsay and Steven Kull. "Pakistani Public Opinion on Democracy, Islamist Militancy, and Relations with the U.S." (Washington D.C.: PIPA, USIP, January 7, 2008).

[18] The Political Parties Act of 1962 (amended in 2002 with the Political Parties 2002) regulates the activities of political parties and their members. In the absence of the political parties act in FATA, political parties are not authorized to campaign, hold rallies or meetings that are typically considered to be quotidian party practices. As such, religious parties are at a distinct advantage in that they need not conduct "party" gatherings as they have ready access to religious institutions from which they can run their political campaigns and associated political outreach. The Frontier Crimes Regulation (FCR) is a colonial-era legislation that exists in FATA and is the framework for rule of law in the tribal areas. The FCR enshrines a number of problematic principles such as "collective responsibility," by which innocent family members can be punished for the crimes of near and distant relatives and tribesmen. Under the FCR, the political agent serves as the apex person for the execution of most

first exercised in the 1997 elections, the residents of FATA overwhelmingly and without precedent elected religious scholars (ulema) to represent them in the national assembly. Since 1997, FATA has consistently voted for Islamist in the general elections. Without legal reform and political liberalization, I am skeptical that economic investments will help bring the hapless residents of FATA into Pakistan's mainstream society. At some point, FATA must become part of Pakistan's legal, political and social structure. FATA must have functioning police and courts and other amenities that Pakistanis elsewhere enjoy. Thus economic investments need to be accompanied by political liberalization and legal reform.

Another area of recent focus is expanded military assistance to Pakistan's Frontier Constabulary, a paramilitary organization that operates in the FATA. While its officers are seconded from the Pakistan army, its cadres are drawn from the local Pashtun population. The Frontier Corps has played an important part of Pakistani operations in FATA because of their local language skills and familiarity with the local train. Yet the Frontier Corps is inadequately trained and equipped and has been ill-prepared for counterinsurgency operations in FATA. Numerous defections and refusals to fight and follow orders have taken place within the Frontier Corps. Thus belated moves to help resource the Frontier Corps are welcome and urgently needed. However, it should be kept in mind that the Frontier Corps' myriad problems are not completely resource-related. This organization was used to train the Taliban in the 1990s and many are suspected of having ties to that organization. Second, they are deeply infiltrated and/or sympathetic to the local militants. Third, even if they are not sympathetic to the militants, Frontier Corpsmen are often hesitant to fight due to fear of sparking a sanguinary blood feud in which they or their families may be ensnared. Training, equipping and professionalizing a competent Frontier Corps is fraught with multidimensional problems and will take years—not months—to do so.

Pakistan's Military

Since 9/11 numerous concerns have been voiced about the Pakistan army in particular. Some have raised the specter of an inner cabal of Islamist officers who can split away from the rest of the army. This scenario has typically included the possibility of officers absconding with nuclear weapons and/or missiles or some transfer of technology or know-how to militant groups or other undesirable state or non-state entity. Regarding

state activities associated with law and order Persons convicted under the FCR have no recourse to Pakistani jurisprudence. Pakistani high court rulings have on several instances ruled that the FCR is unconstitutional to no avail. Pakistani human rights organizations have also registered sharp complaints similarly without state action.

command and control and the security of Pakistan's nuclear weapons, most dedicated Pakistan analysts have no reason to believe that existing policies and procedures are inadequate at this juncture.[19]

There are—and should be—persistent concerns about nuclear safety in Pakistan. Concerns also persist about the prospects for a conventional Indo-Pakistan conflict to escalate or for some misunderstanding about movements of dual-use assets that could precipitate an accidental exchange (among other worrisome scenarios in the context of the Indo-Pakistan security competition). Thus nuclear safety should remain a focus of U.S-Pakistan military-to-military engagement to the greatest extent possible.

As is well-understood, the A.Q. Khan network is a known source of proliferation and indeed, his network was an important means by which Pakistan obtained its nuclear and missile technologies in the first instance. Proliferation will, and should, remain a concern for the United States and the international community. As Pakistan has declined to allow the IAEA or other non-Pakistani officials access to Dr. Khan and members of his network, doubts will continue to linger about the nature of his network, its expanse and the degree to which parts of it remain functional. This will remain a major irritant in the U.S.-Pakistan relationship that is unlikely to change irrespective of the February electoral outcome.

There is consensus that the Pakistan army is a professional organization and that the nuclear program is the most important priority for the army. As such, the army takes the protection of these assets very seriously. Recent attacks on Pakistan military and leadership targets have involved penetration of the armed forces' military and civilian ranks; however, these remain the exception, not the rule. But the Pakistan army has undergone considerable, but poorly understood change. At independence it continued the British practice of recruiting its officer corps from elite land-owning families of the northern Punjab. Since independence, it has become more urban, increasingly middle-class and ever-more representative of Pakistan's population. In other words, it has come to increasingly resemble Pakistani society from which it draws. Many longtime observers of Pakistan note that the country has become more conservative and suggest that this is likely to be true of the officer corps as well as the enlisted and non-commissioned officers. It is also the case that many officers today took their commissions during the Zia ul Haq's efforts to Islamize the country and the army and many officers came up through the ranks after the 1990 U.S. military cutoff.

---

[19] Institute for National Strategic Studies, National Defense University, "Roundtable Summary U.S. Strategy Toward Pakistan," 30 November 2007.

Thus there are numerous reasons to believe that the Pakistan army may be more anti-American and more conservative than one would like to countenance. Unfortunately recruitment data on the military is virtually non-existent and thus it is difficult to say with any confidence whether and how this institution is changing. However, these historical trends should caution U.S. policy against tightly aligning itself with an institution it does not and indeed cannot understand.

Moving Forward

In the short term, the United States must work to help achieve a democratic transition in Pakistan—not a democratic patina by which to legitimize President Musharraf. This will involve creating incentives for the Musharraf government to remove the barriers to maximally free and fair elections and to pursue conciliation with the political parties and civil society. This should include reinstating the judiciary; forging an acceptable election commission and securing a voters registration list acceptable to all parties; lifting restrictions on the political parties, the media and election observers; working to minimize electoral violence; and to refrain from using the intelligence agencies and local functionaries to interfere in the election. Musharraf is very unlikely to take these steps without a clarion statement—in public and in private—from the administration and Congress that such measures are expected.

The United States should work to support institutions and processes and demure from supporting or undermining particular persons or institutions. Both Benazir Bhutto and Musharraf were tainted in the eyes of Pakistanis for their association with Washington while U.S. failure to support institutions such as the media and the judiciary has vexed Pakistanis. The United States must make a commitment to securing a democratic Pakistan and Pakistanis must be reassured that this is the case. As the political situation will remain turbulent for the foreseeable future, it is important that the United States reach out to all political parties, key civilian institutions and civil society groups while sustaining a working relationship with Pakistan's armed forces.

In coming months, there will be a temptation to restrict or condition aid and military assistance to Pakistan, particularly if the elections prove illegitimate. However, one must be mindful of the history of U.S. aid to Pakistan. While the conventional wisdom about the "Pressler Amendment" is false, the United States has done little to address pervasive and erroneous accounts of the cutoff of military assistance in 1990 in both the United States and in Pakistan.[20] As such, moves towards cutting aid or

[20] While the historical record shows that the Pressler Amendment was forged with Pakistani input to accommodate the administration's interest in continuing to provide military assistance to Pakistan

conditioning it will likely reinforce Pakistani perceptions that U.S. is only episodically interested in Pakistan for utilitarian purposes. More dangerous is the belief in Pakistan that the U.S. cuts aid when there is a transition to democracy.

However, over the medium and long term, there is urgent need to structurally re-shape the terms of U.S. assistance to Pakistan. The U.S. should continue to expand programs that enable the Pakistani armed forces to fight their and our war on terror more effectively. Military educational programs should be expanded. While IMET is important, there may be other means of expanding the engagement with Pakistan's armed forces through public and private educational institutions. Higher-end equipment that is desirable for Pakistan's strategic purposes should increasingly be contingent upon demonstrable evidence of greater alignment of U.S. and Pakistani interests in counter-terrorism and sustained disengagement from the political management of the country.

While re-optimizing the assistance to the Pakistan military, the U.S. must dramatically expand *programmed* assistance to reform all of Pakistan's civilian institutions including the judiciary, police and law enforcement; to train large numbers of politicians; support major civil society institutions such as those dedicated to monitoring human rights, corruption mitigation, political reconciliation, human development and the like through financial resources and capacity building. While education should remain a priority, all initiatives should be sensitive to Pakistani preferences which may not entail secularization of their curriculum. While a seeming bromide, the United States should explore any and all means of expanding people-to-people contact through exchanges of students, journalists, parliamentarians and other politicians, lawyers, police, judges, teachers and other important representatives of Pakistan's civil society and civilian institutions. In short, the U.S. must rapidly transition from supporting one person towards supporting the key institutions and processes of this critical country.

---

despite growing concerns within the intelligence community and congress about Pakistan's progress towards weaponization, most Pakistanis see the Pressler Amendment as a punitive measure that allowed the United States to drop Pakistan when its strategic utility had diminished.

DOCUMENT NO. 26

PAKISTANI PUBLIC OPINION ON DEMOCRACY, ISLAMIST MILITANCY, AND RELATIONS WITH THE U.S.

United States Institute of Peace Report

February 2008

C. Christine Fair
RAND Corporation
Clay Ramsay
WorldPublicOpinion.org
Steve Kull
WorldPublicOpinion.org

About This Report

This report is based on the results of a survey conducted from Sept. 12–18, just before President Pervez Musharraf declared a six-week state of emergency and before the assassination of former Prime Minister Benazir Bhutto. The sample included 907 Pakistani urban adults, selected using multi-stage probability sampling, who were interviewed at home in 19 cities.

C. Christine Fair, Clay Ramsay, and Steven Kull designed the questionnaire and wrote the analysis for this study, with contributions from Stephen Weber, Evan Lewis, and Ebrahim Mohseni. Mary Speck, Abe Medoff, Melanie Ciolek and Melinda Brouwer managed the editing and production of the report.

WorldPublicOpinion.org also received support from the Ford Foundation and the Circle Foundation. The survey was conducted by WorldPublic Opinion.org in collaboration with, and with financial support from, the Center for Conflict Analysis and Prevention at the U.S. Institute of Peace.

About This Series

USIP Working Papers are unedited works in progress and may appear in future USIP publications, peer-reviewed journals, and edited volumes. This product is only distributed online and does not have a hard copy counterpart.

Introduction

Over the past year, Pakistan has endured a series of traumatic events that have brought increasing stress to its people and its political classes, as well as to American policymakers and the international community.

In March 2007 President Musharraf suspended the Supreme Court's chief justice, a move which sparked a movement of lawyers and professionals in opposition to the government's action. In July, the army retook the Lal Masjid ("Red Mosque") from militant groups in an assault that brought numerous casualties. This led to the breakdown of a tenuous accord between the government and pro-Taliban groups in Waziristan, who resumed attacks on government forces—attacks that have expanded since into settled areas.

In October, the opposition leader Benazir Bhutto returned to Pakistan to campaign in upcoming National Assembly elections; on the day of her return, an attempt was made on her life that killed 149 others. In November, President Musharraf declared a state of emergency that lasted six weeks, purged the Supreme Court, and put new controls on broadcast media. Finally, in December Benazir Bhutto was killed, precipitating a new situation that seems to be moving—tortuously—toward new elections.

In this fierce succession of events, it is important to not lose a broader perspective. The Islamic Republic of Pakistan has gone through many crises in its 60 years, and its resilience has been often underestimated. One source of this resilience has been, necessarily, the Pakistani public. Thus it is vital to ask what are the strengths and weaknesses, the areas of agreement and polarization that characterize the public's attitudes.

Naturally a key concern, especially from an American perspective, is how Pakistanis view the proper role of Islam in society. Central to the US "war on terror" is concern about militant groups, such as al Qaeda and the Taliban, who seek to create an extremely conservative and theocratic Islamist state. How responsive are Pakistanis to the siren song of such ideas? The Pakistani government has taken a number of steps in recent years to reform the madrassahs and laws related to the treatment of women: how do Pakistanis view these developments?

Conversely important is the question of how Pakistanis view democracy. How important is democracy to them and how do they assess the reality of democratic functioning in Pakistan? Likewise, how do they value the independence of the justice system, which has been sorely tested over the last year?

Perhaps most centrally, does the majority feel there are contradictions between democratic governance and Islam's social role, or do they see these as essentially in harmony? Does the current political turmoil arise from deep-seated ideological conflicts on these questions, or do they primarily arise from political power struggles?

The army has long taken the central role among Pakistan's governmental institutions. How do Pakistanis really feel about the army? Is there a single view of the army held by a majority, whatever role the army takes—or do they see its many different roles in different ways?

Over the last year the Taliban and other militant groups consolidated themselves in the Federally Administered Tribal Areas (FATA) and reached increasingly into the Northwest Frontier Province, much to the concern of the United States and its NATO allies in Afghanistan. A key part of this situation is the fact that the FATA is only loosely integrated with Pakistan as a whole. How do Pakistanis view this longstanding arrangement?

How do Pakistanis look on military action in FATA against Islamist militant groups? When Pakistanis think about Islamist militancy, how do they perceive it? How aware are they of these organizations' actual methods and activities? Do they think of such groups as a threat to Pakistan?

The United States has made major investments in its relationship with Pakistan's government and military. The events of the last year have led to an American debate—likely to grow only more intense—over what direction the United States should take now. Should the United States continue to focus on its relations with the governing elite? Should it engage with Pakistan in a wider and perhaps riskier way, one that includes Pakistan's people and civil society? What do Pakistani public attitudes suggest about the prospects of different possible US courses of action?

To seek answers to these and many other compelling questions, WorldPublicOpinion.org and the U.S. Institute of Peace collaborated on a far-ranging study of Pakistani public attitudes. The survey was conducted from Sept. 12 to 18, just before President Pervez Musharraf declared a six-week state of emergency and before the assassination of former Prime Minister Benazir Bhutto. The sample included 907 Pakistani urban adults, selected using multi-stage probability sampling, who were interviewed at home in 19 cities. The margin of error is +/– 3.3 percent.

The key findings of the study are:

1. Role of Islam

There is strong public support for giving Islam a wider role in Pakistan. A large majority feels it is very important to live in a country that is governed according to Islamic principles. A majority says it would like to see Shari'a or Islamic law play a larger role in their country than it does today.

At the same time, there is little support for a shift towards extreme religious conservatism. Instead there is significant support for some reforms in the opposite direction. Only a small minority—even among those who want a greater role for Shari'a—wants to see the "Talibanization" of daily life increase. About two-thirds support a recent government plan to reform the madrassahs, including strong support among those favoring Shari'a. A plurality supports the Women's Protection Act, which modifies existing law in the direction of greater women's rights.

2. Views of Democracy

A large majority of Pakistanis endorse democracy. Most Pakistanis say it is very important to live in a country governed by elected representatives. Among those who want a greater role for Islam, support for democracy is even higher than among the population as a whole. Likewise, a large majority supports an independent judiciary.

3. Assessment of Pakistani Democracy

Pakistanis are lukewarm about how well their government lives up to democratic principles. A plurality is not confident that the next elections will be free and fair, and few think the courts are independent of political or military influence. Assessments of Pakistan's protection of human rights are also lukewarm.

4. Views of the Government

Majorities express little confidence in the national government's political institutions including the president, the National Assembly, the Provincial Assemblies, and the police. However, views are mixed about the Nazims and the justice system.

5. Views of the Military

In sharp contrast to their negative views of many civilian institutions, Pakistanis express substantial confidence in the armed forces and give the army high ratings for performing traditional military functions. However, when it comes to the army's role in the ongoing governance of the country, views are complex. While the army is seen as capable, few believe that it has a positive influence on Pakistan's economy and politics. A plurality says that the role of the army should be limited to military matters.

6. Islamist Militant Groups

A large majority of Pakistanis have negative views of Islamist militant organizations such as al Qaeda, local Taliban, and Pakistani militant groups. The activities of these groups are seen as threats to Pakistan and the use of violence against civilians is overwhelmingly rejected. However, a majority also rejects the government's recent military assault to retake the Red Mosque from Islamist extremists and their militant associates. Awareness of Pakistani militant groups' activities appears to be low: few perceive that their operations have targeted civilians, that they have relations with the Pakistani army and intelligence agencies, or that they provide social services.

7. The Federally Administered Tribal Areas (FATA)

A large majority of Pakistanis want to phase out the FATA's special legal status and to integrate the areas into the country's overall legal structure. Few want this to happen abruptly, however; a plurality favors a gradualist approach. Pakistanis strongly prefer negotiating with the Taliban rather than fighting them. Only a small minority supports using military force to exert control while a plurality favors a negotiated approach. The current policy of limited military action while pursuing negotiations with local forces receives plurality approval.

A plurality believes the army should pursue and capture Taliban insurgents and al Qaeda forces crossing into Pakistan from Afghanistan. But overwhelming majorities oppose allowing foreign forces to enter Pakistan in order to do so. Almost no Pakistanis appear to believe Osama bin Laden is in Pakistan, and even if his location were to be established in the FATA, a plurality thinks the government should not try to capture him.

8. Relations with the United States

Majority opinion toward the United States is negative. Large majorities say that the United States cannot be trusted to act responsibly and also believe that it has extraordinary influence over Pakistan. US military presence in the region is viewed as a threat to Pakistan. A large and growing majority believe it is a US goal to weaken and divide the Muslim world. A plurality disapproves of how Pakistan's government has handled relations with the United States. Only one in four feels that security cooperation with the United States has brought Pakistan any benefit.

9. Relations with Afghanistan

Majorities see the tensions with Afghanistan as a threat to Pakistan's interests and approve of the way Pakistan's government has handled relations with its neighbor. Views of the Taliban's activities in Afghanistan are quite mixed: nearly half show at least some sympathy for their attacks on NATO troops, while one in three show some sympathy for Taliban attacks on Afghan police and troops. Only one in three believe that the Pakistani government is seriously trying to prevent the Taliban from operating in Afghanistan.

10. Ranking of Perceived Threats

Asked to evaluate a series of possible threats to Pakistan's vital interests, the Pakistani public rates US military presence in the region as a critical threat by the largest percentage. Other threats regarded as critical by majorities include tensions with India and violence between Pakistani religious and ethnic groups. Slightly fewer regard the activities of al Qaeda, local Taliban, and jihadist militants as critical, or the activities of ethnic nationalist movements. Only half see the possibility of Iran acquiring nuclear weapons as threatening. A majority considers the rise of China to be no threat to Pakistan.

11. Trade and Globalization

Large majorities endorse international trade and see it as beneficial for Pakistan, though only a plurality are positive about the idea of globalization.

12. Pakistan's Economy

Two thirds feel that Pakistan's economy has gone off on the wrong track. Nonetheless, a majority approves of how the government is handling the economy.

13. Education

Majorities express confidence in the educational system and approve of the government's policies. Pakistanis put the highest priorities on teaching children religious values and good citizenship, followed by basic skills, problem-solving, and independent thinking.

Findings

1. Role of Islam

There is strong public support for giving Islam a wider role in Pakistan. A large majority feels it is very important to live in a country that is

governed according to Islamic principles. A majority says it would like to see Shari'a or Islamic law play a larger role in their country than it does today.

At the same time, there is little support for a shift towards extreme religious conservatism. Instead there is significant support for some reforms in the opposite direction. Only a small minority—even among those who want a greater role for Shari'a—wants to see the "Talibanization" of daily life increase. About two-thirds support a recent government plan to reform the madrassahs, including strong support among those favoring Shari'a. A plurality supports the Women's Protection Act, which modifies existing law in the direction of greater women's rights.

Support for a Greater Role for Islam

Majorities of Pakistanis would like to see Islam playing a wider role in the public life of their country. When asked to use a 10-point scale to rank the importance of living "in a country that is governed according to Islamic principles," 61 percent picked 10 (meaning "absolutely important"), and 81 percent chose 8 or higher. Only a miniscule 4 percent said 4 or less. The mean response was 9.0.

Respondents were then asked to use another 10-point scale to rank how much Pakistan is currently governed by Islamic principles, with 0 meaning "not at all" and 10 meaning "completely." This time 61 percent picked scores of 5 or less. Only 17 percent answered 8 or higher. The mean score was just 4.6.

A clear majority thinks that Shari'a should play a more important role in Pakistan. Asked whether "Shari'a should play a larger role, a smaller role, or about the same role" compared to current Pakistani law, 60 percent said

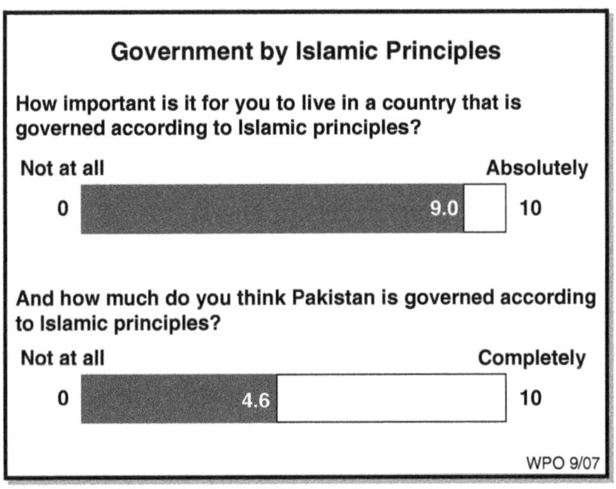

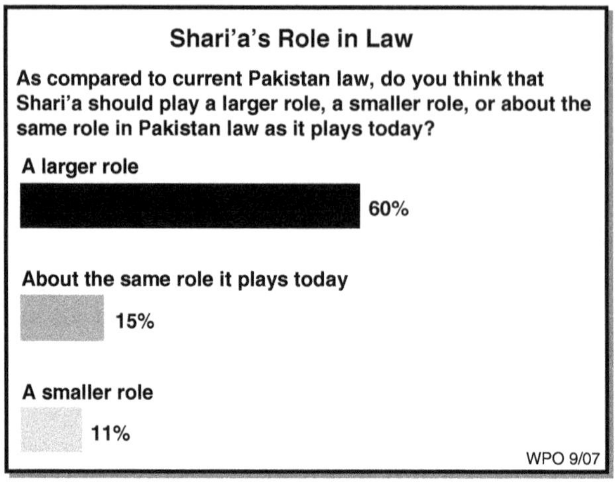

a larger role. Only 11 percent thought the role of Shari'a should be smaller, and 15 percent thought it should stay the same.

Pakistanis also consider Islam more vital to their identity than ethnicity or nationality. The survey asked respondents to choose which of five identities—Pakistani, Muslim, individual, citizen of the world, member of your ethnic group—was "most central to your sense of self or identity." Sixty-one percent said being a Muslim was the most central (another 31 percent said this was their second choice.) The next most popular was, being Pakistani, which was the first choice of 29 percent (56 percent second choice).

Asked about the "secularization of daily life," only 13 percent said they would like to see more, while 69 percent expressed opposition. A striking 52 percent refused to answer the question as posed and volunteered that that there should be no secularization at all. Another 17 percent said they would like to see secularization decrease.

The question of Islam having a greater role does not appear to be a divisive issue—rather, support cuts across key political lines. Support for a greater role for Islam extends to supporters of all of the major Pakistani leaders, including Pervez Musharraf. Respondents were asked who they thought was best to lead Pakistan (Benazir Bhutto was the most popular at 27 percent while Musharraf and Nawaz Sharif were tied at 21 percent). Though there was some variation, supporters of all leaders mostly favored a greater role for Islam and Shari'a and opposed increased secularization. Mean ratings for the importance of Pakistan being governed by Islamic principles were approximately 9 (on a 0-10 scale) for all groups. Those favoring a larger role for Shari'a varied only slightly: 55 percent among Musharraf supporters, 62 percent among Sharif supporters. Interestingly, opposition to secularization was highest among Musharraf supporters (76%), followed by Sharif supporters (68%) and Bhutto supporters (63%).

Rejection of Extreme Religious Conservatism

A number of poll questions revealed that the Pakistani public's support for Islam playing a larger role in their country does not signify support for extreme religious conservatism. Majorities of all Pakistanis—even majorities of those who favor a greater role for Shari'a—oppose an increase in Talibanization and support reforming structures of a conservative character dating from the time of General Zia

Respondents were asked about the "Talibanization of daily life," a term widely used by Pakistani media at the time of the poll, which is generally understood to signify extreme religious conservatism and even militancy. Just 15 percent said they would like to see this increase (11% "a little," and only 4% "a great deal"). Fifty-nine percent expressed opposition: A plurality (38%) said that such "Talibanization" should decrease (20% a great deal) and 21 percent said it should stay about the same.

Interestingly, support for Talibanization was no greater among those wanting a greater role for Shari'a.

Perhaps the most important indication that Pakistanis have little interest in extreme religious conservatism is their strong majority support for a recent government plan to regulate the madrassahs, or Islamic schools. About two-thirds (64%) said they would support a plan requiring "madrassahs to register with the government and to spend more time in class on subjects like mathematics and science." This included one third (36%) who said they strongly supported the plan. Only 17 percent opposed such reforms. Interestingly, those who wanted a larger role for Shari'a were slightly *more* likely than others to strongly favor these reforms: 40 percent favored them strongly and only 16 percent were opposed.

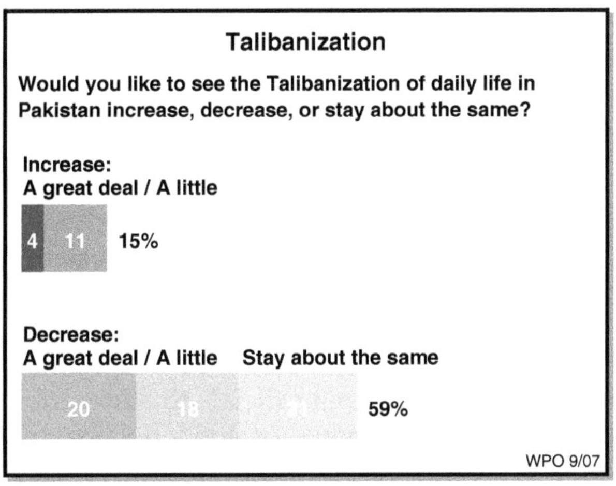

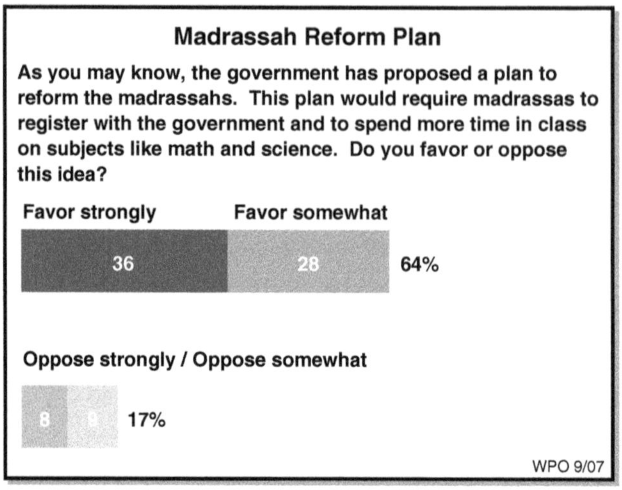

Another indication of majority disinterest in extreme religious conservatism is Pakistani reaction to the government's Women's Protection Act, which made the laws on adultery and rape from the Zia period (the Hudood Ordinances) less harsh for women. A 38 percent plurality—and a clear majority of those who answered—supported the Women's Protection Act while only 27 percent opposed it. Another 16 percent volunteered they had not heard of the Act and 19 percent declined to answer.

Pakistanis overwhelmingly reject the attacks on religious minorities carried out by some extreme fundamentalist groups in Pakistan as part of an ideology that demonizes such minorities. Three quarters (75–78 percent) said that attacks on specific religious minorities (Shi'a and Ahmadiyya) were never justified. Only 5–8 percent said protection of minorities was not important or that such attacks were sometimes justified.

Four out of five (81%) also say it is "important for the unity of Pakistan to protect religious minorities in Pakistan" A large majority perceives that "religious minorities get such protection" either "almost always" (38%) or "most of the time" (31%). Twenty-one percent believe minorities are protected only "some of the time" (15%) or "hardly ever" (6%).

Why do Pakistanis say they want more Shari'a even though they resist extreme religious conservatism and support reforming certain Islamic laws? It is important to note that Pakistan was founded as an Islamic republic and second that Shari'a has been part of the court system since the 1970s, when it was introduced under General Mohammad Zia ul-Haq. Thus when Pakistanis say they want Shari'a to play a greater role, they may be expressing a desire for the system to work better, not for fundamental change. They may simply want government officials to show more wisdom and piety or want their courts (known for long delays) to operate more efficiently.

2. Views of Democracy

A large majority of Pakistanis endorse democracy. Most Pakistanis say it is very important to live in a country governed by elected representatives. Among those who want a greater role for Islam, support for democracy is even higher than among the population as a whole. Likewise, a large majority supports an independent judiciary.

Most Pakistanis want their government to be democratic. Asked to assess, on a 10-point scale, "How important is it for you to live in a country that is governed by representatives elected by the people," a large majority indicated that it was very important, choosing 8 or higher, and 50 percent chose 10, meaning "absolutely important." The mean score was 8.4. Only 7 percent chose a score of 3 or lower.

Interestingly, those who wanted a larger role for Islam had an exceptionally strong desire for greater democracy. Among the 60 percent majority who support a larger role for Shari'a compared to current Pakistani law, 64 percent give the importance of democracy a 10; among those who want the role of Shar'ia to decrease or stay the same, only a quarter (25–26 percent) give the importance of democracy a 10. Similarly, among the 31 percent for whom it is extremely important to live in a country governed by Islamic principles, *and* who give Pakistan a low rating in this regard, 72 percent give the importance of democracy a 10–22 points higher than the full sample.

Pakistanis also consider it very important to "live in a country where the decisions of the courts are independent from influence by political and military authorities." Asked to assess the importance of this on the 10-point scale, a large majority (71%) chose a score of 8 or higher. The mean score was 8.6. Only a tiny minority (3%) considered this unimportant, giving it a score of less than 3.

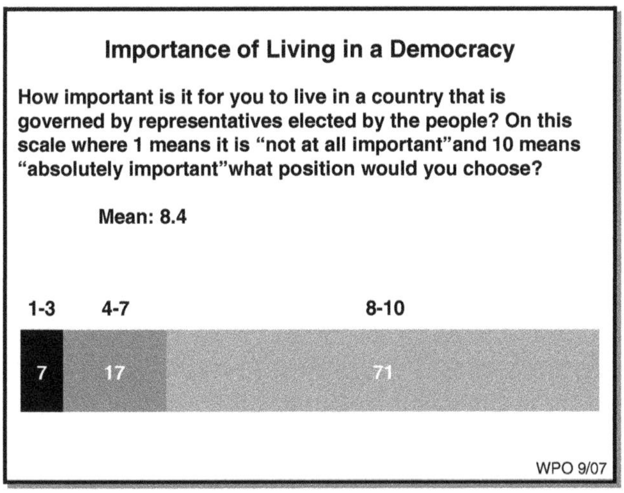

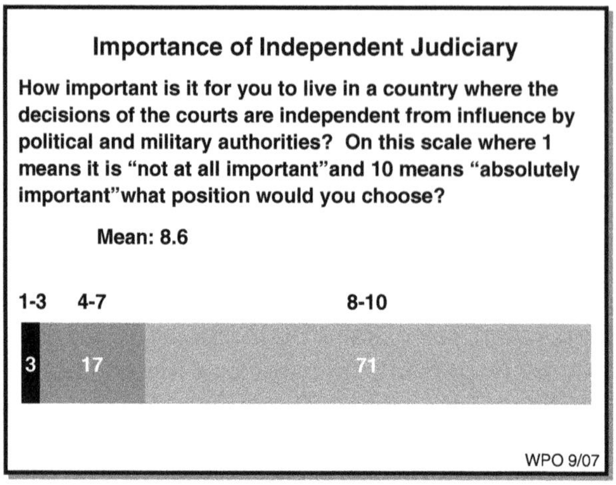

Support for democracy and an independent judiciary is also very strong among supporters of all the various Pakistani leaders. Those saying democracy was important varied only moderately from a mean of 8.1 out of 10 among Sharif supporters to 8.6 among Musharraf supporters (Bhutto supporters, 8.4), while those favoring an independent judiciary varied even less, at 8.4 among Sharif supporters and 8.6 among Bhutto and Musharraf supporters.

3. Assessment of Pakistani Democracy

Pakistanis are lukewarm about how well their government lives up to democratic principles. A plurality is not confident that the next elections will be free and fair, and few think the courts are independent of political or military influence. Assessments of Pakistan's protection of human rights are also lukewarm.

When asked to assess, on a 10-point scale, "how much do you think Pakistan is governed by representatives elected by the people," with 1 meaning "not at all" and 10 meaning "completely," the mean response was 4.8. Thirty-two percent gave a score of 3 or lower. Only 18 percent said Pakistan rated an eight out of 10 or higher. Polling was conducted before Pakistani president and army chief Pervez Musharraf declared a state of emergency on Nov. 3. It also took place before the Dec. 27 assassination of former Prime Minister Benazir Bhutto.

Pakistanis show skepticism about the quality of elections in their own country. Asked how confident they were that the upcoming elections would be "free and fair," only 39 percent said they were either somewhat (28%) or very confident (11%), while a plurality of 44 percent said they were not very confident (27%) or not at all confident (17%). Nonetheless, a majority of Pakistanis (60%) said they thought there would be elections in 2007, though this was still an open question at the time of the poll.

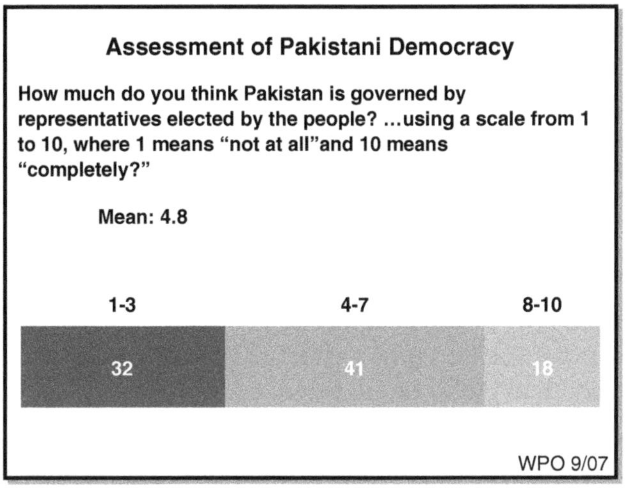

Only 17 percent said they thought there would not be a vote, while 23 percent would not answer.

Relatively few think their own country is fulfilling the ideal of an independent judiciary. Asked to use a 10-point scale to assess how much "the decisions of the courts are independent from influence by political and military authorities" (with 1 meaning "not at all" and 10 meaning "completely"), only 26 percent gave their country a score of 8 or higher while nearly as many (23%) gave it a score of three or lower. The mean score was 5.6.

Similarly, few Pakistanis think their country consistently protects human rights. Only one in four (24%) said that there was "a lot of respect for individual human rights in our country. Another fourth (26%) said there was "some respect." Forty-two percent said there was either "not much respect" (21%) or "no respect at all" (21%).

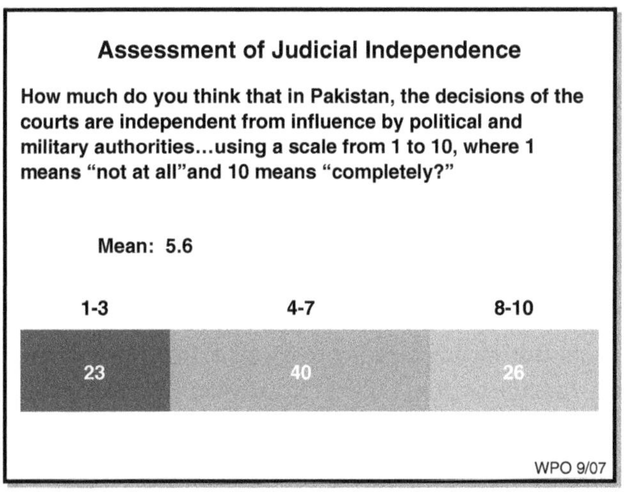

4. Views of the Government

Majorities express little confidence in the national government's political institutions including the president, the National Assembly, the Provincial Assemblies, and the police. However, views are mixed about the Nazims and the justice system.

Asked about national institutions—the government as a whole, the president and the legislature—strong majorities in Pakistan express little or no confidence. Two out of five Pakistanis (59%) said either that they did not have very much faith in their "national government as a whole" (48%) or that they had none (11%). Only a third (33%) said they had "quite a lot" (25%) or a "great deal" (8%) of confidence.

There was a similar lack of confidence in the "office of the president." Fifty-five percent had either little (42%) or no confidence (13%) while only 30 percent had quite a lot (22%) or a great deal (8%).

The National Assembly scored even lower. Fifty-nine percent had little (45%) or no confidence (14%) while 29 percent had quite a lot (23%) or a great deal (6%). The same was true of the Provincial Assemblies: 58 percent had little (44%) or no confidence (14%) in them, while 29 percent had quite a lot (23%) or a great deal (6%).

The police received the worst ratings. Two-thirds of those polled said they had either not very much (53%) or no confidence (13%) in the local police.

Local governments, such as Nazims, at least garnered a divided assessment. The Nazims, local administrators (akin perhaps to mayors) who came into being under President Musharraf's Devolution of Power Plan of August 2000, run for election on a non-party basis. Less than half of those polled (47%) showed little (37%) or no confidence (10%) in local authorities, while nearly as many (44%) said they had quite a lot (30%) or a great deal (14%) of confidence.

Pakistani views of their country's justice system are also mixed: Nearly half (47%) expressed little (37%) or no confidence (10%), almost as many (43%) expressed quite a lot of confidence (30%) or a great deal (13%).

Another question asked respondents where they would turn if they were the victims of a crime, giving them a range of formal, traditional or religious options: "If someone in your family suffered from a serious crime, which of the following would you have the most confidence to effectively deal with it in the right way?"

"The courts" was the most popular response, but only 34 percent chose it. Next came "my family or clan" (25%), followed by "the local police" (14%). Very few—only 9 percent—selected any of the religious or semi-religious

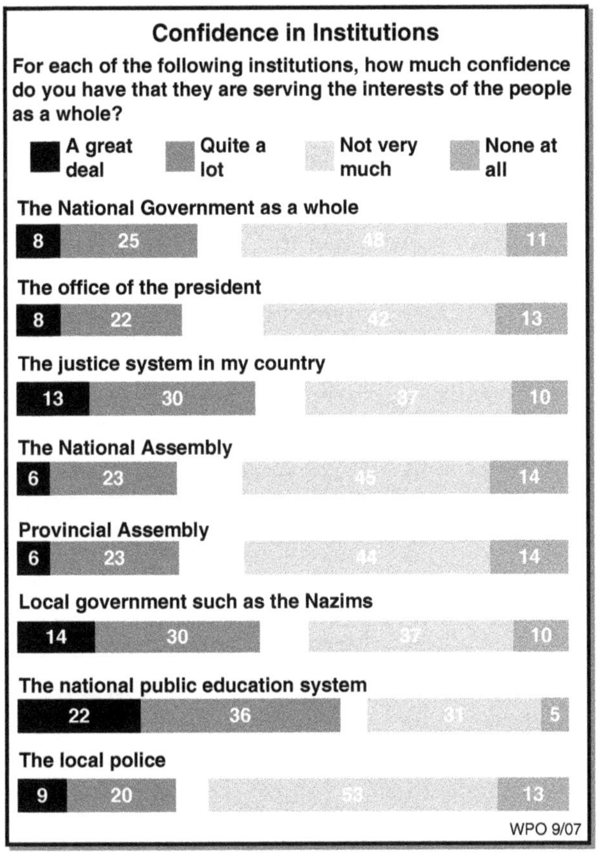

authority offered ("a local religious leader," 2%; "a jirga," 2%; "a panchayat," 2%; "a mohalla committee," 3%).

This suggests that for many Pakistanis, formal means of justice (police and courts) are seen as the primary source of redress. However, for important minorities, traditional forms of justice (including family and clan and other local religious and cultural institutions) remain appealing.

Pakistani attitudes about public officials do not seem to reflect personal experience with corruption. An overwhelming 88 percent of those polled answered "No," when asked "have you or someone in your family been personally affected by an act of corruption by government officials in the past 12 months." Only 3 percent said they had been affected by corruption.

5. Views of the Military

In sharp contrast to their negative views of many civilian institutions, Pakistanis express substantial confidence in the armed forces and give the army high ratings for performing traditional military functions.

However, when it comes to the army's role in the ongoing governance of the country, views are complex. While the army is seen as capable, few believe that it has a positive influence on Pakistan's economy and politics. A plurality says that the role of the army should be limited to military matters.

Although they exhibit little trust in many government institutions, a majority of Pakistanis express confidence in the military. Two-thirds said they had either a great deal (34%) or quite a lot (35%) of confidence in the army and other armed forces. Only a quarter said they had not very much (18%) or no confidence (5%).

This approval is especially high when Pakistanis are asked about the military's performance of traditional military functions. More than four out of five (84%) said the Pakistani army was doing either an "excellent" (56%) or a good job (28%) "defending Pakistan's borders and territory." Only 12 percent said its performance was fair or poor.

When asked to evaluate the army's role in the governance of Pakistan, views are complex. Asked to rate the army's performance in "how Pakistan is governed", a modest majority (53%) considered military participation in governance to be excellent (25%) or good (28%). But large numbers (36%) thought that the army's role in governing their country was either only fair (21%) or poor (15%). Two out of three (66%) also said the army did an excellent (31%) or good (35%) job of "helping with economic growth and development," while 28 percent said these efforts were fair (22%) or poor (6%).

But though the army is seen as capable, there is little enthusiasm for the impact of the army on political and economic aspects of the country. Less than a quarter viewed that army as having a "mostly positive" influence

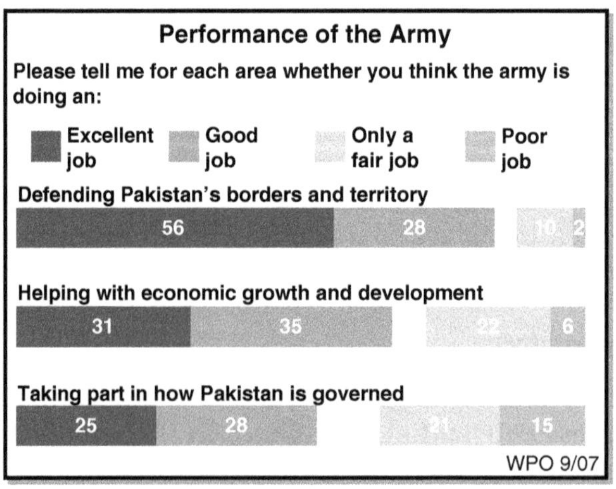

on Pakistan's economy, justice system, education and the rule of law, with more or equal numbers choosing "mostly negative." For each question in the series, 45 percent or more of the respondents either declined to answer or volunteered other responses ("both," "neither," "it depends").

Only one in four (23%) called the army's influence on the economy mostly positive while one in three (32%) called it negative. Pakistani assessments of the army's influence on the justice system were even less favorable: just 17 percent said positive while 27 percent said negative. About the same number said the army's influence on the constitution and rule of law was positive (18%), while one fourth (24%) had a negative view. Less than one in four rated the army's influence on the public education system as mostly positive (23%) and just as many rated it mostly negative (23%). About one in five considered the army's influence on the press, radio and television to be positive (21%) while one in four called it negative (26%).

The highest percentage of "mostly positive" responses (29%) concerned the army's influence on "national reconstruction, as instituted by the National Reconstruction Bureau," an entity established by General Musharraf in November 1999, just one month after his military coup, to formulate policies for national reconstruction, promote good governance and strengthen democratic institutions. Only 19 percent considered the military's influence on the Bureau to be mostly negative.

A plurality of Pakistanis believe that "as a general rule" the armed forces should "be limited to strictly military matters," rejecting the idea that they should "take a wider role in the country's affairs." Forty-one percent said the armed forces should handle only military matters, compared with 33 percent who favored a wider role.

6. Islamist Militant Groups

A large majority of Pakistanis have negative views of Islamist militant organizations such as al Qaeda, local Taliban, and Pakistani militant groups. The activities of these groups are seen as threats to Pakistan and the use of violence against civilians is overwhelmingly rejected. However, a majority also rejects the government's recent military assault to retake the Red Mosque from Islamist extremists and their militant associates. Awareness of Pakistani militant groups' activities appears to be low: few perceive that their operations have targeted civilians, that they have relations with the Pakistani army and intelligence agencies, or that they provide social services.

The degree to which militant groups find sympathy and resonance among the Pakistani public is a primary question for policymakers and analysts. Pakistan's ability to override Islamist militancy and strengthen democracy and the rule of law depends in large measure upon the Pakistani polity's willingness to combat—militarily, politically and through law enforcement mechanisms—the various militant groups fighting in and from Pakistan. Without such willingness, it is unclear whether Pakistan will be able to develop into a stable, democratic state at peace with itself and with its neighbors.

Large majorities of urban Pakistanis view the activities of al Qaeda, local Taliban, and Pakistani militant groups as threats to Pakistan's vital interests. Respondents were asked whether they saw the activities of these various groups "as a threat or not to the vital interests of Pakistan in the next ten years," and, if so, whether they saw it "as a critical threat, or as important but not critical?"

Sixty-two percent said al Qaeda's activities threaten Pakistan, and 41 percent saw this threat as critical. Only 14 percent thought al Qaeda was not a threat. Sixty percent said the "activities of Islamist militants and local Taliban in FATA [the Federally Administered Tribal Areas] and settled areas" threaten Pakistan, and 34 percent saw the threat as critical; 18 percent said these activities were not a threat. Finally, 61 percent thought the activities of domestic militant groups (*askari tanzeems*) were a threat to Pakistan, with 38 percent calling them a critical threat (17% said these were not a threat).

Supporters of all the various Pakistani leaders view Islamist militant groups as threats to Pakistan. Al Qaeda was seen as a threat by 76 percent of Musharraf supporters, 60 percent of Bhutto supporters and 62 percent of Sharif supporters. Similar perceptions were held for other Islamist militant groups.

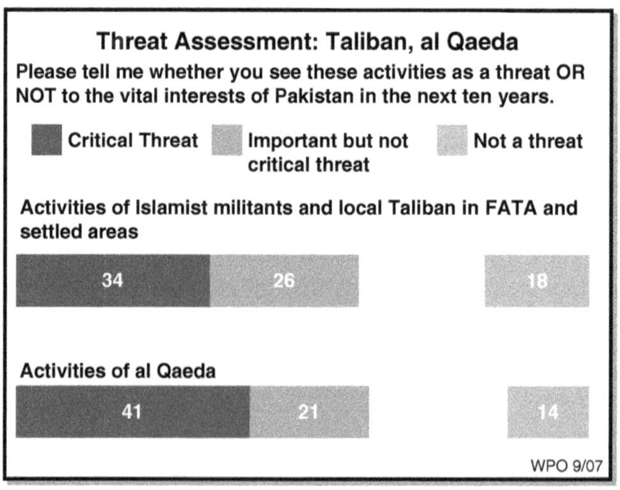

Rejection of Attacks on Civilians

Substantial majorities also repudiate the tactic of attacks on civilians in general, including those directed against India by Pakistani extremist groups. Respondents were asked:

Some people think that bombing and other types of attacks intentionally aimed at civilians are sometimes justified while others think that this kind of violence is never justified. Do you personally feel that such attacks are often justified, sometimes justified, rarely justified, or never justified?

Two thirds (66%) said such attacks were either "never justified" (55%) or "rarely justified" (11%). Only 15 percent called such attacks "sometimes" (8%) or "often" (7%) justified.

Respondents were then asked whether specific types of attacks were sometimes or never justified. Sixty-four percent said "Attacks conducted against government institutions (like the national Parliament in Delhi and state assemblies)" were never justified while 15 percent said sometimes justified. Sixty-seven percent said "attacks in India on families of Indian military personnel" were never justified while 13 percent said they were sometimes justified. And 68 percent condemned "attacks conducted against Indian targets like subways, stock exchanges, and tourist sites" while only 12 percent said these attacks were sometimes justified.

Thus, only a minority of about 15 percent showed any support for the tactic of targeting civilians in general or in specific cases.

Pakistan has long justified its support for militant groups battling India over Kashmir with the argument that because it was founded as the home for South Asia's Muslims, Pakistan has an obligation to protect the Muslims of South Asia. To determine whether Pakistanis believe their country has such an obligation to protect Muslims in Kashmir and elsewhere,

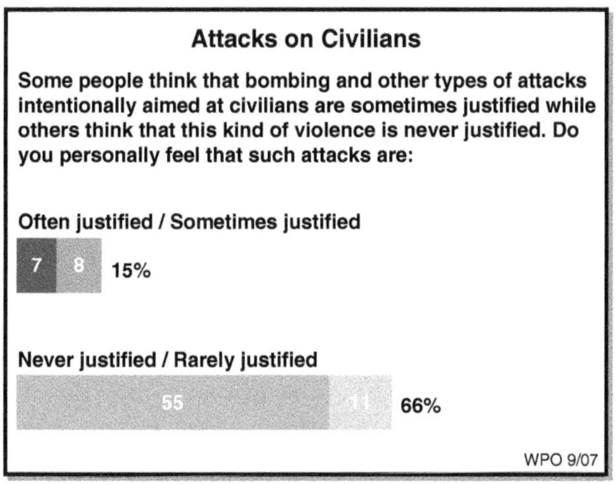

respondents were asked whether they agreed or disagreed with the statement: "Pakistan has a moral obligation to protect Muslims anywhere in South Asia." Sixty-six percent agreed (36% strongly); only 21 percent disagreed (13% strongly).

Those who agreed were then asked: "To protect Muslims in South Asia, do you think Pakistan should use any means, including force, or do you think Pakistan should only use peaceful means?" Fifty-one percent of the whole sample thought Pakistan should use only peaceful means; only 12 percent thought Pakistan should use any means, including force. Thus overall, 72 percent rejected the idea that Pakistan should use force beyond its own territory in defense of Muslims.

Attack on Red Mosque

Pakistani perceptions of Islamist extremist and even militant groups as a threat does not translate necessarily into support for using military-style force against them, as in the Pakistani military's attack on the Red Mosque or Lal Masjid in July. The Red Mosque and its affiliated Jamia Hafsa seminary are Deobandi institutions situated in the heart of Islamabad that have been long associated with sectarian militant groups. In recent years, the leadership of the Red Mosque and its seminary engaged in vigilante violence against such targets as women who chose not to wear the veil and stores selling music and movie CDs and DVDs. Throughout 2007, they confronted the Pakistani government by seizing state assets, kidnapping police officers and capturing purported prostitutes. The Pakistani government's military offensive against the mosque and seminaries resulted in the death of the head cleric and a number of students. The exact death toll remains controversial, with wildly varying estimates offered by government and non-government sources.

When asked, "Do you think the Pakistani security forces should have used force to take over the Red Mosque, or do you think that this was a mistake?" nearly two out of three (64%) agreed that it was and only 22 percent disagreed. Another question asked whether respondents approved of "the way Pakistan's government is handling . . . religious extremism such as the Lal Masjid [Red Mosque]." A majority disapproved (56%) while only 31 percent approved.

Awareness of Activities of Militant Groups

The Pakistani public does not appear to be very informed about the activities of Pakistani jihadist groups. Few think that their operations have targeted civilians, that they have relations with the Pakistani army and intelligence agencies, or that they provide social services to Pakistani communities.

Pakistanis were asked about three militant groups that are known to have conducted operations in Kashmir—Jaish e Mohammad, Hizbol Mujahadeen, and Lashkar e Taiba. Respondents were asked whether each group "has intentionally targeted civilians in attacks" in Kashmir, or "has never intentionally targeted civilians?" In each case, about the same number—40 to 42 percent—said that the group "has never intentionally targeted civilians," while a miniscule 6 percent said they had. But a majority of respondents would not answer.

Most observers of Pakistan agree that there are substantial linkages between militant groups that operate in Kashmir and India and the Pakistani army and intelligence services. This study sought to learn whether Pakistanis believe that there is such a relationship and, if so, how close it is.

Respondents were offered four options: 1) "no relationship;" 2) "some contacts;" 3) "some elements within the army and intelligence agencies provide support, such as money, training, advice and weapons;" and 4) "the army and intelligence services as a whole work closely with these groups." One in four respondents said "there is no relationship at all." Another 24 percent chose an option indicating some relationship: 14 percent thought there were some contacts; 5 percent believed the army and intelligence provided support; and five percent thought the army and intelligence services worked closely with the militant groups. About half (51%) did not provide an answer.

These groups also claim that they that they provide social and community services in many parts of Pakistan. To find out whether these services might influence Pakistani views, respondents were asked, "thinking about groups like Lashkar-e-Taiba, Jamaat ul Dawa, Hizbol Mujahadeen, and Jaish e Mohammad among other tanzeems, do you think they provide social and community services, or are these not part of their activities?" Less than a quarter of Pakistanis believe that these services are even offered. Only 23 percent said the groups provided such services; a plurality of 42 percent said they did not; and 35 percent did not answer.

The 23 percent who said the groups offered some community services were then asked to name some of them. Nearly all (22% of the whole sample) mentioned religious *madaris* (the plural of *madrassah* or religious school). The next best-known services were humanitarian assistance during disasters (19%), medical care (16%), schools that do not primarily offer religious training (15%), and financial help with marriage and burials (11%).

7. The Federally Administered Tribal Areas (FATA)

A large majority of Pakistanis want to phase out the FATA's special legal status and to integrate the areas into the country's overall legal structure. Few want this to happen abruptly, however; a plurality favors

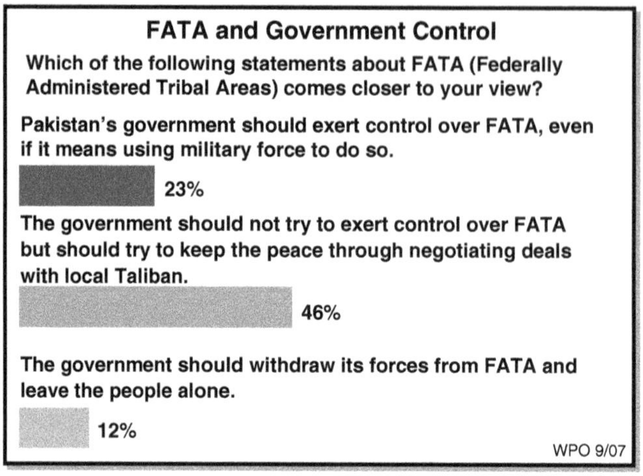

a gradualist approach. Pakistanis strongly prefer negotiating with the Taliban rather than fighting them. Only a small minority supports using military force to exert control while a plurality favors a negotiated approach. The current policy of limited military action while pursuing negotiations with local forces receives plurality approval.

A plurality believes the army should pursue and capture Taliban insurgents and al Qaeda forces crossing into Pakistan from Afghanistan. But overwhelming majorities oppose allowing foreign forces to enter Pakistan in order to do so. Almost no Pakistanis appear to believe Osama bin Laden is in Pakistan, and even if his location were to be established in the FATA, a plurality thinks the government should not try to capture him.

A large majority favors the phasing out of the FATA's special legal status and its integration into Pakistan's legal structure. Respondents were offered three statements about the FATA and asked which came closer to their own views.

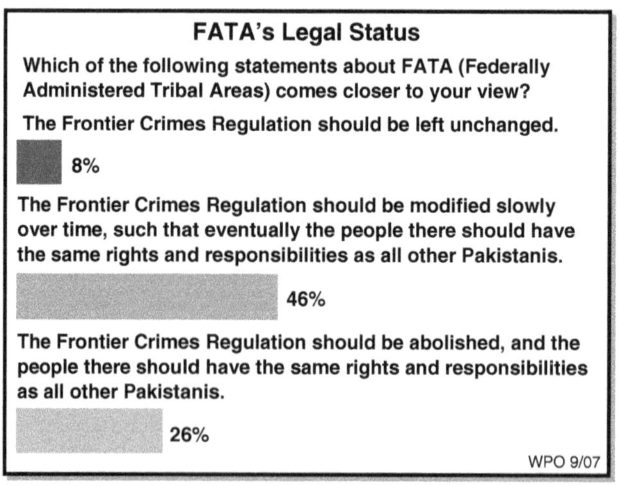

The least popular statement—chosen by only 8 percent—was that "the Frontier Crimes Regulation should be left unchanged." Instead 72 percent agreed that these regulations should be modified so that people in the FATA "have the same rights and responsibilities as all other Pakistanis." Only 26 percent thought that "the Frontier Crimes Regulation should be abolished." Instead 46 percent said these regulations should be "modified slowly over time." Thus although there is wide majority support for changing the FATA legal system, which was codified by the British in 1901, a plurality favors a gradualist approach.

Pakistanis express similar caution when asked about other approaches to dealing with militancy in the FATA. Only 23 percent said that "Pakistan's government should exert control over FATA, even if it means using military force to do so." The largest numbers (46%) say "the government should not try to exert control over FATA, but should try to keep the peace through negotiating deals with local Taliban." Another 12 percent said the "government should withdraw its forces from FATA and leave the people alone."

A plurality approves of the way the government is handling the situation in the FATA, a policy combining limited use of military strikes and more extensive negotiations with local forces. Forty-eight percent approved of "the way Pakistan's government is handling" the FATA (14% strongly), while 34 percent disapproved (12% strongly).

Dealing With the Taliban and al Qaeda

As discussed above, 60 percent saw "the activities of Islamist militants and local Taliban in FATA and settled areas" as a threat to Pakistan, and 34 percent regarded this threat as critical. However, only a 48 percent plurality favored "allowing the Pakistani army to pursue and capture Taliban insurgents who have crossed over from Afghanistan," while 34 percent were opposed. The same pattern was evident when respondents were asked about al Qaeda using the FATA as a sanctuary. A plurality (44%) favored "the Pakistani army entering federally administered tribal areas to pursue and capture al Qaeda fighters," with 36 percent opposed.

Taken together, these findings suggest considerable ambivalence among Pakistanis about the best way of handling the cross-border problems with Afghanistan. There is overwhelming opposition to *outside* forces coming in to fight either the Taliban or al Qaeda, however. When asked "what about allowing foreign troops to pursue and capture Taliban insurgents who have crossed over into Afghanistan," 77 percent thought the Pakistani government should not allow this, and only 9 percent disagreed. Similarly, only a miniscule 5 percent thought "the Pakistani government should . . . allow American or other foreign troops to enter Pakistan to pursue and

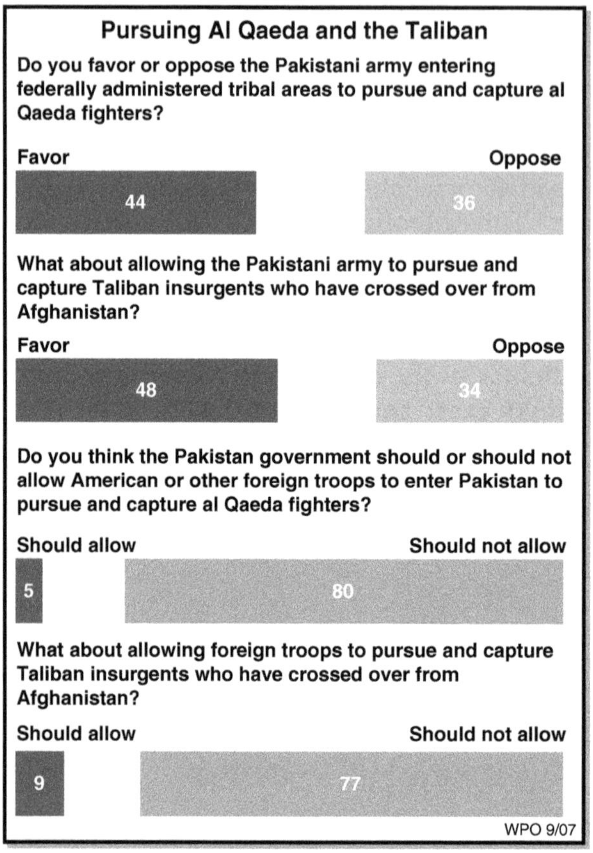

capture al Qaeda fighters," while an overwhelming 80 percent opposed such foreign intervention.

Almost no Pakistanis say they believe Osama bin Laden is in Pakistan, and even if authorities could establish his location in the FATA, a plurality thinks the government should not try to capture him. Respondents were asked to guess bin Laden's whereabouts: "Which do you think is more likely to be true: Osama bin Laden is somewhere in Pakistan; somewhere in Afghanistan; or in some other country?" Only 2 percent said they thought he was in Pakistan, while 18 percent picked Afghanistan. Thirteen percent supposed he was in some other country, and another 8 percent volunteered that he was in the United States. A majority declined to venture a guess.

Next, respondents were asked to "suppose the Pakistani government learned that Osama bin Laden was in the Federally Administered Tribal Areas (FATA) and found his exact location." Even under these circumstances, a 39 percent plurality thought the government should not attempt his capture; only 24 percent thought the government should.

8. Relations with the United States

Majority opinion toward the United States is negative. Large majorities say that the United States cannot be trusted to act responsibly and also believe that it has extraordinary influence over Pakistan. US military presence in the region is viewed as a threat to Pakistan. A large and growing majority believe it is a US goal to weaken and divide the Muslim world. A plurality disapproves of how Pakistan's government has handled relations with the United States. Only one in four feels that security cooperation with the United States has brought Pakistan any benefit.

Pakistanis view the United States as an untrustworthy superpower. A majority (64%) expressed doubt that the United States could be trusted "to act responsibly in the world," including 49 percent who answered "not at all" and 16 percent who said "not very much."

This mistrust is coupled with the perception that the United States is exerting extraordinary influence over what happens in Pakistan. Asked to consider "recent major events happening in Pakistan," a majority of respondents (56%) said that most (32%) or nearly all of these events (24%) were controlled by the United States. Only 26 percent thought events in Pakistan were controlled some (22%) or very little (4%) by the United States.

Most Pakistanis believe the United States' military presence in their region puts their country's "vital interests" at risk. Eighty-four percent said that the US military presence in Asia was either a "critical" (72%) or an "important" (12%) threat to Pakistan's interests. About as many—83 percent—said that the US presence in neighboring Afghanistan was a critical (68%) or important (15%) threat to Pakistan.

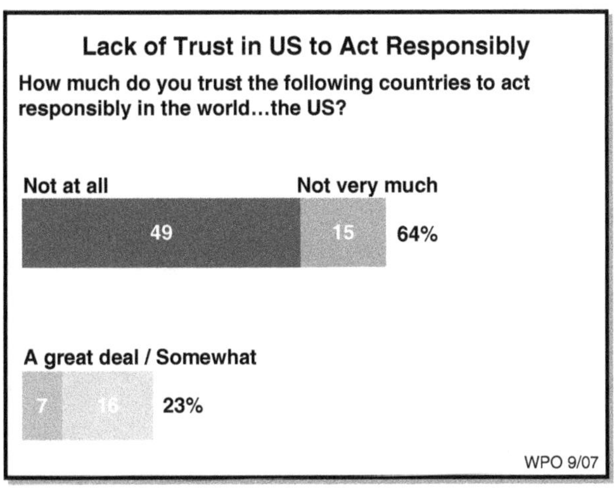

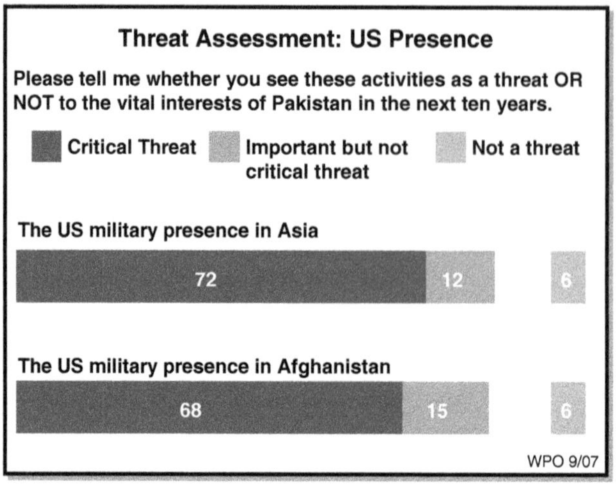

A majority of Pakistanis give some credence America's stated goal of defending itself from terrorist attacks. A majority (63%) said that it is a goal of the United States to "prevent more attacks such as those on the World Trade Center in September 2001" (definitely a goal, 41%).

However, larger majorities perceive other, more perfidious, goals. About three-quarters (78%) also said that the United States wants to "maintain control over the oil resources of the Middle East" (definitely a goal, 59%).

Perhaps most strikingly, an overwhelming majority believes that the United States has goals that are hostile to Islam itself. A remarkably high 86 percent agreed that it was a US goal to "weaken and divide the Islamic world" ("definitely" 70%, "probably" 16%). Furthermore, this

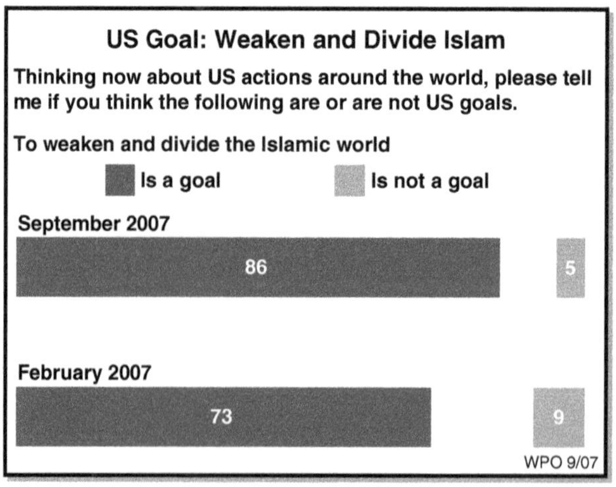

view appears to be growing substantially—up 13 points from February 2007 when 73 percent said it was a US goal (definitely, 55%).[1]

Three out of four even believe that it is a US goal to "spread Christianity in the Middle East." Seventy-five percent said this was definitely (53%) or probably (22%) a US goal, while only 10 percent said that it was not.

A plurality of Pakistanis disapproves of the way their government has handled its relations with the United States. Nearly half of those polled (47%) said they did not like the way their government handled these ties, including 25 percent who said they "disapprove somewhat" and 22 percent who said they "disapprove strongly." Thirty-nine percent said they approved somewhat (29%) or strongly (10%).

Few Pakistanis think their government's collaboration with US anti-terrorism efforts has helped their country. Asked about "the cooperation in the last few years between Pakistan and the US on security and military matters," only one in four (27%) said that it had brought any benefits to Pakistan. This includes 12 percent who said it had benefited both countries, 9 percent who said that although it had "mostly benefited the United States" it had also helped Pakistan, and 6 percent who said that it had "mostly benefited Pakistan." Nearly one third said US-Pakistani cooperation had actually hurt Pakistan (29%), and an additional 11 percent said it had benefited neither country.

[1] This question was first asked by WorldPublicOpinion.org in a study conducted with the National Consortium for the Study of Terrorism and Responses to Terrorism (START). The February 2007 result cited above is for the urban portion of that sample, parallel to the urban sample in the present study. WorldPublicOpinion.org's report on the policy-related aspects of that study ("Muslim Public Opinion on U.S. Policy, Attacks on Civilians, and al Qaeda") can be found at http://www.worldpublicopinion.org/pipa/pdf/apr07/START_Apr07_rpt.pdf

Supporters of all leaders were also united in their negative views of the United States and its motives. Majorities of all supporters said they did not trust the United States to act responsibly in the world, including 68 percent of Sharif supporters, 65 percent of Bhutto supporters and 55 percent of Musharraf supporters. More than seven in 10 of all supporters view the US military presence in Asia as an important or critical threat to Pakistan—varying from 78 percent among Musharraf supporters to 70 percent among Bhutto supporters. About seven in 10 of all supporters—71 percent of Musharraf and Sharif supporters and 69 percent of Bhutto supporters—also believe the United States is definitely trying to weaken and divide Islam.

9. Relations with Afghanistan

Majorities see the tensions with Afghanistan as a threat to Pakistan's interests and approve of the way Pakistan's government has handled relations with its neighbor. Views of the Taliban's activities in Afghanistan are quite mixed: nearly half show at least some sympathy for their attacks on NATO troops, while one in three show some sympathy for Taliban attacks on Afghan police and troops. Only one in three believe that the Pakistani government is seriously trying to prevent the Taliban from operating in Afghanistan.

A large majority of Pakistanis believe the tensions between Afghanistan and Pakistan threaten the vital interests of Pakistan. Two thirds (67%) said they saw these tensions as either critical (40%) or important (27%). Twenty-one percent said tensions with Afghanistan were not a threat to Pakistan.

At the same time, Pakistan's government receives good marks for how it has been handling relations with Afghanistan. Sixty percent approved of its performance (17% strongly) and only 25 percent disapproved (5% strongly).

Views of the Taliban's Activities

Views of the Taliban's activities are remarkably mixed and poorly defined. When asked about the Taliban's attacks on "Afghan troops and police in Afghanistan," only 18 percent said they approved of such attacks (5% strongly). But only 29 percent disapproved (15% strongly) and 14 percent said they had mixed feelings. A large 38 percent did not take a position. Thus about one in three (32%) show some sympathy for such attacks.

When asked about the Taliban's attacks on NATO troops, approval rose to 30 percent (12% strongly), disapproval dropped to 15 percent (9% strongly), and 18 percent expressed mixed feelings. Once again a large 37 percent did not take a position. Thus nearly half (48%) view them at least somewhat favorably.

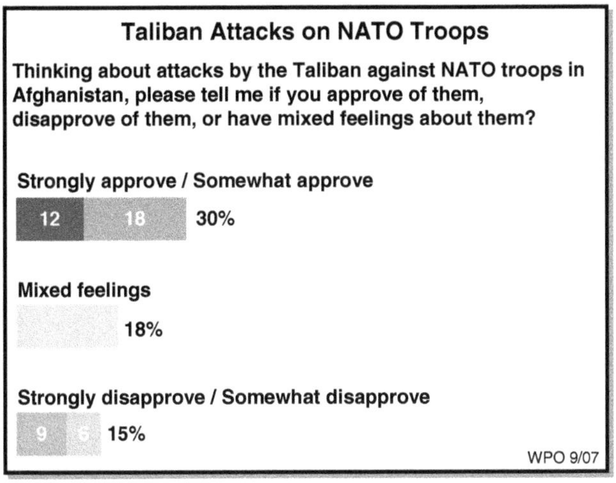

Thus it appears that Pakistanis' views of the Taliban are colored by various factors. As discussed above, Pakistanis perceive US military presence in Afghanistan as a critical threat, thus potentially engendering some sympathy for their attacks on NATO troops.

Also, about a third of Pakistanis have some sympathy for Taliban. Respondents were asked: "Thinking about the current Afghan government and the former Taliban government, which one do you think has had the best approach to governing Afghanistan?" Thirty-four percent said the former Taliban government, and only 9 percent said the current Afghan government. A quarter (24%) said "neither" and the rest declined to answer.

Perception of Pakistan Government's Efforts to Counter the Taliban

When asked whether the Pakistan government was seriously trying to stop the Taliban from operating in Afghanistan or whether instead it was "allowing the Taliban to operate in Afghanistan," only 33 percent thought the government was seriously trying to stop the Taliban while 4 percent said the government was allowing the Taliban to operate. Another 3 percent volunteered that it was actually helping the Taliban. This means that just 7 percent believed the government was enabling the Taliban in some way. Another 25 percent said "it depends" or "neither," implying they thought the government's policy could not be summed up in either alternative. A third (36%) declined to answer.

The same question was asked in Afghanistan in November 2006. Among Afghans, a very large majority—79 percent—thought Pakistan's government was allowing the Taliban to operate in Afghanistan. Only 15 percent thought Pakistan was seriously trying to stop the Taliban.

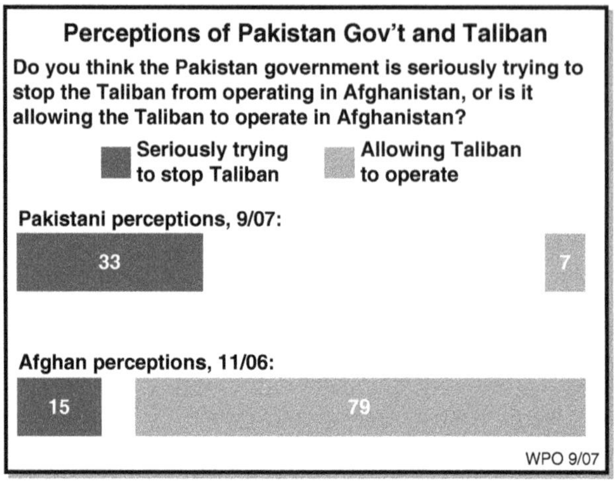

Durand Line

Only a small minority of Pakistanis know of the Durand Line and its disputed status as a boundary between the two countries. Sir Mortimer Durand, the foreign secretary of British colonial India, demarked the border in 1893, inducing the then king of Afghanistan to agree. Following partition in 1947, Pakistan accepted the line as its international border, though subsequent Afghan governments have not.

The current study asked: "Are you aware of the Durand Line, dividing Pakistan and Afghanistan?" Only 15 percent said yes, while 63 percent said no. The 15 percent answering yes were then asked whether Afghanistan accepted the line as an international border. Eight percent (of the whole sample) thought Afghanistan did not, while 5 percent thought it did. Thus, despite the dispute's importance for Pakistan's leadership, it seems to have almost no resonance in the general public.

10. Ranking of Perceived Threats

Asked to evaluate a series of possible threats to Pakistan's vital interests, the Pakistani public rates US military presence in the region as a critical threat by the largest percentage. Other threats regarded as critical by majorities include tensions with India and violence between Pakistani religious and ethnic groups. Slightly fewer regard the activities of al Qaeda, local Taliban, and jihadist militants as critical, or the activities of ethnic nationalist movements. Only half see the possibility of Iran acquiring nuclear weapons as threatening. A majority considers the rise of China to be no threat to Pakistan.

In order to better understand Pakistani views of what could endanger their country, the study asked an extensive series of questions—17 in all—about "possible threats to the vital interests of Pakistan in the next ten years." The questions included international, regional and domestic threats. Examining them as a group throws light on how the Pakistani public views the world around them and clarifies some of the attitudes discussed in other sections of this report.

The US military presence in the region is rated as a critical threat by the largest percentage of respondents. Almost three in four—72 percent—call the US military presence in Asia a critical threat; another 12 percent call it important but not critical. Almost as many Pakistanis view the US military presence in Afghanistan as threatening. Sixty-eight percent call it a critical threat, and another 15 percent say it is important but not critical.

Somewhat smaller majorities regard tensions with India and violence between Pakistani religious and ethnic groups as potential dangers. Fifty-three percent said "tensions between India and Pakistan" were a critical threat, and another 26 percent called them important. The growth of "closer relations between India and the United States" were viewed similarly, with 53 percent seeing them as a critical threat and 24 percent as important. "India's growing influence in the world" raised a little less concern (44% critical, 27% important).

About the same numbers are concerned about "violence between different religious groups in Pakistan" (51% critical, 26% important) and violence between different Pakistani ethnic groups (49% critical, 25% important).

While many in the West perceive the activities of al Qaeda, the Taliban, and other militant groups as Pakistan's greatest problem, the Pakistani public regards these as meaningful threats, though less severe than those presented by the United States, India, and the country's own centrifugal forces.

A 41 percent plurality sees the "activities of al Qaeda" as a critical threat, and another 21 percent see them as important; only 14 percent says they are not a threat. The related "tensions between Afghanistan and Pakistan" are a critical threat for 40 percent (27% important), but 21 percent says these tensions are not a threat. Only 38 percent sees the activities of militant organizations (*askari tanzeems*) in Pakistan as a critical threat, while another 23 percent sees them as important (17% not a threat). Likewise, "activities of Islamist militants and local Taliban in FATA and settled areas" are viewed as a critical threat by only 34 percent (26% important; 18% not a threat).

The activities of ethnic separatist groups with nationalist ambitions cause relatively little concern to Pakistanis. Only 22 percent saw Mohajir nationalists as a critical threat, with another 33 percent seeing them as important. About a third (32%) said they were not a threat. There was even less concern about Sindhi nationalists (18% critical) and Baluch nationalists (17% critical).

Pakistanis show little concern about the possibility that neighboring Iran is developing nuclear weapons and may become the second Muslim nation, after Pakistan, to join the nuclear club of nations. Only 16 percent viewed such a development as a critical threat to Pakistan. Another 34 percent called it important, while 37 percent said it was not a threat to Pakistan.

A majority sees the rise of China as no threat at all to Pakistan. Fifty-one percent said that "the development of China as a world power" was not a threat. Of the 42 percent who saw it as a threat, only 10 percent called it critical. There was a little more anxiety over the growth of "closer relations between India and China," with 23 percent calling this a critical threat and 37 percent important.

11. Trade and Globalization

Large majorities endorse international trade and see it as beneficial for Pakistan, though only a plurality are positive about the idea of globalization.

Three in four Pakistanis view international trade positively. By 77 percent to 13 percent, respondents said international trade was positive for the economy and 67 percent that it was positive for Pakistani companies. Large majorities also see international trade as good for creating jobs in Pakistan (68%), job security for Pakistani workers (63%), and for their own standard of living (61%). More modest majorities see international trade as good for "consumers like you" (57%), and for the environment (52%). In all of these areas, no more than 25 percent saw international trade as bad.

The Pakistani public's response to the idea of globalization is more hesitant than their response to international trade. Asked whether they believe that "globalization, especially the increasing connections of our economy with others around the world, is mostly good or mostly bad for Pakistan," a 48 percent plurality said it was mostly good, 16 percent that it was mostly bad, and 36 percent declined to answer. Some respondents may have been aware of the cultural aspect of globalization and were more reluctant to endorse such changes.

12. Pakistan's Economy

Two thirds feel that Pakistan's economy has gone off on the wrong track. Nonetheless, a majority approves of how the government is handling the economy.

Two thirds of Pakistanis are dissatisfied with how the country's economy is performing. Sixty-eight percent said Pakistan's economy "has . . . gone off on the wrong track," while only a quarter (26%) thought it was "moving in the right direction."

Further, a majority perceives (correctly) that India is experiencing faster growth. When asked, "As compared to Pakistan, do you think India's economy is growing much faster, a little faster, about the same speed, a little slower, or much slower," a 56 percent majority said India was growing faster (30% much faster). Only 27 percent believed that India was growing at either the same speed as Pakistan (11%), a little more slowly (7%), or much more slowly (9%).

Despite this dissatisfaction, the public shows little inclination to blame Pakistan's government for the country's economic performance. Fifty-five percent said they approved of how the government had handled the economy, either strongly (23%) or somewhat (32%). About a third (34%) disapproved, but only 9 percent disapproved strongly. Perhaps many Pakistanis are conscious that there has been sustained growth in the last few years but are looking for a higher level of economic performance.

13. Education

Majorities express confidence in the educational system and approve of the government's policies. Pakistanis put the highest priorities on teaching children religious values and good citizenship, followed by basic skills, problem-solving, and independent thinking.

Foreign observers and policymakers have expressed concern about Pakistan's educational system, saying that its curriculum has significant Islamist and Islamic content, espouses narrowly nationalist tendencies and does not prepare the poor for better jobs. However, a majority of Pakistanis want to see their schools inculcate a religious and patriotic outlook along with the rest of the curriculum.

A majority views the national public education system positively, with 58 percent saying they have a great deal (22%) or quite a lot (36%) of confidence. Only about a third—36 percent—said they did not have very much (31%) confidence in education or that they had none at all (5%). Almost two thirds (64%) said they approved "of the way Pakistan's government is handling the educational system" (30% approve strongly). Only 28 percent say they disapprove somewhat (21%) or strongly (7%).

To better understand what the Pakistani public wants from public education, the study asked questions used originally by Matthew J. Nelson in his research on Pakistani parents' preferences for their children's schools.[2] All respondents were told to choose the most important and second most important of "five things different people sometimes say about what makes a school a good school":

A. Some people say that a good school teaches students how to read and write. In other words, good schools provide students with basic reading skills and basic math skills.

B. Some people say that a good school is a school that creates good Muslims. In other words, good schools provide students with strong values and strong religious beliefs.

C. Some people say that good schools teach students how to solve problems and think for themselves.

D. Some people say that good schools prepare students to provide good jobs.

[2] Matthew J. Nelson, "Muslims, Markets, and the Meaning of a 'Good' Education in Pakistan," *Asian Survey*, vol. 46, no. 5, pp. 699–720. Nelson conducted a survey of parents in and around the city of Rawalpindi.

E. Some people say that good schools make sure that every student becomes a good citizen, showing respect for the laws of their country.

Overall, B—teaching children to be good Muslims—was chosen most often, with 32 percent naming it as their first choice and 21 percent as their second choice. Next most important was E—teaching good citizenship—chosen first by 17 percent and second by 26 percent. These preferences were followed by A—teaching basic skills (25% first choice, 12% second choice), C—teaching problem-solving and independent thinking (14% first choice, 19% second choice), and finally, D—preparing students for good jobs (5% first choice, 15% second choice).

This suggests that Pakistanis want education to combine religious and "worldly" content. Work by C. Christine Fair and others finds that the Pakistani educational market is fast evolving new opportunities that reflect this growing demand.

While parents desire religious content in the public school curriculum, a large majority of Pakistanis also support the government's plans for madrassah reform. This appears to reflect the longstanding debate about the madrassah curriculum, which has remained largely unchanged since the nineteenth century and which relies upon texts that are hundreds of years old. Religious scholars have discussed the need to reform the madrassah curriculum to ensure that the seminaries produce religious scholars whose religious training is relevant for a modern Muslim state.

About the Authors

Steven Kull, editor of WorldPublicOpinion.org, is director of the Program on International Policy Attitudes (PIPA) and the Center on Policy Attitudes (COPA). He directs the PIPA/Knowledge Networks poll of the US public, plays a central role in the BBC World Service Poll of global opinion and the polls of the Chicago Council on Foreign Relations, and is the principal investigator of a major study of social support of anti-American terrorist groups in Islamic countries. He regularly appears in the US and international media, providing analysis of public opinion, and gives briefings to the US Congress, the State Department, NATO, the United Nations and the European Commission. His articles have appeared in Political Science Quarterly, Foreign Policy, Public Opinion Quarterly, Harpers, The Washington Post and other publications. His most recent book, co-authored with I.M. Destler, is Misreading the Public: The Myth of a New Isolationism (Brookings). He is a faculty member of the School of Public Policy at the University of Maryland and a member of the Council on Foreign Relations and the World Association of Public Opinion Research.

Clay Ramsay is Director of Research at PIPA and a CISSM fellow. He co-founded PIPA in 1992. He regularly appears in the US and international media providing analysis of public opinion. With a background in history and psychology, he has focused on the study of ideology and mass psychology. He received his Ph.D. in History from Stanford University, has taught at Oberlin College, and is the author of The Ideology of the Great Fear (Johns Hopkins University Press). He is a faculty member of the School of Public Policy at the University of Maryland.

Christine Fair has just returned from Afghanistan where she worked for the United Nations Assistance Mission to Afghanistan (UNAMA) as Political Officer during which time she authored UNAMA's comprehensive report on suicide attacks in Afghanistan. Prior to leaving for Afghanistan in June, 2007, Fair served as a Senior Research Fellow at USIP. In November, she will return to the RAND Corporation as a Senior Political Scientist. Fair's research centers upon political-military affairs in South Asia, including Afghanistan, Pakistan, Bangladesh and Sri Lanka. She completed her PhD from the University of Chicago, Department of South Asian Languages and Civilizations as well as her MA from the University of Chicago, Harris School of Public Policy. She has authored and co-authored several monographs on South Asian security, written numerous chapters in edited volumes and published many peer-reviewed journal articles. She has authored The Madrassah Challenge: Militancy and Religious Education in Pakistan (USIP, forthcoming); Fortifying Pakistan (USIP, 2006); The Counterterror Coalitions: Cooperation with Pakistan and India (RAND, 2004) among others. Currently, she is co-editing with Sumit Ganguly Treading on Sacred Ground: Lessons Learned from Counter Insurgency Operations on Sacred Space. She is the Managing Editor of India Review.

About the United States Institute of Peace

The United States Institute of Peace is an independent nonpartisan institution established and funded by Congress. Its goals are to help prevent and resolve violent conflicts, promote post-conflict stability and development, and increase peacebuilding capacity and tools. The Institute does this by empowering others with knowledge, skills, and resources, as well as by directly engaging in conflict management efforts around the globe.

About the Program on International Policy Attitudes (PIPA) and WorldPublicOpinion.Org

WorldPublicOpinion.org (WPO) is a project, managed by PIPA, that studies public opinion around the world on international issues. WPO conducts polls through an international network of research partners and maintains a major website with articles and reports analyzing and integrating polls from around the world and from numerous organizations.

The Program on International Policy Attitudes (PIPA) is a joint program of the Center for International and Security Studies at Maryland and the Center on Policy Attitudes. PIPA undertakes research on American attitudes in both the public and in the policymaking community toward a variety of international and foreign policy issues. It seeks to disseminate its findings to members of government, the press, and the public as well as academia.

Related Publications

C. Christine Fair, The Madrassah Challenge: Militancy and Religious Education in Pakistan (Washington, DC: USIP Press, 2008).

C. Christine Fair and Peter Chalk, *Fortifying Pakistan: The Role of U.S. Internal Security Assistance* (Washington, DC: USIP Press, 2006)

Marvin Weinbaum, "Afghanistan and Its Neighbors: An Ever Dangerous Neighborhood," *USIP Special Report*, No. 162 (June 2006).

Touqir Hussain, "U.S.-Pakistan Engagement: The War on Terrorism and Beyond," *USIP Special Report*, No. 145 (July 2005).

Praveen Swami, "Quickstep or *Kadam Taal*: The Elusive Search for Peace in Jammu and Kashmir," *USIP Special Report*, No. 133 (March 2005).

C. Christine Fair, "India and Pakistan Engagement: Prospects for Breakthrough or Breakdown?" *USIP Special Report*, No. 129 (January 2005).

DOCUMENT NO. 27

COMBATING TERRORISM: THE UNITED STATES LACKS COMPREHENSIVE PLAN TO DESTROY THE TERRORIST THREAT AND CLOSE THE SAFE HAVEN IN PAKISTAN'S FEDERALLY ADMINISTERED TRIBAL AREAS

GAO Report
GAO-08-622

April 2008

What GAO Found

The United States has not met its national security goals to destroy terrorist threats and close the safe haven in Pakistan's FATA. Since 2002, the United States relied principally on the Pakistan military to address U.S. national security goals. Of the approximately $5.8 billion the United States provided for efforts in the FATA and border region from 2002 through 2007, about 96 percent reimbursed Pakistan for military operations there. According to the Department of State, Pakistan deployed 120,000 military and paramilitary forces in the FATA and helped kill and capture hundreds of suspected al Qaeda operatives; these efforts cost the lives of approximately 1,400 members of Pakistan's security forces. However, GAO found broad agreement, as documented in the National Intelligence Estimate, State, and embassy documents, as well as Defense officials in Pakistan, that al Qaeda had regenerated its ability to attack the United States and had succeeded in establishing a safe haven in Pakistan's FATA.

No comprehensive plan for meeting U.S. national security goals in the FATA has been developed, as stipulated by the *National Strategy for Combating Terrorism* (2003), called for by an independent commission (2004), and mandated by congressional legislation (2007). Furthermore, Congress created the National Counterterrorism Center (NCTC) in 2004 specifically to develop comprehensive plans to combat terrorism. However, neither the National Security Council (NSC), NCTC, nor other executive branch departments have developed a comprehensive plan that includes all elements of national power—diplomatic, military, intelligence, development assistance, economic, and law enforcement support—called for by the various national security strategies and Congress. As a result, since 2002, the U.S. embassy in Pakistan has had no Washington-supported, comprehensive plan to combat terrorism and close the terrorist safe haven in the FATA. In 2006, the embassy, in conjunction with Defense, State, and U.S. Agency for International Development (USAID), and in cooperation with the government of Pakistan, began an effort to focus more attention on other key elements of national power, such as development assistance and public diplomacy, to address U.S. goals in the FATA. However, this does not yet constitute a comprehensive plan.

Abbreviations

CENTCOM	U.S. Central Command
CIA	Central Intelligence Agency
CSF	Coalition Support Funds
Defense	Department of Defense
DNI	Director of National Intelligence
FATA	Federally Administered Tribal Areas
FCR	Frontier Crimes Regulations
NIE	National Intelligence Estimate
NCTC	National Counterterrorism Center
NSC	National Security Council
ODNI	Office of the Director of National Intelligence
State	Department of State
USAID	U.S. Agency for International Development

United States Government Accountability Office
Washington, DC 20548

April 17, 2008

Congressional Requesters:

The terrorist attacks of 9/11 were planned from an Afghan safe haven, and many of the terrorists who attacked the United States used Pakistan as the main route to travel from Afghanistan to the United States. Since the 9/11 attacks in 2001, the administration and Congress have repeatedly stated that destroying terrorist threats and closing terrorist safe havens are the nation's critical national security goals.[1] As such, the United States has

[1] These goals have been set forth in the 2002 *National Security Strategy*, the 2003 *National Strategy for Combating Terrorism*, the 2004 *9/11 Commission Report*, and endorsed by the Intelligence Reform and

provided Pakistan, which has become a key U.S. ally in the global war on terror, with more than $10.5 billion for military, economic, and development activities in support of these goals. The 9/11 Commission, an independent, bipartisan commission created by congressional legislation in late 2002, concluded in 2004 that it is hard to overstate the importance of Pakistan in the struggle against Islamist terrorism. The commission found that the country's vast unpoliced regions have made it attractive to extremists seeking a safe haven and have reportedly provided a base for terrorist operations against U.S. and coalition forces in Afghanistan. Following the defeat of the Taliban in Afghanistan, al Qaeda and Taliban fighters are believed to have retreated across the Afghan border and into Pakistan's Federally Administered Tribal Areas (FATA) in an effort to reestablish a terrorist safe haven.

Because of the challenges the United States faces in Pakistan in meeting its goals to destroy the terrorist threats and close the terrorist safe haven, we were asked to assess (1) U.S. progress in meeting its national security goals in Pakistan's FATA region, and (2) the status of U.S. efforts to develop a comprehensive plan for the FATA.

This report is the first in a series of reports we plan to issue in response to your interest in U.S. support of the Pakistani government's efforts in the FATA region bordering Afghanistan. We plan to issue an interim product on the use and oversight of Coalition Support Funds (CSF) in May 2008 and a report on CSF in the summer of 2008, followed by a broader report covering security, political, and development assistance activities undertaken by the United States to meet U.S. national security goals in the FATA.

To address our objectives, we reviewed relevant national security strategies, the *9/11 Commission Report*, key congressional legislation, and related documentation from the Departments of Defense (Defense) and State (State) and the U.S. Agency for International Development (USAID), and discussed these issues with relevant department officials in Washington, D.C. We also interviewed Defense officials operating out of the U.S. Central Command (CENTCOM) headquarters in Tampa, Florida. We requested meetings with the Central Intelligence Agency (CIA), the National Counterterrorism Center (NCTC), and the National Security Council (NSC); however, only the CIA agreed to meet with us. To determine progress in meeting national security objectives, we compared the national security goals stated in strategic documents with unclassified assessments conducted by the Director of National Intelligence (DNI), State, and U.S. officials operating in Pakistan. To determine if comprehensive plans were

Terrorism Prevention Act of 2004 (P.L. 108-458, sec 7102 (b)(3)) and the Implementing the Recommendations of the 9/11 Commission Act of 2007 (P.L. 110-53, sec. 2042(b)(2)).

developed and contained the elements recommended by national security documents, legislation, and GAO, we requested all plans addressing U.S. efforts in the FATA from the CIA, Defense, NCTC, NSC, State, USAID, and the U.S. Embassy in Pakistan. CIA, NCTC, and NSC did not provide any plans. We reviewed all plans provided by Defense, State, and USAID, as of April 17, 2008. We also met with members of the International Crisis Group in Washington, including the director of their office in Pakistan.[2] In addition, we conducted field work in Pakistan, where we met with officials from the U.S. embassy and Pakistan's Ministries of Defense and Interior, as well as international donors from Canada, Japan, the Netherlands, and the United Kingdom. We visited Peshawar, near the FATA, to conduct discussions with the U.S. consulate, Pakistan's 11th Army Corps, the Frontier Corps, the FATA Secretariat and Development Authority, and a Pakistani nongovernmental organization with experience working in the FATA. We determined the amount of U.S. funding to Pakistan by analyzing Defense, State, and USAID budget documents covering the period from fiscal years 2002 through 2007 and by verifying the amounts used for the FATA and the border regions through discussions with agency officials. This analysis does not include funding for covert activities in Pakistan.

We conducted this performance audit from July 2007 through April 2008 in accordance with generally accepted government auditing standards. Those standards require that we plan and perform the audit to obtain sufficient, appropriate evidence to provide a reasonable basis for our findings and conclusions based on our audit objectives. We believe that the evidence obtained provides a reasonable basis for our findings and conclusions based on our audit objectives.

Results in Brief

The United States has not met its national security goals to destroy the terrorist threat and close the safe haven in Pakistan's FATA region. Since 2002, the United States has relied principally on the Pakistani military to address its national security goals. There have been limited efforts, however, to address other underlying causes of terrorism in the FATA by providing development assistance or by addressing the FATA's political needs. Of the over $10.5 billion that the United States has provided to Pakistan from 2002 through 2007, we identified about $5.8 billion specifically for Pakistan's FATA and border region; about 96 percent of this funding reimbursed Pakistan for military operations in the FATA and the border region.

[2] The International Crisis Group is an independent, nonpartisan source of analysis on the prevention and resolution of global conflicts.

According to Defense and State Department officials, Pakistan deployed up to 120,000 military and paramilitary forces in the FATA and killed and captured hundreds of suspected al Qaeda operatives. In October 2007, State reported that it had determined that Pakistan was making "significant" progress toward eliminating the safe haven in the FATA. However, we found broad agreement, as documented in the unclassified 2007 *National Intelligence Estimate* (NIE), State and embassy documents, as well as among Defense, State, and other officials, including those operating in Pakistan, that al Qaeda had regenerated its ability to attack the United States and had succeeded in establishing a safe haven in Pakistan's FATA.

No comprehensive plan for meeting U.S. national security goals in the FATA has been developed, as stipulated by the *National Strategy for Combating Terrorism*, recommended by the independent 9/11 Commission, and mandated by congressional legislation.[3] Since 2003, the administration's national security strategies and Congress have recognized that a comprehensive plan that includes all elements of national power—diplomatic, military, intelligence, development assistance, economic, and law enforcement support—was needed to address the terrorist threat emanating from the FATA. Furthermore, in 2004, a provision of the Intelligence Reform and Terrorism Prevention Act of 2004 (Intelligence Reform Act) established the NCTC to develop comprehensive plans to combat terrorism that included clear objectives, the assignment of tasks among executive branch departments, and interagency coordination. We have previously reported on the need for these and other elements to enhance interagency cooperation and improve effectiveness.[4] The NCTC also was tasked with monitoring each department's efforts. However, neither the NCTC, the NSC, nor the other executive branch departments have developed a comprehensive plan that integrates the capabilities of the executive agencies and the intelligence community. As a result, since 2002, the embassy has had no Washington-supported, comprehensive plan to combat terrorists and close the terrorist safe haven in the FATA. In 2006, the U.S. government, in conjunction with the government of Pakistan, began an effort to focus

[3] The administration's 2003 *National Strategy for Combating Terrorism*, the independent *9/11 Commission Report*, and Congress's (1) Intelligence Reform Act and Terrorism Prevention Act of 2004 (P.L. 108-458, sec. 7120) and (2) the Implementing the Recommendations of the 9/11 Commission Act of 2007 (P.L. 110-53, sec. 2042 (c)) all support the development of a comprehensive plan that uses all elements of national power.

[4] We reported that strategic plans should clearly define objectives to be accomplished, identify the roles and responsibilities for meeting each objective, ensure that funding necessary to achieve the objectives is available, and employ monitoring mechanisms to determine progress and identify needed improvements. See GAO, *Combating Terrorism: Law Enforcement Agencies Lack Directives to Assist Foreign Nations to Identify, Disrupt, and Prosecute Terrorists*, GAO-07-697 (Washington, D.C.: May 25, 2007); GAO, *Results-Oriented Government: Practices That Can Help Enhance and Sustain Collaboration among Federal Agencies*, GAO-06-15 (Washington, D.C.: Oct. 21, 2005); and GAO, *Combating Terrorism: Observations on National Strategies Related to Terrorism*, GAO-03-519T (Washington, D.C.: Mar. 3, 2003).

more attention on other key elements of national power, such as development and public diplomacy, to address U.S. goals in the FATA. In support of this effort, Defense, State, and USAID began to develop department-specific plans and hold interagency meetings to address security and development issues in the FATA. However, this effort has not yet resulted in a comprehensive plan. As of April 2008, not all of these efforts have been approved in Washington, funding shortfalls exist, and support from the recently elected government of Pakistan is unknown.[5]

We are recommending that the National Security Advisor and the Director of the NCTC, in consultation with the Secretaries of Defense and State, the Administrator of USAID, the intelligence community, and other executive departments as deemed appropriate, work to develop a comprehensive plan using all elements of national power to combat the terrorist threat and close the associated safe haven in Pakistan's FATA region. The comprehensive plan should also include key components called for in the Intelligence Reform Act and components that we have previously reported as being needed to improve the effectiveness of plans involving multidepartmental efforts to combat terrorism.

State, the Office of the Director of National Intelligence (ODNI), Defense, and USAID provided written comments on a draft of this report, which are reproduced in appendixes I, II, III, and IV.

State and ODNI did not comment on our recommendation, while Defense and USAID concurred. In general, they all commented on their individual planning efforts and interagency meetings to coordinate these efforts that began in 2006. This, however, was not the focus of our review; our report assessed whether a comprehensive plan had been developed that incorporated all elements of national power.

State's comments asserted that embassy and U.S. government efforts to date have resulted in a comprehensive strategy. We disagree, and note in our report that while the initiatives begun by Defense, State, and USAID are being coordinated by the embassy, they have not been fully approved or integrated into a formal, comprehensive plan.

ODNI's comments stated that they agreed with our finding that the United States had not met its national security goals in Pakistan's FATA; however, they disagreed that the United States lacks plans to combat terrorism. Our report does not state that the U.S. lacks agency-specific plans; rather, we found that there was no comprehensive plan that integrated the combined capabilities of Defense, State, USAID, the intelligence community, and

[5] We will continue to monitor the status and progress of the U.S. government's effort in the FATA and report on the matter in a subsequent report.

others, as called for by the 2003 national security strategy, the 9/11 Commission report, and Congress.

We also received technical comments from Defense and USAID, which we have incorporated throughout the report where appropriate.

Background

The FATA is mountainous and shares a 373-mile border with Afghanistan known as the Durand Line (see fig. 1). The FATA, which has a population of 3.1 million people, is one of Pakistan's poorest regions, with high poverty, high unemployment, and an underdeveloped infrastructure. Most of

Figure 1: Map of the Federally Administered Tribal Areas, Pakistan

Source: GAO; USAID and Map Resources (maps).

the population depends on subsistence agriculture. The FATA's per capita income is $250 per year, which is half of the national per capita income; about 60 percent of the population lives below the national poverty line. Per capita public development expenditure is reportedly one-third of the national average. Social development indicators are also poor. The overall literacy rate is 17 percent, compared with 56 percent nationally, with male literacy at 29 percent and female literacy at 3 percent. The FATA has just 41 hospitals for its population of 3.1 million, and a doctor to population ratio of 1 to 6,762.

The FATA is governed by an administrative system and a judicial system different from the rest of Pakistan—the Frontier Crimes Regulations (FCR) of 1901, codified under British rule.[6] Because Pakistan retained the colonial administrative and legal structures of the British, as codified in the FCR, the FATA populations are legally separate from and unequal to other Pakistani citizens. Examples of these differences under the FCR follow:

- FATA residents do not have access to national political parties, and political parties are forbidden from extending their activities into the agencies of FATA.
- The FATA is under the direct executive authority of the President of Pakistan. Laws framed by the National Assembly of Pakistan do not apply in the FATA unless so ordered by the President, who is empowered to issue regulations for the tribal areas.
- FATA residents do not have the right to legal representation, to present material evidence, or to cross-examine witnesses in Pakistan's judicial system. Those convicted are denied the right of appeal in Pakistan's courts.
- The President's representatives to the FATA, who are called political agents, can punish an entire tribe for crimes committed on the tribe's territory by issuing fines, making arrests, implementing property seizures, and establishing blockades.

In response to the draft, Defense noted that the FCR is a culturally acceptable recognition of the tribal structure of the FATA, where the population is ethnically different from the majority of Pakistan's citizens, and precludes forced assimilation. Further, Defense noted that removing the FCR without a replacement mechanism that is accepted by the indigenous population has the potential to create a vacuum that could result in negative consequences. A recent announcement by Pakistani Prime Minister Yousaf Raza Gillani regarding the repeal of the FCR drew mixed reactions from

[6] The information on foreign law in this report does not reflect our independent legal analysis but is based on interviews and secondary sources.

tribesmen and political leaders, some of whom called for amendments to the FCR, rather than its repeal.

The U.S. Government Has Not Met National Security Goals in Pakistan's FATA

The United States has not met its national security goals to destroy the terrorist threat and close the safe haven in the FATA, despite more than $10.5 billion in U.S. support to Pakistan since 2002. Various national security strategies have called for the use of all elements of national power, such as diplomatic, military, intelligence, development assistance, economic, and law enforcement support, to meet these goals; however, the United States has relied principally on supporting the Pakistani military to meet these goals. According to Defense and State, the Pakistani government deployed up to 120,000 military and paramilitary forces to combat terrorism in the FATA. Despite this effort, the 2007 NIE, State and embassy documents, and Defense and State officials, including those operating in Pakistan, have concluded that al Qaeda has regenerated its ability to attack the United States and succeeded in establishing a safe haven in Pakistan's FATA.

Although State Has Reported Some Progress in Pakistan's FATA, Other Sources Indicate Resurgence of an al Qaeda Threat and the Establishment of a Terrorist Safe Haven in the FATA

On October 1, 2007, State provided Congress with a report in response to a requirement in the Implementation of the 9/11 Commission Act of 2007 (9/11 Commission Act).[7] The report stated that it had determined that Pakistan was (1) committed to eliminating from Pakistani territory any organization, such as the Taliban, al Qaeda, or any successor engaged in military, insurgent, or terrorist activities in Afghanistan; (2) undertaking a comprehensive military, legal, economic, and political campaign to achieve the goal described; and (3) making demonstrated, significant, and sustained progress toward eliminating support or safe havens for terrorists. Notwithstanding State's report to Congress, we found broad agreement that al Qaeda had established a safe haven in the FATA and reconstituted its attack capability. In particular, the unclassified versions of the 2007 NIE and 2008 *Annual Threat Assessment* state that al Qaeda has regenerated its attack capability and secured a safe haven in Pakistan's FATA.[8] These conclusions are supported by a broad array of sources, including Defense, State, and senior U.S. embassy officials in Pakistan.

---

[7] P.L. 110-53, sec. 2042(d), Aug. 3, 2007.

[8] The DNI's 2007 NIE and its 2008 *Annual Threat Assessment* are designed to help U.S. civilian and military leaders develop policies to protect U.S. national security interests and represent the combined judgments of 16 U.S. intelligence agencies, according to the NIE.

The NIE and other sources have found that al Qaeda has established a safe haven in Pakistan. The DNI's 2008 assessment stated that the safe haven in Pakistan provides al Qaeda with many of the same advantages it had when it was based across the border in Afghanistan. According to the assessment, the safe haven in the FATA serves as a staging area for al Qaeda's attacks in support of the Taliban in Afghanistan. Further, it serves as a location for training new terrorist operatives for attacks in Pakistan, the Middle East, Africa, Europe, and the United States. U.S. government officials in Washington and Pakistan also acknowledge that al Qaeda has established a safe haven near Pakistan's border with Afghanistan. For example, State's April 2007 *Country Reports on Terrorism* states that Pakistan remains a major source of Islamic extremism and a safe haven for some top terrorist leaders, including those of al Qaeda.

The NIE, *The Terrorist Threat to the U.S. Homeland*, also found that al Qaeda had effectively found replacements for many of its senior operational planners over the years. The NIE stated that, in the past 2 years, al Qaeda's central leadership regenerated the core operational capabilities needed to conduct attacks against the United States. It also found that al Qaeda's central leadership, based in the border area of Pakistan, is and will remain the most serious terrorist threat to the United States.

The 2008 DNI *Annual Threat Assessment* and other sources have concluded that the resurgence of al Qaeda terrorists on the border between Pakistan and Afghanistan now pose a preeminent threat to U.S. national security. The assessment also examines the impact of not meeting the national security goals. It states that al Qaeda is now using the Pakistani safe haven to put the last element necessary to launch another attack against America into place, including the identification, training, and positioning of Western operatives for an attack. It stated that al Qaeda is most likely using the FATA to plot terrorist attacks against political, economic, and infrastructure targets in America "designed to produce mass casualties, visually dramatic destruction, significant economic aftershocks, and/or fear among the population."

DNI's 2008 assessment found that al Qaeda and other Pakistan-based militants now also pose a threat to Pakistan. The assessment found an unparalleled increase in suicide attacks against Pakistan's military and civilians over the past year, with total casualties in 2007 exceeding all such attacks in the preceding 5 years. These attacks were ordered by Pakistan-based militants, many of whom are allied with al Qaeda. It found that the terrorist assassination of former Prime Minister Benazir Bhutto could encourage terrorists to strike the Pakistani establishment anywhere in the country. The assessment concluded that radical elements now have the potential to undermine Pakistan itself.

The United States Has Relied Primarily on the Pakistani Military to Accomplish Its Goals in Pakistan's FATA, with Little Focus on Economic Development and Improving Governance

Since 2002, the United States has relied principally on the Pakistani military to address U.S. national security goals in the FATA. There have been limited efforts, however, to address other underlying causes of terrorism in the FATA, such as providing development assistance or addressing the FATA's political needs. For example, although the FATA has some of the worst development indicators in Pakistan and is ruled under colonial administrative and legal structures dating from 1901, the United States has devoted little funding to address these issues in the FATA.

From fiscal years 2002 to 2007, the United States has provided Pakistan with more than $10.5 billion in funds and assistance.[9] Approximately $5.8 billion of this amount has been directed at efforts to combat terrorism in Pakistan's FATA and the border region. As figure 2 shows, about 96 percent of this amount was used to reimburse the Pakistani government through CSF[10] for military operations in support of Operation Enduring Freedom in Afghanistan, most significantly against terrorists in Pakistan's FATA and border region. We identified only two nonmilitary activities that occured in the FATA and border region: State's Border Security Program, which received about $187 million, and USAID development activities, which amounted to about $40 million.

According to a State Department report, Pakistan's military forces have had some tactical successes in the FATA. The Pakistani government stationed military and paramilitary forces along the border with Afghanistan, and security operations in the FATA disrupted terrorist activity by targeting and raiding al Qaeda and other militant safe havens.[11] According to State, Pakistan has helped kill or capture hundreds of suspected terrorists, including al Qaeda operatives and Taliban leaders. In addition, Pakistani military operations have resulted in the deaths of approximately 1,400 members of its security forces.

[9] GAO arrived at this figure by analyzing Defense, State, and USAID documents. We identified major sources of U.S. funding to Pakistan, including $5.56 billion in CSF reimbursed through June 2007, $1.98 billion in development assistance (through December 2007), $1.6 billion in economic support fund cash transfers to support basic government operations, $1.22 billion for the purchase of military equipment, $9 million in international military training, and $202 million in border security assistance.

[10] CSF reimburses Pakistan for a variety of activities in support of the global war on terror, the majority of which consists of Army and Air Force operations against terrorists in Pakistan's FATA and the border region. However, some of the CSF also supports Pakistani Navy and Air Force activities outside of this area. Defense was unable to quantify what was reimbursed for activities outside the FATA and the border region at the time of our report, and therefore, we included all CSF funds in figure 2 as funds going toward the FATA and the border region.

[11] Department of State report to Congress, pursuant to Section 2042 of the Implementing Recommendations of the 9/11 Commissions Act of 2007 (P.L. 110-53).

Figure 2: Percentage of U.S. Funding Directed toward Military, Border Security, and Development Activities in Pakistan's FATA and Border Region from Fiscal Years 2002 to 2007

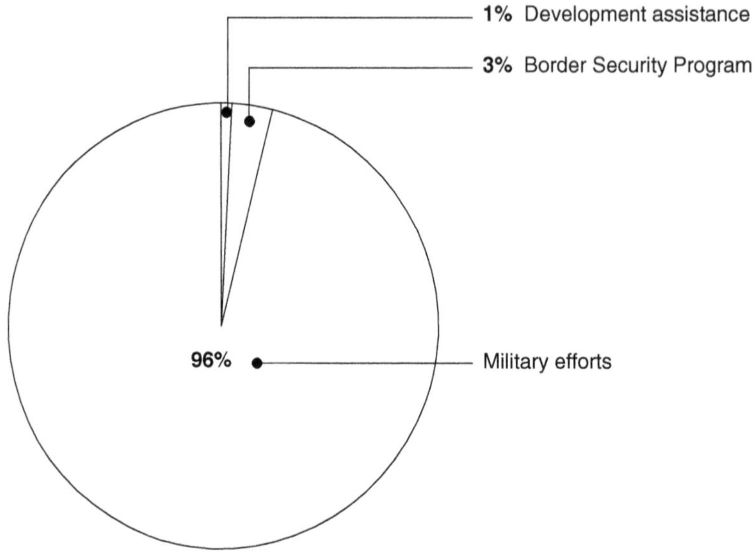

Source: GAO analysis of Defense, State, and USAID data.

Key Government Stakeholders Recognize That a More Comprehensive Approach Is Needed

Defense, State, U.S. embassy, and Pakistani government officials recognize that relying primarily on the Pakistani military has not succeeded in neutralizing al Qaeda and preventing the establishment of a safe haven in the FATA. State's April 2007 *Country Reports on Terrorism* states that, despite having Pakistani troops in the FATA and sustaining hundreds of casualties, the government of Pakistan has been unable to exert control over the area. The report concluded that Pakistan has now recognized that military operations alone will not restore security and stability to the FATA. Similarly, U.S. embassy officials in Pakistan stated that Taliban and al Qaeda elements have created a safe haven in the FATA and have used it to plan and launch attacks on Afghan, Pakistani, U.S., and coalition forces in Afghanistan and Pakistan. The embassy further noted that al Qaeda and the Taliban continue to recruit, train, and operate in the FATA.

According to senior embassy officials, U.S. reliance on Pakistan's military stemmed from the lack of a comprehensive plan to guide embassy efforts and the sense that the Pakistani military was the most capable institution in Pakistan to quickly undertake operations against al Qaeda immediately after the attacks of 9/11. Senior embassy officials stated that this may have led to an "over-reliance" on the Pakistani military to achieve U.S. national security objectives in Pakistan.

No Comprehensive Plan for Guiding U.S. Efforts in the FATA Has Been Developed, as Called for by the Administration and Congress

Despite the recognition of U.S. government officials, including the U.S. President and Congress, that a comprehensive plan employing all elements of national power—diplomatic, military, intelligence, development assistance, economic, and law enforcement support—was needed to combat terrorism and close the terrorist safe haven in Pakistan's FATA region, a comprehensive plan to meet U.S. national security goals in the region was never developed. Recognizing in 2006 that military efforts alone would not succeed in the FATA, the embassy, with Defense, State, and USAID support, and in conjunction with the Pakistani government in power at that time, began an effort to focus more attention on the other key elements of national power, such as development and public diplomacy, to address U.S. national security goals in the FATA. However, this effort has not been formally approved by U.S. government stakeholders who would play a key role in the funding and implementation of such an effort, and support from the recently elected Pakistani government is uncertain.

Presidential Powers for Implementing National Security Strategies and Developing a Comprehensive Plan

The President of the United States has primary responsibility to ensure that his national security strategy is carried out effectively. The President has the authority to task executive branch departments to develop comprehensive plans that use all elements of U.S. power—diplomatic, military, intelligence, development assistance, economic, and law enforcement support—toward meeting U.S. national security goals. As a result, the President can task key national security agencies, such as Defense, State, USAID, the Departments of Homeland Security, Justice, the Treasury, and intelligence agencies, to develop a comprehensive, integrated strategy and to use their combined capabilities to combat terrorism, as called for in the national security strategies. The President can also use the NSC[12] and the NCTC[13] to assist in developing, coordinating, and monitoring these plans.

[12] The NSC is charged with more effectively coordinating the policies and functions of the departments and agencies related to national security. The NSC advises the President with respect to the integration of domestic, foreign, and military policies relating to national security to enable the departments and agencies to cooperate more effectively in matters involving national security.

[13] The NCTC is charged with conducting strategic operational planning for counterterrorism activities, integrating all instruments of national power—including diplomatic, military, intelligence, development assistance, economic, and law enforcement support—within and among agencies, with the

Despite Executive, Congressional, and Independent Calls for Comprehensive Plans to Combat Terrorism and Close Terrorist Safe Havens, Such Plans Were Never Developed

As table 1 shows, the need for the development of comprehensive plans employing all elements of national power—diplomatic, military, intelligence, development assistance, economic, and law enforcement support—to combat terrorism and close terrorist safe havens has been recognized by the President's national security strategies (2003), the independent 9/11 Commission (2004), and by Congress in repeated legislation (2004 and 2007). As it became clearer that al Qaeda had retreated from Afghanistan into Pakistan and was creating a safe haven in the FATA, Congress increased its demands on the U.S. administration to develop comprehensive plans to help Pakistan combat terrorism and close the FATA safe haven.

Despite recommendations by the President's own national security strategy, by the independent 9/11 Commission, as well as legislative mandates from Congress, a comprehensive plan to destroy the terrorist threat or close the safe haven in the FATA was never developed. Even after the creation of the NCTC, an organization specifically intended to develop, implement, and monitor multidepartment plans to combat terrorism, the embassy has yet to receive any such plan to combat terrorism in Pakistan's FATA. In addition, the administration did not report to Congress on its plans for assisting Pakistan in (1) combating terrorism and (2) closing terrorist safe havens, as required by both the 2004 and 2007 legislation.

As a result, the embassy has lacked a Washington-approved, comprehensive plan that combines the capabilities of Defense, State, USAID, intelligence agencies, and other U.S. departments to combat terrorism in the FATA. According to senior embassy officials in Islamabad, the embassy had not received a comprehensive plan from the CIA, Defense, State, the NCTC, the NSC, the White House, or any other executive department. Further, these officials stated that they had not received any strategic guidance on designing, implementing, funding, and monitoring a comprehensive effort that would use all elements of national power to combat terrorism in Pakistan. According to senior embassy officials, given the strategic threat to America, the United States should have a comprehensive strategy to defeat terrorists that uses all elements of national power.

Defense, State, the DNI, USAID, and the government of Pakistan recognize that a comprehensive approach is needed to meet U.S. national security goals in Pakistan. For example, in its 2007 *Country Reports on Terrorism*,

ultimate goal of preventing future attacks against the United States and its interests worldwide. Both report directly to the President.

Table 1. Key Recommendations by Executive, Independent, and Congressional Sources to Combat Terrorism and Close Terrorist Safe Havens

Key document	Source	Recommendation
National Strategy for Combating Terrorism, 2003	President Bush and the NSC	• Called for comprehensive plans employing all elements of national power—diplomatic, military, intelligence, development assistance, economic, and law enforcement support—to combat terrorism • Gave State lead to develop coordinated plans; all appropriate departments were to develop supporting strategies • Directed Defense, State, and intelligence agencies to annually assess and develop plans to close safe havens
9/11 Commission Report, 2004	9/11 Commission, an independent, bipartisan study group mandated by Congress in 2002	• Stated that long-term success demands coordinated, comprehensive, multidepartment efforts employing all elements of national power • Recommended that a single entity be responsible for comprehensive, multidepartment planning for U.S. efforts to combat terrorism • Recommended U.S. (1) make a long-term, comprehensive commitment to assist Pakistan to combat terrorism and (2) develop a strategy to close safe havens
Intelligence Reform Act, 2004	Congress	• Authorized creation of the NCTC to develop comprehensive, multidepartment plans to combat terrorism employing all elements of national power • Stipulated that such plans should include (1) the mission, (2) objectives, (3) tasks to be performed, (4) interagency coordination, and (5) roles and responsibilities. It also tasked the NCTC with monitoring each agency involved • Required a report within 180 days of passage of the act on the administration's strategies for (1) closing terrorist safe havens and (2) assisting Pakistan to combat terrorism
9/11 Commission Act, 2007	Congress	• Required the President to submit a report by November 2007 on the strategy, employing all elements of national power, to combat terrorism in the FATA

Source: GAO analysis of key documents.

State indicated that Pakistan recognized that military operations alone would not restore stability to the FATA; instead, a comprehensive strategy was needed that also included economic, social development, political, and administrative efforts to enhance security in the region. The U.S. Embassy in Pakistan also concluded that, while force is a necessary component of an overall strategy to combat terrorism in the FATA, it is not sufficient as the sole component. Similarly, the DNI stated that Pakistan now recognizes it must take a more comprehensive approach to defeating terrorism and that an intensified and sustained effort that combines administrative, economic, educational, legal, and social reforms to defeat the terrorist threat is required.[14]

We have previously reported on the need for plans to combat terrorism to include elements that would enhance interagency cooperation and improve effectiveness. Specifically, in large-scale interagency efforts where collaboration is essential, we have found that agencies should (1) define and articulate a common outcome; (2) establish mutually reinforcing or joint strategies; (3) identify and address funding needs by leveraging resources; (4) agree on roles and responsibilities; (5) establish compatible policies, procedures, and other means to operate across agency boundaries; (6) develop mechanisms to monitor, evaluate, and report on results; (7) reinforce agency accountability for collaborative efforts through agency plans and reports; and (8) reinforce individual accountability for collaborative efforts through performance management systems.[15]

Pakistan and the U.S. Embassy are Encouraging More Focus on Other Key Elements of National Power to Achieve U.S. Goals in the FATA

In March 2006, the President of Pakistan requested that President Bush support Pakistan's effort to support a more comprehensive approach to combating terrorism in the FATA. As a result, the U.S. Embassy in Pakistan began coordinating efforts by Defense, State, and USAID to develop department-specific efforts to support Pakistan's Sustainable Development Plan for the FATA. Pakistan's Sustainable Development Plan is a 9 year, $2 billion effort to provide economic development, extend the influence of the Pakistani government, and establish security in the FATA. To assist this effort, Defense undertook a counterinsurgency assessment in the FATA and began developing its Security Development Plan. At the same time, USAID provided technical assistance to the Pakistani government to help formalize its Sustainable Development Plan, as well as to plan USAID-development activities in the FATA.

---

[14] Annual Threat Assessment of the Director of National Intelligence for the Senate Select Committee on Intelligence, Feb. 5, 2008.

[15] See GAO-07-697, GAO-06-15, and GAO-03-519T.

This approach, if approved by the administration and key U.S. government agency stakeholders, would constitute the U.S. government's first attempt to focus more attention on other key elements of national power to address U.S. counterterrorism goals in the FATA. These elements include development assistance and public diplomacy, as well as counterinsurgency training, which have not been part of the previous military approach. This new approach also calls for greater levels of direct U.S. planning, implementation, coordination, and oversight. However, this new approach does not yet constitute a comprehensive plan, and all of the agencies' individual efforts have not been fully approved in Washington. Furthermore, funding shortfalls exist, and support by the recently elected government of Pakistan is uncertain.

If fully approved, the United States would provide an estimated $956 million between fiscal years 2008 through 2011 for development, security, capacity building, and infrastructure in support of the Pakistani government. This approach represents the first effort by the U.S. embassy to directly plan, implement, coordinate, and monitor a multidepartment effort to combat terrorism in the FATA. According to officials with the U.S. embassy, the Pakistani government, and international donors, this comprehensive approach is critical to addressing the terrorist threat in the FATA and represents a significant departure from the past.

As of September 2007, the embassy planned to spend $187.6 million on this initial effort using fiscal year 2007 funds. The funding has been directed to four areas:

- **Development:** The $99 million development effort would be led by USAID and would include capacity building for the FATA institutions needed to plan, manage, and monitor development projects; efforts to build community and government relations; funding for health and education services; and efforts to increase employment and economic growth.[16]
- **Security:** The $54.1 million Defense and State security effort would include training for military and paramilitary units in the FATA—including the Frontier Corps, special operations forces, and air crews—and for providing night vision goggles, radios, and other equipment.
- **Infrastructure:** The $32.5 million the U.S. embassy has designated for infrastructure improvements related to both its security and development efforts would be used for road construction, the Frontier Corps training center, and border surveillance outposts.

[16] In commenting on this report, USAID stated they received $88 million for these efforts in the Fiscal Year 2007 Supplemental Appropriation.

- **Public diplomacy:** $2 million in funding was allotted for public diplomacy programs.

According to the embassy, the success of this new effort in the FATA will depend on close coordination among an array of institutions within the U.S. and Pakistani governments. The new effort also will involve partner agencies and allies, including the United Kingdom, Japan, and Europe; the Asian Development Bank; nongovernmental organizations; and the Pakistani private sector, civil society, and the tribes of the FATA.

We plan to monitor the status and progress of the U.S. government in developing this effort and provide an assessment in a subsequent report covering security, political, and development activities undertaken by the United States to meet U.S. national security goals in the FATA.

Conclusion

Combating terrorism is the United States' top national security priority at home and abroad. Since 9/11, U.S. national security strategies have consistently called for using all elements of national power to combat terrorism, including diplomatic, military, intelligence, development assistance, economic, and law enforcement support. Because the use of the various elements of national power falls under the authority of numerous U.S. government agencies, the development of a comprehensive plan is needed to ensure that the full capacity of the U.S. government is focused on meeting U.S. national security goals.

We believe that such a plan would help to ensure coordination, integration, and implementation of U.S. efforts to close the terrorist safe haven in the FATA. A comprehensive plan to combat terrorism in the FATA that establishes goals, objectives, priorities, outcomes, and milestones, including specific performance measures, would allow an assessment of progress and help ensure accountability of U.S. efforts. As such, we believe that the administration should develop a comprehensive plan using the full capabilities provided by Defense, State, USAID, and other U.S. agencies and stakeholders to further assist Pakistan in combating terrorism.

Recommendations for Executive Action

We recommend that the National Security Advisor and the Director of the NCTC, in consultation with the Secretaries of Defense and State, and the Administrator of USAID, the intelligence community, and other executive departments as deemed appropriate, implement the congressional mandate to develop a comprehensive plan using all elements of national power to combat the terrorist threat and close their safe haven in Pakistan's FATA region.

The comprehensive plan should also include key components called for in the Intelligence Reform Act, the Implementing Recommendations of the 9/11 Commission Act of 2007, and components that we have previously reported as being needed to improve the effectiveness of plans involving multidepartmental efforts to combat terrorism.[17] The plan should (1) place someone directly in charge of this multidepartment effort to improve accountability; (2) articulate a clear strategy to implement the national security goal to destroy terrorists and close the safe haven in the FATA; (3) clarify roles and responsibilities of each department for implementing the goal; (4) provide guidance on setting funding priorities and providing resources to meet these national security goals; and (5) require a monitoring system and provide periodic reports to Congress on the progress and impediments to meeting national security goals in Pakistan.

Agency Comments and Our Evaluation

State, the Office of the Director of National Intelligence (ODNI), Defense, and USAID provided written comments on a draft of this report, which are reproduced in appendixes I, II, III, and IV.

State and ODNI did not comment on our recommendation, while Defense and USAID concurred with our recommendation. In general, they all commented on their individual planning efforts and interagency meetings to coordinate these efforts that began in 2006. This, however, was not the focus of our review; our report assessed whether a comprehensive plan had been developed that incorporated all elements of national power. We plan to conduct a detailed assessment of the individual agency efforts from 2002 to the present as part of our broader engagement efforts and look forward to working closely with ODNI, Defense, State, USAID, and other agencies in assessing their plans and efforts to meet national security goals in Pakistan.

State's comments assert that embassy and U.S. government efforts to date have resulted in a comprehensive strategy. We disagree and note in our report that, while the initiatives begun by Defense, State, and USAID are being coordinated by the embassy, they have not been fully approved or integrated into a formal, comprehensive plan. While we acknowledge that this effort is a step in the right direction toward implementing the 2003 national security strategy, the recommendations by the 9/11 Commission, and Congress, it is unclear whether the new approach will include all of the key elements of national power, such as intelligence, economic, and law enforcement support.

[17] GAO-07-697, GAO-06-15, and GAO-03-519T.

ODNI's comments stated that they agreed with our finding that the United States had not met its national security goals in Pakistan's FATA and that countering the growth of terrorist safe havens requires all elements of national power. They disagreed, however, that the United States lacks plans to combat terrorism in the area. Our report does not state that the U.S. lacks individual plans; rather, we found that there was no comprehensive plan that integrated the combined capabilities of Defense, State, USAID, the intelligence community, and others to meet U.S. national security goals in Pakistan.

We also received technical comments from Defense and USAID, which we have incorporated throughout the report where appropriate.

As agreed with your offices, unless you publicly announce the contents of this report earlier, we plan no further distribution until 30 days from the report date. At that time, we will send copies of this report to interested congressional committees, to the National Security Advisor of the NSC, the Director of the NCTC, the Secretaries of State and Defense, and the Administrator of USAID. We will also make copies of this report available to others upon request. We will also make copies available at no charge on the GAO Web site at http://www.gao.gov.

If you or your staffs have any questions about this report, please contact me at (202) 512-7331 or johnsoncm@gao.gov. Contact points for our Offices of Congressional Relations and Public Affairs may be found on the last page of this report. GAO staff who made major contributions to this report are listed in appendix V.

Charles Michael Johnson Jr.
Director, International Affairs and Trade

Congressional Requesters

The Honorable Howard Berman
Chairman
The Honorable Ileana Ros-Lehtinen
Ranking Member
Committee on Foreign Affairs
House of Representatives

The Honorable Gary Ackerman
Chairman
The Honorable Mike Pence
Ranking Member

Subcommittee on the Middle East and South Asia
Committee on Foreign Affairs
House of Representatives

The Honorable John F. Tierney
Chairman
The Honorable Christopher Shays
Ranking Member
Subcommittee on National Security and Foreign Affairs
Committee on Oversight and Government Reform
House of Representatives

The Honorable Tom Harkin
The Honorable Robert Menendez
United States Senate

Appendix I: Comments from the Department of State

United States Department of State

Washington, D.C. 20520

APR 07 2008

Ms. Jacquelyn Williams-Bridgers
Managing Director
International Affairs and Trade
Government Accountability Office
441 G Street, N.W.
Washington, D.C. 20548-0001

Dear Ms. Williams-Bridgers:

We appreciate the opportunity to review your draft report, "COMBATING TERRORISM: U.S. Lacks Comprehensive Plan to Destroy Terrorist Threat and Close Safe Haven in Pakistan's Federally Administered Tribal Areas," GAO Job Code 320573.

The enclosed Department of State comments are provided for incorporation with this letter as an appendix to the final report.

If you have any questions concerning this response, please contact Tom West, Desk Officer, Bureau of South and Central Asian Affairs, at (202) 647-6710.

Sincerely,

Bradford R. Higgins

cc: GAO – Charles Michael Johnson
SCA – Richard Boucher
State/OIG – Mark Duda

Department of State Comments on GAO Draft Report

Combating Terrorism: U.S. Lacks Comprehensive Plan to Destroy Terrorist Threat and Close Safe Haven in Pakistan's Federally Administered Tribal Areas
(GAO-08-622; GAO Code 320573)

The Department of State appreciates the opportunity to review the Government Accountability Office (GAO) draft report titled: *Combating Terrorism: U.S. Lacks Comprehensive Plan to Destroy Terrorist Threat and Close Safe Haven in Pakistan's Federally Administered Tribal Areas.*

The study does not acknowledge that the United States had an overall plan for Pakistan, put together in the immediate aftermath of 9/11. That initial plan called for working closely with and supporting the Pakistani military to confront the extremists militarily and working to deny them their safe havens along the Pakistan-Afghan border. To a large extent, the plan worked. From 2001-2006, we – or the Pakistanis – arrested or killed hundreds of al-Qaeda and Taliban extremists, shattered terrorist networks, disrupted their training camps and short-circuited terrorist operations. U.S.-Pakistani cooperation made it more difficult for terrorists to operate in Pakistan. By the end of 2006, 120,000 Pakistani troops were involved in on-going operations against violent extremists along the Pakistan-Afghan border. The GAO draft report acknowledges this but fails to attribute it to a deliberate planning effort.

The immediate post-9/11 plan was, however, largely military and was therefore limited in its effect. Additionally, the plan was undercut by events following the 2006 North Waziristan agreement between the militants and the Government of Pakistan (also unaddressed in the report), during which time terrorists were able to rebuild and regroup.

We and the Pakistanis recognized that a new plan was needed to address the broader conditions that support terrorism; specifically, the abysmal social conditions in the Tribal Areas and the absence of central authority there. A series of interagency meetings in summer of 2006 (Deputies Committees meetings on July 16 and August 22, specifically) laid further groundwork for what became our current FATA strategy and our support for the Pakistani Sustainable Development Plan for the Tribal Areas. This strategy brought together security assistance for the local Frontier Corps, economic and development assistance for the Tribal Region, private sector development programs, and our proposal for Reconstruction Opportunity Zones for job creation in border areas of both Pakistan and Afghanistan. Taken together with complementary military and intelligence participation, this became our comprehensive, integrated strategy and has been implemented since that time.

The GAO draft does acknowledge the difficult conditions in Pakistan, the vast un-policed territories, the abysmal social conditions in the tribal belt and our need to rely completely upon a Pakistani military under-equipped and under-trained to conduct counter-insurgency operations. It also acknowledges the decades when the Tribal Areas were used as a jihadist training area and jumping off point for the anti-Soviet war in Afghanistan. But the Report fails to acknowledge the continuing efforts that have gone into devising, funding and implementing a broad-based plan to address these conditions.

Appendix II: Comments from the Department of Defense

THE ASSISTANT SECRETARY OF DEFENSE
2700 DEFENSE PENTAGON
WASHINGTON, DC 20301-2700

ASIAN & PACIFIC
SECURITY AFFAIRS

APR 0 7 2008

Mr. Charles Johnson Jr.
Director, International Counterterrorism Issues,
International Affairs and Trade
Government Accountability Office
441 G Street, N.W.
Washington, D.C. 20548

Mr. Johnson:

This is the Department of Defense (DoD) response to the GAO Draft Report, GAO-08-622, "COMBATING TERRORISM: U.S. Lacks Comprehensive Plan to Destroy Terrorist Threat and Close Safe Haven in Pakistan's Federally Administered Tribal Areas," dated March 28, 2008 (GAO Code 320573).

We have enclosed comments addressing the report and its recommendations.

My point of contact is Mr. Eric Lebson, 703-697-3754, or e-mail: eric.lebson@osd.mil.

Sincerely,

James J. Shinn

GAO DRAFT REPORT DATED MARCH 28, 2008
GAO-08-622 (GAO CODE 320573)

"COMBATING TERRORISM: U.S. LACKS COMPREHENSIVE PLAN TO DESTROY TERRORIST THREAT AND CLOSE SAFE HAVEN IN PAKISTAN'S FEDERALLY ADMINISTERED TRIBAL AREAS"

DEPARTMENT OF DEFENSE COMMENTS
TO THE GAO RECOMMENDATION

RECOMMENDATION: The GAO recommends that the National Security Advisor and the Director of the National Counterterrorism Center, in consultation with the Secretaries of Defense and State, and the Administrator of United States Agency for International Development, the intelligence community, and other executive departments as deemed appropriate, implement the congressional mandate to develop a comprehensive plan using all elements of national power, to combat the terrorist threat and close their safe haven in Pakistan's Federally Administered Tribal Areas region. The comprehensive plan should also include key components called for in the Intelligence Reform Act and by GAO to improve the effectiveness of plans involving multi-departmental effort to combat terrorism. (p. 25/GAO Draft Report)

DOD RESPONSE: Concur. DoD supports the development of a comprehensive plan to close safe havens in Pakistan's Federally Administered Tribal Areas. In November 2007 and February 2008, DoD provided to the State Department inputs for a comprehensive strategy. DoD has participated in a wide variety of inter-agency meetings that have addressed the on-going development of this strategy. This includes Deputies Committee meetings on 14 and 20 March 2008 and long-standing weekly informal South/Central Asia inter-agency meetings hosted by the Assistant Secretary of State for South and Central Asia. DoD is continuing to play an active role in the inter-agency effort to develop and coordinate a comprehensive plan to close terrorist safe havens in Pakistan.

NOTE: DoD has forwarded technical comments (context, inaccuracies and additional background) about the report directly to GAO and recommended their consideration for the final version of the report.

Attachment
Page 1 of 1

Appendix III: Comments from the U.S. Agency for International Development

USAID
FROM THE AMERICAN PEOPLE

APR 9 2008

Mr. Charles Michael Johnson, Jr.
Director
International Affairs and Trade
Government Accountability Office
441 G Street, N.W.
Washington, DC 20548

Dear Mr. Johnson:

The U.S. Agency for International Development (USAID) appreciates the opportunity to review and respond to your draft audit report entitled "COMBATTING TERRORISM: U.S. Lacks Comprehensive Plan to Destroy Terrorist Threat and Close Safe Haven in Pakistan's Federally Administered Tribal Areas," GAO-08-622.

In general, we concur with your overall recommendation that the U.S. Government (USG) needs a comprehensive plan for work in the FATA. However, work in the FATA should be guided by the Government of Pakistan's own FATA Sustainable Development Plan, which was developed in consultation with the USG and was completed in 2006. The USAID plan for programs in the FATA was presented to the USG's interagency in December 2006. Prior to the formal presentation, this plan was vetted thoroughly with, and approved by, the country team in Islamabad, and also in the interagency in Washington.

Additionally, please note that:

- USAID is an instrument of "soft power" as opposed to the "hard power" programs with the Pakistani military described extensively in the draft report. Our programs focus on addressing the underlying causes of insurgencies and the development issues which allow for terrorist safe havens. Successful strategies in settings such as the FATA depend on mutually reinforcing hard and soft approaches conducted in tandem.
- The embassy's engagement on strategic development in FATA began in summer 2006 and included reopening a USAID office in Peshawar, launching a

U.S. Agency for International Development
1300 Pennsylvania Avenue, NW
Washington, DC 20523
www.usaid.gov

- 2 -

development strategy in tandem with the GOP and organizing a FATA donor's discussion at the fall 2006 World Bank/IMF meetings in Singapore.

- USAID initially started with small scale programs in education, health and microfinance as pilots which then determined the strategy for our larger programs currently being implemented.

In conclusion, we feel that the GAO should recognize the Government of Pakistan, USAID and the wider country team for advancing strategic thinking on the FATA development program.

Thanks very much for the opportunity to comment on this report and for the courtesies extended by your staff in the conduct of this review.

Sincerely,

Lisa Chiles

Lisa Chiles
Deputy Assistant Administrator
Bureau for Asia

Appendix IV: Comments from the Office of the Director of National Intelligence

OFFICE OF THE DIRECTOR OF NATIONAL INTELLIGENCE
WASHINGTON, DC 20511

April 8, 2008

Ms. Janet St. Laurent
Managing Director, Defense Capabilities
and Management
United States Government Accountability Office
Washington, D.C. 20548

Dear Ms. St. Laurent:

(U) The Office of the Director of National Intelligence and the National Counterterrorism Center appreciate the opportunity to review the GAO report number 08-622 *Combating Terrorism: U.S. Lacks Comprehensive Plan to Destroy Terrorist Threat and Close Safe Haven in Pakistan's Federally Administered Tribal Areas.* Although we agree that the United States has not yet met its national security goals in Pakistan's Federally Administered Tribal Areas (FATA), we disagree that the United States lacks plans to combat terrorism in the area.

(U) Effectively countering the growth of extremism and the emergence of terrorist safehavens requires all elements of national power, to include diplomatic, military, development assistance, financial, law enforcement, and intelligence. The National Security Council, the Department of State, and the Department of Defense, have, therefore, been actively involved in the United States Government efforts to deny our terrorist enemies safehavens such as the FATA. The Office of the Director of National Intelligence, the National Counterterrorism Center, and the Intelligence Community have also been actively involved in such efforts.

(U) The National Counterterrorism Center, for example, produced the landmark National Implementation Plan for the War on Terror, which was signed by the President in June 2006, and was the first-ever United States Government-wide strategic plan for countering terrorism. This war plan does not stand alone. Rather, it complements two types of planning efforts that have long existed and continue to exist: (1) high-level national strategies directed by the President and the National Security and Homeland Security Councils, and (2) very granular and tactical department and agency-specific implementation plans.

(U) The National Counterterrorism Center (NCTC) has also been expanding its ongoing efforts to coordinate near-term department and agency activities at the strategic operational level in certain key regions of the world. NCTC combines regional and functional priorities to ensure its strategic operational planning initiatives, which by definition are interagency in nature, properly balance high-level and mission centric perspectives, and are comprehensive in drawing on all instruments of national power. NCTC has participated in a recently-completed interagency initiative to determine counterterrorism priorities, which, along with other efforts, provide a regional perspective to functional efforts and plans, such as the National Implementation Plan.

- 2 -

(U) I thank you again for the opportunity to review this report and look forward to working with your office in the future.

Sincerely,

Kathleen Turner

Kathleen Turner
Director of Legislative Affairs

Appendix V: GAO Contacts and Staff Acknowledgments

GAO Contact:

Charles Michael Johnson Jr., Director, International Affairs and Trade, (202) 512-7331 or johnsoncm@gao.gov

Staff Acknowledgments

In addition to the individual named above, Hynek Kalkus, Assistant Director; Edward J. George; Claude Adrien; David Hancock; Lynn Cothern; Karen Deans; Mark Dowling; and Jena Sinkfield made key contributions to this report.

GAO's Mission

The Government Accountability Office, the audit, evaluation, and investigative arm of Congress, exists to support Congress in meeting its constitutional responsibilities and to help improve the performance and accountability of the federal government for the American people. GAO examines the use of public funds; evaluates federal programs and policies; and provides analyses, recommendations, and other assistance to help Congress make informed oversight, policy, and funding decisions. GAO's commitment to good government is reflected in its core values of accountability, integrity, and reliability.

Obtaining Copies of GAO Reports and Testimony

The fastest and easiest way to obtain copies of GAO documents at no cost is through GAO's Web site (www.gao.gov). Each weekday, GAO posts newly released reports, testimony, and correspondence on its Web site. To have GAO e-mail you a list of newly posted products every afternoon, go to www.gao.gov and select "E-mail Updates."

Order by Mail or Phone

The first copy of each printed report is free. Additional copies are $2 each. A check or money order should be made out to the Superintendent of Documents. GAO also accepts VISA and Mastercard. Orders for 100 or more copies mailed to a single address are discounted 25 percent. Orders should be sent to:

U.S. Government Accountability Office
441 G Street NW, Room LM
Washington, DC 20548

To order by Phone: Voice: (202) 512-6000
TDD: (202) 512-2537
Fax: (202) 512-6061

To Report Fraud, Waste, and Abuse in Federal Programs

Contact:

Web site: www.gao.gov/fraudnet/fraudnet.htm
E-mail: fraudnet@gao.gov
Automated answering system: (800) 424-5454 or (202) 512-7470

Congressional Relations

Ralph Dawn, Managing Director, dawnr@gao.gov, (202) 512-4400 U.S. Government Accountability Office, 441 G Street NW, Room 7125 Washington, DC 20548

Public Affairs

Chuck Young, Managing Director, youngc1@gao.gov, (202) 512-4800 U.S. Government Accountability Office, 441 G Street NW, Room 7149 Washington, DC 20548

DOCUMENT NO. 28

IAEA REPORT ON PAKISTAN'S NATIONAL LEGISLATION

Information Circular
INFCIRC/636

November 23, 2004

General Distribution
Original: English

Pakistan's National Legislation Entitled: "Export Control on Goods, Technologies, Material and Equipment Related to Nuclear and Biological Weapons and Their Delivery Systems Act, 2004"

1. The Director General has received a letter from the Permanent Mission of Pakistan, dated 4 November 2004, concerning Pakistan's national legislation entitled "Export Control on Goods, Technologies, Material and Equipment related to Nuclear and Biological Weapons and their Delivery Systems Act, 2004".

2. As requested by the Permanent Mission of Pakistan, the letter and the Export Control Act of 2004, are reproduced herein for the information of the Member States.

PERMANENT MISSION OF PAKISTAN
TO THE INTERNATIONAL
ORGANIZATIONS
VIENNA

No.UN-6/04/IAEA

Dear Director General,

I have the honour to submit, on behalf of my Government, a copy of Pakistan's national legislation entitled "Export Control on Goods, Technologies, Material and Equipment related to Nuclear and Biological Weapons and their Delivery Systems Act, 2004" (please see attached).

The legislation entered into force on September 23, 2004, after its adoption by the Parliament and approval by the President of Pakistan.

2. Pakistan shares the international concern regarding threats posed by proliferation of weapons of mass destruction and is fully committed to the objectives of non-proliferation. The new Export Control Act is a major step towards the realisation of these objectives.

3. The purpose of the Export Control Act is to further strengthen controls on export of sensitive technologies, goods, materials and equipment related to nuclear and biological weapons and their means of delivery. Pakistan already has necessary legislation in place for control of transfers relating to chemical weapons, materials and technologies.

4. The salient elements of the new Export Control Act include:-

- Controls over export, re-export, transshipment and transit of goods, technologies, material and equipment covered. Prohibition of diversion of controlled goods and technologies.
- Wide jurisdiction (also includes Pakistanis visiting or working abroad).
- Envisages an authority to administer rules and regulations framed under this legislation. Also provides for the establishment of an Oversight Board to monitor the implementation of this legislation.
- Comprehensive control lists and catch all provisions.
- Licensing and record keeping provisions.
- Penal provisions: Up to 14 years imprisonment and Rs. 5 million fine or both, and on conviction offender's property and assets, wherever they may be, shall be forfeited to the Federal Government. Right of appeal provided for.

5. I would be grateful if you could arrange for the circulation of this letter and the enclosed Export Control Act, 2004, to all the IAEA Member States as an INFCIRC document as a manifestation of Pakistan's support for the objectives of non-proliferation as well as the Statutory responsibilities of the IAEA.

Accept, Sir, the assurances of my highest consideration.

Yours sincerely,

(Ali Sarwar Nagvi)

Dr. Mohamed ElBaradei,
Director General,
International Atomic Energy Agency (IAEA),
Vienna.

REGISTERED No. M - 302/L.-7646

The Gazette of Pakistan

EXTRAORDINARY
PUBLISHED BY AUTHORITY

ISLAMABAD, MONDAY, SEPTEMBER 27, 2004

PART I

Acts, Ordinances, President's Orders and Regulations

SENATE SECRETARIAT

Islamabad, the 25th September, 2004

The following Act of Majlis-e-Shoora (Parliament) received the assent of the President on 23rd September, 2004, is hereby published for general information:

Act No. V of 2004

to provide for export control on goods; technologies, material and equipment related to nuclear and biological weapons and their delivery systems;

WHEREAS the Islamic Republic of Pakistan—

(a) is determined to safeguard its national security and foreign policy objectives and to fulfill its international obligations as a responsible nuclear weapon State;

(b) as a party to the Chemical Weapons Convention has promulgated the Chemical Weapons Convention Implementation Ordinance, 2000 (LIV of 2000); and

(c) is committed to prevent proliferation of nuclear and biological weapons and missiles capable of delivering such weapons;

AND WHEREAS to achieve the aforesaid objectives it is necessary to strengthen controls on the export, re-export, transshipment and transit of goods and technologies, material and equipment related to nuclear and biological l weapons and missiles capable of delivering such weapons;

AND WHEREAS it is expedient to provide for export control on, goods, technologies, material and equipment related to nuclear and biological weapons and their delivery systems;

It is hereby enacted as follows:

1. Short title, extent, application and commencement.—

(1) This Act maybe called the Export Control on Goods, Technologies, Material and Equipment related to Nuclear and Biological Weapons and their Delivery Systems Act, 2004.

(2) It extends to the whole of Pakistan.

(3) It applies to—

(a) every citizen of Pakistan or a person in the service of Pakistan within and beyond Pakistan or any Pakistani visiting or working abroad;

(b) any foreign national while in the territories of Pakistan; and

(c) any ground transport, ship or aircraft registered in Pakistan wherever it may be.

(4) It shall come into force at once.

2. Definitions.—In this Act unless there is anything repugnant in the subject or context.—

(a) "basic scientific research" means theoretical- or experimental work undertaken principally to acquire new knowledge of the fundamental principles of phenomena or observable facts;

(b) "biological weapon" means any weapon designed to kill or harm or infect people, animals or plants on a large scale through effects of the infectious or toxic properties of a biological warfare agent;

(c) "delivery system" means missiles exclusively designed and adapted to deliver a nuclear of biological weapon;

(d) "development" means any activity or phase prior to production and may include or relate to design research, design analysis, design concept, assembly and testing of prototypes, pilot production schemes, design data, the process of transforming designed data into product, configuration design and integration design or layout;

(e) "equipment" means an assembly which may, comprise electrical, electronic, mechanical, chemical and metallurgical components, including those used in manufacturing or pilot plants, used in the production of nuclear and biological weapons;

(f) "export" means—

(i) shipment, transfer or transmission of goods or–technology out of the territory of Pakistan; and

(ii) a transfer of goods or technology within Pakistan with the knowledge or intent that the goods or technology will be shipped, transferred or transmitted to an unauthorized recipient out side Pakistan;

(g) "goods" means any article natural or man-made substance, material supply or manufactured product,-including inspection and test equipment except technology;

(h) "material" means materials used in the production of nuclear and biological weapons and their delivery system;

(i) "nuclear weapon" means any weapon designed to kill or cause destruction or harm people on a large scale through the effects of a nuclear explosion;

(j) "*re*-export" means export of an item from any end user State or entity after having imported any goods or technology covered under this Act from Pakistan to any other State or entity;

(k) "services" means providing training and technical assistance including intangible transfer such as disclosure of technical data relating to the purposes of this Act;

(1) "technology" means any documents including blueprints, plans, diagrams, models, formulae, tables, engineering designs or specifications', manuals or instructions, necessary for the development and production of nuclear or biological weapons and their delivery systems, Including on-the-job training, expert advice and services attached therewith except—

(i) any document or information that is in the public domain or is related to basic scientific research and other peaceful applications of such technology including that related to its application for protective purposes; and

(ii) any application of the grant of a patent or any other form of protection for inventions or for the registration of a design in each case under the law of the Islamic Republic of Pakistan or any other country or under any treaty or international conventions to which Pakistan is a party or any document necessary to enable any such application to be filed, made or pursued;

(m) "transit" means transportation through the territory of Pakistan by land, air or amphibious means of transportation; and

(n) "transshipment" means shipment through ports of Pakistan.

3. **Authority.—**

(1) For the purposes of this Act, the authority-rests with the Federal Government and the Federal Government, as and when necessary, may—

(a) make such rules and regulations as are necessary for implementation of this Act;

(b) delegate authority to administer all activities under this Act to such Ministries, Divisions, Departments and Agencies as it may deem appropriate;

(c) establish a government Authority to administer export controls established under this Act;

(d) designate the agency or agencies authorized to enforce this Act;

(e) establish an Oversight Board to monitor the implementation of this Act; and

(f) require licenses for exports from Pakistan of goods and technology, and the re-export of goods and technology that originated in Pakistan.

(2) Officials of the designated agency or agencies are authorized to inspect consignments declared for export and review, acquire or confiscate records of persons engaged in the exporting or holding an export license under this Act, with the same powers in respect of exports in contravention of any provision of this Act. The Federal Government may vest any investigatory powers and powers of arrest authorized by law in officials of the customs administration or other appropriate agencies.

4. Control Lists.—

(1) The Federal Government shall maintain Control Lists, to be notified separately, of goods and Technologies subject to licensing requirements under this Act.

(2) The control lists shall be reviewed periodically, and revised or updated, as required by the Federal Government and notified accordingly.

(3) The Federal Government shall notify all licensing requirements and procedures.

(4) The Federal Government shall control export, *re*-export, transhipment, transit of goods, technologies, material and equipment, subject to the provisions of this Act, which may contribute to the designing, development, production, stockpiling, maintenance or use of nuclear and biological weapons and their delivery systems.

(5) Nothing in this Act shall be construed to restrict or prohibit basic scientific research in Pakistan or other peaceful applications or relevant technologies.

5. Licensing.—

(1) The Federal. Government shall frame and notify the licenses required under this Act, and also adopt and notify the procedures under which such licenses shall be approved or rejected.

(2) Licenses for export of goods and technologies for peaceful applications may be approved unless the Government determines that the export Would be in contravention of the provisions of this Act.

(3) An exporter is under legal obligation to notify to the competent authority if the exporter is aware or suspects that the goods or technology are intended, in their entirety or in part, in connection with nuclear or biological weapons or missiles capable of delivering such weapons.

(4) Nothing in this Act shall be taken to prohibit the export of licensed goods and technology, provided that all conditions attached to the said license are complied with.

6. **Record keeping.**—

(1) All exporters shall maintain records of all transactions and report these to the designated authorities.

(2) Any Government agency or department involved in export licensing procedure shall keep records of their recommendations and decisions. Such records shall be made available to other agencies or departments involved in export licensing, upon request.

7. **Offences, etc., to be tried by a Court of Session.**—Any person who contravenes any provision, or attempts to commit or abets the commission of an offence, under this Act or any order, rules and regulations framed thereunder shall be tried by a Court of Session only upon complaint in writing made by an officer of the Federal Government authorized in this behalf by the. Federal Government.

8. **Offences and penalties.—**

(1) Any person who contra any provision of this Act or any order, rules and regulations framed thereunder, or provides false information concerning matters governed by this Act to any of the agencies responsible for administering this Act, shall be guilty for an offence punishable on conviction by imprisonment for a term which may extend to fourteen years, or with fine not exceeding five million rupees or both, and on conviction offender's property and assets, wherever they may be, shall be forfeited to the Federal Government.

(2) Any person who attempts to commit or abets the commission of an offence under this Act shall be proceeded against in the manner as if he had committed such an offence.

(3) In case the offence is not serious for criminal proceedings, administrative actions, which may be determined from time to time, shall be taken against the individuals contravening any provision of this Act.

9. **Appeal.**—Any person sentenced under this Act may within thirty days of the decision prefer an appeal before the High Court having jurisdiction.

10. Diversion of controlled goods or technologies to unauthorized use.— Whenever the Federal Government determines that a recipient of controlled goods or technologies has knowingly diverted these goods or technologies to unauthorized use in violation of the conditions of an export license issued by, the Government of Pakistan, the Federal Government⁻ or officials of the appropriately designated agency may deny—

(a) further export to that recipient of goods or technologies for a specified period for each offence; or

(b) the recipient the privilege of exporting products into Pakistan for a specified period for each offence.

11. Act not to derogate from other laws, etc.—The provisions of this Act shall be in addition to, and not in derogation of, any law, rules, orders or notifications for the time being in force.

RAJA MUHAMMAD AMIN,
Acting Secretary.

DOCUMENT NO. 29

REGIONAL IMPLICATIONS OF THE RISE OF ISLAMIC FUNDAMENTALISM IN PAKISTAN

Inistitute for Defence Studies Report

January 2006

Kalim Bahadur

Abstract

Muslims comprise the second largest population after Hindus in South Asia. They are, however, not a monolithic community. The rise of religious fundamentalism in Pakistan and the official patronage it has got has an enormous political and security impact on the region. The terrorist campaign, sponsored by Pakistan and waged by Islamic fundamentalist groups in Jammu and Kashmir and Afghanistan, has wide implications and poses a major threat to the region. Setting up an Islamic state and Jihad are the two objectives of all fundamentalist movements. Religious parties had opposed the Pakistan movement before Independence. After Pakistan came into being, the fundamentalist parties gradually raised Islamic issues and the demand for making Pakistan an Islamic state. Though successive governments in Pakistan used Islamic parties for political objectives, it was under General Zia-ul Haq that a campaign was launched from the top to 'islamise' Pakistan. Gen. Zia's policies led to the growth of Islamic and sectarian violence in the country. Pakistan's intervention in Afghanistan and the Islamic policies at home gradually turned the country into the epicentre of global Islamic militancy. The Mullah-Military alliance has been strengthened during the Musharraf regime. The recent growth of Islamic fundamentalism in the South Asian countries, apart from specific historic and social factors in each country, can be greatly attributed to Pakistan's religious parties and its strategic anti-India policies. After Afghanistan, Bangladesh is one of the larger Muslim counties upon which the threat of Islamic militancy looms large. The involvement of Pakistani agencies can also be clearly discerned in the growth of militancy in India, Nepal and Sri Lanka

Islamic fundamentalism is not a new phenomenon. In recent times, it has acquired a militant and jihadi form. It has grown because of the failure of the ruling elite in South Asian countries in nation building and in constructing democratic polities. Successive regimes, both civilian and military, in some of the countries in the region have used Islam as a means to legitimise their rule. Islamic fundamentalism has been well entrenched in Pakistan's power structure for the last two decades or so, ever since the military rule of General Zia-ul Haq. Pakistan military's alliance with the Mullahs was formed during this period. The conglomerate of six fundamentalist parties, the Muttahida Majlise Amal (MMA), controls the provincial government in the strategic NWFP, where it has already enforced a kind of Taliban rule. The MMA is also part of the government in Baluchistan. Pakistan's military ruler Gen. Musharraf has only strengthened the Mullah-Military alliance.

These developments in Pakistan were bound to have repercussions in other countries of the region. The major Islamic party, the Jama'at-i-Islami of Pakistan, and the Tablighi Jama'at and their militant offshoots have a strong presence in Pakistan, India and Bangladesh. There is a wide network of Deobandi and Wahabi madrassas in almost each South Asian country and many of them are being funded by Saudi and Pakistani sources. Pakistan has been sponsoring a militant terrorist campaign in the Indian state of Jammu and Kashmir for the last two decades. Pakistan's official agencies have been active in promoting militant groups in all countries of the region. In India, there has also been a visible increase in the activities of Pakistani-sponsored militant groups, like Lashkar-e Toiba and Jaish-e Muhammad.

South Asia is the most complex region of the world in terms of religion, and is inhabited by the followers of all major religions. Islam, after Hinduism, is one of the major religions of South Asia. It has the second largest following (29 per cent) after Hinduism (64 per cent).[1] Almost four out of every 10 South Asians are Muslims, and they form the single largest Muslim population in the world. Islam in the region has had to co-exist, ever since its arrival in the Indian subcontinent in the first century of the Islamic calendar, with a bewildering variety of religions and cults.[2] All the countries in the region that emerged after Independence are hence multi-religious, multi-ethnic and multi-linguistic. India is larger, both in size and population, than all the other countries of the region combined. It has also the largest Muslim population in the world after Indonesia. Muslims constitute the majority of the population in three of the seven countries in South Asia, i.e., Pakistan, Bangladesh and Maldives, and they are also a significant minority in India, Sri Lanka, and Nepal. But Muslims of South Asia are not a monolithic community. Even at the height of the Mughal

[1] www.cet.edu/earthinfo/sasai/SApeo.html
[2] www.gort.uscd.edu/newjour/q/msg01736.html

rule in India, the Muslims of the region did not constitute a single harmonious community.[3] They are divided in different Islamic sects, sub-sects and schools of thought. Though a majority of them belong to the Sunni sect, each South Asian country has a substantial number of Shias and other minority sects and schools. Almost every country in the region also faces unresolved ethnic, communal and linguistic tensions that at times lead to major conflicts. The terrorist campaign in Jammu & Kashmir—waged mainly by militant Islamic groups sponsored and trained by Pakistan's agencies—and the disruptive activities of the Islamic fundamentalist parties within Pakistan, therefore have wider implications and pose a major threat to the region.[4] The rise of Islamic fundamentalism in Pakistan has had serious implications for social and political stability in the region and a highly volatile impact on relations among communities adhering to different faiths.

Rise of Islamic Fundamentalism

The origins of Islamic fundamentalism can be traced to the tendency among the Muslims to scrutinise the early origins and scriptures for clues to return to the golden era. The setting up of an Islamic state and jihad are the two objectives of every fundamentalist movement. However, there can be no uniform definition of Islamic fundamentalism since the Quran does not prescribe any particular system of government.[5] The term has hence come to be applied to a wide variety of disparate religious and political movements.[6] It is also called 'resurgent Islam', 'radical Islam' and 'political Islam'. Islamic fundamentalism is commonly used synonymously with 'communalism' and 'religious revivalism'. Fundamentalism is only one of a number of strands of politics and thought in Muslim countries.[7] Islamic fundamentalism is also defined as a religio-political movement, which essentially seeks to return to the original sources and roots of Islam. It advocates adherence to the original beliefs of religion in their literal interpretations as a fundamental and basic principle, thus transcending all social, economic, political and cultural transformations that span a period of 14 centuries.[8] The philosophical roots of Islamic fundamentalism are largely the result of a conscious attempt to revive and restate the theoretical relevance of Islam in the modern world.

The earliest fundamentalist movement in the Indian sub-continent can be traced to the collapse of the Mughal Empire in the early 18th century.

[3] Yoginder Sikand. *The Origins and Development of the Tablighi Jama'at 1920–2000*, Orient Longman, New Delhi, 2002, p. 19.
[4] www.satp.org/satporgtp/southasia/samain.htm
[5] www.ipcs.org/TerrorismSeminars2jsp?action=show/new&Kvalue=668
[6] Lionel Caplan *(ed.) Studies in Religious Fundamentalism*, Macmillan, London, 1987, p. 1.
[7] William Maley *(ed.), Fundamentalism Reborn*, Hurst & Company, London, 1999, p. 17.
[8] Zia-ul Haq; "Islamic Fundamentalism", *Dawn* (Karachi), February 14, 1992

The anarchy that followed the loss of Muslim power created widespread feeling among the Muslims that they lost power because they were no longer righteous and that Islam had been polluted by accretions from non-Muslims practices. The real danger, according to the purists, was the ignorance of newly-converted Muslims of the requirements of Islam in their daily life and their non-Islamic practices and beliefs. One of the critics of these impure practices was Shah Waliullah (1703–1762). He criticised the practice of popular Islam in India.[9] He was followed by his son, Shah Abdul Aziz (1746–1824), and later by his disciple, Sayyiad Ahmed Barelvi (1786–1831).[10] The Faraizi movement led by Haji Shariatullah (1781–1840) and Titu Mir (1782–1831) in Bengal was also a reform movement. These reformers wanted to purify Islam of un-Islamic accretions and return to its basic precepts. Sayyiad Ahmed Barelvi aimed at setting up an Islamic state in India. He also aimed at reconquering India and proclaimed jihad against the Sikh ruler Ranjit Singh. His army was decimated in the battle at Balakot (1831) but the movement survived. His followers were called the Wahabis.[11] Some of his followers later founded the famous Deoband School in 1867. The Jamiat-al Ulema-i-Hind (formed in 1919) and the Jama'at-i-Islami-i-Hind (formed in 1941), apart from some others, though different in religious and political perspectives, were the leading exponents of the fundamentalist movement in pre-partition India in the twentieth century.

Pakistan and the Rise of Islamic Fundamentalism

It is necessary to underline here that the idea of Pakistan emerged not from the desire of the Indian Muslims for an Islamic state but was rooted in socio-economic factors. One important factor was the emergence of educated Muslims in provinces where Muslims were in a minority and faced competition from the well-entrenched non-Muslims. Another reason was that the abolition of the use of Persian as the official language had adversely affected the job prospects of educated Muslims. Religion, much less fundamentalist Islamic ideology, played no role in the politics of the Muslim League, founded in 1906, and the Pakistan movement till the second half of the 1940s. Two major fundamentalist parties of India, the Jamiat-al Ulema-i-Hind, along with the Ulema of the Deoband and the Jama'at-i-Islami actively opposed the demand for Pakistan. Maulana Husain Ahmed Madani, head of the Deoband, had stated that nations are made by homelands.[12] The then head of the Jama'at-i-Islami, Maulana Maududi, had declared that he was opposed to Pakistan because the system of the government would not be based on the sovereignty of God but on the

9 Hardy, P, *The Muslims of British India*, Cambridge University Press, London, 1972, pp. 28–29.
10 Yoginder Sikand, n. 3. Sayyid Ahmed Barelvi was born in Rai Bareli and not in Bareilly.
11 Ram Gopal, *Indian Muslims: A Political History, 1858–1947*, Asia Publishing House, Bombay, 1964, p. 23.
12 P. Hardy, n. 9, p. 244.

sovereignty of the people.[13] The crux of the opposition of the Ulema lay in their traditional conception of Islam, and also because the leadership of the Pakistan movement was in the hands of the Western educated elite.[14] It is not surprising, therefore, that the movement for Pakistan was led by political activists rather than by the Ulema.[15] Many Ulema parties, which, in fact, opposed Pakistan, ironically later claimed that it was Islamic ideology that created Pakistan and they, therefore, had the right to decide its future.[16]

The Muslim League leadership in its early years in power in Pakistan faced the gigantic problem of economic reconstruction in the wake of the migration of non-Muslim businessmen and industrialists to India and influx of Muslim refugees from India. Most Muslim League leaders were migrants from India and had no political base in the new country. They were dogged by the problem of legitimacy and failing political fortunes, and it was in this context that the Muslim League leaders began to raise Islamic issues.[17] On taking over power, the Muslim League found that they had done no homework for building the political system of the new country. While the Muslim League leadership had talked of Islam—in very general and vague terms as being the guiding light for Pakistan, party workers used slogans of Islam and Islamic state to mobilise Muslims for the movement. The Muslim League used the Ulema and an assortment of clerics during the election to the Constituent Assembly in 1946.[18] After independence, the new country had nothing but Islam as the common factor to unite and mobilise the people for carrying out the essential task of nation building. In such a situation, the politicians in Pakistan increasingly used Islam for achieving their political ends. The Ulema parties, which had opposed Pakistan before independence, too were looking for some platform or cause to get back into favour with the common people.

Mohammad Ali Jinnah did not live long after independence to work out any definite outline of the political system for the country. His speech at the inaugural session of the Pakistan Constituent Assembly on August 11, 1947 clearly spelt out the vision of a secular and democratic system for the country. Addressing the people of Pakistan, he had said: "You are free; you are free to go to your temples, you are free to go to your mosques or to any

13 Kalim Bahadur, *The Jama'at-i-Islami of Pakistan: Political Thought and Political Action*, Chetana Publications, New Delhi, 1977, p. 39.
14 Zia-ul-Hasan Faruqi; *Deoband School and the Demand for Pakistan*, Asia Publishing House, Bombay, 1963, p. 230.
15 Keith Callard, *Pakistan: A Political Study*, George Allen & Unwin Ltd, London, 1958, p. 225.
16 Hamza Alavi: "Social Forces and Ideology in the Making of Pakistan". *The Friday Times*, Lahore, December 12, 2002.
17 Seyyed Vali Reza Nasr, *The Vanguard of the Islamic Revolution*, I.B. Tauris Publishers, London, 1994, p. 117.
18 Khalid Bin Sayeed, *Pakistan: The Formative Phase, 1857–1948*, Oxford University Press, Karachi, 1992, p. 203.

other place of worship in the state of Pakistan. You may belong to any religion or caste or creed—that has nothing to do with the business of the state . . ."[19]

His speech shocked the Ulema. After Jinnah died, the political elite of the country was divided and there was no consensus on the political system. References in Jinnah's speech to religion having no role in the business of the state were deleted from its later versions.[20] The Ulema wanted to give an Islamic colour to the new Constitution, which was in the making and they succeeded in getting an objective resolution passed by the Constituent Assembly, which could be interpreted as a resolution for Pakistan to be an Islamic state.[21]

The first opportunity for the Ulema to flex their muscles came in 1951. Punjab Chief Minister Mian Mumtaz Daultana, who belonged to the Muslim League, fomented an anti-Ahmadi[22] agitation mainly for factional reasons. His aim was to bring down the federal government. Widespread violence against the Ahmadi community broke out, which also led to the breakdown of law and order in Punjab. A virulent campaign spearheaded by the various fundamentalist parties was launched, demanding that the Ahmadis be declared non-Muslims and be removed from important positions in the government, including the then Foreign Minister of the country, Zafarullah Khan. The Ulema thus had a cause that could help them seize the ideological initiative, though the Ahmadis were far too few to pose any danger to mainstream Islam.[23] The Punjab government appointed a commission, headed by Justice Munir and Justice Kayani, to inquire into the disturbances. The Munir Commission came to the conclusion after questioning the Ulema of the different schools of Islam that, "Pakistan is being taken by the common man, though it is not, as an Islamic State. This belief has been encouraged by the ceaseless clamour for Islam and Islamic state that is being heard from all quarters since the establishment of Pakistan."[24] The fundamentalist parties did not succeed in getting the Ahmadis declared as non-Muslims but the entire agitation put the Ulema in the centre-stage. For them, the huge problems facing the new state—the rehabilitation of the refugees from India, unemployment and mass poverty were marginal. They carried on a ceaseless campaign for an Islamic state.

[19] Sharif Al Mujahid, *Quaid-i-Azam Jinnah: Studies in Interpretation*, Quaid-i-Azam Academy, Karachi, 1981, p. 248.

[20] Ardesher Cowasji, "In the Name of Religion," at www.dawn.com, October 5, 2003

[21] Hasan Abbas, *Pakistan's Drift into Extremism: Allah, the Army, and the War On Terror*, M.E. Sharpe, New York, 2005, p. 20.

[22] Ahmadis are the followers of Mirza Ghulam Ahmad (1830–1908), who claimed to be a messiah but mainstream Muslims refuted the claim.

[23] Abbas Rashid, "Pakistan: The Ideological Dimension", in Asghar Khan, *Pakistan: State and Religion*, Vanguard Books Ltd., Lahore, 1985, p. 84.

[24] Munir Commission Report, p. 232. Cited in Muhammad Munir, *From Jinnah to Zia*, Vanguard Books Ltd., Lahore, 1980, p. 49.

The Ulema had a confrontation in the early 1960s with the military ruler General Ayub Khan, who was a liberal and wanted to modernise the country. The first clash took place over the Constitution, which Ayub Khan had introduced and which declared Pakistan a republic and not an Islamic republic. Secondly, the new Constitution stipulated that the laws in Pakistan would be in accordance with Islam and not in accordance with the Quran and Sunnah. The Ulema threatened agitation and Ayub buckled down. The Constitution was amended within a few weeks of its enforcement. The Ulema had tasted victory but their happiness was short-lived. In 1961 Ayub faced another challenge from the Ulema, when he introduced a progressive Muslim marriage law. The military ruler reacted strongly by having the Ulema leaders arrested, banning the Jama'at-i-Islami and freezing their funds. Ayub realised that much of the increasing militancy of the mullahs had to do with the madrassas. This was the first time the government sensed the danger posed by the madrassas in promoting militancy.[25]

The trend towards Islamisation picked up once Gen. Ayub was forced to give up power. General Yahya Khan, who took over the reins in 1969, focused on the military's role as the guardian of the 'ideological frontiers' of Pakistan. The election he conducted in 1970 also promoted Islamic elements. The Legal Framework Order, under which the elections were held, prescribed a fundamental role to Islamic ideology. The military went out of its way to provide material and financial help not only to the Muslim League during the election but also to the Islamic parties. The military agencies were actively campaigning to sabotage the secular and liberal parties. The government agencies created the spectre of a threat to Islam and Pakistan.[26] The Jama'at-i-Islami organised the infamous terrorist groups, Al Badr and Al Shams, to kill Bengali nationalists during the liberation movement in East Pakistan. The Jama'at had declared that Bengali Muslims were not good Muslims and the Bengali nationalist movement was sponsored by Hindus, communists and atheists, all of whom were acting as agents of India, Western imperialists and Jews that wanted to eliminate the Muslims.[27] It was during the East Pakistan crisis that a nexus between the Pakistan Army and the fundamentalists was created and this has continued ever since. Later, Zulfikar Ali Bhutto gave a major boost to the fundamentalist forces by passing in 1974 a legislation declaring the Ahmadi community as a non-Muslim minority. It is ironical that a very religious Khwaja Nazimuddin in 1952 had refused to surrender before the religious fundamentalist forces while Zulfikar Ali Bhutto, not known for his religiosity, conceded their demand for declaring the community out of the pale of Islam. It was also extraordinary that a National Assembly elected

[25] Hasan Abbas, n. 21, p. 37.
[26] Husain Haqqani; *Pakistan: Between Mosque and Military*, Vanguard Books, Lahore, 2005, p. 55.
[27] Kalim Bahadur, n. 13, pp.132–133.

on a secular mandate chose to sit in judgement on a question that was purely religious.

Pakistan's Islamisation under General Zia-ul Haq

General Zia-ul Haq toppled the elected government of Zulfikar Ali Bhutto on July 5, 1977. He had no legitimacy whatsoever and from the first day announced his intention to promote an Islamic agenda. Gen. Zia is also seen responsible for making Pakistan the global centre of political Islam. He assiduously worked to turn the country into an Islamic state, which inspired the ideology of jihad and which threatened to destabilise most of the region and the Muslim world.[28] Maulana Abul Ala Maududi, chief of the Jama'at-i-Islami, had welcomed the Islamisation programme of General Zia-ul Haq soon after the military takeover. The Jama'at leaders were happy that for the first time in the history of Pakistan, a ruler was carrying out a programme close to their heart. However, they were also apprehensive, as the experience of the Jama'at with the earlier military ruler Gen. Ayub Khan had not been pleasant, since he had banned the party and jailed its leaders. In fact, it was Gen. Zia who needed the help of the Jama'at, since it had a well-organised cadre that would have countered any political opposition. Thus, while other political parties were banned and not allowed to function, the Jama'at was allowed to function unhindered. Gen. Zia also mobilised the Ulema, mullahs and *pirs* of various Islamic sects. The Army's role was redefined as the 'defenders of Pakistan's ideological frontiers.'[29] Within a few days of taking over power, General Zia-ul Haq had issued Martial Law Order No. 5, which introduced for the first time the Islamic punishment of amputation of the right hand from the wrist for theft, robbery and dacoity.

The politics of Islamisation in the region has often focused on the regulative, punitive and extractive aspects. Islamisation in Pakistan under Gen. Zia was not only the means to acquire legitimacy but it was held to be the *raison d'être* of martial law.[30] Gen. Zia reconstituted the Council for Islamic Ideology to give representation to the conservative and orthodox Ulema. The Constitution was amended to set up Shariat benches for the four High Courts and the Supreme Court. Four laws were issued for Islamic punishments, which are collectively called the Hudood Laws. Interest-free banking was introduced. A compulsory Zakat law was also introduced. Several other measures like compulsory break during work for prayers and restrictions on music, television and cultural activities were imposed.[31] Highly discriminatory laws and rules were imposed against women.

---

[28] Husain Haqqani, n. 26, p. 131.
[29] Hasan Abbas, n. 21, p. 101.
[30] Hasan Askari Rizvi, *Military, State, and Society in Pakistan*, Macmillan, London, 2000, p. 170.
[31] Ibid., p. 172.

Several restrictions were placed on their movement and travel, and a dress code was prescribed. The *Diyat* ordinance was issued, which set the blood money compensation for a female victim at half of that for the male. A Presidential order laid down that the testimony of two women would be equal to that of a man.[32] Gen. Zia's Islamisation was just the precursor to the Taliban in Afghanistan.

There was another dimension to Gen. Zia's Islamisation of Pakistan. He encouraged various sectarian groups, particularly the Deobandi School, and promoted the setting up of madrassas by religious parties and such groups.[33] Many of them were meant for refugees from Afghanistan. This was done in order to create a group of religion-oriented students, who would assist the Afghan Mujahideen to drive out the Soviet Army from Afghanistan.[34] These madrassas ultimately became factories for producing jihadis to fight in Afghanistan, Jammu & Kashmir and Muslims of other sects in Pakistan.[35] Most heads of the madrassas deny that they had anything to do with jihad, though there is enough evidence to show that during the war against the Soviet Army in Afghanistan, training camps were set up in the Pakistani areas bordering Afghanistan. In these camps, apart from training in guerrilla warfare, handling of arms and making bombs, the trainees were given a smattering of religious education mainly to indoctrinate them with the spirit of jihad and to fill them with religious fervour. These madrassas were funded by the CIA and some Muslim countries.[36] It is often suggested that there were only few madrassas imparting extremist training. There is the contrary view that most of the madrassas, which were controlled by the religious political parties, provided the foot soldiers for the extremist groups, which subscribed to the belief that jihad against non-Muslims is mandatory.[37] A Pakistan scholar, Tariq Rahman, on the basis of a survey of different educational institutions in Pakistan, found that 59.86 per cent of the students of the madrassas supported open war for taking Kashmir away from India. The teachers were even more militant than their students. His survey showed that 70.37 per cent of the teachers of madrassas favoured open war for taking away Kashmir from India. According to the author of a book on Osama bin Laden cited by Rahman, "nowhere is bin Laden more popular than in Pakistan's madrassas, religious schools from which Taliban draws many of its recruits."

32 Ian Talbot, *Pakistan: A Modern History*; Oxford University Press, New Delhi, 1998, p. 281.

33 For a study of the madrassa system of education, see Kuldip Kaur, *Madrasa Education in India: A Study of its Past and Present*, Centre for Research in Rural and Industrial Development, Chandigarh, 1990.

34 Kamal Matinuddin, *The Taliban Phenomenon: Afghanistan 1994–1997*, Lancer Publishers & Distributors, New Delhi, 2000, p. 14.

35 Jessica Stern, "Pakistan's Jihad Culture", *Foreign Affairs*, 79 (6), p. 119.

36 Inam Khwaja, "Terrorism and the Madaris" at www. nation.com.pk/daily/aug- 2005/29/columns2.php

37 Zubeida Mustafa, "Reining in the Madressahs" at www.dawn.com/2005/08/24/op.htm

Madrassas, according to Rahman, may be the potential centres of Islamic militancy.[38]

There are different versions of the birth of the Taliban in Afghanistan. They came from the madrassas, which had been set up by the Jamiat-ul Ulema-i-Islam, the Jama'at-i-Islami and other Deobandi groups in Pakistan. The emergence of the Taliban shows the role played by the madrassas in the NWFP and Baluchistan. Most of these schools were being used as hideouts for terrorists attached to foreign agencies, which were funding the institutions.[39] The Taliban was the product of the war against the Soviet Army in Afghanistan and the intense bloodletting by the various Mujahideen factions after the withdrawal of the Soviet Army from that country.[40]

The rise of sectarian conflicts within Pakistan was the direct result of the growth of the jihadi madrassas and sectarian armed groups. Religious terrorism is the principal source of terrorism in Pakistan.[41] Sectarian confrontation between the Sunni and Shia communities has also grown in the country since the Zia regime. Sipaha Sahaba,[42] an extremist Deobandi organisation and its military wing, the Lashkar-e-Jhangvi, have been carrying on their murderous campaign against the Shias. The religious parties were helped by government agencies in setting up militant groups for fighting in Jammu & Kashmir. Pakistan-sponsored terrorist groups like the Lashkar-e-Toiba, Jaish-e-Muhammad, Hizb-ul Mujahideen and others, owing their allegiance to the Jamiat-ul Ulema-i-Islam, Jama'at-i-Islami, Ahle Hadith, etc., are even now active in Kashmir. It was Pakistan's fundamentalist parties that exported Deobandi Wahabi ideology to Kashmir and Afghanistan, both of which were earlier largely free from such ideological currents. Successive Pakistani governments from 1994 onwards, when the Taliban almost controlled 90 per cent of Afghanistan, supported the Taliban regime. The world community later boycotted the Taliban regime for its violation of human rights, treatment of women, persecution of minorities like Shias, public executions as Islamic punishments, and the destruction of the Bamiyan Buddhas. Once in power, the Taliban also began to re-export its brand of Islam to the troubled northern and western frontier areas of Pakistan.

---

38 Tariq Rahman, *Denizens of Alien Worlds*, Oxford University Press, Karachi, 2004, pp. 93–96.

39 Kamal Matinuddin, n. 34, p. 14.

40 Ahmed Rashid, *Taliban: Islam, Oil and the New Great Game in Central Asia*, I.B. Tauris Publishers, London, 2000, p. 23.

41 *The State of Sectarianism in Pakistan*, Asia Report No. 95, April 18, 2005, International Crisis Group, p. 1.

42 For an analysis of Sipah Sahaba, see Afak Haydar; "The Sipah-e-Sahaba Pakistan", in Hafeez Malik, *Pakistan: Founders' Aspirations and Today's Realities*, Oxford University Press, New Delhi, 2001, pp. 263–286.

General Musharraf and the MMA

General Pervez Musharraf, who toppled the elected government of Mian Nawaz Sharif in October 1999, has broadly followed in the footsteps of his military predecessors. For some time, he gave the impression that he would follow a rather liberal policy so far as religious issues were concerned. He gave several indications in his speeches during the first few months after his takeover that he would act decisively against militants and sectarian groups. However, he found that this was easier said than done. The militants and the religious groups were inseparably connected with Pakistan's Afghanistan and Kashmir policies. Soon after he took over power, Musharraf had promised to amend the anti-minority Blasphemy Law and the anti-women Hudood Ordinance. Expectedly, the religious groups raised uproar, and Musharraf backed down within weeks.[43] Later, he banned some sectarian groups and terrorist organisations but they reemerged soon thereafter under different names without much interference from the government. He had promised in his speech in January 2002 that he would not allow terrorists to use Pakistani territory for attacks on neighbouring countries. However, there are credible reports that the terrorist infrastructure is intact and training camps continue to function unhindered even four years after his speech.

The Musharraf regime has been persecuting the mainstream political parties of Pakistan and has forced into exile popular leaders of two major parties, i.e., Benazir Bhutto of the Pakistan People's Party and Mian Nawaz Sharif of the Pakistan Muslim League. The military also manipulated the 2002 elections to ensure that the group of religious parties under the umbrella of the Muttahida Majlise Amal (MMA), which was the mentor of the Taliban and also sponsored the militant groups fighting in Jammu & Kashmir, secured a crucial position in Pakistan's political structure.[44] The MMA was able to form the government in the strategic North West Frontier Province (NWFP) and was a partner in the provincial government in Baluchistan. The MMA supported General Musharraf on the passage of the 17th Amendment to the Constitution, which allowed the military ruler to simultaneously retain two offices—that of the President and the Army chief. In return, the military allowed the MMA chief, Maulana Fazalur Rahman to become the leader of the opposition against all rules of parliamentary democracy, as the MMA was not the second largest party in the National Assembly.[45]

[43] Hasan Abbas, n. 21, p. 193.
[44] *Pakistan: The Mullahs and the Military, Islamabad*/Brussels, ICG Asia Report No. 49, March 20, 2003, pp. 15–16.
[45] Ibid., p. 19.

The nexus between the mullahs and the military that had taken shape during Zia ul Haq's regime has been carried forward and strengthened during the Musharraf regime. Over the past few decades, Islam has been nationalised in Pakistan. The Pakistani state has been completely identified with religion as interpreted by one particular school of Islam. The Federal Ministry of Religious Affairs and the state-sponsored Council of Islamic Ideology propagate, administer, guide, coordinate and finance all religious activities, including public morals and mores.[46] Their worldview can be judged by the fact that the Ministry of Religious Affairs justified the destruction of the Bamiyan Buddhas by the Taliban, saying that there was nothing wrong in destroying them.[47] These institutions are dominated by the Ulema of one particular school and offer patronage to its followers.

Afghanistan and the Rise of the Taliban

Afghanistan was the greatest victim of the rise and growth of Islamic fundamentalism in Pakistan. Islamic fundamentalism in Afghanistan originated in the late 1950s. Cross-currents in Islam in India have influenced Afghan Muslim society, along with their tribal traditions. The Deoband School rejected innovation in Islam and maintained strict orthodoxy but accepted Sufism, which became the hallmark of the Ulema of India as well of Afghanistan, as distinct from the Saudi brand of Wahabism.[48]

The Islamic fundamentalist movement in Afghanistan is of recent origin and owed much more to Ikhwanul Muslimeen (Muslim Brotherhood) of Egypt rather than the Jama'at-i-Islami of Pakistan.[49] There were surprising similarities between Maulana Abul Ala Maududi's writings and the ideology of the Ikhwan.[50] Maulana Maududi had contributed to the strengthening of relations with Afghan Islamists during the 1970s. The current head of the Jama'at, Qazi Husain Ahmed, who is a Pushtun, was a frequent visitor to Afghanistan. In fact, since the early 1970s, most of the Saudi aid to Afghan refugees and terrorists in Afghanistan has been channelled through the Jama'at-i-Islami and the Muslim World League.[51] Pakistan's Afghan policy after the withdrawal of the Soviet Army from Afghanistan was to unite the various Mujahideen groups and to enable them to form a united government. This did not succeed because tribal, ethnic, religious and personality conflicts prevented the Mujahideen from uniting. The Jama'at-i-Islami of Pakistan was deeply involved in running Pakistan's Afghanistan

[46] Ibid., pp. 22–24.
[47] www.dailytimes.com.pk/default.asp?date=1027/2005
[48] Oliver Roy, *Islam and Resistance in Afghanistan*, Cambridge University Press, London,1990, p. 57.
[49] Ibid., p. 69.
[50] Frederic Grare, Political Islam in the Indian Subcontinent: The Jama'at-i-Islami, Manohar, New Delhi, 2001, p. 65.
[51] Mark Huband, *Warriors of the Prophet: The Struggle for Islam*, Westview Press, Boulder CO, p. 9.

policy till the emergence of the Taliban. Gulbuddin Hekmatyar, leader of the Hizb-e-Islami, was the favourite of the Jama'at and also of the ISI. The Taliban did not represent any specific Islamic group or ideology. Their interpretation of Islam, jihad, and social transformation did not tally with any other Islamic trend that had emerged during the anti-Soviet war.[52] The Darul Uloom Haqqania in Akora Khatak, led by Maulana Samiul Haq, has claimed that thousands of students of their institution joined the Taliban. The Taliban was recruited from Afghan refugee camps, indoctrinated in Pakistani madrassas, and learnt its fighting skills from Mujahideen groups based in Pakistan. The families of the Taliban men carried Pakistani identity cards.[53]

The Taliban revived the concept of jihad in the later half of the twentieth century.[54] Its ideology, like that of all fundamentalist movements, revolved around a central key personality, a leader or a cult figure, the *Ameer al Momeneen*, Mullah Omar. The political system constructed by the Taliban could be called totalitarian, as under it, pluralism did not have a place. It was backed by the creation of the religious police, a Taliban innovation in the modern period. The Taliban issued decrees on women's conduct and cultural issues. These decrees imposed stiff restrictions on the movements of women, their visits to hospitals, total ban on music, kite flying and on men shaving their beard. They also abolished all pictures and portraits.[55] Thus, the essence of Taliban ideology was against democracy, secularism and pluralism, and was anti-women. They represented the worst picture of the ideal Islamic life.

In October 2002, the six-party fundamentalist alliance, the MMA, took office at the provincial government in NWFP. It soon thereafter ordered compulsory prayers for the population and created a Taliban-style religious police called the Department of Vice and Virtue. It also introduced a Hisba law, which was, however, declared void by the country's Supreme Court. Pakistani mullahs have been allies of the Army and see the opportunity to turn Pakistan into a theocratic state.[56] The situation in the NWFP and several districts of Punjab indicates that the Taliban have come back to haunt Pakistan.

Regional Fallout

Bangladesh has been a fertile ground for Islamic fundamentalism for a long time, particularly since the assassination of the founder of the nation,

---

52 Ahmed Rashid, n. 40, p. 87.
53 Ibid., p. 185.
54 Ahmed Rashid, *Jihad: The Rise of Militant Islam in Central Asia*, Orient Longman, Hyderabad, 2002, p. 44.
55 Ahmed Rashid, n. 40, pp. 217–219.
56 Ahmed Rashid, "Return to Taliban", 4 June 2003 at www.yaleglobal.yale.edu/display article?id=1766

Sheikh Mujibur Rahman, in August 1975. This was followed by the return of pro-Pakistani elements and politicians. The ISI tightened its hold on Bangladesh using its past connections with Islamic fundamentalists, certain sections of the military and the political establishment. The Jama' at-i-Islami was legalised and its leader, Golam Azam's citizenship restored. He was let off by the BNP Government on the serious charge of being a war criminal despite popular demand for his trial.[57] The ideology of the Jama' at-i-Islami of Pakistan of setting up an Islamic State in Bangladesh is being disseminated through various militant groups and the madrassas. There was a flurry of building of mosques and madrassas with the generous help of Saudi charities, like Al Haramain Islamic Foundation, and funds from Pakistan's ISI, leading to recruitment of youth for jihad. The Pakistani agency had undertaken the training of anti-India militants in Bangladesh. The head of India's Border Security Force had reported that the terrorist groups operating in Jammu and Kashmir were also being trained in Bangladesh. He went on to claim that the ISI is now fully concentrating on Bangladesh.[58] Pakistan's major terrorist groups like Lashkar-e-Toiba and Jaish-e Muhammad coordinate their activities with Bangladesh's militant groups. The 1999 hijacking of an Indian Airlines' plane on a flight from Kathmandu to New Delhi indicated that the ISI had set up facilities in Nepal taking advantage of the porous India-Nepal border. Militant groups from Kashmir have also been active in the area. The small Muslim community in Sri Lanka has become an unwitting victim of the ethnic conflict in the country. The Lashkar-e-Toiba has been showing keen interest in taking jihad to the Eastern province of Sri Lanka. Of late, there have been attempts by Pakistani terrorist groups to extend their activities in India, and some recent incidents show they have begun to succeed.

Bangladesh's Drift into Extremism

Bangladesh is another country in the region after Afghanistan over which the threat of Islamic militancy looms large. Bangladesh emerged as a new state in 1971 after a protracted struggle for autonomy, which evolved into a freedom movement against the Punjabi-dominated military bureaucratic establishment of Pakistan. The initial Constitution of Bangladesh unambiguously enshrined secularism, which was to be realised by eliminating communalism in all its forms, and the establishment of multi-party democracy as fundamental political values.[59] Sheikh Mujibur Rahman had spelt out the meaning of secularism in the context of the Muslim society. He had explained that secularism does not mean absence of religion. The people of

---

[57] Hiranmay Karlekar, *Bangladesh, The New Afghanistan*; SAGE Publications, New Delhi, 2005, p. 55.
[58] www.atimes.com/atimes/South _Asia/FLO90/03.html
[59] Anisuzzman, "Religion and Politics in Bangladesh", in S.R. Chakravarty, *Society, Policy and Economy of Bangladesh*, Har-Anand Publications, New Delhi, 1994, p. 42.

Bangladesh would have the right to religion but nobody would be allowed to use religion as a political weapon.[60] Islam in Bangladesh has been based on three types of religious beliefs: modern, orthodox and popular. A majority of the Muslims of Bangladesh practice 'popular' religion that includes faith in *pirs*, sacred places, Hindu gods and local deities and spirits.[61] The disenchantment with Pakistan among the Bengalis began with the imposition of Urdu soon after independence. Bengalis in Pakistan began to suffer from a sense of frustration and deprivation because of the domination by the Punjabis. The language movement in defence of the Bengali language gave rise to the autonomy movement. The Jama'at-i- Islami had no appeal in the political environment in East Pakistan. In 1947, the Jama'at-i-Islami had only one member in that part of Pakistan. The party was aware of the growth of discontent and alienation among the people of East Pakistan. It also accepted that the imposition of Urdu was resented by the people. The Jama'at leader Maududi in 1956, nonetheless, asserted that Hindus, communists and political adventurers were taking advantage of the problems in the province. What Maududi was saying in other words was that anyone who championed the cause of Bengali nationalism was a communist, a Hindu or a political adventurer.[62] The Jama'at increasingly found itself on the wrong side of history. During the liberation struggle, the Jama'at appealed to the Bengalis to support the Pakistan Army.[63]

The reason for the dilution of secularism after 1975 was not the resurgence of Islam in Bangladesh. As in Pakistan, the military rulers, Gen. Zia-ur Rahman and General H M Ershad, used Islam to strengthen their hold on power as they lacked legitimacy. Bangladesh officially became an Islamic state in 1988 and in the course of time, Islamic extremism became well entrenched.[64] The Jama'at-i-Islami, which had been banned because of its opposition to the liberation movement and support to the Pakistan Army, was legalised and its leader, Prof. Golam Azam, who had been forced into exile and whose citizenship had been cancelled, was given back his rights and political role.[65] The Jama'at won 18 seats in the National Assembly in 1990 and it helped Khaleda Zia to form the government. The Jama'at suffered a setback in the next election in 1996 and could secure only three seats. In the 2001 election, religious rhetoric was a prominent feature. The Jama'at won 18 seats in the National Assembly in alliance with the Bangladesh Nationalist Party (BNP). During this period, new militant Islamic groups emerged in Bangladesh. The fact that the Jama'at-i-Islami

[60] U.A.B. Razia Akter Banu, *Islam in Bangladesh*, E.J. Brill, Leiden, 1992, p. 148.
[61] Ibid., p. 55.
[62] Kalim Bahadur, n. 13, p. 130.
[63] Kalim Bahadur, "The Emergence of the Jama'at-i-Islami in Bangladesh", in S.R. Chakravarty, n. 59.
[64] Yoginder Sikand, n. 3, p. 195.
[65] Kalim Bahadur, "Prof Golam Azam: The Ameer of the Jama'at-i-Islami of Bangladesh", *News Letter*, Maulana Abul Kalam Azad Institute of Asian Studies, Calcutta, 3(1).

and another group, the Islami Oikya Jot, are part of the Khaleda Zia government complicates the situation and is a major reason for the growth of Islamic militancy. A new outfit, the Jama'at-ul Mujahideen, has come into prominence since 2002. Some of the leaders of the militant groups had their training in Pakistan and one of them called 'Bangla Bhai' had participated in the Mujahideen war in Afghanistan. There are reports that Saudi and Kuwaiti funds are coming to these militant groups.[66] Bangladesh today has become a centre for Islamic militants. The emergence of the suicide bomber in December 2005 and the bomb blasts that took place in several cities in November 2005 point to the seriousness of the situation.[67] They indicate the growth of a wide network of Islamic militants and their capacity to strike. It is no secret that the Islamic forces are opposed to democratic values. There has been a proliferation of madrassas in the country. The Jama'at-ul Mujahideen of Bangladesh has declared that it is time to implement Islamic laws in the country. According to it, there is no future for man-made laws.[68] The Tableeghi Jama'at, which in a way is the mother organisation of most militant groups, now has a strong following in the country. Its annual sessions in Tongi near Dhaka are attended by huge crowds.[69] There are 27 militant outfits in India's Northeast that have ties with Bangladesh and its various religio-political groups. The ISI and Bangladesh's DGFI coordinate with ULFA. The influx of migrants from Bangladesh across the border into north-east India and West Bengal certainly poses a threat of Islamic militancy spreading in these regions of India as well.

The Danger in Nepal

Nepal is a Hindu kingdom but not a Hindu state and religious minorities have lived in the Kingdom without any discrimination. Over the last several years, the Kingdom, however, has been in turmoil. It has been plagued by Maoist insurgency. The situation was compounded by the massacre of the royal family in 2000. King Birendra was succeeded by King Gyanendra. The democratic government was dismissed last year and now the King rules the country as an absolute monarch. The political parties, which opposed the anti-democratic stance of the King, have launched a movement for the restoration of democracy. The presence of militant Islamists on the India-Nepal border has been causing concern in the contiguous Indian areas. It may be noted that India has an open, porous border with Nepal, which is 1,859 km-long. There are almost 20 Indian districts that share the border with 27 Nepalese districts. The open border provides

[66] www.ipcs.org/WhatsNewsArticle/1.jsp?action=ShowViewValue=1934&status=article&mod=b
[67] www.dawn.com/2005/12/19/0p.htm#1
[68] www.asianaffairs.com/oct2005/bangladesh.htm
[69] Yoginder Sikand, n. 3, p. 198.

a free field to all kinds of criminal activities, like drug trafficking, smuggling, intelligence activities, fake currency, fugitives, etc. What has caused concern is the emergence of numerous madrassas and mosques on both sides of the border. The number of mosques is certainly not justified by the number of Muslims in the area. The madrassas are largely funded from West Asia.[70] These developments too have serious implications for India. The 1999 hijacking of the Indian Airlines plane on a flight from Kathmandu to New Delhi, which ultimately ended with the release of three top Pakistani terrorist leaders, showed that the ISI had set up an active base in Nepal. Some Kashmiri groups belonging to Hizb-ul Mujahideen have been caught in Nepal trying to send money to Islamic separatists in Jammu and Kashmir. Pakistani presence in Nepal is reflected in the growth of madrassas, increase in Muslim population, floating of fake Indian currency and is helped by an open border and lack of monitoring system.[71]

The Sri Lankan Crisis

Muslims in Sri Lanka are the descendants of the Arabs, who came about a thousand years ago. The origins of Islamic fundamentalism in the country, however, are recent and can be traced to 1990 when the Sri Lankan ethnic Tamils drove away Muslims from the Eastern region under their control. This forced migration increased Muslim population in the districts to which they had migrated. No effort was made by the government to rehabilitate these uprooted Muslim refugees, who had to live in poverty and misery. Over time, madrassas came up, funded by munificent Arabs. Frequent Sinhala-Muslim communal clashes began to take place. Shariat courts were set up and strict rules imposed on Muslim women in the Eastern areas.[72] The situation in the Muslim areas deteriorated and Muslim-Buddhist clashes became a regular feature. Militant camps were set up in the Eastern areas where volunteers were given arms and weapons training in the jungles and they called themselves jihadis fighting a holy war for protecting themselves.[73] Ironically, the government itself had provided arms to the Muslims in the early 1980s to protect themselves against the LTTE. Also, attempts were made on part of the government to use Islamic militancy as a buffer against the LTTE. The country has been facing the threat of Tamil Eelam. The situation in the Eastern province is a potential bloody cauldron.[74]

There have been reports of two Islamic militant bases in Valaichchenai. The formation of an Osama Squad in Batticaloa has also come to notice.

70 www.members.tripod.com/israindia/isr/aug15/nepal.html
71 www.india_seminar.com/2002/517/517%20yubaraj%20ghimre.htm
72 www.morquendi.blogspot.com/2005/04/rise_of_militant_islamic.html
73 www.taipeitimes.com/news/world/archives/2005/05/06/2003253378
74 www.atimes.com/atimes/South_Asia/GE24D102.html

All this indicates growth of extremist elements in the community. In this background, the appointment by Pakistan two years ago of a former director of the Intelligence Bureau as its High Commissioner in Colombo was not without significance. The ISI is keenly interested to collect intelligence about developments in Indian nuclear establishments, many of which are located in Tamil Nadu and Kerala. There has been an increase in the activities of Lashkar-e-Toiba in the Eastern province.[75]

Indian Secularism and Islamic Fundamentalism

The origin of Islamic fundamentalism in the Indian subcontinent has been discussed in the earlier part of this study. There were two main fundamentalist parties in the country, apart from some minor outfits when India became independent. They were the Jamiat-al Ulema-i-Hind and the Jama'at-t-Islami. The Jamiat-al Ulema, which had opposed the creation of Pakistan till the end, withdrew from active politics after the achievement of freedom and the framing of the Indian Constitution, which provided a secular and democratic political system with equal rights to all religious communities. The Jama'at-i-Islami was divided after the emergence of Pakistan in 1947 and some members of the Jama'at, including its founder, Maulana Abul Ala Maududi, migrated to Pakistan. Maududi had declared after the partition plan had been announced that he would try to build Pakistan as an Islamic state. He believed that India would be a secular state, which he equated with an atheistic or anti-religious state.

After independence, the members of the Jama'at, who were left in India, formed a separate Jama'at in April 1948. The leaders of the Indian Jama'at declared secularism as abhorrent since it was no longer a theory or a principle confined to a few aspects of life, but had become an operative principle in all walks of life.[76] They decided that since the secular system was against Islam, they would not participate in elections, in short they decided to opt out of the Indian political system. The Jama'at's opposition to secularism and election did not endure for long. In the 1960s, the Jama'at accepted secularism and the Indian democratic system though with some reservations. The Jama'at's political position promoted Indian Muslim's alienation by detracting from their stake in secularism, democracy and pluralism. The Jama'at members from Jammu & Kashmir have not been part of the Indian Jama'at and formed a separate party in the state. This was done mainly to avoid the legal consequences of its refusal to accept the state of Jammu & Kashmir as a part of India. The Jama'at-i-Islami and its philosophy, however, could never get the acceptance of most Indian Muslims. That is why the efforts of Lashkar-e-Toiba and Jaish-e-Muhammad during

75 http://tamilnet.com/art.html?catid=79&artial=12219

76 Kalim Bahadur; "Jama'at Philosophy", in G.S. Bhalla *et al* (*Eds.*), *India: Nation-State and Communalism*, Patriot Publishers, New Delhi, 1989, p. 95.

the last many years to recruit terrorists in India have mostly not succeeded. However, the December 2005 terrorist attacks in Bangalore prove that radical Islam's presence is no longer located in any particular country. The Indian security establishment has recently accused Pakistan of breeding a new form of jihadi terror aimed at fanning communal tension in India as indicated by the recent bomb attacks in Varanasi. There is a possibility that some Indians are becoming part of the jihadi movement.[77] The Lashkar and other groups are a part of a global web. India clearly has become a target of jihad in the age of globalisation.[78] Islamic fundamentalism is against democracy and equal rights for all citizens, irrespective of caste, creed, or gender. Its further growth will disrupt peace and stability in the country and in the entire region.

Conclusion

The rise of Islamic fundamentalism in Pakistan is not only responsible for the present situation in Afghanistan and Islamic militancy, terrorism and the shaping of the conflict in Jammu and Kashmir, it also has far reaching consequences for all countries of the South Asian region. All South Asian countries are pluralistic and face at different levels, internal tensions and conflicts based on caste, religion, ethnicity, language and community, and these distort their national integrity and unity.[79] Religious nationalism has made a great headway not only in Pakistan but also in Bangladesh and Sri Lanka. It has made Pakistan a haven for Islamic terrorists, including Al Qaida, and it inspires terrorist activity in Kashmir. Some of the features of Islamic extremism in South Asia are: religiously defined national identity, undermining of democracy by promoting majoritarian theory and practice of non-liberal democracy and accentuation of international conflicts on ethno-religious lines, for example, between 'Hindu India' and 'Muslim Pakistan' and 'Hindu India' and 'Muslim Bangladesh'.[80] The fundamentalists aim to turn the Muslim majority states of the region into Islamic states and start jihad in those countries where Muslims are in a minority. There is no accurate information about the exact number of madrassas in Pakistan, Bangladesh, Nepal and India. Many of these madrassas disseminate the militant ideology of Islamic fundamentalism and turn out militants. These contribute to the ongoing destabilisation not only in Pakistan but also in other countries of the region. The potential radicalisation of Indian Muslims is also a cause of concern.[81]

Kalim Bahadur retired as Professor of South Asian studies from the School of International Studies, Jawaharlal Nehru University, New Delhi.

---

[77] *Hindustan Times*, New Delhi, March 20, 2006.
[78] Ranjan Roy, "The Rise of Homegrown Terrorist", *The Times of India*, New Delhi, January 10, 2005.
[79] trinstimte.org/01pcr/2_3bhanot.htm
[80] www.eppc.org/programs/southasian/publications/programID.38pubID.2081/pub_detailasp
[81] www.centerforsecuritypolicy.org/index.jsp?section=status&page=alexiev

DOCUMENT NO. 30

PAKISTAN'S POLITICAL AND SECURITY CHALLENGES

Research Paper 07/68

Septemeber 13, 2007

2007 marks the 60th anniversary of Pakistan's independence. By contrast with the attention that the identical anniversary of its powerful neighbour, India, has received, the international response has been decidedly muted. This reflects the relative uncertainty and pessimism which many observers feel about Pakistan's future prospects.

Pakistan has had a central role as an incubator of militant Islam since the 1980s. Equally, despite the fact that there have been several periods of civilian rule, democracy has failed to put down roots in the country. The military has been a powerful player within Pakistan's polity and economy since independence. Over the next two months, the fate of President Pervez Musharraf, who came to power in a coup in 1999, will be decided. He is currently both President and Army Chief of Staff. With parliamentary elections due by mid-January 2008 at the latest, he appears willing to stand down as Army Chief of Staff but is seeking to retain the Presidency. Two civilian leaders that went into exile, Benazir Bhutto and Nawaz Sharif, are seeking to return to Pakistan. There remains talk of a possible political deal between Musharraf and Bhutto. The political endgame is in sight.

This Research Paper reviews the many threats and challenges facing Pakistan and discusses the current political crisis that is convulsing the country.

See also Research Papers 07/40, An economic introduction to India, and 07/41, A political introduction to India.

Jon Lunn, Claire Taylor and Tim Youngs
International Affairs and Defence Section

Ed Beale
Economic Policy and Statistics Section
House of Commons Library

Summary of Main Points

2007 marks the 60th anniversary of Pakistan's independence. By contrast with the attention that the identical anniversary of its powerful neighbour, India, has received, the international response has been decidedly muted. This reflects the relative uncertainty and pessimism which many observers feel about Pakistan's future prospects. The US Fund for Peace's *Failed States Index* for 2006 placed Pakistan as the ninth most failed state in the world, one place worse than Afghanistan.

Over the next two months, the fate of President Pervez Musharraf, who came to power in a coup in 1999, will be decided. Musharraf is currently both President and Army Chief of Staff and has been highly reluctant to relinquish either role. With parliamentary elections due by mid-January 2008 at the latest, he is seeking to retain the Presidency. Two civilian leaders in exile, Benazir Bhutto and Nawaz Sharif, are seeking to return to Pakistan. Sharif has already tried once, only to be deported. Negotiations between Musharraf and Bhutto over a deal whereby he retains the Presidency but sheds his role as Army Chief of Staff, while she is appointed Prime Minister after the elections, hang in the balance. A host of legal challenges before an increasingly independent Supreme Court could scupper these plans even if a deal is reached.

Pakistan has had a central role as an incubator of militant Islam since the 1980s, for example through its support for armed groups active in Indian Kashmir and, prior to September 11th 2001, for the Afghan Taliban. State control over the frontier areas of the country is tenuous and Pakistan has been facing armed rebellions in Waziristan and Baluchistan. Following September 11th 2001, the Pakistani military expressed its support for the US-led 'war on terror'. However, since 2006 the Government has combined military action in the Federally Administered Tribal Areas (FATA) with efforts to negotiate peace deals with local tribal leaders that will weaken the Taliban and al-Qaeda. Some view this willingness to negotiate as close to appeasement. Others point out that the unwillingness of the Pakistani military fully to break with militant Islam reflects a 'hedging of bets' in the context of fears that the US will turn against Pakistan.

The question of whether Pakistan 'can survive' has long been posed by analysts. There has been a continuous search since independence for ideas that can help to bind the country together. 'Anti-Indianness', above all in relation to Kashmir, has played an important part in doing so, fuelling high levels of military expenditure and the development of its nuclear weapons programme, but it is an essentially negative ideology. General

Zia's policies of 'Islamisation' were in part an attempt to inoculate the country against the threat of ethnic nationalism following the loss of East Pakistan (now Bangladesh) in 1971. However, for some analysts, the 'Islamic cure' has turned out to be as dangerous, if not more so, to the idea of Pakistan, as the original disease. The strongly Sunni character of Pakistan's 'Islamisation' has contributed to the emergence of Sunni-Shia sectarianism. Other religious minorities have also faced persecution.

While some analysts argue that under Musharraf radical Sunni Islam has expanded its power to the point where a 'take-over' of the state is no longer out of the question, others point to the fact that in 2002 its share of the vote was still only 11%. The electoral process appears highly unlikely to deliver power to radical Islamists. Others note that there are now significant Islamist currents within the military. But most observers argue that these currents are not strong enough to warrant fears that the military might spearhead a radical Islamic 'take-over'. One goes so far as to talk about "the myth of an Islamist peril".

Despite the fact that there have been several periods of civilian rule, democracy has failed to put down roots in the country. The military has been a powerful player within Pakistan's polity and economy since independence. For critics of the military, who claim that it has distorted Pakistan's governance and retarded its development, only genuine democracy offers a way forward. But it is hard to believe that liberal-democratic politics can yet be sustained effectively in a country where, even in the cities, relationships continue to operate predominantly on patron-client principles and where conservative forms of Islam still hold strong sway.

The US and EU member Governments have been strong supporters of President Musharraf since September 11th 2001, donating billions to Pakistan in military, humanitarian and development assistance. Today, they appear to have decided that some kind of 'managed transition' of the type currently being discussed by representatives of Musharraf and Benazir Bhutto is the least-worst option available. But this carries with it the danger of further perpetuating a sterile cycle of civilian-military alternation in which radical Islam is as often accommodated as confronted within Pakistan. This would have continuing security implications in Afghanistan and more widely. Furthermore, numerous analysts also claim that a deal of the kind now envisaged could rapidly unravel, plunging Pakistan into further instability. There is no guaranteed match up between Western preferences with regard to Pakistan in the short-term and wider long-term politico-security objectives.

I Background

A. Historical Chronology

Colonial Period	1600	East India Company is formed, operating principally in Bengal
	1700	The Company secures control of Madras (now known as Chennai), Calcutta (Kolkata) and Bombay (Mumbai)
	1756	Battle of Plassey won by Robert Clive
	1857	Indian Mutiny and subsequent transfer of control over India from the East India Company to the British Government
	1885	Indian National Congress (INC) is formed.
	1899	Lord Curzon is appointed Viceroy
	1906	Muslim League is formed
	1917	Edwin Montagu, Secretary of State for India, announces a policy of gradual introduction of home rule
	1919	Wartime measures to allow detention without trial by jury extended by the Rowlatt Acts. I,370 peaceful protesters massacred near the Golden Temple in Amritsar, Punjab.
	1920	Gandhi initiates civil disobedience campaign against British rule
	1927	Simon Commission appointed to recommend further political reform for India. It has no Indian membership and is boycotted by all sides in India
	1930	Gandhi's civil disobedience movement gathers momentum
	1935	The Government of India Act 1935 is passed. Henceforth, central government is controlled by the British while provincial government is partially democratic
	1939	Without consultation with the Indian parties, Britain declares that India is at war with Germany. The INC demands the immediate transfer of power. After failing to get it, it resigns from all provincial governments
	1940	The Muslim League adopts a resolution demanding 'autonomous and sovereign' states in areas where Muslims are in a majority
	1947	Independence on the basis of partition into two states: India and Pakistan. The British Monarch remains head of state and Mohammed Ali Jinnah, leader of the Muslim League, becomes first Governor-General of Pakistan. Hundreds of thousands die in inter-communal violence. 12 million refugees
Post-Independence	1948	First war with India over Kashmir
	1956	New Constitution declares Pakistan to be an Islamic Republic
	1958	General Ayub Khan seizes power in a military coup
	1965	Second war between India and Pakistan over Kashmir
	1969	Ayub Khan stands down and hands over power to General Yahya Khan
	1970	The Bengali nationalist Awami League wins elections but the military refuses to convene the National Assembly

Post-Independence	1971	12 day war with India. East Pakistan becomes the independent state of Bangladesh. Yayha Khan steps down and Zulfikar Ali Bhutto, leader of the Pakistan Peoples Party (PPP), becomes President
	1972	India and Pakistan sign the Simla Agreement
	1973	Zulfikar Ali Bhutto becomes Prime Minister under a new Constitution
	1973–77	The Pakistan military takes on and ultimately defeats a major insurgency in Baluchistan
	1977	General Zia ul-Haq seizes power in a coup
	1979	Zulfikar Ali Bhutto is hanged. The Soviet Union invades Afghanistan
	1980	Mujahideen operations begin against the Soviet occupation of Afghanistan. In Pakistan, the Hudood Ordinance is passed as General Zia pursues policies of 'Islamisation'
	1986	Benazir Bhutto returns from exile to campaign for the restoration of democracy
	1988	General Zia dies in an air crash. The PPP wins election. Benazir Bhutto becomes Prime Minister
	1989	The Soviet Union withdraws from Afghanistan
	1990	Benazir Bhutto dismissed as Prime Minister on charges of corruption. Nawaz Sharif becomes Prime Minister after his Muslim League-led coalition wins election. Pro-independence Kashmiri separatists begin military activities against the Indian army
Events Since 1990	1993	Nawaz Sharif forced to resign under military pressure. Benazir Bhutto becomes Prime Minister for the second time
	1996	Benazir Bhutto dismissed amid corruption allegations. In Afghanistan, the Taliban take power with Pakistan's support
	1997	Nawaz Sharif returns to power after the Muslim League wins election
	1998	India carries out a series of nuclear weapons tests; Pakistan quickly responds in kind
	1999	Further clashes with India over Kashmir (the Kargil operation). General Pervez Musharraf seizes power, overthrowing Nawaz Sharif. Sharif is subsequently sentenced to life imprisonment on hijacking and terrorism charges and sent into exile
	2001	Musharraf names himself President while remaining head of the army. After the 9/11 attacks in the US, Musharraf renounces the Taliban in Afghanistan. Gunmen attack parliament in New Delhi. India suspects Pakistani complicity. The US lifts sanctions imposed after 1998 nuclear tests
	2002	Following a rigged referendum, Musharraf's term as President is extended for five years. Pro-Musharraf faction of the Muslim League leads a new governing coalition following election. Islamic parties form a government in North West Frontier Province. Renewed tension between India and Pakistan over Kashmir.
	2003	Kashmir ceasefire agreed by India and Pakistan, ushering in a period of reduced tension

Events Since 1990	2004	Top nuclear scientist AQ Khan admits selling nuclear technology to North Korea, Iran and Libya. He is placed under house arrest. Major military operations in Waziristan against Islamic militants. Musharraf reneges on an earlier promise to stand down as head of the army
	2005	An earthquake, with its epicentre in Pakistan-administered Kashmir, kills more than 73,000 people
	2007	Pakistan is plunged into political crisis as Musharraf suspends the Chief Justice of the Supreme Court as elections approach, only to be overruled by the Supreme Court itself, leading to the Chief Justice's reinstatement. Bhutto and Sharif both announce their intention to return to Pakistan to contest the election, but their anti-Musharraf alliance appears increasingly fragile, as Bhutto and Musharraf discuss a political deal that would give her the Prime Ministership while leaving him as President

B. Main Political Organisations[1]

1. Parties

Over 70 political parties contested the 2002 parliamentary elections. The following are the main parties operating in Pakistan.

a. Jamaat-e-Islami (JI)

Established in 1941 by Maulana Maududi, JI is the largest Islamist party in Pakistan.[2] It has an estimated five million members. According to its political programme, it is a pan-Islamic party that seeks the peaceful establishment of an Islamic order. The JI opposed the creation of Pakistan in 1947. Despite this, JI has often allied itself with the Pakistani military. There is strong evidence of links between elements within the JI, armed militant groups of Pakistani origin and al-Qaeda. JI's membership has tended to come particularly from the urban middle class.

b. Jamiat-e-Ulema-e-Islami (Fazlur Rehman group)

The JUI-F was formed in 1945 and was a strong supporter of the establishment of Pakistan in 1947. A rigid advocate of conservative Deobandi ideas, it re-entered the political sphere in the 1960s.[3] It has set up more Islamic schools (madrassas) than any other group and has been a strong supporter of the Afghan Taliban. There is also strong evidence of links with armed militant groups of Pakistani origin and al-Qaeda. It has strong support in

---

1 Much of the information used in this section of the paper is drawn from the *Europa Regional Survey for South Asia 2006* (London, 2006), pp. 458–9.

2 'Islamist', as used here, simply means a philosophy that places Islam at the heart of a political programme. There are many different expressions of this philosophy.

3 For a brief discussion of the Deobandi school of thought and the other main traditions within Sunni Islam in Pakistan, see page 20.

Baluchistan and North West Frontier Province (NWFP) amongst the rural Pashtun population.

c. Muslim League (Quaid-e-Azam group)

The Muslim League (Quaid) is currently the largest of four existing factions of the Muslim League. It was established by political forces supportive of President Musharraf and is the dominant party in the present Coalition Government. It contains many defectors from other parties in its ranks. It won 118 seats out of a total of 342 seats in the 2002 National Assembly elections.

d. Muslim League (Nawaz group)

The Muslim League-N is the second largest of the four existing factions of the Muslim League, which, headed by Mohammed Ali Jinnah, led the campaign for the creation of Pakistan during the years up to independence in 1947. It represents supporters of the former Prime Minister Nawaz Sharif, whose Muslim League Government was overthrown by the 1999 coup. It won 19 seats in the 2002 National Assembly elections. Sharif is attempting to return from exile.

e. Muttahida Qaumi Movement[4]

The MQM was established in 1978 as the Mohajir Qaumi Movement. Although it has sought in recent years to broaden its political constituency, it is primarily a movement that represents urban Muslim, Urdu-speaking immigrants from India in Pakistan, known as Mohajirs (Urdu for refugees). The Mohajirs were initially dominant within the Pakistani political and commercial elite but came to resent their demotion as other groups, in particular the Punjabis and Sindhis, subsequently grew in influence and wealth.[5] The MQM's political base is in Sindh Province, in particular the city of Karachi, where it currently is the dominant party within the Provincial Government. The MQM has often allied itself with the Pakistani military. President Musharraf is himself from a Mohajir family. It has a reputation for political violence, although today it denies such allegations. A small break-away group known as the Haqiqi faction has challenged the authority of the MQM's founder, Altaf Hussein, who has been granted political asylum in the UK.

---

[4] For an interesting analysis of the MQM, see F. Haq, "Rise of the MQM in Pakistan: Politics of Ethnic Mobilisation", *Asian Survey*, Vol. 35, No. 11, November 1995.

[5] Reliable figures as to the size of Pakistan's main ethno-linguistic groups are hard to come by and often disputed. According to one source, Punjab is are the largest ethno-linguistic group within Pakistan, comprising about 66% of the total population. Other significant groups are the Sindhis (13%), the Pashtuns (8.5%) and Baluchis (2.5%). The Mohajirs are not recognised as an ethnic group but are estimated to comprise around 7.5%. See *Europa Regional Survey for South Asia 2006*, p. 419.

f. Pakistan People's Party

The PPP was established in 1967 by Zulfikar Ali Bhutto. Avowedly a centre-left party, it first governed Pakistan between 1971 and 1977, following the loss of East Pakistan in the 1971 war with India. It lost power in 1977 following a military coup and two years later Bhutto was executed having been found guilty of murder in a politically-motivated trial. His daughter, Benazir Bhutto, headed PPP-led Governments twice during the 1980s and 1990s and remains the leader of the party. She is planning to return from exile. The party is currently known within Pakistan as the Pakistan People's Party's Parliamentarians (PPPP). It won 81 seats in the 2002 National Assembly elections. There are several small splinter groups of the PPP.

2. Coalitions

There are currently four main political coalitions in existence:

a. The Alliance for the Restoration of Democracy (ARD)

This is an anti-Musharraf coalition formed after the 2002 parliamentary elections by the two civilian parties—the Muslim League-(N) and the PPP—which governed Pakistan prior to the 1999 coup. In 2006 they agreed a 'Charter for Democracy', under which the two parties would work together to end military rule in Pakistan. However, talks between President Musharraf and the leader of the PPP, Benazir Bhutto, have placed this alliance under severe—possibly fatal—strain.

b. The All Parties Democratic Movement (APDM)

Formed by the Muslim League-N, the JI and the JUI-F in July 2007, this new coalition reflects the shifting sands of Pakistani politics. With the Muslim League-N anxious about a possible future political deal between President Musharraf and the leader of the PPP, Benazir Bhutto, it has hedged its bets by joining this coalition.

c. The Muttahida Majlis-e-Amal (MMA)

This is an alliance of Islamist parties, in which the JI and the JUI-F are the largest parties. It won 60 seats in the 2002 elections to the National Assembly. The MMA has been broadly supportive of President Musharraf until recently. It decided not to join the pro-Musharraf Coalition Government led by the Muslim League (Quaid) following the 2002 parliamentary elections, although dissident elements split away from it and did so. The MMA heads the Provincial Government in North West Frontier Province and is part of the ruling coalition in Baluchistan.

d. The National Alliance (NA)

This relatively marginal coalition, in which break-away groups from the PPP are strongly represented, won 17 seats in the 2002 elections to the National Assembly.

II The Current Political Crisis

In July 2006 domestic anxiety about Pakistan's direction led to an intervention by a group of retired generals, former politicians and academics that might normally be relatively sympathetic to President Pervez Musharraf. They called upon him to resign either as President or Army Chief of Staff and to oversee the establishment of a neutral caretaker government that would ensure free and fair parliamentary elections in 2007. One of the signatories of a letter sent to the President stated: "We were motivated by a fear that the status quo is untenable and may be dangerous."[6] So it has proven. As the time for elections approaches, Musharraf is struggling for political survival.

Musharraf, who overthrew the Muslim League Government of former Prime Minister Nawaz Sharif in 1999, is currently both President and Army Chief of Staff and has been highly reluctant to relinquish either role. Campaigning on the basis of a programme of 'enlightened moderation', in 2002 he secured a five-year extension of his term as President through a referendum which it is widely accepted was rigged. Flawed elections held in the same year brought a sympathetic Coalition Government into office.[7] In late 2003 he promised to stand down from his military office, only to renege on that promise a year later, instead passing a Constitutional amendment that allowed him to hold both positions until the end of the 2007.[8] His critics argue that, by holding onto both posts, he has proven conclusively that Pakistan's 'democratic transition' under him has been a sham. Since coming to power, he has constructed a political system that is highly presidential in character.

It has long been reported that Musharraf might try to seek re-election in September or October 2007 for another term as President from the two Houses of Parliament and the Provincial Assemblies, *before* new parliamentary elections are held, while his supporters are still in the majority. Many of his political opponents have pledged that they will resign en masse from Parliament in order to delegitimise such a move. Musharraf's term of office ends in November. The parliamentary term ends on

6 "Generals urge Musharraf rethink", *BBC News Online*, 26 July 2006.
7 O. Bennett-Jones, *Pakistan. Eye of the Storm* (New Haven, 2003), p. xiv.
8 Z. Hussain, Frontline Pakistan. *The Struggle within Militant Islam* (London, 2007), p. 183.

15 November. Normally, new elections would be held before the end of the year. They must be held by mid-January 2008 at the latest unless Musharraf postpones them. A firm electoral timetable has to be announced soon.[9]

Musharraf's apparent determination to hold onto power is the underlying cause of Pakistan's current political crisis. The catalyst for his current political troubles was Musharraf's conflict with the Chief Justice of the Supreme Court, Iftikhar Mohammad Chaudhry, whom he suspended on misconduct charges in March 2007. Some analysts claim that Chaudhry's real offences were to have investigated the cases of people who had been 'disappeared' by the security forces in the context of anti-terrorism operations, to have questioned aspects of Pakistan's privatisation programme and, most importantly, to have given grounds for concern that he might be sympathetic to legal challenges against Musharraf's political plans.[10] Chaudhry contested his suspension and became the focal point of anti-Musharraf protests in key cities across the country, in which lawyers have been prominent.

At the beginning of May 2007 the Supreme Court suspended a special panel formed at the behest of the Government to hear the case against Chaudhry, arguing that it was not properly constituted. Instead, a full bench of the Supreme Court was established to hear the case. On 12 May Chaudhry was prevented from reaching a mass rally in Karachi, which he was due to address, as political violence flared. At least 41 people died in clashes between protesters and militias of the pro-Musharraf Muttahida Qaumi Movement (MQ M) in Karachi during 12–13 May.

Political tensions remained high as the country awaited the verdict of the Supreme Court on Chaudhry's suspension. A Supreme Court official who was due to be a witness in the case was assassinated in mid-May. Then a bomb went off at an Islamabad rally in support of Chaudhry in mid July 2007, killing at least 18 people.

During the first half of 2007 there was also an increased willingness by Islamist militants to challenge the Musharraf Government, not just in the frontier areas but also in and around the capital, Islamabad. This was illustrated by the siege at Islamabad's Red Mosque during June-July, in which at least 108 people died (there are allegations that the authorities covered up the deaths of many more, including women and children).[11] Following the capture of the Red Mosque, there has been a wave of further bomb attacks by militants and a 'peace deal' in Waziristan has collapsed following a decision to move more troops into the frontier areas, leading to renewed clashes between militants and the army (see Part III B). It has been

[9] "Musharraf has timetable to quit army", *Chicago Tribune*, 1 September 2007.
[10] International Crisis Group (ICG), *Elections, Democracy and Stability in Pakistan*, Asia Report No. 137, 31 July 2007, pp. 9–12.
[11] "Pakistan signals red", *Reuters*, 5 July 2007.

claimed that there was also an assassination attempt in mid-July, when a missile was fired at Musharraf's plane (this would be the third known attempt on his life since he seized power). On 4 September at least 24 people were killed in two bomb blasts near the Pakistani military's headquarters in Rawalpindi.[12] On 12 September, 16 people were killed in a suicide bombing in the town of Dera Ismail Khan.

Then, in mid-July 2007 the Supreme Court, in a ruling that surprised many, decided that Musharraf's suspension of Chaudhry was illegal and ordered his immediate reinstatement. Musharraf agreed to abide by the ruling. Musharraf's efforts to secure his own re-election ahead of parliamentary elections now look sure to be challenged before a Supreme Court headed by Chaudhry. The episode left Musharraf gravely weakened.[13]

Despite his many problems with militant Islamist groups, analysts argue that Musharraf's ability to hold on to power for this long has depended on an uneasy accommodation with radical Islamist parties with links to them, such as the Jamaat-e-Islami (JI) and Jamiat-e-Ulema-e-Islami (Fazlur Rehman group) (JUI-F). His ability to establish effective control over the areas of the country bordering Afghanistan has been partly limited by his dependency on these parties. However, the MMA has for some time indicated that its support for him would end as the elections drew near, and that if he did not support a genuinely democratic transition, it too would turn to street protests. Following the outbreak of political violence in Karachi on 12 May, the MMA joined a nationwide strike in protest at continued *de facto* military rule. Since July it has formed an alliance with Nawaz Sharif's Muslim League-N.

Musharraf's most consistent critics since he came to power in a coup in 1999 have been the faction of the Muslim League loyal to Nawaz Sharif (Muslim League-N), whom Musharraf deposed, and the Pakistan People's Party (PPP), led by Benazir Bhutto. While these parties did contest the 2002 elections, both leaders have been excluded from politics and been based abroad. Unresolved charges of corruption and abuse of power hang over Benazir Bhutto, forcing her into exile, while Nawaz Sharif was convicted on hijacking and terrorism charges following his ejection from power; after a brief period of imprisonment, he was sent into exile in Saudi Arabia for ten years. Musharraf and his supporters argue that he went voluntarily. The Muslim League-N and PPP jointly formed the Alliance for the Restoration of Democracy, whose goal has been to end the role of the military in politics and to reduce its considerable hold over the economy. Both stated their intention to return to Pakistan ahead of the coming elections, regardless of the possible consequences.

---

[12] "Blast hit Pakistan garrison town", *BBC News Online*, 4 September 2007.

[13] ICG, *Elections, Democracy and Stability in Pakistan*, pp. 11–12.

For a long time, Musharraf took few substantive steps towards compromise with either of his main political opponents. He regularly asserted that neither Nawaz Sharif nor Benazir Bhutto would be allowed to return to the country ahead of the next parliamentary elections. However, he is now seeking to do a deal with Benazir Bhutto and the PPP. An indication that greater co-operation between the two might be possible came with the PPP's vote in favour of the passage of the Women's Protection Act in the National Assembly in 2006. The Act repealed significant elements of the 1979 Hudood Ordinances, including provisions placing the onus on the woman to prove assault and criminalising sex outside marriage. A Government Bill that would outlaw forced marriage was introduced in Parliament in February 2007. This also has PPP support.

Some claim that a Musharraf-Bhutto deal would involve all charges against her being dropped and her becoming Prime Minister, on the assumption that the PPP performs sufficiently strongly in the forthcoming elections. In return, the PPP would not oppose the re-election of President Musharraf by Parliament prior to the parliamentary elections. However, Bhutto is reportedly insisting that Musharraf must relinquish the post of Army Chief of Staff and that the power of the President to dismiss Parliament (and by extension the Prime Minister and Government) should be removed.

For a while, there were expectations that the May 2007 outbreak of political violence in Sindh Province, the PPP's heartland, might scupper *rapprochement* efforts between Bhutto and Musharraf. Her supporters began to talk about a 'grand governing coalition' involving all the main parties but not including Musharraf. Another sign of his vulnerability came in June, when a series of proposed curbs on the media had to be withdrawn almost as soon as they were announced. European ambassadors in Islamabad joined with Pakistani protesters in criticising the move. However, talks between their representatives resumed over the summer in Dubai and London.

The possibility that the Sharif-Bhutto alliance might fracture led to speculation that Sharif would respond by aligning himself with radical Islamic parties. He worked with them when he was Prime Minister, attempting to extend Shari'a law with their support. In July 2007, as talks between Musharraf and Bhutto resumed, the Muslim League-N, the JI and the JUI-F created the All Parties Democratic Movement.[14]

One of the main potential stumbling blocks to a Musharraf-Bhutto deal is the growing independence of the Supreme Court, backed by a legal profession that has remained mobilised since the Chaudhry case blew up. In August 2007 the Supreme Court gave a strong indication of its increasingly independent spirit when, seven years after he was sent into exile, it ruled

[14] ICG, *Elections, Democracy and Stability in Pakistan*, pp. 8–9.

that Nawaz Sharif and his brother Shahbaz, who also went into exile, were entitled to return to Pakistan. Soon after, Sharif announced that would defy Musharraf and return to Pakistan on 10 September. The authorities promptly revived cases of corruption against Nawaz and there was talk of revoking presidential pardons issued in relation to previous convictions. A court also ordered the arrest of Shahbaz in connection with five murders in the 1990s. As the day drew nearer, at least a thousand Muslim League-N activists were rounded up and detained.[15] When Sharif finally flew into Islamabad, amidst street clashes between the security forces and his supporters in several cities, he was immediately taken into custody, charged with corruption and deported to Saudi Arabia, whose Government has been co-operating in this matter with Musharraf.[16] It seems unlikely that Sharif and the Muslim League-N leadership will meekly accept this outcome. One Western diplomat has commented of Sharif's deportation: "Musharraf has managed to achieve the next to impossible feat of making Nawaz look good."[17]

Analysts expect the Supreme Court will soon have something to say about the flouting of its decision with regard to Sharif's right of return. The Muslim League-N has lodged a petition arguing that his deportation violated the ruling of the Supreme Court. This is just one of several ways in which the Supreme Court could frustrate the plans not just of Musharraf but of Benazir Bhutto too. It could rule Musharraf's re-election by the existing Parliament unconstitutional. It could also uphold the present two-year bar in the Constitution on retired senior military officers standing for public office. The MMA has launched a petition before the Supreme Court arguing that Musharraf is too old at 64 under military regulations to continue as Army Chief of Staff. Prime Ministers are currently barred from serving more than two terms in office. Bhutto has already served on two occasions, although both were cut short. The Supreme Court may decide to uphold this provision.[18]

The question increasingly is whether Musharraf and Bhutto, should they reach a deal, are sufficiently in control of the situation to manipulate it to their advantage. Significant elements within the Muslim League (Quaid), unhappy about Musharraf's attempt to reach a deal with Bhutto that could lead to a loss of many seats in elections, are threatening to vote against him should he come before the present Parliament and seek re-election. Many might defect to Sharif's Muslim League-N, which was their original political home.

---

15 "Pakistan prepares for major confrontation", *BBC News Online*, 10 September 2007.
16 His brother Shahbaz did not travel with him. "Pakistan 'deports' ex-PM Sharif", *BBC News Online*, 10 September 2007.
17 "President set on collision course with the judiciary", *Financial Times*, 11 September 2007.
18 ICG, *Elections, Democracy and Stability in Pakistan*, p. i.

For Benazir Bhutto, her political credibility could also be on the line. Many within the PPP are also unhappy at the prospect of doing a deal with Musharraf. The PPP might lose support in the coming elections should there be a deal, destroying her hopes of becoming Prime Minister.[19] Sharif's announcement that he would seek to return home put pressure on her to finalise her own plans to return, which she has said she will make public on 14 September.

So a deal between Musharraf and Bhutto is not done yet and may never materialise.[20] Another complication is Musharraf's current insistence that a future Bhutto-led government should also include the strongly pro-Taliban JUI-F.[21] Some fear that, should the basis for a deal between Musharraf and Bhutto collapse, Musharraf could be tempted to declare a state of emergency and re-impose untrammelled authoritarian rule. He also has the power to cancel parliamentary elections for a year under the Constitution. The final possibility, should Musharraf be deemed beyond rescue, is another army coup 'in the interests of the nation'.

III Security Issues and the 'War on Terror'[22]

State control over frontier areas of the country is tenuous and Pakistan is facing armed rebellions in Waziristan, which is part of the Federally Administered Tribal Areas (FATA), and Baluchistan. In 2003 the army moved into the FATA, where the Afghan Taliban and al-Qaeda still have bases, as part of Pakistan's contribution to the fight against international terrorism. Over the past three years, the Musharraf Government has combined military action in the FATA with efforts to negotiate peace deals with local tribal leaders that will weaken the Taliban and al-Qaeda. There is no 'peace track' at all in Baluchistan. The International Crisis Group (ICG), a well-known non-governmental organisation, recently warned that there is also rising discontent in the Federally Administered Northern Areas of Gilgit and Baltistan.[23] Following the siege of the Red Mosque in Islamabad, there has been a spate of suicide bombings across the country in recent months.

Pakistan's strategic importance in the 'war on terror' means that the US and the UK have so far given the Musharraf Government the 'benefit of the doubt' in public, despite private reservations over its failure to tackle

[19] Some argue that the subservience of the Election Commission of Pakistan to the Executive could protect the PPP from some of the worst electoral consequences of doing a deal with Musharraf. *Ibid.*, pp. 14–17.

[20] "Musharraf's talks on pact with Bhutto stall", *Financial Times*, 3 September 2007.

[21] "Pakistan crisis 'hits army morale'", *BBC News Online*, 6 September 2007.

[22] Kashmir is discussed in Part IV A of this Paper.

[23] International Crisis Group, *Discord in Pakistan's Northern Areas*, Asia Report No. 131, 2 April 2007. The Federally Administered Northern Areas adjoin Afghanistan, China, India and Central Asia.

Islamic militancy effectively. The role of the AQ Khan network in promoting nuclear proliferation also undermined Western confidence in Pakistan (see Part V B).

A. Combating Armed Militant Groups[24]

According to one commentator, by 2002 there were 24 armed militant groups in Pakistan—that is, groups willing to engage in violent *jihad* to achieve their objectives.[25] A significant number emerged, often sponsored by elements linked to the Pakistani military, including its powerful Inter-Services Intelligence (ISI) agency, in response to the conflict between Pakistan and India over Kashmir. Some have also been motivated by support for the Afghan Taliban. A smaller number have been active in promoting sectarian violence across the Sunni-Shia divide.[26]

Since September 11th 2001 the Pakistani authorities have moved to ban an increasing number of these groups, although some commentators claim that several retain the sponsorship of elements within the military. Many resurface under another name only to be banned once more. Some occasionally conduct operations under different names with a view to confusing the authorities. Most have 'political wings'. The fighting membership of these groups is usually estimated to be in the hundreds at most. Fighters from these groups have travelled abroad to support radical Islamist insurgencies in other parts of the world. In turn, some have had a number of 'foreign fighters' in their ranks. Al-Qaeda reportedly has links with most of the groups and also has small Pakistani affiliates such as Jundullah.

1. Pakistani Armed Militant Groups

Below are the main active armed militant groups of Pakistani origin:[27]

a. Al-Badr Muhajideen

Established in 1998, its main theatre of operation has been Kashmir. It is believed to be a small organisation but has co-operated effectively with other armed militant groups in the past. Its objective is to bring all of Kashmir into Pakistan.

---

[24] Some commentators have argued that the pan-Islamic revivalist movement Tablighi Jamaat, whose world headquarters are in Pakistan, should also be considered as an adjunct to these armed groups, on the grounds that it provides 'cover' for them. However, such claims are strongly disputed by others, including TJ itself. It is worth noting that none of India, the US, the UK or the European Union (EU) has added the group to their list of proscribed organisations.

[25] Hussain, *Frontline Pakistan*, p. 52.

[26] Reliable figures as to the exact size of the Shia population are hard to come by, but there is widespread agreement that it is a maximum of 20%. See *Europa Regional Survey for South Asia 2006*, p. 461.

[27] The information provided in this section is drawn from a wide range of sources, most notably Hussain, *Frontline Pakistan* and Jane's Terrorism and Intelligence Centre.

b. Harakat-ul-Mujahideen

Harakat-ul-Mujahideen (HuM) was formed in 1985. Since the Soviet Union left Afghanistan, its main theatre of operation has been Kashmir. It has strong support amongst Kashmiris in Pakistan-administered Kashmir (known as Azad Kashmir). It has close links with the JUI-F. HuM has also displayed strong hostility towards President Musharraf. It was banned in November 2001, after which it operated under the name Jamiat al-Ansar. Some believe that it may also be the organisation behind armed actions by a group calling itself 'Al-Nasirin'.

c. Jaish-e-Mohammed

Founded in 2000, Jaish-e-Mohammed (JeM) is a breakaway group from Harakat-ul-Mujahideen. The group led an armed attack on the Indian Parliament in December 2001. The Pakistani authorities banned the group, along with Lashkar-e-Taiba (LeT), in January 2002. It began operating under the name Jamaat-e-Furqa. However, unlike LeT, JeM has also sought to intervene in domestic politics. It was reportedly involved in an assassination attempt against Musharraf in December 2003. It was the group responsible for the murder of American journalist Daniel Pearl in 2002.

d. Harkat-ul-Jihad-al-Islami

Harkat-ul-Jihad-al-Islami (HuJI) was formed in 1980 and was one of the organisations that supported the struggle against the Soviet occupation of Afghanistan. In this it reportedly had strong support from the ISI. For a period it merged with HuM, but it has been a separate organisation for the past decade. Since then its activities have spread to India and Bangladesh.

e. Hizb-ul-Mujahideen

Founded in 1989 and closely linked to JI, the organisation's theatre of operation has been Kashmir. It has been less active in recent years.

f. Sipah-e-Sahaba

The Sunni Sipah-e-Sahaba (SeS) was established in 1985, at a time when Sunni-Shia sectarianism was on the rise. Its goal is to force the Pakistani authorities to declare the Shia a 'non-Muslim community'.[28] It has also

[28] This would follow the precedent set by the declaration during the government of Zulfikar Ali Bhutto (1970–77) that the small Ahmaddiya (sometimes also known as Ahmadis) sect, whose followers do not believe that Mohammed is the only prophet, should no longer be considered Muslim. This set the stage for decades of persecution of the sect. For example, see the report by the UK All Party Parliamentary Human Rights Group, "Rabwah: A Place for Martyrs? Report into Internal Flight for Ahmadis", January 2007.

targeted non-Deobandi Sunni groups.[29] It has been less active in recent years. The group was banned in January 2002. Afterwards, it changed its name to Milat-e-Islamia Pakistan.

g. Lashkar-e-Jhangvi

The Sunni Deobandi Lashkar-e-Jhangvi (LeJ) was established in 1996 ostensibly as a break-away group from the Sipah-e-Sahaba (see below), which it felt was failing to pursue its objectives effectively. Some commentators believe that the two are in reality still closely linked. It is reported to have links with both the Taliban and al-Qaeda. It has conducted many attacks against Shias but has also attacked the small Christian community in Pakistan. It was banned by the Pakistani authorities in August 2001.

h. Lashkar-e-Taiba

Founded in 1990, LeT's main theatres of operation have been Kashmir and India. It draws its cadres mainly from Punjab and from the Wahhabi-inspired Sunni Ahle Hadith sect. The group was banned by the Pakistani authorities in January 2002. Despite this, the LeT has apparently maintained relatively cordial relations with the ISI, keeping a low profile within Pakistan itself. It currently operates within the country through its political wing, Jamaat-ud Da'awa. Some observers believe that it has occasionally also carried out operations under the names 'Al-Mansourian' and 'Al-Nasirin'. It operates a large network of schools and hospitals. The group is reported to have close links to Saudi Arabia. It is claimed that some of its fighters have been operating in Iraq.

i. Sipah-e-Muhammad Pakistan

The Sipah-e-Muhammad Pakistan (SMP) is the main Shia armed militant group. Probably established in 1993, it is closely linked to Tehrik-Nifaz-e-Fiqh-e-Jafaria (TNFJ—Movement for the Implementation of Jafaria Religious Law), the main Shia political party. Its objective is to protect the Shia community against attacks by Sunni militant groups and to create a 'pure' Shia society in Pakistan. It was banned in August 2001.

j. 'Pakistan Taliban'[30]

This is not a single armed group in the conventional sense but the term is increasingly used as shorthand to describe the predominantly Pashtun communities in the tribal areas—in particular, North and South

[29] For a brief discussion of the Deobandi school of thought and the other main traditions within Sunni Islam in Pakistan, see page 20.
[30] For further discussion, see Parts III B and C of this Paper.

Waziristan—adjoining Afghanistan which have allied themselves closely with the Afghan Taliban, often taking part in its operations across the border.[31]

2. Operations against al-Qaeda

Over a dozen al-Qaeda operatives, many of them apparently senior, have been arrested by the Pakistani authorities since 2002, with many of them handed over to the US authorities. The Pakistani authorities argue that this demonstrates their commitment to the 'war on terror'. Some have claimed that the arrests of key al-Qaeda figures have often come shortly before senior US officials were due to visit Pakistan.[32]

Below is a list of some of the most notable arrests that have taken place:[33]

March 2002	**Abu Zubaydah**. He played a major role in the planning of the September 11th attacks and other al-Qaeda operations. He was captured in Faisalabad and is now held at Guantanamo Bay
September 2002	**Ramzi bin al-Shibh**. He also played a major role in the planning of the September 11th attacks and other al-Qaeda operations. He was captured in Karachi and is now held at Guantanamo Bay
February 2003	**Khalid Sheikh Mohammed**. This senior figure is believed to have been the mastermind behind the September 11th 2001 attacks. He was captured in Quetta, where he was reportedly staying in the house of a JI leader. He is now held at Guantanamo Bay
July 2004	**Naeem Noor Mohammed Khan**. Captured in Lahore, he has been described as a top al-Qaeda IT specialist, acting as one of its main 'information hubs'. He was released without charge by the Pakistani authorities amidst much controversy in August 2007, leading to speculation that he had gained his freedom in exchange for co-operation or had been a double agent
May 2005	**Abu Faraj al-Libbi**. He was captured near Peshawar. He is now being held at Guantanamo Bay
July 2005	**Ahmed Khalfan Ghailani**. A participant in the 1998 US Embassy bombings, he was captured in Gujrat. He is now being held at Guantanamo Bay

[31] For example, see G. Usher, "The Pakistan Taliban", *Middle East Report Online*, 13 February 2007. Available at: http://www.merip.org/mero/mero021307.html.

[32] O. Bennett Jones and F. Shaikh, "Pakistan's foreign policy under Musharraf: between a rock and a hard place", Chatham House Briefing Paper, ASP BP 06/01, March 2006.

[33] Hussain, *Frontline Pakistan*, pp. 125–35.

A significant number of al-Qaeda operatives have also been killed in Pakistan over the past five years as a result of military operations by the security forces.

3. The Role of Madrassas

The dramatic expansion in the number of madrassas over the past 30 years has provided a fertile recruiting ground for militant Islamic groups. There are now an estimated 13,000 madrassas in Pakistan, with up to 1.7 million enrolled in them.[34] The ICG has argued that even those madrassas that do not have direct links to violence "promote an ideology that provides religious justification for such attacks."[35] However, one analyst has claimed that no more than 10-15% of madrassas are linked to terrorism.[36]

Those linked to terrorism are largely (but not exclusively) drawn from Sunni madrassas which espouse a highly rigid Deobandist ideology closely related to the Wahhabism that originates in the Gulf and which underpins the al-Qaeda view of the world.

The main fracture within Sunni Islam in Pakistan is between the Deobandis and Barelvis. The Deobandi sect comprises about 15% of Pakistan's Sunni Muslim population.[37] 60% of Sunni Muslims in Pakistan are Barelvi, whose interpretation of Islam, while also culturally conservative, is on the whole comparatively tolerant and moderate on political matters. Deobandis believe that Barelvi traditions of worshipping at shrines to holy men (pirs) are pagan and un-Islamic. The two groups have often clashed—for example, over the control of Sunni mosques.

The Barelvi also have an extensive network of madrassas, as does the JI and the small but significant Ahle Hadith sect, which broadly shares the radical world-view of the Deobandis.

Since 2001, both the US and the UK have put significant pressure on the Musharraf Government to embark upon a reform programme of the madrassas. In January 2002, in the aftermath of the September 11th attacks on the US by al-Qaeda, President Musharraf announced plans for reform. However, according to the ICG, this programme is now "in shambles."[38]

President Musharraf's reform programme has involved a push by the state to register all madrassas as part of a wider system of regulation and the introduction of a programme to modify their curricula. The ICG, calling for the establishment of a single regulatory authority, claims that no coherent

[34] Hussain, *Frontline Pakistan*, p. 79.
[35] ICG, *Pakistan: Karachi's Madrasas and Violent Extremism*, Asia Report No. 130, 29 March 2007, p. i.
[36] Hussain, *Frontline Pakistan*, p. 79.
[37] Bennett-Jones, *Pakistan*, pp. 10–11.
[38] ICG, *Pakistan: Karachi's Madrassas and Violent Extremism*, Asia Report No. 130, 29 March 2007.

system of regulation has in fact been instituted and that official claims that over 12,000 have now been registered are "misleading". Equally, efforts so far to modernise the curriculum have not, it believes, had much impact. Furthermore, it argues that there has been backtracking on moves to expel all foreign students from Pakistan's madrassas, as announced in July 2005 following the 7/7 bombings in London, and that official claims in this regard that the process is complete are not credible. Finally, the ICG asserts that little has been done to improve the financial transparency of madrassas, pointing out that Pakistan has not yet signed the International Convention for the Suppression of the Financing of Terrorism. The Government has argued that it does not need to do so and that a Bill currently before the National Assembly, the Anti-Money Laundering Bill, will adequately address the issue. The ICG claims that the Bill "fails to comply with the standards established by the Financial Action Task Force on Money Laundering."[39]

Analysts also point out that the madrassas would not be so influential if Pakistan's system of public schools had not been neglected for decades. The ICG and others have called on donors to focus their support much more on reinvigorating that system. The Pakistan Government argues that expenditure on its public schools is now moving significantly upwards.[40]

While President Musharraf received plaudits from many quarters following his firm action to end the stand-off between the authorities and the Red Mosque in Islamabad during June-July 2007, the crisis there confirmed to others that the madrassas remain a serious problem. This was the first time that such a frontal challenge had been mounted in the capital, signalling to more pessimistic observers that Islamist militants are now prepared to challenge the political and moral legitimacy of the authorities beyond North West Frontier Province and the tribal areas.

B. North West Frontier Province and the Federally Administered Tribal Areas

While North West Frontier Province (NWFP) has its own Provincial Government, seven areas adjoining the frontier with Afghanistan are Federally Administered Tribal Areas (FATA).[41] They are Bajaur, Khyber Agency, Kurram Agency, Mohmand Agency, Orakzai, North Waziristan and South Waziristan. In formal terms, this means that they are administered by the Governor of NWFP on behalf of the President. In practice, the

[39] The FATF is an inter-governmental body established by the 'Group of 7' countries in 1989. *Ibid.*, pp. 17–22.

[40] "Madrassas shut amid fears of a new crackdown", *Financial Times*, 13 July 2007.

[41] There are also Provincially Administered Tribal Areas (PATA) that are represented in the provincial structures of the NWFP.

writ of central government barely runs in the tribal areas. The ICG argues this is because central governments have preferred to govern through unelected local proxies, trading control for acquiescence, rather than because the tribal areas are inherently somehow ungovernable. Colonial era laws remain in force, the regular court system does not function and the inhabitants of the tribal areas effectively do not enjoy the civil and political rights set out in the Constitution. President Musharraf has pledged to reform these arrangements but the ICG calls the measures taken to date "cosmetic".[42]

During the 1950s and 1960s there was a significant Pashtun nationalist movement and many Pashtuns in the FATA favoured the creation of 'Pashtunistan'. However, Pashtuns have generally been well represented within the Pakistani state and key institutions such as the army. Nationalism has in recent decades been largely supplanted as a force for political mobilisation among Pashtuns by Islamism, although it remains there beneath the surface.[43] Tribal leaders in the FATA played a major role in Pakistani assistance to the Afghan Mujahideen in the struggle against Soviet occupation and, later, to the Taliban. Such links remain strong today as the Taliban seek to regain power in Afghanistan. Al-Qaeda bases have also been established in the tribal areas since 2002.

Between 2003 and late 2006 the Pakistani army conducted military operations, often suffering significant casualties, to try and flush out Taliban and al-Qaeda militants in Waziristan.[44] However, in early September 2006 the Government signed a peace agreement with pro-Taliban tribal leaders and militants in North Waziristan. Under the deal the tribal leaders agreed to stop crossing the border to fight in Afghanistan in return for a withdrawal of army troops from the area, the freeing of prisoners and compensation for losses experienced. The army also undertook not to make arrests without first consulting tribal leaders. The issue of foreign fighters was left formally undefined. However, tribal leaders agreed not to give foreign militants 'safe haven'.

Initially, there was a mixed response to the peace agreement internationally. However, attitudes quickly soured. By early 2007 some Allied Commanders in Afghanistan, along with the Afghan Government, were declaring that, by agreeing to such a deal, Pakistan had virtually capitulated to the militants, strengthening the hand of the Taliban on both sides of the porous border. Militants were also said to be moving from Waziristan into the main towns and cities of NWFP and challenging the authority of the local administration.[45] There have been a series of explosions in

[42] ICG, *Pakistan's Tribal Areas: Appeasing the Militants*, Asia Report No. 125, December 2006, pp. 2–5.
[43] C. Jaffrelot (ed), *Pakistan. Nationalism without a Nation?* (New Delhi, 2002), p. 25.
[44] One source claims that the army lost 500-700 men between 2004 and mid-2007. P. Brookes, "Peril in Pakistan", *Armed Forces Journal*, June 2007.
[45] "Enough murder, enough mayhem. Tribes vow to fight Talibanisation", *Guardian*, 21 June 2007.

Peshawar, the capital, over the past year or so. In late April 2007 Pakistan's Interior Minister, Aftab Khan Sherpao—a leading figure in the country's 'war on terror'—narrowly survived an assassination attempt while visiting Peshawar, the capital of NWFP. Over 30 people were killed by the suicide bomber, including several MPs.

Supporters of the deal argued that there can be no purely military solution to the problem of Islamic militancy in the frontier areas of Pakistan and that there are differences between more 'moderate' pro-Taliban groups and al-Qaeda—which has bases in Mir Ali and Wana in Waziristan—that should be exploited.[46] Anti-foreigner feeling has led to some fighting between tribal militias and al-Qaeda during the first half of 2007—most notably in March, when at least 160 foreign fighters were reportedly killed.[47]

Following the North Waziristan deal, during October 2006 there were also negotiations aimed at ending fighting between the army and pro-Taliban militants in the tribal area of Bajaur. However, at the end of that month the Pakistani military launched a helicopter-led strike against a madrassa in the area, killing up to 80 people. The authorities claimed that it was being used as a military training camp by militants. This set back peace talks.[48] Within days a Taliban suicide bomber had killed at least 41 Pakistani soldiers undertaking exercises in NWFP as retaliation for the attack in Bajaur.[49]

The US and others have suspected for some time that al-Qaeda's most senior leaders, Osama Bin Laden and Ayman al-Zawahiri, are hiding somewhere in the Bajaur area. In January 2006 a US drone aircraft had bombed a house where al-Zawahiri was believed to be staying. In the event, he was not there. 18 other people were killed. Some claim that the October 2006 attack was also aimed at al-Zawahiri and was based on US intelligence.[50] In late March 2007 the Pakistan Government finally concluded a deal with Taliban-supporting militants in Bajaur. While similar in many respects to the Waziristan deal, it has been reported that this time the army did not agree to pull its troops out of the area.[51]

Critics of Musharraf's relatively 'softly-softly' approach to Islamic militancy also cited the challenge posed to his authority by the Red Mosque in Islamabad during the first half of 2007. Although the Red Mosque was ultimately successfully captured by military force in July, the showdown

46 "Fractious militants united by one thing", *BBC News Online*, 7 March 2007.
47 "New Musharraf deal with militants", *Australian*, 28 March 2007.
48 "Pakistan madrassa raid 'kills 80'", *BBC News Online*, 30 October 2006.
49 "Blast kills dozens at Pakistan base", *Chicago Tribune*, 9 November 2006.
50 "Tribal fury as Pakistan military kills 80 in religious school", *Guardian*, 31 October 2006.
51 "New Musharraf deal with militants", *Australian*, 28 March 2007.

triggered a new wave of militant violence, not just in NWFP and the FATA, but in other parts of the country too, with militant leaders calling for suicide attacks and holy war in retribution for those 'martyred' by the authorities.

The crisis at the Red Mosque and its aftermath seems to have prompted Musharraf to demonstrate more widely that the state cannot be bullied into submission. With the US and UK supporting the move, in mid-July an additional 20,000 soldiers were sent into North Waziristan. They quickly became involved in fighting. Local leaders declared the 2006 peace deal was now redundant.[52] Cynics claimed that the operation was 'for show', rather than representing a serious or sustained change of policy. Nonetheless, there were further clashes in the area in August and September 2007. Tribal militants have taken over 300 soldiers' hostage in recent weeks, many of whom gave up without a fight. One experienced observer has declared that army morale is low.[53]

In July 2007 a US intelligence estimate asserted that the Taliban and al-Qaeda are stronger than ever in North Waziristan. It also reported that Osama Bin Laden remains alive and based in the tribal areas.[54] Recent suggestions by elements within the US Administration that the time may have come for US forces to launch new attacks into Pakistani territory have been met with hostility on the Pakistan side. In late August 2007 it was reported that US-led forces had launched attacks on Taliban positions on the Pakistan side of the border, killing more than a dozen. The US quickly apologised for not requesting prior permission from the Pakistan Government for the attacks.[55] Musharraf is currently under great pressure from the US on the issue. This may lead him to continue with military operations in the tribal areas for a while yet.[56]

Following the flawed 2002 elections, the MMA formed the Provincial Government in NWFP. However, it is possible that the Alliance will struggle to hold on to the gains it made then in the forthcoming elections. The proximity of the MMA to Musharraf has damaged its credibility and its administration has been plagued by corruption. The Muslim League-N is likely to be the main beneficiary of any reduction in support for the MMA in the non-Pashtun areas of NWFP.[57]

---

52 "Taliban end Pakistan ceasefire as bomb attacks kill up to 38", *Associated Press*, 16 July 2007.
53 "Pakistan crisis 'hits army morale'", *BBC News Online*, 6 September 2007.
54 That he is alive was apparently confirmed by his appearance in a video marking the sixth anniversary of September 11th 2001. "Pakistan militants step up bomb attacks", *Daily Telegraph*, 20 July 2007.
55 "Pakistan raid was 'not approved'", *BBC News Online*, 28 August 2007.
56 "Death toll in Pakistan skirmishes at 101", *St Paul Pioneer Press*, 19 July 2007.
57 ICG, *Elections, Democracy and Stability in Pakistan*, Asia Report No. 137, 31 July 2007, p. 8.

C. Baluchistan

In the relatively thinly populated Province of Baluchistan (also sometimes called Balochistan), there has been a rumbling rebellion against the central government for decades. The dominant sentiment amongst Baluchis at the time of the creation of Pakistan was against incorporation. However, these wishes were overridden. The poorest Province in Pakistan, it is nonetheless rich in mineral resources. It is a major supplier of natural gas to the country, accounting for 36% of its total production.[58] Baluchi nationalists have long complained that its 6 million people do not benefit from the revenues that its economic assets have generated. One analyst claims that Baluchistan receives only 12.4% of the royalties due to it for supplying gas.[59] A new port is being built at Gwadar, with Chinese assistance, despite local opposition. The Iran-Pakistan-India gas pipeline currently under discussion would probably have to go through Baluchistan if built. The military has a heavy presence in the Province. There are a range of important bases in Baluchistan, including nuclear weapons testing facilities.

The Pakistan Government claims that foreign interests—India and Afghanistan—have provided support to the Baluchi resistance. The accusation against India is, in part, retaliation for longstanding Indian claims that Pakistan arms and finances Islamist extremists in Kashmir. Most commentators argue that the problems of the Province are essentially local in origin and require a political solution.[60]

Following outbreaks of armed conflict in 1948 and 1958, between 1973 and 1977 discontent exploded into a full-blown nationalist insurgency in which thousands died. It was defeated only after a major army operation in the Province. Subsequently, the Baluchistan Liberation Army, which has since been banned by both Pakistan and the UK, was established in the 1980s by the chief of the largest tribe in the east of the Province, Khair Bux Marri, to carry on the struggle. In recent years, another tribal leader, Akbar Bugti, has joined the fight at the head of a group of tribal insurgents. Other Baluchi nationalists today are less convinced of the merits of armed struggle, preferring peaceful political action. Many of them are grouped in the Baluch National Party (BNP). Another similar grouping is the Baluch National Movement. One of the primary strategies deployed by the centre to defeat nationalist sentiment has been to support the strengthening of Islamist parties in the Province. This strategy has had some success, assisted by considerable mistrust between the different Baluchi nationalist factions.[61]

---

[58] F. Grare, "Pakistan: The resurgence of Baluch nationalism", Carnegie Papers, No. 65, January 2006, p. 4.

[59] *Ibid.*, p. 5.

[60] "Pakistan's battle over Balochistan", *BBC News Online*, 26 August 2006.

[61] Grare, "Pakistan: The resurgence of Baluch nationalism", pp. 7–9.

Since early 2005 there has been a resurgence of unrest in the Province. There have been several attacks against Chinese workers in the Province. However, in August 2006 the 79 year-old Bugti was killed by an army attack. This seriously weakened the effectiveness of the insurgency that he had led. An analyst concludes:

> In the absence of foreign support, which does not appear imminent, the Baluch movement cannot prevail over a determined central government with obviously superior military strength. Still it can have a considerable nuisance value.[62]

The Taliban are also present in Baluchistan. The Afghan Government suspects that Mullah Omar and other Taliban leaders are currently operating out of Quetta, the capital of the region. Pakistan denies this while claiming that the Taliban is assisting the Baluchi insurgency. Much Afghan opium is smuggled through western Baluchistan.[63] There are over 800,000 Afghan refugees still in Baluchistan, most of them Pashtun.

After flawed elections in 2002, Musharraf's faction of the Muslim League (Quaid) formed a Coalition Government in Baluchistan with the MMA. However, were there to be free and fair elections in the Province, it is possible that Baluchi nationalist parties, with the BNP to the fore, might well garner the most votes and seek to form a government with either the PPP or the Muslim League-N.[64]

D. The Federally Administered Northern Areas[65]

Before independence in 1947, the Northern Areas, which comprise Gilgit and Baltistan, were part of the princely state of Jammu and Kashmir. In 1947 the leaders of the Northern Areas sided with Pakistan. Because Pakistan asserts that the Northern Areas are part of the unresolved Kashmir dispute, successive governments have refused to finalise the constitutional status of the region and have stated that they will do so only once there is a solution to the dispute. Like the FATA, the Northern Areas are not covered by the Pakistan Constitution. However, in contrast to the FATA, they are also unrepresented in the national Parliament. In contrast to neighbouring Azad Kashmir, which enjoys some political autonomy (however notional in practice), the Northern Areas are subject to untrammelled direct rule from Islamabad through the Ministry of Kashmir Affairs and Northern Areas. A 1999 Supreme Court ruling which stated that the people of the Northern Areas should enjoy the full range of civil rights available to

---

[62] *Ibid.*, p. 13.

[63] "Baluchistan an 'administrative nightmare", *Toronto Star*, 22 February 2007. For more information about Afghan opium, see Library Standard Note SN/IA/3831.

[64] ICG, *Elections, Democracy and Stability in Pakistan*, Asia Report No. 137, 31 July 2007, p. 18.

[65] This section draws heavily on the ICG's report, *Discord in Pakistan's Northern Areas*, Asia Report No. 131, 2 April 2007.

citizens of Pakistan and should be granted genuine political autonomy, including provincial status, has so far been ignored.

Some observers believe that Islamabad's preference for unlimited direct rule partly reflects the fact that the Northern Areas are the only part of Pakistan where the Shia are in a majority. The Pakistani military has long promoted the region as a base for Sunni militant Islamic groups active in Kashmir. There have been problems with sectarianism in the region since the 1980s, with significant incidents of Sunni-Shia violence in recent years, particularly in and around Gilgit, the main city. The authorities have been accused of failing to take effective action to bring the perpetrators of such violence to justice. As elsewhere in the country, the PPP and other opposition political parties have been politically marginalised, leaving the religious parties with considerable room for manoeuvre.

According to the ICG, most of the local population—which is linguistically and culturally distinct from Kashmir—today rejects the idea that their fate should be tied to a resolution of the Kashmir dispute; discontented with the region's ambiguous status within Pakistan, there are stirrings of nationalism. Since 1999 a number of organisations have been formed around more-or-less explicit nationalist agendas: the Balawaristan National Front, the Karakoram National Movement and the Gilgit-Baltistan United Alliance. How much popular support such organisations have is impossible to say. The ICG concludes:

> While the nationalists are still relatively weak, their challenge to Pakistan's control should not be dismissed lightly. The longer Pakistan denies the region political freedoms, the more the nationalists stand to gain.[66]

IV Bilateral Relations

A. India

The dominant bone of contention between Pakistan and India since 1947 has been Kashmir. The conflict has two interlocking dimensions. The first dimension has been inter-state rivalry between India and Pakistan over which country is entitled to sovereignty over Indian Kashmir. The two countries have gone to war twice over Kashmir (in 1947 and 1965) and have been close to it on several other occasions. The second dimension has been protest by political organisations on both sides of the border against 'Indian occupation', which since the late 1980s has in some cases extended to taking up arms. Most of the groups that have taken up arms have bases in Azad Kashmir, the Pakistan part of Kashmir, support Pakistan's claim to

[66] *Ibid.*, p. 20.

the whole of Kashmir, and have received support from Pakistan's security establishment. Many also have militant Islamist agendas (see Part III A.1). A minority of armed groups—mainly based in Indian Kashmir (now part of the state of Jammu and Kashmir)—argue for independence for the whole of Kashmir from both India and Pakistan.[67]

In 2002 India and Pakistan again came close to war over Kashmir following the December 2001 attack on the Indian Parliament by two armed militant groups, Lashkar-e-Taiba and Jaish-e-Mohammad. However, since April 2003 there have been renewed efforts by both India and Pakistan to reduce violence and re-start peace negotiations on Kashmir. Full diplomatic relations have been restored and a range of confidence-building measures introduced. In November 2003 a ceasefire was agreed along the current *de facto* border, known as the Line of Control, by Pakistan and India. Since then there have been several rounds of talks at different levels of seniority, which are formally known as 'the composite dialogue'. Since January 2004 India has also held talks with more moderate Kashmiri groups that have been willing to engage bilaterally, following a split within the ranks of the coalition known as the All Party Hurriyat Conference. Pakistan's endorsement of these talks represented a shift in its position as previously it had insisted on it (or the UN) also being involved. But there are parts of the security establishment that remain ambivalent about such shifts. This dialogue has periodically come under strain because Kashmiri groups involved have accused India of failing to rein in its security forces and prevent human rights abuses against civilians, but so far it has not collapsed.[68]

While the talks between India and Pakistan have assisted in promoting significant confidence-building measures and certainly helped to facilitate mutual co-operation following the devastating earthquake in Kashmir in 2005, which killed an estimated 73,000 people in Pakistan, progress on substantive issues has so far been harder to achieve. India sees Kashmir as one of a number of issues that it wishes to resolve with Pakistan but the latter wants real progress on Kashmir first before addressing other issues (such as economic co-operation, the nuclear issue and water sharing). India continues to state that any solution cannot involve a change in its external borders. Pakistan's traditional position has been that the conflict should be resolved by the holding of a UN-sponsored plebiscite of the people of Kashmir. President Musharraf has engaged in periodic exploratory 'thinking aloud', in which he has floated ideas for breaking the impasse—for example, demilitarisation, self-governance or joint Pakistan-Indian control—which would not require a redrawing of borders. In March 2006 the Indian

[67] For a brief discussion of the origins of the conflict between India and Pakis tan over Kashmir, see House of Commons Library Paper No. 272, 11 June 1991, *Kashmir*. For background on subsequent developments, also see Library Paper 04/28, 30 March 2004, *Kashmir*.

[68] "NC pulls out of working groups", *The Hindu*, 26 October 2006.

Prime Minister Manmohan Singh indicated that India was willing to consider initiatives that rendered the Line of Control irrelevant. Pakistan welcomed this announcement.

Periodic outbreaks of violence by Kashmiri-led armed groups continue to occur and appear designed to prevent 'new thinking' from gaining momentum. The most notable pro-independence armed group, the Jammu and Kashmir Liberation Front, has been gravely weakened by the counter-insurgency strategies of the Indian security forces. However, pro-independence sentiment remains strong in the Kashmir Valley. The Kashmiri-led Islamist armed groups have remained active. There were attacks in April 2006 and, most notably, in June 2006, when at least 200 people died in bombings in Mumbai. The bombings were widely attributed to Lashkar-e-Taiba.[69] The April and June 2006 attacks inevitably froze the gradual *rapprochement* between Pakistan and India for a period. Foreign Secretary-level talks were suspended and in August 2006 there was a tit-for-tat expulsion of diplomats for alleged spying.

The militant Islamist armed groups want talks that simultaneously include India, Pakistan and Kashmiri representatives under the auspices of the UN, leading to a plebiscite on the future of Kashmir. They calculate that if levels of violence are raised, bilateral peace efforts of the kind pursued since 2003 will not advance far. This has been the case in the past. For example, Prime Minister Manmohan Singh was due to visit Pakistan in 2006, but he indicated that a date could not be set for the visit while levels of violence were high.

Despite regular setbacks over the past three years, neither side has abandoned the peace track. A brief meeting between Musharraf and Manmohan Singh in September 2006 at the Non-Aligned Movement's summit re-activated it. Known as the 'Havana handshake' in the Indian media, the two men agreed to establish a joint mechanism to address terrorism. The foreign secretaries of the two countries met in mid-November 2006 to put some flesh on the bones of this proposal. In December 2006, Musharraf stated that Pakistan might be willing to give up its claim over all Kashmir in return for autonomy and self-governance for the region, some form of joint India-Pakistan supervision across the Line of Control and a gradual demilitarisation on both sides of the border.[70]

Known as the 'four-point formula', it has provoked an angry reaction in some quarters within Pakistan and from Kashmiri-led armed groups. The Indian Government initially responded warmly to this indication of willingness to compromise, offering Pakistan the possibility of a comprehensive

---

[69] The same group was reportedly involved in an attack in 2001 on the Indian Parliament, which nearly led to war between the two countries.

[70] "Musharraf gives a hint of progress on Kashmir", *International Herald Tribune*, 6 December 2006.

treaty of peace, security and friendship. However, in recent months there have been signs of a cooling in Indian attitudes to the proposals. During talks between the two countries in March 2007, the Indian Government expressed opposition to any ideas of joint supervision across the Line of Control and reiterated that demilitarisation could only become possible towards the end of any peace process.[71] There has been talk of Manmohan Singh travelling to Pakistan during 2007, but the growing political crisis there looks likely to rule such out such an initiative.[72]

Some Kashmiri political forces do accept that the armed struggle for independence has failed and that new strategies are required. But this does not mean that all of them are willing to go as far as Musharraf has now proposed. There have been reports that Pakistan's military intelligence is currently seriously clamping down on the movement of armed groups into Indian Kashmir.[73] Both sides have reiterated their commitment to the idea of a joint mechanism to counter terrorism, although its first formal meeting in March 2007 produced no appreciable result, raising doubts about what it will amount to in practice.[74]

If there has been a Pakistani clamp-down on armed groups, it has some way to go. During the night of 18–19 February 2007, bomb blasts 50 miles west of New Delhi hit the 'Friendship Express' that travels directly between India and Pakistan, killing at least 66 people—mostly Pakistan nationals. Although there is still no certainty about which organisation was behind the attack (for many analysts, the most likely candidate is Lashkar-e-Taiba and its affiliates), it was clearly designed to disrupt the peace process. The 'Friendship Express' is itself a product of that process, symbolising the cautious *rapprochement* between the two countries since 2003. The Indian and Pakistan Governments have both been very measured in their response, in contrast to previous such incidents. No official accusations of culpability have been exchanged, although other commentators have not been as restrained. It has been reported that at least five people have been arrested by the Indian authorities in connection with the bombing. There have been further clashes between militants and the Indian security forces in recent months.

Human Rights Watch published a report in late 2006 on Azad Kashmir which was highly critical of the performance of the Pakistani authorities following the 2005 earthquake.[75] Human Rights Watch accuses the authorities of being more preoccupied with maintaining their control over the region than with assisting reconstruction. Indeed, they allegedly encouraged

---

[71] "Musharraf's plan gets a thumbs down", *Times of India*, 10 March 2007.
[72] "PM offers Pak treaty of peace and friendship", *Times of India*, 21 December 2006.
[73] "Kashmir militants feel the squeeze", *BBC News Online*, 7 February 2007.
[74] "India-Pak terror pact sinking fast", *Times of India*, 12 March 2007.
[75] As discussed in Part VI of this Paper.

radical Islamic groups to take a lead role in reconstruction efforts, thus bolstering their legitimacy.[76]

There have been some hopeful signs that the Indian authorities may be prepared to adopt a less heavy-handed approach to security issues. In early February 2007, responding to a general strike on the Indian side of the border in protest against extra-judicial killings and other human rights abuses by the security forces, the Jammu and Kashmir State Government acknowledged for the first time that there is evidence to support such allegations.[77] In late February seven policemen were charged with killing a Kashmiri carpenter who they falsely claimed had been an Islamic militant.[78]

Neither the US nor the EU considers Kashmir to be the lodestone of its policies towards India and Pakistan. Both are encouraging peace efforts and the apparent flexibility currently being shown by both sides. Pakistan would like to see greater international engagement but is more pragmatic about this than in the past. India is happy for the issue to be addressed through bilateral channels.

As we approach the 60th anniversary of the birth of the dispute over Kashmir, expectations have been rising of a dramatic breakthrough. This may be over-optimistic. There is strong opposition on both sides of the border to any idea of compromise. Further terrorist operations in India by Kashmiri-led armed groups could change the dynamics again. On issues of substance, the two countries remain far apart. But the apparent willingness of both India and Pakistan to begin thinking in different terms about possible solutions does offer growing hope.

Despite some signs of potential progress, Kashmir continues to cast the largest shadow over relations between India and Pakistan. A successful resolution of the conflict over Kashmir is integral to achieving a real sea-change in relations between the two countries. As stated earlier, India is dangling the possibility of a comprehensive treaty of peace, security and friendship between India and Pakistan should the Kashmir issue be resolved. However, the seeming intractability of the conflict over Kashmir has recently prompted greater efforts on both sides to build mutual confidence by addressing other important disputes between them—partly in the hope that an improved atmosphere will ultimately lead to a breakthrough over Kashmir itself.

There have been efforts to make progress on issues that are not wholly dependent on an overall resolution of the conflict over Kashmir but which are nonetheless 'Kashmir-related'. The two countries have sought to

[76] "Emperor's new clothes", *Guardian*, 31 October 2006.
[77] "Restoring faith", *Times of India*, 7 February 2007.
[78] "Kashmir: police charged in civilian killing", *New York Times*, 1 March 2007.

address the specific border dispute between them over the 74 kilometre Siachen glacier in the strategic heights of Kashmir. The status of the Siachen glacier as part of the Line of Control has never been resolved. In 1984 Indian troops took control of the previously unoccupied glacier, fearing moves by Pakistan to seize it. Pakistan then moved its own troops and claimed to have seized part of the glacier too. India disputes that there are any Pakistani forces on the glacier. Indian and Pakistani forces have clashed in the area on several occasions, most notably in 1999 (known as the Kargil operation). India has accused Pakistan of seeking to push their troops off the glacier.

There appears to have been some progress on the issue in recent years, although a resolution still seems some way off. Both sides have agreed to the principle of demilitarising the glacier. Pakistan has given undertakings that it would not seize the glacier if Indian troops were to withdraw. India is reported to be removing detritus from the glacier. However, India has demanded that Pakistan must give full details of its troop positions in the area before it begins to withdraw and that such details should be part of any final agreement. Pakistan is prepared to do so only if India agrees not to use such information to make a legal claim over the glacier in future.[79]

Both countries' arrival as nuclear weapon states has greatly raised the stakes for the world whenever conflict between them is threatened, usually over Kashmir. However, the two countries have signed two agreements on nuclear issues to reduce the likelihood of resorting to the use of nuclear weapons. The most recent agreement was signed in February 2007. Neither is in the public domain.

In late July 2006 there were reports that Pakistan was intensifying its nuclear collaboration with China. This was viewed as in part a response to increased US-India co-operation on nuclear power.[80] India indicated that it did not view this development with any great alarm.[81] When Pakistan tested a new version of on e of its nuclear-capable missiles in February 2007, the response of the Indian authorities was extremely muted by previous standards.[82]

One incentive for improved relations with Pakistan is India's growing energy needs. It has been discussing the building of an oil pipeline between it and Iran since the 1990s. This would need to travel through Pakistan. However, this proposal currently remains on paper only.[83] The two countries are working together in discussions with Iran about a proposed pipeline

[79] "India doesn't buy Pak 'promise' on Siachen", *Times of India*, 12 February 2007.
[80] "As India debates N-deal, China and Pak move close to rival pact", *Indian Express*, 17 August 2006.
[81] "India OK with China-Pak N-deal", *Times of India*, 28 November 2006.
[82] "Pakistan stages new missile test", *BBC News Online*, 23 February 2007.
[83] Oral Evidence of Matthew Nelson, School of Oriental and African Studies, to the Foreign Affairs Select Committee Enquiry on *South Asia*, 31 January 2007, HC 55-iv, Q209 Available at: http://www.publications.parliament.uk/pa/cm/cmfaff.htm#uncorr.

that will bring natural gas from there to India, again via Pakistan. The prospects in this regard appear more favourable.[84]

Kashmir is not the only area where there are border disputes between India and Pakistan. Negotiations have advanced in the dispute over the land and maritime boundary between India and Pakistan in Sir Creek, which is a narrow 96 kilometre strip of marshland between Sindh in Pakistan and Gujarat in India. Both sides have agreed to a joint survey. Maps were exchanged in March 2007.[85] An incentive for co-operation is the fact that if the two countries have not resolved their disagreement over Sir Creek by 2009, the maritime area would be open to exploitation by any party under the UN Convention on the Law of the Sea. The area is rumoured to have gas and oil deposits.[86]

Control over natural resources has also been a key issue in relations between India and Pakistan. Water is a good example. There has been a long-running dispute about the proposed Baglihar dam on the river Chenab in Jammu and Kashmir. However, in February 2007 both countries accepted the binding judgment of a neutral expert appointed by the World Bank under the 1960 Indus Waters Treaty to arbitrate between the claims of the two sides. The Treaty allocated the three eastern rivers originating in Punjab for India's exclusive consumption and the three western rivers for Pakistan's exclusive consumption. However, India was allowed to use the western rivers for hydroelectric power generation so long as this did not deplete the water supply. Pakistan had alleged that the dam, with which India planned to supply electricity to Indian Kashmir, would do so. The project will now go ahead on a modified basis.[87] The two countries are still in dispute about the Wular Barrage.[88]

Indian allegations about Pakistan's support for terrorism go beyond the conflict over Kashmir. India has also accused Pakistan's security agencies of supporting the United Liberation Front of Assam over the three decades of its existence.[89] Pakistan counters by accusing India of providing assistance to Baluchistan insurgents in its North-West Frontier Province, an accusation India denies.[90]

Both India and Pakistan currently appear more willing to resolve—or at least mitigate—the areas of conflict that have shaped their relationship in the past. But their *rapprochement* remains fragile. India's rise to great power

[84] "India, Pakistan discuss tri-nation gas pipeline project", *BBC Monitoring South Asia*, 22 February 2007.
[85] "Sir Creek maps exchanged", *The Hindu*, 24 March 2007.
[86] "Sir Creek model for Siachen?", *Hindustan Times*, 5 January 2007.
[87] "Baglihar award a finely balanced verdict", *The Statesman* (India), 22 February 2007.
[88] C. Bajpaee, "Asia's coming water wars", *Power and Interest News Report*, 22 August 2006.
[89] "Trouble brews in India's northeast", *Gulf News*, 3 February 2007.
[90] "India denies role in Balochistan insurgency", *Times of India*, 8 March 2007.

status will be difficult for Pakistan to swallow. Pakistan has always insisted to the world that it and India should be treated as equals. While formally this will always remain the case, many observers argue that in practice this is increasingly a myth. The growing power asymmetry could itself have a destabilising impact on relations between the two countries in the future.[91]

B. Afghanistan

Relations between Pakistan and Afghanistan have oscillated sharply over the past 60 years. Some analysts argue that Pakistan's main strategic goal throughout the period has been to create a pliant neighbour which will ensure that it has 'strategic depth' in relation to its primary adversary, India.[92]

Regardless of who has been in power in Afghanistan, there has always been a structural tension between the two countries over their highly porous border. Every Afghan Government has refused to recognise the Durand Line drawn during the colonial period, which still delineates the border between the two countries, and retains a territorial claim over parts of NWFP, where it sponsored a separatist movement in the 1950s. However, Afghan and Pakistan Governments over the decades have shared a common interest in combating Pashtun nationalist sentiment. However, support for 'Pashtunistan' appears to have declined since the 1970s.[93]

Formal relations between the two countries reached their nadir during the Soviet occupation of Afghanistan between 1979 and 1989. They were at their peak during the rule of the Pashtun-dominated Taliban, of which Pakistan was the main sponsor, until September 11th 2001, after which, following a US ultimatum, Pakistan announced that it was ending its support. One commentator has argued that, under the Taliban, it was Afghanistan which enjoyed the greater 'strategic depth' in its relations with Pakistan, preparing the ground for Pakistan's progressive 'Talibanisation'.[94] Despite its post-September 11th *volte-face*, doubts remain over whether elements within the Pakistani military, including a number of prominent retired Generals, have completely ended their backing.[95]

---

[91] S. Cohen, "Pakistan and the Crescent of Crisis", in I. Daalder, N. Gnesotto and P. Gordon (eds), *Crescent of Crisis. US-European Strategy for the Greater Middle East* (Washington DC, 2006), p. 186. For further discussion of how Pakistan's relationship with India shapes its idea of itself and its future, see Part VII.

[92] Hussain, *Frontline Pakistan*, p. 29.

[93] *Ibid.*, p. 30.

[94] Hussain, *Frontline Pakistan*, p. 30.

[95] For relations between Afghanistan and Pakistan post-September 11th, see also House of Commons Library Research Paper RP 01/72, *11 September 2001: The Response* and RP 05/72, *Afghanistan and the Culmination of the Bonn Process.*

Over the past 18 months, there have been serious tensions between Islamabad and Kabul over how best to tackle the Taliban's renewed insurgency. The Pakistan Government has called on its Afghan counterpart to initiate peace talks with the Taliban, or at least those factions which are open to negotiation. This has reflected its own strategy on the Pakistan side of the border, which has involved attempts to secure peace deals interspersed with bursts of military action. The Afghan Government has so far rejected these calls, accusing Pakistan of failing to take effective action against Taliban and al-Qaeda bases on its side of the border. The Pakistan Government occasionally retaliates by claiming that Afghanistan is supporting Baluchi nationalists.

In April 2007 there were small-scale clashes between the armed forces of Pakistan and Afghanistan along the border.[96] The US and UK took steps to mediate between the two countries to ensure that tensions did not escalate further. Such efforts helped to calm relations, at least on the surface.

In August 2007 Presidents Karzai and Musharraf attended a 'peace jirga' in Kabul which brought hundreds of delegates from both countries together.[97] Although there were disagreements on a range of issues, the jirga was widely judged to have assisted in reducing tensions between Afghanistan and Pakistan. A Declaration was issued, which stated that both parties would wage a "tireless ... campaign against terrorism" and would not provide sanctuary for terrorists. There was also a renewed commitment to combating drug cultivation and trafficking. It was agreed to set up a smaller, regular jirga to take cooperation forward, including promoting dialogue with "opposition". It was not stated to whom this referred. There were no representatives at the jirga of the Taliban or of their sympathisers in Pakistan's border areas, leading some to question what the meeting could in practice deliver.[98]

C. The US

Pakistan was viewed as a crucial ally by the US during the Cold War. Its anti-communist credentials were strong and contrasted with India's policy of non-alignment. Close economic and military ties developed during this period, reaching their most intense while Pakistan was sponsoring the Afghan Mujahideen during its struggle against Soviet occupation. The alliance continued afterwards, driven in part by the need of the US to counter the influence of Shia Iran within the Muslim world and the belief that Chinese support to Pakistan required a response. However, the relationship progressively became more ambivalent, as Pakistan's role as an alleged

[96] "Many killed in Pakistan bombing", *BBC News Online*, 15 May 2007.
[97] A jirga is a gathering of political and tribal leaders.
[98] "Was the 'peace jirga' a success?", *BBC News Online*, 13 August 2007.

'incubator' of militant Sunni Islam rose up the list of US foreign policy concerns. Some arms sales were cut and Pakistani officers were no longer offered training opportunities in the US. Pakistan's nuclear programme also became a point of dispute, provoking US economic sanctions. Pakistan's nuclear tests in 1998 (held after India had undertaken its own tests) led to further economic sanctions by the US, which also pushed successfully for the World Bank, IMF and other donors to suspend their programmes of assistance.

September 11th 2001 provoked a 'moment of truth' between the two countries. Despite considerable reluctance within parts of the Pakistani military, President Musharraf pushed through an agreement to abandon the Afghan Taliban and ally itself unambiguously with the US in the 'war on terror'. One analyst concluded that this proved that, when forced to choose, the Pakistani military values access to the advanced military hardware that the US offers more highly than its relationships with radical Islamist groupings.[99] Had Pakistan not taken this path, it could itself have become the location of major US military action against the Afghan Taliban and al-Qaeda. Musharraf also feared that a refusal would trigger a shift on the part of the US towards India as its main ally in South Asia.

This remains an anxiety on the part of the Pakistan Government today. In recent years, the US and India have undertaken a *rapprochement* that may extend to civil nuclear cooperation in future years. However, it has not yet led to US moves to align itself with India over Kashmir; it retains an even-handed position on the issue. Musharraf's decision after September 11th has opened the way for a massive programme of US economic and military assistance. This has included a US$1 billion loan write-off, $600 million in budgetary support and $12.5 million debt rescheduling, which has helped to rescue Pakistan's ailing economy. All economic sanctions were also lifted. A recent estimate of the total value of US assistance since 9/11 put the figure at over $10 billion.[100]

The US has also engaged in military sales that have helped Pakistan to refurbish its fleet of F-16 aircraft and upgrade its counter-insurgency capabilities.[101] In August 2007 it was announced that the US planned to sell up to 36 F-16 aircraft to Pakistan.[102] Despite this largesse, the Pakistan Government has retained some 'red lines' in terms of US prerogatives. While it did open up its territory to US military forces during the period leading up to the overthrow of the Taliban, since then it has repeatedly

[99] S. Cohen, "Pakistan and the Crescent of Crisis", in I. Daalder, N. Gnesotto and P. Gordon (eds), *Crescent of Crisis. US-European Strategy for the Greater Middle East* (Washington DC, 2006), p. 186.

[100] D. Markey, "False choice in Pakistan", *Foreign Affairs*, July/August 2007, p. 88.

[101] O. Bennett Jones and F. Shaikh, "Pakistan's foreign policy under Musharraf: between a rock and a hard place", Chatham House Briefing Paper, ASP BP 06/01, March 2006.

[102] Markey, "False choice", p. 89.

rejected requests by the US to allow its combat troops to operate in the tribal areas on the Pakistan side of the border. It has also refused to allow US personnel to deal directly with local tribal leaders.[103] There are growing voices in the US suggesting that Pakistan has not done enough to combat Islamic militancy, whether home-grown, Afghan or al-Qaeda related. Mistrust of Pakistan in the US has been further increased by revelations up to 2004 about the AQ Khan network, which has been shown to have played a major role in fuelling nuclear proliferation around the world, most notably in relation to North Korea and Iran (see Part V B.2). Some fear that the network may still be partially intact.[104]

According to one commentator, many Pakistanis—particularly those opposed to military rule—view the US as a "disloyal, inconstant friend" which cannot be relied upon.[105] Predictably, radical Islamists view the US with unalloyed hostility, blaming Musharraf personally for the post-September 11th *volte-face*. As for the military itself, it too is cautious about US support. It fears being abandoned. Some analysts believe that Pakistan's security services have maintained their links with radical Islamists as a "hedge against abandonment". If this is so, they argue, abandoning the military could be counter-productive.[106]

Despite mounting domestic challenges to his power and authority during 2007, US backing for Musharraf remains strong—at least in public. But it is becoming increasingly difficult for the Bush administration to ignore those in Congress who are questioning whether the US has been wise to downgrade the importance of restoring democracy in Pakistan, while pinning its hopes entirely on Musharraf and the military to deliver on security.[107] There are calls to block the planned sale of F-16 aircraft to Pakistan. Behind the scenes, the US is seeking to encourage Musharraf and the leaders of the main civilian political parties which he has sought to marginalise, the PPP and the Muslim League-N, to find some form of compromise way forward (see above).

D. China

China is a longstanding ally of Pakistan. It has greatly assisted Pakistan in the development of its nuclear weapons and ballistic missile programmes and has generally taken its side in disputes with India.[108] Some believe that

---

[103] On occasions, the US has nonetheless gone ahead and covertly done both. Hussein, *Frontline Pakistan*, pp. 49-50, 120-22.
[104] S. Cohen, "Pakistan and the Crescent of Crisis", in I. Daalder, N. Gnesotto and P. Gordon (eds), *Crescent of Crisis. US-European Strategy for the Greater Middle East* (Washington DC, 2006), p. 187.
[105] Bennett-Jones, *Pakistan*, p. xxiv.
[106] Markey, "False choices", p. 92.
[107] Cohen, "Pakistan and the Crescent of Crisis", p. 192.
[108] Bennett-Jones, *Pakistan*, p. 217.

China tested nuclear devices for Pakistan in the 1990s. This favour has been returned by Pakistan with regard to Sino-Indian border disputes. Defence and wider economic cooperation continues. For example, China is assisting in the building of a major naval base and deep-sea port at Gwadar. In return it will be allowed berthing rights there for its ships and submarines. Gwadar will also afford China a sea-land alternative passage for energy imports should its access to the Arabian sea or the Strait of Malacca be disrupted in the future.[109] But China has concerns about the security of Chinese workers in Pakistan following attacks by Islamic militants angry about its treatment of the Uighur Muslim population in Xinjiang Province. It is unclear whether China is still providing much support to Pakistan in terms of its nuclear weapons and ballistic missile programmes, but in recent years there have been discussions between the two countries about the purchase of as many as six nuclear reactors.[110]

Despite such close relations, Pakistan is nervous—as it is with regard to the US—about the implications of a gradual *rapprochement* between China and India as those countries advance towards great power status. But China is likely to avoid being forced to choose between India and Pakistan.

E. The UK

The overarching framework for relations between the two countries was formally set out in a December 2004 Joint Statement by the then Prime Minister Tony Blair and President Musharraf. The full text is set out below:[111]

> UK—PAKISTAN A PARTNERSHIP FOR PEACE AND PROSPERITY JOINT STATEMENT
>
> The Rt Hon Tony Blair MP & President Pervez Musharraf: 6 December 2004
>
> His Excellency General Pervez Musharraf, President of the Islamic Republic of Pakistan, paid an official visit to the United Kingdom on 5–7 December 2004 at the invitation of the Rt Hon Tony Blair, Prime Minister of the United Kingdom. At the conclusion of their talks, they issued this joint statement.
>
> 1. Pakistan and the UK are bound together by strategic ties. The two countries already enjoy close and fruitful cooperation in diverse areas within

[109] "Gwadar port—a Pakistani 'pearl' but a Chinese Gibraltar", *Indo-Asian News Service*, 26 March 2006.

[110] O. Bennett Jones and F. Shaikh, "Pakistan's foreign policy under Musharraf: between a rock and a hard place", Chatham House Briefing Paper, ASP BP 06/01, March 2006.

[111] Foreign Affairs Select Committee, *South Asia*, Fourth Report, Session 2006–7, HC 55, Ev 56–7. Available at: http:*//www.publications.parliament.uk/pa/cm200607/cmselect/cmfaff/55/55.pdf*. Annex 6 (Ev 57-62) of the Committee's report provides information about visa/consular operations in Pakistan and a summary (Ev 133-4) of UK-Pakistan economic ties. See also Part VI B.1 of this Paper for a survey of the aid relationship and Part VI C.1.a for UK humanitarian support to Pakistan following the 2005 earthquake.

several institutional frameworks. President Pervez Musharraf and Prime Minister Tony Blair agreed to broaden the relationship between their countries into a reenergised partnership for peace and prosperity in the 21st century.

2. Pakistan and the United Kingdom are close allies in countering terrorism in all its forms and manifestations. The Prime Minister thanked the President for his courage in standing firm against terrorism, which is a serious threat to international stability. The President and the Prime Minister agreed that no terrorism is acceptable, whatever the cause, and agreed to seek further ways to enhance bilateral cooperation in combatting terrorism, especially terrorist networks spanning the UK and Pakistan.

3. The President shared with the Prime Minister his vision for Enlightened Moderation in the Islamic World. He also detailed the far-reaching measures taken by Pakistan to eliminate extremism and militancy in the country. They agreed on the need for a concerted international effort to tackle the root causes of terrorism and extremism, including through addressing poverty and injustice, and by providing people with a greater stake in the democracy and development of their own societies. They agreed on the need for judicious resolution of conflict, including in the Middle East and South Asia.

4. The Prime Minister welcomed President Musharraf's commitment to continuing the process of democratisation in Pakistan, and Pakistan's readmission to the Councils of the Commonwealth. They both affirmed their commitment to the Commonwealth Harare principles.

5. The President and the Prime Minister welcomed the political cooperation which both countries have enjoyed in the United Nations over the last two years while Pakistan has been a member of the UN Security Council, and looked forward to continuing to work together in the United Nations and other multilateral forums.

6. The two leaders also agreed to work towards the objective of non-proliferation of weapons of mass destruction and their means of delivery. They agreed to initiate a bilateral strategic dialogue on these issues.

7. The President and the Prime Minister agreed on the need for a fairer international trading regime, providing, inter alia, for greater market access in a way which allows developing countries to reap the substantial benefits of an increasingly open world economy. They pledged to work closely for a successful conclusion of the WTO Doha Development Agenda.

8. The President and the Prime Minister discussed the situation in Iraq and agreed on the need for continued UN and multinational efforts to bring lasting peace and stability to the country. They welcomed the communiqué issued at the end of the conference in Sharm el-Sheikh which underlined the continued commitment of the international community to support the political process in Iraq.

9. The President and the Prime Minister reaffirmed their commitment to support Afghanistan's democratic process and its development. They welcomed

President Karzai's election and recognised that a stable, peaceful and prosperous Afghanistan will have benefits for the whole region. The Prime Minister commended Pakistan for its constructive role in the elections, especially the arrangements for refugee voting in Pakistan.

10. The Prime Minister emphasised the UK's long-term commitment to Afghanistan. The President reaffirmed his commitment to cooperation with Afghanistan and its neighbours in the context of the Good Neighbourly Relations Declaration of December 2002, including the counter narcotics declaration and action plan agreed this year. Both agreed to intensify their efforts to clamp down on the growth, processing, tracking and abuse of opiates in the region which have such serious effects on our societies and economies.

11. The Prime Minister praised President Musharraf's statesmanship in seeking to resolve Pakistan's outstanding issues with India, and welcomed the progress made by both sides since January 2004 in the ongoing Composite Dialogue process. The Prime Minister encouraged further efforts to find a lasting resolution to these issues, including over Jammu and Kashmir, taking into account the wishes of the Kashmiris. They agreed that resolution of the Kashmir issue would help to establish durable peace in the region.

12. The Prime Minister and the President agreed to work closely towards achieving the Millennium Development Goals. The President warmly welcomed the United Kingdom's commitment of up to £144 million over two years in development assistance to help support Pakistan's long-term development and poverty reduction initiatives. The Prime Minister acknowledged the turnaround in Pakistan's economy, making it one of fastest growing economies in the world with an annual growth rate of over 6.5%.

13. The President and the Prime Minister praised the ongoing work of the Pakistan-Britain Trade and Investment Forum and the Pakistan-Britain Business Advisory Group in helping to promote the already close trading links between their countries. The UK is the second largest foreign investor in Pakistan. They welcomed the success of the two trade missions which visited Pakistan in September and October 2004 and the plans for further trade missions in February 2005.

14. The President and the Prime Minister welcomed the deepening defence relationship between their countries, including through the success of the annual meetings of the Defence Cooperation Forum. They agreed on the importance of further evolving the Forum into a wide-ranging dialogue, including discussions of global and regional security, and defence equipment. They also agreed to enhance cooperation through both countries' continued involvement in UN Peacekeeping Operations, to which Pakistan currently contributes more troops than any other country in the world, and actively to explore opportunities to learn from each other's experiences, such as through dialogue, training and peacekeeping exercises between the two countries.

> 15. They also reviewed the constructive work of the Pakistan Britain Joint Judicial Cooperation Working Group in helping to improve the operations of law enforcement agencies affecting both countries.
>
> 16. The Prime Minister expressed his appreciation of the ongoing links between Pakistan and the approximately one million people of Pakistani heritage living in the UK, and both welcomed the reopening of the visa issuing service in the British High Commission in Islamabad and the British Deputy High Commission in Karachi. They agreed on the need to encourage bona-fide travel between their countries as a means of fostering strong people-to-people links, but to clamp down on those who try to cheat the system.
>
> To this end the leaders agreed to conclude as soon as possible a Memorandum of Understanding on immigration issues, re-documentation and resolution of cases.
>
> 17. The President and the Prime Minister agreed to hold an annual summit-level meeting between their countries and to explore new areas of bilateral cooperation.

The importance of Pakistan to the security of the UK has been underscored by the role of British citizens of Pakistani origin in the 7/7 and 21/7 bombing attacks in London in 2005 and by other terrorist plots that have been uncovered subsequently. While there has been considerable media attention on the training that some of those involved received in Pakistan, President Musharraf has argued that Pakistan cannot be held responsible for their actions. According to one recent source, the security services are currently tracking "more than 20 plots, involving as many as 200 terrorist cells, and watching more than 1,500 people associated with them in the United Kingdom—most of whom are of Pakistani origin."[112] The two countries have concluded a prisoner transfer agreement with regard to nationals held in each other's prisons. It will come into force once both countries have ratified it.[113]

While the fact that Musharraf combines the positions of Head of State and Army Chief of Staff means that the UK does not yet consider the process of democratisation in Pakistan to be "irreversible", the public stance of the UK Government remains one of strong support for Musharraf as a key ally in the 'war on terror'.[114] However, behind the scenes there has been considerable concern about his strategy in the border areas and about whether he can survive the wider political challenges facing him during 2007. The UK

[112] P. Brookes, "Peril in Pakistan", *Armed Forces Journal*, June 2007.

[113] There are more than 800,000 British citizens of Pakistani origin in the UK and at least 80,000 residents in Pakistan of British nationality. HC Deb 11 June 2007 c632; HC Deb 17 July 2007 c270W.

[114] The concept of "irreversibility" comes from the 2005 Commonwealth Heads of State/Government Declaration in Malta. Pakistan was suspended from the Commonwealth between 1999 and 2003. See HC Deb 11 June 2007 c632.

Government has been maintaining its contacts with Benazir Bhutto and Nawaz Sharif with a view to being in a position to support moves towards orderly political change in Pakistan. The Department for International Development (DFID) has allocated £3.5 million in support of the coming electoral process.[115] The then Prime Minister, Tony Blair, visited Pakistan in late 2006.[116] During his visit he described relations between the two countries as "at their highest point, I think, than they have been for many, many years."[117]

The Foreign Secretary, David Miliband, made his first foreign visit in the post to Pakistan in July 2007. After a meeting with President Musharraf, he said:

> Britain ha s a strong interest in the stability of Pakistan, in defeating extremism and in the development of tribal areas. Our approach . . . is that the right way forward is one based on partnership between different countries. The abiding theme is that economic, social, and political development has to go together.[118]

A resolution was passed in Pakistan's National Assembly in June 2007 demanding the withdrawal of the knighthood conferred upon the writer, Salman Rushdie. There were also street protests. The UK Government has stressed that the award was not intended as an insult to Islam or the Prophet Muhammed.[119]

The UK Government has also been active, along with the US, in trying to improve relations between Musharraf and President Karzai of Afghanistan (see Part IV B).

F. The EU

Despite being by far the largest trading partner and provider of aid to Pakistan, the EU and its Member States are less important to the country than its alliance with the US. Accordingly, the US takes the lead in the politico-military and security spheres. This does not mean that the EU's 'soft power' is without influence, although concerns have been expressed by some that it does not make full enough use of the leverage that it has over Pakistan to promote human rights and democracy.

Issues of human rights and democracy have had to compete with serious concerns over security and terrorism since September 11th 2001.[120] But they

[115] HC Deb 5 June 2007 c446W.
[116] For details of some of the outcomes of the visit, see HC Deb 23 November 2006 c73-4WS.
[117] "Press Conference with the Pakistani President", No. 10 Press Release, 19 November 2006. Available at: http://pm.gov.uk/output/Page10443.asp.
[118] "Miliband support for Musharraf", *BBC News Online*, 26 July 2007.
[119] HC Deb 25 June 2007 c215W.
[120] For the EU's own description of EU-Pakistan relations see: http://ec.europa.eu/external_relations/pakistan/intro/index.htm.

have not disappeared from the EU agenda. The EU delegation to Pakistan, EU missions and the European Council have all regularly expressed public concern about human rights and democracy issues, including President Musharraf's insistence on combining the roles of both Head of State and Army Chief of Staff. In July 2007 the European Council publicly welcomed the decision of the Supreme Court to reinstate the Chief Justice:

> The Presidency, on behalf of the EU, welcomes the decision of the Government of Pakistan to respect the ruling of the Supreme Court of Justice to reinstate Chief of Justice Iftikar Chaudhry. Independence of the judiciary and the rule of law are key elements of democracy. The EU hopes Pakistan will continue to abide by these principles, on the path towards enhanced legitimacy of political institutions and democratic consolidation, in particular in the view of the forthcoming elections.[121]

The EU has also called for Nawaz Sharif to be allowed to return to Pakistan and be given the opportunity to defend himself against any charges that might be laid against him.[122]

A Third Generation Co-operation Agreement was signed by the EU and Pakistan in November 2001. The Agreement contains a clause calling for respect for human rights and democratic principles as its basis. The Agreement entered into force in September 2004. However, concerns about democracy and human rights have held up its implementation. A Joint Commission, set up under the Agreement to meet annually to oversee the Agreement's implementation, did not meet for the first time until May 2007.

The decision to allow the Joint Commission to meet was taken at an EU-Pakistan meeting of ministers in February 2007. The Joint Statement following the meeting went on to say:

> Beyond this, the EU and Pakistan express their resolution to develop relations in areas not covered by their 2004 Cooperation Agreement. In particular, the two sides undertake to develop a broad, formalised political dialogue, aimed at improving mutual understanding through regular contacts, exchanges and consultations. This shall particularly take the following forms:
>
> - Regular ministerial level dialogue to discuss strategic and other issues.
> - In between the ministerial meetings, senior officials from both sides (Political and Regional Directors, as appropriate) will meet to ensure follow-up.
> - Expert level meetings in a variety of policy areas, including:
>   - interfaith dialogue;
>   - counter-terrorism;

[121] See: http://www.delpak.cec.eu.int/WHATSNEW/Council-Supremecourtpdf.pdf.
[122] "EU appeals for Sharif return", *Irish Examiner*, 10 September 2007.

  - counter-narcotics;
  - non-proliferation;
  - human rights and good governance.
- Encouraging development of contacts at parliamentary level.

> The EU and Pakistan have agreed to exchange experience in the fields of political and economic governance, as well as human rights and the rule of law. Furthermore, both sides have agreed to cooperate in the promotion of regional peace, stability and security. To this end, the EU and Pakistan reaffirm their commitment to the settlement of disputes by peaceful means, in accordance with international law, bilateral agreements and the principles of the UN Charter. Both sides are also committed to the elimination of poverty in Pakistan, in accordance with the Millennium Development Goals.[123]

The EU observed the October 2002 elections to Provincial and National Assemblies with an 88-person strong Election Observation Mission (EOM). The mission declared that the polling day itself had gone relatively smoothly but described the electoral process as seriously flawed, referring to restrictions on political parties and their candidates and misuse of state resources. The EOM recommended support to strengthen the electoral process in preparation for the forthcoming parliamentary elections.[124]

A recent report by the Foreign Affairs Committee of the European Parliament, sponsored by Baroness Nicholson of Winterbourne, caused some controversy in Pakistan due to its opposition to the longstanding idea of holding a plebiscite to decide Kashmir's future and by its focus on the continuing lack of democracy in Azad Kashmir.[125]

G. Other Countries

In 2005 President Musharraf initiated diplomatic talks with Israel. After nearly 20 years of informal contacts, this was the first time that the Pakistani authorities had held talks with Israel in the glare of the public eye. While it provoked anger amongst Pakistan's radical Islamists, Musharraf's main aim, according to one analyst, was to broaden support in the US for future arms sales.[126]

Relations with Shia-dominated Iran have been cool since the 1979 revolution—with the exception of the period 1989-95, when the AQ Khan network shared nuclear weapons technology with the country at a time when the US had imposed sanctions on Pakistan for pursuing a weapons

---

123 EU-Pakistan Joint Declaration, Berlin, 8 February 2007. Available at: http://www.consilium.europa.eu/ueDocs/cms_Data/docs/pressData/en/er/92681.pdf.

124 EU-Pakistan Joint Declaration, Berlin, 8 February 2007.

125 "Europe snubs Pak over Kashmir", *Hindustan Times*, 24 May 2007.

126 O. Bennett Jones and F. Shaikh, "Pakistan's foreign policy under Musharraf: between a rock and a hard place", Chatham House Briefing Paper, ASP BP 06/01, March 2006.

programme.[127] Iran's hostility towards the Afghan Taliban and its pursuit of closer relations with India led to a renewed deterioration in diplomatic relations. Since the fall of the Taliban, relations have improved but Pakistan is careful not to step out of line with the US again with regard to Iran's nuclear programme. Pakistan has also accused Iran, which has its own population of Baluchis, of promoting unrest in Baluchistan.

Relations with Bangladesh—formerly East Pakistan—have gradually improved since the 1971 war between Pakistan and India that led to its creation. Diplomatic relations between Pakistan and Bangladesh were established in 1976. This improvement has been made possible by the relative loosening since then of the ties between India and Bangladesh, which is wary of its powerful neighbour. Although there remain scars on both sides due to the circumstances of Bangladesh's birth, Pakistan is keen to ensure that Bangladesh does not become too close an ally of India again in the future.

V Military and Nuclear Capabilities

A. Military Capabilities

Primarily regional concerns, including Pakistan's relationship with India and issues arising from shared borders with Afghanistan and China, shape the country's military posture, from both a conventional and a nuclear perspective. Yet internal security issues such as religious extremism and sectarian violence have also been a significant factor in the development of Pakistan's defence and security policies and the subsequent configuration of its armed forces.

1. Military Expenditure

In 2005 Pakistan achieved its highest level of economic growth in over a decade due largely to robust growth in the agricultural and manufacturing sectors coupled with the supportive macroeconomic policies of the Pakistan's Government. In 2006 economic growth remained at over 6%. As a result, military expenditure has risen over the last few years. In 2006–07 the Government allocated Pakistani Rupees (PKR) 250bn to the defence budget, a rise of 3.7% on the previous year; whilst in 2007-08 the defence budget is expected to increase by a further 10% to PKR 275bn, approximately 15% of the overall national budget.[128] For comparison, Pakistan's defence expenditure equates to approximately one fifth of India's overall

[127] *Ibid.*

[128] Figures taken from the International Institute for Strategic Studies (IISS), *Military Balance 2007*, and "Pakistan bids to boost defence budget for FY07", *Jane's Defence Weekly*, 20 June 2007.

defence budget, although defence spending does represent a higher percentage of Pakistan's GDP.

However, it is widely acknowledged that Pakistan's official defence budget is not a true reflection of its military spending as it excludes some major areas of expenditure, including military pensions, foreign military aid, foreign credit assistance for military procurement and income generated by the military's own business interests. For example, in 2003 the US agreed a five-year military and economic assistance package to Pakistan worth US$3bn, with approximately half of that package earmarked for military procurement under the US Foreign Military Sales programme.[129] As a result of this lack of transparency, prominent analysts have failed to agree on the exact nature of Pakistan's defence spending. The International Institute for Strategic Studies has estimated the Pakistan's defence budget as follows:

Military expenditure—Pakistan: 2000 to 2006

	2000	2001	2002	2003	2004	2005	2006 (est)
Pakistani rupees (billion) (cash terms)	Rs 131	Rs 152	Rs 160	Rs 180	Rs 193	Rs 241	Rs 250
US dollars (billion) (cash terms)	$2.5	$2.5	$2.7	$3.1	$3.3	$4.0	$4.1
% gross domestic product	4.0	4.1	4.4	4.5	3.5	3.6	3.5

Source: International Institute for Strategic Studies *Military Balance*

The Stockholm International Peace Research Institute (SIPRI) on the other hand has provided the following expenditure figures:

Military expenditure—Pakistan: 2000 to 2006

	2000	2001	2002	2003	2004	2005	2006
Pakistani rupees (billion) (current prices)	Rs 154	Rs 170	Rs 188	Rs 210	Rs 240	Rs 270	Rs 290 (est)
US dollars (million) (2005 prices)	$3,320	$3,553	$3,819	$4,138	$4,399	$4,534	$4,572 (est)
% gross domestic product	3.7	3.9	3.9	3.7	3.6	3.5	. . .

Source: SIPRI Yearbook 2007; see also http://www.sipri.org/contents/milap/milex/mex_data_index.html

Despite the disparity, both sets of figures show a clear upwards trend in defence expenditure. However, this significant rise has prompted criticism

129 That aid began in 2005 with annual instalments of $600 million. $300 million per annum is directed toward military assistance.

within Pakistan's legislature. In response to the government's most recent budget request opposition politicians within the Upper House, the Senate, called for a cap to be placed on the defence budget, citing concerns over other domestic spending priorities and the potential for an "arms spending race" with India to develop.[130]

2. Conventional Capabilities

Given Pakistan's defence and security priorities, its conventional forces are sizeable.[131] They are configured with an emphasis on territorial defence and power projection against its main regional adversary—India. This is reflected in the balance between each of the respective Services. From a total active manpower strength of 619,000 personnel, approximately 550,000 (88.9%) of those are army personnel.[132] In addition, the army reportedly has approximately 200,000 reserve personnel.[133] A further 302,000 active paramilitary forces have responsibility for internal and border security. Of those paramilitary forces, the National Guard form the majority at approximately 185,000 personnel, followed by the forces of the Frontier Corps (65,000) and the Pakistan Rangers (40,000), which are at the disposal of the Ministry of the Interior. By contrast, the Pakistan Navy, whose main role is to protect Pakistan's maritime interests and maintain the security of its sea lanes,[134] has a manpower strength of 24,000 active personnel, including 1,400 marines and a further 3,200 reserves. The Air Force consists of 45,000 active personnel and approximately 10,000 reserve personnel.[135]

Since independence in 1947 Pakistan's military capabilities have largely developed as a result of considerable military assistance from foreign governments. In contrast to many countries during the Cold War period which aligned themselves with either the West or the Soviet Union and China, Pakistan's preoccupation with the perceived threat from India prompted the country to seek military assistance from both the US, China and to a lesser degree from France and the UK at differing points during that period. In the 1950s and early 1960s the US, which was keen to counter the possibility of Soviet expansionism into South Asia, was the main donor of

[130] "Pakistan bids to boost defence budget for FY07", *Jane's Defence Weekly*, 20 June 2007.

[131] Pakistan has the second largest conventional force in the Central and Southern Asia region and the fifth largest in Asia as a whole behind China, India, North Korea and South Korea.

[132] See the *Military Balance 2007* for a breakdown of forces by role.

[133] Some sources have suggested that the reserve contingent of the Pakistani Army could be significantly higher at approximately 500,000 personnel.

[134] Due to Pakistan's topography almost 95% of Pakis tan's trade is transported by sea. *Jane's Defence Weekly*, 2 May 2007.

[135] Figures are taken from the IISS, Military Balance 2007, and *Military Technology: World Defence Almanac 2007*.

military assistance to Pakistan.[136] However, that assistance was suspended at the start of the Indo-Pakistan war in 1965 and only periodically reinstated during the next twenty five years until 1990 when assistance was suspended entirely in protest at Pakistan's development of a nuclear weapons programme.[137] In 2001 US military assistance was once again reinstated in response to Pakistan's key role in the fight against terrorism.[138]

Due to the inconsistency of relations with the US from the mid-1960s onwards Pakistan subsequently turned to China as the main supplier of both arms and other types of military aid. Over the last few decades China has played an important role in developing Pakistan's indigenous defence manufacturing capability through collaborative programmes and licensed production agreements and in modernising its armed forces with the supply of complete weapons systems at discounted prices.[139] That relationship was strengthened after the imposition of US sanctions on Pakistan in 1990. More recently, Beijing and Islamabad have signed a number of defence accords designed to boost bilateral co-operation. Yet it has been acknowledged that China's relationship with Pakistan has always been one of mutual benefit. Whilst China has been, and continues to be, the main supplier of conventional weapons systems to Pakistan, that assistance has been attributed to China's desire to maintain a strategic regional ally and prevent India from establishing a position of overwhelming conventional military superiority in the South Asia region.

Despite some efforts to achieve a degree of self sufficiency in defence manufacturing, Pakistan remains heavily dependent on external assistance. Therefore, since 2001 Pakistan has maintained relations with both the US and China, and to a lesser extent other arms exporting countries such as Sweden, France, the UK, Ukraine and Russia. According to SIPRI, between 2002 and 2006 Pakistan imported US$2bn worth of military equipment, making it the 14th largest recipient of major conventional arms in the world during this period.

Pakistan's current military equipment inventory is a subsequent reflection of these historical ties.[140] Its 313 combat capable fixed-wing fighter aircraft are a mixture of French Mirage III and Mirage V jets, US F-16s and Chinese F-7PG and F-7MG's equipped with requisite missiles. Its helicopter fleet

---

[136] Between 1953 and 1961 Pakistan received nearly $2bn in US assistance, one quarter of which was military aid. See Congressional Research Service, *Pakistan-US Relations*, 23 July 2007. Available at: http://italy.usembassy.gov/pdf/other/RL33498.pdf.

[137] Most notably, the suspension of aid resulted in the non-delivery of F-16 fighter aircraft that had been purchased by Pakistan in 1989.

[138] See also Part IV C of this Paper.

[139] China is also believed to have assisted in the development of Pakistan's nuclear weapons programme (see also Part IV D of this Paper).

[140] A comprehensive breakdown of Pakistani military equipment, by Service, is available in the IISS's *Military Balance 2007*.

consists mainly of French Alouette III and American Bell utility helicopters, American AH-1F Cobra and Russian Mi-24 Hind attack helicopters, and French Puma and Russian Mi-8 support helicopters. Pakistan's naval fleet is relatively small and consists of five French designed tactical submarines,[141] six ex-UK Type 21 frigates, three French mine countermeasures vessels and several domestically built patrol vessels. The Army's 2,461 combat capable main battle tanks are largely of, or based on, Soviet (T-80, T-54, T-55), Chinese (T-85, T-69, T-59) and US (M-48) design, although an increasing number are of the MBT2000 Al-Khalid design which has been produced domestically in collaboration with China. In addition, the Pakistan Army's armoured infantry fighting vehicles are a mixture of domestically produced vehicles along with US-designed and manufactured M-113's and the Soviet BTR-70.

Regardless of the extent of foreign military assistance provided to Pakistan and the size of its conventional forces, particularly its land forces, it is worth noting that with 1.3 million personnel in active service[142] and significantly more military assets, India retains considerable conventional military superiority over Pakistan.[143] As a result Pakistan has consistently relied on the deterrent effect of its nuclear capabilities as a means of offsetting that advantage.

3. Military Modernisation Programme

Motivated by India's extensive modernisation programme of its own conventional forces, in the last few years Pakistan has embarked upon an ambitious acquisition programme in an attempt to upgrade its own military forces.[144] Military and foreign credit assistance from overseas, particularly from China and the US, is central to that agenda, although in keeping with the trend of the last few years Pakistan has continued to maintain diversity in its supplier base.

The main recipients of modernisation thus far have been the Pakistan Air Force and Navy. In 2005 the US announced that it would resume the sale of F-16 aircraft to Pakistan, which had previously been halted in 1990. Under the deal, the Pakistan Air Force will acquire 18 new F-16C/D fighter aircraft equipped with AMRAAM missiles (with an option to acquire 18 more) and 26 used F16-A/B aircraft by 2008-2009. Pakistan is also understood to be planning the acquisition of 36 J-10 fighter aircraft from China in a deal worth US$1.2bn. In addition, 150 JF-17 fighter aircraft are being

[141] The majority of which were built under licence in Karachi.

[142] India also has 1.2 million reserves, 1.3 million paramilitary forces and a further 1 million paramilitary reserves.

[143] Further information on India's military capabilities is available in House of Commons Library Research Paper RP07/41, *A Political Introduction to India*.

[144] *ibid*.

manufactured domestically under a collaborative Pakistani-Chinese programme. In November 2006 China and Pakistan were also reported to have signed an agreement to jointly develop an AWACS aircraft.[145]

The Pakistan Navy is also set to acquire four F-22 light frigates from China, one of which is expected to be manufactured domestically under licence, in order to replace its ageing Type-21 fleet. The deal signed in 2005 is worth approximately US$600m, with the first vessel expected to be commissioned in 2009 and the remainder by 2013. At present, negotiations are also underway to acquire at least four new corvettes and to pursue a next-generation submarine capability following the recent decommissioning of the navy's four Daphne-class vessels. The vessels are expected to be produced domestically under licence and based on either French or German designs.

The development of a second generation of the Al Khalid main battle tank is also underway and is expected to become the backbone of the Army's fleet from 2012.

Since 2001 Pakistan has also received under the US military assistance programme six C-130 military transport aircraft, tactical radios, an air traffic control system, Harpoon anti-ship missiles, eight excess P-3C Orion maritime patrol aircraft and eight AH-1F Cobra attack helicopters.[146]

B. Nuclear Capabilities

Pakistan has been a self-declared nuclear weapon state since it, along with India, conducted a publicised series of nuclear tests in May 1998. The country's nuclear weapons programme began in the early 1970s following the 1971 war with India that led to East Pakistan becoming Bangladesh, although it was not until the late 1980s that the US concluded that Pakistan had acquired the capability to build a primitive nuclear device. US officials believe the Pakistani programme received material and technical assistance from China, although key information on uranium enrichment was also obtained by a leading Pakistani scientist working in the Netherlands during the mid-1970s.[147]

Nuclear weapons play a crucial role in Pakistan's military doctrine, being viewed as an essential safeguard to offset India's conventional superiority. Pakistan's comparatively small territory and 'lack of strategic depth' would give its military little defensive room for manoeuvre in the event of a major Indian attack. Possession of nuclear weapons is also a source of great

[145] IISS, *Military Balance 2007*, p. 306.
[146] Further detail is available in Congressional Research Service Report, *Pakistan-US Relations*.
[147] *'Pakistan Profile: Nuclear Overview'*, *Nuclear Threat Initiative* (NTI) website, last updated February 2006.

national pride, not least because Pakistan was the first, and thus far only, Muslim nation to acquire such a capability.

Despite its self-declared nuclear status, Pakistan is not recognised as a nuclear weapon state under the 1968 nuclear Non-Proliferation Treaty (NPT) and has consistently declined to join the treaty as a non-nuclear weapon state.[148] In its view, the NPT represents an attempt by the five recognised nuclear weapon states to cement in place an unfair advantage over the non-nuclear weapon states.[149]

Pakistan is generally assumed to have sufficient stocks of highly enriched uranium to build between 30 and 50 fission bombs.[150] By way of comparison, India is believed to have sufficient weapons-grade plutonium to produce between 40 and 90 weapons, depending on the sophistication of the warhead design.[151]

1. Ballistic Missile Development Programme

Pakistan's nuclear posture is predicated on two methods of delivery: by offensive strike aircraft such as the F-16 or Mirage and/or by land-based ballistic missiles.

Like its nuclear programme, Pakistan's ballistic missile development programme (BMDP) is driven by regional security imperatives and the fact that its conventional air forces are quantitatively inferior to those of the Indian Air Force. Pakistan has therefore focused on its BMDP as the most effective means of establishing a minimum deterrent against Indian conventional superiority. As Brigadier Naeem Ahmad Salik observed in an article in 2002:

> As is the case with nuclear weapons, Pakistan does not need to match India missile for missile. As long as it can field a modest missile force and can ensure its survivability against a surprise pre-emptive strike it has no cause for concern.[152]

---

[148] The NPT defines a nuclear weapon state as one that manufactured and exploded a nuclear weapon or other nuclear explosive device prior to 1 January 1967. India's first nuclear test, which it characterised as "a peaceful nuclear explosion experiment", was in 1974.

[149] The five nuclear weapon states recognised under the NPT are China, France, the Russian Federation, the United States and the United Kingdom. The other states parties—referred to as non-nuclear weapon states—are allowed to access peaceful nuclear technology but must forego nuclear weapons. A safeguards system under the auspices of the International Atomic Energy Agency (IAEA) is used to verify compliance and to prevent the diversion of fissile material for use in weapons.

[150] There are two main types of nuclear weapon: those that rely on nuclear fission (colloquially known as atomic bombs) and those more powerful devices that use nuclear fission and fusion (commonly referred to as thermonuclear or hydrogen bombs).

[151] Sources: '*India Profile*', updated September 2006, and '*Pakistan Profile*', updated April 2007, *Nuclear Threat Initiative* website.

[152] Brigadier Naeem Ahmad Salik, "Pakistan's ballistic Missile Development Program—Security Imperatives, Rationale and Objectives", *Strategic Studies*, Spring 2001.

In tandem with the nuclear programme, Pakistan embarked upon its BMDP in the 1980s and, like its nuclear programme, is widely believed to have benefited from extensive technical assistance from China. Co-operation with North Korea has also been highlighted.

Initial capabilities focused on the development of the short-range Hatf-1 and Hatf-2/Abdali missile, believed to have been based on the Chinese M-series of missile.[153] Each has a range and payload of 80-100km/500kg and 190km/500kg respectively. However, it was the test firing of the Ghauri-I missile, developed in co-operation with North Korea, in April 1998 that was considered a major breakthrough.[154] With a range of 1,500km and a payload of 700kg, the nuclear-capable Ghauri-I essentially provided Pakistan with a real deterrent capability, matching the abilities of the Indian Agni missile and giving Pakistan the ability to strike strategic targets throughout a substantial part of India.

Since 1998 Pakistan and India have embarked upon a tit-for-tat testing programme of their ballistic missile capabilities. In response to Indian testing of its intermediate-range Agni-II in 1999, Pakistan immediately conducted tests of an improved, longer-range version of the Ghauri-I (Ghauri-II) [155]and its newly developed Shaheen-I missile, believed to have been 'reverse engineered' with Chinese technical assistance from either the Chinese M-9 or M-11 missile.[156]

Subsequent tests of both the Ghauri-I and Ghauri-II took place in 2000, 2002, 2004, 2006 and more recently in February 2007. Testing of the Shaheen-II began in March 2005, with the most recent tests conducted in early 2007. Tests of the Hatf-2/Abdali missile were also conducted in March 2007.[157]

More recently, Pakistan has been reported to be developing a third generation Ghauri missile which has a range of 3,000km and an unspecified payload. Some analysts have suggested that the Ghauri-III is based on the North Korean Taepodong missile.[158] To date, it is understood that the missile has yet to be tested.[159] Further developments in Pakistan's ballistic missile inventory are also considered likely given the current emphasis by India on acquiring conventional military technologies that will enhance

153 On this basis, ongoing technical assistance from China has been considered likely. See Center for Defense Information, *Nuclear Weapons Database: Pakistan*. Available at: http://www.cdi.org/issues/nukef&f/database/panukes.html.

154 The Ghauri-I is believed to be based on the Nodong-1 missile. See: http://www.globalsecurity.org/wmd/world/pakistan/hatf-5.htm.

155 The Ghauri-II is believed to have a range of 2,300km and a payload of 700kg.

156 *SIPRI Yearbook 2006*.

157 In November 2005 India and Pakistan finalised an agreement to notify each other in advance of any ballistic missile tests in an attempt to reduce tension between the two countries.

158 *SIPRI Yearbook 2006*.

159 Centre for Nonproliferation Studies, *Pakistan's missile tests highlight growing South Asia nuclear arms race*, April 2007.

both its nuclear weapons delivery capabilities (next generation strike aircraft and unmanned aerial vehicles) and anti-ballistic missile defence systems. Such acquisitions could go some way to neutralising Pakistan's minimum deterrent. Some Pakistani analysts consequently believe that:

> The most cost effective means to counter New Delhi's strategic advantage and saturate its missile defenses is to improve Pakistan's missile arsenal, qualitatively and quantitatively.[160]

Indeed, in the last few years Pakistan's attempts to develop nuclear-capable cruise missile capabilities in addition to its ballistic missile inventory have been noted. Since 2005 Pakistan has been testing a short-range missile, codenamed 'Babur', which is capable of carrying either conventional or nuclear warheads. More recently in August 2007 Pakistan began initial testing on its latest Raad cruise missile. Although limited to a range of approximately 350km, the missile is capable of being launched from an airborne platform such as the Mirage.

2. Proliferation Concerns and the AQ Khan Network

Pakistan set up an extensive and covert international supply network during the 1970s and 1980s to support its nuclear weapons programme.[161] The public face of the nuclear programme was Dr. Abdul Qadeer (AQ) Khan, a scientist who had obtained centrifuge designs for uranium enrichment while working in Europe during the 1970s. By the early 1990s the black market supply network was increasingly working in reverse, with Khan engaging in the illicit transfer of nuclear enrichment and weapons technology to other countries. He is known to have sold technology to Iran, Libya and North Korea and to have offered it to Iraq and possibly to other, as yet unknown, countries.

Western intelligence agencies had become increasingly aware of those activities during the 1990s, although it was not until 2000 that it became clear the activities were not isolated incidents, but part of a concerted programme of proliferation. Attention increasingly focused on Libya, as Western concern grew about the potential spread of not only enrichment technology, but also the capability to build nuclear warheads for missiles. Intelligence gathering continued during 2001 and 2002 as Western Governments sought to uncover the full extent of the network and to identify the various financial and transportation links in the supply chain. Investigations revealed that Khan's network had transferred

[160] *ibid.*

[161] This section draws on information from the *Review of Intelligence on Weapons of Mass Destruction*, HC 898, 14 July 2004 (commonly known as the Butler Review), Chapter 2.2, paras 64–75; Wyn Q. Bowen, *Libya and Nuclear Proliferation: Stepping back from the brink*, IISS Adelphi Paper, Vol. 46, 380, 2006; and the IISS Strategic Dossier *Nuclear Black Markets: Pakistan, A.Q. Khan and the Rise of Proliferation Networks, A Net Assessment*, 2 May 2007.

weapons-related technology, centrifuge parts and blueprints, with little or no oversight from the Pakistani authorities.

By mid-2003 Western Governments had concluded that the risks of inaction were too great and steps were taken to intercept the transfer of centrifuge materials to Libya and to halt Khan's activities in Pakistan. AQ Khan, who is revered in Pakistan as a national hero, was arrested on 31 January 2004. He subsequently confessed on television in Pakistan to having undertaken the illicit transfer of nuclear weapons technology to a number of states, and was reported to have received millions of dollars from the transfers. Pakistani officials said Khan had claimed he had been motivated by a desire to enhance the security of other Muslim countries.[162] In return for cooperation with the investigation, AQ Khan received a presidential pardon but was placed under house arrest. Over two dozen of his associates were detained, although few appear to have received significant punishment for their role.[163] Pakistan says it has taken all the required steps to tighten its export control legislation and to prevent such incidents from happening again.

The AQ Khan network represented the first known case of a private enterprise offering a complete range of services to enable a customer to acquire highly enriched uranium for nuclear weapons. The revelations damaged Pakistan's international reputation and raised doubts about its ability to secure its own nuclear arsenal and to prevent further proliferation in the future. Some fear that the network may still be partially intact.[164] By contrast, India has come to be seen as a "responsible" state that has shown a strong commitment to combating nuclear proliferation. That reputation has earned India a pledge from the United States that civilian nuclear cooperation will resume after a hiatus of three decades.[165]

VI Development and Humanitarian Aid to Pakistan

Donors are aware that Pakistan's political and security challenges cannot be understood in isolation from those it simultaneously faces in the humanitarian and development spheres. Pakistan is one of the poorest countries in the world. In 2005 its per capita income was $670 and 24% of the population lived below the national poverty line in 2004/05.[166] Furthermore, in

162 'AQ Khan confesses to leaking nuclear secrets to Iran, Libya', *Agence France-Presse*, 2 February 2004
163 IISS Strategic Dossier *Nuclear Black Markets: Pakistan, A.Q. Khan and the rise of proliferation networks*, p. 8.
164 S. Cohen, "Pakistan and the Crescent of Crisis", in I. Daalder, N. Gnesotto and P. Gordon (eds), *Crescent of Crisis. US-European Strategy for the Greater Middle East* (Washington DC, 2006), p. 187.
165 For a fuller discussion of the US-India nuclear deal, see Library Standard Note SN/IA/4127, *US-India Nuclear Co-operation*.
166 Sources: *World Development Indicators Database*; DFID, *Pakistan Factsheet*, July 2007.

2004 only 52% of the population aged 15-64 was classed as economically active while unemployment stood at 7.7%.[167]

Some additional headline statistical indicators for Pakistan are shown in table 1 below:

Table 1. Selected Indicators: Pakistan

	2002	2003	2004	2005	2006	2007	2008
IMF data (a)							
Gross Domestic Product, current prices ($ million)	71,854	82,592	98,094	110,970	128,996	141,378	154,677
Gross Domestic Product, constant prices (annual % change)	3.2%	4.9%	7.4%	8.0%	6.2%	6.5%	6.5%
Inflation, consumer prices (annual % change)	2.5%	3.1%	4.6%	9.3%	7.9%	6.5%	6.0%
Current account balance ($ million)	2,833	4,061	1,811	−1,534	−4,996	−5,637	−5,600
Population (million)	143	147	150	153	155	158	161
World Bank data							
Gross National Income per capita, current prices ($)	490	520	600	670			
Exports of goods and services (annual % growth)	10.3%	32.9%	0.9%	−0.3%	0.9%		
Imports of goods and services (annual % growth)	4.5%	13.9%	16.3%	6.5%	4.5%		
External debt, total (current $ million)	33,672	36,345					

Note: (a) IMF data for 2006 onwards are estimates except inflation for which 2007 and 2008 data are estimates only.
Sources: World Bank, World Development Indicators Database; IMF, World Economic Outlook Database

[167] ILO, LABORSTA database: http://laborsta.ilo.org/. Unemployment rate is for all economically active aged 10 and over.

The World Bank's Country Assistance Strategy for Pakistan highlights the following key development challenges for the period to 2009:[168]

- Sustaining recent growth performance in order to generate significant poverty reduction
- Investing in infrastructure in order to support Pakistan's growth and service delivery goals
- Accelerating human development to ensure the poor participate in and benefit from Pakistan's growth
- Addressing Pakistan's poor social indicators compared with other countries at similar levels of per capita income and development
- Addressing governance challenges and combating corruption in order to improve the investment climate and strengthening the delivery of public services

A. Performance against the Millennium Development Goals

The Millennium Declaration, agreed at the UN Millennium Summit in September 2000, includes targets aimed at reducing world poverty and improving lives by 2015. These aims were subsequently translated into a set of eight goals (the Millennium Development Goals, or MDGs) with over 40 indicators used to assess progress; July 2007 marked the half-way point of progress towards the MDGs.

Pakistan has made steady progress towards most of the MDGs since 2000. However, DFID reported in a 2006 progress update that due to a low starting point and slow progress during the 1990s, many of the targets will be difficult to reach by 2015.[169]

Similarly, a 2006 report on progress towards the MDGs in Asia expressed concern that there was a "lack of effort" by Pakistan in key areas, which meant that the country was falling behind on some of the targets.[170] A particular problem highlighted was the fact that public expenditure on health and education as a proportion of GDP is low compared with other countries in the region and, in both cases, had fallen over the period since the late 1990s. Low expenditure in these areas was linked directly to the fact that the country's primary enrolment rate is the lowest in the region (68.1% in 2005) and its girls to boys ratio at the primary and secondary level are also among the region's lowest (around 0.75 in 2005); similarly, Pakistan has among the highest under-5 and infant mortality rates in the region (99 and 79 deaths per 1,000 live births respectively in 2005).[171]

[168] World Bank, *Country Assistance Strategy for the Islamic Republic of Pakistan for the Period FY06-09*, April 2006, pp. 2-7.
[169] DFID, *Pakistan and the MDGs*, August 2006, p. 1.
[170] UNDP, The Millennium Development Goals: Progress in Asia and the Pacific 2006, 2006, p. 11
[171] *ibid*. Data taken from MDGs database available at: http://mdgs.un.org/unsd/mdg/Default.aspx.

Table 2 below displays progress made towards some of the MDG indicator targets by Pakistan. As a result of data limitations, the table does not cover all the MDGs or all indicators towards the MDGs.[172]

Table 2. Progress towards the Millennium Development Goals in Pakistan

GOAL 1: Eradicate extreme poverty and hunger	
Proportion of population below $1 per day	Early achiever
Prevalence of underweight children under five years of age	Slow progress
GOAL 2: Achieve universal primary education	
Net enrolment ratio in primary education	On target
GOAL 3: Promote gender equality and empower women	
Ratio of girls to boys in primary education	Slow progress
Ratio of girls to boys in secondary education	On target
Ratio of girls to boys in tertiary education	Regressing
GOAL 4: Reduce child mortality	
Under-five mortality rate	Slow progress
Infant mortality rate	Slow progress
GOAL 6: Combat HIV/AIDS, malaria and other diseases	
HIV prevalence	On target
Prevalence and death rates associated with malaria	Early achiever
Prevalence and death rates associated with tuberculosis	Early achiever
GOAL 7: Ensure environmental sustainability	
Proportion of land covered by forest	Regressing
Ratio of area protected to maintain biological diversity to surface area	Early achiever
Carbon dioxide emissions per capita and	Regressing
Consumption of ozone depleting CFCs (OPD tons)	Regressing
Proportion of population with access to an improved water source, urban	Early achiever
Proportion of population with access to an improved water source, rural	Early achiever
Proportion of population with access to an improved sanitation, urban	Early achiever
Proportion of population with access to an improved sanitation, rural	On target

Source: UNDP, Millennium Development Goals: Progrwess in Asia and the Pacific 2006
http://www.mdgasiapacific.org/files/shared_folder/documents/MDG-Progress2006.pdf

[172] It should be noted that MDG targets apply irrespective of starting points and that some targets, in particular those under goals 1, 4, 5 and 7 are formulated in relative terms. Therefore, while Pakistan has by far the lowest primary enrolment rate in the region, it is classified as on track for this indicator because of its even lower enrolment numbers in the early 1990s.

Early achiever—Has already met the target
On target—Target is expected to be met by 2015 if prevailing trends continue
Slow progress—Target is expected to be met, but after 2015
Regressing—Slipping backwards or stagnating

B. International Development Aid

1. UK Assistance

Total UK aid disbursments to Pakistan since 2002/03 are displayed in table 1 below. Notably, in 2004/05 Pakistan received £23.1 million in debt relief from the UK, while the large increases in humanitarian assistance since 2005/06 are accounted for by the UK response to the earthquake in Pakistan in October 2005 (further details of which are provided in section 3 below). In 2005/06, Pakistan was the sixth largest recipient of UK bilateral aid, accounting for 2.2% of the total.

In December 2006, the UK Government signed a long-term Development Partnership Agreement with the Government of Pakistan.[173] Alongside this, the then Prime Minister Tony Blair announced a doubling of UK aid to Pakistan, from £236 million for the period 2005 to 2008, up to £480 million for the period 2008 to 2011. This assistance is in addition to humanitarian assistance provided for post-earthquake reconstruction (see Part VI C.1 below). The priorities for the increased aid to Pakistan will be set out in a new DFID Country Assistance Plan for Pakistan which is currently being consulted on.[174]

2. International Assistance

Total Official Development Assistance (ODA) to Pakistan is shown in table 4 below:

Pakistan was the 11th largest recipient of ODA in 2005, receiving $1.7 billion (1.6% of total ODA to developing countries and 3.7% of total ODA to Asia). In 2005, the US was the largest country donor to Pakistan accounting for 21.7% of total ODA to the country, while the UK was the fifth largest country donor (accounting for 3.8% of total disbursals). The largest overall donor was the World Bank (31.0% of total disbursals).

[173] See: http://www.dfid.gov.uk/countries/asia/pakistan/pakistan-dpa%20.pdf.
[174] The current DFID Country Assistance Plan for Pakistan which runs for the period 2005 to 2007 is available at: http://www.dfid.gov.uk/pubs/files/cappakistan.pdf.

Table 3. UK bilateral aid to Pakistan

£000s

	Financial aid								
	General poverty reduction budget support	Sector poverty reduction budget support	Other financial aid	Technical cooperation	Grants and other aid in kind	Humanitarian assistance	Total DFID bilateral programme	Aid from other UK official sources (a)	Total bilateral gross public expenditure
2002/03	20,000	0	11	8,579	9,498	226	38,314	8,538	46,852
2003/04	35,000	15,000	6	6,589	9,337	308	66,240	59	66,299
2004/05	0	7,500	5	9,680	14,051	140	31,377	23,901	55,277
2005/06	20,000	22,500	6	6,228	9,830	38,849	97,413	275	97,688
2006/07	20,000	15,000	25,471	11,943	13,006	15,699	101,118	..	..

Notes (a) Includes CDC investments, non-DFID debt relief, contributions from Other Government Departments to CSOs, British Council and Global Conflict Pool, and small amounts of drug related assistance funded by the Home Office and FCO.

. . . Denotes data not yet available.

Sources: DFID, Statistics on International Development 2005/06; DFID, Provisional Total DFID Bilateral Aid Expenditure 2006/07, 12 July 2007

Table 4. Total ODA to Pakistan

Current prices					
	Level ($ million)	Ranking (1 = largest recipient of ODA)	% of total ODA to Asia	% of total ODA to developing countries	UK as a % of total ODA to Pakistan
2000	692	14	4.3%	1.4%	3.4%
2001	1,942	1	11.6%	3.8%	1.4%
2002	2,128	2	11.2%	3.5%	3.1%
2003	1,062	13	5.3%	1.5%	10.6%
2004	1,424	10	6.2%	1.8%	6.4%
2005	1,666	11	3.7%	1.6%	3.8%

Source: OECD, DAC database, table 2a

C. Humanitarian Aid

1. Response to 2005 Earthquake

On 8 October 2005 an earthquake measuring 7.6 on the Richter scale struck with the epicentre close to Muzaffarabad, Pakistan. There was severe damage in North West Frontier Province and Pakistan-administered (Azad) Kashmir and some damage in Indian-administered Kashmir and Afghanistan. Some 3.5 million people and 500,000 families have been affected, with nearly 2.5 million people losing their houses and 2.3 million at risk of not being able to meet their own food needs. The estimated death toll in Pakistan was around 73,000 people, with 70,000 injured.

a. UK Response

The UK Government pledged an initial £58 million to assist with the humanitarian relief effort and a further £70 million over three years to help with the rebuilding as part of a total of $5.8 billion in aid from the international community.

Support included grants to UN agencies, the Red Cross Movement and nongovernmental organisations. Also, RAF Chinook helicopters were deployed and other military support, including Royal Engineers, was provided.[175] Assistance included:

- UK Search and Rescue teams—84 experts with 4 dogs—who rescued 13 of the total 24 survivors pulled from the rubble

[175] *HC Deb 24 November 2005 c138-9WS; HC Deb 17 March 2006 c2578-80W.*

- relief supplies including 9,000 winter tents, 165,000 tarpaulins, 40,000 sleeping mats and 204,000 blankets
- more than £10 million to support essential United Nations (UN) helicopter operations in areas with limited road access, including a cash grant, staff support, three Chinook helicopters for immediate airlift assistance and four Mi-8 helicopters that will operate until the end of April
- £13 million to non-governmental organisations such as Christian Aid, Islamic Relief, Merlin, World Vision, Oxfam and Save the Children for shelters, stoves, blankets, safe water, latrines and healthcare
- more than £4 million for 73 flights to help these organisations and the British Red Cross to fly relief items out to Pakistan
- £19.5 million to UN agencies for activities ranging from food distribution and shelter to helicopter and plane logistics and co-ordination activities
- £6.5 million to the Red Cross for a wide range of assistance; and
- a team of 89 Royal Engineer Commandos worked with Pakistani guides to reach remote mountain villages and build winter shelters[176]

On reconstruction, the UK's pledge of £70 million over three years includes:

- £5 million which has already been disbursed to reconstruct critical bridges, train teachers and administrators so as to get the education sector running effectively, detect and treat TB, and provide mental health support services
- £9 million which has already been disbursed to improve the Government's capacity to deal with the reconstruction effort, and to support the World Health Organisation in establishing an effective early-warning system for disease
- The remaining £56 million will be disbursed to the Government of Pakistan's Earthquake Reconstruction and Rehabilitation Authority in three parts. The first £17.5 million was released on 30 March 2007 for reconstructing housing, health, education and other facilities[177]

On 14 August 2006, the UK Government received the Sitara-i-Eisaar (Star of Sacrifice) award from Pakistan for its contribution to the relief effort.[178]

---

[176] *Investing in the future: Pakistan earthquake 6 months on* , DFID Press Release, 7 April 2006; http://www.dfid.gov.uk/news/files/emergencies/pakistan/pakistan-earthquake-sitrep44.pdf.

[177] *Pakistan Earthquake—Budget Support Begins*, DFID Press Release, 30 March 2007.

[178] *On Pakistan independence day UK receives award for Pakistan Earthquake relief effort*, DFID Press Release, 14 August 2006; *Pakistan Earthquake: What the UK did and what we're doing now*, DFID Press Release, 14 August 2006.

The Disasters Emergency Committee Asia Quake Appeal received pledges of more than £60 million from the UK public for the relief operation.[179]

b. International Response

To 14 August 2007, the United Nations Flash Appeal for the earthquake had received $367 million, 65.5% of the $561 million required, while a further $7.3 million has been pledged.[180] The UK is the third largest country donor to this appeal, behind the US and Norway. Donations from private individuals and organisations were more than any country except Norway.[181]

During the period immediately following the earthquake relief agencies commented that the international funding target had not been reached and that the response was slow. Oxfam said that the relief operation had been "hampered" by a lack of funds.[182] In November 2005, the then UN Secretary General, Kofi Annan, criticised the speed of the response:

> "I think there is no doubt that donors' response has been weak and tardy," he said ahead of today's donors conference in Islamabad. Mr Annan, who returned to Islamabad from a day-long trip to areas in Kashmir under Pakistan's control and parts of the northern region, said: "When the tsunami struck, at the 10-day point we have 80 per cent of the money we needed. In the case of Pakistan, at the 10-day point we had 12 per cent. Today, we have 30 per cent."[183]

Both the World Bank and Asian Development Bank have made over $1 billion available for reconstruction and rehabilitation, most of it as loans. In total, more than $6.5 billion has been pledged while $5.1 billion has been committed, of which around half as loans on concessional terms. In addition to the US and UK, Saudi Arabia, China, Japan, Iran and the United Arab Emirates are among the countries providing the most assistance.[184]

2. Response to 2007 Floods

Severe storms and cyclones in South Asia in June and July 2007 led to extensive flooding in Pakistan, where DFID estimate that 296 people have died, 377,000 have been made homeless, and 2.5 million affected in total.

---

[179] *DEC Press Release 6 October 2006.*

[180] ReliefWeb, *SOUTH ASIA—Earthquake—October 2005, Financial Tracking System.*

[181] ReliefWeb, *Flash Appeal: South Asia Earthquake 2005, Table G: Total Funding per Donor*, 14 August 2007.

[182] http://www.oxfam.org.uk/press/releases/asian_quake_160106.htm.

[183] "Annan chides earthquake response", *Financial Times*, 19 November 2005, p. 7.

[184] DAD Pakistan, *Earthquake-related Pledges and Commitments by Funding Source*, accessed on 14 August 2007.

The UK Government has committed up to £2.2 million to help with flood relief in Pakistan.[185] This has been allocated as follows:[186]

- £250,000 to the (Pakistani) Rural Support Programme Network
- £500,000 to the UN Food and Agriculture Organisation
- £250,000 to the UN, for them to allocate to urgent priorities
- £500,000 through the IFRC
- £600,000 to Oxfam, Mercy Corps and Islamic Relief (£200,000 each)
- £100,000 spent on key UN and Red Cross field experts

DFID has also provided human resources to assist the Pakistan Government and NGOs in responding to the floods.[187]

Internationally, the UN launched the Pakistan Cyclone and Floods Flash Appeal 2007 which, to August 14 2007, had received $7.7 million of the $38 million requested, with a further $3 million having been pledged.[188] The UK is the largest country donor to this appeal.[189]

Overall, total humanitarian assistance in response to the Pakistan floods currently stands at $16.6 million while a further $7.2 million has been pledged. The UK is again the largest country donor followed by Australia and then Canada, while donations from private individuals and organisations total $1.6 million.[190]

VII Conclusion: Future Prospects

The US Fund for Peace's *Failed States Index* for 2006 placed Pakistan as the ninth most failed state in the world, one place worse than Afghanistan.[191] The question of whether Pakistan 'can survive' has long been posed by analysts.[192] However, previous reports of its 'death' have proven premature.

Pakistan has been described as a case-study of "nationalism without a nation". An 'anti-India' ideology helped bring it into being in 1947. Some have argued that since then Pakistan has been bound together by what it is not, rather than by a positive vision of what it is. Many of its future

[185] *South Asia Floods: UK offers help*, DFID Press Release, 25 July 2007.
[186] *ibid.*
[187] *ibid.*
[188] ReliefWeb, *PAKISTAN—Floods/Cyclone—July 2007, Financial Tracking System.*
[189] ReliefWeb, *Flash Appeal: Pakistan Cyclone and Floods Flash Appeal 2007, Table G: Total Funding per Donor*, 14 August 2007.
[190] ReliefWeb, *PAKISTAN—Floods/Cyclone—July 2007*, Table B: Total Humanitarian Assistance per Donor, 14 August 2007.
[191] Available at: http://www.fundforpeace.org/programs/fsi/fsindex2006.php.
[192] For example, see Tariq Ali's *Can Pakistan Survive?* (Harmondsworth, 1983).

citizens, particularly those who did not live in states where Muslims were in a minority, were lukewarm about or hostile to the idea of Pakistan during the 1940s. The fragility of Pakistan was underscored by the loss of East Pakistan in the 1971 war with India. Some Pashtuns have hankered for an independent Pashtunistan composed of territory on both sides of the Afghan-Pakistan border. In Sindh, some Sindhis have flirted with the idea of their own state. In Baluchistan, the authorities have faced armed rebellions since 1947; there was a full-blown insurgency during the mid-1970s. Each of these ethnic nationalisms gained momentum from perceptions that Pakistan was becoming increasingly 'Punjabised' during the 1950s and 1960s.[193] These perceptions also contributed to the rise of 'Mohajir' (refugee) as an oppressed category during the 1980s.

Pakistan's civilian and military elites have been highly preoccupied since 1947 with maintaining equality and parity with India. This has become increasingly hard to sustain in recent decades as India's economy has expanded rapidly. If one issue has shaped the fragile ideology of 'anti-Indianness' that has sustained Pakistan, it is Kashmir.[194] Despite the many economic incentives that exist today to defuse if not resolve the conflict over Kashmir, some wonder how Pakistan would cope with the loss of this unifying cause.[195] This may partly help to explain why both civilian and military elites have often appeared reluctant in the past to engage in fresh thinking on the issue. For the military, Kashmir has also been the alibi it needed to justify high levels of defence spending year after year. For radical Islamists, Kashmir has become their most potent recruiting sergeant. President Musharraf has gone further than his predecessors towards trying to reframe Pakistan's relationship with India, but there is still a long way to go.[196]

By the 1970s, it looked as if the greatest threat to the survival of Pakistan was ethnic nationalism. However, while ethnic nationalist sentiments have far from wholly vanished, the threat does appear less acute today. Scholars point to the waning appeal of 'Pashtunistan' as confirmation that Pakistan

> [. . .] can defuse separatist movements, like India, even though it does not have the same culture of democracy and federalism: access to power—socioeconomic as well as political—are powerful factors of integration.[197]

---

193 Scholars have argued that the domination of Punjab is virtually unavoidable during periods of democratic rule in Pakistan, given that over half the constituencies in the National Assembly are located there. They also point out that Punjab itself is divided by linguistic group and along socio-economic lines. C. Jaffrelot (ed), *Pakistan. Nationalism without a Nation*? (New Delhi, 2002), pp. 31–2.

194 *Ibid.*, p. 38.

195 K. Shamsie, "How Pakistanis see India", *Guardian*, 14 August 2007.

196 *Ibid.* To a significant extent, Pakistan has played a similar ideological role with regard to India until recently. However, the existence of other unifying narratives—for example, 60 years of democratic government—has meant that India's national identity has been less wholly dependent on the threat of the 'other' next door..

197 C. Jaffrelot (ed), *Pakistan. Nationalism without a Nation?* (New Delhi, 2002), p. 25.

However, Pakistan, despite some successes in this regard, remains less effective overall than India in defusing separatist threats. The case of Baluchistan demonstrates this—as does recent evidence of growing discontent in the Federally Administered Northern Areas. The army, unsurprisingly, has tended to prefer military solutions to political ones. Its excesses have often reinforced separatist currents rather than diminished them.[198] The threat of ethnic nationalism is far from extinguished in Pakistan.

General Zia's policies of 'Islamisation', which ran deep both within the military and across significant sections of Pakistani society, were in part an attempt to inoculate the country against the disease of ethnic nationalism. While he did not invent the strategy of appealing to Islam as a force for order and unity when faced by nationalist threats, he took matters to a new level. Subsequent leaders, including Benazir Bhutto and Nawaz Sharif, were able or inclined to do little to counter his legacy.[199] Here too, Musharraf has arguably done more than they did when in power. For some analysts, the 'Islamic cure' has turned out to be as dangerous to the idea of Pakistan as the original disease.

While the idea of Pakistan still has resonance for many Pakistani radical Islamists, it is often as the means to an end—the spread of Islamic law, values and beliefs—rather than as the end in itself. When Pakistan ceases to be viewed as a reliable means to these ends, radical Islamists are prepared to turn against its present rulers. However, there are few signs yet that concepts of going 'beyond Pakistan', such as those espoused by some 'transnational jihadis', are gaining much appeal.

A further limitation upon the deployment of an ideology of 'Islamisation' as a unifying force in Pakistan has been its overwhelmingly Sunni character. While to an extent this simply reflects the fact that the Sunnis are in the majority in Pakistan, it has opened the way for growing Sunni-Shia sectarianism, not to mention the persecution of those minorities that profess non-Islamic religious beliefs.[200] Cynics might claim that this was not entirely accidental. History is full of examples where internal enemies have been 'manufactured' in the context of efforts to bind majority communities more strongly together. Sunni-Shia sectarianism has also been fuelled by "socio-economic rivalries between the Sunni urban middle class and the Shia landed elite."[201]

---

198 Grare, *Pakistan: The resurgence of Baluch nationalism*, p. 3.

199 Bennett-Jones, *Pakistan*, p. 17.

200 For a good report on this issue, see Amnesty International, *Pakistan: Insufficient Protection of Religious Minorities*, May 2001. Available at: http://web.amnesty.org/library/index/engASA330082001?OpenDocument. For a 2002 report by the Minority Rights Group, see: http://www.minorityrights.org/?lid=1034.

201 Bennett-Jones, *Pakistan*, p. 34.

While religious sectarianism is a major problem in Pakistan today, it does not currently pose a threat to the survival of the state itself. Nevertheless, some analysts see it as potentially the greatest threat of all to the idea of Pakistan:

> It puts the very notion of Pakistan into question since it demonstrates that Islam cannot be the only cementing ideological force behind the nation. This development is more challenging than ethnic separatist movements because it takes place in the heartland of Pakistan—the NWFP and Punjab—and amounts to a kind of ethnicisation of Islam.[202]

So while the question, 'can Pakistan survive?' is a valid one, an equally important question is: if Pakistan does survive, what are its likely prospects? It is certain, in the short- to medium-term, to remain a 'weak state', given the factors outlined above. Paradoxically, it is this structural weakness that has provided the rationale since independence for supporters of a strong role for the military in the country's politics and economy. Pakistan has been ruled by a series of civilian-military alliances since its birth. Sometimes these have taken the form of periods of direct military rule. However, these have alternated with periods of civilian rule. It is possible that today Pakistan is heading for what some have called "indirect rule" by the military through an alliance with part of the civilian elite. This could involve the PPP if negotiations between Musharraf and its leader, Benazir Bhutto, bear fruit.[203]

It is possible that the cycle will be broken this time around. However, neither Nawaz Sharif, the other opposition civilian leader who has been in exile, nor the Islamic political parties are likely candidates to lead such a break with the past; both have previously been closely allied with the military when it suited them. The present strains in the long-established alliance between the 'mullahs and the military' centre mainly on the person of Musharraf rather than on the military as an institution. While some analysts argue that under Musharraf radical Islam has expanded its power to the point where a 'take-over' of the state is no longer out of the question, others point to the fact that in 2002 its share of the vote, while increased, was still only 11%. The electoral process appears highly unlikely to deliver power to radical Islam. Others note that there are now significant Islamist currents within the military. These have been increased by the changing social composition of the army, which has drawn more heavily upon the lower middle class in recent decades. But most observers argue that these currents are not strong enough to warrant fears that the military might

202 Bennett-Jones, *Pakistan*, p. 36.
203 Hussain, *Frontline Pakistan*, p. 23.

spearhead a radical Islamic 'take-over'.[204] One goes so far as to talk about "the myth of an Islamist peril", stating:

> No Islamic organisation has ever been in a position to politically or militarily challenge the role of the one and only centre of power in Pakistan: the army . . . Although the military remains opaque, there is so far no evidence that it has been widely infiltrated, much less controlled, by the Islamists . . . Although Islamists are undoubtedly present, there is no reason to believe that their numbers are significantly greater than in the rest of Pakistani society.[205]

For the military, one important reason for supporting the radical Islamic parties has been to keep the pressure on more secular opposition parties which potentially pose a much greater political threat to its power and legitimacy. Some go so far as to allege that the spectre of an 'Islamic threat' also helps to keep Western support coming in—above all, arms sales—and persuades both Pakistanis and international donors that only the military can contain it.[206]

Increasing numbers of Pakistanis appear to be questioning whether the military's image of itself as the sole guarantor of the country's security and stability really holds up under scrutiny.[207] One analyst has anatomised the stranglehold that the military has over the economy and the way in which this has promoted rampant corruption and retarded development. She has written:

> Pakistan's military today runs a huge commercial empire. Although it is not possible to give a definitive value of the military's internal economy because of lack of transparency, the estimated worth runs into billions of dollars. Moreover, the military's two business groups—the Fauji Foundation and the Army Welfare Trust—are the two largest business conglomerates in the country. Besides these, there are multiple channels through which the military acquires opportunities to monopolize national resources.[208]

She argues that the extent of the military's interests in the economy reflects the fact that it is a "predatory institution". These interests also strengthen its determination to retain political control over Pakistan. She adds that civilian elites have in general acquiesced in, and often benefited from, their links to the military's 'internal economy'.[209]

---

[204] Although Bennett-Jones questions whether the army would fire on civilians in the event of an 'Islamic revolution'. *Pakistan*, pp. 257–61.

[205] F. Grare, "Pakistan: The Myth of an Islamist Peril", *Carnegie Policy Brief No. 45*, February 2006, pp. 1–3.

[206] *Ibid.*, pp. 4–5.

[207] T. Ali, "The General in his labyrinth", *London Review of Books*, 4 January 2007.

[208] A. Siddiqa, *Military Inc. Inside Pakistan's Military Economy* (London, 2007), p. 2.

[209] *Ibid.*, pp. 2, 29 and 107.

In the political sphere, there are currently two main symbols of the entrenched role of the military. First, there is the National Security Council, the creation of which the military has long campaigned for. Finally established under Musharraf, it is chaired by the Head of State. Aside from the Prime Minister and the Chief Ministers of Pakistan's four Provinces, its members also include the heads of the army, airforce and navy. Second, there is the constitutional power of the Head of State to dismiss Parliament—and by extension, an elected government. Overall, Musharraf has established, through a series of political and constitutional manoeuvres, a presidential system of government during his period in power. The support of the radical Islamist parties has been crucial to this endeavour.

For critics of the military, only genuine democracy offers a way forward for Pakistan. In the light of the 'faustian bargains' that civilian elites have been willing to strike with the military over the decades, some analysts have begun to talk recently of a possible 'democratic revolution from below'. The mass protests that followed the suspension of Chief Justice Chaudhry in mid-2007 are seen as a possible portent. There are certainly developments that provide hope for supporters of this idea. The senior judiciary and legal profession are increasingly independent and assertive and Pakistan's media is now remarkably diverse; the last five years has seen the emergence of a vibrant private broadcasting sector. Civil society groups could yet have a major role to play in ending Musharraf's hopes of remaining President. But liberal-democratic forms of politics are still a long way from being dominant in a country where political relationships continue to operate predominantly on patron-client principles and where conservative forms of Islam remain powerful. One commentator has argued that "the educated middle class—which in India gained control in 1947—is in Pakistan largely excluded from the political process."[210]

An important constraining factor in terms of the likelihood of a 'thoroughgoing democratic transition', although it is sometimes overlooked, is the enduring political and economic power of Pakistan's feudal landlords in Sindh and Punjab. Not only are these landlords usually very wealthy, they effectively are the law at local level, responsible for functions that in most other countries would be carried out by the state—for example, meting out punishments for alleged crimes and conducting divorce proceedings. Past attempts at limiting their power, including through redistributive land reform, have been ineffective—perhaps not least because they have always been strongly represented within Pakistan's political elite.[211] The Bhutto family is a major landowner in Sindh Province. There are few signs yet of

[210] William Dalrymple goes so far as to call Pakistan's democracy a "form of elective feudalism". "A friend of feudalism", *Guardian*, 1 September 2007.

[211] President Musharraf promised land reform after seizing power in 1999 but, like his military predecessors, has not really been able to deliver. Bennett-Jones, *Pakistan*, pp. 242–9.

the emergence of social movements that might be able significantly to reduce the power of the feudal landlords while potentially offering a stronger base for genuine pro-democratic currents in society.

A 2006 report by the Carnegie Endowment for Peace predicted that neither the US nor EU Governments would seriously protest f Musharraf successfully bent the rules to ensure his re-election.[212] The US and EU member Governments, preoccupied above all with Pakistan's security role, appear to have decided that some kind of 'managed transition' of the type that has been discussed by representatives of Musharraf and Benazir Bhutto over recent months is the least-worst option available. But this carries with it the danger of perpetuating a sterile cycle of civilian-military alternation in which radical Islam is as often accommodated as confronted within Pakistan.[213] Numerous analysts also claim that a 'stitch up' between them could rapidly unravel, plunging Pakistan even further into instability.[214] In short; there is no guaranteed match-up between Western preferences with regard to Pakistan in the short-term and wider long-term politico-security objectives.

A. Appendix Map of Pakistan

Please note: Map intended for briefing purposes only and should not be taken as necessarily representing a particular view on boundaries or political status.

[212] "Emperor's new clothes", *Guardian*, 31 October 2006. For the report, see F. Grare, "Islam, the Military and the 2007 elections" (July 2006). Available at: http://www.carnegieendowment.org/publications/index.cfm?fa=view&id=18553&prog=zgp&proj=zsa.

[213] Frederic Grare proposes an alternative approach in "Rethinking Western Strategies toward Pakistan: An Action Agenca for the United States and Europe", *Carnegie Endowment for International Peace*, 2007.

[214] Tariq Ali, "The lifeline thrown to Musharraf could sink him", *Guardian*, 31 August 2007; "The scramble for power in Pakistan", *Financial Times*, 31 August 2007.

Map No. 4181 Rev 1 UNITED NATIONS
January 2004

Department of Peacekeeping Operations
Cartographic Section

DOCUMENT NO. 31

A MESSAGE FROM SHEIKH AYMAN AL-ZAWAHIRI TO PAKISTAN

August 10, 2008

[This document is the transcript of a statement obtained by NEFA investigators on behalf of the NEFA TerrorWatch subscription service. This transcript is provided for educational and informational purposes only. For more statements from Al-Qaida's leadership, see: http://www.nefafoundation.org/documents-aqstatements.html.]

"My Muslim brothers and sisters in Pakistan, I want to speak to you today regarding the miserable condition to which Pakistan has deteriorated. I have decided to speak to you today in English, the thing I dislike not from a nationalistic point of view because Allah knows that we are among the fiercest enemies of nationalists and their like, who believe in the Western democratic system and British judicial and legislative system instead of the Law of Allah, (to whom be ascribed all perfection and majesty) and who have divided the Muslim Ummah and been the cause of some of the worst catastrophes the Ummah has faced in her modern history. But rather, I don't like to speak in English for a number of other reasons."

"First of all, it isn't the language of the Holy Quran, which should be the language of communication between Muslims or at least, it is not one of the languages of the Muslims which can be alternative language of communication. I hope that one day the Westerners embrace Islam and their languages become part of the family of Muslim languages. But till that day comes the English language is the language of the Muslims' enemies who have occupied their lands forcibly implanted Israel in their midst looted their resources tortured, deported, and killed them and aided, supported, and enforced the corrupt tyrant regimes which are sucking our blood and replacing our divine (Shariah) with manmade laws. It is the language which we didn't choose but are forced to use due to our weakness and dependency."

"Secondly; it is not my mother tongue through which I am able to express my ideas in the best possible manner keeping in mind that the Arabic language is considered to be one of the richest broadest and most beautiful languages on Earth. But unfortunately, most of you don't understand the Arabic language and sadly, I am unable to speak in Urdu that charming language otherwise, I wouldn't hesitate to speak in it."

"Therefore, and in spite of all that I have mentioned I have decided to speak to you today in English in order to communicate directly with you and draw your attention as much as I can to the imminent and grave dangers which are facing Pakistan. So from the start I beg your pardon for my weak English language which I have only partially mastered."

"The second thing I wish to beg your pardon for; is that for me and for all my brothers who have lived in Pakistan for some time it is difficult to remain detached and neutral on issues relating to Pakistan because we have a deep emotional and sentimental relationship with this land and its peoples. All of us have enjoyed the warm welcome and the caring attitude of most Pakistanis which has been so evident during the current crusade being carried out in Pakistan by Pervaiz and his hunting dogs in compliance with the orders of their masters in Washington."

"And for me personally Pakistan is an old love from my childhood days because my grandfather Professor Abd-ul Wahhab Azzam was a great lover of Allama Iqbal. He was the first to translate his poems into Arabic poetry and among his many books was one about Allama Iqbal. I read that book and much of his Arabic translations of Piam-e-mashriq, Armaghan-e-Hijaz, Zarb-e-Kaleem and other divans early in my life and as I grew up Pakistan represented for me as well as for many millions of Muslims a hope and a dream of establishing a strong independent Muslim government after the colonial era. I came face to face with that hope in reality in the summer of 1980 when I came to Pakistan for the first time, to treat the Afghan muhajireen and mujahideen."

"And from that time until I along with thousands of other sincere Muslims supporting the Afghan jihad was forced to leave Pakistan at the behest of the Crusader Americans in the early nineties I stayed no less than six years in Pakistan mostly in Peshawar that charming city which I still admire greatly. And during my time there I came to know its ins and outs like any real Peshawarite. Throughout that time I, like thousands of my brothers, mixed thoroughly with Pakistani society and I was blessed to have at that time some fine Pakistani friends and brothers whom I hope still remember me today."

"As I said before, I came into actual contact with what I considered to a hope. And by living in Pakistan I was given the opportunity by the grace of Allah to develop a deep understanding of the complex goods and evils of Pakistan. Moreover, I was able to compare the common powers and ills of many different Muslim societies. And after all those years and experiences I still consider Pakistan to represent a hope and a bastion for the establishment of a strong independent Muslim country not only in the post-colonial era but also in the face of the contemporary Zio-Crusader campaign. This hope is not based on the so-called 'Theory of Pakistan' which has now vanished particularly after the engagement of the Pakistani army and security agencies in the American war against Islam and the massacre of the Red Mosque. Rather, it is based on my belief that there are millions of Muslims in Pakistan ready to sacrifice all that can be sacrificed for the victory of Islam."

"When I was living in Pakistan it was difficult for me to imagine that one day we would be thrown out of Pakistan or that the liberators of Afghanistan and the defenders of Pakistan would be overnight declared the so-called Terrorists and pursued in every nook and cranny of the country. To this day there lies next to the border gate of Turkham a silent graveyard containing the remains of approximately two hundred Arab mujahideen and standing as a living material witness to how the rulers of the rulers of the so-called Islamic Republic of Pakistan betrayed their Muslim brothers who inflicted no harm on Pakistan and committed no sin other than sacrificing their souls (in Allah's path) to liberate Afghanistan. After that, life taught me to be more realistic and I stumbled upon the bitter reality that these greedy rulers were not only prepared to betray their Muslim brothers and deport them from Pakistan but were also prepared to kill and arrest their innocent and cooperative Muslim neighbors and to help and support the neo-crusaders in occupying their lands bombing and burning their villages and overthrowing their honest Islamic Emirate and replacing it with a corrupt anti-Pakistan puppet regime made up of traitors and drug traffickers many of whom are loyal to India and Russia."

"And not only that but they are also prepared to kill their own citizens and demolish their houses over the heads of their women and children. They are even prepared to destroy mosques and madrassas and kill thousands of innocent male and female students just to appease and please their masters who pay them the neo-crusaders in the White House. This greedy gang worships its salaries benefits and bribes and if you pay them enough they are prepared to do whatever you would like them to do however dirty it might be and not in the dark or behind the scenes but in the full light of day, in uniform and under the motto (Faith, Allah fearing, Jihad in Allah's path)."

"Therefore, my message today to every Pakistani Muslim sincere in his love for Islam and his Prophet (peace be upon him) is to rise up to his religious and moral responsibility and to ask himself specific serious crucial questions. Is the Pakistan Army an army defending Muslims? Or merely a security service agency or a band of mercenaries which kills Muslims to please those who pay it the neo-Crusaders in the White House? And what do these American masters really think of the Pakistan Army? Can any Pakistani serving in such an army or directly contributing to his government's criminal role in the modern anti-Islam crusade the so-called 'war on terror,' really be a sincere Muslim? Or is he simply an enemy of Islam violating the fundamental principles of Quran and Sunnah? Does anything by the name of 'the Theory of Pakistan' still exist? Or has it drowned in the innocent blood spilled in the name of the war on terror or perhaps been crushed under the ruins of the Red Mosque?"

"Regarding the first question it is evident that for years the Pakistan Army's primary duty has been to take part both directly as well as indirectly in the killing of Muslims from Kabul to Islamabad. It has through the orders of its greedy commanding officers been transformed into an army which, instead of acting as the defender of the Ummah is in fact posing the greatest of dangers to the dignity, safety and property of Muslims in South Asia and the Middle East and is even threatening the very existence of Pakistan."

News Footage

"Just compare the practices of the Pakistan Army with its famous motto and you will discover that the writing of such a motto on army buildings is nothing more than a silly joke. Let me, my brothers and sisters remind you here of just some of the crimes committed by Pervaiz and his bribe seeking gang against Muslims inside and outside Pakistan. Pervaiz has proven himself to be one of the biggest enemies of Islam in Pakistan, if not the biggest. He declared in his first statement after his takeover of the presidency as he hugged his two dogs that his ideal and role model is Ataturk who destroyed the Khilaafat killed the Ulamaa, banned the Hijab and forcibly imposed secularism upon Turkey."

"In accordance with the orders of the neo-Crusaders Pervaiz offered all the support necessary to topple the Islamic Emirate in Kabul and with that the government of Pakistan killed the hope the Muslim Afghan nation fought twenty years to achieve and for which millions of Muslims and thousands of Mujahideen laid down their lives an Islamic state in Afghanistan and with that it accomplished the old objective of America and the West which they had tried their best to realize after the Russian defeat to establish a broad-based government made up of secularists, atheists, Communists, war lords, and agents of the West. It was an objective which they themselves had failed to achieve despite all their attempts but the Pakistani government was able to accomplish it for them."

"Pervaiz has tried his best to put as many obstacles as he could in the path of the Islamic madrassas in Pakistan. And he invented a new religion devoid of jihad, (Enjoining of good and forbidding of evil) and adherence to the rules of (shariah) a religion which he described as 'enlightened moderation,' thus presenting a new American-sponsored Qadyaneiah to revive the old British-sponsored one."

"Almighty Allah says, '*Who, then, is more unjust than he who forges a lie against Allah that he should lead astray men without knowledge? Surely Allah does not guide the unjust.*;' And Allama Iqbal said: 'He may change the Ka'aba into a Magian fire home if he wishes or may install the European idol in it if he wants. He may make of Quran a plaything of interpretation. And invent a new Shariah if he wants'."

"Pervaiz destroyed the very grounds for the existence of Pakistan and shattered the 'Theory of Pakistan' when he joined the war on terror in which he assaulted his own Muslim people their Muslim neighbors and their Supporters and when he massacred the students of the Red Mosque by demolishing it over their heads, Lest we forget, dividing Pakistan continues to be a permanent joint Indian-American aim and the leadership of the Pakistan army has helped extensively to achieve this goal by launching military operations against the people of Pakistan."

"As regards the Red Mosque what did its destruction and the massacre committed within it expose? It exposed the corruption which prevails in the Pakistani military, bureaucracy and political establishment It was and is a bleeding wound in the conscience of every free, sincere Muslim. Beneath the ruins of the Red Mosque the 'Theory of Pakistan' was buried and the goal of its creation was lost and over the dead bodies of those martyrs the American, Zionist and Indian flags were raised high."

"The assaults on the Red Mosque and the tribal areas exposed the ugly anti-Islamic face of the military leadership of Pakistan. In the tribal areas, it partially succeeded in concealing the real crimes but in the Red Mosque the bomb's fumes mixed with the smell of the student's charred flesh, spread to every corner of Pakistan and the massacre was covered by both the local and foreign media."

"The massacre at the Red Mosque exposed the ugliness and hypocritical double standards of Western civilization for had a single church been attacked and a single American or Briton killed a violent wave of protest would have flared up perhaps ending with Security Council sanctions but when the Red Mosque is stormed and those inside it are killed and the exact number of victims and even the location of their remains is concealed, it's treated as being nothing more than a security operation, to pacify some fanatics."

"The massacre at the Red Mosque by the Rangers, elite commandos, regular Army and agents of the ISI and Military Intelligence is a disgrace for every officer and soldier in Pakistan. And it provokes a very serious question: Is the Pakistani army defending Islam in Pakistan and South Asia? Or attacking it for the benefit of the Muslims' enemies? Does it represent the shield of Muslims in Pakistan or is it the criminal heir to the British Indian Army? Pervaiz has seriously threatened the national security of Pakistan. Pervaiz is the one who fully supported the Americans in toppling the Islamic Emirate in Kabul and replacing it with the regime loyal to India and hostile to Pakistan."

Brief News Footage

"As a result of that, Indian intelligence sneaked into the Afghan-Pakistan border region and opened its consulates in the cities adjacent to Pakistan. With the Islamic Emirate's departure from Kabul the Pakistani army's loss was twofold. First, it lost the strategic depth which Afghanistan with its high altitude terrain and mountains can afford during any confrontation with India."

"Secondly, the back of the Pakistani army became exposed to a hostile regime loyal to its enemies. And if you add to this the success of India in making use of air bases in Tajikistan and her efforts to expand military cooperation with the Central Asian states the extent of the strategic blunder the Pakistani army committed becomes apparent Pervaiz is the one who has put Pakistan's nuclear program in jeopardy by allowing it to fall under American surveillance thus making Pakistan's national secrets available to Jewish and Indian intelligence. The American accusations against Abdul Qadir Khan were used as an excuse to justify that."

News Interview and Footage

"However, is it logical that Abdul Qadir Khan was outside the surveillance of Pakistani intelligence? Whether or not that is really the case the first ones to be tried in the Abdul Qadir Khan case should be the high commands of the Pakistani army and intelligence with Pervaiz at their head. But Abdul Qadir Khan was used as a scapegoat to appease the Americans."

News Interview

"Pervaiz is the one who has ignited civil war inside Pakistan by indulging in a fruitless bloody struggle in the tribal areas in blind obedience to American orders resulting in catastrophic harm to Pakistan national security. The worst situation any army could possibly imagine is to be responsible for defending its borders even as it is entangled in an internal civil conflict Pakistan's collective memory has not yet forgotten the dire consequences of the civil war in East Pakistan."

"And everything that Pervaiz and his generals have done in Waziristan, Bajaur, Swat and Balochistan they will not hesitate to repeat in Karachi, Lahore, Peshawar and any other place the Americans order them to strike. Pervaiz is the one who has tried to change the combat doctrine of the Pakistani armed forces by repeatedly insisting that the real threat against Pakistan lies within and doesn't come from outside. The enemy is not outside, the enemy is within. We will have to handle the inside enemy."

"That is to say, he is urging the Pakistani armed forces to concentrate on fighting their own people and ignore the Indian threat. And when the combat doctrine of any army is corrupted and its service becomes merely for the sake of post and salary this army will without a doubt flee the battlefield at any real confrontation. How can the Pakistani officer or soldier be convinced that he is protecting Islam when he has enabled the Americans to kill tens of thousands of Muslims in Afghanistan and helped them to remove the Islamic Emirate from Kabul? How can the Pakistani officer or soldier be convinced that he is protecting the honor of the Pakistani people when he is being ordered by his superiors to kill women and children inside his own country? How can the Pakistani officer or soldier be convinced that he is safeguarding the dignity and high repute of Pakistan when he receives orders from his commanders to launch a new massacre with every visit of a senior American official?"

"Thus, Pervaiz has dealt severe blows to the morale of the Pakistani army twice the first time was when he ordered it to launch an immoral anti-Islam war against its own people as mercenaries under the American flag and the second was when he exposed the army to repeated humiliating defeats at the hands of the brave Islam-defending tribal fighters. Pervaiz is trying to sell Kashmir at any available price."

"He stated in March 2004 that he wants to conduct a national dialogue about possible solutions for Kashmir including local autonomy joint Indo-Pak administration and UN supervision! He has strangled the jihadi resistance to India. He has offered and is still offering repeated concessions in the Kashmir issue, whereas India has not retreated a single inch from its obstinate stance. He is trying to mislead the Muslim Ummah in Pakistan by falsely claiming that the problem with India will be solved through confidence-building measures in an attempt to end the struggle for the liberation of Kashmir the core issue between India and Pakistan. And he is the one targeting the Arab mujahideen and their brothers from all over the Muslim world who are considered to be one of the most important keys to the liberation of Kashmir just as they played a crucial part in the liberation of Afghanistan before."

"I wish to stress here the vital fact that the jihad to liberate Kashmir should first be liberated from the ISI because corrupt governments spoil jihads.

These governments defer to the wishes of the superpowers, and no jihad will succeed unless it is freed from the wishes of the enemies of Islam. Pervaiz has practically recognized Israel in an attempt to mentally prepare the Pakistani people for the recognition of a non-Muslim state in Kashmir. Pervaiz has insulted and compromised Pakistan's sovereignty by allowing the CIA and FBI to operate freely in Pakistan and arrest, interrogate, torture, deport, and detain any person whether Pakistani or not for as long as they like thus turning the Pakistani army and security agencies into hunting dogs in the contemporary crusade."

News Interview

"It is no secret that the Americans have exclusive control of many Guantanamo-like detention centers on Pakistani soil. Pervaiz and his greedy gang have committed all the crimes because of which Pervaiz claimed he took power so he could save Pakistan from their evils. If you were to read his memoirs you would find no single sin of which he accused Benazir and Nawaz which he himself has not committed subsequently. And because Pervaiz is thirsty for money and a bribe-seeker he is always trying to convince the people of Pakistan to look out only for their own material interests regardless of any Islamic or moral consideration"

"What do we want in Afghanistan?"

"We want peace in Afghanistan."

"Why do we want this?"

"I have said before; 'First comes Pakistan.'"

"What is Pakistan's interest? Pakistan has the greatest interest in it."

"When there will be peace in Afghanistan?"

"The economy of the central Asian Republics that I explained before . . . their trade, their oil, their gas . . . all this will come here and go through Pakistan . . . go through Afghanistan and Pakistan. When there will be peace and development in Afghanistan, Pakistan's Foreign exchange will increase, Pakistan's economy will uplift. This is exactly the same logic of drug traffickers, white slavery mafias spies and traitors."

"Almighty Allah has said: 'Shaitan threatens you with poverty and enjoins you to be niggardly and Allah promises you forgiveness from Himself and abundance and Allah is Ample-giving, Knowing.' But you will see those in whose hearts is a disease Hastening towards them saying: 'We fear lest a calamity should befall us but it may be that Allah will bring the victory or a punishment from Himself, so that they shall be regretting on account of what they hid in their souls'."

"Now another 'Pervaiz' namely, Pervaiz Ishfaq Kiyani has taken over the same duties that the old 'Pervaiz' used to perform for the US and accordingly we see him as an equally hostile enemy of Islam."

News Footage

"In all the aforementioned examples we shall be fools, if we don't recognize the American factor in the politics of Pakistan which is virtually ruled from the American embassy. And now, and after all those services provided by Pervaiz and his greedy gang to the Americans, let us take a look at how the Americans view the Pakistani army and security agencies."

News Interview

"Let me remind my brothers and sisters of the cartoon which appeared in the American press after the arrest of brother Abu Faraj Al-Libi may Allah release him soon showing an American soldier patting a hunting dog and asking him to bring Osama Bin Laden may Allah protect him. The American may like his dog play with it, feed it, smile at it and may even kiss it."

"But after all is said and done it is still a dog."

"Let me remind my brothers and sisters that the present army chief Pervaez Kiyani was the senior hunter of Abu Faraj may Allah release him soon. That's the American psychological perception of the Pakistani army and security agencies in spite of all the smiles and compliments. In contrast, we have solid proof of American alignment with India in their advanced cooperation with it, particularly in the nuclear and high technology field, as as well as in military training."

"The parable of all those who take guardians besides Allah Is as the parable of the spider that makes for itself a house and most surely the frailest of the houses is the spider's house, did they but know."

"And whoever takes the Shaitan for a guardian rather that Allah he indeed shall suffer a manifest loss. He gives them promises and excites vain desires in them; and the Shaitan does not promise them but to deceive."

"As regards, the second question is any Pakistani serving in such an army or taking part with his government in the contemporary crusade which they call 'the war on terror' a true and sincere Muslim or is he an enemy of Islam violating the very principles of the Quran and Sunnah?"

"Almighty Allah has said: ;O you who believe! do not take the Jews and the Christians for friends they are friends of each other and whoever amongst you takes them for a friend then surely he is one of them surely Allah does not guide the unjust people'."

"Imam Al Tabari said in his tafsir commenting on this verse: 'Whoever supports and champions the Jews and Christians against the Muslims becomes a follower of their religion and faith because no one supports someone else unless he is pleased with him and his religion. And if he is pleased with him and his religion then he has hated and become hostile to that which opposes him and his status becomes the same as his'."

"And Imam Al Jassas Al Hanafi, commenting on the same verse said: 'the speech here is directed either to the Arab Mushrikeen (Polytheists) or to the Muslims and that in the latter case, it is a notice that [you are] a kafir (Infidel) like them because of [your] championing of them'."

"This is why I warn each and every officer and soldier in the Pakistani army and security forces of the grave consequences Almighty Allah has prepared for those assisting the kafirs against the Muslims. And each one of them particularly from the lower ranks should know that Pervaiz does not care about them at all and is throwing them into the hell of civil war carelessly and is prepared to sacrifice thousands of low-ranking personnel in order to guarantee the continuous flow of America bribes. I request each Muslim in Pakistan to remember the glorious history of their noble scholars who resisted fiercely any and all cooperation with or support for the British Indian Army."

"Sheikh ul Hind Maulana Mehmood ul Hasan said in his fatwa to the students of Aligarh University: 'You have no choice but to abandon supporting and championing Islam's enemies whether in practice or in belief And the religious basis of this matter is undeniable.' And he wrote in his letter to the Jamiat-i-Ulamaa meeting in Amritsar: 'The fiercest enemies of Islam and Muslims are the British so it is mandatory to stop supporting them'."

"And his student Sayyed Hussain Ahmad Madni stood up in court to say: 'Joining the British army; helping another to join it or advising him to join; and supporting the British army or giving it loans for war: all are haram'."

"He also said: 'Mr. Lloyd George, during the invasion of Bait-ul-Maqdas named this war a crusade Mr Churchill also called it a crusade. Therefore I declare now in plain and clear words that any Muslim who champions Christianity not only commits a sin but also become a kafir'."

"He also stated that: 'The second form of killing a Muslim is when a person considers killing Muslims as permissible (Halaal) and does not feel sorry or repent for this act. For example, if there is a Muslim army which says, 'Fighting is our job, so even if Muslims come in front of us, we will fight them,' as if raising a sword against a Muslim is no sin; or they say, Our masters have ordered us to fight Muslims, and we are fed by their money, so we should obey their orders,' as if there is nothing wrong in obeying someone's orders to kill Muslims as long as he keeps feeding you . . . thus in such a condition, it is the agreed upon verdict (Ijma') of the entire Ummah that the person committing such an act is surely and verily a Kaafir, and has committed the type of kufr that expels him from the Ummah."

"His ruling according to the Law of Allah is the same as that of Kuffar and the Mushrikeen, both in this work and the hereafter No Muslim is allowed to consider such a person to be a Muslim or deserving of being dealt within the manner in which we deal with other Muslims . . . "

"The third possible form of killing a Muslim is when a Muslim fights alongside Kuffar against other Muslims or aids them in war so that the Kuffar attain success and victory, and when a war is waged between Muslims and non-Muslims, he sides with Kuffar. This form of the said crime embodies the gravest type of Kufr and transgression, and represents such an extreme condition of the death of a person's belief and annihilation of his Islam, that no worse form of infidelity and disbelief can possibly be imagined. All the sins, offences and impurities of the world and each and every kind of disobedience which a Muslim can commit in this world or can think of committing are nothing when compared to this crime! Any Muslim who commits this crime surely becomes a Kaafir; and is the worst kind of Kaafir. He has not only committed the sin of killing a Muslim, but has also aided and strengthened the enemies of the Truth in their fight against Islam. And there is no doubt that this is such an explicit and definite form of Kufr that it expels a person from the realm of Islam."

"When Islam, in such a condition, does not permit keeping merely a relationship of love and affection with the non-Muslims, how then can someone's faith and Islam remain intact after giving explicit support [to the Kuffar in their] war against Islam and after directing his weapon towards Muslims."

"My brothers and sisters in Pakistan, don't you notice how the words of Sheikh-ul-Hind Maulana Mehmood-ul-Hasan and his student Sayyed Hussain Ahmad Madni may Allah bless their souls, describe exactly the behavior of those who are aiding the Americans and British today in Pakistan and Afghanistan?"

"Don't you see how the Indian armies which were killing Muslims yesterday at the orders of the British, are themselves the forces of Pervaiz what are today killing Muslims in Afghanistan and the tribal areas of Pakistan at the orders of the Americans? Don't Pervaiz's forces provide the Crusaders with information, bases, airports, and even detention and torture centers? Don't they supply them with food and fuel to kill, detain, torture, and humiliate Muslims in Pakistan and Afghanistan?"

"Don't you notice how when Sayyed Hussain Ahmad Madni quoted the statements of past British politicians about their crusade, he was quoting word for word Bush, when he declared his new crusade against Muslims? Isn't is clear that the Malta detention center, in which Sheikh-ul-Hind and Sayyed Hussain Ahmad Madni were jailed, is comparable to the Guantanamo camp? Isn't it clear that we are fighting a new battle in an old war? It is the same struggle against the same enemies. The facts are the same, only the names and faces have changed."

"The king's viceroy in Delhi has become the American ambassador in Islamabad, the British Indian Army has become the American Pakistani Army, the prime minister in London has become the president in Washington, and Sayyed Ahmad Shaheed and Shah Ismail Shaheed and their mujahideen are today the mujahideen fighting to expel the neo-crusaders from Afghanistan, Pakistan and the entire sub-continent. But the difference is that the jihadi awakening of today is by the grace of Allah much stronger, wider spread, and not limited to the sub-continent and the American crusader empire is facing by the grace of Almighty Allah humiliating defeats in Afghanistan and Iraq. And now after this painful description of the degenerating situation in Pakistan, the crucial question comes: what to do?"

"First, before discussing the answer to this question, I wish to remind every Muslim of the consensus, Muslim scholars, that when a non-Muslim enemy invades a Muslim country, it becomes the individual duty of every Muslim, to rise up and resist the invaders by all available means, and this duty extends to the other Muslim countries from the nearest to the farthest until the Muslim Ummah is able to expel the invaders from its lands. This is exactly the same as the fatwas issued by the scholars of Pakistan during the Russian invasion of Afghanistan."

"So what's the difference? The Russians have gone, but the Americans have come to Pakistan and Afghanistan! So, coming back to the answer to the crucial question of what to do? Let me put the answer in a few short, straightforward points: Create Awareness We should first be aware of the real nature of the conflict. We are facing a zio-crusader campaign aided by our corrupt rulers and executed by their hunting dogs; then this awareness must be spread to the whole nation, Although this is the duty of every Muslim in Pakistan, it is particularly the duty of the Ulamaa in Pakistan. They must explain the facts of the Quran, in order to encourage the Muslims to resist the Crusaders and their agents; and they should revive the glorious history of their ancestors: Shah Abd-ul-Aziz, Sayyed Ahmad Shaheed, Shah Ismail Shaheed, Shah Abd-ul-Hai and Sheikh-ul-Hind. Don't kill or help in killing Muslims, nor aid or support killers of Muslims."

News

"We had received a questionnaire from Mr. Mehmood-ul-Hasan and he had asked answers to his questions from our Mufti in the light of Quran and Sunnah. As an answer of which the Mufti of our Dar-ul-Ifta of Lal Masjid, Mufti Abdul Diyan issued this fatwa that is absolutely according to the Quran and Sunnah and there is no sort of ambiguity in it whatsoever. Hazrat Qazi Abdul Rasheed will elaborate on this subject . . . It is the primary duty upon the Ulema to guide Muslims according to the Quran and Sunnah, to convey them correct instructions . . . where and to what extent the ruler shall be obeyed . . . plain instructions are present regarding this subject. Where the Quran has commanded that obey Allah His Messenger and the those in authority . . . the commentators have clearly stated here that such obedience will only be observed in good: 'There shall be no obedience of the Created beings in the disobedience of the Creator' . . . as it is related in the Hadeeth that it is unlawful to obey any created being in the disobedience of the Creator . . . almost all of the prominent Dar-ul-Ifta in the country the Jamiat-ur-Rasheed in Karachi likewise, the Dar-ul-Uloom Haqqania of Akora Khatak the Jamiah Ashrafia and Jamiah Farooqia and the Dar-ul-Ifta's of Islamabad and Rawalpindi . . . thousands of Ulema of the country have approved this Fatwa and the attestation with the signatures of hundreds of Muftis has reached us and is present with us. All of them have stated without any disagreement they are 100% agreed upon the statement that it is against the Quran and Sunnah to shower bullets at Muslim brothers and harm them in order to please kuffar or under their pressure or to gain their pleasure this is unlawful."

"Every soldier and officer should absolutely disobey any order to kill Muslims or aid their killers. I am also asking here anyone who has committed any of those sins to immediately repent and stop serving the devils of our age. Join and support the Mujahideen. It is the personal duty of every Muslim in Pakistan to perform jihad against the crusaders invading Afghanistan and Pakistan but if he is unable to do so, he must at the very least support and aid the Mujahideen. Examine yourselves: Are you really following and practicing Islam personally, socially and politically? Or you are deviating from Islam in one way or another? Are you really championing Islam? Or you are siding with the secular pro-Western, anti-Muslim forces cooperating with America in its crusade against Islam, the so called war on terror?"

"I know that among you are those who sacrificed their jobs when Pervaiz decided to support America in its war against the Islamic Emirate in October of 2001, and that among you are those who refused to kill their brothers in Waziristan, costing them their jobs. But are you really ready to sacrifice everything (in Allah's path) or are you wasting your time and effort in the tiresome shows of the Pakistani political circus. Let there be no doubt in your minds that the dominant political forces at work in Pakistan today are competing to appease and please the modern-day Crusaders in the White House, and are working to destabilize this nuclear-capable nation under the aegis of America. So don't allow the fruits of the victory achieved through the sacrifices of the Mujahideen fighting in Afghanistan, Iraq and the tribal belt of Pakistan to be highjacked by the politicians, who sat passively while the girls and boys of Jamia Hafsa and the Red Mosque perished and burned."

"These are the same politicians who follow the tenets of an alien Western democratic system and judiciary, and exploit Islam to fulfill their own greedy aims. This is why I address here everyone possessing a remnant of intelligence and conscience in the armed forces of Pakistan Be aware that many among the Muslims continue to hold onto a glimmer of hope that among you are some decent and Allah fearing individuals who refuse to soil their hands with Muslim blood and who don't agree with the direction Pakistan is being taken in, and are prepared to take it upon themselves to ensure that the reins of power in Pakistan either remain in the hands of Pervaiz and his supporters in the army, nor in the hands of the present lot of politicians; but are taken over by leaders who believe in implementing the Law of Allah who believe in legislating and judging according to the Laws of Allah who shun the Western democratic system and judiciary; who refuse to be slaves of the Crusaders and Jews, and who believe in the command of Allah. 'And that you should judge between them by what Allah has revealed and do not follow their desires'. and his statement: ' And it behooves not a believing man and a believing woman that they should have any choice in their matter when Allah and His Apostle have decided a matter; and whoever disobeys Allah and His Apostle he surely strays off a manifest straying'."

"I must warn you, however, that if you fail to discharge your duty to Islam, then Allah is in need of no one's help, and He, will send His sincere soldiers to rule this Ummat of Islam, whether you like it or not!"

"'And most surely Our host alone shall be the victorious ones'."

"'O you who believe! whoever from among you turns back from his religion then Allah will bring a people, He shall love them and they shall love Him lowly before the believers, mighty against the unbelievers they shall fight in Allah's way and shall not fear the censure of any censurer this is Allah's grace, He gives it to whom He pleases and Allah is Ample-giving, Knowing'."

"You may be asking yourselves, 'What will happen to Pakistan if we support the Mujahideen and confront America?' But rest assured that if you rise up against the Taghut, then Allah, will give you the power to overcome the might of the Great Taghut, America, or He Himself may stop it Allah has said to his prophet: 'Fight then in Allah's way; this is not imposed on you except In relation to yourself, and rouse the believers to ardor maybe Allah will restrain the fighting of those who disbelieve and Allah is strongest in prowess and strongest to give an exemplary punishment'."

"And I don't have to remind you, my brothers and sisters, of the losses, suffering and casualties of the modern-day Crusaders in Afghanistan and Iraq at the hands of the mujahideen (those who rely on Allah alone) and reject the hypocritical and subservient tactics of Pakistani politicians in the same way they reject the cowardly and greedy miscalculations of the Pakistani military junta. Neither freedom, nor justice, nor dignity nor independence can ever be achieved without the full and proper implementation of (shariah) and the expulsion of the neo-Crusaders, their agents and their influence from Pakistan and Afghanistan."

"Otherwise, we shall get nothing except the trifles the prisoners get from their jailer. And here I wish to add a few words for the heroes of Pakistan, be they well-known or unknown: those who have sacrificed and are still sacrificing their lives, property, wealth, homes, posts, jobs and everything they could possibly sacrifice for the glory and victory of Islam I want to assure these heroes that their sacrifices are never neglected nor overlooked, and I want to remind them of what Almighty Allah said to his Prophets (Moses) and (Aaron) when they told their God that they were afraid of the excesses and tyranny of (Pharaoh)."

"Both said: 'O our Lord! Surely we fear that he may hasten to do evil to us or that he may become inordinate'. Almighty Allah assured them that they shouldn't be afraid, because He is with them listening and seeing He said: 'Fear not, surely I am with you both I do hear and see'." So these brothers should have full confidence that during every moment of suffering they have passed through, Almighty Allah was with them listening and seeing He was with them at each and every moment of exhaustion, fear, stress, torture, deprivation, pain, injury and migration listening, seeing and counting for them their (good deeds). So they should be sure that they by the grace of Allah are winning, not losing. With their suffering and sacrifices, they are pioneering the victory of Islam in Pakistan and following in the footsteps of the Prophets (peace and bless be all upon them) and their followers (Allah was pleased with all of them)."

"Finally, I request every Muslim in Pakistan to ask himself seriously: Does he want Pakistan to truly become Pakistan? Or is he going to stand by idly and passively until it becomes part of Greater Hindustan?"

DOCUMENT NO. 32

VIOLENCE IN PAKISTAN: TREND ANALYSIS

IDSA Report

December 02, 2008

Alok Bansal, T. Khurshchev Singh

The number of violent incidents in Pakistan increased from 309 in September 2008 to 346 in October 2008. Yet, casualty figures decreased from 1342 to 1081.[1] This shows that Pakistan's security forces have succeeded in controlling the level of violence, even though current levels are still unacceptably high. 582 suspected militants, most of them from the North West Frontier Province (NWFP) were also arrested by the security forces during the month, in military operations as well as during searches in various areas. This relative "success" of the security forces has succeeded in frustrating the militants to some extent. However, as a result, the number of suicide attacks during October 2008 went up to nine from five in the previous month. 142 lives were lost and over 317 others were injured in these suicide attacks. The prevalence of violent incidents continues to be the highest in NWFP. At the same time, incidents of violence were lower in the Federally Administered Tribal Areas and Balochistan.

Continuing the trend that emerged in September 2008, NWFP recorded the most number of violent incidents—from 126 in September to 160 in October 2008. And unlike in the rest of Pakistan even the number of lives lost in the province registered a sharp rise to 405 from 292 in September; and some 182 persons were injured. 223 militants were killed in October 2008 as against 161 in September. At the same time, 136 civilians died in October 2008 as against 102 in September; and 46 security personnel as against 29 lost their lives in the violence within the province. Among the injured 100 were civilians, 46 security personnel and 13 militants. Given that accurate inputs about casualties among militants are generally not available, the number of militants injured could well be higher.

Large tracts of Swat valley continued to remain under militant control and the district which is the epicentre of violence in the province saw heavy exchange of fire between security forces and militants. Pakistan Air Force jets and helicopter gunships pounded alleged militant strongholds on a daily basis. In rest of the province militants targeted CD shops, police stations and educational facilities, especially those for girls and women. Low level functionaries of the Awami National Party and security forces personnel bore the brunt of the terrorist ire. In a new development, security personnel from the region and on leave were also targeted.

NWFP also witnessed four suicide attacks during October 2008. In a high-profile act, a suicide bomber attempted to kill Asfandyar Wali Khan, the president of ANP, by blowing himself up just a few feet away when Wali Khan was greeting his supporters on occasion of Eid-ul Fitr at his residence. This was the fifth suicide attack against top political leaders of the NWFP in the last one and a half years; four of these attacks took place in Charsadda district, while the fifth one was in Peshawar. The other three suicide attacks during October targeted security personnel—the targets being a military check post, a police station and the office of a police DIG. Militants also kidnapped a large number of security personnel and other government functionaries.

Security forces arrested 456 alleged militants in NWFP during the month, apart from confiscating a large cache of arms and ammunition. 200 of these militants were arrested after a major operation launched on October 16 and 17, and among them were 40 Uzbek militants arrested in Kohat. The high number of arrests of terrorists in the province shows the resolution of the provincial administration to deal with the menace of terrorism and is in sharp contrast with the performance of other administrative units in Pakistan. As a result of pressure eight militants surrendered in Peshawar on October 22 and swore on the Holy Qura'an to refrain from terrorist activities in future.

As in the past, the highest casualties in violent incidents occurred in FATA, a region that has emerged as the epicentre of global Islamic terrorism. As in September 2008, more than half of the lives lost in Pakistan as a result of violent incidents were in the region. Though the number of violent incidents declined marginally from 103 in September 2008 to 101 in October 2008, the killings reduced quite considerably and declined from 892 to 605. Among these, 455 (539 in September) were alleged militants, 149 (336 in September) were civilians, and only one was a security personnel (17 in September). 227 civilians, 3 security personnel and 60 militants are believed to have been injured during October, though the figure for militants could be higher. Only 29 alleged militants were apprehended by the security forces, clearly indicating that security forces operations were mainly confined to aerial attacks. There were three suicide attacks in different parts of

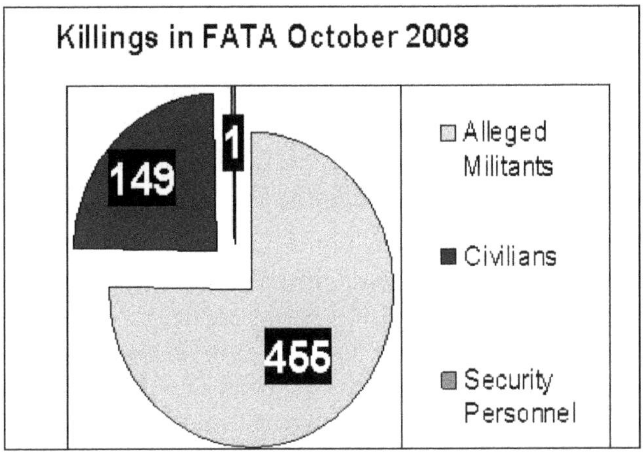

FATA which claimed 96 lives and injured 205 others. Two of these attacks were directed against security forces while one targeted an anti-Taliban tribal jirga.

The security forces confronted the militants mainly in Bajaur Agency, where militant strongholds were continuously pounded by helicopter gun ships and fighter jets, as part of an operation that had begun with an attack on Lowi Sam on August 7. While security forces, supported by armour and artillery, claimed to have captured the town of Lowi Sam on October 24, fighting continued unabated in other parts of the agency. In the eleven weeks of operations in Bajaur Agency to regain control of Lowi Sam, the security forces claimed to have killed 1,500 Taliban whilst losing 73 troops and 95 civilians. They also claimed to have arrested 950 Taliban during the operation that began in August, including 300 foreign terrorists who were mainly from Uzbekistan, Tajikistan and Afghanistan.

In addition security forces raised and armed numerous tribal militias to take on the Taliban not only in Bajaur but also in neighbouring Mohmand and Orakzai Agencies. Most of the deaths in the region were on account of aerial bombings and clashes between Taliban and tribal militias. The ongoing strife between the Taliban and tribal Lashkars supported by the government might get aggravated as both sides have dealt with each other rather brutally. The Taliban have beheaded tribal leaders collaborating with the government and tribal lashkars with over 20,000 'volunteers' have also dealt with Taliban sympathizers similarly. In fact over 250,000 people from Bajaur and the adjoining Mohmand Agency have been displaced from their homes. Interestingly, the Tehrik e Taliban Pakistan (TTP) on October 22 indicated its willingness to lay down arms if the government ended the ongoing military operation. Its spokesman Maulvi Omar said that the allegation that the Taliban movement was destabilising Pakistan was baseless and added that they would lay down their arms if the government ended its military operation, but refused to do so before talks. Some local Taliban and supporters of militants in the Mamoond tehsil of Bajaur Agency surrendered to a jirga (local Lashkar) on October 28 and 29. It showed that the Taliban was under some pressure in Bajaur and wanted to have a breather in the garb of talks, but the security forces refused to bite the bait and fighting continued as October came to an end.

Although fierce fighting continued in Bajaur agency and adjoining areas throughout the month, the militant citadels in North Waziristan and South Waziristan were not touched by Pakistani security forces. They were left for US drones and missiles. There was also mortar fire on militant positions from across the border. There were at least 12 such attacks from across the border. There were instances when militants fired at Army helicopters, US jets and drones. Militants also targeted with impunity personnel believed to be close to the government. In Khyber Agency, NATO supplies were targeted and there were skirmishes between the Taliban and security forces as well as between the security forces and Mangal Bagh led Lashkar-i-Islam.

In Balochistan, there was a further reduction in violence and the number of incidents declined from 32 in September to 22 in October 2008. Only 17 people were killed and 43 were injured as against 59 deaths and injuries to 61 in September. All those killed or injured during the month were civilians. Security forces claimed to have arrested 53 militants and captured huge caches of arms and ammunition within the province. The violence level in Baloch areas came down considerably and was confined to Dera Bugti district and Quetta. There were some instances of attacks on gas pipelines and railway tracks.

At the same time, activities of Islamic militants increased in Northern Balochistan especially along the province's border with Afghanistan. Supplies to Afghanistan being sent by a National Logistics Cell trailer through Chaman were seized by militants on October 9. Four would-be suicide bombers were arrested at Zhob on October 12. The month was characterised by a significant reduction in the intensity of the Baloch insurgency, although there was some increase in the activities of pro-Taliban elements in Pakhtoon areas.

October 2008 also witnessed an expansion in the activities of militants in other parts of Pakistan, namely, Punjab, Sindh and Islamabad, where there was an increase in incidents of violence during the month to 63 as against 48 in September 2008. However, in the absence of any major incident like the attack on the Marriot, the casualty figures reduced considerably and only 54 lives were lost and 138 received injuries as against 99 killings and injuries to 265 in September. Apart from the two suicide bombers, all those who were killed and injured were civilians. Almost half the casualties were sustained in the two suicide attacks, which resulted in the loss of 25 lives and injuries to 68, the targets being the house of a parliamentarian in Bhakkar in Punjab and the building of the Anti Terrorism Squad in Islamabad. There were a number of hoax calls made reporting bombs in numerous public buildings in Islamabad and cities in Punjab and Sindh. Tribal clashes as well as ethnic and sectarian clashes were reported from rural Sindh and Punjab during the month.

During October 2008 violence spread to newer areas, although the casualties reduced, as security forces mainly concentrated on taking on militants in Swat valley and Bajaur Agency, while leaving the militants in other parts to themselves. The Taliban claimed that they now have cadres in Karachi and the MQM chief seemed to agree with them on this count.

Capt. Alok Bansal is Research Fellow at the Institute for Defence Studies and Analyses, New Delhi. T. Khurshchev Singh is Research Assistant at the Institute for Defence Studies and Analyses, New Delhi.

Table of Casualty Figures in Pakistan—October 2008*

Region	Incidents	Militants			Civilian		Security Forces		Total	
		Killed	Injured	Arrested	Killed	Injured	Killed	Injured	Killed	Injured
FATA	101 (103)	455 (539)	60 (82)	29	149 (336)	227 (158)	1 (17)	3 (0)	605 (892)	290 (240)
NWFP	160 (126)	223 (161)	13 (45)	456	136 (102)	100 (99)	46 (29)	59 (38)	405 (292)	172 (182)
Balochistan	22 (32)	0 (25)	0 (0)	53	17 (26)	43 (56)	0 (8)	0 (5)	17 (59)	43 (61)
Rest of Pakistan	63 (48)	2 (2)	0 (0)	24	52 (92)	138 (265)	0 (5)	0 (0)	54 (99)	138 (265)
Total (Pakistan)	**346 (309)**	**680 (727)**	**73 (127)**	582	**354 (556)**	**508 (578)**	**47 (59)**	**62 (43)**	**1081 (1342)**	**643 (748)**

* Based on media reports. Injury figures are approximate. Figures in patenthesis indicate September 2008 figures.

SUBJECT INDEX

Doc/Pg

Afghanistan

Durand Line Agreement, November 12, 3793
Khan, Amir Abdur Rahman; Durand, Sir Henry Mortimer 1/1
Expert Testimony in United States v. Hamid Hayat
Kohlmann, Evan F. 20/459
Indictment of Sabri Benkahla
McNulty, Paul J.; Spencer, Robert; Kromberg, Gordon D.; Gibbs, John T., United States Attorney; Assistant United States Attorney Chief, Criminal Division; Assistant United States Attorney; Department of Justice Trial Attorney. 22/507
Pakistan and Terrorism: A Summary, Congressional Research Service Report, RS22632
Kronstadt, K. Alan, Specialist, Foreign Affairs, Defense and Trade Division, Congressional Research Service. 24/533
Pakistani Public Opinion on Democracy, Islamist Militancy, and Relations with the U.S., United States Institute of Peace (USIP) Report
Fair, C. Christine; Ramsay, Clay; Kull, Steve, Rand Corporation; WorldPublicOpinion.org; WorldPublicOpinion.org. 26/555
Resolving the Pakistan-Afghanistan Stalemate, United States Institute of Peace (USIP) Special Report
Rubin, Barnett R.; Siddique, Abubakar, Chair, Afghanistan Working Group; Fulbright Scholar 21/477
United States of America v. Sabri Benkahla 23/519

Doc/Pg

Arms Proliferation

IAEA Report on Pakistan's National Legislation entitled: "Export Control on Goods, Technologies, Material and Equipment related to Nuclear and Biological Weapons and their Delivery Systems Act, 2004", International Atomic Energy Agency Information Circular, INFCIRC/636
Amin, Raja Muhammad, Acting Secretary 28/625

Asia, South

A Message from Sheikh Ayman al-Zawahiri to Pakistan
al-Zawahiri, Sheikh Ayman 31/723
Durand Line Agreement, November 12, 3793
Khan, Amir Abdur Rahman; Durand, Sir Henry Mortimer 1/1
Pakistan-U.S. Relations, Congressional Research Service Report, IB94041
Kronstadt, K. Alan, Specialist, Foreign Affairs, Defense and Trade Division, Congressional Research Service 16/335
Pakistan's Political and Security Challenges, Research Paper 07/68
Lunn, Jon; Taylor, Claire; Youngs, Tim; Beale, Ed, International Affairs and Defence Section; Economic Policy and Statistics Section, House of Commons Library 30/653
Regional Implications of the Rise of Islamic Fundamentalism in Pakistan, Institute for Defence Studies Report
Bahadur, Kalim 29/633
Tashkent Declaration
Shastri, Lal Bahadur; Khan, Mohammad Ayub, Prime Minister of India; President of Pakistan 2/5
Terrorism in South Asia, Congressional Research Service Report, RL32259
Kronstadt, K. Alan, Specialist, Foreign Affairs, Defense and Trade Division, Congressional Research Service 18/381
Vaughn, Bruce, Specialist, Foreign Affairs, Defense and Trade Division, Congressional Research Service 18/381
UN Resolutions on Kashmir 15/319

Congressional Research Service (CRS) Reports

Pakistan and Terrorism: A Summary, Congressional Research Service Report, RS22632
Kronstadt, K. Alan, Specialist, Foreign Affairs, Defense and Trade Division, Congressional Research Service 24/533

Doc/Pg

Pakistan-U.S. Anti-Terrorism Cooperation, Congressional Research Service Report, RL31624

Kronstadt, K. Alan, Specialist, Foreign Affairs, Defense and Trade Division, Congressional Research Service. .17/355

Pakistan-U.S. Relations, Congressional Research Service Report, IB94041

Kronstadt, K. Alan, Specialist, Foreign Affairs, Defense and Trade Division, Congressional Research Service. .16/335

Terrorism in South Asia, Congressional Research Service Report, RL32259

Kronstadt, K. Alan, Specialist, Foreign Affairs, Defense and Trade Division, Congressional Research Service. .18/381

Vaughn, Bruce, Specialist, Foreign Affairs, Defense and Trade Division, Congressional Research Service. .18/381

Counterterrorism

Anti-terrorism (Amendment) Ordinance

Musharraf, Pervez, President of Pakistan 4/13

Anti-terrorism (Second Amendment) Act, Act No. II of 2005

Khan, Shahiq A., Secretary 5/17

Combating Terrorism: The United States Lacks Comprehensive Plan to Destroy the Terrorist Threat and Close the Safe Haven in Pakistan's Federally Administered Tribal Areas, GAO Report, GAO-08-622. . . . . .27/593

Expert Testimony in United States v. Hamid Hayat

Kohlmann, Evan F. 20/459

India-Pakistan Joint Statement

Qureshi, Makhdoom Shah Mahmood; Mukherjee, Pranab, Foreign Minister of Pakistan; External Affairs Minister. 7/23

Pakistan Anti-Terrorism (Amendment) Ordinance

Tarar, Rafiq, President of Pakistan. 3/7

Pakistan-U.S. Anti-Terrorism Cooperation, Congressional Research Service Report, RL31624

Kronstadt, K. Alan, Specialist, Foreign Affairs, Defense and Trade Division, Congressional Research Service. .17/355

Pakistan-U.S. Relations, Congressional Research Service Report, IB94041

Kronstadt, K. Alan, Specialist, Foreign Affairs, Defense and Trade Division, Congressional Research Service. .16/335

Doc/Pg

Pakistan's 2002 Report to the UN on Its Counter-Terrorism Efforts, UN Security Council Resolution S/2004/21

Arias, Inocencio F.; Khalid, Masood, Chairman, Counter-Terrorism Committee; Acting Permanent Representative of Pakistan to the United Nations 11/81

Pakistan's 2003 Report to the UN on Its Counter-Terrorism Efforts, UN Security Council Resolution S/AC.44/2004/(02)/22 . . . . 12/91

Pakistan's 2004 Report to the UN on Its Counter-Terrorism Efforts, Part 1, UN Security Council Resolution S/2005/524

Sardenberg, Ronaldo Mota; Akram, Munir, Acting Chairman of the Security Council Committee; Permanent Representative of Pakistan to the United Nations 13/103

Pakistan's 2004 Report to the UN on Its Counter-Terrorism Efforts, Part 2, UN Security Council Resolution S/AC.44/2004/(02)/22/Add. 1. . . . . 14/113

Pakistan's 2005 Report to the UN on Its Counter-Terrorism Efforts, Part 1, UN Security Council Resolution S/2001/1310

Greenstock, Jeremy; Ahmad, Shamshad, Chairman, Counter-Terrorism Committee; Permanent Representative of Pakistan to the United Nations 8/27

Pakistan's 2005 Report to the UN on Its Counter-Terrorism Efforts, Part 2, UN Security Council Resolution S/2002/797

Greenstock, Jeremy; Akram, Munir, Chairman, Counter-Terrorism Committee; Permanent Representative of Pakistan to the United Nations 9/39

Report of Pakistan to the UNSC on Implementation of UNSC Resolution 1373, UN Security Council Resolution S/2003/307

Greenstock, Jeremy; Akram, Munir, Chairman, Counter-Terrorism Committee; Permanent Representative of Pakistan to the United Nations 10/71

Terrorism in South Asia, Congressional Research Service Report, RL32259

Kronstadt, K. Alan, Specialist, Foreign Affairs, Defense and Trade Division, Congressional Research Service. 18/381

Vaughn, Bruce, Specialist, Foreign Affairs, Defense and Trade Division, Congressional Research Service. 18/381

U.S.-Pakistan Engagement: The War on Terrorism and Beyond, United States Institute of Peace (USIP) Special Report

Hussain, Touqir, Senior Fellow, U.S. Institute of Peace. 19/435

Doc/Pg

Government Accountability Office (GAO) Reports

Combating Terrorism: The United States Lacks Comprehensive Plan to Destroy the Terrorist Threat and Close the Safe Haven in Pakistan's Federally Administered Tribal Areas, GAO Report, GAO-08-622. . . . . 27/593

House Foreign Affairs Committee

U.S.-Pakistan Relations: Assassination, Instability, and the Future of U.S. Policy, Testimony Before the Foreign Affairs Committee Subcommittee on the Middle East and South Asia
Fair, C. Christine, Rand Corporation 25/541

India

Durand Line Agreement, November 12, 3793
Khan, Amir Abdur Rahman; Durand, Sir Henry Mortimer 1/1
India-Pakistan Joint Statement
Qureshi, Makhdoom Shah Mahmood; Mukherjee, Pranab, Foreign Minister of Pakistan; External Affairs Minister. 7/23
Tashkent Declaration
Shastri, Lal Bahadur; Khan, Mohammad Ayub, Prime Minister of India; President of Pakistan 2/5
UN Resolutions on Kashmir. 15/319

International Atomic Energy Agency (IAEA)

IAEA Report on Pakistan's National Legislation entitled: "Export Control on Goods, Technologies, Material and Equipment related to Nuclear and Biological Weapons and their Delivery Systems Act, 2004", International Atomic Energy Agency Information Circular, INFCIRC/636
Amin, Raja Muhammad, Acting Secretary 28/625

International Cooperation

Durand Line Agreement, November 12, 3793
Khan, Amir Abdur Rahman; Durand, Sir Henry Mortimer 1/1
India-Pakistan Joint Statement
Qureshi, Makhdoom Shah Mahmood; Mukherjee, Pranab, Foreign Minister of Pakistan; External Affairs Minister. 7/23
Pakistan-U.S. Anti-Terrorism Cooperation, Congressional Research Service Report, RL31624
Kronstadt, K. Alan, Specialist, Foreign Affairs, Defense and Trade Division, Congressional Research Service. 17/355

Doc/Pg

Pakistan's 2002 Report to the UN on Its Counter-Terrorism Efforts, UN Security Council Resolution S/2004/21

Arias, Inocencio F.; Khalid, Masood, Chairman, Counter-Terrorism Committee; Acting Permanent Representative of Pakistan to the United Nations 11/81

Pakistan's 2003 Report to the UN on Its Counter-Terrorism Efforts, UN Security Council Resolution S/AC.44/2004/(02)/22 . . . . . 12/91

Pakistan's 2004 Report to the UN on Its Counter-Terrorism Efforts, Part 1, UN Security Council Resolution S/2005/524

Sardenberg, Ronaldo Mota; Akram, Munir, Acting Chairman of the Security Council Committee; Permanent Representative of Pakistan to the United Nations 13/103

Pakistan's 2004 Report to the UN on Its Counter-Terrorism Efforts, Part 2, UN Security Council Resolution S/AC.44/2004/(02)/22/Add. 1 . . . . . 14/113

Pakistan's 2005 Report to the UN on Its Counter-Terrorism Efforts, Part 1, UN Security Council Resolution S/2001/1310

Greenstock, Jeremy; Ahmad, Shamshad, Chairman, Counter-Terrorism Committee; Permanent Representative of Pakistan to the United Nations 8/27

Pakistan's 2005 Report to the UN on Its Counter-Terrorism Efforts, Part 2, UN Security Council Resolution S/2002/797

Greenstock, Jeremy; Akram, Munir, Chairman, Counter-Terrorism Committee; Permanent Representative of Pakistan to the United Nations 9/39

Report of Pakistan to the UNSC on Implementation of UNSC Resolution 1373, UN Security Council Resolution S/2003/307

Greenstock, Jeremy; Akram, Munir, Chairman, Counter-Terrorism Committee; Permanent Representative of Pakistan to the United Nations 10/71

Resolving the Pakistan-Afghanistan Stalemate, United States Institute of Peace (USIP) Special Report

Rubin, Barnett R.; Siddique, Abubakar, Chair, Afghanistan Working Group; Fulbright Scholar 21/477

Tashkent Declaration

Shastri, Lal Bahadur; Khan, Mohammad Ayub, Prime Minister of India; President of Pakistan 2/5

U.S.-Pakistan Engagement: The War on Terrorism and Beyond, United States Institute of Peace (USIP) Special Report

Hussain, Touqir, Senior Fellow, U.S. Institute of Peace 19/435

UN Resolutions on Kashmir 15/319

Doc/Pg

Islam

A Message from Sheikh Ayman al-Zawahiri to Pakistan
al-Zawahiri, Sheikh Ayman 31/723

Pakistani Public Opinion on Democracy, Islamist Militancy, and Relations with the U.S., United States Institute of Peace (USIP) Report
Fair, C. Christine; Ramsay, Clay; Kull, Steve, Rand Corporation; WorldPublicOpinion.org; WorldPublicOpinion.org 26/555

Regional Implications of the Rise of Islamic Fundamentalism in Pakistan, Institute for Defence Studies Report
Bahadur, Kalim 29/633

Military – Role of

North West Frontier Province Government's Agreement with the Taliban 6/21

Violence in Pakistan: Trend Analysis, Institute for Defence Studies and Analysis, IDSA Report
Bansal, Alok; Singh, T. Khurshchev, Research Fellow, Institute for Defence Studies and Analyses, New Delhi; Research Assistant, Institute for Defence Studies and Analyses, New Delhi. 32/739

Nuclear Terrorism

IAEA Report on Pakistan's National Legislation entitled: "Export Control on Goods, Technologies, Material and Equipment related to Nuclear and Biological Weapons and their Delivery Systems Act, 2004", International Atomic Energy Agency Information Circular, INFCIRC/636
Amin, Raja Muhammad, Acting Secretary 28/625

Pakistan-U.S. Relations, Congressional Research Service Report, IB94041
Kronstadt, K. Alan, Specialist, Foreign Affairs, Defense and Trade Division, Congressional Research Service. 16/335

Pakistan

A Message from Sheikh Ayman al-Zawahiri to Pakistan
al-Zawahiri, Sheikh Ayman 31/723

Anti-terrorism (Amendment) Ordinance
Musharraf, Pervez, President of Pakistan 4/13

Anti-terrorism (Second Amendment) Act, Act No. II of 2005
Khan, Shahiq A., Secretary 5/17

Doc/Pg

Combating Terrorism: The United States Lacks Comprehensive Plan to Destroy the Terrorist Threat and Close the Safe Haven in Pakistan's Federally Administered Tribal Areas, GAO Report, GAO-08-622. . . . . 27/593

Durand Line Agreement, November 12, 3793

Khan, Amir Abdur Rahman; Durand, Sir Henry Mortimer 1/1

Expert Testimony in United States v. Hamid Hayat

Kohlmann, Evan F. 20/459

IAEA Report on Pakistan's National Legislation entitled: "Export Control on Goods, Technologies, Material and Equipment related to Nuclear and Biological Weapons and their Delivery Systems Act, 2004", International Atomic Energy Agency Information Circular, INFCIRC/636

Amin, Raja Muhammad, Acting Secretary 28/625

India-Pakistan Joint Statement

Qureshi, Makhdoom Shah Mahmood; Mukherjee, Pranab, Foreign Minister of Pakistan; External Affairs Minister. 7/23

Indictment of Sabri Benkahla

McNulty, Paul J.; Spencer, Robert; Kromberg, Gordon D.; Gibbs, John T., United States Attorney; Assistant United States Attorney Chief, Criminal Division; Assistant United States Attorney; Department of Justice Trial Attorney. 22/507

North West Frontier Province Government's Agreement with the Taliban 6/21

Pakistan Anti-Terrorism (Amendment) Ordinance

Tarar, Rafiq, President of Pakistan. 3/7

Pakistan and Terrorism: A Summary, Congressional Research Service Report, RS22632

Kronstadt, K. Alan, Specialist, Foreign Affairs, Defense and Trade Division, Congressional Research Service. 24/533

Pakistan-U.S. Anti-Terrorism Cooperation, Congressional Research Service Report, RL31624

Kronstadt, K. Alan, Specialist, Foreign Affairs, Defense and Trade Division, Congressional Research Service. 17/355

Pakistan-U.S. Relations, Congressional Research Service Report, IB94041

Kronstadt, K. Alan, Specialist, Foreign Affairs, Defense and Trade Division, Congressional Research Service. 16/335

Pakistani Public Opinion on Democracy, Islamist Militancy, and Relations with the U.S., United States Institute of Peace (USIP) Report

Fair, C. Christine; Ramsay, Clay; Kull, Steve, Rand Corporation; WorldPublicOpinion.org; WorldPublicOpinion.org. 26/555

Doc/Pg

Pakistan's 2002 Report to the UN on Its Counter-Terrorism Efforts, UN Security Council Resolution S/2004/21

Arias, Inocencio F.; Khalid, Masood, Chairman, Counter-Terrorism Committee; Acting Permanent Representative of Pakistan to the United Nations 11/81

Pakistan's 2003 Report to the UN on Its Counter-Terrorism Efforts, UN Security Council Resolution S/AC.44/2004/(02)/22 . . . . . 12/91

Pakistan's 2004 Report to the UN on Its Counter-Terrorism Efforts, Part 1, UN Security Council Resolution S/2005/524

Sardenberg, Ronaldo Mota; Akram, Munir, Acting Chairman of the Security Council Committee; Permanent Representative of Pakistan to the United Nations 13/103

Pakistan's 2004 Report to the UN on Its Counter-Terrorism Efforts, Part 2, UN Security Council Resolution S/AC.44/2004/(02)/22/Add. 1 . . . . . 14/113

Pakistan's 2005 Report to the UN on Its Counter-Terrorism Efforts, Part 1, UN Security Council Resolution S/2001/1310

Greenstock, Jeremy; Ahmad, Shamshad, Chairman, Counter-Terrorism Committee; Permanent Representative of Pakistan to the United Nations 8/27

Pakistan's 2005 Report to the UN on Its Counter-Terrorism Efforts, Part 2, UN Security Council Resolution S/2002/797

Greenstock, Jeremy; Akram, Munir, Chairman, Counter-Terrorism Committee; Permanent Representative of Pakistan to the United Nations 9/39

Pakistan's Political and Security Challenges, Research Paper 07/68

Lunn, Jon; Taylor, Claire; Youngs, Tim; Beale, Ed, International Affairs and Defence Section; Economic Policy and Statistics Section, House of Commons Library 30/653

Regional Implications of the Rise of Islamic Fundamentalism in Pakistan, Institute for Defence Studies Report

Bahadur, Kalim 29/633

Report of Pakistan to the UNSC on Implementation of UNSC Resolution 1373, UN Security Council Resolution S/2003/307

Greenstock, Jeremy; Akram, Munir, Chairman, Counter-Terrorism Committee; Permanent Representative of Pakistan to the United Nations 10/71

Resolving the Pakistan-Afghanistan Stalemate, United States Institute of Peace (USIP) Special Report

Rubin, Barnett R.; Siddique, Abubakar, Chair, Afghanistan Working Group; Fulbright Scholar 21/477

Doc/Pg

Tashkent Declaration

Shastri, Lal Bahadur; Khan, Mohammad Ayub, Prime Minister of India; President of Pakistan 2/5

U.S.-Pakistan Engagement: The War on Terrorism and Beyond, United States Institute of Peace (USIP) Special Report

Hussain, Touqir, Senior Fellow, U.S. Institute of Peace...............19/435

U.S.-Pakistan Relations: Assassination, Instability, and the Future of U.S. Policy, Testimony Before the Foreign Affairs Committee Subcommittee on the Middle East and South Asia

Fair, C. Christine, Rand Corporation 25/541

UN Resolutions on Kashmir...15/319

United States of America v. Sabri Benkahla 23/519

Violence in Pakistan: Trend Analysis, Institute for Defence Studies and Analysis, IDSA Report

Bansal, Alok; Singh, T. Khurshchev, Research Fellow, Institute for Defence Studies and Analyses, New Delhi; Research Assistant, Institute for Defence Studies and Analyses, New Delhi...............32/739

State Sponsors of Terrorism

Pakistan's Political and Security Challenges, Research Paper 07/68

Lunn, Jon; Taylor, Claire; Youngs, Tim; Beale, Ed, International Affairs and Defence Section; Economic Policy and Statistics Section, House of Commons Library 30/653

Regional Implications of the Rise of Islamic Fundamentalism in Pakistan, Institute for Defence Studies Report

Bahadur, Kalim 29/633

U.S.-Pakistan Relations: Assassination, Instability, and the Future of U.S. Policy, Testimony Before the Foreign Affairs Committee Subcommittee on the Middle East and South Asia

Fair, C. Christine, Rand Corporation 25/541

Taliban

Indictment of Sabri Benkahla

McNulty, Paul J.; Spencer, Robert; Kromberg, Gordon D.; Gibbs, John T., United States Attorney; Assistant United States Attorney Chief, Criminal Division; Assistant United States Attorney; Department of Justice Trial Attorney.......................22/507

North West Frontier Province Government's Agreement with the Taliban 6/21

Doc/Pg

Pakistani Public Opinion on Democracy, Islamist Militancy, and Relations with the U.S., United States Institute of Peace (USIP) Report
Fair, C. Christine; Ramsay, Clay; Kull, Steve, Rand Corporation; WorldPublicOpinion.org; WorldPublicOpinion.org 26/555
Resolving the Pakistan-Afghanistan Stalemate, United States Institute of Peace (USIP) Special Report
Rubin, Barnett R.; Siddique, Abubakar, Chair, Afghanistan Working Group; Fulbright Scholar 21/477
Violence in Pakistan: Trend Analysis, Institute for Defence Studies and Analysis, IDSA Report
Bansal, Alok; Singh, T. Khurshchev, Research Fellow, Institute for Defence Studies and Analyses, New Delhi; Research Assistant, Institute for Defence Studies and Analyses, New Delhi. 32/739

Terrorism – Criminal Prosecution

Anti-terrorism (Second Amendment) Act, Act No. II of 2005
Khan, Shahiq A., Secretary 5/17
Indictment of Sabri Benkahla
McNulty, Paul J.; Spencer, Robert; Kromberg, Gordon D.; Gibbs, John T., United States Attorney; Assistant United States Attorney Chief, Criminal Division; Assistant United States Attorney; Department of Justice Trial Attorney 22/507
Pakistan Anti-Terrorism (Amendment) Ordinance
Tarar, Rafiq, President of Pakistan. 3/7
United States of America v. Sabri Benkahla 23/519

Terrorism – Financing of

Pakistan's 2004 Report to the UN on Its Counter-Terrorism Efforts, Part 1, UN Security Council Resolution S/2005/524
Sardenberg, Ronaldo Mota; Akram, Munir, Acting Chairman of the Security Council Committee; Permanent Representative of Pakistan to the United Nations 13/103
Pakistan's 2005 Report to the UN on Its Counter-Terrorism Efforts, Part 1, UN Security Council Resolution S/2001/1310
Greenstock, Jeremy; Ahmad, Shamshad, Chairman, Counter-Terrorism Committee; Permanent Representative of Pakistan to the United Nations 8/27
Pakistan's 2005 Report to the UN on Its Counter-Terrorism Efforts, Part 2, UN Security Council Resolution S/2002/797
Greenstock, Jeremy; Akram, Munir, Chairman, Counter-Terrorism Committee; Permanent Representative of Pakistan to the United Nations 9/39

Doc/Pg

Report of Pakistan to the UNSC on Implementation of UNSC Resolution 1373, UN Security Council Resolution S/2003/307
Greenstock, Jeremy; Akram, Munir, Chairman, Counter-Terrorism Committee; Permanent Representative of Pakistan to the United Nations 10/71

Terrorism – International

A Message from Sheikh Ayman al-Zawahiri to Pakistan
al-Zawahiri, Sheikh Ayman 31/723

Expert Testimony in United States v. Hamid Hayat
Kohlmann, Evan F. 20/459

Indictment of Sabri Benkahla
McNulty, Paul J.; Spencer, Robert; Kromberg, Gordon D.; Gibbs, John T., United States Attorney; Assistant United States Attorney Chief, Criminal Division; Assistant United States Attorney; Department of Justice Trial Attorney 22/507

North West Frontier Province Government's Agreement with the Taliban 6/21

Pakistan and Terrorism: A Summary, Congressional Research Service Report, RS22632
Kronstadt, K. Alan, Specialist, Foreign Affairs, Defense and Trade Division, Congressional Research Service 24/533

Pakistan-U.S. Anti-Terrorism Cooperation, Congressional Research Service Report, RL31624
Kronstadt, K. Alan, Specialist, Foreign Affairs, Defense and Trade Division, Congressional Research Service 17/355

Pakistan's 2002 Report to the UN on Its Counter-Terrorism Efforts, UN Security Council Resolution S/2004/21
Arias, Inocencio F.; Khalid, Masood, Chairman, Counter-Terrorism Committee; Acting Permanent Representative of Pakistan to the United Nations 11/81

Regional Implications of the Rise of Islamic Fundamentalism in Pakistan, Institute for Defence Studies Report
Bahadur, Kalim 29/633

Resolving the Pakistan-Afghanistan Stalemate, United States Institute of Peace (USIP) Special Report
Rubin, Barnett R.; Siddique, Abubakar, Chair, Afghanistan Working Group; Fulbright Scholar 21/477

Doc/Pg

Terrorism in South Asia, Congressional Research Service Report, RL32259

Kronstadt, K. Alan, Specialist, Foreign Affairs, Defense and Trade Division, Congressional Research Service.......18/381

Vaughn, Bruce, Specialist, Foreign Affairs, Defense and Trade Division, Congressional Research Service.......18/381

U.S.-Pakistan Engagement: The War on Terrorism and Beyond, United States Institute of Peace (USIP) Special Report

Hussain, Touqir, Senior Fellow, U.S. Institute of Peace.......19/435

United States of America v. Sabri Benkahla.......23/519

Terrorism – Policy

Anti-terrorism (Amendment) Ordinance

Musharraf, Pervez, President of Pakistan.......4/13

Anti-terrorism (Second Amendment) Act, Act No. II of 2005

Khan, Shahiq A., Secretary.......5/17

Combating Terrorism: The United States Lacks Comprehensive Plan to Destroy the Terrorist Threat and Close the Safe Haven in Pakistan's Federally Administered Tribal Areas, GAO Report, GAO-08-622.......27/593

Pakistan Anti-Terrorism (Amendment) Ordinance

Tarar, Rafiq, President of Pakistan.......3/7

Pakistan and Terrorism: A Summary, Congressional Research Service Report, RS22632

Kronstadt, K. Alan, Specialist, Foreign Affairs, Defense and Trade Division, Congressional Research Service.......24/533

Pakistan's Political and Security Challenges, Research Paper 07/68

Lunn, Jon; Taylor, Claire; Youngs, Tim; Beale, Ed, International Affairs and Defence Section; Economic Policy and Statistics Section, House of Commons Library.......30/653

U.S.-Pakistan Engagement: The War on Terrorism and Beyond, United States Institute of Peace (USIP) Special Report

Hussain, Touqir, Senior Fellow, U.S. Institute of Peace.......19/435

U.S.-Pakistan Relations: Assassination, Instability, and the Future of U.S. Policy, Testimony Before the Foreign Affairs Committee Subcommittee on the Middle East and South Asia

Fair, C. Christine, Rand Corporation.......25/541

Doc/Pg

Terrorism – Threat Assessment

Violence in Pakistan: Trend Analysis, Institute for Defence Studies and Analysis, IDSA Report

Bansal, Alok; Singh, T. Khurshchev, Research Fellow, Institute for Defence Studies and Analyses, New Delhi; Research Assistant, Institute for Defence Studies and Analyses, New Delhi. 32/739

Terrorist Incidents

Bansal, Alok; Singh, T. Khurshchev, Research Fellow, Institute for Defence Studies and Analyses, New Delhi; Research Assistant, Institute for Defence Studies and Analyses, New Delhi. 32/739

Terrorist Organizations

A Message from Sheikh Ayman al-Zawahiri to Pakistan

al-Zawahiri, Sheikh Ayman 31/723

Combating Terrorism: The United States Lacks Comprehensive Plan to Destroy the Terrorist Threat and Close the Safe Haven in Pakistan's Federally Administered Tribal Areas, GAO Report, GAO-08-622. . . . . 27/593

Expert Testimony in United States v. Hamid Hayat

Kohlmann, Evan F. 20/459

North West Frontier Province Government's Agreement with the Taliban 6/21

Pakistani Public Opinion on Democracy, Islamist Militancy, and Relations with the U.S., United States Institute of Peace (USIP) Report

Fair, C. Christine; Ramsay, Clay; Kull, Steve, Rand Corporation; WorldPublicOpinion.org; WorldPublicOpinion.org 26/555

Pakistan's Political and Security Challenges, Research Paper 07/68

Lunn, Jon; Taylor, Claire; Youngs, Tim; Beale, Ed, International Affairs and Defence Section; Economic Policy and Statistics Section, House of Commons Library 30/653

Terrorism in South Asia, Congressional Research Service Report, RL32259

Kronstadt, K. Alan, Specialist, Foreign Affairs, Defense and Trade Division, Congressional Research Service. 18/381

Vaughn, Bruce, Specialist, Foreign Affairs, Defense and Trade Division, Congressional Research Service. 18/381

U.S.-Pakistan Relations: Assassination, Instability, and the Future of U.S. Policy, Testimony Before the Foreign Affairs Committee Subcommittee on the Middle East and South Asia

Fair, C. Christine, Rand Corporation 25/541

Doc/Pg

United Nations – Security Council Resolutions

Pakistan's 2002 Report to the UN on Its Counter-Terrorism Efforts, UN Security Council Resolution S/2004/21

Arias, Inocencio F.; Khalid, Masood, Chairman, Counter-Terrorism Committee; Acting Permanent Representative of Pakistan to the United Nations 11/81

Pakistan's 2003 Report to the UN on Its Counter-Terrorism Efforts, UN Security Council Resolution S/AC.44/2004/(02)/22 . . . . 12/91

Pakistan's 2004 Report to the UN on Its Counter-Terrorism Efforts, Part 1, UN Security Council Resolution S/2005/524

Sardenberg, Ronaldo Mota; Akram, Munir, Acting Chairman of the Security Council Committee; Permanent Representative of Pakistan to the United Nations 13/103

Pakistan's 2004 Report to the UN on Its Counter-Terrorism Efforts, Part 2, UN Security Council Resolution S/AC.44/2004/(02)/22/Add. 1. . . . . 14/113

Pakistan's 2005 Report to the UN on Its Counter-Terrorism Efforts, Part 1, UN Security Council Resolution S/2001/1310

Greenstock, Jeremy; Ahmad, Shamshad, Chairman, Counter-Terrorism Committee; Permanent Representative of Pakistan to the United Nations 8/27

Pakistan's 2005 Report to the UN on Its Counter-Terrorism Efforts, Part 2, UN Security Council Resolution S/2002/797

Greenstock, Jeremy; Akram, Munir, Chairman, Counter-Terrorism Committee; Permanent Representative of Pakistan to the United Nations 9/39

Report of Pakistan to the UNSC on Implementation of UNSC Resolution 1373, UN Security Council Resolution S/2003/307

Greenstock, Jeremy; Akram, Munir, Chairman, Counter-Terrorism Committee; Permanent Representative of Pakistan to the United Nations 10/71

UN Resolutions on Kashmir. 15/319

Weapons of Mass Destruction

IAEA Report on Pakistan's National Legislation entitled: "Export Control on Goods, Technologies, Material and Equipment related to Nuclear and Biological Weapons and their Delivery Systems Act, 2004", International Atomic Energy Agency Information Circular, INFCIRC/636

Amin, Raja Muhammad, Acting Secretary 28/625

Doc/Pg

Pakistan's 2003 Report to the UN on Its Counter-Terrorism Efforts, UN Security Council Resolution S/AC.44/2004/(02)/22 . . . . 12/91

Pakistan's 2004 Report to the UN on Its Counter-Terrorism Efforts, Part 2, UN Security Council Resolution S/AC.44/2004/(02)/22/Add. 1 . . . . 14/113

www.ingramcontent.com/pod-product-compliance
Ingram Content Group UK Ltd.
Pitfield, Milton Keynes, MK11 3LW, UK
UKHW051348240926
475595UK00048B/163

9 780195 383072